THE AMERICAN MUSICAL

AND THE PERFORMANCE OF PERSONAL IDENTITY

Contrasting performances of personal identity

Raymond Knapp

THE AMERICAN MUSICAL

AND THE PERFORMANCE OF PERSONAL IDENTITY

PRINCETON UNIVERSITY PRESS   .   PRINCETON AND OXFORD

Copyright © 2006 by Princeton University Press
Published by Princeton University Press, 41 William Street,
Princeton, New Jersey 08540
In the United Kingdom: Princeton University Press, 3 Market Place,
Woodstock, Oxfordshire OX20 1SY

Library of Congress Cataloging-in-Publication Data

Knapp, Raymond.
The American musical and the performance of personal identity / Raymond Knapp.
p.   cm.
Includes bibliographical references (p.   ) and index.
ISBN-13: 978-0-691-12524-4 (hardcover : alk. paper)
ISBN-10: 0-691-12524-4 (hardcover : alk. paper)
1. Musicals—United States—History and criticism. 2. Musicals—Social aspects—
United States. 3. Personality and culture. 4. Motion pictures—United States—
History. I. Title.
ML2054.K6   2006
782.1′40973—dc22   2005038029

British Library Cataloging-in-Publication Data is available

Publication of this book was supported in part by a grant from the H. Earle Johnson Fund
of the Society for American Music.

This book has been composed in Sabon Typeface

Printed on acid-free paper. ∞

pup.princeton.edu

Printed in the United States of America

10   9   8   7   6   5   4   3   2   1

To my children,

RACHEL, DASHIELL, AND GENEVIEVE

CONTENTS

FIGURES

EXPLANATORY NOTE ABOUT AUDIO EXAMPLES

AUDIO EXAMPLES for this book are available online at http://epub.library.ucla.edu/knapp/americanmusical/. Each example is keyed to its appropriate place in the text and numbered sequentially within each chapter, using the following marginal notation (this particular indication is for the eighth audio example for chapter 6):

♫ **6.8**

To hear an example, simply click on the appropriate icon on the website. You must have RealAudio installed on your computer; a link on the main website will direct you to a source for this program if it is not already installed.

In some cases, you will simply hear the example. In other cases where it might be useful, other visual matter may appear, such as musical notation detailing all or part of the example, or perhaps a picture. These may not appear if the appropriate plug-in is not installed. A link on the main website will direct you to a source for the missing plug-in to allow you to view these images.

The website also includes, for each of the musicals covered separately in the main text, a list of songs (in almost all cases according to the original production) and lists of nonwritten source materials, including recordings, films, and video recordings. I have not tried to be comprehensive in these lists, confining myself to what is readily available and/or particularly interesting.

ACKNOWLEDGMENTS

AS WITH MY FIRST VOLUME, *The American Musical and the Formation of National Identity*, my deepest thanks for the present volume go to Rose Rosengard Subotnik and Mitchell Morris, who were, if anything, even more generous this time around with their readings and detailed comments. The book is much richer, and certainly less inaccurate, for their contributions. Indeed, it would be hard for me to imagine undertaking a book of this kind without them—or, for that matter, without the ongoing conversations with my daughters, Rachel and Genevieve, whose readings, observations, peculiar predilections, and sometimes off-the-wall dialogues have exerted an inescapable (but entirely welcome) influence. This time around, I was especially fortunate that Genevieve (aka Zelda), on vacation from NYU's Tisch School of the Arts, was able to devote her considerable energy and insight to a careful reading of my entire first draft in the summer of 2004. And Dan Sallitt's astute and tough-minded observations helped me to reshape many of my arguments, especially in chapters 2 and 3. The final form of the book also owes much to Geoffrey Block's careful reading of the first full draft, for which I am extremely grateful.

Among the many in UCLA's academic community—including undergraduates, graduates, and faculty—whose interactions regarding various subjects addressed in this book have proven invaluable, I wish to thank especially Elizabeth Upton, who read substantial chunks of the book and made many useful observations and suggestions, and Holley Replogle, whose expert work on the index and website of the first volume extended into many useful discussions that have helped inform this volume, and I am grateful for her work, as well, on the musical examples and index. Other specific—and gratefully received—assistance came from several of my UCLA colleagues, including Paul Attinello, Tanya Bertram, Ewelina Boczkowska, Peter Broadwell, Tara Browner, Kelsey Cowger, Francesca Draughon, Robert Fink, Philip Gentry, Jonathan Greenberg, John Hall, Gordon Haramaki, Marcus Desmond Harmon, Ljubica Ilic, James Kennaway, Cheryl Keyes, Elisabeth LeGuin, Tamara Levitz, Olivia Mather, Elizabeth Morgan, Louis Niebur, Stephan Pennington, Graham Raulerson, Marcie Ray, Steven Rothstein, Erica Scheinberg, Yara Sellin, Eva Sobelevski, Timothy D. Taylor, Robert Walser, and Griffin Woodworth. And I am especially grateful to Susan McClary and Philip Brett, whose pioneering work—along with that of Elisabeth LeGuin, Mitchell Morris, and Robert Walser, already mentioned—provides the indispensable foundation for most of what I deem valuable in this book.

Within a wider sphere at UCLA, Gordon Theil and Stephen Davison have been especially useful allies, along with their associates in the UCLA Library community, Timothy Edwards, David Gilbert, Julie Graham, and Bridget Risemberg; and, as my activities have continued to draw me into the catacombs of Murphy Hall, I have benefited (in ways they have probably not noticed) from enthusiastic interchanges with, among others, Lucy Blackmar, Robin Garrell, Greg Kendrick, Judith Lacertosa, Paula Lutomirski, and Judi Smith. More concrete help has been provided, at UCLA, by Larry Loeher and the Office of Instructional Development, Joseph Vaughan and the Center for Digital Humanities, the Academic Senate Committee on Research, the Music Library, and the Department of Musicology. Fred Appel at Princeton University Press has been tremendously supportive and enthusiastic, so that this book, like its predecessor, owes much to his intelligent guidance; I also wish to thank Frank Mahood, Jennifer Nippins, and Terri O'Prey at Princeton University Press, and Dalia Geffen for her excellent and sympathetic editing. For help with the illustrations, I am especially grateful to Miles Kreuger and Eric Davis of the Institute of the American Musical. For his design of the frontispiece, I am, as with the first volume, in Jonathan Hofferman's debt. Other important contributions and support came from Byron Adams, Rachel Bindman, Loretta Fox, and Howard Pollack. And I remain grateful, for the fostering of my early interest in musicals both within my parents' home and without, to my siblings, parents, friends, and especially Ken Sherwood and Doug Fosse. To all of these, and to those many I have forgotten to mention, I am profoundly grateful, but to no one more than to my wife, Ahuva Braverman, whose psychological insights and occasional operatic offerings have probably had as much to do with the issues and concerns of this book as anyone else's.

About the Frontispiece

The collage presents a quartet of musical-based identities, each in its way celebrating the freedoms and opportunities promised by the Statue of Liberty (background):

1. immigrant Frank-N-Furter, late of Transsexual, Transylvania (Tim Curry, *The Rocky Horror Show*, left; photograph courtesy of Miles Kreuger and the Institute of the American Musical, Inc.);
2. Dorothy Gale, as a young Kansas girl before she became the heroic liberator of the Land of Oz (Judy Garland, *The Wizard of Oz*, bottom; movie still courtesy of Miles Kreuger and the Institute of the American Musical, Inc.);
3. fellow liberator Sir Percy Blakeney, inspiring prospective recruits for the League of the Scarlet Pimpernel with "Into the Fire" (Douglas Sills, *The Scarlet Pimpernel*, top; photograph © Joan Marcus, used with permission); and

4. dance hall hostess Charity Hope Valentine, who is still pursuing an elusive happiness (Gwen Verdon, *Sweet Charity*, right; publicity photograph, Billy Rose Theatre Division, the New York Public Library for the Performing Arts, Astor, Lenox and Tilden Foundations).

(Collage design by Jonathan Hofferman.)

THE AMERICAN MUSICAL

AND THE PERFORMANCE OF PERSONAL IDENTITY

ENTR'ACTE

THIS IS THE SECOND VOLUME of my two-part thematic history of the American musical. Subdividing my subject in this way has allowed me to treat with approximately equal weight both the work the American musical has done in helping Americans shape their collective identity (volume 1)[1] and the role it has played for many people, whether Americans or not, as they develop and perform their own personal identities (volume 2). But this deceptively simple structure cloaks an important difference between these two thematic emphases. As categories, "national identity" and "personal identity" tend in opposite directions, the former toward a single, relatively stable abstraction, and the latter toward a multiplicity of possibilities expressed and experienced in more concrete terms. Moreover, that multiplicity of possibilities operates on a multiplicity of levels as well, not only mapping out inner self and outer persona, but also helping to negotiate, within a dynamic of reciprocal influence, the sometimes treacherous terrain that lies between these two frontiers. In tracing the ways the American musical has contributed to personal identity formation, the present volume thus undertakes a more complex task than its predecessor. Nevertheless, as with the first volume, I have found it useful to structure the book in two unequal spans, the first laying out specific generic types that have been central both to the development of the genre and to its furthering of the larger thematic category, and the second (and larger) span exploring a broadly scaled range of more specific themes, considered individually. My principal task in this "Entr'acte" will be to lay out the rationale for this approach and for its specific components and ordering.

The American Musical reached what may fairly be termed its first maturity near the beginning of the twentieth century. Most notable among the events that marked this arrival were the emergence of the first auteur of the American musical, George M. Cohan, and the beginning of a series of fitful attempts to displace the blackface minstrel tradition with something more directly representative of African American life, music, and characteristic modes of theatrical performance. Neither of these events may be construed as definitive, however. Minstrelsy maintained a strong presence in some areas of the country until the civil rights movement of the 1960s and even beyond, and its imprint continues to be felt in the persistence of its stereotypes and attitudes. Moreover, most early landmarks in the establishment of a viable black presence and sensibility in the American musical initially had little effect on the mainstream development of the genre, and even when blacks emerged more forcefully several decades later, most notably with *Show Boat* (1927) and a variety of projects in the 1930s and into the 1940s, it was mainly under the oversight of existing mainstream white control.[2] For his part, Cohan—important as he may have been—was scarcely the first to present a successful series of shows written and composed primarily by their lead performer(s);[3] moreover, his shows have not remained in the repertory, nor did he prove to be a model for later Broadway auteurs, who generally worked in teams. Indeed, as first maturities go, turn-of-the-century American musical theater seems particularly unrewarding of extensive study within a general history of the genre, since its most important legacy consists of the many memorable songs it introduced, which have long since been merged into a more general category of American popular song.

Nevertheless, both the emergent presence of black Americans and Cohan's string of successes represent important milestones along the path to maturity. Each development in its way is a strong indicator of the genre's coming of age, demonstrating that at least some of those involved were taking the measure of its past and established habits, and striving energetically to alter its course of development. True, the American musical would accumulate many such critical moments in its later history, moments of reappraisal and renewal, with resultant paradigmatic shifts that have left a more secure legacy of enduring works behind them than did this historical moment. Yet, with the first full emergence of blacks into mainstream venues, the biggest blemish in American theatrical history was at last being addressed—even if that blemish stubbornly refused to fade except by increments, its nature and extent could thereafter no longer be so easily ignored. And Cohan's shows marked another kind of arrival, as his combination of a specifically American sensibility with more careful attention to the integration of story and song managed to both Americanize and elevate the blend of German *Singspiel*, French and English operetta, English music hall, and American variety and/or extravaganza that had become standard fare on Broadway. If Cohan did not exactly change the ingredients, nor even appreciably alter the blend, he did demonstrate the potential for bringing these diverse types into line behind a more definitively American manner of storytelling, and demonstrated as well the potential for making good money while doing so.

In my first volume, I traced some of the antecedents to this "first maturity" and followed several strands of nationalist and related race-based themes as they were developed in American musicals across the twentieth century. Significantly, the specific markers that I identify here for the genre's level of maturation approximately one century ago—racial embodiment and Cohan's Americanization of the musical stage—were core to that book's structure and focus. Here, however, what is most important is the generic arrival itself, for it marks a point from which we must begin noting tributary influences that make a substantial impact on an existing type, rather than formative influences affecting the development of a still-embryonic genre (cf. the "models and topics" discussed in chapter 2 of the first volume). In part 1 of the present book, I will consider two of these later influences—Viennese operetta and film musicals—as each charts its own path of development, both separate from and somewhat coextensive with that of the American musical.

The American musical, as it took shape in the early twentieth century, was in core ways specifically Americanist and thus concerned with collective identity-formation. Given this early emphasis, one may most easily gauge the influential strength of operetta and film musicals by noting how, in the main, they effectively shift the focus of the musical toward the personal and away from larger political issues. Often closely coordinated with this shift toward the personal is the developing focus in musicals on exploring different kinds of identities and relationships, already a growing trend by the time of its first maturity. Consequently, Viennese operetta and film musicals figure profoundly in what will be the main focus of the book, the four separate "Personal Themes" of part 2, and may, at least through this lens, be themselves understood as "Personal Genres."

At issue with both operetta and film musicals are important distinctions of genre and venue, which raise the question of whether these types should, in the broader view, simply be absorbed into a larger conceptualization of the American musical or set apart as closely related but separate genres. Both alternatives make a great deal of sense, which is a good indicator that it is more useful to ask the question than to attempt a definitive answer. In this book, I will take the fairly pragmatic approach of posing the question of genre separation at key moments, but leaving it mostly unanswered, in part so as to reserve the possibility of considering these generic types almost as themes in themselves, each with a legitimate place within my thematic history of the American musical. My wish to consider these tributary genres together within the broadened rubric of the American musical—even when the basis for distinguishing among them seems the most clear-cut, as with staged and filmed musicals—rests on the observation that these different types offer their substantially overlapping audiences alternative versions of the same things. From this perspective, film musicals must be considered together with staged musicals rather than placed to the side, however entrenched the latter convention might be. Accordingly, in the later stages of the book, beginning with part 2, I will move fairly freely between the two; likewise, I will note operetta's influence without insisting that such influences mark generic ruptures.

Viennese operetta and the film musical exerted important influences over the development of the American musical theater, but those influences were very different in kind and arose from different points of origin. Viennese operetta made its most intense impact almost concurrently with Cohan's emergence as a major force on Broadway, and we may usefully characterize its influence as a long series of reverberations set off by the one great American success of Franz Lehár, *The Merry Widow* (1905, 1907 in New York). As a foil to Cohan's brash Americanism, Viennese operetta offered a world of sexuality and intrigue (aka romance), cloaked in modes of playful nuance and buoyed by the lilt of frothy orchestrations and dance idioms, that nevertheless often served serious themes. Viennese operetta's foreign point of origin was never altogether forgotten even as the type was adapted to American subjects; indeed, its admixture of Old-World styles and sensibilities was central to its charm. Movies, however, were decidedly American and seemingly determined from the start of the sound era either to extend the purview of staged musical theater or to partly displace it, depending on one's point of view. The symbiotic relationship between the two venues has sometimes been one of fierce rivalry, sometimes of frank emulation (in both directions), and sometimes of pretended indifference—all to be expected, considering that one of the principal motivations for developing and working with the cumbersome equipment needed for synchronized sound in its early stages was the desire to preserve (and, of course, market) staged musical performances.

These two externally constituted influences on the American musical may be contrasted with a third influence to be addressed in the epilogue of this book: operatic ambition. The ambition to make something loftier of the American musical, often codified as the desire to create an American version of European opera,[4] was largely an internally generated quest, driven by ambitions of the genre's practitioners and the exhortations of a variety of kibitzers, including both reviewers and the self-appointed guardians of high culture. This ambition has a long but largely subterranean history across the twentieth century, emerging occasionally to exert a strong influence on the genre's evolution. Notable at such emergent moments were those shows that coupled this ambition with important and difficult topics, as with such race-themed shows as *Porgy and Bess* (1935) and *West Side Story* (1957), each discussed under the rubric of "Race and Ethnicity" in the first volume. Yet, as we will see in chapter 7 ("Operatic Ambitions and Beyond"), racially charged subjects were scarcely the only spur for this line of development.

Accompanying these three generic influences, in addition to the more direct impact each had on the development of the mainstream tradition of staged musicals, was a significant interactive dynamic with the other two. Operatic ambitions, for example, were fed both by operetta's gesture toward something a little grander and more redolent of European sensibilities and by film's more negative example, which inspired some to try to widen the gap of sensibilities they perceived between stage and screen. But the field of interaction was more complex than even this dynamic suggests. The most important shows stemming from the aspiration toward American opera were, with few exceptions, neither particularly like operetta, despite its upwardly mobile impulse, nor removed from the possibility of emulating filmic realism, whatever the latter's role as a more negative spur. Nor did the development of narrative film in the direction of naturalistic realism distract attention from the possibilities, in film, of exploring and exploiting increasingly unrealistic modes of musical representation, and this dimension was pursued aggressively not only in specifically filmic ways but also in a hugely successful revival of the American operetta tradition, on film, beginning in the 1930s. This revival both fed immediate interest in the genre and reinforced a nostalgic perspective on it, thereby ensuring that operetta's impact on staged musicals would remain vital, if neither central nor in any way definitive. Indeed, given this film-driven renaissance of operetta and the longer trajectory of influence that it helped to maintain, it will prove instructive in the first chapter to consider not only *The Merry Widow* and a fairly early imitation of the style, but also these later filmic repercussions (if more briefly), along with referential returns to the style still later in the twentieth century in both comic and more serious contexts.[5]

All three of these influences tended to increase the perceived level of artificiality in American musical theater, even allowing for their frequently fostering an enhanced realism in at least some dimension, as well. Again, however, there were significant differences in the *mode* of artificiality among the three. Operetta tended to pull away from what seemed "natural" to Americans— that was largely the basis for the genre's American success, after all—and it did this in several ways. Stylistically, it departed from more obviously American types and encouraged a more performance-based (operatic) musical style, the kind of "putting on airs" that American popular song has often aimed to displace. To the extent that operetta evoked earlier sentimental traditions (for example, the nineteenth-century parlor song), it would have seemed both reassuring and quaintly nostalgic already in the first decade of the twentieth century. But it also encouraged an interesting stylistic confrontation, since the Viennese waltz idiom in particular was both very familiar and oddly different from the American type. The Viennese rhythmic device of slightly anticipating the first of the two offbeats in the characteristic accompaniment pattern, especially as combined with its more flexible approach to tempo more generally and its lingering over arrival points through the exaggerated use of the *Luftpause* (hold), produced a dynamic lilting effect with a strong whiff of sexuality absent in the more mechanical American idiom, where the accompaniment tended toward a more even oom-pah-pah pattern.[6]

The impulse toward opera, like Viennese operetta, resulted in considerably higher demands being placed on singers, even when the basic idiom remained both "popular" and "American." More signally artificial in opera, however, was the convention of recitative, of singing not only songs but also dialogue, in a plainer, less songlike (but often more overtly dramatic) fashion. This had already become a frequent feature of the English operetta tradition (that is, Gilbert and Sullivan) and its American derivatives, where it was sometimes employed to heighten the drama or evoke the urgency of melodrama, but was more often deployed for comic effect precisely because of its perceived artificiality (e.g., Buttercup's entrance in *Pinafore*, discussed in chapter 2 of the previous volume, pp. 40–41). The dual potential, in the speculative genre of American opera, for recitative to become a dangerous flirtation with comedy on the one hand and an enrichment of the musical fabric on the other was obvious. That the seriousness of *Porgy and Bess* manages to keep its "unnatural" recitative from seeming overtly funny to most audiences may help explain why such serious topics seemed almost to be a prerequisite for operatic success on the American musical stage. But there was a reverse side to that coin, too, since *Pinafore* and other shows that used recitative for comic effect thereby also enhanced their musical profiles by involving music more often and with a greater range of styles, arranged hierarchically. Thus, recitatives—even comic ones—set the songs they introduce in higher relief, while using their own artificiality to divert attention from the more basic artificiality of bursting into song at all.

In employing more elaborate vocal styles, both operetta and operatic musicals drew important emphasis to the performative dimension of the musical, a dimension that was also brought into greater relief, albeit somewhat differently, in film musicals. In film, the artificiality of song and dance was often placed against a more naturalistic setting than the stage could provide, which helped open up an interpretive space for camp and other related strategies of layered interpretation in both performance and reception, so that one and the same artifact could serve two seemingly very different theatrical modes. The most salient enabling feature in film, in this regard, is our increased awareness of the performer *as performer*, rather than as the character being portrayed. The camera's often loving engagement with the performer as a moving body or singing head, seen from a variety of angles, made of the performer in a film musical a literally larger-than-life icon, foregrounded against an often irrelevant dramatic background—a dimension of musical films that was often all the more exaggerated in musical numbers so as to provide more visual excitement during an extended moment when the dramatic action otherwise seems to stop.

Also contributing to the effect of artificiality was a particularly problematic dimension of the film musical: the difficulties in welding musical sound to moving image. While many who watch film musicals either do not notice or have learned to ignore the awkward artificialities that result from trying to match action to prerecorded sound (or, more rarely in sung musical numbers, overdubbing music to an already filmed scene), the artificiality must surely register on some level for nearly all listeners, given the sheer variety of ways in which musical numbers in films can seem artificial. Thus, most viewers will be aware of poor lip-synching, whether occasional or pervasive, and many will also note (often with some amusement, especially in the wake of Mel Brooks's 1974 *Blazing Saddles*) the obvious visual absence of the orchestra we are hearing.[7] Still others might notice some aspect of improbability in the joining of audio to visual, as, for example, when evident vocal strain does not have a visual corelative or when another actor's voice is used. A more subtle disparity, painfully obvious to many even if it does not register for others, occurs when music recorded in a closed acoustical space is matched to an outdoor setting. And so on; the aggregate of these markers of artificiality, perhaps even the mere knowledge of them, highlights the evident fact—easily forgotten during those parts of a film when it seems merely to record what comes before its camera and microphone—that a filmed musical number is *constructed*, and therefore does not qualify fully as *authentic*, that is, as a faithful record of a human performance, based in experienced emotions resonant with the surrounding dramatic sequence.

As I discussed in the introductory chapter of the first volume, the addition of music to spoken drama does not simply heighten emotions. Rather, it also imposes a kind of mask that both conceals and calls attention to the performer behind the persona; in film, for the reasons given, this kind of artificiality is all the more evident. Whereas in staged musicals an audience may pretend through the convention of "suspending disbelief" not to notice how artificially the emotional level suddenly shifts through song into a higher gear, film makes this convention harder to adhere to. Film musicals, even more readily than stage musicals, generate a kind of expressive double image, in which a heightened sense of reality is enacted through the brazenly artificial, making the film musical a particularly ripe arena for camp (a capacity that is greatly enhanced by the opportunity, especially with the technologies developed in recent decades, to view performances in film many times over).

Camp, understood broadly, always involves exaggeration and an expressive lack of proportion, either through investing enormous expressive energy in the seemingly trivial or by seeming to trivialize the most serious of subjects. (This is true whether or not we view camp through the particular lens of gay subculture, where it has become most fully developed as an interpretive and communicative mode.)[8] The dimension of camp may accrue to dramatic presentation through intention (as a matter of performance) or through modes of reception, or both; film, in particular, permits an easier separation between the performance and reception of camp, although performers' intentions are not always easy to read. To some extent, all musicals, whether on stage or in film, become camp the moment they become *musical*, for the first notes that sound under the dialogue are like a set of arched eyebrows serving as quotation marks around whatever is ostensibly being expressed, whether musically or dramatically. In film, where music often serves as part of an unnoticed background, this particular effect may be muted, but the larger effect of performed artificiality is much greater; in either venue, the element of camp shifts sudden attention to the performed nature of the drama. But if, as I noted in the introduction to the first volume, camp thus calls into question the specific content of what is being performed through this use of expressive quotation marks, it is also capable of standing back to reveal that those quotation marks are themselves set off in quotation marks, allowing us to reconnect with the content, but at a much higher emotional pitch than could have been achieved otherwise. In this way, camp can revert to a more normally accepted mode of performance, in which it serves primarily as a vehicle, a realization and embodiment of specific aesthetic content. And the manipulation of the performer's mask gives us in the audience access and permission: access to a heightened emotionality and permission either to feel the moment more deeply or to laugh at it—or, somehow, to do both at once, in which case we are also laughing at and with ourselves and, perhaps, more fully embracing our humanity.

Within the traditions and conventions of the American musical—and in this sense I include film, operetta, and the operatic musical—the potentialities of camp are often invisible to large segments of the audience, who have no difficulty accepting, as background, the convention of actors launching into song at a moment's notice and, indeed, will wait with some degree of impatience if this does not happen fairly regularly. Moreover, so as to encourage this acceptance, the writers, director, and actors often go to imaginative lengths to make the transition to singing seem as natural as possible, to weld inevitable exaggeration to its dramatic moment as securely as they can— and thus, seemingly, to move as far away from camp as possible. Yet the mechanisms of camp are always present. No one thinks for a moment that singing happens, fundamentally, for any reason other than that in musicals people sing as well as talk; the resulting artificiality may be generic, but that does not make it natural. And, however more "natural" the result would be, few who attend musicals would prefer *not* to have song when it is called for, even if sometimes a good effect can be achieved by delaying (but rarely altogether withholding) the inevitable song. In a curious way, audiences not only relish the heightened dramatic effect that song can create but also seem to need the comforting artificiality that comes with it. Through precisely the same mechanisms that operate in camp, the inherent exaggeration of interpolated song allows audiences to experience more deeply the dramatic situation and characters on stage and screen because music, singing, and often dancing decisively remove that situation from anything even remotely like the real world. Artificiality thus provides essential protection from the dangerous, potentially destructive effect of emotions felt too deeply.

How this dimension of the musical is enhanced and fostered by the added artificialities of operetta and film may be seen most vividly in what is probably the most intense conflation of the two: the filmed versions of operetta in the 1930s and 1940s. For the most part, these film versions were played (and taken) very seriously, so that their pretensions to an operatic dimension were actively encouraged in a variety of ways. In reception and over the years, however, alongside this more serious mode of reception, an alternative viewing mode developed, which understood this generation of operettas revived on film as pure camp.[9] Nelson Eddy's earnestly wooden acting makes him a perfect foil for this receptive mode, but it is really the diva aspect of Jeanette MacDonald's bravura performances (even when—or, perhaps, especially when—her vocal equipment is not fully up to the task) that provides the most important payoffs, precisely because her performance "works" much better than Eddy's within a straight reading. What seems key to these films' fitting comfortably within both straight and camp viewing environments is the very fragility of MacDonald's performance, the nervy way that she takes her quasi-operatic delivery into places where it simply doesn't belong, whether that place is construed as the specific locale in the film's world or as the inauthentic world of filmed musical numbers more generally. In dramatic terms, the signal effect is at least partly one of personal courage, merging the personae of MacDonald and the character she plays more firmly. Yet, from a camp perspective, the function of that courage is in part to sustain the fragile structure of the musical in question, with all its delicious inadequacies, and in part to give access to a somewhat different dimension of ecstatic exaggeration. In the latter, the brazenly artificial suddenly becomes very real indeed, a sustaining, life-giving force attainable only through a process of abjection, through which inadequacies of performance come into sharp focus and then become, at the same time, both irrelevant as such and vital tokens of human aspiration.

The camp dimension of musicals, in different ways enhanced by both operetta and film, may itself be better understood as a separate "personal theme" closely allied to those taken up in part 2, in the sense that it provides a mode of embodiment that may be partaken of widely by performers and audiences alike. Musicals have proven to have an extraordinary capacity to overlap significantly with the lives and souls of their various constituencies, who learn to express themselves, to act, to conceive of themselves and the world around them, and often even to *be* themselves more fully and affirmatively by following their rhythms, living out versions of their plots, and singing their songs. But engaging with this capacity obliquely—that is, through camp, which ostensibly denies the value of whatever content it advances even as it finds that content infinitely nourishing—is only one possibility.

For many constituencies, the most valuable dimension of American musicals is what they provide, permit, and facilitate on a personal level. As I put it in the final chapter of the first volume (which served in part to anticipate and introduce this volume):

> American musicals—through their characters, stories, and songs; through the memorable performance of those characters, stories, and songs by charismatic stars; and through the varied ways and degrees to which wider populations merge with those characters, live out their stories, and sing or move to their songs—have given people, in a visceral way, a sense of what it *feels* like to embody whatever alternatives that musicals might offer to their own life circumstances and choices. On a surface level, singing (or, perhaps, lip-synching) the songs from a musical can be empowering, providing a sense of what being a Broadway star might be like. But this kind of reinforcement and projected embodiment reaches much deeper than celebrity identification, engaging on the most fundamental level with what it means to be *human*. On this level, American musicals teach people in powerful ways what and whom to care about, and how to go about caring about them. And they teach these things all the more effectively for giving audiences the opportunity to experience— almost, to taste—what it is like to do so.[10]

Part 2 considers separately four personal themes advanced by American musicals. The first two, "Fairy Tales and Fantasy" and "Idealism and Inspiration," are easily related themes that point mainly in opposite directions, respectively to child and adult orientations, and to filmic and staged worlds. The first of these themes draws significantly on the filmic resurrection of Viennese operetta, whose escapist fantasies were often reoriented toward a younger generation as they were brought to film, opening up another expressive duality in addition to the camp-straight receptive modes already discussed: the contrasting but coexisting receptive modes of child and adult. Idealism, however, points more broadly to questions of aspirational ambition within the development of the musical; thus, the concerns in this chapter point ahead to those of the epilogue ("Operatic Ambitions"), since both, especially in the second half of the century, attempt not only to lay claim to cultural prestige but also to deepen the treatment of important subjects in musicals from within the tradition.

The final two themes, "Gender and Sexuality" and "Relationships," represent a two-step approach to one of the most vital contributions that American musicals have made to those whose lives they have affected, through their routine engagement with the formation of problematic romantic relationships. In the first volume, my focus was directed mainly outward, to the larger problems that these romantic relationships often point to. There I invoked the "marriage trope" to explain how musicals have embedded larger issues within their lead characters, so that the success or failure of their personal relationship(s) might serve as a marker for the resolution or continuation of conflicts between larger antagonistic forces.[11] Within this paradigm, relationships provide a readily adaptable dramatic "surface" for musicals, with marriage standing allegorically for the resolution of seemingly incompatible peoples or ideas into a stabilized partnership. The trajectory of a successful if rocky courtship provides a convenient vehicle for larger themes, replete with standardized modes of expression and the firm expectation of successful resolution, since optimistic comedies have long been the mainstay of the American musical.

Yet, successful musicals are always first and foremost about the characters on the stage or screen, and for most people who are drawn to the genre, those characters are what matter on a personal level. Thus, the familiarity of the marriage trope should not obscure the fact that musicals also directly model relational behavior, even if they may sometimes seem to be "really" about something else. In this realm, musicals often reveal possibilities that echo, extend, and shape our existing attitudes and prejudices about the risks and possibilities of human connection. My final theme, "Relationships," will therefore revisit more directly one of the most frequently encountered stratagems of the American musical in order to consider it at face value; thus, to play off the Freudian bon mot ("sometimes a cigar is just a cigar"), I will consider the possibility that sometimes in musicals sex is just sex, and a relationship is just a relationship. Because the sexual-societal configuration of the individuals involved is basic to the very possibility of relationships, I will first discuss, in the penultimate theme, the extraordinarily rich capacity of musicals for exploring the multifaceted thickets of "Gender and Sexuality."

These two themes bear the strong imprint of the "Personal Genres" considered in part 1. Operetta as a type—and especially Viennese operetta—in a curious way already represents an inversion of the marriage trope, frequently taking political situations and revealing that, after all, it is indeed "really" the personal relationships that count. Even in the highly politicized *H.M.S. Pinafore* (discussed in chapter 2 of the first volume), it is the preordained alignment of the couples that compels our acceptance of the absurd denouement. What Viennese operetta, more particularly, provides for the final theme of part 2 is a high degree of nuance, grounded specifically within musical discourse, through which we might observe the subtle ways in which relationships take shape, develop and blossom, and sometimes fail. And although musicals have always modeled gender roles and helped define sexuality, the growing wider awareness in recent decades of how diverse this realm of human development actually is, *by nature* on the one hand and *by construction* on the other, has made film musicals, with their enhanced artificialities, an increasingly potent site for their fuller exploration. In this respect, camp, both because of its close association with male homosexuality—the touchstone and flash point for considerations of sexual alternativity—and because of its established modes for emphasizing the constructedness of personae, will provide, especially in connection with film, a particularly useful focal point.

But these two themes also provide part of a larger frame, echoing in reverse order the first themes I considered in the first volume: "Defining America" (subdivided there into "Whose (Who's) America?" "American Mythologies," and "Countermythologies") and "Race and Ethnicity." Specifically, the latter two themes also explored the ways that musicals have considered questions of interpersonal relationships and identity, but on the level of politics and within a specific social-historical context. Here again, the marriage trope provides a useful pivot between the two perspectives, since it operates as just such a pivot within individual shows, allowing us to shift easily between personal and larger issues and concerns. Importantly, however, the primary focus shifts dramatically as we move from considering a background, group identity, to considering more closely the individuals occupying the foreground. Although race and ethnicity will continue to matter here in our consideration of personal identity, they take a decidedly secondary position relative to the primary focus on "Gender and Sexuality."

———————

In the introductory chapter of the first volume, I considered at some length the paired issues of what, precisely, the American musical *is*, and how and why it ought to be considered an important object of study. There, I compared the American musical to jazz and American film, art forms with a similar trajectory and intertwined histories, while acknowledging that these art forms are also profoundly different from each other, because they refer, respectively, to a genre, a style, and a medium. My basic working definition for the American musical remains much the same: I am here, as there, most interested in the tradition of theatrical presentation that evolved by the third decade of the twentieth century into the semblance of an original, integrated artwork intended for a specifically American audience, involving both naturalistic spoken drama and some combination of singing and dancing. As already indicated, and as will be clear from my choice of specific musicals, however, the thematic basis of this volume has made it imperative that I broaden the scope of this definition from its implicit basis onstage to include film and, on one occasion, television. Thus, the present volume provides me with the opportunity to consider more fully some of the concerns I raised near the end of my earlier introduction, regarding the interaction of the staged American musical with other related traditions (particularly in part 1), and most particularly the problematic relationship between film and stage.

Although my focus has shifted, my approach will in many respects be quite similar, especially regarding the materials of study and the emphasis I give to the musical dimension of the shows I discuss. As I noted in the first introduction, American stage musicals have left us many and various traces, which typically include the written music and book, and various preserved traces of particular performances, ranging from films and videos, to "original cast" or "soundtrack" recordings, to still photographs, to similar traces of later performances and revivals, to anecdotal accounts of the show in preparation or performance, to arrangements and recordings made separately of songs from a show. Whereas film musicals may be definitive artifacts, for stage musicals no one component in this mix is necessarily privileged over the others. The central artifacts of stage musicals are the book and score on the one hand and show-based audio and video recordings on the other; while each is authoritative in some way, however, they represent either side of the work-performance divide. Moreover, our experience of the show through its recorded artifacts, however immediately felt, is heavily mediated by the mechanical aspects of camera and microphone placement, by the montage and mixing of the results, and more fundamentally by the sensibilities of those who are more or less self-consciously "documenting" the work, or trying to compensate for media-based shortcomings by adding explanatory words and sound effects (in sound recording) or by cutting to focus on significant detail or to introduce perspectives not available to a live audience (in film or videotape). More fundamentally, these artifacts *do not change* (except to deteriorate);[12] the more we hear or see them, the less they are *a performance* and the more they become—as with film musicals—*the work* with which we are concerned.

We must, of course, depend heavily on those things we can study—book, score, films, recordings, and so on.[13] For this book, as for the first volume, I am effectively limited, in discussions of individual musicals, to referring to the written record and to readily available documented performances. As there, I will be fairly circumspect in my references even to the score and will most often give descriptive accounts that may be verified through listening, while occasionally providing a clarifying excerpt from the score for those readers who do read music. Above all, with regard to stage musicals, our dependence on the concrete as a basis for discussing something much more fluid and ephemeral must be acknowledged up front and reaffirmed as we go along.

Finally, because this book, like the first volume, is designed so that it might serve as a textbook, it is important to underscore one of the basic strategies in my presentation: to provide a rather fuller slate of musicals as exemplars of my chosen themes than might be practical to teach in a single course, particularly if that course deals with more themes than are included here. In this, I am mindful of many contexts and needs, as well as a pitfall or two. For the instructor, I wish to include a fair range of choice regarding which musicals to focus on and to leave some room for further elaboration; I expect that only some of the musicals I have selected will be studied in any given course, and hope that I have included most of those that a given instructor might find essential to a course dealing with personal themes in the American musical. For the student, I wish both to provide some discussion of musicals that she or he might wish to study beyond what a particular course can usefully include and to indicate how the various themes being studied are worked out in musicals other than those taught in that course. For the independent reader, I wish simply to provide as full and wide-ranging an account as is practical in this format. And to all I apologize for leaving out many a favorite musical or song and for focusing more obsessively on what I consider central issues at the expense of what might well be the lifeblood of the tradition for particular readers and approaches, such as the intriguing lives and individual achievements of its many colorful practitioners. But regarding the latter, I may say with some assurance that readers who care deeply about those aspects do not probably need me to tell them more (but in case they do, I have provided an extensive bibliography); moreover, it is these readers who may potentially benefit most from this attempt to provide a richer context for what they already know.

Part One

PERSONAL GENRES

The Viennese Connection

Franz Lehár and American Operetta

THE AMERICAN MUSICAL has sometimes been understood as the American answer to European operetta, or as an extension of the European tradition. A good case for these and similar claims is easy enough to make, given the impact of Gilbert and Sullivan on late nineteenth-century American musical comedy and of Franz Lehár a few decades later. Moreover, the case need not be overwhelming in order to be fairly convincing. Thus, divergences from these formative influences may be readily accounted for; after all, important differences also evolved between and among the principal European forms, so that one might simply argue that Americans, like their European predecessors, evolved their own distinct type of operetta, according to local tastes and interests. Or, to summarize the scenario that Gerald Bordman argues for, one might trace how an American type of musical comedy has been periodically enriched by returns to its European models, with Rodgers and Hammerstein, in particular, representing one of the most vigorous of these later returns, if seldom recognized as such.[1]

But it is just as easy to argue the other side of this issue. European operetta was largely a reaction against more serious operatic traditions, which by mid-nineteenth century had evolved into something quite serious indeed in the three main traditions that then flourished: Italian and German romantic opera, Wagnerian *Musikdrama*, and French grand opera. America had no comparable tradition to react against, although many attempted, often with some success, to transplant these European traditions to America, so that European opera did in fact provide a frequent foil for humor on the American musical stage. But in the main, American musicals took shape, as a genre, within a context almost diametrically opposed to the European situation. Instead of reacting against a thriving higher tradition—opera—they quite often strove to elevate an already "low" tradition into something more elevated, if not fully operatic. Regarding Viennese operetta in particular, American reception seemed oddly dissonant with European reception, even if both sides of the Atlantic came to an enthusiastic accord over *The Merry Widow* (1905, 1907 in London and New York). Thus, although Americans embraced the Gilbert and Sullivan operettas as (almost) their own—and here we might well remember that England also had no native high-art operatic tradition of any consequence—they did not similarly embrace either the French or the Viennese operetta traditions in the nineteenth century. Moreover, when they did respond enthusiastically to *The Merry Widow*, it was largely because of the show's greater sophistication relative to American fare, and not merely because of the escapist fun that the show offered (which was the basis of its appeal in Europe, in retrospect already well on its way to the cataclysm of World War I, a cataclysm that was first of all Vienna's).

This greater sophistication had a number of facets, all of them easily associated with Europe. Musically, the show was deftly realized by Franz Lehár, a trained composer who had tried his hand at opera (if unsuccessfully) and had already composed popular waltzes and achieved mixed success with a handful of operettas before *Die lustige Witwe* (*The Merry Widow*) became the most widely performed operetta ever, playing across Europe with huge success before it was brought to America. But musical sophistication was only part of what *The Merry Widow* had to offer, for its story of sexual and political intrigue was presented with both frankness and a suave grace rich in nuance, with the latter serving to partly deflect the former, offering a face-saving interpretive strategy of deniability about just how much (if any) illicit sex the audience was supposed to be winking at. This blend of a frankly acknowledged sexuality with modes of graceful deflection became an important topic for Americans, who sometimes referred to it as "worldly" or "sophisticated," but often enough located its origin more specifically, with descriptive terms such as "European," "continental" (thus, as opposed to the presumably more respectable British), "Parisian," or "Viennese"—the latter two referring to the setting and original venue of *The Merry Widow*, respectively.

This one signal success of Viennese operetta in America set off a long series of reverberations across the twentieth century, first in the spate of American offshoots that followed it (even if few other Viennese shows, including Lehár's, had much success in America). But this initial wave of enthusiasm was short-lived. Many blame World War I for the sudden lapse in America's enthusiasm for Viennese operetta so soon after *The Merry Widow*'s American success; Vienna was, after all, the seat of the Austro-Hungarian Empire, the referential flashpoint—and our eventual enemy—in the Great War, as it was then called. But the genre did not simply disappear, as the leading American practitioners—Rudolf Friml and Sigmund Romberg—continued to have great success throughout the 1920s, with their authenticity seemingly guaranteed by their names (although Friml was born in Prague, and Romberg, like Lehár, in Hungary; Victor Herbert, their prominent older colleague who died in 1924, was born in Dublin but raised—and trained—in Germany).[2] When synchronized sound made film musicals a practicality by the 1930s, operettas provided a rich body of source material, particularly since—however daring they might once have seemed—they had by then acquired an important patina of respectability, with their music being generally viewed as more elevated, and stemming from a more reputable tradition, than more "American" jazz-influenced styles.[3] Many important operettas from earlier in the century were filmed, often substantially altered, several with Jeanette MacDonald (with still others being refashioned as vehicles for the child actress Shirley Temple). As color became more standard after World War II and into the 1950s, a new wave of film musicals included another large dose of revived operettas, most often with newly revised plots. Alongside this development, television provided yet another venue for keeping early works in the genre before a wide public, if often drastically cut.

The operettas I've chosen for the first part of this chapter reflect this history fairly well. *The Merry Widow* was filmed with a vastly reworked plot by Ernst Lubitsch in 1934, with Jeanette MacDonald and Maurice Chevalier,[4] and was filmed again in 1952, similarly unrecognizable in its refashioned plot and spare use of songs from the original; a live television version of the show was broadcast in 1958. *Naughty Marietta*, the most important of the early American operettas that followed *The Merry Widow*, was filmed with Jeanette MacDonald one year after she starred in Lubitsch's *The Merry Widow* and was broadcast live on television in 1955. (For other representative film versions from the 1930s and 1940s, and "second-wave" revivals as color films and in televised versions from the 1950s, see the list at the end of this chapter.)

The quaintness of both these live televised performances and the lavish MGM operetta films of the 1950s inspired the hugely successful off-Broadway parody-operetta *Little Mary Sunshine* (1959), which makes many specific references to *Naughty Marietta* and other well-known operettas (including, most prominently, the 1924 *Rose-Marie*, filmed in 1936 and 1954). One may well argue that *Little Mary Sunshine*, in its affectionate campiness, was oblivious to the large dose of camp appeal already long recognized in the genre, but the show deftly struck a chord with audiences, who loved much of what operetta had to offer but winced at its dated sentimentality; it thus provides us with a useful gauge for assessing the devices and contrivances of operetta, as seen from the vantage point of the late 1950s. Certainly the success of the show confirms the separateness of the American musical from operetta by that stage of development. Indeed, for many who may not otherwise be familiar with the American operetta tradition, *Little Mary Sunshine*, enduringly popular in revival, is a surer point of reference than more traditional fare.

If *Little Mary Sunshine* refers mainly to the American operetta tradition—although, surely, the assonance between the titles *Little Mary Sunshine* and *The Merry Widow* is no accident—the older European tradition serves as the most useful background for considering Stephen Sondheim's *A Little Night Music* (1973), with its confrontation between Old-World sensibilities and modernity, and its dance-infused score. Besides completing a usefully symmetrical frame for this chapter, *A Little Night Music*, in its very title, manages both to refer obliquely to Vienna (specifically, to Mozart's *Eine kleine Nachtmusik*, composed in Vienna and often used emblematically, as "background music," to represent Vienna's rich musical past) and to complete a string of verbal assonances that might also include *Rose-Marie*; thus, *The **Merry** Widow–Naughty **Marietta*** (or, perhaps, "Naughty **Little Mary**"?)–*Rose-**Marie**–**Little Mary** Sunshine–A **Little** Night Music.* More-

over, the words that accompany this string independently articulate a sexually suggestive symmetry (especially remembering that Little Mary Sunshine,
among its many associations, refers to a particularly striking flower, a
bearded iris): *Widow–Naughty / Rose–Sunshine / Night Music.*

   The Merry Widow, as it was presented to American audiences in 1907, was performed with its songs in rhymed translation, with a
few minor cuts to its score, two interpolations of musical numbers in Act III
(added by Lehár himself; see the website for the complete English-language
song list), and some minor adjustments to its plot and comic byplay. In most
respects, the English adaptation by Adrian Ross (the one most often staged
in America, first performed in London earlier in 1907) is close enough to
the original that it will not be necessary here to draw a particularly sharp
differentiation between them, beyond noting a series of name changes and
occasionally observing other concessions made to its English-speaking audiences in London and New York. Inevitably, of course, something is lost in
translation, even with a fairly faithful adaptation such as this one, both because of the forced rhymes that such translations often produce (which, besides sounding quaint, also often result in an awkward fit between text and
music) and because it is difficult to know with any precision what, in musical
terms, would have seemed exaggerated and mannered about performance
styles in 1905 Vienna versus 1907 New York. To some extent, something of
The Merry Widow slips between the cracks that open between different levels of familiarity and perceived strangeness. Nevertheless, in the present context, Ross's adaptation of *The Merry Widow* may usefully be taken as *the*
representative of the Viennese tradition in America, for that is indeed how
it functioned historically.
   Because of the numerous versions of *The Merry Widow* that have since
proliferated on film, all of them with plots wildly different from that of the
original stage show, it will be useful to sketch the story here.[5] Although the
basic plotline remains much the same as in the Viennese original, Ross's
English adaptation makes a number of name changes, the most important
of which are as follows:

>   die lustige Witwe **Hanna Glawari** becomes the merry widow **Sonia Sadoya;**
>   the kingdom of **Pontevedro** becomes **Marsovia;**
>   **Baron Mirko Zeta** becomes **Baron Popoff;**
>   **Valencienne** (the baron's wife) becomes **Natalie;**
>   **Camille de Rosillon** (her lover) becomes **Camille de Jolidon;**
>   and **Count Danilo Danilowitsch** becomes **Prince Danilo.**[6]

   The entire action takes place in Paris, where Baron Zeta (Popoff), who is
afraid that the recently widowed Hanna's (Sonia's) fortune will be lost to
Pontevedro (Marsovia) if she is to remarry with a foreigner—with catastrophic results for the small kingdom—enlists the help of fellow countryman
Danilo, a notorious womanizer who was once romantically involved with

Hanna. Meanwhile, Zeta's own wife, Valencienne (Natalie), is conducting an affair with Camille, of which only the Baron seems ignorant; although Valencienne seems to be trying to break off the affair (or, perhaps, end it before it truly begins), her behavior can be interpreted as "playing hard to get." Danilo agrees to help keep Hanna from marrying a foreigner but refuses to court her himself, since, although he has long been in love with her, he feels betrayed by her, believing she married her late husband for his money; this is why (we are given to understand) he now habitually spends his free time at the Parisian nightclub Maxim's. Hanna also loves him, but knows she will have to finesse their oddly oblique courtship. She flirts with a number of suitors at a ball before choosing Danilo as her partner for a "Ladies' Choice" waltz number, only to be outraged when he offers to auction the dance off among her would-be suitors, all of whom abandon the field. The first act ends with a bare rapprochement between them, as eventually she joins him in dancing the "Ladies' Choice" waltz ("Oh, Come Away").

Act II begins with musical entertainments from Pontevedro hosted by Hanna, including characteristic dances and two parable-like folk songs, "Vilja" (or "Vilia") and "The Cavalier," both obviously resonant with the situation at hand, with the latter presented as a playful duet between Danilo and Hanna. In "Women," the men alternate celebrating and disparaging the opposite sex, ending in an all-male, cancan-inflected chorus line, after which Danilo and Hanna come together and dance to what is now known as "The Merry Widow Waltz." The progress of their rekindled relationship is disrupted, however, by the culmination of Camille's dalliance with Valencienne (the passionate duet, "Love in My Heart," concluding with their entering the pavilion together for a "farewell kiss"). When Zeta discovers his wife's apparent infidelity with Camille, Hanna rescues the situation by taking Valencienne's place and announcing her own engagement to Camille. Act II then ends with alternations of Hanna's description of a modern marriage of convenience ("In the Modern Style," or "In the Parisian Style," sung with the chorus) and another "parable song" ("The Prince and the Princess") delivered by a furious Danilo.

The third act is quite short if we do not count the standard interpolations, sometimes augmented with an extensive waltz ballet (reminiscent of the long-standing custom of interpolating the entire *Blue Danube Waltz* into Johann Strauss's *Die Fledermaus*). The setting is again Hanna's residence, now fashioned into a semblance of Maxim's (or the actual Maxim's, in the American version) and introduced by the "show girls" (Grisettes) led by a slumming Valencienne (in some performances by Hanna herself). After Hanna explains why she pretended to become engaged to Camille, Zeta, again convinced of his wife's infidelity, announces his intention to divorce her, offering to marry Hanna himself. Hanna then plays her trump card, announcing that, according to her late husband's will, she will lose her fortune if she remarries, which prompts Zeta and her other suitors to withdraw and Danilo to propose to her; as she accepts Danilo, she further explains that she loses her fortune only because it devolves to her husband. Danilo accepts this news with some resignation, but is content that he has proven he loves her and not her money, while she has proven her desire to wed for love rather than money. Resolution is nearly complete: Pontevedro is saved; Zeta and Valencienne reconcile; and Danilo, still unable to confess his love for Hanna in words, lets "The Merry Widow Waltz" say it for him.

The scenario and musical structures of *The Merry Widow* deftly lay out a number of landscapes, the subtleties of which are often lost when they are tampered with. We may usefully think of these interlocking landscapes on either a quasi-literal level, referring to actual political geographies, or a figurative level, mapping a terrain of public and personal lives and describing against that terrain contrasting trajectories of romantic intrigue.

The musical geography includes some fairly straightforward markers and a few contradictory ones. Vienna maintains a benign control over the whole even though it is nowhere to be seen, simply because all truly important events in the show are accompanied by waltzes, with many of the other dances borrowing the dynamic energy of the Viennese waltz, as well. Paris, the official setting, is well represented by the frequent galops performed in the raucous style of the cancan, often replete with cymbal crashes; the most obvious of these are at the very opening of the show and in the women's "Grisette" number in Act III, but the style also permeates the all-male show-stopper in the middle of Act II, "Women," and the "laughing" concluding section to Act II ("In the Modern Style").[7] Slightly trickier is the precise location of Pontevedro, whose name hints strongly at the often victimized country of Montenegro, one of the Balkan states located on the Adriatic Sea between Bosnia-Herzegovina (then part of the Austro-Hungarian Empire), Serbia, and Albania (the latter still under Turkish control in 1905) and absorbed after World War I into Yugoslavia. The change in name obliquely pokes affectionate fun at the lofty pretensions of such small countries by converting the imposing "Black Mountain" of "Montenegro" into the more homey image of "Cheerful Bridge." Much else in *The Merry Widow* points to an identification of Pontevedro with Montenegro, including the names of Baron Mirko Zeta, whose surname is the name of a river in Montenegro and an old name for Montenegro itself, and Danilo, who takes his name doubly from the first in the line of a later theocratic dynasty (Petrović, 1697–1851)[8] and from an especially important (and, in 1905, still fairly recent) Montenegrin prince (also Petrović) who effected a shift to a secular state. (The second Danilo—Danilo Danilowitsch?—ruled from 1852 to 1860, when he was assassinated; his older brother Mirko was a famed military strategist.)[9]

But the music associated with Pontevedro spreads out in a wide scatter shot across Eastern Europe, with strong doses of Polish, Czech, and Russian, along with a hint of Hungarian (or, perhaps, Gypsy) worked in. Thus, Hanna's opening number is a mazurka (a Polish folk dance);[10] Valencienne introduces Camille to Hanna as a potential suitor in the first-act finale with a

♪ 1.1
♪ 1.2
♪ 1.3

polka (a Czech dance with Polish associations); Act II begins with a polonaise to introduce the celebration of Pontevedro's heritage (the polonaise,
although Polish, has strong Russian associations, particularly when introduced with fanfares such as Lehár uses) and continues with a set of country
dances redolent of Hungary, Russia, or both at once, with generic "folk-
song" elements added to the mix, including both a lyrical "folk legend"
("Vilja") and its rustic counterpart ("The Cavalier"). Despite this rather   ♪1.4
wanton mix of types, however, what they sing during one of the dances is   ♪1.5
(in both the original and English-language versions) indeed Serbo-Croatian,   ♪1.6
the language of Montenegro: "Mi velimo dase veslimo! Hei a ho!" (in more   ♪1.7
standard spelling: "Mi volimo da se veselimo!"—roughly, "We like to make
merry!"). Moreover, the Russian cast to some of this music may easily be   ♪1.8
justified—indirectly, at least—by the fact that many Montenegrins have a
common heritage with the Baltic region of Russia.[11] And just before they
dance "The Merry Widow Waltz" later in the second act, Danilo and Hanna
dance a *kolo*, which they identify as the national dance of Pontevedro, and
which is indeed the most important dance type native to Montenegro, even
if it is just as important to other Balkan states, such as Croatia and Serbia.[12]   ♪1.9

It is important to note the orientalizing aspect of Lehár's musical strategy,
since what binds the music of Pontevedro together is its Eastern European
"otherness" in relation to Vienna (even recalling that Vienna is farther east
than Prague); also involved is a strong imperialist streak, which looks down
on the extreme vulnerability of (most of) the lands referred to, all of them
except Russia functioning historically as buffers between larger and more
powerful neighbors on all sides, forced to form compromising alliances with
those powerful neighbors in order to achieve some measure of stability.[13]
Montenegro itself was caught directly between the Austro-Hungarian Empire and the Ottoman Empire, protected more by its strategic inconsequen-
tiality and mountainous inaccessibility than by its own strength or alliances—
even if, historically, Montenegro boasts a truly impressive history of fierce
resistence to the Turks, maintaining some degree of sovereignty during centuries of being completely surrounded by the Ottoman Empire. Since shortly
after the Napoleonic Wars in the early nineteenth century, the Czech lands
had been under Austrian control and most of Poland under Russian control;
Hungary was also a secondary power to Vienna within what was ostensibly
a ruling partnership, and Gypsies, by definition, have no specific homeland
(although in musical terms they are most often linked with Hungary).

If all this might have been lost on American audiences in 1907, particularly
with the shift to "Marsovia" (it is in any case definitely lost on most audiences today), what is *not* lost is the shift to the kolo, the last "ethnic" dance
introduced in the show, early in Act II. Of all the ethnic dances, this is the
least universalized. The mazurka, despite its specific origins, had long since
become a familiar type, given Chopin's series of piano works in this idiom
earlier, in the nineteenth century. The polonaise and polka already had a
kind of mixed currency. The Russianist and "Hungarian" dances are not

identified as types. Suddenly, however, we are drawn inward, with the kolo, into the shared heritage between Hanna and Danilo, this time more intimately than in the playful folk-song duet heard shortly before, "The Cavalier." It hardly matters that their kolo is inauthentic or that it doesn't coordinate very well with the other ethnicities being suggested; what does matter is that this move aligns with a larger strategy that shrinks the dramatic focus from the public and political to the personal and intimate. This strategy is evident throughout the show, especially with regard to the three parable-like folk legends in Act II and the treatment of the famous "Merry Widow Waltz," whose subsequent fame tends to obscure its careful deployment in the show.

Most memorable of the three parable songs is Hanna's "Vilja," which tells of a wood nymph ("Vilia" is a "witch" in Ross's translation) who seduces and then abandons a hunter, a scenario resonant with Danilo's perspective on Hanna's behavior toward him. Musically, the folk element is first established rhythmically, in the verse, through simple repetitions of a duple-meter "canzona" rhythm (long, short-short), which the haunting chorus then takes up in an expansive gesture based on the "gapped" or pentatonic scale (a five-note scale without half steps often used to evoke folk music) that climaxes, however, on an aching major seventh above the tonic before falling back (see also example 1.1 below):

♪1.10
♪1.11

> Vilia, O Vilia! the **witch** of the wood!

The upper pitch of this archlike trajectory (on "witch") departs from the pentatonic vocabulary, so that its bittersweet failure to attain the upper tonic note is all the more poignant, an emblem for the apparent unattainability of Vilja herself (although the upper tonic is reached and lingered over when the musical phrase repeats).

The second parable reverses perspective; in "The Cavalier," sung by Danilo and Hanna, it is the man who is fickle, unwilling to commit to his beloved, preferring his freedom and thus missing his chance for romantic happiness. As before, the verse tells the story, this time with a rhythmic snap over characteristic "rustic" accompaniment (a grace-note inflection to the upper note of an open-fifth drone),[14] a combination that well expresses the haughty horseman's impatience; the chorus mocks this prideful hauteur with a flighty "Silly, silly cavalier!" contemptuously sending the uncomprehend-

♪1.12

ing horseman on his way. Important here is the woman's perspective, which takes in much more than that of the man, who sees only that she has spurned him and congratulates himself that he has retained his freedom. Implicitly, we know from this that Hanna sees both past and future more clearly than does Danilo, whose vaunted "freedom" mainly involves escape to Maxim's.

The third parable, "The Prince and the Princess," is the most transparent; here, in Danilo's story of a prince who has finally had enough of his beloved princess's tricks, his rage overcomes him, so that he is barely able to distinguish between himself and the prince of his story. But between "The

Cavalier" and "The Prince and the Princess" (which serves as a kind of "trio," or middle section, to "In the Modern Style"), comes "The Merry Widow Waltz," where begins the true trajectory of his and Hanna's rekindled romance.

"The Merry Widow Waltz" contrasts vividly with the other, much louder waltzes that have come before it (such as "Oh, Come Away" in Act I), all very public in their orientation. One of Lehár's principal concerns from the start, it would seem, is to set up this sudden shift to extreme intimacy for maximum dramatic effect; this is undoubtedly why he does not begin the show with this most famous of his waltzes,[15] but rather begins the first act with "Parisian" music, provides ample ballroom music along the way (often as background), and closes the act with the couple finding their private way within a public waltz. Within Act II, he creates "public" frames for two related moments of private intimacy. First, as the trio to the fast and furious "Mi velimo dase veslimo!" he introduces the extended lyrical interlude of "Vilja." Across the second half of the act he creates a larger-scale frame based on the even more raucous Parisian idiom, extending from "Women" to "In the Modern Style," with its repeated episodes of musical laughter and cancan effects. Between these framing numbers, the trajectories of the show's two love stories meet and cross, with Hanna and Danilo's "Merry Widow Waltz" interlude and Camille and Valencienne's final impassioned duet; thereafter, the latter's affair will terminate, and the former's will continue to flourish (after an initial setback).

"The Merry Widow Waltz" episode is thus situated in parallel to "Vilja," as a suddenly intimate moment within a raucous, public frame, and Lehár underscores this connection by beginning each with the same four-note musical gesture (and in the same key), borrowing as well from "Vilja" the characteristic move to the upper leading tone that does not resolve to the upper tonic (see example 1.1). But these two recollections make somewhat opposite points. The striking opening gesture is immediately arresting with its recollection of Vilja's siren song—the overpowering voice of true love—but the suspended leading tone in this case does not "ache," since it is harmonized not against the dissonant tonic but within a conventionally descending sequence that comes to rest comfortably in the lower octave.

♪1.13
♪1.14

Indeed, part of what makes this waltz so satisfying is its fairly systematic conversion of the early tune's poignancies into something more comfortably assured. From the beginning, the open-ended gesture of "Vilja" is absorbed into a more compact waltz idiom, the opening four-note phrase repeats, reaches benignly up a half step (thus departing from the eerie pentatonicism of "Vilja"), and immediately cycles back down to begin again. Meanwhile, the waltz idiom returns us to the moment at the end of Act I, when Hanna and Danilo are virtually compelled by the waltz to come together as a couple, if only for the duration of the dance. In this way, "The Merry Widow Waltz" suddenly brings together the necessary ingredients of a successful resolution: the overpowering love and shared heritage of "Vilja," and the idiom of the

Example 1.1a. *The Merry Widow*: excerpt from "Vilja"

Example 1.1b. *The Merry Widow*: excerpt from "Merry Widow Waltz"

waltz, with a comforting sense of trust evoked by the familiar formulas of romantic dance (especially important for Danilo). The only missing ingredient is verbal articulation. The first step toward this is taken during this initial episode, which moves from an instrumental waltz to their humming in unison while they dance (a broad hint that has been particularly well received: this has indeed been a tune that people have chosen to *hum*, usually quite comfortable about not knowing the words). But verbal articulation does not come until the plot is comfortably resolved, when, near the end of Act III, words added to the tune complete the trajectory from instruments to expressed love (and here I offer a literal translation, since the Ross translation is not entirely successful in conveying this element):[16]

♩1.15
♩1.16

Lippen schweigen, 's flüstern Geigen:	Lips are silent, the violin whispers it:
Hab mich lieb!	Love me!
All die Schritte sagen: Bitte,	All the steps say: Please,
Hab mich lieb!	Love me!
Jeder Druck der Hände	Each press of the hands
Deutlich mir's beschrieb,	Describes it to me plainly,
Er sagt klar: 's ist wahr, 's ist wahr,	It says clearly: It's true, it's true,
Du hast mich lieb!	You love me!
[middle section]	
Bei jedem Walzerschritt	With every waltz step
Tanzt auch die Seele mit,	Dances the soul as well,

Du hüpft das Herzchen klein,	You make my small heart leap,
Es klopft und pocht:	It knocks and pounds:
Sei mein! Sei mein!	Be mine! Be mine!

Und der Mund, er spricht kein Wort,	And the mouth, it speaks no word,
Doch tönt es fort und immerfort:	Yet it sounds on and on:
Ich hab' dich ja so lieb . . .	I love you so . . .
Ich hab' dich lieb!	I love you!

Even when words are placed against the tune, they insist that the real message remains unspoken, sounding within the music and experienced in the responsive dance. And these lines of communication, too, are intimate in the extreme, for it is not what even the music *says aloud* but rather what it *whispers* (through its solo strings) as the hands press together in secret, the soul dances along, and the heart within leaps in response.

This insistence on the intimate and personal over the public, expressed so eloquently in the music of *The Merry Widow*, is ultimately the "message" of the show. The larger fate of Pontevedro does not really matter; neither Danilo nor Hanna expends a moment's energy on this issue, one way or the other. Even the clichéd dichotomy of love versus money becomes part of this theme; only when all considerations of money—the loudest and most public of the world's "talkers"—are put aside is Danilo able to "speak" of his own love for Hanna, and then only through music and dance. The raucous, very public clamor that especially the Parisian music offers is thus a foil for the more private resolution—even if that foil is indulged in with shameless abandon at nearly every turn. Within the dynamic of the music's "geography," Paris is the real world, the noisy exterior; Pontevedro—not as a real place, but as a nostalgic memory—provides the path to a quieter and more vital interior; and Vienna (through the waltz) inflects each dimension with romance (i.e., the potential for coupled sexuality).

But the trajectory of Hanna and Danilo's reconciliation does not in itself provide a fully satisfactory romantic trajectory within the established idioms of romantic musical theater. The ardor against a perhaps feigned resistance and the interplay between the dangerous unknown and the safely known—that is, the emblems of a romance in its early stages—are part of their prehistory and not relived except through the mediation of their parable songs. Camille and Valencienne, however, provide precisely this dimension of romance and disappear as a romantic couple only as—and precisely when—the viability of Hanna and Danilo as a romantic pairing is proven. Symbolically, the shift between the two romances occurs when we see Valencienne enter the pavilion and Hanna emerge to launch the second-act finale. But before that shift, we get three musical numbers that provide the fully launched trajectory of a romance: the resisted intitial thrust ("A Dutiful Wife," early in Act I); the jesting interplay of a projected domestic tranquillity ("The Charm of Domesticity," later in Act I, often cut), which offers the playful cut and thrust that operetta recovered from Mozart's Da Ponte collaborations;[17] and, in Act II, the overwhelming ardor of Camille's romance, "Love in My Heart," sung in a waltzlike idiom just before they enter the pavilion for what is ostensibly a farewell kiss. When, as in some English-language performances, the second of these ("The Charm of Domesticity") is given to Hanna and Danilo instead of Valencienne and Camille—following the logic that it is the second duet in Act I for the latter couple, whereas the ostensible stars have no real duet until Act II—it clearly violates the dramatic logic of Lehár's schematic of interlocking romantic trajectories, and more particularly undermines the awakening of their dormant love during "The Merry Widow Waltz" episode in Act II.

♪1.17
♪1.18
♪1.19

Yet on a broader level, following another kind of logic, it scarcely matters which couple sings what, just so it all gets sung in the right order, for the combination of the two barely interlocking romantic trajectories provides precisely one fully satisfying romance, with the disappearance of Valencienne and Camille behind the closed doors of the pavilion providing the visual equivalent of the unspoken intimacies of "The Merry Widow Waltz" moments before. Lehár thereby makes it easy for us to follow our natural inclination to splice these two separate stories together as we take in the show, allowing the truncated romance of Valencienne and Camille to substitute, implicitly, for the missing "back story" of Hanna and Danilo. In the special logic of Viennese operetta, there is really only one love story, however rendered. Nor can it be otherwise if we in the audience are to believe that their romances might also be ours if we can but learn to dance their waltzes and sing their songs (or even, in this particular case, to wear their clothing; both the original American production and the 1952 film led to fashion crazes, for the "Merry Widow Hat" in the first instance [see figure 1.1] and the "Merry Widow"—the type of corset worn by Lana Turner in the film—in the second).[18]

The Merry Widow thus figures prominently in a developmental strand of the American musical of particular importance to the themes to be taken up later in this book: the relentless focus in musicals on the individual, at the expense of the larger issues redounding to the world at large. Tangentially related to this dynamic is another to be taken up in the epilogue (chapter 7): the halfway status *The Merry Widow* and other operettas have traditionally inhabited between high and low culture, at least in America. This relationship is perhaps more than tangential, since European operetta itself was born in a reactive move away from the grandeur of opera, in order to inhabit a more intimate space. But in America, the position of operetta has been less well defined, functioning both to mock high-art pretensions (as in Europe) and as something with the potential to elevate the more mainstream tradition. It is interesting to note, for example, that when *Little Mary Sunshine* sets out to mock operetta—albeit with doting affection—half a century after *The Merry Widow*, it can do so only by being itself an actual operetta, or that *Kiss Me, Kate*'s equally gentle mockery of operetta in "Wunderbar" (1948; see chapter 6) is set within a complicated mix of high and low: back-

Figure 1.1. The craze for "Merry Widow hats," with wide brims and elaborate feathers, inspired Bobby Heath and Gus Benkhart's "Under My Merry Widow Hat," published the same year that *The Merry Widow* opened in New York (1907; this publication thus predates what the *Oxford English Dictionary* reports as the first written use of the phrase "Merry Widow hat," in 1908). The song's lyric proposes the sheltering brim of the hat as a substitute for the bamboo tree in Bob Cole and J. Rosamond Johnson's popular 1902 song, "Under the Bamboo Tree" (discussed in chapter 2, pp. 98 and note 69), and its music refers clearly to both the "Merry Widow Waltz" and "Under the Bamboo Tree." Typical for the time, the sheet-music cover carries photographs not only of the song's authors and publishers but also of a noted singer.

stage of the elevated Shakespeare's rather low comedy *The Taming of the Shrew*, as part of Cole Porter's most complexly realized score for a "mere" musical, in which the song functions as an "authentic" moment between two major poseurs.

More specific to *The Merry Widow* are the intriguing moments when symphonic music by major "classical" figures seems to allude to its tunes, which constitutes an exceedingly rare response to operetta. Mahler, virtually on the heels of the show that had so recently taken his adopted city of Vienna by storm (even if he was to abandon the city shortly after *The Merry Widow* had nearly completed its conquest of Europe),[19] seems to allude to "Women" in a much-repeated passage in the third movement of his Ninth Symphony (composed 1908–1909), in a passage that Mahler's most serious interpretive critic, Theodor Adorno, singles out as particularly significant.[20] Better known are Shostakovich's apparent borrowing from "Maxim's" in his 1941 *Leningrad* Symphony and Bartók's notorious "response" in his 1943 *Concerto for Orchestra*.[21] That some or all of these references might have been satirical should not distract us from noticing that their source material was itself presented with satirical intent, with a sophistication rivaling that of these more venerated "classical" figures, all of them noted satirists. The childish "Maxim's," for example, with its infantilizing refrain of "Lolo, Dodo, Joujou, Cloclo, Margot, Froufrou," provides a portrait of a regressed Danilo that repeats (and repeats) whenever he wants to escape painful realities, and serves as a foil for the later emergence of a more adult Danilo, who can once again trust his more mature response to Hanna. And "Women," however much it may masquerade as a rebuke to its subject, more fundamentally rebukes the characters who are singing by revealing them in a similarly regressed state—again as a foil, this time for the first "Merry Widow Waltz" sequence, immediately following. The number offers not only a sophisticated topical play on the cancan but also, in one passage, an almost Mahlerian blend of satire and musical sophistication, when a canonic descending chromatic scale ("Women, women, women, women") produces a harshly comic series of descending augmented triads (see example 1.2). The very longevity of *The Merry Widow* in the repertory bears witness to its ability to play both sides of the fence, whether as low comedy masquerading as high art or vice versa.[22]

Emblematic of *The Merry Widow*'s ability to play both sides of this divide, whether in Europe or America, is its double-edged treatment of its diva. In a manner highly characteristic of operetta more generally, *The Merry Widow*—named, as in so many operettas, for its female lead—is built around a female star persona who is accustomed to being the center of attention and given ample opportunities for vocal display, but who in the end needs the love of a man to whom she must accommodate, one who is often both less advantageously placed socially and more truly independent. Danilo is, to be sure, an important man (*Prince* Danilo in the Anglo-American version), yet in this situation not as important as Hanna, who ultimately makes conces-

♪1.20
♪1.21

♪1.22
♪1.23
♪1.24

♪1.25

Example 1.2. *The Merry Widow*: excerpt from "Women"

sions to win *him* (albeit in the form of a subterfuge), not the reverse. Importantly, this characteristic structure entails yet another shift from public to personal; more on the surface, it indulges an audience's taste for feminine vocal display while putting that element "in its place."

Both sides of this situation of "having one's cake and eating it too" are crucial to the success of operetta in America. Perhaps the fullest expression of this dynamic occurs in the tradition of the "laughing song," which in the case of *The Merry Widow* ends the second act ("In the Modern Style"). As in many such numbers, the heroine introduces extravagant material with much virtuosic work on repeated syllables (in this case "Tra la la la la . . . la!" and "No! Oh, no! Oh, no, no, no . . . no!"), which the chorus takes over while she "improvises" above them, creating a feeling of virtuosic overabundance. In *The Merry Widow*, that effect is enhanced by a kind of virtuosic competition between Hanna and Valencienne, with each reaching her high A in turn, so that at every moment of the passage in question one of them is either sustaining the climactic pitch or singing rapid syllables below (Hanna, of course, "wins" the contest in the end). But implicit in this overabundance is the sense that it is, indeed, *too much*, a giddy moment of feminine (and operatic) ascendancy that must eventually be reversed.   ♪1.26

Naughty Marietta (1910) is widely regarded as the best work of the first great American composer of serious music, Victor Herbert (who also wrote, performed, and conducted concert music and operas; moreover, as is fairly rare in American musical theater, he mostly did his own orchestration). The show exemplifies the "in-between" aspect of American operetta, as it was the first work mounted by the impresario Oscar Hammerstein (grandfather to the eventual partner of Richard Rodgers) after he was "persuaded" through a large settlement not to stage operas in competition with the Metropolitan Opera Company, and since the show featured, in vocally demanding roles, the Italian opera singer Emma Trentini (who specialized in soubrette roles; see figure 1.2) and Orville Harrold, known as the

American Caruso. Despite a weak libretto by Rida Johnson Young, *Naughty Marietta* was a major success both in New York and on tour. Several of its tunes remain well known today, even if they have become to some extent laughable clichés. Thus, "Ah, Sweet Mystery of Life" served as the punch line to a crude joke at the end of Mel Brooks's *Young Frankenstein* (1974),[23] quite a comedown from its function within *Naughty Marietta* as the celebrated climax of a kind of musical treasure hunt. "Italian Street Song," too, has become irretrievably campy in performance, with men prancing around the stage, at one point booming the following lines with only the deeper instruments accompanying them in unison, and the women responding after each line:

♪ 1.27

MEN:	Mandolinas gay	Dancing as we play
WOMEN:	Zizzy, zizzy, zing, zing, zing	Zizzy, zizzy, zing, zing, zing

When staged with any skill and combined with a bravura performance by a capable coloratura (in male drag), the number provides a particularly potent mix for high camp, but only because it is no longer as familiar as "Ah, Sweet Mystery of Life."

Numbers such as these two have in fact become emblematic of the other "in-between" position operetta has come to occupy, especially in later decades, when it acquired two overlapping audiences: those who took its absurdities seriously and relished the occasion they provided for beautiful virtuoso singing in the grand manner, and those who savored the campy mixing of overelaborate plots, setting, staging, and costumes—and of course virtuoso singing—with the laughably melodramatic situations they ostensibly supported. Two conclusions seem credible about this potential bifurcation of audience, which has long been a substantial component of Broadway shows more generally. Often, the assumption has been that the campy disjuncture between expressive means and dramatic substance is to be explained wholly in terms of historical distance; according to this assumption, these laughable artifacts would have been taken seriously in their day, as seriously as their extravagant accoutrement would suggest. Although this is certainly and obviously true—many did take them quite seriously, and many have continued to do so, even in revival—the historical validity of this receptive mode does not rule out the possibility that operetta's expressive disjunctures were even in their day quite deliberate.

Indeed, the notion that all who enjoyed *Naughty Marietta* in 1910 took its melodrama seriously is on the face of it insulting to those early audiences; moreover, there is ample evidence that the show was played rather broadly even then. Thus, while to some extent the well-documented "acting up" or "clowning" of the original Marietta was a byproduct of performing the same material up to eight times a week, it was also a way of suggesting to an audience that it need not take everything seriously. It may be difficult to show—and for many to believe—that in 1910 "Mandolinas gay / Dancing as we play" was an inside joke, and that Herbert himself might have been

Figure 1.2. Italian-born Emma Trentini rose to stardom in New York as the original Marietta in *Naughty Marietta*, but her temperament so alienated Victor Herbert that he refused to compose for her again. She appears here in "Italian Street Song," disguised as a Gypsy boy. (Photograph courtesy of Miles Kreuger and the Institute of the American Musical, Inc.)

in on it. But it seems foolish, and insulting to Herbert, to rule out that possibility. With Herbert, indeed, we are caught between his high-art aspirations (presumably *not* an appropriate background for indulging in camp) and his extremely competent and knowing deployment of musical tropes. Did his basic aesthetic preclude deliberate engagement with the 1910 equivalent of camp? Or did his knowingness extend to his management of a camp dimension, so that later generations merely rediscovered what he had deliberately fashioned, as part of the show? Perhaps the best way to respond to this dilemma is to note, once again, that the two audience perspectives on operetta *overlap* to a significant extent, for it is indeed possible to take operetta's content seriously and laugh at it, *both at the same time*—and it seems, moreover, an admirably human capacity to be able to respond in precisely this way.

From one perspective, *Naughty Marietta* marks the Americanization of Lehár's Viennese confections, a process that entails a kind of coarsening of the genre. Here, the show's plot contrivances and the other inadequacies of Young's libretto, when considered along with the obvious connections between this show and *The Merry Widow*, offer important evidence. Indeed, *Naughty Marietta* makes an overt mention of the earlier show during a conventional "Jewish shtick" number interpolated late in the second act ("It's ♪1.28 Pretty Soft for Simon"; the "he" in question is Adonis): "Ant he danced der Merry Vidow Valse / Mit Frau Demosthenes." But there are many more substantial connections, as well. Like *The Merry Widow*, *Naughty Marietta* indulges a taste for the exotic musical colors offered by Gypsy music, Parisian cancan, and Viennese waltz. Also evocative of *The Merry Widow* are a raucous second-act men's number to establish a locale where respectable women normally do not venture ("New Orleans Jeunesse Dorée") and an "ethnic" segment of songs and dances that ranges much more widely than geography and history might reasonably allow ("Loves of New Orleans"), in this case concluding in a ragtime version of a melody first given as a seductively chromatic "quadroon" melody in thirds,[24] following episodes styled ♪1.29 after a Spanish waltz, a dreamy "Island" number, and a French cancan. More ♪1.30 basically, "Ah, Sweet Mystery of Life" in *Naughty Marietta* borrows the ♪1.31 dramatic profile of the "Merry Widow Waltz," which is transformed from ♪1.32 a mysterious melody to an actual song only at the end of the show, where ♪1.33 it serves to enforce the union of the main romantic couple (a device also ♪1.34 prominently featured in *Rose-Marie*, centering around "Indian Love Call" and later adapted to trace the central psychological journey of the heroine in *Lady in the Dark*, discussed in chapter 6). And, as in *The Merry Widow*, that couple earlier sings of the impossibility of their union; if "It Never, Never Can Be Love" seems considerably less subtle than the series of parable songs in *The Merry Widow*, such is only par for the coarsening many see in the American derivatives of Viennese operetta more generally.

Yet, the more basic way in which *Naughty Marietta* points to an Americanization of Viennese operetta concerns its conversion of the latter tradition's emphasis on personal issues and relationships into a thoroughgoing exploration of human slavery and freedom, quite daring and sophisticated in its way, even if placed at a safe remove from 1910 America and seldom dealing overtly with the racial component of the issue in America. At every turn and with every situation in *Naughty Marietta*, personal freedom is the basic concern. Already in the opening sequence, in a "daybreak" number based largely on the street cries of early-morning vendors, we hear them proclaim their commitment to freedom in response to watching the Creole convent girls on their way to prayer:

♩ 1.35

> To Smile they are afraid.
> Oh! la! la!
> Oh! la! la!
> I wouldn't be a convent maid!

Since basing musical numbers on the street cries of "costermongers" (street vendors) partakes of a long European tradition dating from the thirteenth century, the number foregrounds New Orleans's cultural connection to the Old World, but it also Americanizes that tradition in its emphasis on personal freedom.[25]

With the main characters, the fierce commitment to freedom is even more overt. Marietta (the disguised Italian Countess d'Altena, rendered French in both the 1935 film and the 1955 televised version)[26] escapes one kind of servitude in Europe—in which she would be forced to marry against her will—for another, disguising herself as a "casket girl" (or "casquette girl"), sent from France to New Orleans with a small dowry on condition that she marry someone among its female-starved population (which Marietta refuses to do). Richard Warrington (Captain Dick) and his "rangers" eschew allegiance to any particular government (touting themselves as "Planters and Canucks, / Virginians and Kaintucks"), preferring to work as freelance mercenaries. The commission they have undertaken is to capture another "freelance" adventurer, the notorious pirate Bras Piqué (the name refers to his "needled"—or tattooed—arm), who in reality is Etienne, the son of the Lieutenant Governor, plotting to establish an independent Louisiana. Etienne is romantically involved with Adah, a quadroon who is also his slave, whom he threatens to sell when he tires of her. The symbolic image of the puppet, obviously relevant to the underlying theme, occurs throughout. Thus, Marietta joins a marionette troupe to escape detection and performs in "Dance of the Marionettes," which in turn inspires Etienne to sing "You Marry a Marionette," whose title describes the only way to remain free while committing oneself to a woman, who will otherwise pull the strings.

The frequent claim that the plotline of *Naughty Marietta* is confusing—fair enough as far as the claim goes—stems partly from a certain ineptitude on the part of the librettist and partly from a habit carrying over from opera more generally, but more importantly from two exterior sources, both deriving from an unwillingness on the part of the show's critics to credit the show with a guiding intelligence. First of these is the failure to grasp the show's thematic consistency, thereby missing the point of its otherwise odd refusal of a conventional conclusion. According to the conventions of melodrama, which we tend to assume must apply to operetta automatically, Etienne, who has seemed amply villainous in his treatment of Adah and who plans to escape prosecution by forcing himself on the highborn Countess d'Altena (Marietta), must obviously be either captured or killed by Captain Dick. Instead, Warrington recognizes in Etienne a kindred free spirit—whose larger political aims are pointed after all in the direction of political freedom for his adopted land—and so allows him to escape, thereby also refusing to accept the will of existing governmental authority. The second basis for faulting the show's plot stems from a more basic failure to accept one of the governing principles of operetta: to wit, its focus on the personal dimension, which means, ultimately, that its apparent ties to real situations in the real world (or to history) are in the end beside the point. American operetta, like its Viennese antecedent, points to reality and history, but in a deliberately vague way, so as not to be held accountable to either. Thus, to reject *Naughty Marietta* because its New Orleans setting never existed in any particular historical moment—its events officially take place between the American and French Revolutions, but the show borrows situations (and, of course, musical modes) from both later and earlier times—is to miss entirely the point of American operetta's elaborately evasive dance with reality.[27]

We might in this regard usefully contrast operetta with French grand opera, which also mixes the historical and the personal. In the latter, produced mainly in the middle decades of the nineteenth century, as in many operettas, historical settings typically provide the backdrop for a personal drama, yet the dynamic between the two is almost precisely the opposite. In French grand opera, history functions as a determining force that overwhelms the lives of its foregrounded individuals with a sense of inevitable fate; for this dynamic to work well, the history in question must be fairly accurate, at least according to the preconceptions of its audience. In operetta, however, which insists on the ability of the individual to determine his or her own fate, it helps tremendously both to evoke the powerful imperatives of history and geography and to blunt their controlling power through a variety of devices, which might include precisely the kind of historical conflations we find in *Naughty Marietta*.[28]

Another intriguing point of reference for operettas, particularly those that trade in disguises to make political points, is Rossini's *Barber of Seville* (1816), an *opera buffa* (derived from the same series of political comedies by Beaumarchais as Mozart's earlier *Marriage of Figaro*) in which the Count, with the aid of Figaro, disguises himself in order to woo his future Countess. While the situation in *Barber* is seemingly resonant with the disguises undertaken by Countess d'Altena in *Naughty Marietta*, or Sonia (Hanna) in the later film versions of *The Merry Widow*, there is again an important difference: whereas in *Barber* the Count's authority, as Count, is

Example 1.3. *Naughty Marietta*: excerpt from "Ah! Sweet Mystery of Life"

a necessary adjunct to the successful resolution of the plot, in operetta the restoration of the "real world" through the stripping away of a character's disguise represents the single most potent threat to the only resolution that truly matters.

In *Naughty Marietta*, the emphasis on the personal is couched, musically, within two kinds of "quest" scenarios, realized side by side. In the most obvious of these, Marietta, haunted throughout by a fragment of a melody, whether sung as vocalise or presented instrumentally, seeks to find its completion, both as a melody and as a song with meaningful words. This quest reaches its completion in the finale, led by Captain Dick in rhymes as forced and sentiments as banal as in most translations of *The Merry Widow*'s "I Love You So." If the arrival point is the same—that is, "Love" as "The Answer"—the point is made much less subtly; nevertheless, Herbert does a creditable job of emphasizing key words by rendering them as dissonant appoggiaturas (i.e., accented nonharmonic tones that resolve downward into alignment with the harmony; these syllables are emphasized here in bold italics, and the dissonant appoggiaturas correspond to the texted arrivals in example 1.3):

♫ **1.36**
♫ **1.37**

> Ah! sweet *mys*tery of *life*, at last I've found thee,
> Ah! I *know* at last the secret of it all.
> All the *long*ing, seeking, *striv*ing, waiting, yearning;
> The *burning* hopes, the joy and idle tears that fall!

> For 'tis *love*, and love a*lone* the world is seeking;
> And 'tis *love*, and love alone, that can repay!
> 'Tis the answer, 'tis the end and all of living,
> For it is love alone that rules for aye!

This familiar tune is built out of a string of simple melodic units, each of which might function as a dissonant appoggiatura; since only a few of them actually function that way, what emerges is a clear progression: "*my*stery of *life*"—"I *know* at last" / "*long*ing"—"*striv*ing"—"*burning*" / "*love . . . a*lone*"—"*love*." The rest tends to fade into the generalized unison concordance of arrival, particularly in the final two lines, where the long-avoided cadence to the tonic actually occurs.

If we might here observe, as in music more generally, the frequent banality of actual resolution after an extended and significantly more engrossing quest for resolution, that pattern is even more deliberately realized within the other quest scenario, in which an early "striving" chromatic movement upward is finally brought to resolution within a conventional waltz idiom. Examples of this chromatic "questing" motive (generally three notes) are legion early on, including most prominently "Tramp, tramp, tramp," which begins the overture and soon after introduces Captain Dick and his men (bracketed words in bold indicate rising chromatic motion; braced italics ♩ 1.38   indicate its inverted or retrograde form, a falling chromatic motion):

> [Tramp, tramp, tramp] along the {highway
> [*Tramp*}, tramp, tramp], the [road is free]

The motive appears in many contexts, such as the beginning of "Taisez-Vous," where the men's ardor provokes the response of "taisez-vous" ("be ♩ 1.39   quiet") from the Casket girls:

> MEN: [Oh! Maiden fair, oh, maiden fair],
>   Won't you marry me? Won't you marry me?
> WOMEN: Taisez-vous, taisez-vous, we'll see!

More playful hints of the motive, where it is "resolved" through its inverted form, occur in Dick and Marietta's duet, "It Never, Never Can Be Love," which traces the upward-chromatic motion within questions ("You'll never try just to kiss my hand?") and offers pat reassurances that reverse the chro- ♩ 1.40   matic motion into a three-note repeating motive:

> {Then I'm sure}, / {if you're sure},
> {And I'm sure}, / {I am sure},
> {That we mu}tually understand.

The climax of this quest scenario occurs shortly before the finale, with Captain Dick's "I'm Falling in Love with Some One," where symmetrical chromatic motion yields to a simple, even, stepwise descent in waltz time, directly reminiscent of the phrase endings of "The Merry Widow Waltz" (beginning here with the repeated words "some one"):

♪ 1.41

[**For I'm fall**]*{ing in love}* with some one, some one . . .

Here, the musical profile is a deft realization of the text, turning from the "quest" motive to its realization on the second syllable of the word "falling." Aligning the descending version of the motive with the actual word "falling" is an example of "word painting," a kind of musical literalism that on its own might seem almost comic (especially since the word "falling" is set to a *rising* fifth). But here the gesture also encapsulates the larger motivic progression, balancing with one simple gesture the rising chromatic opening. Moreover, the chromatic descent, in performance (where it is often slowed down), comes across as an initial reluctance, which then yields to a more accepting free fall regulated by the waltz idiom ("some one, some one"); here Herbert is taking advantage of the typical Viennese waltz pattern of holding back before arrivals—the *Luftpause*—which gives a feeling of release to the return of the faster tempo.[29] (Significantly, the overture is built around these two quest scenarios, beginning with "Tramp, tramp, tramp," which resolves into "I'm Falling in Love with Some One," and ending with the same pairing that will conclude the finale, "Ah, Sweet Mystery of Life" and "Italian Street Song"; the latter song does not, however, otherwise figure in either quest scenario.)

As with *The Merry Widow*, the larger romantic trajectory receives implicit support through the secondary romantic interest, in this case through " 'Neath the Southern Moon," sung by Adah; the song also indirectly helps to validate Etienne, who would in most respects otherwise come across as simply bad (as opposed to "complicated bad, with possibilities for redemption"). And again, the two romantic trajectories are interwoven sufficiently that this ultraromantic number, with its chromatically inflected harmonic shifts by thirds, might serve partly as Marietta's background, by association, and so displace both the sauciness of the number that officially introduces her ("Naughty Marietta," which imagines two Mariettas inside her heart, one well behaved, the other more hotly tempered: "So when I am good, I am very good indeed, / But when I am bad, I'm horrid!") and the frivolity of her more elaborate numbers, such as "Italian Street Song." [30]

♪ 1.42
♪ 1.43

The critical musical number that serves to intertwine the two stories is the impressive quartet "Live for Today," just before "I'm Falling in Love with Some One," in which both Adah and Marietta, motivated by feelings of betrayal by their respective lovers, insist on a wanton indulgence in the moment. Although Captain Dick (but not Etienne) stands somewhat apart from this sentiment, the number insists, as does operetta more generally, on the here and now over the supposedly larger context. Not for nothing is "Live for Today" the most exaggeratedly "Viennese" number in the show, with its supple waltz idiom pausing to dwell deliciously on one anticipatory moment

♩1.44   after another. In dramatic terms, the intertwining of the two stories within this number both deepens the main love story and provides the necessary (and specifically musical) motivation for Captain Dick's decision to allow Etienne to escape at the end.

Little Mary Sunshine (1959), with book, music, and lyrics by Rick Besoyan, marks an important point of articulation in the historical management, within operetta, of its coexisting "straight" and "camp" dimensions. As with nearly all staged musical traditions in New York, going well back into the nineteenth century, a variety of modes of reception were available for Viennese operetta and its American offshoots. Thus, operetta might be taken to be either high art or "mere" entertainment, or both at once; either serious or campy, or both at once; either a musical drama to be taken more or less at face value or a heavily coded performance of a variety of tropes and double entendres—or both at once. In more recent decades, operetta has become most accessible to gay readings through its camp dimension (although other dimensions continue to matter), but even here, gay associations are rarely made explicit, since the multivalent interpretive possibilities of operetta depend on the genre's refusal to acknowledge, through explicit content, the very possibility of gay readings. As Matthew Bell puts it regarding the gay presence in American musical theater more generally, "Perhaps no other modern art form succeeds so thoroughly in appealing, at the level of reception, to a gay (and implicitly male) 'sensibility,' and in refusing, at the level of denotation, gay content."[31]

A central marker for this disjuncture between reception and the lack of explicit gay content in American operetta is the genre's frequent use of the word "gay" as part of a heavy emphasis on long-A rhymes in its lyrics. One striking example of the latter is the overuse in American operetta of the affected phrase "for aye" (meaning "forever"), which seems at times to stand as a verbal sign for the exaggerated vocal dimension of the genre. Thus, the phrase ends "Ah, Sweet Mystery of Life" in *Naughty Marietta* (see above) and is almost immediately echoed in the final syllable of the brief reprise of "Italian Street Song" that ends the operetta. Although it might be debated just how much the "gaiety" of American operetta was being read both ways as early as 1910, the word itself—a particularly useful "hinge" for the kinds of double meanings gay readings must depend on—has a prominence in this repertory that is difficult to ascribe to chance. Rather, it seems to point to an environment in which the word "gay" was, in a sense, still fully closeted, completely innocent to some, and an open secret to others.

By the mid-1930s this particular verbal closet was beginning to open. It was on the heels of the film-operetta revival that Cary Grant (as the sexually repressed David Huxley in the 1938 film *Bringing Up Baby*) famously answers the door in a spectacularly feminine negligee, for which his only explanation is "I just went *gay*, all of a sudden!" accompanied by a dancelike leap on the word "gay." Given Grant's previous career on the musical stage (which began not that long after *Naughty Marietta*) and other bits of recently recovered evidence, it seems reasonable to conclude that "gay" had a fairly long history as a code word for homosexual, at least within New York's theatrical circles.[32] In any case, the potential to associate operetta with gay sensibilities was both indulged and guarded against in the operetta films of the mid-1930s, whether by using them as Shirley Temple vehicles (which was both a guarantee of innocence and a shameless indulgence in itself) or through the naturalizing that took place in the drastic revisions made to their situations and plots. The latter process, a common feature of the Jeanette MacDonald adaptations, provided a contextual foil that could (depending on the viewer's predisposition) either mask or accentuate Nelson Eddy's prettiness and the coded "male bonding" within the group of men he led, who in their quaint costumes and behavior tended to resemble a theatrical troupe more than a military troop. Nelson Eddy, in particular, is fascinating to watch in these films. With familiarity (or, perhaps, the right perspective), his infamous "woodenness" as an actor often comes across as a bemused reaction to MacDonald's curious obliviousness to her principal dramatic function, as the "serious" center for camped-up melodrama, a function not that different from Margaret Dumont's in the Marx Brothers' films of the same era.[33]

The revisions to the plots of these shows in their film revivals stemmed partly from a felt need to make them more "cinematic," to remove them from the stage into a semblance of the real world. But the impulse to revise was probably also based on a growing uneasiness about their double nature. Although elevated above mere "musicals," operettas were, for some, made suspect by their appeal to a gay-inflected theatricality and seemed, to others who may have been oblivious to this dimension, simply laughable in their conceits and pretensions. These disquietudes reflect a strong tendency, especially for "straight" audiences, to see such things as relics of a bygone aesthetic, so that what once might have functioned as quasi-natural conventions appears stilted and artificial to later audiences. And this perception was true as far as it went, since these "artificial" components were indeed more readily accepted as generic conventions by similarly mainstream audiences of an earlier generation. Yet this rather complacent view of things, also common among later gays, is naive in its failure either to notice the important payoff of such "conventions" for much of their earlier audiences or to imagine that this payoff was actually intended.

If the 1930s operetta films achieved some success in wrestling with this duality, by the 1950s operetta had come to seem impossibly quaint and old-fashioned to mainstream sensibilities, with two seemingly inevitable consequences. Already in the 1940s (as Gerald Bordman has argued), much of the tradition had been salvaged and brought back into the mainstream, most notably by Rodgers and Hammerstein, whose reliance on operetta was disguised somewhat through an apparent newness of approach and a much ballyhooed aspiration to elevate the American musical. But performances of

older operetta in revival meanwhile lost a dimension vital to the genre's
ability to maintain its double audience, as fewer and fewer could take them
seriously, both because of the alternative Rodgers and Hammerstein were
industriously providing and through the rise of "method" acting, which
made operetta's theatricalities seem all the more absurd. Simply put, performances of operetta tended increasingly to give audiences permission to laugh
at them, and so they did. Thus, the scrolling (and pompously recited) text
that introduces the 1955 televised version of *Naughty Marietta* reads:

> *New Orleans*
> *1790*
>
> *While the Paris*
> *of the New World*
> *still flew the flag*
> *of Louis the XVI*
> *of France,*
> *America had*
> *just won it's* [sic]
> *independence*
> *from England!*
> *The Old City*
> *was a cauldron*
> *of intrigue,*
> *hot tempers,*
> *cold steel and*
> *fiery passions,*
> *which can only*
> *lead to one thing*
>
> *Operetta!*

Thus, operetta itself bifurcated into a set of features central to Rodgers
and Hammerstein's "elevation" of the mainstream musical, on the one
hand, and an increasingly ridiculous genre that mixed operatic singing and
woefully outmoded melodrama, on the other. The latter development provides the direct basis for *Little Mary Sunshine*, which, by frankly leaving
aside all possibility of being taken seriously as drama, managed nevertheless to maintain the bifurcation of the remaining audience into those who,
within a camp dynamic, might or might not "get" the gay component. Key
to the show's ability to do this is its deft engagement with the operetta
tradition, extending especially to its music, which to a large extent thereby
continued to yield the pleasures of "serious" operetta in significant measure.
Perhaps most important, the show safely removed American operetta from
the awkwardness of having to feign serious engagement with its situations
and plots in order to satisfy those audience members who could not easily
relinquish the heroic dimension of its dramatic action—a dimension that

outside a camp context was absolutely required as a justification for the extravagant singing.

Markers for those inclined toward understanding *Little Mary Sunshine* as specifically gay are plentiful. Within the song lyrics, for example (given here in the order they appear in the show), the Rangers "march on, man to man, to man, to man, / To man" ("The Forest Ranger"); Mary encourages them to "Please be gay" ("Look for a Sky of Blue"); "Big Jim" Warington recites a long list of flowers for Mary, including "frilly Phlox," "Poppies of fairy gold," promiscuously "teasing Tulips," and "pampered Pansies" that "bring us to our knees" ("You're the Fairest Flower"); Mme Ernestine von Liebedich hopes to make each "precious little nutting" "gay," ending with the admonishment to "[t]ake it vile you may" ("Every Little Nothing"); Nancy Twinkle substitutes "men" for "eats," "dainty little sweets," "drinks," and "frill" in a song celebrating a particularly "gay" party ("Such a Merry Party"); and Mary asserts that "the world is for the birds," with their "merry song" that is "like a fairy song" ("Coo Coo"). If only some of the early examples register, we might well begin to wonder what Mme Liebedich's German pronunciations are really about (including her name, if one really wants to be wicked), so that "nutting" becomes a genuine gerund to which we can apply her later suggestion to "take it vile." Moreover, the recurrence of key words, by association, quickly spreads the double meaning of "gay" over virtually everything. "Merry," for example, already a synonym for "gay" in a straight context and ostentatiously used that way in one song ("Such a Merry Party"), is rhymed later with "fairy" in another song extolling birds, which brings to mind the "gay" congruence of "fay" (derived from "fairy") and the common Yiddish term for male homosexual, *fagele* (pronounced "fay-ge-lay" or "fay-ge-la" and variously spelled, deriving from the German "Vöglein"); both terms also have an obvious assonance with "faggot." Once "merry" is thus given a securely gay connotation, the game becomes an especially easy one, since the title character's name is but a normalized version of her Indian name, Little Merry Sunshine (who, in the song "Little Mary Sunshine" is deemed to be "very merry all the time"). Suddenly, the whole tradition is marked as gay through verbal association, from *The Merry Widow* through *Naughty Marietta* and *Rose-Marie*, and including a great many other operettas along the way.[34]

All of which is, of course, eminently deniable. As with most gay camp, *Little Mary Sunshine* does not have to be understood as in the least bit gay. As D. A. Miller notes in a discussion of Alfred Hitchcock's *Rope* (1948), "Until recently, homosexuality offered not just the most prominent, it offered the only subject matter whose representation in American mass culture appertained exclusively to the shadow kingdom of connotation, where insinuations could be at once developed and denied, where . . . one couldn't be sure whether homosexuality was being meant at all, but on the chance it was, one also learned, along with the codes that might be conveying it, the silence necessary to keep about their deployment."[35] And connotation can

♩ 1.45
♩ 1.46

♩ 1.47

♩ 1.48

♩ 1.49
♩ 1.50

be particularly slippery when the gay dimension is not made concrete enough to raise questions about dramatic identity (thus, "Are they or aren't they homosexual?" in the case of *Rope*) but is instead heavily mediated, dramatically impossible, or fairly occasional. For example, in operetta, a gay sensibility can easily be embodied through a woman, and it is much safer to do so than it would be to present a possibly gay man. Nancy Twinkle in *Little Mary Sunshine* is not a man and is not homosexual, yet she easily channels gay attitudes and sensibilities because of the overall campy context, the specific choice of name (both evoking the gay designation "Nancy-boy" and suggesting, through "Twinkle," a parallel to Little Mary's "Sunshine"), and the over-the-top expression of admiration for men (as in "Such a Merry Party"). Moreover, she doesn't have to sustain this dimension consistently in order to serve it; indeed, it is again safer if it emerges only at key moments, preferably within particularly "safe" sequences of song and dance, where exaggeration is already to be expected. Dramatically, Nancy "redeems" herself, in terms of either her channeled "gayness" or her promiscuous heterosexuality, by assuming great personal risk to rescue her beloved Billy—no matter that this takes her to a moment in which she, Billy, and Yellow Feather, identically clothed, circle each other in a "Shell Game"!

Accordingly, the gay associations suggested here are in each case and in each particular easily denied. In a strictly literal sense, none of these means what a gay sensibility might take it to mean. "Man to man to man" is merely a comically extended cadence. "Gay" means "happy and carefree." Flowers are flowers (even "Poppies of fairy gold" and "pampered pansies"). And Mme Liebedich's "nutting" means nothing, both literally and figuratively. Nor does the show as a whole have to be understood as camp, since other categories also apply, such as the respectably straight designations "spoof" and "parody." Indeed, much of the charged verbal play in *Little Mary Sunshine* is very specifically overdetermined. For example, its overuse of the word "gay" on one level simply reproduces an element of the genre's quaintness (along with such phrases as "Our love today / Shall rule for aye" at the end of the second-act reprise of "Colorado Love Call"). And Mme Liebedich is there to evoke the Old Country and specifically Vienna (in "Do You Ever Dream of Vienna"), with "unintentional" wordplay manifest mainly in idiomatic nonsense, such as when the American phrase "precious little"— which would normally mean "extremely little," with a sarcastic emphasis— emerges to undermine the saccharine sentiment of "Every Little Nothing." In this way, *Little Mary Sunshine* manages to be both safely and scandalously funny at the same time, with very few of those awkward moments when only part of the audience laughs.

But the show's basic means for keeping both parts of the operetta crowd happy is the adroitness with which it refers to the tradition. In its many knowing references to American operetta's best-known shows (mainly *Naughty Marietta* and *Rose-Marie*), *Little Mary Sunshine* rewards all fans of the operetta tradition, whether gay or straight, by addressing them as insiders, and thereby also may slightly mollify those who object to the very idea of spoofing a venerated tradition. In this context, another bifurcation of audience takes place, between those who know the tradition and those who don't, or have only the vaguest sense of what operetta is about. With *Little Mary Sunshine*, "straight" operetta fans are in this respect as much on the inside as gays, if sometimes uneasy or in denial about that closeness of sensibility. Moreover, in its thoroughgoing parody of the type, the show also encourages relative outsiders in the audience to believe they might come to know the American operetta tradition inferentially (or at least what they need to know of it), by extrapolating back from the show's exaggerations. It is, however, important to note that *Little Mary Sunshine* spoofs much more than the operetta tradition, repeatedly referring as well to later, more mainstream shows. Although this is probably little more than shameless opportunism, it may also be seen as a way of "playing safe," by ensuring a somewhat larger "in" component to the audience; it may also be construed as an implicit commentary on how much the mainstream musical theater in America has been influenced by operetta.

Although the plot of *Little Mary Sunshine* can hardly be said to matter in a conventional sense, it does bring together quite well a number of important points of reference in its characters and situations. The name of the male lead, Captain "Big Jim" Warington, derives from his counterparts in *Rose-Marie* and *Naughty Marietta*—Jim Kenyon and Captain Richard Warrington (Captain Dick), respectively—a cross-referencing that confirms, for those who might need such confirmation, what precisely is meant by the "Big Jim" nickname. Mary is, of course, an Americanized derivative of both earlier titles, and "Little Mary Sunshine" has become a generic term of mockery akin to "Pollyanna," a usage that may have come specifically from the name of a very popular 1916 silent film that starred Baby Marie Osmond, the Shirley Temple of her day (a film and personage still well known within some gay circles). Even more intriguingly in the present context, the name Mary Sunshine seems to have served at times as a transgender cover: thus, it is the "sob-sister" byline of a male reporter in the 1932 Frank Capra film *Forbidden*, and a cross-dressing role in the 1975 musical *Chicago* (also a reporter).[36] Indeed, by some reports "Mary Sunshine" had additional currency in the 1950s within some gay communities, where one might use it to refer sarcastically to a "Mary" who is less than "gay" in the mainstream meaning of the word; perhaps, though, that currency was more broadly based, owing to the sustained popularity of a children's song, "Good Morning, Merry Sunshine," which figured in many morning rituals.[37]

The Forest Rangers themselves also seem to refer to 1950s realities, in that they more clearly evoke the Boy Scouts of America—an organization that is both homophobic and a well-known refuge for closeted gays—than any historical reality. Thus, the "Scout Law," a list of a dozen attributes for Boy Scouts to aspire to ("trustworthy, loyal," etc.), is virtually recited in "The Forest Ranger," if sometimes out of order and not quite complete:

Figure 1.3.
Eileen Brennan, as
Little Mary, in a
publicity photo-
graph for *Little
Mary Sunshine*.
Her pose on a
flower-bedecked
swing recalls a
similar publicity
still, of Jeanette
MacDonald and
Nelson Eddy, for
Maytime (a 1937
operetta film by
Robert Leonard
with a composite
score drawing on
the music of nine-
teenth-century
composers Léo
Delibes, Giacomo
Meyerbeer, Robert
Planquette, and
Pyotr Ilich Tchai-
kovsky, as well as
twentieth-century
operetta compos-
ers Sigmund Rom-
berg and Herbert
Stothart). (Photo-
graph courtesy of
Miles Kreuger and
the Institute of the
American Musi-
cal, Inc.)

Stout hearted is the Forest Ranger / He's a scout:
He's thoughtful, friendly, courteous and kind,
> He's reverent and grave
> He's healthy and he's brave
He's clean in soul and body and mind / Yes, Sir!
He's cheerful, honest, thrifty and obedient.[38]   ♪1.51

But operetta aficionados will recognize the troop as a conflation of Captain Dick's rangers and the Mounties of *Rose-Marie*, even if the style of their marching tune, especially through its 6/8 meter, is more evocative of the Sousa-derived "Seventy-six Trombones" from Meredith Willson's *The Music Man*, which was then halfway through its four-year run. Similarly, *Little Mary Sunshine*'s Indians derive from *Rose-Marie*, although its two scenarios of Indian adoption (for both Mary and Corporal Billy Jester) are more clearly referential to the 1946 Irving Berlin musical *Annie Get Your Gun* (cf. the latter's "I'm an Indian, Too" and "Me a Heap Big Injun," the latter left off the original cast album of *Little Mary Sunshine*). "Naughty, Naughty Nancy" seems more purely operetta, mainly because it virtually steals the conceit and melodic profile of the title song of *Naughty Marietta* (see example 1.4). The most impressive dual borrowing—that is, from both   ♪1.52
Broadway and operetta—is the three-part combination song "Playing Cro-   ♪1.53
quet," "Swinging," and "How Do You Do?" The principal target of this tour de force, however, is unmistakably the Victorian sensibilities basic to American operetta, even predating the influence of *The Merry Widow*. Thus, the specific point of reference here is "Sweet" Rose Maybud of Gilbert and Sullivan's *Ruddigore* (1887), who lives her life according to a book of etiquette; more generally, the larger sequence spoofs the Gilbert and Sullivan penchant for bringing together rather unlikely groupings of men and women for the purposes of group courtship, evoking in particular the first-act combi-   ♪1.54
nation songs of *Pinafore* and *Ruddigore*.[39] (Thus, in this extended number,   ♪1.55
the Forest Rangers meet up—and pair up—with a vacationing group of   ♪1.56
young women from the "Eastchester Finishing School.")   ♪1.57
Intriguingly, the shadow of Cole Porter's 1948 *Kiss Me, Kate*—Porter's   ♪1.58
homosexuality had long been an open secret, at least among gays—hangs   ♪1.59
over many numbers in the show, although there are ample ties to the older operetta tradition in each instance. Among the most prominent Porter derivations are *Little Mary Sunshine*'s archly retrospective look at Viennese operetta (cf. Porter's "Wunderbar" and *Little Mary Sunshine*'s "In Izzenschnooken on the Lovely Essenzook Zee" and "Do You Ever Dream of Vienna"); the situation explored in "Once in a Blue Moon" between the second male lead (Billy) and his promiscuous love interest, Nancy Twinkle (cf. Porter's "Always True to You" and possibly also Rodgers and Hart's "Blue Moon"); and the overblown "Colorado Love Call," whose lyrics often seem to parody Porter (thus: "And for your sake / My lonely heart will ache /

Example 1.4a. *Naughty Marietta*: excerpt from "Naughty Marietta"

Example 1.4b. *Little Mary Sunshine*: excerpt from "Naughty, Naughty Nancy"

And quake and break. / If you do not return, / My heart will yearn, / And burn, / So please return").

In the case of "Colorado Love Call," it is seemingly Porter's influence that transforms an obvious allusion to "Indian Love Call" (from *Rose-Marie*) into a posturing, melodramatic love anthem—with a little help from the hackneyed device of modulating upward by half step, which the number does, ostentatiously, three separate times, so that we hear the big tune in D, E♭, E, and F, each time more majestically than the last. Although the style of "Colorado Love Call" is much more ponderous, its motivic derivation from "Indian Love Call" is clearly stated, as it moves up to the sixth scale degree in a dramatic opening arpeggio and settles back through the same scale steps (five and three), with a hint of its predecessor's distinctive chromaticism and vocalizing on the syllable "you." (See example 1.5; note that "Indian Love Call" falls back, echolike, from D to C to A, with the latter move stretched out chromatically [C–B–B♭–A]; whereas "Colorado Love Call" falls back more quickly through the same basic pitches, subsequently adding its chromaticism in a lower octave [D–D♭].) Related to this process of generic aggrandizement is Mary's song, "Look for a Sky of Blue," introduced fairly innocently, but then converted at a moment of duress into a rather inadequate inspirational "hymn" to close the first act, and recalled once again, with a patriotic overlay, to close the show—all of which clearly evokes one of Rodgers and Hammerstein's borrowings from operetta, the heroic "inspirational" number.

Notwithstanding copious references to later Broadway, *Little Mary Sunshine* maintains its primary allegiance to American operetta in various ways: through its many waltz songs, its recurring Indianist element (that is, clichéd "American Indian" music, such as may be heard in *Rose-Marie*, but also, by 1959, in countless film Westerns), its enchantment with disguise, and its idiomatic "laughing" songs. The first example of the latter type sets the tone for the whole, as Mary interpolates her "Ha, ha, ha, has" a shade too neatly between the lines of the Forest Rangers' "Little Mary Sunshine," just miss-

Example 1.5a. *Rose-Marie*: excerpt from "Indian Love Call"

Example 1.5b. *Little Mary Sunshine*: excerpt from "Colorado Love Call"

ing—and probably intentionally so—the sense of overabundance typical of operetta's laughing songs at their best. Regarding the enchantment with disguise, it is significant that Nancy's big number, "Mata Hari"—in which she evokes "European" intrigue as she adopts her Indian disguise—appropriately combines an East European exoticism redolent of *The Merry Widow*'s "The Cavalier" with Indianist idioms.[40] Governing all this is a plot that combines the least believable aspects of its two principal models, so that Yellow Feather, who has waited (rather gallantly) to make his move on Mary until the Forest Rangers are around to defend her, is destined not to die or otherwise pay for his villainy but rather to remain in custody only "until the Forest Rangers have returned him to the world as a useful member of society."

♩1.65

♩1.66
♩1.67

The key to *Little Mary Sunshine* is provided, up-front, in Rick Besoyan's opening instruction to the performers:

> It is absolutely essential to the success of the musical that it be played with the most warm-hearted earnestness. There should be no exaggeration in costume, make-up or demeanor; and the characters, one and all, should believe, throughout, in the perfect sincerity of their words and actions.

And thus are the precarious dualities of American operetta to be maintained, as camp that refuses to acknowledge that it is camp, even at the rather late date of 1959.

    A Little Night Music (1973) seems in many ways designed
to be the end piece of the Viennese operetta tradition in America, to serve
as the summation and culmination of the European tradition while ignoring
the American tradition in between.[41] This summational quality, typical of
Sondheim's work more generally, may be seen most vividly in the show's
nearly strict adherence to triple meter (often compound), which led many to
claim it as a return to the Viennese "waltz musical."[42] But its actual waltzes
are relatively few,[43] and the tradition it supposedly returns to used duple
meters quite often. Thus, the return is a *stylized* return, entirely retrospective,
yet using that perspective to great advantage in its idiosyncratic focus on the
individuals caught in its plot machinations.

    But the show was first and foremost a fairly faithful adaptation of Ingmar
Bergman's 1955 film *Smiles of a Summer Night*. Bergman's title refers most
immediately to the stratagem of explaining its plot developments in terms of
three "smiles" of the seemingly perpetual twilights characteristic of Swedish
summers (thus Sondheim's lyric for the "Night Waltz": "The sun won't set.
. . . It's dark as it's going to get").[44] But it also refers obliquely to Shakespeare's *Midsummer Night's Dream*, in which the long *English* summer evening (however short by Scandinavian standards) similarly provides the backdrop for a game of romantic mix and match among the main characters, a
connection acknowledged by Woody Allen in the title of his much looser
adaptation of the Bergman film, *A Midsummer Night's Sex Comedy*
(1982).[45] Characteristic of all of these is a plot dynamic that Mozart had
already shown to be particularly well suited for musical comedy, especially
in his 1790 *Così fan tutte*. In "sex comedies" generally, the configuration of
the couples tends to be such that an audience will anticipate an inevitably
"natural" alignment, which the characters generally do not see quite so
clearly or in the same way, with some of them resisting the inevitable or
angling for a different alignment.[46]

    Thus, in the best examples of this genre, we are made intensely aware of
both the neatness of the inevitable outcome and the human need to protest
against that deadening neatness, to resist being reduced to a mere pawn in
a sexual game of chess. In *Così fan tutte*, Mozart not only showed just how
human such chess pieces can be made to seem through their music, but also
proved how disturbing the result can be for an audience to watch; thus, even
today, wonderful and admired as it is, *Così fan tutte* has relatively few ardent
fans. Viennese operetta, taking its cue from Mozart—but from a different
page of the score, as it were—places less emphasis on resistance and pain
and more on what actually compels humans to behave like chess pieces,
arguing through its music that there is no alternative, and that we should be
glad of it, whatever the resulting pain. It is no wonder, then, that in Bergman's film, Fredrik Egerman (the central male character) whistles a bit of
"Là ci darem la mano" from Mozart's 1787 *Don Giovanni* (the instructions
in the script of the musical are to whistle "a bit of Mozart"). And, more
generally, this is why the waltz became so central to Viennese operetta, a

genre that already overlaps significantly with the sex comedy in its typical plot dynamic. While virtually compelling its characters to "dance" to its tunes, Viennese operetta softens the pill by making dance seem the most delicious imaginable activity, offering a means to experience more fully not only the exquisite loveliness of the music but also one's basic humanity.

In his introduction to the published play of *A Little Night Music* (book by Hugh Wheeler), Sondheim's orchestrator, Jonathan Tunick, produces a neat diagram of the triangular relationships that determine the situation and plot of *A Little Night Music*, which in this respect has a structure nearly identical to that of Bergman's film:

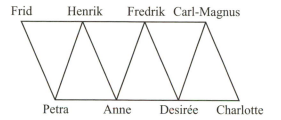

Thus, at the beginning, each of the main male characters is inclined in the wrong direction (Henrik toward Petra, Fredrik toward Anne, and Carl-Magnus toward Desirée), so that resolution can come only through a reorientation to an already available choice.

Useful as this chart is, it is still more useful to adapt the chart so as to distinguish the nature of the developing connections among the characters.[47] Thus, the opening condition for the story is pointedly imbalanced and dysfunctional:

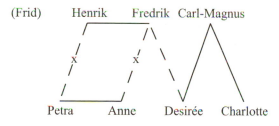

As indicated, Frid (the Armfeldt butler) is not yet a "player," and the horizontal lines have for the most part not been activated. Neither Fredrik Egerman (a successful lawyer) nor Henrik (his eighteen-year-old son) has made real headway with, respectively, Anne (Fredrik's very young wife) or Petra (their maid). Fredrik's affair with the famous (but now touring) actress Desirée Armfeldt is long a thing of the past. And Carl-Magnus (Count Malcolm, a dragoon) is openly unfaithful to Charlotte (his wife), in an obviously mismatched affair with Desirée. Yet, once Frid makes his first move on Petra, the "solution" to the puzzle becomes as obvious as if a switch has been thrown:

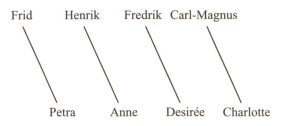

But this is, of course, neither a chess game nor a logic puzzle, and although the romantic issues are clear enough on this schematic level, the situation becomes a good deal more complex once Fredrik tries to reactivate his connection with Desirée (an attempt consummated in *A Little Night Music*, though not in the original film), and other considerations and plot machinations have been added to the mix:

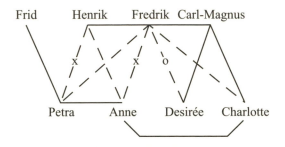

In the original film (but less so in the musical), Petra flirts openly with Fredrik, in a bit of saucy verbal byplay and a series of speculative glances.[48] Much later, Charlotte, too, will flirt with Fredrik, in an effort to make Carl-Magnus jealous. Desirée, as it turns out, has a child by Fredrik, of whom he has been unaware (Desirée is coy about this, but her boy in the film is named Fredrik, and her daughter in the musical is named Fredrika). And although Anne and Desirée form no bond, it turns out that Charlotte is the older sister to a childhood friend of Anne, so that they easily become co-conspirators. (Although Desirée and Charlotte are the main co-conspirators in the film, the musical does not develop the connection; I have therefore left that line out of the chart.) And (not shown), Fredrika becomes Henrik's confidante in the musical, reinforcing the potential for them to fall easily into their roles as half siblings (a potential already suggested by their parallel introductions, playing the piano and cello, respectively).

Aside from Fredrik's obviously pivotal position within this precarious set of intertwined relationships (notwithstanding the "end run" of Charlotte to Anne), it is clearly a very messy situation indeed. In fact, each line in the chart, as indicated, makes the situation more tangled for the two involved, so that Fredrik, who connects with every other character (except Frid), has the messiest life of all. Desirée's choice is easier, at least in theory, yet her apparent isolation, as shown in the chart, is counterbalanced by her interactions with her mother and her daughter, a dimension much expanded in the musical, which also includes pivotal dialogue between Fredrika and her grandmother.[49] But Desirée's isolation is nevertheless quite real, and sharply contrasted with the situation of the other women, each of whom has a close relationship with at least one other woman, to the extent of indulging (especially in the Bergman film) in a touch of homoeroticism. The latter, in turn, sharply contrasts with the extremely contentious relationships among the male characters.

In converting Bergman's scenario into a musical, Wheeler and Sondheim made many adjustments, two of which are particularly important to the special dynamic of the show as a sex comedy. In Bergman's film, Desirée is the main conspirator, inviting both parties (the Malcolms and Egermans) for a weekend so as to unfold her scheme for winning Fredrik back; there is even a strong suggestion that she has enlisted Frid's help so as to pry Petra away from Henrik, which will in turn pry Anne away from Fredrik. Addressing the other end of the schematic, she enlists Charlotte's help to make her husband (Carl-Magnus) jealous through Charlotte's flirting with Fredrik, with the aim of forcing the count to give up his affair with Desirée. In the film, then, the tidiness of the outcome is conceived initially as a scheme engineered by Desirée, reinforced as "natural" through Frid's explanations to Petra about the three "smiles" of the summer night; to chart the relationships in the film, then, one would need to draw lines linking Desirée to both ends of the chart, through which she sets up two dominolike chain reactions with herself as the beneficiary.

But in the musical, where Desirée is more isolated, there is no mastermind for the plot, only a series of missteps that somehow manages to come right by the end.[50] Thus, Desirée invites only the Egermans, who have determined not to go until Charlotte's intervention. Charlotte, desperately unhappy, subsequently (but still within the same song, "A Weekend in the Country") tries to make Carl-Magnus jealous by telling him about the invitation, which backfires when he insists that the two of them also go, unannounced. The plot to seduce Fredrik is not Desirée's but Charlotte's (with the collaboration of Anne), but it seems to produce no effect beyond increasing her own humiliation. As in Bergman's film, Henrik's immediate response to his witnessing Petra with Frid is not to pursue Anne but to attempt suicide (an attempt that is diverted in the film with particular charm). And Fredrik is unable to make the choice of Desirée over Anne, even though he knows it is his familial obligation and perhaps his only path to personal salvation (hence, "Send in the Clowns")—until he sees Anne running off with Henrik, which initially sends him into such despair he almost welcomes the opportunity to play Russian roulette with Carl-Magnus. In the musical, no one is orchestrating these events, so that their elaboration comes across much more as an unraveling of plots than as a progression toward resolution.

What the musical offers instead of a mastermind is a master perspective: that of Desirée's mother, who watches everything with exaggerated disapproval, knowing that the only way the game can come out right is if all the players gracefully accept their roles within it, which they mainly refuse to do through most of the show. In the musical, she and the benign providence of the "summer night" seem to merge; as the night comes to a close and the couples have aligned properly—last of all her daughter and Fredrik—she dies. While Mme Armfeldt's elevation within the story's hierarchy eliminates Frid's pivotal function (leaving him with nothing to do beyond seducing Petra, scarcely a challenge), it gives both an increased presence to an older sensibility and an authoritative voice to the ache for something irretrievably lost. The symbolic point of the smiles also changes to accommodate this changed configuration, in part to reflect Mme Armfeldt's personality (as opposed to the more generous Frid), and in part to align with the thematic texture of the show and its retrospective view of operetta. In the film, the smiles—which seem to bestow an unearned happiness on their recipients—correspond to three stages in the coupling process: the first is for young love (Henrik and Anne), the next is for fools (Petra and Frid, Charlotte and Carl-Magnus), and the last is for the sad and lonely (Fredrik and Desirée).[51] In the musical, the smiles trace a similar but importantly different trajectory: the first is for the "young, who know nothing" (not quite the same as young love; this smile is for Fredrika), the second is for the "fools who know too little" (all four sets of lovers; in Mme Armfeldt's words at the end of the show, "The smile for the fools was particularly broad tonight"), and the third is for the "old, who know too much"; thus, with the final smile, Mme Armfeldt dies knowing that her daughter and granddaughter are on course toward a more fulfilling future.

The nostalgic perspective of Mme Armfeldt, tinged with a profound regret for a lost world and sensibility, is echoed within the personal perspective of the most agonized member of each "natural" couple: Charlotte, who desperately wants to become once again the focus of her husband's romantic attention; Henrik, who is trying too hard to be older and is caught between his religious training and his "sinful" impulses; and Petra, whose fertile mind and fervent spirit imagine more possibilities than really exist for her ("The Miller's Son"). Naturally enough, Mme Armfeldt's perspective is echoed most importantly within the angst of the lead couple, Desirée and Fredrik, each equally agonized, who know they have let their lives slip away and do not until the very end fully believe in the possibility of their personal redemption through a shared future. Mme Armfeldt's perspective is echoed as well on a larger scale, as the entire show seems to ache for the return to the world it evokes (the beginning of the twentieth century) and the musical modes then operative. The questions that seem to hang over the show are, Can we go back? Can we return to the blithe assurances of happy endings? Can we recover the optimism of youth? Can we still waltz? Can we, in these senses, go back to operetta?[52] And the answer Wheeler and Sondheim pro-

Example 1.6a. *A Little Night Music*: excerpt from "Night Waltz"

Example 1.6b. *The Merry Widow*: excerpt from "Merry Widow Waltz"

vide—characteristically ambiguous—is something between "No, but . . ." and "Yes, but . . ."

The "No" is perhaps most clearly stated in the ache of the music, whose eminently singable melodies, some of which would be right at home in *The Merry Widow*, are trapped within bittersweet minor-mode harmonies laced with pungent dissonances. Thus, the first melodic phrase of the "Night Waltz" reproduces the contour of the repeated culminating gesture of "The Merry Widow Waltz" (see example 1.6), but within a more veiled harmonic idiom, slanted toward the minor mode. More specifically, the "veiled" nature of these dissonances derives from Sondheim's use of a device known as a double tonic, in which (in this instance) the established orchestral key of D♭ major is at odds with the melodic key and its most immediate support, in F minor, creating a layered harmonic effect and enhancing the sense of a troubled distance between gesture and reality.

1.68
1.69

Confronted with this conjunction of allusion and dissonance, one may wish to recall that the Viennese-oriented Arnold Schoenberg and Gustav Mahler were working with such dissonances as these at precisely the time of *The Merry Widow*—indeed, Mahler was a bit of a specialist in the use of double tonics—so that profound existential doubt had, through them, already found a musical voice at the same historical moment as the second great flowering of Viennese operetta. And one might also wish to recall that Mahler's and Schoenberg's contemporary Richard Strauss—the composer of such disturbing operas as *Salome* (premiered in 1905, the same year as *The Merry Widow*) and *Elektra* (1909)—managed, shortly afterward, to score a huge success with his contemporary operatic response to operetta,

Der Rosenkavalier (1911), which also looked back to Mozart and which "A Weekend in the Country," "Now–Later–Soon," "Remember," and "Perpetual Anticipation" all seem to refer to.[53]

But if *A Little Night Music* nevertheless has seemed to be the first real attempt to conflate a modernist musical temperament with operetta, it is because it does so from the perspective of a musical tradition—the American musical—that had not found a place for such dissonances until the renewal of modernism after the Second World War—and then only occasionally, most notably with Marc Blitzstein and Sondheim's early collaborator, Leonard Bernstein. However easily we might imagine Lehár writing the tune to the "Night Waltz" or Lehár's contemporaries providing its dissonant harmonies, context tells us that those harmonies come from a much later age. Because the show is grounded in the musical comedy traditions of Broadway, the felt perspective of *A Little Night Music* fuses with that of Mme Armfeldt in yet another way, as the ache for something lost seems neither borrowed nor imposed from without, but *remembered*. Through her persona, through Sondheim's own progression from the musicals of the 1940s on, and through his working securely within the generic traditions of Broadway, Sondheim seems to put us in the presence of an operetta sensibility that has somehow survived the evolution into modernism and is now reaching back for that lost world through the dissonant haze that has evolved around it.

But the possibility of answering "Yes" to the questions posed earlier is also implied throughout the show, first through the important *act* of remembering, and last through the equally important *fact* that the plot does, after all, work out—not because its characters deserve it in any real sense, but because of a natural benevolence that continues after all this time to smile benignly on them (and also, presumably, on us).

The importance of memory is established at the outset and maintained throughout. The overture, sung rather than played—by the "Liebeslieder singers," a chorus of five commentators who are at once the ghosts of operetta and the innermost thoughts of the "real-life" characters in the show—begins with "Remember" (after a vocal "warm-up") before reversing temporal directions with "Soon" and taking us directly into the moment with "The

♪1.70   Glamorous Life" (with its imperative "Bring up the curtain").[54] But what that curtain opens to is a danced instrumental number, "Night Waltz," which looks back to *The Merry Widow* not only in the specific way already mentioned but also in its device of introducing its central song as an intimate wordless dance; notably, the "Night Waltz" ends, in its first appearance in the second act, with a hummed version of the tune, and returns as an instrumental number at the end of the show (Sondheim eventually backed away somewhat from this concept, adding words to the opening waltz number

♪1.71   for the 1977 film version of *A Little Night Music*).[55] Throughout the show,
♪1.72   memory will be seen to be key, denied to the Egerman family at the opening
♪1.73   in the elaborate tour-de-force "Now–Later–Soon"—an unusual combination song that knows no past tense—and to Desirée in her mad rush into the

future ("The Glamorous Life"). Both the quintet's "Remember" and Mme Armfeldt's "Liaisons" counteract these with their phantasmal series of vignettes—ending with the latter's regretful pronouncement:

♩1.74
♩1.75

> In a world where the kings are employers,
> Where the amateur prevails and delicacy fails to pay,
> In a world where the princes are lawyers,
> What can anyone expect except to recollect
> Liai . . . (she falls asleep).

Her last full word, "recollect," echoes the quintet's "Remember" and emphasizes that the point of the song is not its ostensible content (that is, the remembered liaisons) but the act of remembering itself. Significantly, Sondheim guards against our hearing the complete word "liaisons" in his setup of the final rhyme, since the lyric is complete with the second syllable; even on this level, what is being remembered is not as important as the activity of remembering.

Time is the central issue throughout the show, which amounts to an extended fermata on twilight. Always, the show looks forward or back, rooted in its moment, imprisoned by its characters' seeming inability to find their way to a coherent link between past and future. And nearly all the songs reflect this temporal hiatus, not only in those already mentioned (and "The Glamorous Life" is no exception), but in such obvious anticipatory songs as "A Weekend in the Country," "Perpetual Anticipation," and "The Miller's Son," which are in turn balanced by the redemptive backward look of "Send in the Clowns," with its rueful consideration of bad timing and opportunities missed. And yet, there are two important mitigating considerations—pulling in opposite directions, of course—that the show elaborates for us. First, the past as it is reconstructed in memory turns out to be as negotiable as the future. Throughout "Remember," for example, the details seem oddly disjunct from the larger shapes of the memories, ready to reattach themselves to an entirely different situation with entirely different players (thus such concluding lines as "I *think* you were there"). Second, the story embodies a fundamental irony: only by letting go of the past—symbolically realized through Mme Armfeldt's death—may the future be enabled. Put differently, time may seem to stop, in a perpetual twilight, but it can never rewind. And death—the final proof of this—has been a preoccupation throughout, offering ultimate resolution to a series of intolerable situations. Charlotte sings "Every Day a Little Death" to a mostly uncomprehending Anne—and it is the touch of actual death she means, not the "little death" by which sexual coitus was once euphemistically referred to (except, perhaps, in the release, when she sings "but first I die")—whereas both Henrik and Fredrik come uncomfortably close to succeeding in their respective suicide attempts.

Particularly deserving of attention in Sondheim's score is the unusual joining together of "Now" (sung by Fredrik), "Later" (Henrik), and "Soon" (Anne). This is the first and most literal of several "triangle" songs in the

show; although not restricted to the triangles in the earlier charts, these songs do map that terrain fairly thoroughly, since they include "You Must Meet My Wife" (Fredrik and Desirée, about Anne), "In Praise of Women" (Carl-Magnus, about Desirée and Charlotte), "Every Day a Little Death" (Charlotte and Anne, whose disconnect stems from a double image regarding the third member, Carl-Magnus for Charlotte, and Fredrik for Anne), and "It Would Have Been Wonderful" (Fredrik and Carl-Magnus, about Desirée). Each individual song in the "Now–Later–Soon" complex details both musically and verbally the managerial style of its singer. As with Carl-Magnus's prosaic managerial style,[56] Fredrik's suits his profession, as he judiciously considers nested possibilities for seducing Anne in the best lawyerly fashion, a series of nested As and Bs that reduce in the end to the default position of an afternoon nap.[57] Musically, the song proceeds as a series of patter-song bursts describing alternatives within alternatives, well within the tradition of Gilbert and Sullivan and on the same level of verbal cleverness (reminding us, perhaps, that Gilbert was a lawyer by training)—all in counterpoint with Anne's seeming nonsense, which is, however, clearly designed both to tease
♫ 1.76   and to fatigue him. Henrik's song "Later" also proceeds against a controlling counterpoint, in his case provided by his own playing of the cello ("It isn't gloomy, it's profound"), which has already been established through dialogue with Anne as a stand-in for the strict Lutheran training he is receiving from Pastor Ericson.[58] Caught between that training (the cello), the urges of the flesh, and being perpetually put off by Anne, Petra, and his father, Henrik, in this ruminative song, proceeds in a series of fitful bursts, reaching two agonized climaxes; for the second of these, he reverses roles with the cello,
♫ 1.77   imagining himself lying on his deathbed after a long life of unrelieved "later."

Both father and son, in their different but similarly ruminative ways, express frustration at the endless tease of their lives, seeking "now" but always getting "later." With Anne's "Soon," however, we first hear the perspective of control as she puts off "now" with a softer, seemingly more yielding form of "later." Perhaps surprisingly, her insistence on the indefinite is endorsed as the "right" response to badly managed passion. Thus, hers is the most songlike of the three; it is also the most spontaneous in effect, changing rhythmic style and key several times as an emblem of impetuous femininity (which finds an echo in other songs in the show that originate from a youthful feminine perspective: Fredrika's "Ordinary Mothers," which introduces the various tempi and perspectives of "The Glamorous Life," and Petra's "The Miller's Son"). And it actually manages to *manage*, which neither Fredrik's "Now" nor Henrik's "Later" can seem to do. Thus, when the songs combine, hers is the only one that emerges intact and assured, with Henrik's plaint bending to its changing moods and Fredrik's dream version of "Now" drifting in and out of focus, at a slower pace, at times incoherent, and (as appropriate for a dream that turns out to be about Desirée) more graphic in
♫ 1.78   its sexual images. Sondheim's combination song therefore becomes a matter
♫ 1.79   not just of presenting two or more contrasting points of view simultaneously

(according to the conventions of the type) but also of projecting a hierarchy between and among them that is at once against the grain of assumed masculine control and "natural," since Anne is singing the upper, most "melodic" part. Moreover, there is a dramatic reason that Anne's control should seem complete at this point, since the payoff of the song is the shattering of that control—and with it Anne's sense of security—at its end, when Fredrik sings the name Desirée where he had previously sung Anne.[59]   ♪ 1.80

Hierarchy is also an important consideration in Carl-Magnus's "In Praise of Women," set to the rhythms of an imperial polonaise, in which he tries, somewhat confusedly, to sort out the possibilities after he discovers Fredrik in Desirée's rooms, dressed in his (Carl-Magnus's) dressing gown.[60] First, of course, there is the simple lawyerly management of facts and testimony, which seems beyond him but which we already know to be Fredrik's stock-in-trade. More subtly, the song denies him the strongest military possibility—the march, proscribed here by virtue of its being in duple time—by taking the form and style of a polonaise. The latter type befits Carl-Magnus's position and demeanor and is even historically accurate, as by the late nineteenth century (through Chopin and the Russian imperial tradition) it had acquired a strong ceremonial role supported, as here, by fanfarelike figures. Moreover, its traditionally "softer" middle section (its "trio") allows Carl-Magnus to express, in counterpoint to his growing mistrust of Desirée, his generalized admiration of "Capable, pliable, women." But the polonaise setting denies him the possibility of dynamic action, freezing him, temporally,   ♪ 1.81
within the inactivity of ceremony and posturing, rather than motivating him   ♪ 1.82
into activity in the way that a march might. As it happens, Sondheim will soon enough provide him with at least the semblance of such a march in "A Weekend in the Country," which serves as the first-act finale. Set to a rollicking 6/8 meter just slightly slower than, for example, Meredith Willson's "Seventy-six Trombones" (and the Sousa marches that the latter recalls), "A Weekend in the Country" has the effect of a march on Carl-Magnus, finally galvanizing him into action, however blundering it might be.[61]   ♪ 1.83

Of all the backward looks in the show, that of "Send in the Clowns" is the most important, even though its engagement with the past is quite oblique.[62] Introduced in the second act as a "false resolution" of the main couple's story, the song mirrors the "bad timing" of its subject in two ways, through placement, in coming too soon within the plot structure, and through musical detail, in its insistent duple-meter countermelody placed against the triplets in the melody and accompaniment (see example 1.7). Its immediate successor, "The Miller's Son," also indulges in duple meter (in fact, these are the most prominent duple-meter passages in the entire score), as if to ground its fanciful dreams within the realities of sexual encounters: ♪ 1.84

> It's a wink and a wiggle and a giggle on the grass
> And I'll trip the light fandango,
> A pinch and a diddle in the middle of what passes by.

Example 1.7. *A Little Night Music*: excerpt from "Send in the Clowns"

But in "Send in the Clowns" such realities seem remote, leaving us with a wistful duple-meter descent in the clarinet, lamenting lost opportunities. Thus, the song's evocations of the characteristic pauses of the Viennese waltz anticipate their ecstatic arrivals in vain and are simply left hanging, like unanswered questions.[63] Even more vividly, the song's tracing and retracing of such pauses and arrivals betray Desirée's natural affinities for the world of operetta (much like, for example, Adelaide's bump-and-grind "Lament" in *Guys and Dolls* betrays her milieu),[64] pulling against the resigned text with a taste of the sexual release being denied. And the point is scarcely lost on Fredrik, who hears both words and musical gesture, unable to contradict the former or partake of the latter. The song, introduced late in the second act, is nonetheless the first in the show to behave like a love duet—there is, for once, no third party being discussed—but he is unable to join in, and she is left to finish the song on her own.

Wrenching as this song is in itself, it is the key to Fredrik's and Desirée's redemption in two ways. First, it reveals them as self-acknowledged fools ("clowns"), unable to do what is best for them, however sad and lonely the alternatives might prove to be; surely they are in line for the second of the night's smiles. Second, it sets up its own reprise—arguably its most important function within the show—by establishing an extended moment that can be returned to from a more satisfactory vantage point. Thus, shortly after the song, the requisite sequence of recouplings flies by in rapid order, accompanied by brief reprises from the first act, courtesy of the Liebeslieder singers: "Soon" (Anne and Henrik), "You Must Meet My Wife" (Fredrik, with Charlotte, observing Anne and Henrik leaving together), "Liaisons" (Carl-Magnus seeing Fredrik with his wife), "A Weekend in the Country" (the Russian roulette challenge), and "Every Day a Little Death" (Charlotte's realization that Carl-Magnus has "become a tiger" for her). Suddenly, the quickly unfolding plot leaves Fredrik and Desirée no choice but to embrace their chance for happiness—against all odds, but according to the laws of musical theater, which demand that they reprise their big tune, and this time together, as a genuine duet. And in the enhanced orchestration of "Send in

Figure 1.4. The inspired artwork for *A Little Night Music* (used, with slight varia-tions, for playbills, posters, and the covers of sheet music and cast albums) hides its panoply of nudes and lovers—the latter in various poses ranging from pre- to postcoitus—within the branches of a silhouetted tree (easier to spot here than in the original, with its dark blue, starlit background). While providing a suitable icon for a sex comedy set in Sweden, with the summer sun hovering low in the sky, the image also evokes the Tree of Knowledge from the Garden of Eden. Thus, the bright orb of the perpetually setting sun substitutes for Eve's apple (both as an image and by revealing Eve's nudity), and the serpentine interweaving of the tree's lovers and oda-lisques proffers, as the tree's forbidden fruit, a knowledge that is specifically sexual (that is, "knowledge" in the biblical sense).

the Clowns," the wistful clarinet obbligato countermelody is transformed
♪1.87   into an assured part of an enriched orchestral fabric.

In presenting a stylized version of Viennese operetta, *A Little Night Music*
serves to some extent to idealize operetta, imagining it to be something it
never was. In place of the inadequate translations of actual Viennese operetta
or the somewhat coarsened American product that took its place, Sondheim
offers his own exquisite verbal control, and he bypasses altogether the characteristic laughter of operetta—its cherished gaiety, in both senses of the
word—which has little place in *A Little Night Music*. Thus, once the warm-
up exercises conclude at the beginning of the show, we are virtually finished
with the element of vocal display indulged for its own sake, and there is no
hint of the traditional laughing song (except, perhaps, in "The Glamorous
Life"—the point of which is how bereft of laughter Derirée's life actually is,
a perspective rendered musically by the labored offbeat awkwardness of the
♪1.88   repeated refrain "la, la, la"). In fact, we have, especially in Glynis Johns,
who created the role of Desirée, a diva who does not really sing, at least
according to the standards of operetta, notwithstanding the verve and pa-
thos with which she delivers her songs. And as Stephen Banfield has pointed
out, *A Little Night Music* is a "waltz musical" without a ballroom scene.[65]

Yet, in one core respect *A Little Night Music* is unimaginable except as a
latter-day Viennese operetta, and it is fully consistent with the type. In *A
Little Night Music*, as in *The Merry Widow*, it is ultimately the women who
control what is ostensibly a man's world. *A Little Night Music* is framed by
Mme Armfeldt passing her wisdom on to her granddaughter Fredrika. The
Liebeslieder singers are overbalanced in favor of the women.[66] Early on, the
Anne-dominated trio of "Now–Later–Soon" gives way to the daughter-
mother-grandmother dynamic of "The Glamorous Life." Even the men's
songs are about the women ("You Must Meet My Wife," "In Praise of
Women," "It Would Have Been Wonderful"—all essentially versions of *The
Merry Widow*'s "Women," if considerably less raucous). Given traditional
societal hierarchies, it is perhaps inevitable that operetta, in its pulling the
focus from larger concerns to a more personal dimension, must also shift its
focus to the exercise of womanly control.

Equally intriguing is operetta's tendency to focus on the past, and here it
is useful to note yet one more parallel between *A Little Night Music* and
The Merry Widow. In both shows, the seemingly impossible undertaking of
the lead romantic couple is to recover a love they once shared. In *A Little
Night Music*, there simply is no story if Fredrik and Desirée have no past
together, or if that past is happily *in* the past. And precisely the same can be
said regarding Danilo and Hanna. Already with *The Merry Widow*, our gaze
is directed toward something lost in a seemingly irretrievable past. And so
also does *A Little Night Music* look back, its longing amplified by improbability and distance, from beneath a veil of melancholy dissonance prescribed
by modernity and the unstoppable passage of time.

For Further Consideration

El Capitan (1896), *The Fortune Teller* (1898), *Babes in Toyland* (1903, films 1934 and 1961), *The Dollar Princess* (1909; originally *Die Dollarprinzessin*, 1907; German film 1971), *The Chocolate Soldier* (1909, film 1941, television 1955), *Gypsy Love* (1911; originally *Zigeunerliebe*, 1910), *Alma, Where Do You Live?* (1910), *The Pink Lady* (1911), *The Firefly* (1912, film 1937), *The Merry Countess* (1912; based on Johann Strauß's *Die Fledermaus*, 1874), *The Count of Luxembourg* (1912; originally *Der Graf von Luxemburg*, 1909), *Sweethearts* (1913, film 1938), *Sari* (1914; originally *Die Zigeunerprimas*, 1912), *Maytime* (1917, film 1937), *Apple Blossoms* (1919), *Blossom Time* (1921; based on melodies of Franz Schubert; film 1934), *Rose-Marie* (1924, films 1936 and 1954), *The Student Prince* (1924, films 1927 and 1954), *The Vagabond King* (1925, films 1930 and 1956), *Countess Maritza* (1926; originally *Gräfin Mariza*, 1924), *The Desert Song* (1926; films 1929, 1943, and 1953; television 1955), *A Connecticut Yankee* (1927), *Show Boat* (1927; films 1929, 1936, and 1951; television 1989), *The Three Musketeers* (1928), *The New Moon* (1929, films 1930 and 1940, television 1989), *Bitter Sweet* (1929, films 1933 and 1940), *San Francisco* (film 1936), *The Girl of the Golden West* (film 1938), *Oklahoma!* (1943, film 1955, television 1999), *Song of Norway* (1944, film 1970), *Yours Is My Heart* (1946; based on Lehár's *The Land of Smiles*, 1929; films 1930 [in German], 1952 [in German], and 1974 [in German]), *Brigadoon* (1947, film 1954, television 1966), *Kiss Me, Kate* (1948, film 1953, television 1958, 1968, and 2003), *Kismet* (1953, film 1955), *The Girl in Pink Tights* (1954), *My Fair Lady* (1956, film 1964), *Candide* (1956, television 1986 and 1989), *Gigi* (film 1958, staged 1973), *The Sound of Music* (1959, film 1965), *On the Twentieth Century* (1978), *Into the Woods* (1987)

See Also

Regarding operetta in America generally, see Gerald Bordman's *American Operetta: From* H.M.S. Pinafore *to* Sweeney Todd, chapters 4, 6, and 20 in Ethan Mordden's *Better Foot Forward: The History of the American Musical Theatre;* "American Operetta" and "Broadway," in Richard Traubner's *Operetta: A Theatrical History* (pp. 356–421); and, from *The Cambridge Companion to the Musical*, Orly Leah Krasner's "Birth Pangs, Growing Pains and Sibling Rivalry: Musical Theatre in New York, 1900–1920" and William A. Everett's "Romance, Nostalgia and Nevermore: American and British Operetta in the 1920s."

Regarding operetta films, see chapter 6 of Rick Altman's *The American Film Musical* and pp. 58–60 in Everett's "Romance, Nostalgia and Nevermore."

Regarding *The Merry Widow*, see "The Merry Widow and Her Rivals," in Traubner's *Operetta: A Theatrical History* (pp. 242–73) and pp. 35–40 of Krasner's "Birth Pangs, Growing Pains and Sibling Rivalry."

Regarding *Naughty Marietta*, see Frederick S. Roffman's extensive and illuminating notes to the Smithsonian complete recording, pp. 354–62 of Edward N. Waters's *Victor Herbert: A Life in Music*, and pp. 20–21 of Ethan Mordden's *Broadway Babies*.

Regarding *A Little Night Music*, see especially chapter 18 of Craig Zadan's *Sondheim & Co.*, chapter 7 of Stephen Banfield's *Sondheim's Broadway Musicals*, chapter 5 of Steven Swayne's *Hearing Sondheim's Voices*, chapter 13 of Meryle Secrest's *Stephen Sondheim: A Life*, and chapter 5 of Joanne Gordon's *Art Isn't Easy: The Achievement of Stephen Sondheim*; see also pp. 200–12 of Stephen Citron's *Sondheim and Lloyd-Webber: The New Musical*, pp. 101–06 of Ethan Mordden's *One More Kiss*, and, for a discussion of the Liebeslieder singers (as chorus), pp. 230–34 of Barbara Means Fraser's "Revisiting Greece: The Sondheim Chorus."

The Movie Musical

THE AMERICAN MUSICAL has maintained a double life, between Broadway and Hollywood, ever since it reached its full "maturity" with *Show Boat* in 1927. That very year, *The Jazz Singer* introduced the era of the "talkies" (movies with synchronized sound),[1] which from the beginning were often as much "singies" as "talkies" (to borrow Andrew Sarris's distinction)[2] and have remained partial to musicals ever since, whether through re-creating staged musical numbers or shows or through exploring ways in which film musicals could and should differ substantially from staged musicals. Overall, the interaction between stage musicals and film musicals, between Broadway and Hollywood, has been an extremely productive one, if sometimes contentious.

Synchronized sound was one of two major technological enhancements to film under development in the 1920s, the other being color. Both were prohibitively expensive in their early development and involved complex mechanical arrangements to maintain reliably steady camera and projection speeds, although both the incentives toward development and the prospects of unmanageable expense were much greater with sound. The greater expense of sound was due to the dual needs to produce a synchronized product (difficult enough in itself) and to upgrade theaters to accommodate it; indeed, because of the latter difficulty, both sound and silent versions were made for many films during the transition.[3] But the incentives for developing synchronized sound were even stronger than the disincentives, stemming in large part from the fact that the "silent" films were not actually silent but accompanied throughout by music performed live in the theater (or, in later days, by recorded sound tracks), so that music, unlike color, had long been an expected part of seeing a film. It was only later, when the art of accompanying film had all but died out, that these films became (and became known as) "the silents."[4]

The constant presence of music during the screening of a "silent" film was deemed necessary to enhance the drama and increase the sense of continuity, the latter especially after the wide adoption of montage techniques—that is, cutting between shots—after 1915. But this accompanying music also provided a near-constant reminder of its own clumsiness as a device, continually underscoring (so to speak) how crudely it performed these tasks. The accompanist (sometimes a full orchestra, but more often an organist or pianist), however well prepared or skilled, was awkwardly placed, neither part of the film nor merely part of the audience, but forced to simulate the first

while being in reality the second. As a result, music was too obviously something layered over the film, which was particularly distressing when people
on-screen were either producing music or responding to it. Indeed, with the
advent of synchronized sound, music's importance in film briefly began to
diminish somewhat (except in musicals) so as to make room in the sonic
foreground for speech and other sounds added to give more reality to the
filmic world.[5] Even so, it was song—which an accompanied "silent" film
was particularly inadequate in representing—that sold the new technology
in its early stages (that is, in the wake of *The Jazz Singer*) and forced the
hand of those reluctant to take the expensive plunge into sound film.

Four things about *The Jazz Singer* seem surprising to those who know it
only by its historical position as the first successful "sound" film. First, well
over half of the film was "silent"; the new technology was exploited mostly
in the musical numbers. Second, beyond experiencing the initial gratifying
shock of seeing Al Jolson perform, many of its early viewers were even
more viscerally engaged by the moments in which he spoke, particularly the
lines he ad-libbed: "Wait a minute—wait a minute—you ain't heard nothin'
♩2.1   yet!" Third, its technology was not the one that ultimately held sway for
synchronized sound, which shortly thereafter and ever since has placed the
recorded sound directly on the film to ensure synchronicity. Instead, *The
Jazz Singer* relied on a rival technology (Vitaphone) in which wax records
were played while the film was screened. Although this approach allowed a
higher sound fidelity at that time—an important marketing consideration,
since Jolson's recorded voice was well known—it created enormous difficulties of synchronization, which were solved, at least in theory, by using the
same motor to drive both projector and turntable. The fourth surprise is in
its way the most disturbing today, although then it was simply taken for
granted: Jolson's casual use of blackface. The long tradition of blackface
minstrelsy has since been so thoroughly "edited out" of American cultural
life that, even given the often unacknowledged racial stereotypes that still
persist from the heart of that tradition, blackface has come to seem particularly repellent, especially in the wake of the civil rights movement of the
1960s. Thus, often what is most shocking to later viewers of *The Jazz Singer*
is not the use of blackface itself but the complete absence of any sense that
there was something wrong with the practice.[6] But while the technological
and racial dimensions of *The Jazz Singer* are in themselves quite important
(and the latter will be reconsidered here in relation to *Stormy Weather*), our
more immediate concerns are with the first two surprises, which highlight the
importance of musical numbers in early sound films and offer an intriguing
perspective on how those numbers interface with the perceived "naturalness" of a film's world.

Although the prospect of being able to preserve musical performance on
film was one of the principal incentives for developing the supporting technology, singing came fairly early on (in fact, already in *The Jazz Singer*) to
become associated with a kind of staginess that seemed to violate the new

standard of naturalness taking shape in American sound film. Many of those making nonmusical sound films sought to avoid such obvious artificialities along with the melodramatic acting styles of the silent era, favoring instead a more understated and natural-seeming style. More than might have been expected, musical numbers jumped out within a film as something artificial and alien, especially as musicals, too, began quickly to favor a less melodramatic style. In *The Jazz Singer*, this aspect was additionally emphasized first through the "silent" film that surrounded the musical numbers and, even more significant, by Jolson's spontaneous spoken outburst, quoted earlier. Thus were established the twin but antagonistic pulls of musical performance in film, toward the spontaneity and enhanced realism of live performance and toward an overt artificiality. Significantly, color, too, seemed an artificial enhancement when it first became a more widely used technology, and so it occasioned the same polarized impulses, toward a more "natural" muted quality and a more artificial vibrancy. The extreme instance of the latter polarity is *The Wizard of Oz* (1939; see chapter 3), a musical that, in a kind of primitive synesthesia, used black-and-white (actually, sepia-tone) sequences for the "real world" of Kansas and color for the "not-in-Kansas-anymore" land of Oz (see also the later discussion of the black-and-white sequences in *Singin' in the Rain*). In parallel fashion, musical numbers in film became occasions for escaping the real world and its constraints and were valued—but also derided—accordingly.

Thus, if sound films made it possible to create a fuller sense of the world, they also made music, especially when sung on-screen to unseen accompaniment, seem an artificial intrusion. Yet, there were powerful incentives to make musical numbers in films work. First, of course, were the commercial considerations: musicals were popular; their songs could both make money on their own and advertise the film; and their stars were often either already known as singers or eager to become so known. But even putting aside these considerations, an honest concern for naturalness had to allow for the fact that people in the real world do, in fact, sing and dance, although not typically with the skill and technological advantages afforded by Hollywood or Broadway. Moreover, a long tradition onstage (in opera and its derivatives) had reinforced the idea that music gave access to a reality beyond the "naturalness" of a "real world" simulated through scenery and spoken drama. In response to this situation, film musicals often adopted a two-pronged approach, setting up musical numbers as "naturally" as possible (the "backstage musical" was particularly good for this, or other scenarios that involved characters who were also performers) but moving fairly quickly into what I will here term a Musically Enhanced Reality Mode (henceforth MERM), which permitted both audio and visual violations of what might actually be possible.[7]

The trick—already common in staged musicals, where the urgencies were not so pronounced—was first to sneak into song or dance as a small extension of natural reality: sitting down to accompany oneself or another at a piano or introducing—if one had the grace of a Fred Astaire—elements of dance into mere walking or more "natural" physical contact. Once an audience accepted that first step, they were ready to move into MERM, whether accomplished in similarly gradual increments or all at once; moreover, in this kind of sequential evolution, MERM could even seem to constitute direct personal expression. MERM could take many forms, separately or in combination; thus, for example, MERM almost always involved lip-synching to studio-based singing with nondiegetic instrumental and/or vocal support, but it could also include overdubbing taps to a dance routine or any other invisible enhancement to the performance the audience is ostensibly witnessing, even when that performance is diegetic (that is, when we know its source within the filmic world).[8] But more central to our concerns than these technical considerations are the heightened sense of reality that MERM imparts to the musical number, and more specifically the extra charge it gives to a sung performance, as if shining a sonic spotlight on the singer (an effect enhanced by the frequent use of close-ups in such numbers).

Decisions about how readily to indulge in MERM ranged from virtually refusing to do so to doing so whenever possible, sometimes seeming to switch approaches within a single film; for this and a variety of other reasons, MERM is not generally a useful criterion for developing typologies of film musicals. Rather, typologies of film musicals tend to make distinctions based on featured performance mode, story line, and style; a list of this kind might include "dance" musicals, "backstage" musicals, "singing cowboy" musicals, and operetta, among others.[9] Although such distinctions are not our principal concern, one type does seem important to distinguish here: some film musicals are adaptations of stage musicals, whereas others are not. In the previous chapter I considered briefly one type of adaptation among the former, the operetta film, where the process of adaptation often "naturalizes" the surroundings within a full-scale transformation. Yet, in many important ways, even the most straightforward adaptations create a fundamentally different artifact from the original stage show, even if, as stated in "Entr'acte," filmed adaptations are immensely useful to us in providing latter-day or continued access to what started out as stage musicals.[10] Nevertheless, although intriguing differentiations might be made among adaptations, and between them and their staged versions, adaptations cannot be our principal concern here. Nor can this single chapter of a book on a more general topic provide a full-scale treatment of the film musical as a type distinct from the stage musical. Rather, what seems a reasonable approach here is to explore the dynamic between MERM and filmic realism within a very few specific films, with eye and ear directed to the emergent personal dimension of this dynamic, while at the same time noting relevant aspects of film musicals as they evolved historically.

I have, partly for convenience, chosen two musicals that purport to tell focused histories of musical performance and at the same time to re-create, in part, the critical period in American history that provided the backdrop for Hollywood's early sound era. The first choice is obvious; *Singin' in the Rain* has long been regarded as the definitive treatment of the early evolution of the film musical. A less obvious choice is *Stormy Weather*, since its background is neither the mainstream American musical nor the film musical, and its purported time frame is much broader, taking in the entire period between the two world wars; yet it thereby provides a good foil for *Singin' in the Rain*. Its situation as an all-black musical film made during the Second World War requires, however, a foil in itself—in fact, two foils. Thus, in tandem with *Stormy Weather*, I will consider the treatment of similar material in Spike Lee's *Bamboozled* and then turn to a near contemporary of *Stormy Weather*, *Meet Me in St. Louis*, which was one of the most perfectly realized film musicals of its era—and which, like *Singin' in the Rain*, came out of the celebrated Freed Unit at MGM.[11] Finally, in a paired exploration of MERM, I will consider together two much later celebrations of that dimension, *Moulin Rouge* and *Chicago*, the latter being the only adaptation I will consider in this chapter. As will become evident, the general direction here will be from considerations of the history of film musicals in the first half of the chapter to considerations of how filmic MERM creates a vehicle for personal identity formation and expression.

Some dimensions of the history of the American film musical are inevitably short-changed by this structure, but that can only be lamented, not remedied. In perhaps the most critical among these lapses, the first fifteen years of film musicals are represented only indirectly, by two films that tell very different histories of the era, each with a mix of authenticity and inaccuracy. Both build implicitly on the coincidence of this era with the Great Depression and link musicals to America's attempt, through the offerings of its "entertainment industry," to escape into a world of fantasy. This coincidence has a secure foundation in the many overt musical "escapes" that proliferated in this period, which certainly did try to dance and sing America's troubles away. But the actual historical pattern belies an easy casting of early film musicals as America's escapist answer to the Great Depression. Film musicals began with great success well in advance of the stock market crash in October 1929; thus, Al Jolson's hugely successful follow-up to *The Jazz Singer*, the 1928 *Singing Fool*, outsold all the Depression-era live-action musicals (it is believed to be the top grossing live-action sound film in America before *Gone with the Wind* in 1939).[12] While 1929 and 1930 were big years for film musicals, the public then seemed to lose interest in them until a few years later, when Busby Berkeley's elaborately campy, MERM-based extravaganzas (beginning especially with *42nd Street* in 1933 and *Dames* in 1934) helped to reestablish a market for them, soon to be exploited by a variety of stars and star combinations.[13] The early success of filmed operetta, and its central star Jeanette MacDonald, tapered dramatically after 1930, until both enjoyed a renaissance around mid-decade, first with Lubitsch's *The Merry Widow*, in 1934, but more dramatically with the teaming of MacDonald and Nelson Eddy, which began the following year (see chapter 1).[14]

Fred Astaire (a stage star from the 1920s, often appearing then with his sister, Adele) made a new beginning in film with Ginger Rogers, first in *Flying Down to Rio* (1933), where they shared second billing, and continuing with a five-year run of successes launched with *The Gay Divorcee* in 1934. Shirley Temple, after a series of often (perhaps unintentionally) campy appearances (especially in the Baby Burlesk series), began her own slightly longer run of feature successes in 1934 as well and for several years was the most bankable star in Hollywood (from 1935 to 1938). After Judy Garland had displaced Shirley Temple by the end of the decade, the "child star" was eventually given the chance to grow up during the war years, as we will see in *Meet Me in St. Louis*. (Although her role in the latter represented a slight step back from her adult role in *For Me and My Gal* of 1942, it nevertheless allowed her a graceful position between youth and a sometimes overtly maternal adulthood.)[15]

Nor are the 1930s the only decade effectively left out in the following explorations, which involve certain thematic bases for film musicals—especially as supported by MERM—more centrally than the history of the genre. The extensive list "For Further Consideration" given at the end of the chapter, even though it omits adaptations and includes only a handful of some other genres or star vehicles, gives some indication of how great the loss is. Quite clearly, however, the film musical requires either separate, more extensive treatment or, as here, a highly circumscribed treatment that places it within a larger consideration of the American musical, whatever the corresponding loss.

Singin' in the Rain (1952) did not have quite the noble origins one might imagine for a film destined to become a classic film musical, perhaps *the* classic film musical. It was first conceived as an extreme case of avoiding royalty payments by reusing songs by Nacio Herb Brown (music) and the film's producer, Arthur Freed (lyrics), which were already owned by the studio (MGM). Freed hired the veteran writing team of Betty Comden and Adolph Green, who developed their script as a potential vehicle for Gene Kelly while he was still filming *An American in Paris* (dir. Vincente Minnelli, 1951), having already worked with Kelly and his codirector, Stanley Donen, on Leonard Bernstein's *On the Town*. Choosing mostly songs from two films, *The Hollywood Revue of 1929* and *The Broadway Melody* (1929), Comden and Green fashioned their story as a kind of backstage musical about the early days of the film musical, interweaving familiar themes regarding the difference between appearance and reality, and implicitly noting the important roles that fantasy, celebrity, and generalized glitter—the mythology of Hollywood—played in America's response to the Great Depression.[16]

Comden and Green thus used budget necessities to their advantage, grounding the show securely within its "authentic" time frame, and at the same time banking on their audience's nostalgic affection for the recycled tunes. Moreover, they had, in their title song, the key to both parts of this strategy: a particularly well-known song that expressed metaphorically the film's main theme of turning misfortune into its obverse, celebrating America's capacity for "singin'" during the "rain" of the Great Depression. In an elegant thematic saturation, the song also expressed both the improvisatory adroitness of its principal characters, who repeatedly use the materials at hand as they adapt to changing times (mainly adjusting to the advent of sound film), and, more privately, the similar adroitness of the show's writers, who made efficient use of a constricted repertory of songs, in some cases exploiting and even exaggerating their formulaic basis, rather than trying to disguise it. Although initially *Singin' in the Rain* was not as successful as *An American in Paris*, which had the added advantage of a more distinguished score (using Gershwin tunes), similarly assembled so as to appeal to America's nostalgia for a more innocent age, its more perfectly realized alignment of songs and story has helped make it more enduringly popular.[17]

Singin' in the Rain draws knowingly on a number of well-known situations and legends of Hollywood, especially but not exclusively connected to the era just before and after the conversion to synchronized sound. Thus, the film presents identifiable types—a variety of stars with distinctive personalities, their fickle fans, the chorus girl hoping to be "discovered" (Kathy Selden, played by Debbie Reynolds, herself only recently discovered and virtually untrained as a dancer), the gossip columnist (Madge Blake as Dora Bailey, who according to the script "bears an unmistakable resemblance . . . to Louella Parsons"), the harried director (Douglas Fowley as Roscoe Dexter, a thinly disguised Busby Berkeley), the all-powerful head of the major studio, Monumental Pictures (Millard Mitchell as R. F. Simpson), and so on. In the latter case, one may detect specific references to MGM's power management team of Sam Goldwyn and L. B. Mayer (by that time replaced as head of the studio by Dore Schary), both in Simpson's use of initials in lieu of a first name and in his occasional Jewish locution (referring to *The Jazz Singer*: "Yeah, what a freak—we should have such a freak at our studio"—not, however, delivered with a Jewish inflection). But the real target in this case is the film's actual producer, Arthur Freed (thus, Ar[thur] F[reed]), who was notoriously clumsy (hence the malapropism, à la Goldwyn, "We're going to put our best feet forward").[18] The female megastar from the silent era, Lina Lamont (Jean Hagen), with her doubled initials in imitation of countless "sex symbol" stars, is shadowed throughout the film by Zelda Zanders, the "It Girl" played by Rita Moreno, referred to in the film as "the well-known 'Zip Girl' " (thus putting a more graphic spin on the already sexually charged "It Girl"). Lamont is drawn dually from the many stories of stars whose uncultured or otherwise unpleasing voices kept them from making the transition to sound film and (to put the audience at ease about Lina's failure in particular) the many stories of stars, directors, and producers who abused their power both arbitrarily and to further their careers.[19] And Cyd Charisse's turn in "Broadway Ballet" as a balletic version of Louise Brooks, replete with the latter's trademark pageboy hairdo,[20] is oddly intertwined with the ominous presence of a coin-tossing scar-faced gangster (played by Carl Milletaire), who combines the roles played by Paul Muni and George Raft in Howard Hawks's 1932 *Scarface*. These specific references, along with reasonably accurate accounts of some early difficulties of the talkies, help ground the film in historical reality; those difficulties include technical problems of microphone placement and synchronization, inadequacies of early dialogue (whether stemming from overzealous writers or improvising actors), the expense of outfitting theaters with sound equipment, and the cumbersome procedure for making wax records.[21]

But the more basic reality that broadens and deepens these specifics is the unique ability of film to create its own reality. Early on, we see through a film montage that the verbal autobiographical account given by star Don Lockwood (Gene Kelly) is grossly inaccurate, as it shows him hoofing (with sidekick Cosmo Brown, played by Donald O'Connor) in poolrooms rather than attending the "finest schools" he describes, or clowning in burlesque and taking falls as a stuntman while he speaks of "dignity, always dignity" (see figure 2.1). But we also see film's ability to create the illusion of elegance from the crude materials of Don Lockwood's melodramatic acting and Lina Lamont's sensibilities, a team whom Dora Bailey aptly describes as "like Bacon [i.e., Ham] and Eggs—Lockwood and Lamont." Significantly, we see the result of this Hollywood magic in the screening of their newest film, *The Royal Rascal* (a film that, despite Dora Bailey's gushy prediction, is *not* destined to be "the outstanding event in 1927," not even in Hollywood), before we hear Lina give herself away through speaking in an exaggeratedly grating voice and accent: "What's *wrong* with the way I talk? *What's* the big idea, am I *dumb* or something?"[22]

Equally explicit about the importance of illusion is Lockwood's first romantic number with Kathy, "You Were Meant for Me." After his fumbling beginning—"I'm trying to say something to you, but I . . . I'm such a ham. I guess I'm not able to without the proper setting"—he takes her to an empty soundstage, where he enlists the help of a romantic backdrop, lighting, stepladder, a mist generator, and a wind machine, with which he constructs the proper mood. The elaborate setup is really about establishing a context for MERM, of course, by taking us to a place where a song with dance is all but required, where music can substitute for the words that elude him. Notably, the background music begins to make itself felt first when each "special effect" is turned on (in the kind of musical support that became known as Mickey Mousing, after Walt Disney's Silly Symphonies, produced between 1929 and 1939); the extended number also provides an example of the walk-into-dance transition. (Also, significantly, Kathy does not sing in this number, and her dancing is less than a convincing match for his, even though we have seen her already as an effective part of a chorus line.)

Given the film's frank acknowledgment of the divide between appearance and reality, especially in film—and here, the key sequence is also the linchpin

♪2.2

Figure 2.1. Cosmo Brown (Donald O'Connor) and Don Lockwood (Gene Kelly) ham it up as a vaudeville team in "Fit as a Fiddle," in an early montage sequence from *Singin' in the Rain* that gives the lie to Don's voice-over narrative of a more refined theatrical background. (Photograph courtesy of Miles Kreuger and the Institute of the American Musical, Inc.)

for the plot, the overdubbing of Kathy's voice for Lina's—one might suppose the film's own manipulations of fact and circumstance to be more obvious than they are. But the generalized "magic show" of the movies makes those manipulations seem to disappear behind a semblance of familiarity—much as the ostentatious use of special effects in "You Were Meant for Me" cloaks the fact that it is all just a pretext and enhancement for the song. This process of "cloaking through familiarity" may be noted early on, when we see the orchestra accompanying the gala premiere of *The Royal Rascal* but actually hear a soundtrack fashioned after a later practice, replete with at least one splicing to match a scene change. The real reason for the orchestra's presence, however, seems to be less historical accuracy than the need to establish a precedent for the presence of an orchestra at the premiere of *The Dancing Cavalier* at the end of the film, where it is completely unwarranted in historical terms but absolutely required for the dramatic denouement. Thus, it accompanies the reprise of "Singin' in the Rain," where Lina Lamont is unmasked (or, rather, unvoiced), and "You Are My Lucky Star," which seems to be a reprise of "You Were Meant for Me" but isn't (a deft substitution

♩2.3
♩2.4

that removes the latter's destiny-driven imagery from the past tense so as to project a blessed future). And, midway between these framing sequences, the "out-of-sync" passage from the abortive tryout of *The Dueling Cavalier* more closely resembles what a later audience would have experienced, when an improperly maintained "loop" between the audio pickup and the projector light results in a visual "delay"—even though the technology in question supposedly involves wax records rather than sound on film.[23] And, sandwiched between these screenings, all of which are in black and white—seemingly an inversion of the effect in the *Wizard of Oz*, where fantasy aligns with color—we see two extended sequences that purport to show us "period" film musical sequences ("Beautiful Girl" and "Broadway Ballet") but that are in vibrant color.

But the more important historical lapses in the film derive from the problem of trying to suggest a more extensive history while ostensibly remaining within the "snapshot" of time between the two premieres that frame the main action of the film. The inevitable violations of the film's time frame are already evident in the montage for "Beautiful Girl," which establish two late-1920s styles, with "flappers" dancing to "I've Got a Feeling You're Fooling" and an imitation Rudy Vallee crooning "Should I Reveal Exactly How I Feel?" into a megaphone, only to intermix those styles with one that emerged long after the time frame of the film (about half a decade later, well into the 1930s): Busby Berkeley's directorial style. The latter is evident not only in the general use of montage and the aggressive use of "assembly-line" dancers for the "flapper" number, but also in the marching "toy soldiers" of "Wedding of the Painted Doll," the ending group choreography filmed from above in a kaleidoscopic "crane" shot, earlier specialty shots involving moving cameras and tilting perspectives, and a more complex crane shot superimposed onto the interior of the crooner's megaphone. Given how much of this depends on postproduction and perspectives unavailable on the set—which is ostensibly our perspective as well—it is especially amusing to hear Simpson's reaction to the number: "That's stupendous. . . . This'll start a new trend in musical pictures." Simpson's line seems (incorrectly) to suggest, as do Comden and Green in their description of the ending as "a pioneering, pre–Busby Berkeley overhead shot,"[24] that this early musical (from 1927–1928) was part of a more continuous development into the early 1930s.

The telescoping of film-musical history in this number, oddly contradicted a few scenes later in the extremely inept deployment of microphones during the filming of *The Dueling Cavalier*, is then extended into the 1950s with "Broadway Ballet," based mainly on two songs, "Broadway Rhythm" and "Broadway Melody." This later number uses stylized settings of Broadway derived from those of Times Square in the 1950 show *Guys and Dolls*, whose choreographer, Michael Kidd, seems also to have been an inspiration for the stylized dancing in the number. "Broadway Ballet" is fairly obviously meant to be a counterpart to the extended ballet in *An American in Paris* of the previous year, telling a similar story of betrayed love, yet the number remains grounded in the late 1920s through Cyd Charisse's portrayal of a vamp resembling Louise Brooks and its references to "Roaring Twenties"–style gangsters (even if the latter derive, as already noted, from a 1932 film). The use of the coin toss in this number reflects a somewhat different kind of iconic slippage; originally used in *Scarface* to indicate a casually contemptuous indifference to human life and death (the flipped coin would often end up on the bodies of murder victims), the gesture here aligns with the lure of material wealth, and by extension suggests the rampant commercialism of Broadway, which in this number resembles Las Vegas more than Times Square.

Singin' in the Rain also indulges, in its central plot device of dubbing singers' voices, in an intriguing blend of fiction and historical reality. The 1929 film *Broadway Melody*, whose title tune is used to frame the "Broadway Ballet," was indeed pivotal in the pioneering technique of lip-synching musical numbers, originally conceived as a way out of the cumbersome procedures then being used for filming with sound. Prior to that film, camera movement had been restricted so as not to interfere with simultaneously recording the sound, which resulted in a very static visual dimension. By recording the musical numbers first and then filming to what became known as "playback," filmmakers freed themselves to pursue more imaginative camera manipulations, which quickly became an indispensable component of MERM. But such is neither the rationale nor the procedure for the dubbing that occurs in *Singin' in the Rain*, where it is done to displace an inadequate voice with a more suitable one and takes place after the actual shooting, so that it is dubbed over an existing soundtrack, rather than the reverse.[25]

In the development of its love story, *Singin' in the Rain* follows a particular plotline that came to have a great deal of currency in Hollywood films, especially in "buddy" films (and most especially those directed by Howard Hawks), involving a kind of "love triangle" in which the long-standing friendship of two men (often a hero and his sidekick) is threatened by the attraction of one of them to a woman introduced early on (the ingénue, although often not exactly an innocent).[26] Generally, this plot situation may be taken to carry homosexual overtones, so that the story becomes a parable about embracing heterosexual love. This interpretation is, of course, quite easily avoided, since most sidekicks have next to no discernible sex drive, at least during the film's story,[27] but it is surely significant that, in more recent times, the asexual sidekick is often replaced by a homosexual friend. And even the latter development may be explained away, given the utility of the sidekick plot situation and recent shifts in what audiences might accept as either "natural" or interesting wrinkles on the device. Nevertheless, the homoerotic tension in some of these relationships is significant enough to lay the entire tradition open to this interpretive avenue.

There were a number of ways in which the homosexual dimension of these stories could be disguised or seemingly eliminated. For example, the obstacle to the heterosexual romance might be presented not as the love between the two men but as a shared attitude toward women, whether as contempt (often disguised as womanizing), distrust, or some other aversive reaction. In musicals, where double readings are nearly always possible, these kinds of "disguises" will seem either fully effective (from resolutely "straight" perspectives) or sure signs of a hidden subtext (for those inclined and equipped to read them).[28]

In *Singin' in the Rain*, the male friendship between Don Lockwood and Cosmo Brown may well have been patterned on *An American in Paris* (although potential models are legion), with Donald O'Connor's dancing adding a spirited physical dimension to the cynical, wisecracking, piano-playing sidekick of Oscar Levant in the earlier film. The homoerotic overtones are somewhat more overt in the earlier film, especially given Levant's narcissism and insinuating delivery, which always seems to hint at unspoken meanings.[29] In *Singin' in the Rain*, Lina Lamont provides both an effective "beard" for Don and Cosmo and a foil, representing both the reason for Don's "unattached" state and the basis for their mutual contempt for women. Yet the signs are all there to be read for those interested in reading them: Cosmo and Don performing as a burlesque team, in which they sit on each other's laps and play each other's violins; Cosmo's comment to Lina after the premiere of *The Royal Rascal*, "Yeah, Lina, you looked pretty good for a girl";[30] and their bullying, in "Moses Supposes," of the fogyish diction coach, figuratively drawn out of his closet only to be ridiculed as an asexual "pansy" who can't sing and dance (thus both confirming and denying homosexuality at the same time).[31] On a broader scale, Kelly's career as a dancer, offering a more masculinized style of athletic dance (in opposition especially to the stylized grace of Fred Astaire), represented a similar balancing act between, in this case, the feminized occupation of balletic dance and a strong claim of heterosexual masculinity.

Significantly, the process of exclusion they use with the diction coach is precisely what Cosmo proposes they apply to Lina in converting *The Dueling Cavalier* into a musical: "It's easy to work the numbers. All you have to do is dance around Lina and teach her how to take a bow." But they also apply the strategy to Kathy, who is only just learning to "dance" in this sense (conveniently so, since Debbie Reynolds had had but little dance training, as noted).[32] Early on, we see her dance competently in "All I Do Is Dream of You," but she then seems extremely tentative in "You Were Meant for Me," immobile for much of the number, not joining in the singing, and dancing only as Don draws her in (which is, of course, consistent with her character's development at this point). With "Good Mornin'," though, she seems to "arrive" as part of the Don-Cosmo team, even though for part of the number she serves as a kind of mannequin—much like the voice teacher in "Moses Supposes," except that she sings the song proper while Don and

Cosmo "improvise" tongue-twisting elaborations between the lines. As the number evolves, their emerging positions within the group become clear. Thus, during their solo clownish dance bits, using their raincoats as props, Kathy and Don present themselves as fetishized love objects, Kathy as an "Island girl" and Don as a matador, while Cosmo dances with a "dummy," recalling his earlier solo turn in "Make 'em Laugh."[33] At the end of the scene, when Kathy kisses Don, Cosmo objects, thereby provoking Kathy to kiss him as well, to which he responds with girlish abashment (the exchange replays the part of "Good Mornin'" when Kathy sits first on Don's knee, then on Cosmo's).

♪2.5
♪2.6
♪2.7

Yet Don and Kathy do not yet engage fully as romantic partners, which becomes clear during the following number, Kelly's famous solo rendition of the title song, "Singin' in the Rain," introduced by his deliberately isolating himself (kissing Kathy good night and then waving off the cab driver). Alone on the rain-drenched sound stage (assuming we have learned to recognize it as such from "You Were Meant for Me"), he clarifies the MERM-related function of such effects, which seem in themselves to demand that he sing. The coordination of MERM and Hollywood-style special effects is particularly close in this number, as he soon leaves the song behind, first to explore the sets and props conveniently at his disposal, and then to match the music's crescendo with an expansive embrace of the larger space. Here, the camera cranes outward, and Kelly breaks through into a moment of "dancing-sublime," when his dancing seems either to revert or to come full circle, returning to the primitive urge that gave it birth (thus his stomping and jumping in the puddle like an adolescent boy).[34] But the number, through its supreme narcissism, actually does more to inhibit than to advance the plot.

Surprisingly, the true linchpin for the film is not "Singin' in the Rain" but "Broadway Ballet." Despite the latter's seeming superfluity to the plots of either Singin' in the Rain or The Dueling/Dancing Cavalier, and the absence in the number of either Kathy Seldon or Lina Lamont, it is core to both the romantic plot and the implicit theme of the film: the displacement of Broadway with Hollywood as the ultimate American fantasyland.

In terms of the romantic plot, the number gives Lockwood more heterosexual credibility than his scenes with either Seldon or Lamont could, as he meets the sexual challenge offered by Cyd Charisse. Thus, after he arrives at her feet to retrieve his hat from her outstretched leg, his eyes rising in awe to the cigarette she smokes through an elaborate holder, she blows smoke in his face, rubs his glasses on her inner thigh, kicks his hat and then his glasses away, and sticks her cigarette in his mouth—which finally provokes him to an intensely sexual response, as he throws the cigarette aside and pulls her to him for the beginning of what is obviously, however stylized, a prolonged sexual encounter, replete with highly suggestive body language and phallic leg extensions. Then, in the later stages of the ballet, after a brief montage of his evolving career, he imagines her in idealized form, now with long hair and long train, and dancing classical ballet on her toes, all without her losing the sexual charge of their earlier coupling, which is still notable, for example, in the iconic unfurling of her long train after it is "stroked" by his body. But the stage for their imagined interaction is no longer public, shifting in his imagination to a sound set, obviously evocative in its wind and moonlit effects of the set where he (as Don) had earlier sung "You Were Meant for Me" to Kathy.[35] In an odd transmutation, then, when Cyd Charisse renounces Don's character (she is last seen flipping a coin to him as she departs with "Scarface"), she leaves both her sexualized and idealized images vacant for us to insert Kathy Seldon. In this sense, Cyd Charisse functions as Kathy's stunt double, although officially it is Lina Lamont's inadequacies as a dancer that she is covering for, since the sequence is purportedly part of *The Dancing Cavalier*.[36] Also facilitating this mental substitution are the apparent separateness of this sequence from either *Singin' in the Rain* or *The Dancing Cavalier*, and the recurring theme of substitution, which is elaborated both in Don's early career as a stunt double and in Kathy's dubbing of Lina's voice for *The Dancing Cavalier*. (In an additional twist to this shell game of film-based substitutions, Jean Hagen's voice, and not Debbie Reynolds's, was reportedly used in some of the "dubbed" sequences.)

Notably, however, after Don's character imagines an idealized Cyd Charisse on a Hollywood sound stage, it is to a vulgarized version of Broadway that he returns. In fact, the stylized Broadway that we see throughout this number is often, as noted, more evocative of Las Vegas than what might typically be understood to represent Broadway. The most prominent neon sign reads "Casino" (first seen directly over Kelly's head after his vocal introduction), and we later see roulette wheels as a prominent part of the setting. Musically, the central variation of Broadway Rhythm, in the first of Kelly's duets with Cyd Charisse, layers a Vegas bump-and-grind rhythm onto the tune in a literal transmutation of "Broadway rhythms" into Vegas rhythms. Systematically, then, the image of Broadway is cheapened and made to seem cynically engaged with material wealth, so that Hollywood may be seen to provide the more idealistically inspired escape into fantasy.[37] Although this may seem to fly in the face of the "normal" hierarchy, which regards Hollywood musicals as a cheap, dolled-up imitation of a venerated Broadway tradition, the credibility of the construction is compelling on one central level: Broadway, now jaded and decadent, needs the rejuvenating spirit of Hollywood youthfulness. If that youthfulness is phony to the core, well, that too is part of the American "make-do" process of converting rain into smiles. Phoniness is merely artful exaggeration.

The negotiation between Broadway and Hollywood is nevertheless a precarious one; when Kelly sings at the beginning of the ballet, "Don't bring a frown to Old Broadway, / Ah, you gotta clown on Broadway," the disparaging "Old" and "clown" are offered up through a pretense of affection. And even though the ballet as a whole reads most easily as a scenario to justify the move from Broadway to Hollywood, since the former has let the hero down through its cynicism, it ends with the promise of youthful regeneration on Broadway itself. But the larger point is securely made. Turning the dross of the "silent" era's melodramatic excess into the exaggerated glamour of a film musical seems a natural move given the capacity of film to enhance MERM. It is after all MERM, combined with Hollywood's technological ingenuity, that makes the idea of dubbing Lina's voice seem a brilliant stroke in the first place, leaving little room to consider the problematic disjunctures of the visual and audio dimensions that commonly result from such dubbings in actual film musicals. Since creating illusion as an alternative to reality is both a Hollywood thing and a Broadway thing, it seems eminently reasonable that the former should assert to the latter, "You Were Meant for Me," and to claim, throughout a long period of involvement, "You Are My Lucky Star."

Stormy Weather (1943) and *Bamboozled* (2000) provide very different perspectives on what is in some cases very similar material. It will be interesting to probe here both parts of this relationship, but first it is important to establish more fully the context to which both respond. This is especially pressing after considering *Singin' in the Rain*—a musical about the development of the Hollywood musical following the release of *The Jazz Singer*, but which makes only extremely oblique references to the latter's use of blackface, one of its most salient and culturally important features.[38] Behind this outwardly strange circumstance is the pervasive marginalization of blacks in Hollywood, which both permitted the perpetuation of blackface and systematically denied blacks a central place within mainstream films—just as if this were the natural order of things.[39] Although Hollywood did not invent blackface and race-based hiring practices, it both perpetuated them within a medium that produced more lasting and widely distributed artifacts than minstrelsy, vaudeville, or burlesque and, after this heritage became an embarrassment, conspired to conceal the extent and lasting effects of those practices, while to a large extent continuing them, albeit less obviously.

Especially in the 1930s, but well into the 1940s, blacks were consigned within the major studios mostly to comic and servant roles or to musical numbers—often enough in films in which whites applied blackface and perpetuated the full range of pernicious stereotypes associated with the minstrel stage. Perhaps the most nefarious practice in Hollywood's cynical history of managing the racial divide between blacks and whites involved separating black musical entertainers as fully as possible from the substance of the mainstream films—usually with otherwise all-white or predominantly white casts—that they sometimes appeared in, so that their footage could be excised for screening in the American South. Thus, most typically, performances by black entertainers in these films would be framed by such devices as an applauding audience, making their removal more easily pass unnoticed when such films were screened in cut versions for audiences who would have been shocked and outraged by the appearance of black performers in a "white" picture.[40]

This despicable but entrenched way of doing business, reinforced by the oligarchic structures of the studio system, could not have persevered for as long as it did without a fair amount of complicit behavior from those involved creatively in making films, whether producers, directors, screenwriters, songwriters, choreographers, singers, dancers, or actors. But assigning responsibility is difficult. To begin with, this was only one of many seemingly intractable restraints placed upon filmmakers, which also included, most notoriously, the prudish and dictatorial Hays Code, established in the mid-1930s to maintain standards of "decency" in American films, and the politically repressive atmosphere that followed the late-1940s probe of Communists and their "sympathizers" in the movie industry by the House Un-American Activities Committee (HUAC).[41] Considering the intended audience for *Singin' in the Rain*, and how accustomed its makers were to Hollywood's various repressive and unnegotiable prohibitions, it would have made as little sense for them to probe the African American roots of its dance numbers—to choose a particularly fraught example—as it would have for them to lay bare its closeted homosexual dimension. On one level, it *does* seem reasonable to hold those we see on the screen—or, perhaps, the writers, choreographers, and directors who shaped the films—at least partly responsible for the ill-treatment of blacks in the film industry and the perpetuation of that ill-treatment, since they had learned so much from black performers and yet occupied places, with few outward signs of bad conscience, that were systematically denied to blacks. But individual agency in the suppression of blacks was minimal, since attempts to balance the books would have been accompanied by great personal risk and little chance for measurable success.

One of the difficult lessons to learn from such cases of institutionalized societal bigotry is that assigning retroactive blame to its easiest available targets is a losing game, tending to turn them into scapegoats for a widespread practice that already existed and would have persisted with or without their participation. Worse, this sort of scapegoating draws attention away from just how pervasively supported the practice was. The reality was that many in Hollywood felt various degrees of guilt about Hollywood's racist policies—a guilt that they sometimes admitted but more often hinted at, left unspoken, or simply denied—yet nothing substantial was done about it for a very long time. Thus was American racial bigotry indulged and its policies ingrained until the civil rights era began to erode its power and legacy—a process that still has far to go a half century after the Supreme Court ruled in 1954 that public schools must be desegregated (which is when many date the beginnings of the civil rights movement).

There are many dimensions to the incalculable damage done to blacks through the racist practices of the studio system. Many enormously talented individuals who attempted careers in the mainstream film industry found those careers severely curtailed and their contributions artificially kept on the margins, since they were unable to exercise the kind of options available to other disadvantaged or maligned groups. There is a big difference in circumstance between the homosexual or Jewish performer, writer, or director—who could adopt the outer mask of white, heterosexual "normalcy" while perhaps covertly including elements that might mean something quite different to an audience "in the know"—and a black man or woman who had no such opportunity, very little agency, and almost no power. Most often denied a legitimizing place within mainstream films, many blacks sustained their careers by making "race films," produced by black-owned companies and distributed mainly to "colored" theaters; of these companies, only the Micheaux Company, run by Oscar and Sean Micheaux, survived into the 1930s after the stock market crash of 1929, although others would later appear. Within the Hollywood studio system, however, blacks had only a very few opportunities to create filmic worlds of their own, and these were heavily circumscribed.

Stormy Weather is one of only three feature films made by the major Hollywood studios with all-black casts between 1930 and 1954.[42] All three were written and directed by whites, and none is without serious problems when considered as a possibly viable alternative to the more common all-white film. *The Green Pastures* (1936, directed by William Keighley and Marc Connelly), for example, is a retelling of biblical stories by a black southern preacher in an "Uncle Remus" mode, using heavy dialect (with coaching provided by a white actor) and locating its situations within a landscape familiar to his purported audience. Although many have found the result uplifting and humanizing, it does not fully escape its origins in *Ol' Man Adam and His Chillun*, a 1928 collection of stories by white humorist Roark Bradford, as patronizing to its characters and setting as it may have been intended affectionately.

The Green Pastures remained the only all-black film from a major studio during this period until 1943, when, after considerable lobbying by blacks and under pressure from the United States government as the country prepared to enter World War II, the studios responded with two all-black musicals, MGM's *Cabin in the Sky* (the directorial debut of Vincente Minnelli)[43] and Twentieth-Century Fox's *Stormy Weather* (directed by the less distinguished Andrew Stone). *Cabin in the Sky*, despite its all-star cast and its being based on a successful Broadway show, received a mixed reception. In particular, some critics found little to redeem its perpetuation of black stereotypes; the film's black community comprises a simple, primitive, superstitious folk (as in *The Green Pastures*), and its male protagonist (Eddie Anderson, by then already teamed with Jack Benny as "Rochester") is unable to give up his shiftless, sinful ways, nor resist the temptations of Georgia Brown (Lena Horne), despite the pure Christian love of Petunia Jackson (Ethel Waters).[44] *Stormy Weather*, for its part, offers an impressive panoply of star turns by Bill "Bojangles" Robinson, Lena Horne, Ada Brown, Fats Waller, Mae E. Johnson, Cab Calloway, the Nicholas Brothers, and Katherine Dunham and her Troupe. But it has seemed to many somewhat hollow at its center, with a hackneyed plot that celebrates the fictionalized career of Robinson—who outside the film was criticized for being an "Uncle Tom," too willing to ingratiate himself with whites—and mismatches him romantically with Horne, with neither character receiving any real development.[45] Moreover, the larger point of the film, or at least of the elaborate musical sequences that frame its central narrative, seems wholly cynical: to celebrate black contributions to the earlier war effort in order to "support," in advance, their contribution in the second. If all three films achieved moderate success in their day, they did not lead to significantly greater involvement by blacks in film, at least not immediately or directly.

One of the seemingly odd features of *Stormy Weather*, given its basic rationale as an alternative to white perspectives on blacks, is its use of images and tropes associated with blackface minstrelsy. Thus, for example, it opens with Robinson (as Bill Williamson) tap-dancing with black children, accompanied by a harmonica, on a plantation-style porch reminiscent of the old South, and the extended concluding number of the film reproduces a semblance of that porch onstage. Another early number, ostensibly celebrating African American heroism in World War I, is a cakewalk based on two tunes familiar from late nineteenth-century minstrelsy, Stephen Foster's "Camptown Races" and Kerry Mills's "At a Georgia Camp Meeting"; although the dancing is less clownish than its nineteenth-century counterpart might have been, the women's wide bonnets become, when seen from behind, blackface ♩2.8 caricatures that seem almost obscene in this context. Somewhat later, on a riverboat bound for Memphis, we hear such minstrelisms as "educated feet" during a "challenge number" ("Linda Brown"), introduced by the "miraculous" revival of an exhausted Robinson, whose feet respond to the sound of the minstrel band. Primitive "jungle" settings provide the background for two successive stage-production numbers, "Diga Diga Do" (Lena Horne) and "African Dance," which provides the occasion for a Robinson specialty number (dancing on multileveled tom-toms, a variation of his trademark staircase tap routine). Dooley Wilson plays a shiftless bootblack (Gabriel) specializing in "promoting" the appearance of great wealth. And Williamson's own show includes a blackface number by "The Shadracks" (played by Ned Stanfield and Johnny Horace), a classic "indefinite talk"[46] routine in ♩2.9 which each member of the comedy team interrupts the other:

A whole dozen'll cost about . . .

> That's too much money. I can't afford it. I got to get some that don't cost no more . . .

You can't get 'em that cheap.
. . .
Can you make it on next . . .

> No, I'll be busy then.

Well, when can you make it?

                            Let's see, the best day for me . . .

That suits me. What hour?

                            Anytime between . . .

That's a little early, but we'll be there.

Spike Lee's *Bamboozled* recycles much of this material—a plantation porch (peopled by a band called the Alabama Porch Monkeys), the "educated feets" (*sic*) of its tap-dancing superstar, a miraculous revival of that star through his animalistic response to outer stimuli (using watermelon instead of music as the agent of revival), an indefinite talk routine, and even a cakewalk by the "Pickaninnys," a collection of black stereotypes including Aunt Jemima, Topsy, Sambo, and Jungle Bunny—but places it all within a much harsher light.[47] By frankly borrowing the device, from Billy Wilder's *Sunset Boulevard* (1950), of having a dead man narrate the story, the film inverts the more traditional mechanism employed by *Stormy Weather*, of recounting a successful career from its humble beginnings, narrated by the star. The satirical plot premise of *Bamboozled* is that its protagonist (Pierre Delacroix, played by Damon Wayans), an angry television writer, tries to get himself fired through the outrageous idea of mounting *The New Millennium Minstrel Show* (TNMMS) as a television series—a scheme that backfires when his white producer (Dunwitty, played by Michael Rapaport) loves the idea, and the show becomes a huge success after a briefly rocky start. This premise, too, is a pointed borrowing, recalling Mel Brooks's *The Producers* (1968) in its presentation of a show so outrageously offensive that it seemingly must fail (yet doesn't), but substituting the resurrection of blackface minstrelsy for *The Producer*'s "Springtime for Hitler." Implicitly, *Bamboozled* thereby claims that American slavery, the institution minstrelsy romanticized, is America's Holocaust, a comparison Spike Lee makes explicit in his voice-over commentary for the DVD issue of the film.

       ♪**2.10**

Thematically, *Bamboozled* explores the love-hate relationship many whites have with black culture, both through the white producer—who claims to be "blacker" than Delacroix, has a black wife, and collects black sports memorabilia—and through the whites in the mixed-race audience who respond to the show, eager to embrace the opportunity to belong to the semblance of black culture it presents. By the end of the film, the television audience is also wearing blackface, and its members enthusiastically claim that they, too, are "niggas," in response to the repeated chant of the emcee, (Huneycutt, played by Thomas Jefferson Byrd), "Niggas is a beautiful thing." Yet the images from the past that are sprinkled throughout the film almost exclusively express the hatred of whites for blacks, or at least their attempt to confine blacks to a well-circumscribed role within white culture, where they were patronized as curiosities and something considerably less than human. Thus, Delacroix gives his genuinely talented stars (Manray and Womack, played by Savion Glover and Tommy Davidson) the stage names

Mantan and Sleep'n Eat, and we see, as counterpoint to the main story, a stupefying collection of racist memorabilia, along with images documenting the perpetuation of blackface and black stereotypes in films and on TV. (The latter includes footage of the original Mantan Moreland, most active between 1936 and 1949, whose specialty was simulating a quivering, wide-eyed, superstitious cowardice; there was also an original Sleep 'n' Eat, Willie Best's stage name beginning in the 1930s.)

Curiously, though, the actual performances for TNMMS tell a somewhat different story. Filmed more vividly than the rest of the film (using film rather than digital video), TNMMS presents its exaggerated stereotypes, as might be expected, as offensively as possible; thus, its black performers appear in full blackface and resurrect every racist cliché of the tradition. Yet it also shows vividly the basis for a positive response: the resilience and zest, the sly subversion of authority, the verbal cleverness based in "uneducated" dialect, the physical grace and sheer musical talent, for which whites celebrate "blackness"—all of which emerge even (or perhaps especially) in the context of minstrelsy. Moreover, the film believably traces the audience's progressive reaction, by showing the live audience's "takes" on the show, beginning with a confused disgust mitigated by rueful appreciation for the show's audacity, humor, physicality, and musical appeal, but gradually transforming, through the "permission" granted by the positive response of some blacks in the audience, into open enjoyment and full identification. It is, in many ways, a frightening transition to watch, intertwined as it is with the various ways the film's audience may be responding, which could range from a parallel progression toward acceptance, perhaps mitigated by a more distant perspective or persistent reluctance, all the way to an implacable, visceral rejection out of hand. The latter response is also given expression in the film, through both Delacroix's assistant, Sloan Hopkins (played by Jada Pinkett-Smith), and the extremist Mau-Maus, a wanna-be gangsta rap group (a genre that constitutes, according to Spike Lee in his spoken commentary, the "real twenty-first century minstrel shows"), who kidnap and kill Mantan on live television—another pointed borrowing, this time from Sidney Lumet's 1976 *Network*. Sloan's response, too, results in murder, as she shoots Delacroix, who dies watching a video montage Sloan has prepared of minstrelsy's legacy (compiled with the help of archivist Judy Aley).

On another level, *Bamboozled* probes black complicity in the perpetuation of minstrelsy and its lingering stereotypes. Ironically, this has a good deal of historical validity, since—surprise, surprise—once blacks were allowed to appear on the minstrel stage after the Civil War, it turned out that they were on the whole much better than whites at simulating blackness and making it seem appealing, thereby transforming an increasingly moribund genre back into a thriving business, which remained for a long time one of their few readily available means to pursue a stage career (another was vaudeville, although opportunities there were somewhat more limited).[48] Until film took even that away from them, restoring the tradition of whites performing in blackface, blacks were for a time the mainstay of blackface minstrelsy.[49] Moreover, as the compilation of clips in *Bamboozled* argues, blacks, through their own performances and even into the era of "black" television shows such as *The Jeffersons*, continued to perpetuate the negative stereotypes of minstrelsy, which provided a ready source for situational humor and, in this partly muted form, continued to appeal to both white and black audiences.

It is with this question of black complicity that I return now to the minstrel legacy evident in *Stormy Weather*. If the film is understood, as it usually is, as a slender, cliché-ridden story contrived only to provide an excuse for a series of what are, indeed, sometimes amazing performances by its singers, dancers, and musicians, then its reversion to minstrelsy cannot but offend, even if the relevant numbers are in themselves creditably performed. Yet, on inspection, the film shows a careful integration of story and musical numbers, even if all of the music is diegetic, performed within an acknowledged performance space rather than (merely) as a MERM-based extension of a character's self-expression. Specifically, the most tainted of the minstrelsy-based numbers are without exception connected with the film's villains, whose villainy is signaled through their willingness to pander to prevailing (white) tastes. Thus, the cakewalk, "Diga Diga Do," and "African Dance" are part of the milieu of the shifty and manipulative showman Chick Bailey (played by Emmett "Babe" Wallace), who will hire Williamson under false pretenses, only to fire him when his talent upstages Chick's own more modest abilities. Later, the blackface Shadracks prove their callous villainy when they nearly sabotage Williamson's breakthrough show by unmasking the show's benefactor ("Angel," whom they finally remember as the shiftless bootblack Gabriel) at a critical juncture. The consistency of this association of villainy and minstrelsy tropes (with an admixture of the "jungle" themes in Chick Bailey's show) should encourage us to understand the film as "integrated" in the sense that its songs and other numbers are to some extent situational and not merely a succession of hits, and to take its governing sensibility as more subtle than is usually surmised. ♪2.11 ♪2.12

Yet, the effectiveness of this careful plotting is severely undermined by Robinson's performance as Williamson. Most descriptions of the film see his role as a version of himself, and the career he recounts as a slight variation on his own career. This is, however, quite mistaken, except in the sense that his limitations as an actor restrict him to a relatively narrow character range, with his own public persona at the center. As noted, the film is framed by the two world wars in order to highlight the contributions of black soldiers to each war effort. Although Robinson's own dancing career began well back in the nineteenth century, the film opens with an adult Williamson, just back from fighting in France, who somewhat tentatively decides to pursue a career as a dancer. More important, however, the persona that Robinson projects in the film derives significantly from the series of films he made a few years earlier with Shirley Temple, in which he presents himself, in Donald Bogle's terms, as a "cool-eyed Tom." Adding to this accustomed role of a "well-behaved, mannerly Negro attendant,"[50] Robinson, in musical performance, maintains a wide, toothsome smile reminiscent of the "coon" performance styles for which figures such as Louis Armstrong were sometimes criticized. Both onstage and off, then, Robinson projects a performance history that belies his appearance throughout the film in exclusively black settings; this is clearly someone who has learned how to behave, as an actor and dancer, for white audiences and within predominantly white contexts. And this, far more than the age discrepancy between him and Lena Horne, or his wooden delivery of lines, makes the film's dramatic dimension unviable.

As a fictional "biopic," *Stormy Weather* nevertheless helps Robinson (seventy years old at the time of filming) lay claim to his position within the history of tap dance, a position already widely acknowledged, perhaps most notoriously by Fred Astaire in his controversial "Bojangles" number in *Swing Time* (1936, dir. George Stevens), done in blackface. And, in doing so, the film provides at least one salient point of reference for the two-footed stomping climax of Gene Kelly's "Singin' in the Rain" (discussed earlier), a "step" with which Robinson celebrates his "challenge" victory in "Linda Brown" (which we may thus add to Carol J. Clover's list of dance borrowings in *Singin' in the Rain*; see note 33). But there is nevertheless a doubly obverse side to this claim, not only because the image he projects in the film is oriented toward whites every bit as much as the minstrelsy tropes associated with the film's "villains," but also because his dancing in the film reinforces the frequent criticism that he (unlike his white successors Astaire and Kelly) danced only from the waist down,[51] and is in any case dramatically upstaged by the exuberant acrobatic dancing of the Nicholas Brothers, who seem almost to be exacting revenge for Robinson's apparently bogus claim that he was their teacher.[52]

If Robinson himself is somewhat inadequate to his central role, the situations he progresses through, and the succession of numbers that accompany his career trajectory, effectively carry the story. The opening framing device, of Williamson telling his story to the kids he is teaching to dance (at the very beginning and near the end of the film), recalls Robinson's work with Shirley Temple, establishing a gentleness of soul absent in the devious Chick Bailey, the posturing Gabe, and the more worldly Fats Waller and Ada Brown (who, like Cab Calloway, play themselves). The opening flashback sequence centers around the return of Jim Europe's Infantry Jazz Band after the First World War, focusing immediate attention on valorous participation of African Americans in the war,[53] and most particularly on their musical contributions. The easy sanguinities of the lyric and style of Lena Horne's first number (as Selina Robins, the sister of Williamson's fallen comrade in arms), "There's No Two Ways about Love," project the only possible conclusion to the film (that is, her pairing with Williamson) but contradict her own indecisiveness. Across the film, she will first occupy a triangular position between Chick

♫2.13

Bailey and Williamson, and then pursue a career in Paris (presumably in response to the decline of vaudeville, although this is not made explicit), before finally settling down with Williamson in Southern California.[54] Because of this situational disjunction, this song, alone among the film's many hits, will require a brief reprise, at the point when Selina inevitably returns to Williamson. During the first half of the film, "Linda Brown," the challenge number performed on the riverboat to Memphis, establishes Williamson's credentials as a dancer, and the two numbers performed in "Ada Brown's Beale St. Café" ("That Ain't Right" and "Ain't Misbehavin' ") parallel and inflect Williamson's own estrangement from Selina.

After Williamson's escape from Chick Bailey's "jungle" show (in Chicago), the numbers we see from Williamson's own show (in New York) again run parallel to his circumstances, establishing an uneasy arrival after a geographically circuitous route. Thus, Mae Johnson's performance of "I Lost My Sugar in Salt Lake City," sung to persuade a potential "Angel" (Gabriel) to finance the show, refers to New Orleans and Kansas City in addition to Salt Lake City and (implicitly) New York, and there is a blatant discrepancy between the subject and setting of Selina's duet with Williamson, "I Can't Give You Anything but Love," since its lyrics offer love without wealth, while its elegant setting vividly projects the wealth and sophistication that the words deny.[55] For the final sequence, we move to the here and now (and ♫2.14 another show for the benefit of black soldiers), where all is resolved under ♫2.15 Cab Calloway's stage management. Thus, Calloway sings of homesickness in "Geechy Joe," after which Selina sings the title song, "Stormy Weather," as an expression of her own unhappiness, setting up her reconciliation with Williamson in the reprise of "There's No Two Ways about Love," which is celebrated in the concluding paired numbers, "My, My, Ain't That Somethin'" and "Jumpin' Jive."

Of particular interest among the musical riches of *Stormy Weather* are the performance personae of both Fats Waller (in his two "Beale St. Café" numbers) and Cab Calloway (in the final sequence of numbers), the intricately conceived and rendered title song, and the spectacular dancing of the Nicholas Brothers in "Jumpin' Jive." I will consider each in turn.

"That Ain't Right," the first of the Beale St. Café numbers, sung by Ada Brown and accompanied by Waller and his band, is a complex twelve-bar blues number in which a typical blues progression ("Baby, baby, what is the matter with you? . . . You got the world in a jug, and you've got nothin' to do") gives way after only one statement to a harder-edged complaint, still in twelve bars, but less regular in its phrasing. The basic blues dynamic of heading each phrase with a complaining lyric is maintained throughout, so as to leave room between phrases for supportive, quasi-contrapuntal responses, which might typically come from either the audience or instrumental backup. But here those gaps are taken over by Waller's own mocking repartee, offered from his position at the piano, including his trademark "One

never knows, do one?" (in response to "What is the matter with you?").
Waller indulges in saucy wordplay along the way (Waller, after Ada Brown's
"havin' yourself a ball": "Baby, I was born bawlin' and I'm gonna ball the
rest of my life") and delivers a final zinger after freely admitting that everything she sings is true, that he only wants her money, not her: "Suffer. Suffer,
♪2.16 excess baggage, suffer." What is perhaps most remarkable about this exchange is how much Ada Brown's performance stands on its own, its dignity
and generic integrity intact, despite (and partly because of) being constantly
undermined by Waller. Thus, within the same musical space, this otherwise
standard blues offering is presented within carefully managed quotation
marks, so that we may simply listen to her plaint with sympathy or share
fully in Waller's mockery, or perhaps both at once, which her own interactions with Waller and the audience encourage us to do.

But whence those quotation marks? Surely, Waller's repartee also derives
from minstrelsy, whose classic lineup featured a stuffy "Mr. Interlocutor" at
the center, ostensibly the authoritative leader, who is nevertheless constantly
undermined by the end men, Mr. Tambo and Mr. Bones (the percussionists).
In this sense, then, Waller serves as the "end men" to Ada Brown's interlocutor. But his interjections also partake of a typical sense of play that operates,
almost generically, within many jazz interchanges (which may also, by the
same token, derive from minstrelsy), in which variations on the given tune
might seem almost to mock the tune while also honoring it, first by giving it
pride of place and then by exploring its contours. Similarly, in performed
jazz both mockery and respect can frequently be seen and heard within the
interchanges of the instrumentalists.

This last type of exchange, managed visually through Waller's facial expressions and offhand piano delivery, is beautifully captured in the filming of
"Ain't Misbehavin' " (the second Beale St. Café number) when the drummer
enters suddenly, silencing a seemingly surprised Waller just as he completes
the chorus ("savin' my love for you"). In amused response, Waller then
seems musically to "flirt" with the drummer, tossing in scraps of the tune,
in short bursts, as the latter proceeds with his bravura performance. But
what is being undermined in this flirtatious exchange—the sentiment of the
lyric, which claims absolute fidelity despite the absence of the singer's beloved ("I'm happy on the shelf")—has long since been mercilessly mocked,
by the insinuating interpolations of the trombone and clarinet and by Waller
himself. In a remarkable visual counterpoint to the song, Waller (while simultaneously accompanying himself at the piano and singing) bats his eyes and
simpers throughout the verse in a simulation of coquettish "innocent" flirtation, a kind of playacting that has either led to or seemed to confirm rumors
that he was gay (along with the insinuating "One never knows, do one?"
referred to earlier). In a particularly playful moment, at the end of the first
phrase—"Ain't misbehavin', I'm savin' my love for you"—he thrice repeats
the final two words, looking pointedly and suggestively at a different place
♪2.17 in the audience with each repetition.[56]

The girlishness of Waller's performance seems to find a brief echo in Cab Calloway's danced vocal for the twelve-bar blues number "Geechy Joe," in which he minces, undulates in hulalike motions, and adds provocative Vegas-style hip gyrations that anticipate Elvis Presley. But these feminizing moves are balanced by the deeper, more masculine notes of the song, which he dwells on, and his trademark scat-singing, in imitation of the instrumental riffs that set up and punctuate his delivery ("I'm **never-never-never** . . . comin' back"). He is thus, seemingly, a kind of three-in-one: woman, man, and virtuosic instrument.[57] This chameleon-like balance helps Calloway establish himself easily as the godlike "emcee," not only for the show, but also for the film's denouement, which intertwines with the show's staged progression of numbers. It of course helps that we have at this point moved from Williamson's narration into the film's present, which reinforces the "live" dimension of the concluding sequence, a dimension that will be further reinforced by the Nicholas Brothers' dance number and the exciting free-for-all celebration that they launch. But the danced mobility of Calloway himself, ostensibly conducting the orchestra as he slides gracefully between roles—between feminine and masculine personae in "Geechy Joe," between conductor and dancer, between onstage and off, and so on—places Calloway "above" the action, giving us confidence in the happy ending and allowing him to serve as a kind of benign deus ex machina, orchestrating the plot's resolution as if from on high.[58] Also relevant here is the impression American tap dance creates that it is the dancer who controls the music rather than the reverse (which is of course closer to the reality). Calloway's performance as a dancing conductor, moving easily between stage and pit, "taps" adroitly into this perception, extending it to both a literal and a figurative dimension as he simultaneously dances, sings, and "conducts" both the orchestra and the romantic denouement.

♪2.18

If *Stormy Weather*'s concluding sequence borrows the eighteenth-century *opera seria* device of a deus ex machina, personified by Cab Calloway, an internal number within the final sequence—the title song itself, sung by Lena Horne's Selina—imaginatively borrows from a frequent aria trope from the same era, the "storm" aria, a type of simile or metaphor aria in which an outer storm resonates with an inner turmoil. Here, the "Stormy Weather" in question clearly refers to the turbulence in the singer's own life; we (if not the soldiers in the film's audience) understand through this song that Selina has not been happy away from Bill. The staging carefully maintains both literal and figurative dimensions of the song's imagery, using one to inflect the other. Thus, she sings next to a window, through which we see a storm raging outside. She is seemingly secure "indoors" but deeply unhappy; her security, it would seem, comes only at the price of a kind of imprisonment. This movement inward is well reflected in the musical gestures of the song, which play with the "blue notes" of the scale (notes that lie between the pitches represented on the piano, on the third and seventh degrees), which produce the swirling chromatic figures that are typically used to represent wind-driven rain in orchestral traditions but are here given in slow motion, hypnotically retracing the same blue-note figure (in bold) and occasionally inverting it (in italics):

> **Don't know** why
> **There's no** sun up *in the sky,*
>   **Stormy** weather,
> Since my man and I ain't together
> Keeps rainin' **all the ti**-ime.

Similarly, the characteristic "lightning" motive of musical storms, a sudden accented drop of an octave (or more), is re-created here, but again in slow motion, on the word "weather" (thus, the title phrase, "Stormy weather," combines both characteristic "storm" features). The languor here is both sad—an internalized storm—and extremely sexy, the latter owing in part to another set of conventions that associates obsessive repetition, chromatic excess, and expressive swoops downward with sensuousness. The sensuous effect is here further reinforced through the throaty quality on the second syllable of "weather," which is then echoed, with the same arrival pitch ("together"), before the voice swoops even lower ("**Keeps** rainin' . . ."), dwells poignantly on the blues-inflected "all," and finally resolves with a plaintive

♫ **2.19** sliding figure on "the time."[59]

The carefully etched internalized storm of this song, eloquently delivered by Lena Horne as she stands immobile—first by the window, and then away from the window, transfigured by Bill's presence in the audience—becomes the occasion for an extended ballet by Katherine Dunham and her Troupe (who, like Lena Horne, also appeared in *Cabin in the Sky*). On one level, this is yet another indulgence in the film's seemingly endless parade of African American musical talent, in this case partaking of a general trend to incorporate classical ballet into naturalized American settings, since Dunham and her company were in some ways an all-black counterpart to the dance ensembles of such contemporary figures as Martha Graham, Lincoln Kirstein, and Agnes de Mille.[60] Yet the release into dance seems almost a necessary extension of the song, whose singer is brimming with the need to move but is apparently unable to. Ostensibly, the dance sequence takes us outside, right through the window we see onstage (incongruous at a live performance, of course, but common enough in filmic extensions of live performances). But we are quite clearly going *inside*, into a world projected by the singer's memory and imagination, marked by the layered progression, first to the scene outside, suddenly energized as dance, and then beyond that (or farther inside) to a more balletic and idealized dance sequence. The doubleness of this presentation directly parallels the dance extensions that later support her counterpart Williamson, when Cab Calloway's danced scat-singing in "Jumpin' Jive" similarly awakens an even more extreme dance extension, as the Nicholas Brothers respond in kind from the audience before

♫ **2.20** leaping into action.

The latter "audience-response" device partakes of another Cab Calloway signature, most famously using the phrase "Hi-De-Ho" (with which he earlier established his "gentle soul" credentials during interactions with the kids Williamson is telling his story to). Moreover, the device represents yet another parallel with *Bamboozled*, whose emcee, Honeycutt, dressed in elaborate costumes ranging from Uncle Sam to Abraham Lincoln (in blackface, of course), incites his audience to respond in kind to his "ooo-wee" (once again an acknowledged borrowing on Spike Lee's part, from Andy Griffith's trademark hillbillyism in the 1957 *A Face in the Crowd*, dir. Elia Kazan). ♪2.21 And, here again, the perspective is diametrically opposed to that of *Stormy Weather*, where Calloway actually does run things, be they instrumental music, song, dance, or personal lives. By contrast, Honeycutt is clearly a fraud, in the end unable to hold together the forces unleashed by the show he is ostensibly in charge of.

And this difference is critical, speaking to the fundamental fracture between the two films' takes on the American musical as a genre. *Bamboozled* seems only critical, finding musicals to be escapist and shamelessly commercial, and built directly on the backs of African Americans. Indeed, notwithstanding important European roots for the American musical, what makes it distinctively American is its use of American "vernacular" music and dance styles, all intricately intertwined with minstrelsy, jazz, blues, spirituals, and tap dance. The basic question, then, for both films, is, How viable is the genre itself for African Americans?

In this context, *Bamboozled* is an antimusical, in the most basic way. Although it presents its musical entertainments as if they successfully transcend their problematic roots, in the end they do not, and at no moment along the way do their key performers feel at ease, no matter how skilled they are in making their mostly white *audience* feel at ease—hence the close-ups of Savion Glover, smiling his broad blackface smile but sweating profusely, his face pulling at the edges of his smile, showing the strain of it all. Arguably, *Stormy Weather* betrays a similar discomfort in trying to fit the generic mold of the American musical with resistant content, so that its hollow central characters, emptied of genuine humanity except while performing, may seem analogous to the sweat on Glover's brow, a telltale sign of something very basically wrong.[61]

Yet there are other sides to the black experience represented in *Stormy Weather*, times when it enthusiastically engages with the genre, taking it over and making it into something that both affirms "blackness" and achieves a comfortable sense of ease with the mix. The film's larger arch, for example, is framed at one end by the problematic cakewalk; yet, tainted as it is, this number provides the point of reference for the "My, My, Ain't That Somethin' " / "Jumpin' Jive" combination at the end. Features common to both—surely deliberately so—are a similar fusion of two numbers into one (as in a minuet-trio), a unison strut by a mixed chorus wearing wide-brimmed hats, and a generalized feeling of infectious celebration. But the change in vehicle, from a nineteenth-century cakewalk to a modern swing number, with fashionable hats replacing the obnoxious bonnets of the earlier number, carries with it a sense of great release. Key here is the demonstrated ability to make things over, to refashion something tainted into something more palatable, and thereby bring it under control. And the key element in this process is jazz, which transforms and controls its source material through a process of inflection. Thus may something be both embraced and controlled, as Fats Waller demonstrates in "That Ain't Right," with respect to a traditional blues number. And the point of "Jumpin' Jive," more particularly, is just this kind of process, applied (as the title suggests) to both speech and dance.

In the previous scene, we had been prepared for the introduction of jive (the new, jazz-based figures of speech, a type of discourse that obliquely refers to and displaces both its minstrelsy-based cousin, the indefinite-talk routine, and the "jungle" language of "Diga Diga Do"), which Calloway now combines with syllabic scat-singing. But the danced equivalent by the Nicholas Brothers makes its point both more subtly and more forcefully, first by recalling in their initial emergence Williamson's "miraculous" dancing response to the music on the riverboat, and then by referring visually (and thus, obliquely) to Williamson's earlier dance on the African drums and recasting it in modern terms. The Nicholas Brothers, by dancing on the music desks of the band players (see figure 2.2), and later on the piano itself—and in tuxedos rather than war paint—eclipse the "jungle" association of Williamson's earlier breakout number while also recalling, in their interactions with the pianist, Waller's earlier interactions with his drummer during "Ain't Misbehavin'." Even more subtly (well, perhaps not all that subtly), they also eclipse Robinson's famous "staircase" dance by doing their own trademark splits, leapfrogging down oversize stairs, to bring the number to a close, just minutes after Robinson has performed his own stairway routine in a particularly quaint setting, on the plantation-style porch as he musters his courage to knock on Selina's door. But most telling about the ways the Nicholas Brothers upstage Robinson is their full bodily involvement, with expressive arm and hand movements, and their manner of interacting with the music and with the musicians playing the music, in several instances of "trading" rhythmic figures and in suspended moments of "listening" before responding, whether to the music or to each other. This quality of inflected response transforms their dancing into an integrated component of the music; unlike Robinson's, theirs is a species of jazz dance that truly partakes of jazz.

Yet, the very woodenness of Robinson's acting (and Lena Horne's is only marginally better) puts the generic basis of *Stormy Weather*, as a musical, into question. Musicals tend to ground their sentimental excursions within the action of the story, as the extension of feeling and situation; in *Stormy Weather*, however, there is, until the final sequence of numbers, a fairly complete disconnect between story and music, even though they have been con-

Figure 2.2. Fayard and Harold Nicholas dance on music desks during *Stormy Weather*'s "Jumpin' Jive." This doubly autographed still is inscribed, "To Miles / Here's Dancing For You / Fayard Nicholas" and "To Miles / Keep a Smile on your face / Harold Nicholas." (Autographed photograph courtesy of Miles Kreuger and the Institute of the American Musical, Inc.)

ceptualized together. To be sure, this disconnect has its uses, signaling, perhaps, that the genre itself is being played with and inflected, and giving room for the controlling presences of Waller and Calloway to perform their transformative magic, capped by the sheer exuberance of the Nicholas Brothers. Yet, there is a curious price to be paid in the process, stemming both from the blatancy with which the core story of *Stormy Weather* is discounted and from the fact that none of the musical numbers happens solely as a natural outgrowth of feeling. While the succession of songs relates directly to the film's characters and situations, as shown, the words and music of those songs do not engage fully with its unfolding plot, simply because they are all performed *as songs* rather than *as feeling*. To put it in the terms of the larger discussion, no one steps out of the film's real world for even a moment's worth of undiluted MERM. And on this level, *Stormy Weather* seems to join with *Bamboozled* in refusing to "buy into" the reality of its musical alternatives. Yet, in another sense, by staying within the mode of musical performance, *Stormy Weather* makes that mode the one that matters, so that the transformative story told through its musical trajectory takes on additional power, using the film's principal inadequacies as a foil of sorts. Thus, its wooden acting and its early reliance on minstrelsy and "jungle" tropes provide the base material, which the alchemies of jazz and jive transform into pure gold.

Meet Me in St. Louis (1944) was the first big hit for director Vincente Minnelli, whose stylish sensibility, generosity to his players, and meticulous care for detail established him by the mid-1940s as one of Hollywood's major directors, particularly of musicals. The film also features one of Judy Garland's most appealing performances (as eloquent testimony to the budding romance between the star and her director) and provided child actress Margaret O'Brien with her signature role, a wickedly macabre—yet charming—imp child. Moreover, it has proven to be one of the most durably enjoyable and genuinely moving musicals ever filmed, a deftly realized wartime consideration of what America was fighting for, which manages both to temper its nostalgia with a full confrontation of the pain felt by separated loved ones and to present its wrenching uncertainties alongside fervently expressed hope, however desperately. One of a slate of musical films (including Michael Curtiz's 1942 biopic of George M. Cohan, *Yankee Doodle Dandy*, and the 1943 *Stormy Weather*) that rather self-consciously supported the war effort through a show of nostalgic patriotism,[62] *Meet Me in St. Louis* stands apart for its vivid focus, within a musical, on the familiar realities of domestic life, which are both idealized through meticulous attention to historical accuracy and used as a plausible grounding for nearly all the musical numbers. Most remarkably, perhaps, given its credentials as a sterling representative of its genre, *Meet Me in St. Louis* runs its course, structurally and thematically, as a musical gone sour, whose initial optimism is fully spoiled and extravagantly lamented before being restored in the final sequences, in the meantime managing almost to forget, save for its stylish exaggerations,[63] that it is a musical at all.

Meet Me in St. Louis is based somewhat loosely on a series of autobiographical stories published during 1941–1942 in *The New Yorker* ("5135 Kensington," by Sally Benson, who was the real-life Tootie) and unfolds, with deliberate quaintness, as a series of four "greeting cards," labeled "Summer 1903," "Autumn 1903," "Winter 1903," and "Spring 1904," each centered around the activities of the Smith family as they anticipate the 1904 opening of the Louisiana Purchase Exposition (better known as the St. Louis World's Fair).[64] The Smith family itself—Mr. and Mrs. Smith (Alonzo and Anna), Grandpa, Katie the maid, and the five children, Lon (Alonzo Jr.), Rose, Esther (played by Judy Garland), Agnes, and Tootie (Margaret O'Brien)—is made to seem mildly dysfunctional owing to Mr. Smith's lack of involvement with the rest of the family and Tootie's taste for the macabre. On the whole, however, the family seems otherwise blithely content throughout the first segment, which includes nine of the film's eleven sung musical numbers and centers around a dance party hosted by Rose, which in turn provides the occasion for a budding romance between Esther and John Truitt ("The Boy Next Door"). In the second "greeting card," introduced appropriately with an extended Halloween sequence, both of the family's potential sources of trouble erupt: first, an injured Tootie gives a lying account of John Truitt trying to kill her, followed soon after by Mr. Smith's announcement of a promotion that will take him and the family to New York. Halloween generally, and Tootie's "accident" and fabrications in particular, leave everyone especially vulnerable to the father's announcement, which portends disaster for the family. Nevertheless, they come together by the end of the evening, reconciled through the only song in this segment, "You and I" (a song that was added late by producer Arthur Freed and his long-standing song partner, Nacio Herb Brown, and sung for the film by Freed himself). Through most of the third segment, "Winter," the Smiths seem gamely ready to move to New York, but Esther's "Have Yourself a Merry Little Christmas"—the only song in this segment—unleashes a hysterical reaction from Tootie, allowing her father finally to see that the prospect of moving to New York has brought his family to the brink of catastrophe and despair. In the concluding segment of "Winter," stability and optimism return with Mr. Smith's resolution to stay in St. Louis, a decision that is briefly celebrated in the short (and songless) "Spring 1904" episode, when the family visits the newly opened World's Fair.

Throughout the film, music springs naturally from the home setting. Agnes launches the opening song, "Meet Me in St. Louis," after hearing someone outside whistling the tune; as she skips through the house, she is interrupted by Grandpa singing the same song (in a different key) from behind the bathroom door; and, as he emerges, waltzing into his own room while humming and mumbling past the places where he "forgets" the words, he is in turn interrupted by Esther and her friends, whom he hears singing the same song across the lawn as they return from playing tennis. While the orchestra fills   ♪2.22 in lightly behind each singer, the effect is of a home resonating with its spontaneously singing occupants. Later in the first segment, the older sisters will perform the same song once again, with Rose at the family's piano, interrupted at the cadence by their father returning home from work, instantly marked as an outsider in his own home by his abrupt silencing of the home's music.[65] Later, the family piano will also provide the accompaniment for   ♪2.23 "Under the Bamboo Tree" and "You and I" (in the "Autumn" sequence), the latter with Anna rather than Rose at the piano, subtly underscoring the bond between mother and oldest daughter (since, clearly, Anna has seen to it that her eldest daughter, Rose, also learn piano, as well as French).

Other songs are presented in similarly naturalistic fashion. John Truitt, in trying to remember an "old song" ("Over the Banister"), encourages Esther to sing it, which she does, taking up where he left off in his recitation of the lyric; the awkwardness of the setting—she sings, he doesn't (in fact, oddly for a musical, he never sings)—is symbolic of the one-sided courtship, and

Garland's performance underscores that awkwardness when she cringes slightly at the lines "the loveliest face in town" (which after all he should

♪2.24 sing to her). Tootie sings "Brighten the Corner Where You Are" (Ina Duley Ogdon and Charles H. Gabriel Jr., 1912) from the back of the ice wagon on her way home—a seemingly random choice that is nonetheless consonant with the film's theme, of a family's blithe acceptance of its given situation— and will give a similarly unaccompanied rendition later of "I Was Drunk Last Night, Dear Mother," offering a child-based critique on the rather clean

♪2.25 fun being indulged by the young adults at Rose's party.[66] There is, naturally,
♪2.26 music at the film's two dance parties, Rose's party at the Smiths' home (traditional square dancing) and the Christmas ball in the third sequence (couple dancing, including waltz, two-step, and polka); at the former, we even see the guests bring their instruments, take them out, and begin to play. And the two big song hits from the film are sung as responses to "naturally" occurring musical stimuli, with "The Trolley Song" taking its cue from the actual sounds of the trolley, and "Have Yourself a Merry Little Christmas" being heard first as the melody of a music box, which Esther then plays more slowly to accompany herself. In nearly all cases, the orchestra eventually fills in behind the "diegetic" accompaniment, but only after the song's grounding in the scene is secure.

The only song in the film that is overtly MERM-based—thus, not grounded in a naturally evolving occasion—is the early "The Boy Next Door," sung by Esther about someone she has yet to meet but has already imagined as a romantic partner. The rhythmic and melodic profile of the song deftly recalls "The Merry Widow Waltz," another important reference to the turn of the century, reinforced by the girls' wide-brimmed hats in the later "Trolley Song"; the musical resemblance is especially obvious when

♪2.27 one combines the opening lines with the close:

> How can **I ignore the boy next door?**
> **I love him more** than I can say . . .
>
> And though **I'm heart-sore, the boy next door**
> **Affection for** me won't display . . .
>
> **The boy next door.**

Although the song offers other subtle reminders of this important European model, as well, its most important reference is probably stylistic, evident more in performance than on the page, but drawing inspiration from the yearning appoggiatura on the rhyming syllables (-nore–door–more, etc.), a melodramatic enhancement to the borrowed melodic contour. Departing from the steadier rhythms of "Meet Me in St. Louis," which is performed both just before and just after "The Boy Next Door," and which also recalls the opening of the "Merry Widow Waltz" (thus, "Meet Me in St. . . . "),[67] "The Boy Next Door" has a European lilt, a rhythmic ebb and flow that bespeaks a deeply personal romantic feeling, a budding sexuality that seems oddly contradictory of the song's safely domestic subject matter. Emblematic of the contrast between this pair of waltzes is the innocuous handling, in the title song, of such sexually charged lines as "We will dance the hoochee-coochee, / And I'll be your tootsie-wootsie," whereas even the prosaic line that ends the verse of "The Boy Next Door"—a simple recitation of street addresses that doesn't fit into the poetic structure—accrues an underlying sensuousness in Garland's performance.

The song "Meet Me in St. Louis" (Andrew B. Sterling, 1904) is sung throughout the film only as a chorus, but in its original setting, that chorus is set up, in the verse, as a note to "Louis" from his wife, Flossie, who has run off to the fair, taking most of their household goods with her; various alternate verses detail similarly cheeky situations, so that the chorus's syncopations typically give it a taunting quality, often with a distinct sexual charge. Within the chorus, "hoochee-coochee" refers to the famed "Little Egypt" attraction at the Chicago World's Fair a decade before the St. Louis Fair, which according to some accounts saved the fair financially and according to others introduced the institution of the "exotic dance" (better known as the striptease) to mainstream America.[68] The follow-up phrase, "I'll be your tootsie-wootsie," in the context of a wife's note to her husband, clearly promises sexual favors (as opposed to "I'll be your girl friend" or something similar), especially considering that "tootsy"—a slang expression meaning "prostitute" (or "party girl")—was of fairly recent vintage in 1904. Yet, beyond a casual hip thrust from Judy Garland, none of the performances of the title song betrays any awareness of these meanings; indeed, Grandpa can't even remember the exact words to this part of the song.

On the other hand, the seemingly innocuous line at the end of the verse to "The Boy Next Door" seems inordinately sensual in performance, in large part because it remains hypnotically (if also playfully) on a single pitch for most of its duration (repeated notes are in bold):

> So it's clear to see
> There's no hope for me
> Though **I live at 5135 Kensington Avenue and he lives at 5133.**

This fascination with his tantalizing closeness, however, also forms part of a typical European waltz gesture discussed in the previous chapter (see p. 39): the *Luftpause*, in which an expected arrival is delayed through an exaggerated fermata, employed especially in moments such as this and carrying, in its European context, a distinctly erotic charge. That charge may be less distinct here, since the "fermata" stems from the amateurish versification, which requires a large number of syllables to be repeated on the same pitch before resolving on the last syllable of his address. But the charge is there nonetheless, especially as performed and when heard against the parallel moment in the first part of the verse, when Esther frankly expresses her desire, and where her monotone delivery comes across as a mode of a private confession (repeated notes are again in bold): ♪ **2.28**

My only regret
Is we've never met
For **I dream of him all the while.**

The kind of "forgetfulness" through which the song "Meet Me in St. Louis" becomes, in retrospect, no more than an innocent flirtation is endemic to the treatment of the "period" numbers included in the film. Thus, the clowning rendition of "Under the Bamboo Tree," which Tootie and Esther perform as a cakewalk (see figure 2.3), conveys no sense that either the cakewalk or the song itself, which belongs to the tradition of the "coon" song popular in turn-of-the-century America, are at all problematic, even though both are based in the obnoxious tradition of blackface minstrelsy.[69] Yet the song's primitivisms ("If you lak-a-me lak I lak-a-you") overtly link race ("Down in the jungle lived a maid / Of royal blood though dusky shade") to an easiness in sexual matters, even if the stylized choreography of the Smith sisters suggests American Indians more readily than African natives. And the film elsewhere seems to point to these associations, perhaps inadvertently; as would *Singin' in the Rain* nearly a decade later, it includes an episode of seemingly inconsequential blackface (in this case, burnt cork being applied to Agnes's and Tootie's faces and hands as they prepare for Halloween). Moreover, the song has, like all the "historic" songs in the film, a thematic point to make, for it contains a not-so-subtle message from Esther to John Truitt and comes on the heels of the "Skip to My Lou" medley, whose lyrics are recast to emphasize anew the prominent intimations of sexual promiscuity already present in the original ("I'll find another one, / Prettier than you"). Thus, Esther at one point sings:

I'll be glad to go with you,
So prithee do not tarry,
But if I do,
It's up to you
To let me Dance with Harry. . . .
    (ensemble): Skip to my Lou
Charlie . . .
    (ensemble): Skip to my Lou
Johnny . . .

In this way, the film knowingly plays both sides of the fence in its historical borrowings, taking sexual meanings fully into account and at the same time allowing audiences to ignore them.[70] Yet, often enough, we are guided to take in a familiar song's implications well beyond its appeal to nostalgia. Thus, for example, at the end of the Christmas dance medley, just as Esther is rescued and restored to the arms of John Truitt, we hear "No Place Like Home" and its segue into "Auld Lang Syne," which together perform a similar act of restoration and anticipate the resolution to come (at the same

Figure 2.3. Tootie (Margaret O'Brien) and Esther (Judy Garland) perform an impromptu cakewalk while singing "Under the Bamboo Tree" during the "Summer 1903" sequence in *Meet Me in St. Louis*. (Photograph courtesy of Miles Kreuger and the Institute of the American Musical, Inc.)

time seeming utterly natural within the context of a Christmas ball coming to a close).

The remaining three new songs for the film, each painstakingly constructed as a faux period song, may be considered a trilogy of personal redemption within community, presented in what might seem by this way of reckoning to be reverse order. The first ("The Trolley Song") includes an entire scenario of self-exclusion and restoration, the second ("You and I") serves to heal a serious breach, at least partly, and the third ("Have Yourself a Merry Little Christmas") obliquely addresses the breach itself. Since these songs are so critical for the narrative arch of the film, it is imperative both that each be convincing as a shared memory, so that its basis in the film will be secure, and that it be newly composed, so that it belongs more to the specific filmic world of *Meet Me in St. Louis* than to the world as remembered more generally by the film's audience.

According to Hugh Martin, "The Trolley Song" was written because producer Arthur Freed insisted there be a "trolley song"; for the song's basis,

he and Blane drew inspiration from a period poster with the inscription
" 'Clang, clang, clang,' went the jolly little trolley."⁷¹ Although almost simplistic in its prepackaged nostalgia, the song was hugely successful even before the film was released. The song comes across as a modernized "Jingle
Bells" (beginning with precisely the same three-note motive, repeating the
third degree of the scale) but involves the more varied sound palette of the
"modern" trolley car, including, besides the "clang, clang, clang" of the trolley, the "ding, ding, ding" of its bell, the "chug, chug, chug" of its motor,
the "bump, bump, bump" of its brakes, the "plop, plop, plop" of its wheels,
and the "buzz, buzz, buzz" of its buzzer (signaling the end of the ride). But
the point of these stimuli is what they help to stimulate: the sympathetic
vibrations—a kind of sexual awakening—within the singer, the "zing, zing,
zing," "thump, thump, thump," and "stop, stop, stop" of her "heart-
strings," all in response simultaneously to the vibrant physicality of the ride
itself and to the experience of falling in love ("When he smiled I could feel
the car shake"—a precursor, perhaps, to Carole King's "I Feel the Earth
Move" [1971]). Within the film, John Truitt is late for the trolley, and the
song begins with Esther feeling excluded; when he appears, she becomes the
song's center, vibrating with the kind of energy only Judy Garland could
♩2.29   bring to a song. Thus the trolley provides the vehicle not only for a journey
into love but also for a demonstration of the symbiosis between larger community and the pairing of individuals within it. The song was to have been
followed by another song ("Boys and Girls Like You and Me," dropped from
Rodgers and Hammerstein's *Oklahoma!* the year before), once the trolley
reached its destination. But it is probably important that the later sequence
was cut, so that in the released film the trolley never reaches its ostensible
destination; after all, its real destination is the reuniting of John and Esther,
which needs no second song.⁷²

  We know "The Trolley Song" to be a "period" song because no one would
conceive a song about a trolley in 1944. With "You and I," a fairly nonde-
script (and therefore "timeless") song, it is rather Mr. Smith's recognition of
the song from a few bars of his wife's playing it on the piano that tells us its
vintage; thus, even in 1903, it is an old song, remembered from their past,
perhaps from their courtship. In the course of its performance we see all that
it restores, redeeming both sides of the two central conflicts. First, there is
the restored romance between the parents (the basis for the family): her initial gesture of playing the tune, both as a personal assertion of her own role
in the household and as an oblique invitation that he could either accept or
ignore; his memory of the song and urge to sing it, and so to reconnect with
her; her ready accommodation to his limitations ("I'll put it down in your
key"); his gratitude as the deeper register allows his voice more comfort and
authority; her sure knowledge of when he'll need her to prompt him ("From
my heart"); and their conclusion in harmony, with her allowing him the
melody (a traditional bow to mastery that actually quietly asserts the greater
♩2.30   musical skill). But we also see, in the background, the restoration of the

family, who come back, one by one, drawn to the familiar music; even Esther forgives Tootie for her lies about John Truitt, instinctively slapping her hands away when she reaches for Esther's cake, but then feeding her the first bite with seemingly automatic maternal warmth.

"Have Yourself a Merry Little Christmas" is supposedly old enough in the film's 1903 that it has found its way into the workings of a music box, but it could never have convinced us of its vintage with its original lyric, which was much too specific to the situation of the film (the replacement text is in bold, below the original):[73]

> Have yourself a Merry Little Christmas, it may be your last.
> **let your heart be light**.
> Next year we may all be living in the past.
> **all our troubles will be out of sight**
> Have yourself a Merry Little Christmas, make the yuletide gay.
> Next year we may all be many miles away.
> **all our troubles will be**
> No good times like the olden days, happy golden days of yore.
> **Once again, as in**
> Faithful friends who were dear to us will be near to us no more.
> **once**
> But at least we all will be together if the fates allow.
> **Some day soon**
> From now on we'll have to muddle through somehow.
> **Until then,**
> So have yourself a merry little Christmas now.

The doctoring of the lyric was reportedly at the insistence of Judy Garland, who argued (according to Hugh Martin), "If I sing that to little Margaret O'Brien, people will think I'm a monster."[74] Others have suggested that her commercial instinct correctly told her that the song could be a huge hit with a less pessimistic lyric; if so, her instinct was at one with the need for the song to be more generally applicable if it were to be convincingly "remembered" by Esther and sung to her sister. In its rewritten form, the song presents itself as Esther's vain attempt to reassure Tootie, which instead underscores, through the song's more generalized theme of separation, how truly desperate their situation is (e.g., with the irretrievably lost feeling of the minor-key arrival on "days of yore"). No one has any trouble believing Tootie's tears, or that she would then, in a fit of hysteria, run out into the yard in her nightshirt to destroy the family of snowmen so lovingly created earlier that day (and no, we don't really need the familiar stories about Margaret O'Brien being told her dog had been or would be killed, stories that were in any case flatly denied by the adult O'Brien).[75] In many ways, the song works all the better for having its words undercut by the music, so that the music points out the reality being denied by the lyric. Thus, for example, the sagging chromatic line in the bass denies the assurance that "our troubles will be out of sight" (line two, replacing "living in the past"), and the aching major-seventh dissonances on "Once again" (which replaces "No good times" in the fifth line), especially as fervidly sung by Garland, flatly deny the reassuring lyric. In each case, and throughout the song, both Esther and Tootie hear—as does the audience, through them—not the false reassurances of the words, but rather the truth expressed in the music. Besides expressing the moment perfectly, of desperate hope flung against the certainty of despair, the song thereby exemplifies the typical experience of a Judy Garland song, one of the best in a long series of heartbreaking, despairing attempts, never fully successful, to sing her way to happiness.

♪2.31

Meet Me in St. Louis is ostensibly about an expected world's fair, but the fair itself is, to borrow Alfred Hitchcock's terminology, a "MacGuffin" that we are never encouraged to care very much about.[76] The World's Fair—which might as well be the swamp that John Truitt claims to prefer—is merely a mechanism for elevating St. Louis, to allow it to serve emblematically in a demonstration of the supreme importance of locality, of the here and now, which takes precedence over worldly significance. In the fantasy of this film, the world comes to the Smiths, but it needn't bother, really. As in operetta, so too in this most poignant of film musicals, the larger story pales in comparison to the personal dimension.

Or does it? Surely it matters that world fairs have played such an important role in the formation of an American identity,[77] so that we (and the original 1944 American audience, then at war) might, because of this setting, more easily see ourselves as fellow Americans and these people as versions of ourselves, part of a shared heritage to be cherished and protected. But the real link is forged through music, not through anticipated images of a carnival midway. Perhaps, then, the real story of "classic" film musicals resides in their habitual grounding of personal stories within a shared musical world, whose music is capable of drawing the film's audience into that world, often by exploiting a shared musical past. In classic film musicals, recycling familiar music as part of a sonic landscape helps to enable the stories of those on the screen to carry our stories as well. There are, however, moments in *Meet Me in St. Louis*, especially in the "Skip to My Lou" medley, when the proliferation of familiar music is almost giddy-making, an excess of the familiar that conveys us to a moment of nostalgic sublime capable of either creating in us a feeling of exhilaration on a par with the exuberance of the on-screen dancing or repelling us with the obvious artificiality of it all, so that we laugh even as we may also admire its virtuosity.

But such moments of giddy excess pale in comparison with the film-long exploration of the nostalgic sublime in the 2001 film *Moulin Rouge*.

Moulin Rouge (2001) and **Chicago** (2002) have together been credited with injecting new commercial life into the movie musical. Just how true this is for the long run may be too early to tell, but the two films do make an intriguing pair, for each positions itself as a kind of meta-movie-musical about the relationship between MERM and real life, but from nearly opposite perspectives. *Moulin Rouge*, with its eclectic mix of familiar stories and familiar songs and its wanton intermixing of "reality" and playacting on various levels, seems to model for us the ways in which we live out what we see on stage and screen, borrowing songs, dialogue, situations, and whole scenarios, careening among a variety of options as we seek out the most congenial fit. If *Moulin Rouge* seems thus to suggest that we learn how to live our lives through musicals, *Chicago* sees reality itself—and quite a cynical and grim reality that is—in terms of elaborate musical numbers, as one solid stream of MERM, where it is the mode of enhancement rather than what is being enhanced that is the whole point of the process. The two films' shared extravagance of musical and cinematic means does little to disguise the fact, however, that the core human content—the raw material with which MERM works its magic—is in each case very differently valued. Whereas *Moulin Rouge* nourishes the spark of redemptive love, paramount among its recycled Bohemian virtues (truth, beauty, freedom, love), and uses MERM only in its service, *Chicago* finds little in its characters worth salvaging beyond their aptitude for MERM, which represents the only path toward redemption in its world, with that redemption conceived only in material terms. In its way, *Chicago* places great store in beauty and freedom, but has no place for the other two Bohemian virtues, and uses the razzle-dazzle of MERM to *counter* truth rather than pursue it.

The two films have other highly profiled similarities. The stars of both films are not known for, nor in most cases even particularly proficient at, the basic skills required for stage-based MERM. Part of the point in each film is the alchemic power of MERM—especially cinematic MERM—to transform the ordinary into the extraordinary, to turn anyone's and everyone's story into the story of Cinderella. The one apparent exception to this, Catherine Zeta-Jones in *Chicago*, surprised those who did not know of her dancer's training, so that even she seems magically transformed. Another similarity—which is also a point of departure—involves a fascination in both cases with decadent female sexuality. Traditionally, fascinations of this kind are justified through either a clearly stated disapproval, ending in the death of the decadent heroine/temptress, or her salvation through the redemptive love of an innocent (or both, which is the path chosen by *Moulin Rouge*). *Chicago*, however, alternates between indulging the decadent sexuality of its female stars and punishing (or threatening to punish) them through incarceration, misery, and death, allowing them to survive only through a shared general cynicism pitted against a tendency, just as widely shared, to believe in the truth of what is clearly fabricated. *Chicago*'s world is peopled entirely by manipulators and chumps, the former who know how MERM works and use it to their advantage, the latter who are taken in by its razzle or blinded by its dazzle. Key to how the two films find their respective ways to manage their shared fascination with the seedy underside of society, with its glitzy charm and promise of easy sex, are the perspectives established from the beginning of each film.

In *Moulin Rouge*, the story is told jointly by the main character and a lisping Toulouse-Lautrec in a kind of double-image narrative. The outer frame is set by the opening song, sung by Toulouse (Eden Ahbez's "Nature Boy"), and the background of the song (as is often the case throughout the film) is entirely relevant to its use here. Ahbez was himself a "nature boy," little more than a vagabond, living out his life in Griffith Park in Los Angeles, who managed to sell this song to Nat King Cole in the late 1940s. Set to a Yiddish waltz tune, "Schweig Mein Herz" ("Still My Heart"—a subsequent lawsuit was settled out of court), the song is performed in accordance with the tradition established by Nat King Cole, in a kind of free-floating rhythm retaining only the faintest hint of its waltz origins, here slightly reinforced by the rotating arms of the Moulin Rouge (the Red Windmill), but given no musical presence (see figure 2.4). The song presents itself, even musically, as a kind of mystically charged vagabond song, floating free of its earthly origins ("They say he wandered very far"), evoking an intense sense of loss at the same time that its final lines proclaim an indestructible human truth, sal-

♪2.32   vaged somehow from the perilous journey of life:

> There was a boy,
> A very strange enchanted boy.
> They say he wandered very far, very far
> Over land and sea.
> A little shy and sad of eye,
> But very wise was he.
>
> And then one day,
> A magic day, he passed my way.
> And while we spoke of many things,
> Fools and kings,
> This he said to me,
> "The greatest thing you'll ever learn
> Is just to love and be loved in return."

As Toulouse reaches the final lines, we move from his evocation of the boy in question (Christian) to the same boy, now bearded and bedraggled, typing those lines into an old Underwood typewriter in a disheveled apartment in the Montmartre district of turn-of-the-century Paris, near the notorious nightclub and brothel the Moulin Rouge. Although it is later explained that Christian had earlier arrived from London to learn about life and love among the Bohemians—against the wishes of his strict father—the evocation of mysterious origins in both the song and, for those who know the story behind the song, of its author suggests powerfully that Christian's origins are more beclouded than that, collapsing both time and distance to become almost ahistorical.

Figure 2.4. Toulouse-Lautrec (John Leguizamo) sings Eden Ahbez's mythologizing "Nature Boy" to open *Moulin Rouge*, as Christian (Ewan McGregor) appears behind the slowly turning arms of the "Red Windmill."

Two things in particular support this suggestion of a collapsed time frame. First, the songs used and referred to throughout the show are blatantly eclectic, mostly very well known, and mostly coming from a time well after the established setting, which is just as blatantly a miragelike fantasy version of fin-de-siècle Paris. Second, moving temporally mainly in the other direction, the stories conflated within the narrative of *Moulin Rouge* are among the most familiar to the musical stage, including those of *La traviata*, *La bohème* (and its recent Broadway reincarnation as *Rent*), and *Cabaret*. Underwriting them all is the figure of Orpheus, whose musically based mythology, as a human whose MERM-like musical abilities were prodigious enough to persuade both gods and beasts as well as humankind, has provided the basis again and again for opera, most famously including the first operatic masterpiece, Monteverdi's 1608 *Orfeo*; Gluck's 1762 "reform" opera *Orfeo ed Euridice*; and Offenbach's satirical operette, *Orphée aux enfers* (1858, rev. 1874).[78] Orpheus's most famous mythological deed is his descent into the underworld to rescue his beloved Eurydice, who has died from a snake's venom; through his persuasive musical prowess he succeeds in securing her release, but then loses her when he looks back at her before they have returned to safety (although retellings vary significantly in how it all ends). In *Moulin Rouge*, Orpheus's purity is signaled by his name, Christian; the underworld in question is that of Paris's seedy underside, peopled by prostitutes, pimps, and struggling Bohemians; and Eurydice is Satine (Satan? Satin? Something in between?), a prostitute (like *La traviata*'s Violetta) dying of consumption (like Violetta and *La bohème*'s Mimì).

Our identification with Christian is secured in large part through the early scene in which he is drafted to write the Bohemians' show, *Spectacular Spectacular*, which they hope to have performed by Satine at the Moulin Rouge.

As Toulouse's Bohemians struggle to find the right words for one of their tunes (the composer is supposedly Erik Satie), we understand fairly quickly that what they are trying to come up with happens to be one of the American musical stage's most famous phrases, albeit from over half a century later. When, after we hear a variety of grossly inadequate transmutations in a crescendo of overlapping suggestions—"the hills animate with the euphonious symphonies of descant," "the hills are vital, intoning the descant," "the hills quake and shake with . . . ," "the hills are incarnate with symphonic melodies," "the hills are chanting the eternal mantra . . . ," and even, most absurdly, "Frank is living in my foot"—we know all too well what they are groping for, so that by the time Christian breaks forth with "the hills are alive with the sound of music," we are in that moment one with him. Here and later, as the characters in *Moulin Rouge* continue to sing (mainly) the songs of twentieth-century American popular culture, we are made to feel a strange tug-of-war between a lost world supposedly being re-created for us and a collective memory that tells us that this is *our* world also, more chaotic and modern in its sensibilities, a familiar landscape strewn (as in the film) with the intermingled songs and song fragments of the century between us and the legendary Moulin Rouge. In partaking of the customary practice of using familiar songs from the past to evoke a particular era—which *Singin' in the Rain*, *Stormy Weather*, and *Meet Me in St. Louis* all do—*Moulin Rouge* directs us continually to reconsider the age the film has immersed us in and to reassess its sensibilities. In the end we are forced to yield to the sense that we have entered a timeless realm whose sensibilities are ageless and simply human, whose musical lifeblood consists of (as Christian continues to sing the title song from *The Sound of Music*) the "songs [they/we] have sung for a thousand years."

♫2.33

Yet, the characters of *Moulin Rouge* never let on that they are singing anyone's songs but their own. Indeed, when Christian later stammers through the slightly inchoate lyric that begins Elton John and Bernie Taupin's "Your Song" (1971), he is merely continuing the mode of noncommunication that has characterized his encounter with Satine, who believes him to be a duke about to put money into the project of turning the Moulin Rouge into a legitimate theater (Satine's elaborately phony, mock-ecstatic, sometimes overlapping interjections are given in italics; both Christian's and Satine's dialogue is spoken to this point):

> It's a little bit funny, —*What?*
> This feeling inside.
> I'm not one of those who can easily hide.
>   (Is this—is this okay? Is this what you want?)—*Oh, poetry. Yes,*
>   *yes. Yes, this is what I want. Naughty words. Oh!*
> I don't—*Oh, naughty*—I don't have much money,—
> But boy if I did, —*Oh, yes.*
> I'd buy a big house where we both could live. —*Oh, I love them. Oh, it's*

so good!
If I was a sculptor, —*Wonderful*—
But then again, no. —*Wonderful, Oh, don't*—
Or a man who makes potions at a traveling show, —*Oh, don't, don't, don't!*
  No, no, don't stop!
I know it's not much, —*Give me more! Yes, yes, yes, yes, oh!*
But it's the best I can do. . . .—*Oh, naughty! Don't stop! Yes, yes, yes!*

But when, on her last "yes," he actually begins to sing, she suddenly stops, wide-eyed in wonder, as if seeing him for the first time. It is the second in a series of Orphean moments, of which his slightly earlier "the hills are alive" was the first; particularly central to the effect this time are the very first sung words, which virtually define the persona of Orpheus ("My gift is my song") and the blessing bestowed by the final line, which redeems an otherwise prosaic lyric, enfolding "you're" within the soft caresses of "wonderful" through its layered alternation of stressed syllables within the semblance of a descending melodic sequence (**won**derful—*life*—**you're**—*world*): ♪2.34

> My gift is my song, and this one's for you.
> And you can tell everybody that this is your song.
> It may be quite simple, but now that it's done,
> Hope you don't mind, I hope you don't mind that I put down in words
> How wonderful life is, now you're in the world.

As the exaggerated clumsiness of Taupin's "ordinary speech" lyric continues past this extended moment of revelation, it is ennobled by two things within the film: the music (MERM) and Satine's response to it. But its special magic for us in the audience has to do first of all with its familiarity—as a lyric that, seemingly, any one of us might have written, and that many will actually know by heart along with the tune, so that they might even have sung it just as well as Ewan McGregor's Christian does, assuming similar access to the technology of MERM. Secondary but crucial, however, is the way that this ordinary and familiar material has been transformed through MERM. As Christian and Satine dance into nighttime Paris, above the clouds and with the Eiffel Tower as a lamppost, even the moon joins in, singing Italian opera (courtesy of Plácido Domingo). And, through this transformation of the ordinary into the extraordinary, we are encouraged to believe in Satine's transfiguration, through Christian's love, into someone actually worthy of the love he is bestowing upon her. (In a subtle but probably unintentional way, we are also encouraged in this by Satine's earlier, insufficiently kinetic performances of "Diamonds Are a Girl's Best Friend" and "Material Girl," trademark songs of Marilyn Monroe and Madonna, who performed them much more dynamically than Nicole Kidman's Satine. Arguably, we believe in Satine's redemption in part because she is not fully convincing as a diva.)

Three numbers allow the predictable denouement to acquire great power. As Satine finally keeps her long-postponed rendezvous with the duke, one of the Bohemians (the narcoleptic Argentinean) dances the tango with a prostitute from the show, describing the inevitable stages of "love" with a woman like Satine: "desire . . . passion . . . suspicion . . . jealousy . . . anger . . . betrayal—where love is for the highest bidder, there can be no trust; without trust, there can be no love." As he begins then to sing "Roxanne" (Sting, 1982), Christian leaves, singing of his own sense of betrayal in counterpoint to the Argentinean's song of betrayed love, enacted through dance. This musical cross-cutting then evolves into a more elaborate montage sequence, which cuts among the increasingly violent tango, Christian's anguished descant, the duke's "seduction" of Satine (which turns into attempted rape after they both see Christian on the street), and various others who are watching ♫2.35 with growing alarm. As with many similar numbers in *Chicago* (see below), the cutting between "song and dance" and "real life" creates a powerful effect, using MERM-based exaggeration to set the film's grim realities in sharp relief. A particularly fraught moment occurs when Satine, seeing Christian on the street below, softly sings lines from the "lovers' secret song" ("Come What May") that Christian has written into the show (and one of the few songs in the film that the audience would be unfamiliar with).[79] In the sudden stillness, the tango's raspy violin tries out sneering versions of the title phrase of "Come What May," allowing us to hear, as well as see, that the duke has finally understood just what the secret song has been keep-♫2.36 ing secret. After the number ends, we learn that Christian has, like Orpheus, temporarily saved his Eurydice through his song; but then Satine, like Eurydice, seems to falter, and he loses her.

The latter development, too, is given a powerful musical presence, through Freddie Mercury's "The Show Must Go On." This song was originally released by Queen in early 1991 and acquired special poignancy when Mercury died of AIDS before the year was out, an illness that was—like Satine's consumption, the "AIDS" of the nineteenth century—kept secret until the end. Zidler begins the song after telling Satine that she is dying, starting partway through the verse ("Another hero, another mindless crime"), establishing his increasingly purposeful stride as a visual motive that aligns with both fate and human resolve. Satine herself adopts this mode as well; as she joins in, at first tentatively, then posed defiantly, she also begins walking forward with a parallel sense of resolution, as if prepared to meet her grimly certain fate. As the song builds, its machinery-evoking instrumental track—another representation of fate and resolve—grows gradually louder, reaching its climax as Satine reaches Christian's door with the requisite courage ♫2.37 to convince him that she wants to stay with the duke at the Moulin Rouge.

The third musical component of the denouement, "Come What May," provides the release we have been anticipating; indeed, this "special song" with its "secret message" functions as an internalized deus ex machina to ensure that Satine's fall will involve neither bodily nor spiritual degradation, enabling her to win back Christian's love before dying, transfigured. The song, which defies reality in favor of a soul-based MERM, comes through this reprise to represent, in retrospect, the guiding spirit of the film (along with the final lines of "Nature Boy") in large part because Eurydice has at this point become Orpheus, empowered by song and empowering those who hear her. Thus, after Christian confronts her with a full public denunciation borrowed intact from *La traviata*, Satine halts his departure from the theater with the first words of "Come What May." As she sings, gathering power as he responds, she includes a part of the song left out when he sang it earlier in the film: "Listen to my heart, can you hear it sing? / Come back to me and forgive everything."[80] And so he does turn back, in a moment that replaces *La traviata* once again with *Orpheus*: in turning back to her, he proves his love, but at the price of losing her. As with "Have Yourself a Merry Little Christmas" in *Meet Me in St. Louis*, "Come What May" must seem of a piece with the film's strategy of borrowing songs from the past, and so, indeed, the reprise explodes into a chaotic quodlibet that combines several of the borrowed songs from the film, including "Children of the Revolution" (Marc Bolan; sung by Toulouse and chorus), "Your Song" (sung by Christian), "One Day I'll Fly Away" (Joe Sample and Will Jennings; sung by Satine), and "The Show Must Go On" (sung by Zidler). But the song must ♪ 2.38 also be a new song, unknown to the film's audience, so that it may function as a private utterance belonging *only* to the world of this film.

Yet this fleeting parallel to *Meet Me in St. Louis* should not mislead, for *Moulin Rouge* stands at a far remove from the former's attempt to naturalize its music. And with that remove comes an extraordinary indulgence in camp that miraculously does not intrude on the possibility of taking it all quite seriously. Indeed, camp is, for many, the most distinctive feature of the film, the key to every exaggerated gesture and indulgence in cinematic and/or MERM-based excess. The film's pervasive campiness can, of course, stand in the way of our full engagement, distracting us and signaling that nothing in the film is to be taken seriously. Yet it need not be so, for camp is first and foremost a *mode* of storytelling, not the story itself. At any given screening of *Moulin Rouge*—and this was especially true when the film was first released, with large segments of the audience seeing it for the first time, wondering what to make of it—one may find genuine weeping across the aisle from delirious, delighted laughter bordering on tears.[81] As a mode of storytelling, camp (at least as employed here) ratchets up the emotional charge of each particular within the story, investing every object, every sentiment, and every person with sufficient exaggeration that they might be taken either "straight," with deepened significance, or as complete jokes, a travesty of what they seem to be. Or both. Surely, for example, Toulouse-Lautrec is both, at once a clichéd caricature and the passionate guiding spirit for the film's underlying idealism. The "bird-in-a-gilded-cage" cliché, attached to Satine in all manner of ways (e.g., the "birdcage" perch of her early "Diamonds" number or her rendition of "One Day I'll Fly Away"), brings an unsettling focus to the critical scene in which Zidler tells Satine she is dying as she stands with her own caged bird, which intrudes with its twittering.

This is, to be sure, a silly distraction that might either be ignored or provide a momentary escape into laughter. Yet it is also capable of pushing the poignancy of the scene up a notch for those who can both see the symbolism as the cliché it is and retain the capacity to find resonance between the trivial and more profound states of emotional involvement.

More generally, camp offers a still deeper resonance between the world of *Moulin Rouge* and our own, for those who care to engage with it. Camp has long provided an important mode of discourse for gay men, a context that has tended, in recent years, to constitute the major critical focus for the study of camp.[82] Scarcely coincidentally, a great many of *Moulin Rouge*'s campy exaggerations involve character-defining traits associated with homosexuality: the effeminate, lisping diction of both Toulouse-Lautrec and the duke, Zidler's asexual buffoonery, the hypersensitive squabbling among the Bohemians (Christian's "sidekicks") and their awestruck response to the film's diva and to Christian's huge "talent," the crotch-grabbing proclivities of the Argentinean, the presence of both an opera-singing moon and the Green Fairy (modeled, as Tinker Bell has often been supposed to be, on gay-diva Marilyn Monroe),[83] the eunuchlike loyalty of Le Chocolat, and the bald heads of both the sensitive Satie and Warner (the duke's thug). The film's Satie is a particularly interesting creation; although he bears little resemblance to the actual composer, Erik Satie—he is here an intense, ultrasensitive man, emaciated enough to be in the early stages of AIDS, eventually conducting an orchestra peopled by his visual equivalents—yet they are alike in affecting many odd traits and mannerisms that may be taken to indicate homosexuality. It is thus almost as if the only definitively straight characters in *Moulin Rouge* are its two stars, who alone maintain the vital illusion that heterosexual relationships are what musicals are about. If this exaggerated homosexual profile parallels a defensible (if mistaken) view of the musical more generally, as *merely* camp, it also offers a durable hierarchy, in which a homosexually inflected MERM supports and enhances a core of normalized "decency" (i.e., heterosexuality). More pointedly, especially with the disturbing multiplicities of wraithlike Saties by the film's end, *Moulin Rouge* implicitly forges a link between AIDS, which hit the gay theatrical and musical communities especially hard, and Satine's consumption (tuberculosis), the debilitating fatal disease of choice for the nineteenth century. (And in this respect the assonance of Satine's name with Satie becomes as important as those of Satine with Satan and satin noted earlier.)

The doubleness of camp plays out much differently in *Chicago*, in large part because the established perspective is nearly opposite from that of *Moulin Rouge*'s Christian: that of Roxie Hart, whose eyes, in close-up, open the film. Yet she, too, is a kind of Orpheus, attracted to the underworld and providing access to a MERM capable of transforming her quite ordinary talents into the makings of a star. Although the film of *Chicago* differs in many respects from its various earlier versions, they all center around Roxie

Hart, whose role as both manipulator and manipulated shifts in sometimes ambiguous ways.

The intriguing alternation of venues, titles, and scenarios that make up the background for the 2002 film begins with the original *Chicago*, a 1926 play by Maurine Watkins, a Chicago reporter who probably facilitated the acquittal of the real Roxie Hart (Beulah Annan, defendant in a 1924 murder trial for murdering her lover) by concocting a story about her being pregnant. Quickly turned into a film (1927, a "silent" also titled *Chicago*), the story was then toned down for the 1942 film *Roxie Hart* (starring Ginger Rogers); to satisfy the Hays Code, Roxie here admits to a murder committed by her husband, hoping thereby to capitalize on the resultant notoriety to further her stage career. The property then languished for more than three decades, reportedly due to Watkins's bad conscience over her role in glorifying murderers; after her death (in 1969), however, Bob Fosse, with Fred Ebb and John Kander, developed the story into the 1975 musical *Chicago*. This version, the basis for a 1996 stage revival and the 2002 film, initially achieved only moderate success, although expectations were high after the film version of Kander and Ebb's *Cabaret*, directed by Fosse three years earlier (1972) and to which *Chicago* owes a significant debt for its technique of (mostly) presenting its musical numbers in ironic parallel to, rather than within, the main dramatic action. The 2002 film refocuses this strategy by deriving the numbers more overtly and specifically from Roxie's imagination, intertwining the staged numbers more securely with the dramatic action by embedding them within the sensibilities of the characters themselves.

Admirers of the stage show (starring Gwen Verdon and Chita Rivera in the original, and Bebe Neuwirth and Ann Reinking in the much more successful 1996 revival) often find little to admire in the film, many of whose performers would not pass muster singing and dancing on Broadway. As a filmic realization of a successful stage show, *Chicago* thus fails in one important dimension: its seeming betrayal of its basis in a dance musical. Yet, from another perspective, that failure is part of the point; the "magic" dimension of cinematic MERM would simply distract from or disappear altogether behind the dancing talents of Verdon, Rivera, et al., but can seem transformative with relative amateurs such as Renée Zellweger and Richard Gere, whose tenuous credibility as dancers becomes integral to the effect.[84] Moreover, the strategic casting shakes the characters loose from the glib dance-based personae of the stage version, allowing them—particularly Roxie—to achieve a kind of reality that the highly stylized Broadway mounting categorically denies them, for the "real world" of more naturalistic film is where they most seem to belong for audiences familiar with their other work.

Establishing the perspective of Roxie Hart has both obvious and subtle dimensions. Most obviously, and early on, a second close-up of her eyes produces a momentary "vision" of herself as Velma Kelly, who is singing "All That Jazz" onstage at Chicago's Onyx Club (see figure 2.5). In the successive numbers, "Funny Honey," "When You're Good to Mama," and "Cell Block Tango" (also known as "He Had It Coming"), real-life situations and encounters become musical numbers in her mind, in the first instance starring her (as the policeman's interrogating flashlight transmutes into a spotlight), in the second starring a bigger-than-life Mama Morton (the corrupt prison matron), and in the third featuring, in a major production number, the six women who, like her, await trial for murdering their romantic partners, whose self-justification takes on musical form in Roxie's mind while she watches from a cabaret table. More subtly, each of these numbers is introduced by the pianist-emcee of the Onyx (Taye Diggs), fresh from Roxie's memory.

♪2.39
♪2.40
♪2.41
♪2.42

More subtle still, however, is the degree to which Velma Kelly, who is not in Watkins's original story, seems to be drawn according to Roxie's sensibilities. To those familiar with Liza Minnelli's Sally Bowles in the film version of *Cabaret*, Velma may seem frankly and even objectionably imitative. But one must remember just how derivative Minnelli's Sally was in the first place, modeled most directly on Louise Brooks, who was, like her version of Sally Bowles, an American who achieved some success in Germany in about 1930, whose famous page-boy hairdo was a direct model for Minnelli (and, of course, for Catherine Zeta-Jones)—and whose 1929 *Pandora's Box* (dir. Pabst) runs directly parallel to *Chicago* (both the 1926 play and the 1927 film) in its portrayal of a jazz-crazed, sexually licentious femme fatale on trial for the murder of her husband.[85] Moreover, the act that Roxie sees Velma perform at the beginning of the film ("All That Jazz") is supposedly a sister act, but because she has just murdered her sister (along with her own adulterous husband, Charlie), the act has a vacancy that Roxie might eventually fill. How ready-made all this seems to be for Roxie may be largely a matter of plot design, but at the same time it entrenches her perspective as the one that matters most, especially in the film.

Since the original stage show was not, however, designed to be quite so embedded in Roxie's jazz-crazed mind, the conceit cannot be sustained fully. With the next number, "All I Care About," we leave Roxie's perspective to move between hers and that of Billy Flynn (Richard Gere), the flashy lawyer whom Roxie will hire through her prize chump of a husband (John C. Reilly). Here, as later, such departures are made to tell; thus, the next number, "We Both Reached for the Gun," conflates their two perspectives, as he becomes the arch-manipulator, for whom Roxie is a mere ventriloquist's dummy and the press corps become puppets on strings. With this number, in fact, we move well beyond the early formula, since the "real-life" referent—a press interview—is already a kind of performance. With the next number, "Roxie," there is no emcee's introduction,[86] but he returns with the following number ("I Can't Do It Alone"), which he bills as "Miss Velma Kelly in an Act of Desperation," adding his seal of validation to the established fact that Velma and Roxie have effectively switched places, with Velma now on the outside looking in, attempting a semblance of MERM but

Figure 2.5. *Chicago*'s Velma Kelly (Catherine Zeta-Jones, top panel), fresh from murdering her sister (who was also her co-headliner), finishes singing "All That Jazz" as soon-to-be murderer Roxie Hart (Renée Zellweger, middle panel) imagines herself onstage in Velma's place (bottom panel). This sequence provides the film's first instance of Roxie's vision serving as the link between the film's realities and its jazz-based fantasies. The stars' hairstyles recall two archetypal looks of the Jazz Age, most familiar from Louise Brooks's black pageboy (Velma) and Marlene Dietrich's blond curls (Roxie).

failing to impress. Variants on the formula continue with Billy's nonsinging narrative of the latest of Chicago's jazz-crazed husband murderers, introduced as a "number" by the emcee ("Chicago after Midnight"); the dropping of the emcee again for Amos's "Mr. Cellophane" (appropriately, he sings only for himself); and the emcee's return, overlapping the reporter Mary Sunshine's "Ladies and Gentlemen," to introduce the chilling hanging death of the Hungarian ballerina Katalin Helinszki (the "Hunyak"), the only

♩2.43 woman on death row who is innocent of murder.

The latter figure is, of course, a brutal reminder that the values in *Chicago* are diametrically opposed to conventional decency; here, the only innocent—and, for that matter, the only "legitimate" dancer—is brutally sacrificed, whereas the obviously guilty are allowed to thrive. This overturning of conventional mores has been understood as cynical, and it surely is that, but it is also a part of *Chicago*'s camp dimension, since the most extreme forms of camp have an overriding concern with presentation and must at least in some way invert expressive expectations in order simply to *be* camp.[87] Many found the element of cynicism too difficult to overlook or absorb in the stage show, seeing it as an amoral indulgence in music's celebratory energies, placed in the service of something reprehensible, almost as if *The Producers*' imaginary camp offering, "Springtime for Hitler," were actually being produced on Broadway. Pure camp will always offend in this way, simply because those who want also (or only) to take the subject seriously will be left out. In this respect, the film performs a major act of rescue, making the reality of Roxie's limited perspective and resultant pain sufficiently vivid, through montage, that we can take her seriously as someone who suffers and may not be discounted as *merely* cynical. To the extent that the game playing in *Chicago* may thus seem to have real, *felt* consequences, the potential doubleness of camp is restored, so that MERM both pulls away from reality and reinforces it. Nevertheless, even the film version of *Chicago* is discomfiting, for while it undercuts its cynicism, it does so by substituting a grim, all-too-believable reality, which confronts us whenever MERM falls away (whereas in *Moulin Rouge* we see instead a core of redemptive love and the capacity for human nobility).

Chicago offers yet another doubleness, similar in kind to the disturbing ways that *Cabaret* has its cake and eats it too, on the one hand celebrating the Kit Kat Klub's carnivalesque escape from reality and using it as a ready platform for social protest, and on the other also suggesting that its decadence makes it directly accountable for fostering the then-incipient horrors of Nazi Germany.[88] In *Chicago*, the idea that jazz and its associated lifestyles have warped Roxie, so that these societal ills and not she herself should be held accountable, is put forth cynically, as a way to evoke public sympathy but not as a real explanation. But if we are not really to believe that account—and to be sure, believing it is somewhat problematic while we are simultaneously indulging our own enjoyment of jazz and its associated lifestyles, if vicariously—then how do we explain away the very clear indications that Roxie's fixation on an imaginary world of MERM has led her to disconnect from the real world, discounting its meanness and the harsh consequences of her own immoral actions? This is, indeed, one of the ways that the show's cynicism seems built in, for MERM here effectively reduces to jazz and its dance forms, so that content and its campy mode of delivery merge: medium thus becomes message, and message medium.

The film version of *Cabaret*, as it happens, also provides one of the most direct links between *Moulin Rouge* and *Chicago*, since it served as an important model for both. The central situational details in *Moulin Rouge*— Christian's pilgrimage from England to a troubled continental European city at a fraught moment in its history (turn-of-the-century Paris), his descent into the underworld of the Moulin Rouge, and his subsequent triangular entanglement with its star, Satine, all watched over by the cynical proprietor, Zidler—find their direct parallels in the film version of *Cabaret*: in the English Brian, continental Berlin, the Kit Kat Klub, Sally Bowles, Maximilian, and the Emcee. And, analogically, the Chicago we see in *Chicago* is the Berlin we see in *Cabaret*, spiraling off into evil excess—although *Chicago*'s version of the Kit Kat Klub is largely a creation of Roxie Hart's imagination. But the real connection among the three runs much deeper. It is not for nothing that all three titles are the names of places fraught with associations of decadence. Each of these concerns a particular *place*, a mecca of decadent excitement that is both enchanted and cursed by its association with MERM, whose problems all cycle around the problematic relationship between MERM and reality. *Chicago* and *Moulin Rouge* function in part as meta-movie-musicals precisely because the same may be said of that most MERM-saturated of "places," the American movie musical.

For Further Consideration

(not including many important adaptations of stage shows)
            The Jazz Singer (1927), *The Singing Fool* (1928), *The Cocoanuts* (1929), *The Love Parade* (1929), *The Hollywood Revue of 1929* (1929), *Broadway Melody* (1929), *Glorifying the American Girl* (1930), *King of Jazz* (1930), *Whoopee!* (1930), *Morocco* (1930), *Dixiana* (1930), *The Smiling Lieutenant* (1931), *One Hour with You* (1932), *Love Me Tonight* (1932), *The Big Broadcast* (1932), *Glad Rags to Riches* (1932), *Blonde Venus* (1932), *Duck Soup* (1933), *Flying Down to Rio* (1933), *She Done Him Wrong* (1933), *42nd Street* (1933), *Footlight Parade* (1933), *Bright Eyes* (1934), *Dames* (1934), *Belle of the Nineties* (1934), *Kid Millions* (1934), *The Gay Divorcee* (1934), *The Littlest Rebel* (1935), *The Little Colonel* (1935), *Top Hat* (1935), *Swing Time* (1936), *The Great Ziegfeld* (1936), *Snow White and the Seven Dwarfs* (1937), *Everybody Sing* (1938), *Rebecca of Sunnybrook Farm* (1938), *The Little Princess* (1939), *The Wizard of Oz* (1939), *Destry Rides Again* (1939), *Moon Over Harlem* (1939),

Down Argentine Way (1940), *Fantasia* (1940), *Pinocchio* (1940), *Dumbo* (1941), *Lady Be Good* (1941), *Smilin' Through* (1941), *Babes on Broadway* (1941), *Yankee Doodle Dandy* (1942), *Bambi* (1942), *For Me and My Gal* (1942), *Holiday Inn* (1942), *Sun Valley Serenade* (1942), *The Gang's All Here* (1943), *Cabin in the Sky* (1943), *Stage Door Canteen* (1943), *Something for the Boys* (1944), *Going My Way* (1944), *Anchors Aweigh* (1945), *The Harvey Girls* (1946), *Song of the South* (1946), *Mother Wore Tights* (1947), *A Song Is Born* (1948), *Easter Parade* (1948), *The Pirate* (1948), *In the Good Old Summertime* (1949), *The Inspector General* (1949), *Summer Stock* (1950), *Pagan Love Song* (1950), *Stage Fright* (1950), *Cinderella* (1950), *An American in Paris* (1951), *Hans Christian Andersen* (1952), *Lili* (1953), *The Bandwagon* (1953), *A Star Is Born* (1954), *The Glenn Miller Story* (1954), *White Christmas* (1954), *Seven Brides for Seven Brothers* (1954), *High Society* (1956), *Love Me Tender* (1956), *The Court Jester* (1956), *Les Girls* (1957), *Silk Stockings* (1957), *Jailhouse Rock* (1957), *Jamboree* (1957), *Pal Joey* (1957), *Gigi* (1958), *Rio Bravo* (1959), *Porgy and Bess* (1959), *Some Like It Hot* (1959), *Sleeping Beauty* (1959), *Can-Can* (1960), *Please Don't Eat the Daisies* (1960), *Flaming Star* (1960), *101 Dalmatians* (1961), *Funny Girl* (1964), *Cinderella* (TV 1964), *Mary Poppins* (1964), *A Hard Day's Night* (1964), *Robin and the 7 Hoods* (1964), *Help!* (1965), *Thoroughly Modern Millie* (1967), *Doctor Dolittle* (1967), *To Sir, with Love* (1967), *The Jungle Book* (1967), *Head* (1968), *The Producers* (1968), *Alice's Restaurant* (1969), *Darling Lili* (1970), *Woodstock* (1970), *Willy Wonka and the Chocolate Factory* (1971), *Bedknobs and Broomsticks* (1971), *Cabaret* (1972), *Lady Sings the Blues* (1972), *O Lucky Man!* (1973), *Tommy* (1975), *Funny Lady* (1975), *At Long Last Love* (1975), *Nashville* (1975), *The Rocky Horror Picture Show* (1976), *Saturday Night Fever* (1977), *The Buddy Holly Story* (1978), *Grease* (1978), *All That Jazz* (1979), *Xanadu* (1980), *The Blues Brothers* (1980), *Fame* (1980), *One Trick Pony* (1980), *American Pop* (1981), *Victor/Victoria* (1982), *Let's Spend the Night Together* (1982), *Flashdance* (1983), *Yentl* (1983), *Staying Alive* (1983), *Footloose* (1984), *Purple Rain* (1984), *Give My Regards to Broad Street* (1984), *This Is Spinal Tap* (1984), *Little Shop of Horrors* (1986), *Dirty Dancing* (1987), *Hairspray* (1988), *Earth Girls Are Easy* (1988), *The Fabulous Baker Boys* (1989), *The Little Mermaid* (1989), *Beauty and the Beast* (1991), *Aladdin* (1992), *Newsies* (1992), *Sister Act* (1992), *Strictly Ballroom* (1992), *The Nightmare before Christmas* (1993), *Swing Kids* (1993), *The Lion King* (1994), *Everyone Says I Love You* (1996), *Waiting for Guffman* (1996), *Brassed Off* (1996), *Cannibal! The Musical* (1996), *That Thing You Do!* (1996), *The Harmonists* (1997), *Little Voice* (1998), *Topsy-Turvy* (1999), *Cradle Will Rock* (1999), *Bring It On* (2000), *Dancer in the Dark* (2000), *High Fidelity* (2000), *Center Stage* (2000), *Almost Famous* (2000), *Billy Elliot* (2000), *Bamboozled* (2000), *O Brother, Where Art Thou* (2000), *A Mighty Wind* (2003)

See Also

Regarding film musicals, see Jane Feuer's pioneering *The Hollywood Musical*, Rick Altman's now fundamental *The American Film Musical*, and Leo Braudy's pithy and insightful essay "Musicals and the Energy from Within." Other useful sources include Richard Fehr and Frederick G. Vogel's *Lullabies of Hollywood*; Miles Kreuger's *The Movie Musical from Vitaphone to 42nd Street*; Graham Wood's "Distant Cousin or Fraternal Twin? Analytical Approaches to the Film Musical"; Jerome Delamater's *Dance in the Hollywood Musical*; Allen L. Woll's *The Hollywood Musical Goes to War*; Jennifer R. Jenkins's " 'Say It with Firecrackers': Defining the 'War Musical' of the 1940s"; Ralph Willett's "From Gold Diggers to Bar Girls: A Selective History of the American Movie Musical"; and John Russell Taylor and Arthur Jackson's *The Hollywood Musical*.

Regarding African Americans in film, see Donald Bogle's *Toms, Coons, Mulattoes, Mammies, & Bucks*, which analyzes how black stereotypes have played out in Hollywood; *Representing Jazz* (Krin Gabbard, ed.), which includes two essays on *Cabin in the Sky*; and Marshall Stearns and Jean Stearns's *Jazz Dance: The Story of American Vernacular Dance*.

Regarding *Singin' in the Rain*, see "Introduction by the Authors" in Betty Comden and Adolph Green's *Singin' in the Rain*; Peter Wollen's useful monograph of the same title, particularly regarding the dancing in the film; and chapter 11 of Hugh Fordin's *The World of Entertainment! Hollywood's Gratest Musicals*.

Regarding *Stormy Weather*, see chapters 3 and 4 of Arthur Knight's *Disintegrating the Musical* and pp. 179–85 in Constance Valis Hill's *Brotherhood in Rhythm: The Jazz Tap Dancing of the Nicholas Brothers*.

Regarding *Bamboozled*, see "Coda" in Arthur Knight's *Disintegrating the Musical* (where the film is considered alongside the contemporaneous *O Brother Where Art Thou*).

Regarding *Meet Me in St. Louis*, see Gerald Kaufman's useful monograph of the same title and chapter 4 of Hugh Fordin's *The World of Entertainment! Hollywood's Gratest Musicals*.

Regarding *Chicago* (the stage show), see chapter 2 in Scott Miller's *Deconstructing Harold Hill* and pp. 127–31 in Ethan Mordden's *One More Kiss*.

Part Two

PERSONAL THEMES

Fairy Tales and Fantasy

THE AMERICAN MUSICAL has, throughout its history, provided a realm of fantasy, and has thus seemed eminently suitable for the retelling of familiar fairy tales or inventing new ones.[1] Already with *The Black Crook* (1866), often described as the first American musical, European fairy tales were being refashioned for American sensibilities.[2] Generally, however, operetta has proven a more reliable vehicle for fairy tales than the more mainstream American musical, since operetta is less concerned with the here and now than with the past and far away, and is thus already one step closer to the reimagined kingdoms of "once upon a time." Magic and generically contrived happy endings are staples of operetta, though scarcely the only possibilities for a genre that also indulged more adult topics and sensibilities (including sexually charged intrigue, which played a role in all the operettas considered in chapter 1).[3] By the early years of the twentieth century, child-oriented operetta had become a viable subgenre, with such landmarks as Sloane and Tietjens's *The Wizard of Oz* and Herbert's much-revived *Babes in Toyland* (both 1903, with film versions of the latter in 1934 and 1961). Indeed, the connection between operetta and fairy tale is sufficiently strong that Rick Altman, in his classic study of the film musical, simply conflates the two, thereby essentializing the "happily ever after" component of operetta.[4]

The alliances that the American musical stage forged with fairy tale and child-oriented fantasy mirrored many precedents and contemporary influences from loftier cultural traditions. These included, during the formative years of the American musical, Tchaikovsky's fairy-tale ballets (see note 2), Humperdinck's opera *Hänsel und Gretel* (1893), Dukas's symphonic scherzo *The Sorcerer's Apprentice* (1897), Dvořák's opera *Rusalka* (1900), Debussy's opera *Pelléas et Mélisande* (1902), Rimsky-Korsakov's opera *Le coq d'or* (1909), Ravel's orchestral suite *Ma mère l'oye* (Mother Goose, 1911) and children's opera *L'enfant et les sortilèges* (1925), and many older works that remained in the repertory, such as Mozart's opera *The Magic Flute*, Weber's opera *Der Freischütz*, and Mendelssohn's Overture and Incidental Music to Shakespeare's *A Midsummer Night's Dream*.[5] But the most secure basis for these alliances was generic: how else but through the state-of-the art stagecraft, costuming, and scenic effects of Broadway, and especially as aligned with singing, dancing, and musically accompanied tableau, could the requisite "supernatural" effects and phantasmagoria of fairy tale and fantasy be produced so well in early twentieth-century America? Well into the 1920s, the answer would obviously have been "Nowhere else," even if films from the silent era had already developed a substantial repertory of what would later be called special effects. The situation changed dramatically, however, with the advent of synchronized sound, which increased film's capacity and appetite for phantasmagoria by providing it with an important ally: MERM ("musically enhanced reality mode"; see my discussion in chapter 2). At around the same time, new developments in animation provided another means to indulge America's growing taste for cinematic fantasy.

Walt Disney and his collaborators are most directly responsible for how securely animation attached itself to child-oriented filmic genres in the late 1920s through World War II. Disney launched his seminal character Mickey Mouse with *Steamboat Willie* in 1928, coordinating sound (including music) and simulated action so imaginatively that the potential for animation seemed newly revealed. And such moments of technical-artistic breakthrough would soon proliferate. Disney launched his series of Silly Symphonies the following year,[6] began developing stronger narratives based on fairy tales with *The Ugly Duckling* in 1931, introduced color to animation in 1932, and achieved a runaway hit in this format—the all-color, animated musical short—with *The Three Little Pigs* in 1933. The latter included an instantly popular song, "Who's Afraid of the Big Bad Wolf" (by Frank Churchill, with Pinto Colvig and Ted Sears), which served as an engagingly flippant response to a variety of ills that then plagued America: the Great Depression and union troubles at home, and the worsening situations in Europe and Asia, which would soon explode into World War II. Fueled by the success of *The Three Little Pigs*, Disney took more deliberate aim at what Frank Thomas and Ollie Johnston term "the illusion of life" in their landmark 1981 book, *Disney Animation*.[7] In the years following *The Three Little Pigs*, Disney established new benchmarks with *The Band Concert* (1935) and *The Old Mill* (1937), before releasing the first full-length animated feature—*Snow White and the Seven Dwarfs*, in development since shortly after *The Three Little Pigs*—just in time for Christmas 1937.

Snow White's position at the head of a series of early Disney animated feature films that would include *Pinocchio* and *Fantasia* (1940), *Dumbo* (1941), and *Bambi* (1942),[8] virtually demands that I give it pride of place here. Because *Snow White* so well exemplifies the often prudish moral tone that soon became a Disney hallmark, it is important here to note also the subversive dimension of many of their animated films, evident during these early years in the defiant insouciance of Mickey Mouse, many of the Silly Symphonies, and *The Three Little Pigs*. Thus, for example, the latter's "Who's Afraid of the Big Bad Wolf" comes into direct conflict with the moral of the tale itself. The tune trades successfully on what would seem to be a glaring weakness: an incomplete lyric that consists entirely of a repeated infantile setup and a missing punch line, the latter replaced by a wordless musical taunt. The implicitly smirking "nyeh, nyeh" of this concluding phrase works precisely because it is wordless, even if that lack resulted more from the songwriters' inability to come up with a satisfying line than from deliberate intent. But in succeeding so well, "Who's Afraid" subverts the seeming point of the story; indeed, it is not clear whether the film as a whole endorses the traditional moral lesson of how astute planning and hard work lead to success, or instead advocates an escapist, nose-thumbing attitude, scorning both danger and overly preachy allies. Certainly the latter attitude is what audiences took away with them, and embodied through repeated singing (and whistling) of the featured tune, as a welcome antidote to the painful realities surrounding them.

This kind of doubleness is endemic to shows and films that give musical voice to perspectives and attitudes that they explicitly censure. Moreover, it is especially prominent in fairy-tale musicals, which must openly court two audiences at once, selling themselves to children and adults alike. Indeed, this doubleness is a large part of the appeal of the genre for many adults, who see past the child-oriented mask to the political allegories of Lewis Carroll's *Alice's Adventures in Wonderland* (1865), L. Frank Baum's *The Wonderful Wizard of Oz* (1900), and Rimsky-Korsakov's *Le coq d'or*, or savor the sexual innuendos endemic to fairy-tale accounts of imperiled youthful innocence, which also often involve the first awakenings of virginal love. The latter potential, for a veiled sexualized dimension, becomes even more evident when we leave the relatively neutered realm of Disney animation.

Alongside Disney's rise to prominence in the 1930s, two related genres of live-action musical film held special and somewhat covert appeal for two very different audience groups. The plucky heroine of American operetta in the 1930s, who most often prevailed through some combination of proto-feminism and the intervention of a strong but annoying male (archetypically played by Jeanette MacDonald and Nelson Eddy, respectively), appealed tremendously to two fetishized tastes: heterosexual men addicted to damsel-in-distress narratives on the order of the silent era's *The Perils of Pauline* (later spoofed by Jay Ward and Bill Scott's "Dudley Do-Right" parodies on television)[9] and homosexual men attracted to campy melodrama and the over-wrought performances they engendered.[10] And, for both of these groups, the appeal often became even stronger if the heroine was a child. Carroll's Alice, Baum's Dorothy, vintage silent-era films such as *Little Mary Sunshine* (1916), and Shirley Temple's hugely successful series of films in the 1930s all traded on this (remember, too, that the latter's early short films were often quite risqué). An important climax of this line of development was MGM's 1939 *The Wizard of Oz*, with newly emergent Judy Garland substituting for an unavailable Shirley Temple (who was also, by some reports, judged inadequate as a singer). The film's greatest success came when it was resurrected for annual television viewing in the 1950s, at which time its thinly disguised homosexual dimension also resurfaced with new and persistent vigor, and the key phrase "Friends of Dorothy" became an insiders' term for "homosexual." Even without its many intriguing affinities with Disney's

Snow White—its original inspiration—*The Wizard*'s presence in this book is thus similarly mandatory.

The increasing access afforded by television to an audience of children—indeed, an audience often consisting nearly entirely of children, especially in the after-school hours—only increased what was already by the 1950s a clear affinity between film and child-based themes. But television, as a substitute for live adult caretakers, also offered the picture-tube equivalents of those missing figures in the form of sympathetic on-screen adults who assumed parental or teacherly roles. Such figures had their roots in older, sometimes racialized cinematic conventions, often reflecting the tendencies of Hollywood to relegate blacks to domestic-service roles (thus, Bill Robinson's "uncle" roles in Shirley Temple films or Hattie McDaniel's "mammy" roles). But daily television personalities, such as *The Mickey Mouse Club*'s Jimmie Dodd (late afternoons, from 1955 to 1959) or Bob Keeshan's "Captain Kangaroo" (mornings, from 1955 to 1991), served as more reliable presences and could provide the same variety of experiences a real adult could provide, entertaining children through stories and singing, taking them on (virtual) outings, screening films, and—of course, less overtly—teaching them something in the process.

Arguably, this function of television stands behind the phenomenal success of two "nanny" films in the mid-1960s, both starring Julie Andrews in roles it would be difficult for her to move beyond: *Mary Poppins* (1964) and *The Sound of Music* (1965). In each, rudderless children whose parents have forsaken their parental roles for a variety of reasons are rescued by a nanny-governess who does for them precisely what television was already doing for countless American children: entertaining them directly, taking them on outings, teaching them to sing, and inviting them to take part in fanciful entertainments (animated chalk drawings and puppet shows, respectively)—all this, plus, in what was the greatest leap of faith, repairing a damaged family unit along the way, by restoring an initially absent parental involvement. Of the two, *Mary Poppins* (with songs by the highly regarded brother team, Richard and Robert Sherman) most clearly falls under the purview of this chapter.[11]

The possibility for fantasies of this kind to partake of more serious subject matter, already clear enough in *Mary Poppins* but even more so in *The Sound of Music*, was to some extent latent to the genre of fairy-tale musicals, a byproduct of its inherent doubleness. Indeed, that doubleness, arising from the need to address children and adults simultaneously, and often embracing large doses of camp, marks a striking difference between the theme of this chapter and that of its successor, "Idealism and Inspiration," which tends to rely on more sincere modes of theatrical expression. Moreover, this difference may in turn help explain the relative advantage film has enjoyed as a vehicle for fantasy and fairy-tale musicals, and the signal failure of the film versions of prominent "idealist" shows such as *Camelot* and *Man of La Mancha*. But across the apparent divide between these seemingly related themes (which I will return to at the beginning of the next chapter), the latent seriousness of fairy-tale musicals provides an important link. My final discussion will address one of the most successful musical bridges between fantasy and adulthood—the more so because it allows its adult audiences to reconnect, and often to connect in new ways, with stories already well known to them from their own childhoods. Stephen Sondheim and James Lapine's *Into the Woods* (1989), in part by partaking fully of its adult theatrical venue, and in part through its adroit, interactive combination of familiar stories (so that they seem, indeed, to "talk" to each other), suitably concludes this chapter and also provides a useful springboard into the theme of the following chapter, idealism and inspiration.

Snow White and the Seven Dwarfs (animated film, 1937), as with many of Disney's animated features, has an odd profile for a musical; many, in fact, think of the film primarily in terms of its animation and only secondarily as an extension of musical theater. Part of the reason for this is generic; like most animation, *Snow White* is heavily saturated with music, so that its musical component may be understood as no more than an expected dimension of animated film. In fact, the film's music comes very close to being "wall to wall," punctuated only twice by nontrivial musical silences (lasting about half a minute each).[12] But the film is also built around a handful of songs (by Frank Churchill) that rank among Disney's most enduring, including "Whistle While You Work" and "Heigh-Ho," and displays a sure sense of how to deploy songs to best effect in a romantic operetta.[13]

As animation, *Snow White* succeeds so well in part because of how it manages its most apparent weakness, the insufficiently naturalistic representations of Snow White and her Prince. This weakness is most apparent in their more conventional songs, where facial expressions and lip-synching are inadequately nuanced, especially according to later standards (above all those set by the Disney studio itself). But the animators' supple treatment of the more cartoonish figures—the dwarfs (straight out of vaudeville), the animals and birds, the Witch, the animated landscape—more often distracts our attention from such defects. When constant activity surrounds a more realistically represented character, an audience is unlikely even to notice that its centerpiece (usually Snow White) is less deftly treated. Indeed, often enough an audience is invited to see that surrounding activity as an extension of the character's inner state—much as background music, both here and in films more generally, seems to create a sense not only of the world but also of its dominant sensibility. When Snow White is at her most characteristic—sunny, buoyant, infectiously cheerful—so also is the world around her flooded with sunlight and animated by fluffy birds and preternaturally buoyant woodland creatures, mostly grouped in contented family units. When Snow White is frightened, the world around her darkens into night, the bare branches of trees become arms with claws to snatch at her clothing, owls and other nocturnal creatures swarm threateningly, and the very ground gives way beneath her, so that she plunges into a subterranean pool where logs become alligators. Are we to understand this as a cinematically collapsed temporality, in which Snow White spends a frightening night in the forest? Perhaps; more likely, though—given that the terrain does not make sense as *actual* landscape, especially when the log-infested pool suddenly lets out into a meadow—the nighttime world is meant to play as an expression of her fearfulness and vulnerability, rather than of actually experienced dangers, in a manner consistent with expressionism, in both its fin-de-siècle and later cinematic guises. It is thus in the fluid world of animation that we may see most vividly a direct link between inner and outer worlds (a link critical to the idealist themes discussed in chapter 4).

This kind of scenic mirroring, which thus serves as a visual extension of background music, is in fact thematic to the story. The evil queen learns of the world by consulting her magic mirror and surrounds herself with the accoutrement of black magic, including ravens, rats, and the skeletons of what seem to have been victims of prolonged torture—all of which may be seen as an extension of her essential nature.[14] The Prince appears to Snow White first as a reflection at the bottom of her wishing well, in direct answer to her expression of her innermost wishes; he is, in essence, part of the world only because she has imagined him, an act of conjuring in its way more powerful than the Queen's later manipulations, and well in line with Snow White's ability to enlist the birds and animals as her allies, as extensions of her own will. This kind of pervasive mirroring is also expressed in sonic ♩3.1   terms, as when Snow White sings a duet with her own echo:

I'm wishing	(I'm wishing)
For the one I love	
To find me	(To find me)
Today.	(Today)

In some traditions of echo songs, the echoes seem to respond as answers to questions rather than as simple repetitions. Thus, as in the Inquisition scene in *Candide* (see chapter 7), the echo song provides an occasion for verbal cleverness and surprise reversals of meaning; here, however, the echo simply repeats obediently, supports Snow White during the vocalizing bridge (in thirds!), and gets out of the way entirely so that the Prince himself can take over for the final echo of "Today."[15] Against this background of mirroring, the nightmarish sequence in the forest may be taken as a "reality" previously held in check by Snow White's unwavering goodness of soul. Until this moment, she has inscribed her own vision onto the more shadowed reality of her life circumstances, in which she, a princess, is forced to do menial household labor in rags. But in the forest, the reality that shadows her projected visions emerges unfiltered: doves and bluebirds give way to owls, flowers to barren, clawlike branches and dry leaves, and her wishing well to an alligator-infested pool.

This kind of interplay between mirroring and shadowing becomes even more vivid in the second half of the film, where literal shadows are used to great advantage, particularly those of the Witch and the two buzzards who follow her, waiting for the kill. But it may also be seen to operate on a broader scale, awakening its American audience to see a version of its own dreams superimposed on a more threatening landscape. It is in such terms that we might best explain (other than as a laughable incongruity) the jarring appearance of specifically *American* woodland creatures, such as the raccoon and bobwhite, in what has already been well established as a medieval *European* landscape, replete with castles and kingdoms, and derived, as the opening credits acknowledge, from the Brothers Grimm.[16] Moreover, it is surely no coincidence that these American creatures appear at precisely the moment in the story when the forest has suddenly become not a threatening place but a place of refuge from the Old-World scheming of the Queen. The allegorical aspects of the story are thus "hidden" right before our eyes, as the forest suddenly becomes a version of America peopled by good, hard-working folk (the dwarfs), and the Queen a version of Nazi Germany, about to plunge Europe's heritage of beauty into the ugliness of war and racially motivated genocide—a reading reinforced by the grotesque image later in the film of the Witch triumphant, cackling over the outstretched arm of a fallen Snow White, "Now *I'll* be fairest in the land." But probably more important than this veiled allegorical message is the way the film's subtle visual resonances with an American landscape combine with an implicit endorsement of what may be understood as America's national religion, a kind of secular Protestantism in which one is rewarded, in this world, according to both the hard work one does and the purity and innocence of one's soul, both of which allow the (at least partial) re-creation of the world in one's own image.

Within this secularized Christianity, God is a benign, often unacknowledged presence—thus, Snow White "wishes" rather than prays at the beginning, and says her bedtime prayers but does not insist on saying grace at mealtime (although the lyrics of "Bluddle Uddle Um Dum" reassure us that washing is "good for the soul"). Nevertheless, it is clearly God who determines the outcome when all else has failed, providing the lightning bolt that finishes off the Queen-Witch and prevents her from crushing her pursuers with a boulder. Similarly, when the Prince appears at the end, he has been guided by the heavenly light that shines in response to the mourned goodness of Snow White and the due reverence shown by the dwarfs, who mourn Snow White with an organ chorale redolent of Protestant religious services. And, although the underscore for his kiss, derived appropriately from "Some Day My Prince Will Come," evolves first into a worldly, European-style waltz (appropriate for fairy-tale operetta), and later into a still more abandoned waltz for the woodland creatures, it culminates, as dictated by the final lines of "Some Day," in sanctifying wedding bells (see figure 3.1). ♪**3.2**

Figure 3.1. The climactic scene from *Snow White and the Seven Dwarfs* is doubly autographed by the women who provided the basis for Snow White's humanizing performance. The inscriptions read, "To Miles with love / Voice of Snow White / Adriana Caselotti" and "And now, the live action model / Marge Champion." (Autographed still courtesy of Miles Kreuger and the Institute of the American Musical, Inc.)

It is in the light of this secularized Protestantism that we might best understand the film's many revisions to the story as related by the Brothers Grimm, in which Snow White is considerably younger and does *not* toil for her stepmother (in the film, she is turned into a Cinderella-like figure); the huntsman responds to her beauty, innocence, and pleading (and the sure knowledge that she will perish anyway), rather than to her evident kindness of heart; she disturbs the ultratidiness of the dwarfs' cottage (à la Goldilocks) rather than its messiness; and the Prince, who does not appear until the end, only accidentally restores her to life (when her bearers stumble and break her glass coffin, thereby dislodging the poison apple from her mouth), rather than through a more directly physical gesture of love. All of these changes establish a sense that Snow White's beauty is greater than the Queen's mostly because it is both reflected by inner beauty and externalized through hard work, so that she is *deserving* of both her beauty and of a kinder fate, according to a specifically "American" sense of justice. That this is a fairly deliberate reshaping of the story based on a careful (rather than simply careless) reading of the original seems clear, judging by the imaginative ways in which the film elaborates on both the original's brief description of Snow

White's tactile horror in the woods, where she is terrified by "every leaf on every tree," and the benevolent presence of the birds who in the original come only in the later stages, to watch over her coffin.[17]

Among the most striking of the many other differences between the two versions are the original's complete lack of differentiation among the dwarfs; its delineation of three attempts by the Queen to kill Snow White after her original failure, during which she only gradually drifts into black magical arts; and its description of her even more gruesome fate at the end, where she is forced, at Snow White's wedding celebration, to put on red-hot iron slippers and dance until she dies. The substitution in the Disney film of divine retribution for the latter punishment follows another American trope (in popular fiction, at least), in which punishment and killing, and the vindictiveness they express, are regarded as inappropriate activities for the innocent of soul, so that evil is almost always punished less directly, ideally as a direct result and reflection of its own dastardliness. The Disney film seems to combine the latter process with divine intervention. Thus, the Queen is done in by two things: the storm her actions have provoked and the misfire of her plot to kill the dwarfs by levering the boulder onto them. And each of these can in turn be read as either divine intervention or reflected evil. Storms are traditionally associated with *either* black magic *or* heavenly wrath (the latter according to traditions dating from the great flood), whereas the lightning bolt that strikes her ledge seems timed specifically to prevent her from succeeding in killing the dwarfs. But her ultimate fate— to have her bones picked by the two buzzards that have become her silent shadows—is more clearly the result of her own dastardliness, to be understood as poetic justice.

All this serves as a kind of frame for the core of the film, directly expressed through song: Snow White's projected romance on the one hand and her interaction with the animals and dwarfs on the other. In the former realm, the songs are fairly conventional, including the opening "I'm Wishing" (a typical AABA), the Prince's shorter "One Song" (ABAC, but in sixteen bars instead of thirty-two), and the more elaborate "Some Day My Prince Will Come" (ABAC, repeated with a new text), couched in a European waltz idiom with a flexible tempo partaking freely of the *Luftpause*. Suitably, then, ♫ **3.3** the romance is presented mostly within songs that individually project a future of "happily ever after," with the most elaborate of them extended into a final celebration of achieved happiness. For each of these, also, and for Snow White's more generally, the songs include introductory dialogue in rhyme, which takes on a teacherly demeanor when Snow White is singing to the animals or dwarfs. This kind of verbal pedestal for the songs marks the principal difference between the dwarfs' most characteristic songs, "Heigh-Ho" and "The Silly Song," both of which are launched directly, with cuts away from contrasting scenes (Snow White at the cottage and the newly transformed evil Queen, respectively).

"Heigh-Ho" offers the sharpest contrast, since its predecessor, "Whistle While You Work," is also a "work" song, but one in which Snow White instructs the animals, taking on a parental (or nannylike) role, using the song to inspire directly, and interrupting it to correct their work habits as needed. "Heigh-Ho," however, seems casually thrown together, with improvised words over music whose primary impulse is rhythmic, first governing the individualized, repetitive motions of work in the verse ("We dig, dig, dig, dig"), and then the coordinated marching home in the chorus ("Heigh-Ho"). Both songs use whistling, but very differently, as Snow White whistles to illustrate her instructive lyric, whereas the dwarfs, reminiscent of "Who's Afraid of the Big Bad Wolf," resort to whistling to cover a spectacularly unimaginative lyric's missing punch line. And even when the dwarfs don't resort to whistling, the lyrics are staggeringly banal, as when "Heigh-Ho" repeats seven times before it reaches its one-word arrival, "Hum." "The Silly Song," which the dwarfs later sing to Snow White, is another kind of specialty number, an old-country yodeling song interspersed with choruses and individual verses in which the dwarfs try to outdo each other's silliness; it, too, seems almost improvised, although more in the manner of a jam session. The fact that it leads to the more directed "Some Day," introduced by rhymed dialogue, reflects a general tendency in the film to redirect the randomizing behavior of the dwarfs and animals into something shaped more rationally, whether within a song or across songs. When the dwarfs are on their own, their music seems fragmentary, sometimes not even quite music (as in their snoring sequence, a "number" that never quite becomes "musical"). The one exception proves the rule, as "Bluddle Uddle Um Dum," while using nonsense lyrics at times, is both conventionally well shaped (AABA) and introduced by rhymed dialogue, the latter two features clearly reflecting the influence of Snow White (who has insisted they wash up before dinner), with the bespectacled Doc channeling her parental, teacherly authority.[18]

The moral lessons of Snow White, unlike those of The Three Little Pigs, are reinforced fully by the film's musical profile. Audiences generally remember vividly the sometimes dark visuals of Snow White, be they Snow White's forest scene or the Queen's evil plans, transformative magic, and eventual destruction in the storm that begins at the moment Snow White bites the apple.[19] Indeed, concern has often been expressed about this darker dimension of the film and its possible negative effect on children. Nevertheless, audiences cannot relive these moments through song, simply because one does not generally sing along with unthematic background music (but see my discussion of the much more leitmotivic score for The Wizard of Oz). Dark as these visions might be, they are easily eclipsed by recalling and singing the actual songs of the film—as, indeed, many have done throughout the six-plus decades after the film's release—thereby evoking either its wistful romantic dimension or its good-clean-fun dimension, the latter made all the more wholesome through the way these songs encourage work, cleanliness, and friendly socializing.

If there is a doubleness that undermines the official "message" of *Snow White* (along the lines of *The Three Little Pigs*), it resides in the persistent appeal of chaos, in the possibility of somehow resisting the tidy order imposed by Snow White. This defiant spirit is perhaps best expressed through the ways in which the sometimes contrary personalities of the dwarfs persist despite her "civilizing" influence. Sleepy drifts off to sleep during the most "classical" of the musical numbers, "Some Day My Prince Will Come"; Grumpy continues to offer a corrective to the film's over-the-top sentimentality, even after his capitulation (thus, his "Heh, mush" during "Some Day"); Sneezy persists in his "involuntary" disruptive behavior; and Doc's verbal ineptitudes continue to ridicule authority figures, if indirectly, in a manner reminiscent of American minstrelsy. Even the animators themselves "act out" at times; it is surely no accident that the "G" on Grumpy's bed is nearly invisible throughout the scene following Snow White's awakening by the dwarfs.[20] But the strongest evidence for the persistent impact made by this dimension of the film is the fact that "Heigh-Ho," despite its virtually nonexistent lyrics, remains by far the most popular of the film's songs.

Yet, the most important dimension of *Snow White*, from the perspective of the larger theme of this book, lies less in its advocacy of either order or disorder than in how centrally *performance* contributes to our sense that the central character is actually there, as a truly *animated* soul. As noted earlier, her visual animation (and that of her Prince) seems much less lifelike than that of the dwarfs and woodland creatures. Elizabeth Upton has convincingly related this circumstance to a phenomenon known as the "uncanny valley" (originally noted in robotics but developed further in connection with computer graphics and animation), in which approaches to the "natural-seeming" human countenance will increase comfort levels in viewers until just before full arrival, when that comfort level drops precipitously (hence, the "uncanny valley"). Upton argues that the failure of the Disney animators to bring a human girl to animated life was the principal reason that *Snow White* had to become a musical, so that song could distract viewers from the awkward near miss of its central character's animation.[21] In our terms, we may extend this observation to claim that it is Snow White's performance of musical numbers that enables us to "see" her as a human presence. True, we see *who* Snow White is through her benevolent impact on her world. But we see *that* she is through her ability to perform herself through song, channeling the most basic way that musicals provide their characters—and us in the audience—with the materials to perform personal identity.

The Wizard of Oz (film, 1939) was, from the beginning, planned as MGM's answer to Disney's hugely successful *Snow White and the Seven Dwarfs*. It now ranks as one of the most widely seen films of all time (perhaps *the* most widely seen), in large part due to its frequent showings on television as it gradually established itself as a beloved classic for both straight and gay audiences. It lost money in its original run, however, owing to a number of factors including a huge budget, fierce competition from a number of highly successful films made in 1939 (several of them now considered classics), and the onset of World War II. It shares many features with *Snow White*: a young girl protagonist who undergoes a traumatic transplantation from her home to a new place where she towers over (most of) the adults; a castle that harbors a wicked witch who consults a magic glass (mirror and crystal ball, respectively) and will die, without being deliberately killed, while attempting to kill the heroine; a dark and frightening forest; a magically produced poison whose potential fatality is averted through the intervention of a benevolent higher power (poison apple and love's first kiss; poppies and Glinda's snow); nearly wall-to-wall music with a handful of directly simple songs that have since entered the vernacular of America's everyday life; and a cohort of companions for the heroine, whose essentialized personalities are defined indelibly through comic exaggeration. But there are many important differences as well. *The Wizard of Oz* is based on a much-beloved, specifically *American* property (the 1900 book by L. Frank Baum, which had many sequels), has no love interest for the heroine and hence no close affinity with traditional operetta (indeed, it avoids even the suggestion of a waltz idiom, except for Glinda's brief "Come Out, Come Out"), employs a naturalistic frame to set off both its imagined kingdom and almost all the central characters that inhabit it (in the sepia-toned Kansas scenes and through those of the Kansas characters who take on central roles in Oz), and, of course, is performed entirely by live actors, with no animation. All of these differences matter, but none more than the latter.

The fact that *The Wizard of Oz* uses real actors instead of animation has a number of important consequences. Despite its over-the-top costumes, settings, and performances, the film's realistic core is omnipresent, with its central characters more empathetic not only because we know them from an opening context (Kansas) that lies "close to home"—all the more so in 1939, with the Great Plains' dust storms of the earlier 1930s a vibrant memory—but also because we invest in them as performers, especially those we recognize from other films. Thus, for example, we connect with Dorothy *and* Judy Garland, who through this role is both making the transition into stardom and delaying the transition into adulthood (see the frontispiece). Similarly, because many of the Oz characters appear more naturalistically in the opening Kansas sequence, we connect more easily with them when they reappear in full costume. Professor Marvel's likable fraudulence extends easily to three smaller roles in Emerald City (the doorman, the cabbie, and the guard) before attaching itself to the Wizard, even if it is a little unclear whether the audience is supposed to notice that these other characters are played by the same actor. (Even assuming that we are expected to notice, it remains unclear if we are to understand this device as making a point within the filmic world or as a stunt; a similar confusion results from having both wicked witches played by the same actress.)

Moreover, in an odd way, some have found Margaret Hamilton's Wicked Witch of the West more sympathetic than Billie Burke's Glinda, at least in part because we recognize her, too, from the Kansas scene, whereas Glinda seems too enigmatic, an authority figure we have trouble reading because she has no Kansas counterpart and because she seems dubiously motivated. Why, for example, does she insult Dorothy by first asking her whether she is a good witch or a bad witch and then, a few lines later, telling her that "Only bad witches are ugly"? Why does she put Dorothy at such risk by transferring the ruby slippers to her feet (although, presumably, this also protects her), and then pretend not to know they could take her home to Kansas—which, at the end of the film, it turns out she clearly *does* know?[22] Her patronizing "good fairy" manner, so full of smarmy condescension, wears thin in a way Hamilton's in-your-face evil does not, especially as she presides over the Munchkins as if they were merely cute children pretending to be grownups—an expressed attitude that connects all too easily to the affronts that the adult men and women who played the Munchkins had to endure in the real world because of their shortness.[23]

On a broader level, the transformation of the three farmhands into Dorothy's Oz companions, all in elaborate costumes and makeup, and with more exaggerated mannerisms based on their Kansas personae, makes us even more acutely aware of the performers beneath, facilitating their transmutation into "Friends of Dorothy" in all senses. Thus, within the film, their costumes bring them closer to Dorothy and her desires for sympathetic companionship, so that they are indeed friends in a way the farmhands could not be. And, beyond the film, and especially for the growing homosexual audience for the film in more recent decades, their elaborate drag and exaggerated modes of behavior give them a distinctly gay aspect; thus the Scarecrow's desire to be "conferrin' with the flow'rs"; the Tin Man's interest in "the boy who shoots the arrows" and his shyly giggling "We do" in answer to Dorothy's "We know each other now, don't we?"; or the Cowardly Lion's lament about having been "born to be a sissy," his "dandy-lion" gestures and tail-swishing walk, and his penchant for operatic singing and overly precise locution ("If I Were King of the Forest," where we also hear him, fresh from getting "a permanent just for the occasion," preoccupied with the fabric of his projected regal robes: "satin, not cotton, not chintz"). Because of the easy identification these three provide for many gay men, "Friends of Dorothy" and the film's central rainbow image have long since acquired specifically homosexual connotations. (And, of course, from this perspective Judy Garland is herself in a kind of drag, pretending to be a little girl despite that big voice and her tightly wrapped bosom.) While Dorothy's Oz companions may be framed as her imaginary wish projections, they become the cinematic equivalent of flesh and blood through the campy performances of three grown men shamelessly playing dress-up with a young girl. It is, frankly, hard to see how the film's hints at a homosexual dimension could have escaped mainstream notice for so long, or how even today they

♩3.6
♩3.7

can seem invisible to so many. This dimension has seemed especially obvious in the wake of the Stonewall Rebellion, which occurred in the immediate aftermath of Judy Garland's tragic death in 1969 (by then she had become a major gay diva and icon).[24] From this perspective, Oz seemed to project a pointedly gay land, where Glinda's "Come Out" could seem to have more pointed meaning and where having the courage to admit to being a "Friend of Dorothy"—to "come out" as a homosexual—could seem more widely empowering.

But the doubleness endemic to fairy tales provides access from many other perspectives as well, however dominant among such alternative perspectives the homosexual dimension has become. From the beginning, the "yellow brick road" carried a political message, originally addressing the gold standard in Baum's turn-of-the-century America and newly relevant in the context of the Great Depression, which was itself the extended aftermath of a burst speculative bubble. "Ding-Dong, the Witch Is Dead" and "You're out of the woods" (the opening line of "Optimistic Voices") also seemed to many to refer to the Depression, which by 1939 appeared to be ending. The dropped "Jitter Bug" number (see below) would have carried an implicit critique of modern dance crazes. More subtle is the pronounced Russian aspect to the Wicked Witch of the West's Winkie army, who wear elaborate "Eastern" uniforms with high fur "Cossack" hats; chant "Yo-*ee*-oh, ee-*Ohh*-oh" in what sounds like imitation Russian, in artificially deepened voices that recall the melodic contours of "The Volga Boat Song";[25] and are accompanied by an orchestral sound reminiscent of Russian music from the late nineteenth century, including an excerpt from Musorgsky's *Night on Bald*

♪ 3.8   *Mountain*. Only when the Witch dies, releasing them from her spell, does it become clear that they have been enslaved by her—at which point it also becomes clear what political point their Russian profile makes. Thus, in the late 1930s, America was facing the prospect of a Europe in which entire nations and peoples had been enslaved through tyrannically held power; if the film seems to point specifically to Stalin in Russia (in power since 1929), it might as easily have applied to Mussolini in Italy (since 1922) or Hitler in Germany (since 1933).

One of the most striking "double images" regarding *The Wizard of Oz* has involved the mapping of drug-induced experiences onto the colorful phantasmagoria of Oz, beginning in the late 1960s and involving a generation who had grown up with the film on black-and-white television and were only recently (or occasionally) witness to the film's central sepia-to-color effect. The mind-altering-drug dimension of the story was already present in Baum's original, with the Witch's use of poppies to distract Dorothy and her group, but it achieves a higher profile in the film, if indirectly, through its indulgence in surreality, including animate apple trees, transmutations of characters into other characters, fantastical flowers (so that the Munchkins seem to anticipate "flower children"), the triplike "horse of a different color" in Emerald City, and even Glinda's use of "snow" to rescue the group

Figure 3.2. Friends of Dorothy (Judy Garland)—the Tin Man (Jack Haley), the Cowardly Lion (Bert Lahr), and the Scarecrow (Ray Bolger)—seek admittance to the Emerald City in *The Wizard of Oz*. The initially belligerent doorman is played by Frank Morgan, who also plays several other characters in the film, including the Wizard. (Photograph courtesy of Miles Kreuger and the Institute of the American Musical, Inc.)

from the effects of poppies.[26] It is with this dimension, especially, that Dorothy's famous first line as she steps into Oz—"Toto, I've a feeling we're not in Kansas anymore"—has the most pointed resonance. It is perhaps also from this perspective that we might best understand the odd partitioning of the soundtrack from the visuals, creating two separate "tracks" either literally or in the imagination. This partitioning has worked in both directions, to different ends, with a strong tendency of the visuals, considered in isolation, to support drug-based "readings" of the film and the soundtrack to support a gay dimension (although by no means exclusively).

The former case is the more extreme and was institutionalized with the discovery that playing Pink Floyd's album *Dark Side of the Moon* (1973) produced a host of eerie synchronicities if *The Wizard of Oz* were screened simultaneously with its sound turned off, an effect that enhanced the album's status as a suitable accompaniment for an "acid test" (that is, for neophytes taking their first LSD trip). But this was only one side of the partition and occurred long after many had, through repeated viewings, committed the soundtrack to memory. Indeed, perhaps because its soundtrack is so familiar, *The Wizard of Oz* has become one of the most quoted films of all time, even apart from its music. Among its more familiarly quoted lines are the repeated "if any"; the Witch's "I'll get *you*, my pretty—and your little dog, too"; Glinda's echoing response to Dorothy's "Toto, too?"; the Wizard's "Pay no attention to the little man behind the curtain"; the group's (minus the Cowardly Lion) "Lions and tigers and bears, *oh my*"; and the Witch's final "I'm melting —melting! Oh, what a world, what a world!" As if to support this process of memorization, *The Wizard of Oz* is one of the few films whose soundtrack (including dialogue and background music) has been marketed separately from the film. But whereas druggies on the other side of the partition were sitting back to experience disembodied sound and voiceless images coming in and out of phase with each other, on the "audio" side of the partition audiences were, in a sense, *performing* the film. This kind of performance happens whenever people quote from *The Wizard of Oz* while adopting the appropriate personae (as is common practice when quoting from recordings or film), but it takes on a *participatory* dimension when audiences recite lines while the film is being screened. The latter type of audience participation reached its apex with *The Rocky Horror Picture Show* (1975; discussed in chapter 5), which, especially as a film, linked the resurgence of *The Wizard of Oz* to other tropes shared by the 1930s and the 1950s, including dance crazes and campy science fiction. Indeed, *Rocky Horror*'s connection to *The Wizard of Oz* was at one point to have been made more explicit, by borrowing the latter's device of switching to color at the moment of entering its alternative world.[27] The *Rocky Horror* phenomenon was possible in large part because much of its audience was already prepared, through its engagement with *The Wizard of Oz*, to memorize a film through obsessive viewing and then to "interact" with it in "reel time."

Corresponding directly to both gay and drug-based identifications with Oz was the sense fostered by the film more directly that Oz (minus the Witch)

♪3.9

was on the one hand a reconstitution of Dorothy's dreary Kansas according to her imagination and wishes, and on the other an enticing place peopled by friendly and familiar faces, to the extent that it seemed to constitute a near-death experience. Thus, after Dorothy is hit on the head during the tornado, Oz attempts to seduce her away from life itself (providing another reason not to like Glinda, who seems to be the guiding spirit behind this seductive dimension of Oz). All three of these readings (along with various political messages) are oriented around more mature understandings of what the fantasy of Oz is "about," with the near-death reading most outwardly reinforced by the filmmakers themselves. Dorothy's desire to return to Kansas may thus be understood as her desire not to die, so that her struggles with the Witch take on the aspect of mortal combat, with her principal allies including her transmuted Kansas companions and Auntie Em, who calls to her during her moment of greatest peril (through the Witch's crystal ball), attempting to pull her back to the land of the living. This reading permits an "adult" understanding of the film to exist alongside its child-oriented adventure story in a land of enchantment and provides, for those who do not engage with the film's drug and homosexual reception histories, a mode of engagement that takes the film seriously as narrative film. (This capacity has also been central to the film's camp success, since it enhances the affective discrepancy between the trivial and more serious meanings audiences have found in the film.)

As a narrative film, *The Wizard of Oz* is extremely careful in its placement of music. The film proceeds in six segments of fourteen to twenty minutes each (see table 3.1), with each segment organized very differently in musical terms. As with *Meet Me in St. Louis* (see chapter 2), the musical numbers become less frequent in the later stages of the film. The final two segments have no songs at all, which is partly due to dramatic concerns and partly due to the use of the Kansas setting as a framing device. In the first segment, an exaggerated sense of crisis sets up its only musical number—"Over the Rainbow"—as a kind of escape, both from the oppressive bustle of crisis-ridden farm life, where no one has time for Dorothy, and from Miss Gulch, who seeks to "destroy" Dorothy's dog, Toto. But the escape is above all a sonic one. As the song begins ("A place where there isn't any trouble"), the sounds of the farm and the frenetic background music fade, and Dorothy loses her breathless sense of urgency, soothed by the gently oscillating instrumental introduction to the song; although the farm animals (cows, chickens, and a horse) are still visible in the background, we stop hearing them once Dorothy starts "Over the Rainbow," even though we do hear the bluebirds referred to in the song. Thus, the song—which won an Academy Award for the film's veteran songwriters Harold Arlen and Yip Harburg—like the later land of Oz, represents a projection of Dorothy's wishes and sets up the more elaborate projection to come. Specifically, the broadly arching opening phrase projects the rainbow of the title, and the song then draws its possibilities close through less extreme "reaching" gestures and suggests, in musical terms, an abundance of color notably lacking in the landscape we see around

Table 3.1 *The Wizard of Oz* segments, with approximate timings and song lists

2:00	Kansas	(18 minutes)
	Over the Rainbow	
19:30	Munchkinland	(14 minutes)
	Come Out, Come Out / It Really Was No Miracle	
	Ding-Dong! The Witch Is Dead	
	The Lullaby League / The Lollipop Guild / We Welcome You to Munchkinland	
	Follow the Yellow Brick Road / You're Off to See the Wizard	
33:45	Collecting friends	(20 minutes)
	If I Only Had (a Brain) / We're Off to See the Wizard (reprise)	
	If I Only Had (a Heart) (reprise) / We're Off to See the Wizard (reprise)	
	If I Only Had (the Nerve) (reprise) / We're Off to See the Wizard (reprise)	
53:15	On to the Emerald City	(20 minutes)
	Optimistic Voices	
	The Merry Old Land of Oz	
	If I Were King of the Forest	
72:45	Vanquishing the Wicked Witch of the West	(14 minutes)
87:00	Rewind: back to Emerald City and Kansas	(14 minutes)

Dorothy and Toto.[28] Moreover, in its relative quietude, the song also anticipates Dorothy's eventual return to Kansas, when, indeed, she will become
the focus of all the (friendly) adults' indulgent attention.

♪3.10

Partly because of the relative absence of song in the opening and concluding segments, we are more acutely aware there of the leitmotivic scoring in
the film, the contribution of Herbert Stothart (a journeyman composer in
Hollywood, especially of operetta). Some of his scoring is a matter of using
familiar melodies, such as the urgent rendition of Schumann's "The Happy
Farmer" at the opening of the film, which converts the relaxed bucolic attitude generally associated with the tune (especially, and already by 1939, in
cartoons) into something more troubled; or, as a leftover of "silent" film
accompaniments, we may note the aforementioned quotation of *Night on
Bald Mountain*, and the use of "Home, Sweet Home" during the final seg-

♪3.11
♪3.12

ment.[29] As is common in musicals (especially film musicals), reprises of various tunes also function like leitmotivs (or, more precisely "reminiscence motives") in the later stages, while also substituting for more conventional song
reprises—literally so in the case of "Over the Rainbow," once Dorothy's
tearfully ironic reprise of this song in the Witch's castle was cut. But this
kind of generic blending, between the conventions of narrative film music
and musicals, can work in the other direction as well, for it is from these

framing segments that many memorable musical (and quasi-musical) quotations of the film derive, including the Witch's music that follows "Over the Rainbow" ("Dun-de-un-de-*Ahh*-duh, Dun-de-un-de-*Ahh*-duh," first heard accompanying Miss Gulch on her bicycle, one of the true leitmotivs in the film), the Cowardly Lion's "I *do* believe in spooks," and the Winkies' "Yo-*ee*-oh, ee-*Ohh*-oh." ♪3.13

The second segment of the film, set in Munchkinland, also helps to set up this tendency of the film to collapse actual song, chanting, generic film scoring, instrumental reprise, and leitmotivic work into one fluid category. Like most of the dwarfs' songs in *Snow White*, the Munchkinland music consists mainly of fairly short tunes that do not complete traditional Tin Pan Alley shapes, and sometimes as well devolve into nonsense filler or empty repetition, as in "Follow the Yellow Brick Road / You're Off to See the Wizard" and "Ding-Dong! The Witch Is Dead" (and again later, in the Emerald City's "The Merry Old Land of Oz"). Many of the most memorable "numbers" ♪3.14 in Munchkinland are not songs at all, such as the recited "We Thank You ♪3.15 Very Sweetly" and "As Mayor of the Munchkin City," which occur, like ♪3.16 the sung "As Coroner, I Must Aver," as episodes within and between other numbers. The payoff for this fluidity is twofold. First, it sets up the parallel ♪3.17 episodic structures of the next segment (which "rhyme" with the Munchkinland segment by ending in each case with the short chorus "We're Off to See the Wizard"). Second, and more far-reaching, it ensures that the film's best-remembered tunes encompass not only these less elaborate but clearly identifiable numbers but also the Witch's leitmotivic music and the not-quite-songs, "Lions and tigers and bears, *oh my*" and "Yo-*ee*-oh, ee-*Ohh*-oh."

The tendency for *The Wizard of Oz* to fragment its tunes along these lines is very strong, with only four fully realized songs in the film ("Over the Rainbow," "Ding-Dong! The Witch Is Dead," "If I Only Had . . . ," and "The Merry Old Land of Oz"; another song, "If I Were King of the Forest," achieves its sense of completeness only through its faux-operatic style and extended presentation). This tendency has two main derivations: from the film's fairy-tale aspect, so that the songs its most childlike characters sing are more on the order of ditties than songs, and from its sense of dramatic unfolding, which more elaborate songs would tend to disrupt. "Over the Rainbow," of course, is *meant* to disrupt; it is not the concerns of the Kansas farm that will end up mattering dramatically. The other full-scale songs all mark moments of dramatic relaxation, celebrating first the death of one wicked witch before the other appears, then the acquisition of each new "Friend of Dorothy," and finally the travelers' arrival in the Emerald City. This helps explain why the "Jitter Bug" number, slated for the haunted forest, had to be cut—although, too, its reference to a contemporary dance craze may have seemed inappropriate for a film ostensibly directed toward young children.[30] Whatever its virtues, the song—in part because it unfolds *as* a fairly elaborate song, with a healthy dose of verbal and musical wit—doesn't really convey fear very well and suffers in this regard when compared with the chanted fragments "Lions and tigers and bears, *oh my*" and "I *do* believe in spooks, I do I do I do I do I *do* believe in spooks." By this time in the film, dramatic concerns trump the profile of the film as a musical, so that even the denouement must rely only on underscoring to establish a sense of resolution.

Despite such concerns for drama, and despite its many other avenues for interpretation and reception, *The Wizard of Oz* always engages first according to its fairy-tale orientation, and its fragmented musical profile must also be understood from this perspective. Indeed, many children tend not to like its longer numbers, such as "Over the Rainbow" and "The Merry Old Land of Oz," and engage primarily with the farcical dimension of "If I Were King of the Forest," relating its operatic parody to such cartoonish moments as the Cowardly Lion's earlier bravado and his later motoric running in place (escaping after the first audience with the Wizard and while held suspended between the Scarecrow and Tin Man). Throughout, Oz functions as a fairy-tale land, with its penchant for color both emphasized verbally (thus its catalog of color references: to the rainbow, blue skies, bluebirds, ruby slippers, yellow brick road, Emerald City, and the latter's "horse of a different color") and exaggerated visually, along the lines of color cartoons.[31] Although the film, including its extended fantasy sequence, is set in a relatively modern era, both the appearance of Emerald City from afar and the Witch's castle recall the castle-based kingdoms from older fairy tales, familiar to any child. And the verbal play is as often as not what would tickle a child's fancy, such as the Munchkins' "You'll be hist- [hissed], you'll be hist-, you'll be history," and "You'll be a bust, be a bust, be a bust, in the hall of fame"—which use a device familiar from summer-camp "clapping" games (which, however, more typically flirt with using "bad" words).[32]

♪3.18

The function of Oz, within the larger story, is to provide its child a place of empowerment—not just a prettier, less threatening place (which it offers only part of the time), but more importantly a place where she can be taken seriously and can fight back against adults who threaten her and wrong her. Moreover, it is from this perspective that the film often engages its adult audience as well, since they, too, may feel empowered by it. In this regard, the Wicked Witch is to some extent both a cliché and a cipher—someone who simply *is* bad, unpleasant, and powerful, with little concern expended about why she is that way—so that audience members, whether child or adult, can more easily "fill in the blank" from their own experiences of being wronged without sufficient reason or recourse. This aspect of the film is, as much as is its camp dimension, foundational to its appeal to gays, many of whom feel empowered, through a complicated process of identification, by the image of a Judy Garland on the brink of adulthood, playing a girl who gamely fights for her place in the world. This is also what allows this film to function as an *American* fairy tale: it is here not enough just to *be* good and deserving (as in Snow White); one must also *act*. But in acting, one must nevertheless be more righteous than self-serving—which explains the odd collective of mutually needful personages in the film, individually lacking something essential, who together, by acting on each other's behalf, constitute a functioning whole. Despite the size of this entourage, however, our sympathetic orientation remains centered squarely throughout on Dorothy/ Judy, who, earnest and breathless, plays to both children and adults, desperate to reassure us that the film's more purely moral lessons are the point of it all.

Mary Poppins (film, 1964), like *The Wizard of Oz*, takes its name from the adult who commands its fantasy realm, but that honor is in this case justified, since Mary Poppins, as a character, remains the dramatic and expressive focus of the film throughout. She is the first and last person we see (like Dorothy in *The Wizard of Oz*), perched on a cloud waiting to be summoned in the beginning and returning there in the end. She represents the "Over the Rainbow" projection of a better alternative by the Banks family's untended children ("The Perfect Nanny"). Yet she does not so much empower them to become protoadults (like Dorothy) as allow them to accept and enjoy their childhood; moreover, she provides them with an appropriate home environment in which to do so, by reintegrating them with their parents into a functioning family unit. *Mary Poppins* is thus a fairy tale of successful intervention, built around a fairy-godmother figure who remains the focus but not the center of the action, her role being to facilitate and to provide access to the magic of childhood. And while she provides that access to everyone involved who doesn't already have it, she does not, like traditional fairy godmothers, intervene directly in the real world, even temporarily. As a result, because Jane and Michael's parents never see direct evidence of her magic, they "own" their changed behavior more completely than would be the case in more typical fairy tales with magic fairy godmothers.

Mary Poppins has been both celebrated and reviled as a film, and many of its attributes come into play on both sides of this receptive history. However beloved the film has been, the case against it seems easy to make. It sentimentalizes where its literary source cuts against the grain of sentiment. It sugarcoats childhood. Its presentation of 1910 London is shamelessly "Disneyfied," with perhaps the worst approximation of a cockney accent on record (from Dick van Dyke). And it resolves deep-set family-versus-career issues much too easily, by letting Mr. Banks have his sugar cake and eat it, too, choosing to spend time with his children *and* keeping his job (in fact, getting a promotion in the bargain). For many, these are irreparable flaws, with the most unforgivable of them being Julie Andrews's transformation of the main character from a stern, unsentimental woman to someone who tries to be stern but can't seem to manage it, who is nearly always gentle of voice, and whose features soften fairly often into an indulgent smile and occasionally slide perilously close to simpering. Yet, from the opposite perspective, these "flaws"—particularly the transformation of its central character—are the film's great strengths, for they allow it to connect widely and deeply with its American audience in a way that would surely have been impossible, for example, with a filmic re-creation of the original Mary Poppins, who comes across in the books as a sadistic and tyrannical woman who denies the existence of the very magic she brings, at the same time teasing the children unmercifully with the threat of withholding it. The other complaints may be similarly countered; thus, the valorization of childhood is a fundamental theme of the film, and the precious quaintness of its setting—including the atrocious cockney accent—places its American audience at a useful remove from the situations it presents. Despite the tidiness of the resolution, which indeed provides some reason to distrust the film's unfettered sentiment, we should perhaps think twice before dismissing the film on the basis of what it is generically, especially since it succeeds so well on its own terms.

The musical score for *Mary Poppins* may well be the crowning achievement of the Sherman brothers, Richard M. and Robert B., long-time collaborators with Disney who later also worked successfully independent of the studio. The score is impressive not only for its many fine individual songs but also and especially for the way those songs work with each other and within the story. The integration of songs and story is so well wrought that it is sometimes difficult to tell whether the story seems as effective and affecting as it does because of the songs, or whether the evident craft behind the songs and their deployment is a response to a particularly congenial set of situations and characters. In this respect, the most important songs are those that act as the adult characters' "theme songs": Mrs. Banks's "Sister Suffragette," Mr. Banks's "The Life I Lead," Bert's "Chim Chim Cher-ee," and Mary Poppins's (and the children's) "A Spoonful of Sugar." Through these songs and their many reprises each of these characters asserts his or her perspective on the story. Thus, three of the songs are marches, and each comes to stand for the motivational force behind its character, whereas Bert's melancholy waltz tune, in its simple circularity, establishes an alternative way of being in the world—separate yet permeating everything, and gesturing, through its underlying sadness, toward the eternal.

The most straightforward is "Sister Suffragette," a 6/8 inspirational march in the mold of the combination of "Ya Got Trouble" and "Seventy-six Trombones" in *The Music Man*, set just two years later than *Mary Poppins* (1912) and whose film version had recently been released (1962). Particularly striking is the way Glynis Johns's Mrs. Banks occasionally seems, gesturally, to channel Robert Preston's Harold Hill, especially in her trombonist arm extensions, her inspirational heaven-pointing poses, and the "shocking" attention she draws to the issue of bared knees. As in *The Music Man*, the march models successful recruitment; after the particularly inspirational bridge (within an extended Tin Pan Alley form: ABAC-bridge-AC), the domestics join her for the remainder, evoking future generations—"Our daughters' daughters"—who will "sing in grateful chorus, 'Well done!' " The alliance of this number with the manipulative flimflam of Harold Hill underscores the ambivalence *Mary Poppins* exhibits toward Mrs. Banks's involvement

♪3.19

with the women's suffrage movement, endorsing it to the extent that it empowers the disenfranchised, diverts through harmless playacting, and subverts Mr. Banks's smug belief that his world is secure and well ordered (thus aligning it with the film's valorization of childhood)—yet seeing it also as a distraction from Mrs. Banks's responsibilities as a mother, equivalent to Mr. Banks's work obsession.

While "Sister Suffragette" is deployed only once and referred to only occasionally thereafter, the other three "theme songs" are deployed often and centrally. "Chim Chim Cher-ee" helps reinforce the pivotal position of Bert, who interacts with virtually all the other characters, at the same time providing a relatively "neutral" point of view for the audience. Within the film more broadly, the waltz idiom offers a significant alternative to the many marches in the score, less directed in its impulse and falling into two broad categories, the circus or carnival variety, suitable for accompanying a merry-go-round, and an even more lighthearted kind more suitable for skipping than a romantically charged dance. In the former category are a brief quotation from Rosas's waltz "Over the Waves" (while Bert mimes a high-wire circus act inspired by one of his chalk pavement pictures),[33] a waltz variation of "Jolly Holiday" (to accompany a merry-go-round), and Uncle Albert's "I Love to Laugh," with its circus-band instrumentation apparently inspired by the singers' "acrobatics" on the ceiling, functioning also as a musical laugh track, swelling at punch lines. All of these waltzes involve Bert in the ♪ **3.20** children's fantasy activities, as do many versions of his "Chim Chim Cher-ee"; even the climactic skipping waltz song, "Let's Go Fly a Kite," initiated by the restored Banks family and led by Mr. Banks, is overseen by Bert as a benignly observing presence who, naturally enough, takes the second verse. ♪ **3.21** But while Bert thus acts as the source for the film's liberating waltz idiom, his own "Chim Chim Cher-ee" is tinged by a deep and seemingly eternal sadness. It is the only minor-mode song in the film (except for "Feed the Birds," which ends in the major; see below), and this alone pulls its focus back from the "real" people of the film, hinting at Bert's connection to something beyond. Thus, during "Room 'Ere for Everyone"—the first use of "Chim Chim Cher-ee" in the film proper, although it is also sung over the opening credits—he is momentarily distracted by that other realm: ♪ **3.22**

> Dear Miss Persimmon,—(*Pause*)—wind's in the east—there's a mist coming in,
> Like something is brewing and 'bout to begin.
> Can't put my finger on what lies in store,
> But I feel what's to 'appen all 'appened before.

The song is extraordinarily simple, a sixteen-bar antecedent-consequent phrase framed by a four-bar introduction and a four-bar sung extension. What gives it its haunting feel is both on the surface and somewhat hidden. Immediately felt is the affective discrepancy between its buoyant rhythms and the minor mode itself, which seems to tug downward against the lilting rhythmic impulse after a brief touch of the major mode halfway through each phrase. Less obvious is the basis for both its projection of the eternal

Example 3.1. *Mary Poppins*: excerpt from "Chim Chim Cher-ee" (accompaniment only)

and the hazy indefiniteness with which it both hints at an underlying bleakness and flirts with the major mode. Hidden in an inner voice, and cycling as a hypnotic ostinato through every phrase, is a line descending chromatically from the tonic, producing the odd magic of an augmented triad in the second bar, a double image of minor and relative major in the third, an unexpected major triad in the fourth, and an inevitable fade to the minor in the fifth (see example 3.1). It is this line, derived from a centuries-old lament tradition, that produces the song's sad undertow, making it seem poised between possibilities—much like Bert, the song's abject personification—an enigmatic presence that hangs over the film like an unanswered question, before it is eclipsed in the end by the more upbeat alternative, "Let's Go Fly a Kite." In this sense, just as Mary Poppins frames the film visually, Bert does so musically. Thus, "Chim Chim Cher-ee" is not only the first tune we hear in the film proper but also the only sung portion of the overture, displaced by a choral version of "Let's Fly a Kite" for the closing credits.

♪3.23

The other two "theme songs" represent and resolve the central conflict of the film. Although seeming opposites, "The Life I Lead" and "A Spoonful of Sugar" are both empowering marches, most often accompanied by actual marching. Mr. Banks's "The Life I Lead" is filled with smugly grandiose verbal images: "Much as a king astride his noble steed," "I'm the lord of my castle, the sov'reign, the liege," "the heirs to my dominion," and (in the first reprise) "A British nanny must be a gen'ral! / The future empire lies within

♪3.24

her hands." "A Spoonful of Sugar," on the other hand, thinks small; it is this song that introduces the theme of small things (such as children) holding the key to big things: the "spoonful of sugar," of course, but also the "element of fun," and the "merry tune" that keeps one going—as, indeed, this song does throughout the rest of the film, quickly becoming the children's

♪3.25

marching song. What will eventually serve as the central image for its theme of smallness, however, is introduced only later, with the "tuppence" of the bird woman in "Feed the Birds," a word echoed soon after in "Fidelity Fiduciary Bank" (which, like "The Life I Lead," is chock-full of laughable grandiosity) and used again to launch "Let's Go Fly a Kite" ("With tuppence for paper and strings"). But these two seemingly opposite and fully energized viewpoints must come together if the film's central problem is to be solved convincingly. And because these viewpoints are expressed musically, resolu-

Figure 3.3. Competing family units in *Mary Poppins*: caretakers Bert and Mary taking Jane and Michael on an impromptu outing up the chimney (Dick van Dyke, Julie Andrews, Karen Dotrice, and Matthew Garber, top panel, just before Bert and his fellow chimney sweeps launch into "Step in Time"), resolving not long after into the film's first image of a happily united family, in the film's finale ("Let's Go Fly a Kite," with David Tomlinson and Glynis Johns as parents George and Winifred Banks, bottom panel). Both sequences, like the opening credits, use striking images of the London sky. However, whereas the first indulges childish "acting-out" fantasies (thus, soot-smeared faces and dangerous cavorting across rooftops), the second celebrates more conventional joys, deriving its sense of wonder mainly from the transformation of George Banks, whose attire still bears the scars of his recent "sacking" even as his corsage marks his restoration into his firm's good graces.

tion requires that the songs themselves somehow merge, and that this merger seem natural and inevitable. The fact that they are both marches helps, but only in retrospect, serving more to endorse the connection after it is made than to initiate it. More important in the early stages is a disguised melodic-harmonic link between the two songs, all the more effective for its being "under the surface" of the music.

As befits their opposing thematic functions, the two songs are much differently shaped, with "The Life I Lead" filling out a full AABA in an expanded Tin Pan Alley form (in sixty-four bars instead of thirty-two) and "A Spoonful of Sugar" unfolding as a simpler verse-chorus structure, with each component running to only sixteen bars. But each song approaches its main arrival—the return to the final "A" in "The Life I Lead" and the chorus of "A Spoonful of Sugar"—in a similar fashion, with a chromatic harmonic shift accompanying a melodic move from the tonic to the minor third above, with the tune continuing thereafter to climb chromatically to the dominant (to set up the following formal arrival). Thus (with their parallel melodic moves given in bold), the bridge of the former begins "It's grand to be an Englishman in **nineteen ten**," and the lead-in to the chorus of the latter begins ♫3.26 "And ev'ry task you under**take**." In part because the harmonic environments for these moments are actually quite different from each other, while trading in the same general harmonic vocabulary (shifting chromatically by thirds), these passages provide the means through which Mary Poppins (or her song) can enter into Mr. Banks's world—which is exactly what happens at the two pivotal dramatic moments in the film.

In the first of these, Mary Poppins, in the process of being fired, instead takes over Mr. Banks's song at precisely this moment ("They must feel the thrill of totting up a **balanced book**"), turning the song around to her own advantage and using it to manipulate Mr. Banks into taking his children to ♫3.27 work with him. Then, when that outing ends disastrously, and Mr. Banks's anthem has become a funeral dirge ("A Man Has Dreams"), it is Bert who uses the very same musical moment as a hinge to lead naturally into "A Spoonful of Sugar." Before Bert's entry, Mr. Banks indulges in some of the loftiest language of the film, at once evoking a deeply felt despair and revealing, in his wanton mix of metaphors and incompatible images, the discrep- ♫3.28 ancy between his pretensions and his realities:

> A man has dreams of walking with giants;
> To carve his niche in the edifice of time.
> Before the mortar of his zeal has a chance to congeal,
>> The cup is dashed from his lips, the flame is snuffed aborning.
>> He's brought to wreck and ruin in his prime!

We might well laugh at his odd juxtaposition of metaphoric images. Is he carving into an existing edifice or building a new one with "the mortar of his zeal"? Is the flame, perhaps, snuffed aborning by liquid sloshed from the dashed cup? But the underlying despair nevertheless resonates deeply, recalling in its depth the suicidal depression of another filmic George, also a banker (of sorts) who has endured a bank run and faces professional shame and ruin at a climactic moment: George Bailey in *It's a Wonderful Life* (dir. Frank Capra, 1946).[34] If this assonance helps to enforce an American perspective on a British property, it also helps anticipate the redemption, later in the film, of failed dreams through family; implicitly, in both films, the abject failure of adults is redeemed by the promise embodied by children.[35] Even before Bert's intervention, Mr. Banks's abjectness makes him seem childlike, and his lyric provides a verbal opening for "A Spoonful of Sugar" through a telling reference to medicine: "It's quite a bitter pill to take."

Bert's subsequent transition into "A Spoonful of Sugar" unfolds in two stages. He first layers references to the song onto the bridge of "The Life I Lead," so that the key shift and slight increase in tempo, coupled with a brief orchestral quotation of the head motive from the chorus of "A Spoonful of Sugar," allow us to hear the two songs as a musical double image, even though Bert's vocal melody and the supporting harmonies are wholly those of "The Life I Lead":

> A spoonful of sugar, that is all it takes;
> It changes bread and water into tea and cakes.
> A spoonful of sugar goes a long, long way.
> 'Ave yourself an 'ealthy 'elpin' ev'ry day.[36]

Then, after a mocking repetition of the bridge ("You're a man of high position"), Bert sings through the two songs' arrivals in turn: the "A" phrase of "The Life I Lead" ("You've got to grind, grind, grind at that grindstone, / Though child'ood slips like sand through a sieve") and, immediately following, the chorus of "A Spoonful of Sugar." The fact that "A Spoonful of Sugar" begins on a dominant rather tonic harmony facilitates this final transition tremendously, making it seem almost as if "A Spoonful of Sugar" is, after all, the logical conclusion to "The Life I Lead." In concluding Mr. Banks's song, Bert continues, like him, to trade in oddly matched verbal images, suggesting that the grist of a mill's grindstone relates somehow to the sands of childhood. But the latter image ("like sand through a sieve") turns out to be especially effective, for several reasons: it derives from a childhood sandbox activity; it recalls the film's "small is good" theme by likening children to grains of sand; and it also recalls—perhaps as no more than a timeworn trope of childhood—the precious sand falling all too rapidly through Dorothy's hourglass in the Witch's castle of *The Wizard of Oz*. ♪3.29

The latter association is one of a series of subtle (and some not-so-subtle) assonances between *Mary Poppins* and the landmark films discussed earlier in this chapter. "A Spoonful of Sugar" recalls not only "Whistle While You Work" (in its larger sentiment and in its interactions with birds) but also the echoing reflection of "I'm Wishing," which here (in Mary Poppins's mirror) actually becomes even more independent after breaking apart to sing harmony in thirds. As the children flee from the bank, they run into a crone ♪3.30

whose language ("Granny'll hide you") recalls that of *Snow White*'s Queen-Witch ("Granny knows a young girl's heart"). *The Wizard of Oz* is also recalled, in the "good witch" trope (thus the children's exchange upon first seeing Mary Poppins descending from the sky: "Perhaps it's a witch"; "Of course not, witches have brooms"), the facilitating power of wind (which blows away the other nannies here and causes the death of the Wicked Witch of the East in *Oz*), and the creation of an alternative land of colorful magic, in this case by combining real actors and animation (in the chalk-pavement-picture outing). An odder assonance, given that Julie Andrews was to move directly from this film to *The Sound of Music* (dir. Robert Wise, 1965), is Admiral Boom, who with his nautical whistle and concern for punctuality seems almost a caricature of Captain von Trapp.

Parallels between *Mary Poppins* and *The Sound of Music* center ultimately on the similar yet contrasting roles played by Julie Andrews, raising the question of whether Mary Poppins's status as a magical being precludes a normalizing sexual dimension. In *The Sound of Music*, the issue of sexuality is problematized by religion and her association with the children, whereas in *Mary Poppins* magic substitutes for religious vows, and the relationships are configured much differently. Yet, in P. L. Travers's original book, Mary goes on an outing with Bert on her day off (into a chalk pavement picture, without the children), among other hints of a private life. In the film, however, she does not spend her day off with Bert, arriving after he (now a chimney sweep) has taken over her role as caretaker, so that we are left to wonder just what business she might have been taking care of. Moreover in "Jolly Holiday" she spends an inordinate amount of time extolling Bert's "forbearance," continuing at such length that it becomes uncomfortably emasculating. Consistent with the "family values" the film shares with *The Sound of Music*, the sexual charge in *Mary Poppins*, such as it is, belongs wholly to the parental couple (which in *The Sound of Music* includes the Julie Andrews role, of course). Thus, "Sister Suffragette" refers explicitly to a private realm ("Though we adore men individually") and carries an oddly sexualized charge in its implicit transgendering. More dramatically, Mr. Banks's reconversion to active parenting also involves a reawakening of sexual passion. When he emerges from the cellar after mending the children's kite, his first impulse is to kiss his wife for what seems a very long time for a "children's movie"—the kiss is, to be sure, stretched out for comic effect and mostly offscreen, as the constable describes it over the phone—and then to embrace her passionately and more than once. In sexual matters, too, Mary Poppins would thus seem to be more a facilitator than an active participant.

Nestled among the mix of character-based marches and waltzes in *Mary Poppins* and its fair share of music-hall numbers (such as "Jolly Holiday" and "Supercalifragilisticexpialidocious"), two numbers place Mary with the children at bedtime, providing the kind of moment that calls attention to the Disney Studio's odd dance around the expression of religious feeling in its films. In *Snow White*, for example, a planned scene in which the heroine teaches the dwarfs to say their bedtime prayers was dropped, although she says her own prayers the night before her confrontation with the Queen-Witch. Here, the second of the two lullabies, "Feed the Birds," provides the occasion for a careful deflection of religious sentiment. The song describes a religious setting, the steps of Saint Paul's Cathedral, but centers attention on the archetypal figure of the bird woman selling crumbs for "tuppence a bag." The musical setting is also oblique; for this number, the loveliest in the score, the Sherman brothers adopted a folklike manner, shifting modally between tonic minor and relative major within a slow but lilting triple meter, recalling fairly directly the familiar carols "What Child Is This" ("Greensleeves") and "We Three Kings"—the latter of which, like "Feed the Birds," begins in the minor but ends in the parallel major. If this modeling hints of Christmas, and thus of Christianity, it also hints of a mythical past (as does the image of the ancient bird woman herself); evokes the old tradition of the costermonger song in its echoing call, "Tuppence, tuppence, tuppence a bag"; and connects, through its hint of a minor-mode waltz idiom and its emphasis on a "lower" profession, with Bert's "Chim Chim Cher-ee."[37]

The high point of religious feeling in "Feed the Birds" occurs—suitably for its oblique approach to the topic—during the bridge:

> All around the cathedral the saints and apostles
> Look down as she sells her wares.
> Although you can't see it, you know they are smiling
> Each time someone shows that he cares.

For these lines, the key changes dramatically back to the relative minor, from which it reemerges into the major for the third line ("you know they are smiling") before sinking back to the minor, one last time, in order to reproduce (on the word "cares") the earlier melting effect between verse and chorus, as the harmony shifts to prepare the main tune. Throughout the bridge, a choral backup group (presumably the saints and apostles) sings untexted syllables, bestowing the unspoken blessing described in the lyric. ♩3.31 During the similarly wordless reprise of the song that accompanies Mr. Banks as he walks to the bank (where he will be fired), he stops at the cathedral, just in time for a repeat of the bridge. The bird woman is now gone, so that it is unclear whether his pause is simply to recall the earlier scene (remembering that he now carries Michael's tuppence in his pocket) or to seek heavenly guidance. While his pause before the cathedral surely includes the latter—this is clearly a moment of unstated prayer—the dynamic of the earlier song allows a more secularly grounded interpretation as well.

In such evocations of the eternal, it is the child (or the childlike) that seems most eternal while also, paradoxically, most urgently vulnerable. Despite the broad appeal of the film for children, as a fairy tale, it also reaches, by suggesting these depths of meaning, for something more: to close the circle between adulthood and childhood, which fairy tales traditionally leave deliberately broken (often to facilitate the kinds of double readings I explored in relation to *The Wizard of Oz*). As Bert explains to the frightened children running from the bank, they—unlike their father—always have someone to look after them. Although the film hints that something or someone beyond might indeed watch over their father and protect him as well, it is ultimately up to the children to take care of him. Gesturally, this happens in the sequence just before that upward glance, when Michael gives his father the tuppence he earlier withheld.

But *Mary Poppins* is also, beyond its deliberate crafting and its gestures toward the eternal, a product of its historical moment in the early 1960s, when increasing numbers of America's youth, abandoned to television nannies in the 1950s, determined *not* to enter the adult world of their parents. The film, like Mr. Banks, has it both ways, endorsing the entitlements of childhood as all-supreme, but then finding a solution to the resulting chaos within the restored family unit. But such happy resolutions of unsolvable problems are, after all, the mainstay of fairy tales.

Into the Woods (1987) interweaves several familiar fairy tales with one new one and endeavors to carry those tales into an adult realm without stripping their archetypal characters of their (initially) child-based sensibilities. To do this, James Lapine (who wrote the book) and Stephen Sondheim (music and lyrics) adopt a mosaic approach to both plotting and musical construction and then, gradually, allow the individual characters within that mosaic to take some measure both of their own selves and of the complex world to which they all belong. The intricate dramatic-musical mosaic unfolds in the first act almost like a puzzle, recalling Sondheim's offstage predilection for puzzles of all kinds. As its familiar fairy-tale components connect with each other in unexpected ways, an audience might anticipate with relish an expected tidy resolution of its various plotlines. But an audience might also wonder if perhaps the show's "once upon a time" basis will eventually be compromised by its adult venue and attendant sensibilities, a possibility hinted at through, among other things, a sprinkling of knowing references to sexuality in the early stages, which—owing to the sexually repressive practices of both Disney and the Hays Code, and to long-standing tropes of childhood innocence—call attention to themselves as intrusions into the genre of fairy tales. These references are all the more significant because *Into the Woods* includes no conventional expressions of romantic love—a central preoccupation of most prince-based fairy tales—and virtually restricts the use of the term "love" to its bad or insincere characters (the Witch, Cinderella's Prince, and the stepmother), who apply it most often to parent-child relationships.

From the outset, both Little Red Ridinghood and Jack (of "Beanstalk" fame), though nearly "of age," seem too simple minded to deal with the fact that they even have sexual identities. In each case, we see both their innocence and a more adult perspective on that innocence. Jack's affection for his cow, along with his confusion regarding the cow's gender, leads his exasperated mother not only to unexpected flights of wit—noting, regarding the cow's rapid aging, that "her withers wither with her"—but also to observe, with special emphasis, "Children can be very queer about their animals." And Red Ridinghood responds to the Wolf much as an innocent girl might to sexual advances from a stranger, initially flattered but eventually disgusted by the physical messiness of the act itself (literally being eaten, but enacted and described in sexualized terms). For his part, the Wolf is played by the same actor as Cinderella's Prince and exhibits a similarly habitual lechery, performing "Hello, Little Girl" to Red as a seductive soft-shoe and, in the original production, sporting well-developed abdominal muscles, genitalia, and a shiny tailcoat such as might be worn by an unsavory "man about town" in a burlesque show.[38] And, within the newly invented fairy tale, as the Witch describes to the Baker how his father stole from her garden, she refers to his thievery as rape and illustrates the import of her retaliatory curse—that his "family tree / Would always be / A barren one"—by "zapping" the Baker's crotch.

♩ **3.32**

But more central than the introduction of sexuality in establishing a more mature perspective is the very act of combining stories. When fairy tales place their stories "once upon a time in a far-off kingdom"—to quote both the Narrator at the opening of the show and the Baker at its close—they enforce an insulating distance not only between them and the here and now but also between each other. If some characters and situations in one fairy tale share features with those in another, each story is nevertheless complete and self-sufficient, framed entirely by its formulaic "once upon a time" and "happily ever after." That one such story should have the power to affect the outcome of another violates the integral nature of fairy tales, and an audience may well note with some measure of relief—if partly because the show's plotting is thus easier to follow—that the various tales we see interacting in *Into the Woods* do not tamper with each other's core events as traditionally recounted.[39] For its part, Lapine and Sondheim's newly invented story serves as a catalyst for bringing the others together. Thus, to appease the Witch, the Baker and his wife seek something from each of the lead players in the other tales: Red's cape, Jack's cow, Cinderella's slipper, and Rapunzel's hair (although the latter proves unusable, requiring a last-minute substitution of corn hair). But in acquiring these items, the couple in no way interferes with the stories the items belong to, although they sometimes threaten to do so; indeed, the Baker actually plays out preexisting roles in two of the other stories, rescuing Red from the Wolf (and thus receiving the cape in gratitude) and buying Jack's cow for five magic beans.

The insular nature of traditional fairy tales plays an essential part, as well, in assisting them to convey their moral lessons. Typically, an individual fairy tale is, in part, a clear demonstration of cause and effect, presenting actions and their consequences within a closed system in which those consequences will last "ever after." Fairy tales allow children to "see what happens" (at least according to the adults telling the tales): to see rewards distributed according to personal worth and punishment rained down on misbehavior and misdeeds within a more perfectly arranged world.[40] In combining its tales, *Into the Woods* also opens up this dimension of its multiple fairy tales and thereby complicates their pat moral lessons along several dimensions.

First, *Into the Woods* appears to give considerably more agency to its characters than do traditional fairy tales, so that they are not simply the embodiment of abstract character traits but become instead genuine personages, who choose actions after weighing them carefully, and thereafter have to deal with the consequences, often unintended. Yet, in giving their characters a heightened sense of agency and responsibility, Lapine and Sondheim draw initial inspiration whenever possible from the characters as given in the Brothers Grimm and elsewhere. Understanding Cinderella's running away from the festival on three successive nights as an expression of ambivalence, for example, they find occasion to display that ambivalence at a deeper level. Cinderella thus weighs her mother's admonition to be "good" (from the Grimm version) against her father's admonition to be "nice" (invented) and wonders why, if her goodness continues to go unrecognized and unrewarded, she should continue to be nice (in the prologue, before the "Witch's ♪3.33   Rap," as she braids her stepsister's hair):

> Mother said be good, / Father said be nice,
>   That was always their advice.
> So be nice, Cinderella, / Good, Cinderella,
>   Nice good good nice—
> What's the good of being good / If everyone is blind
>   Always leaving you behind?
> Never mind, Cinderella, / Kind Cinderella—
>   Nice good nice kind good nice—

This distinction between "good" and "nice," which Cinderella is the first to make, will be a recurring trope for the show. For example, slightly later, Red will conclude that, while the Wolf "seemed so nice," "Nice is different than good" ("I Know Things Now"); and, much later, the Witch will castigate the other characters before deserting them (in "The Last Midnight," which ♪3.34   interrupts "Your Fault" in the second act):
♪3.35

> You're so nice. / You're not good, / You're not bad, / You're just nice.
> I'm not good, / I'm not nice, / I'm just right.
> I'm the witch. / You're the world.

At this earlier stage, however, when Cinderella first puzzles over the distinction, she expresses above all a seed of ambivalence basic to her character, which will play out in her thrice running away from the Prince, an action that acquires augmented dramatic weight because of her encounters with the Baker's Wife as she flees, and because we have seen no interactions between her and her Prince that might provide an additional context for her actions. Her ambivalence, which will bear even more fruit in the second act, thus comes across as basic to her nature (although her description of her Prince as "nice" will perhaps already signal an absence of goodness).

Across the show, an important set of numbers give voice to what the characters learn from their adventures, and it is easy to mistake this device for the conventional moralizing of fairy tales. When Red sings "I Know Things Now" after emerging from the Wolf, it is a soliloquy and might be taken as a rather didactic account of what has happened, offered up so that *we* might understand the recently dramatized difference between "nice" and "good." But the number is nothing more (nor less) than *her* developing perspective and so constitutes an actual dramatic event in the plot, rather than a stoppage of the action. The song allows us to hear her "processing" what has happened in psychological terms, making the mental transition from her mother's admonition ("Mother said / 'Straight ahead,' / Not to delay / Or be misled") to her own realizations and conclusions. And the song functions as a kind of enabling therapy (without an actual therapist); immediately thereafter, she offers her cape to the Baker, who had earlier seized it and then returned it when she threw a tantrum. Other "processing" numbers include, ♪3.36 after Red's soliloquy (during a span with few intervening numbers), "A Very Nice Prince" (Cinderella, with the Baker's Wife), "Giants in the Sky" (Jack), "Agony" (the two princes), "It Takes Two" (the Baker and his Wife), and "On the Steps of the Palace" (Cinderella, concluding her "Nice Prince" processing).[41] The second act continues in this vein, if less exclusively, offering a reprise of "Agony" and concluding with the final installment of the Witch's evolving "Children Will Listen" (with roots in her first-act rant "Stay With Me" and her second-act "Lament," both of which address her loss of Rapunzel, whom she has raised as a daughter); in between, we hear the Baker's Wife's "Moments in the Woods" (after her tryst with Cinderella's Prince) and the Baker's "No More" (in which he makes his peace with his father; see figure 3.4). In these numbers, too, the fairy tales "open up" by revealing each character's dynamic inner life, so that the pat resolutions and formulaic assurances of "happy ever after" at the end of the first act—however desired and celebrated—might seem premature and slightly false, even at that point.

But the most important way that the show undermines the closed systems of traditional fairy tales is by demonstrating how different real life is from imagined life in these insular far-off kingdoms. Life as *we* know it, after all, continues beyond the achievement of specific goals, with unforeseen and inadvertent consequences arising from nearly any choice or action. Critical to the way *Into the Woods* presents this aspect of life is, again, the way its various tales "talk" to each other, setting off ripples of influence that affect larger outcomes. The conversations between the Baker's Wife and Cinderella feed their individual fixations on the Prince, beyond what can be resolved through their achieving their immediate goals in the first act. Red goads Jack into making his fateful third trip up the bean stalk, which turns him from a (perhaps justified) thief into a (perhaps justified) killer. The show's (and the audience's) investment in conventional resolutions of familiar tales makes

Figure 3.4. The Baker (Chip Zien) and his father, the "Mysterious Man" (Tom Aldredge), reconcile in "No More" as part of *Into the Woods*'s second-act "processing." Critical here is the father's ability to convey to his son the futility of running away as a coping mechanism, ensuring that his own mistake will not be repeated by his son as a continuing legacy of irresponsibility. The key exchange involves their mutual recognition of shared consequentiality: "*MM*: We disappoint, / We leave a mess, / We die but we don't . . . *B*: We disappoint / In turn, I guess. / Forget, though, we won't . . . *Together*: Like father, like son." (Still reproduced from the 1990 video recording, made for television.)

the growing ruthlessness and self-absorbed meddling of the Baker and his wife seem a constant threat to the basic equilibrium of the plotting. Even though by the end of the first act they play a (mostly) benign part in those resolutions, we may well continue to harbor doubts about their moral standing; after all, we know that, particularly in fairy tales, ends ought not to justify the means (or rather, "the beans," as the Baker's Wife puts it in "Maybe They're Really Magic"). But as we watch the Baker and his wife manage their moral dilemmas while gradually growing together as a couple ("It Takes Two") and falling into the rhythm of the other tales, we are led to forgive—or, perhaps, just to forget—that they have compromised their own "goodness" along the way, however "nice" they might remain.

But that is only the first act. In the second act—and specifically through its songs—we learn both that psychological growth cannot be resolved into a steady-state "happy ever after" and that actions tend to outlive their imme-

diately planned consequences. Already in the first act, we learn that the
"Mysterious Man" who haunts the woods and occasionally intervenes in
the action is the father of the Baker and Rapunzel; when his spirit continues
to "live" beyond his death near the end of the first act,[42] it serves as a figure
of the fact that consequences live on past the actions and actors that generated them. The most disturbing songs in the second act, along with the pair
of songs that bring it to a close, make this point in a variety of ways. The
vitriolic rage expressed in "Your Fault," for example, is as much about how
actions and consequences intertwine inseparably as about the all-too-human
impulse to find scapegoats to blame for collective disasters. The number
derives its bitter humor from the fact that all the characters singing *are* in
some way responsible for the disaster (that is, the giant's wife's arrival in the
kingdom, wreaking destruction as she seeks revenge for the death of her
husband). The Baker was unscrupulous in his dealings with Jack. Jack was
also unscrupulous and becomes greedy, boastful, and rash as well, and so he
is unable to counter Red's jibes except to prove her wrong without regard
for consequences; moreover, it is he who actually kills the giant. Red was
envious and mocking, and perhaps a little manipulative as she goaded Jack.
Cinderella was disdainful of the Baker's Wife's offering of a magic bean for
her slipper and so carelessly discarded it, providing the means for the giant's
wife to descend from the sky. And the Witch was vain (not to mention amoral
in a conventional sense), sacrificing all her magic powers in pursuit of beauty.
All of these failings either contributed to the sequence of events that led to
the giant's death or enabled the giant's wife to enter and despoil the kingdom
unchecked—yet neither of the latter consequences was intended or foreseen
by the characters, whose actions seem in some sense a direct result of going
into the woods "in the first place" (of which, more below). ♩3.37

In "No More," we confront with the Baker both the undying nature of
actions taken—hence the Mysterious Man's refrain "We die but we don't"—
and the impossibility of flight (figure 3.4). And here we have the first of a
series of interpretive inversions that will rescue the show from the despair
that underlies the second act. As the Mysterious Man echoes his son's de-
spondency—"Where are we to go? / Where are we ever to go?"—his "We
die but we don't" refrain points not only to the tendency for actions to live
on but also to potentially painful memories, which similarly do not die. His
lyric indirectly reminds the Baker of his infant son ("what you've left behind"), and so pulls him back from the impulse to run away.[43] This is the ♩3.38
first in a series of ever more elaborate verbal twists—which, however, carry
considerable dramatic resonance, especially in aggregation—that will remind us of how legacy matters, of the role that children play within our
sense of legacy, and of the consequent responsibilities of adults to children.
"No One Is Alone" makes a similar move, reconsidering the clichéd meaning
of the title phrase—which offers reassurance—in order to confront the fact
that no one *acts* alone; while we may take comfort in the fact that "No One
[of us] Is Alone," we must by the same token act responsibly, since our ac-

♩3.39   tions affect others now and in the future. And "Children Will Listen" not only offers hope in its conversion of the Witch's earlier rants—"Children should listen" in the first act ("Stay with Me") and "Children won't listen" in the second ("Lament")—but also advises caution and a sense of responsibility regarding what we communicate to children through our words, choices, and actions: "Careful the things you say . . . the things you do . . .

♩3.40   the wish you make . . . the spell you cast . . . the tale you tell."

In fusing together several tales, then, *Into the Woods* explodes the insularity of each and thereby confronts the infinite complexity of human interactions and mutual responsibilities. Although much of this depends on plotting, dialogue, and lyrics, it is also a function of how the music works within the show. The music's mosaiclike construction, echoing the show's plotting, on the broadest level relates the characters to each other while allowing each to retain his or her individuality, both of perspective and of expressive mode. The opening sung motive, "I wish," for example, functions as much as an initiating *musical* gesture—thus a "motive" in both senses of the word—as a particular watch cry for the always ambivalent Cinderella.[44] Many of the "processing" songs begin with the same basic melodic gesture or recall earlier "processing" songs in other ways, but they remain nevertheless individually coherent and independent songs.[45] And "Into the Woods," like the animating "I wish," is sung with parallel feeling, pulsed musical impetus, and accompanying activity, but without undermining the individual perspectives of those singing. This is particularly important for "Into the Woods" because the song is both similar and dissimilar to "Follow the Yellow Brick Road" in *The Wizard of Oz*; it brings the disparate aims of its characters to a mutual focal point, yet here there is no road to follow, and those aims remain mostly separate from each other (which is largely the point of both the song and the show that bears its name).

Sondheim's mosaiclike approach to the music in *Into the Woods* superficially resembles the leitmotivic-technique approach of Wagnerian opera and many film scores, and which he himself employed throughout his 1979 *Sweeney Todd* (discussed in the epilogue). Similar to leitmotivs, highly profiled musical figures recur throughout *Into the Woods*, forming much of the musical substance of the show without exerting control over its more overt formal structures. Yet, in *Into the Woods*, these musical figures vary greatly in duration and do not seem reliably to carry specific meanings, which differentiates them from leitmotivs. To be sure, some of these musical figures do have fairly direct "meanings," such as the Witch's "spell" chord or the mobi-

♩3.41   lizing rhythms of "Into the Woods," but this is by no means the rule. Some

♩3.42   entire numbers are little more than highly profiled epigrams, such as the

♩3.43   exchanges between Cinderella and her birds or between her and her mother. But even these are treated like pieces of mosaic, which may or may not combine with other such pieces, and thereby help establish the show's unusual flexibility regarding what constitutes a musical number. This makes constructing a song list for this show, such as that given on the book's website, considerably more difficult than for most shows, although the flexible deployment of musical numbers here is similar in kind to that of the Munchkinland sequence in *The Wizard of Oz*. Thus, "I Guess This Is Goodbye" (Jack's brief "love song" to Milky White, his cow), which seems at once a fragment and a complete number, is not nearly the anomaly it might be in another score, although many similar fragments nevertheless do not seem quite worthy of being listed as separate numbers.

♪ 3.44

As noted, many recurring motives do not carry obviously consistent referential meaning. Most striking in this regard is the five-note "beans motive," sounded by the xylophone as the Baker counts out the beans for Jack.[46] This motive may well be argued to be a "family" signifier, since it serves as the basis for the Baker's sister's (that is, Rapunzel's) wordless song, concludes the Baker and his Wife's duet, "Maybe They're Really Magic," is quoted by Rapunzel's Prince in "Agony," and is echoed by the Witch when she sings to Rapunzel in "Stay with Me" (bold type indicates the five-note motive): "**Don't you know what's out** there in the woods?" But it also seems more narrowly related to the beans or their associated magic; thus, it serves as underscoring for Jack's "I Guess This Is Goodbye," reappears melodically as Jack "processes" his first trip up the bean stalk ("There are **giants in the sky**"), appears again as underscoring when Jack returns with the golden harp (just after Cinderella discards the sixth bean) and yet again during the "potion" scene, and, much later, melodically supports allusions to the bean stalk, during "Your Fault." Or, perhaps, it might betoken an element of the grotesque, which could be understood to link its initial appearance (when it accompanies the Witch's entrance, the first of many times it introduces the Witch), Jack's experiences up the bean stalk, Rapunzel's derangement, her Prince's "Agony," and the Witch's obsession with keeping her "protected" from the world.

♪ 3.45

Yet, leitmotivs—"leading motives"—do not withstand this kind of negotiation of meaning and still function effectively as such, since they do not then "lead" our dramatic associations reliably or consistently. Moreover, this particular five-note motive has an especially chameleonlike expressive quality, sounding alternately lyrical, dramatic, beseeching, and ultimately a little maddening (deliberately so, it would seem) in being repeated so often by Rapunzel, for whom its wordless repetition serves as an emblem of her inability to grow as a character. Indeed, its specific deployment often blurs into the basic "sound" of the show, sometimes through intervallic deformities (as during the "Witch's Rap" or in the music of the golden harp), but more often through recombinations, as when these five notes provide the basic material for Cinderella's invocation of magic at her mother's tree ("Shiver and quiver, little tree," recalled frequently thereafter) and her "A very nice prince" (both melodically and in the accompaniment), or at the beginning of the finale.[47]

♪ 3.46

While the construction of much of the score from musical bits of this kind helps create a consistent musical profile for the show (as would leitmotivic technique),[48] it does so in a way that allows its constituent parts to shift their apparent significance easily and often. And, in this, it is precisely consonant with the way more tangible tokens within the drama function, so that, for example, a red cape and a golden slipper might be distinctive identifying features of particular characters in one context and (somewhat arbitrary) ingredients for the Witch's potion in another; a cow might be both a beloved friend and a vehicle for magic; and a handful of apparently worthless beans might be capable of changing the world in manifold ways, making the Witch ugly (when they are lost to her), making Jack rich, and causing the kingdom to be laid waste by enabling the giant's wife to descend from the sky. Or, on another level, a vaudevillian soft-shoe style might work equally well for the "connective" segments of the Wolf's "Hello, Little Girl" *and* the Baker and his wife's "It takes two," even if it thereby forges a seemingly inappropriate connection between two quite different woods-based couplings. That a musical motive might not "mean" something consistent is thus precisely the point; this is a score in which, as in the show's plotting, anything and everything might be reconsidered at some later point.[49]

This kind of associative "shape shifting" also aligns particularly well with the cleverness of Sondheim's lyrics. As already noted, his witty wordplay acquires unexpected depth when clear verbal meanings suddenly seem to reverse themselves, as in the key phrases "No one is alone," "We die but we don't," and "Children [should/won't/will] listen." But even when he seems to be doing no more than indulging his penchant for adroit wordplay for its own sake, there is generally a thematic component operating as well, particularly during the cut-and-thrust dynamic of sung verbal exchanges. The reprise of "Agony," for example, converts the princes' first-act complaints about not being able to reach their hearts' desires into the dual realization that it is that craving, not the objects themselves, that they crave most, whereas attaining their earlier romantic goals has proven stifling. ♪3.47 Thus, we hear, during one stretch of the reprise:

BOTH PRINCES:	Always in thrall most / To anything almost, / Or something asleep.
CINDERELLA'S PRINCE:	If it were not for the thicket—
RAPUNZEL'S PRINCE:	A thicket's no trick. Is it thick?
CINDERELLA'S PRINCE:	It's the thickest.
RAPUNZEL'S PRINCE:	The quickest / Is pick it Apart with a stick—
CINDERELLA'S PRINCE:	Yes, but even one prick— It's my thing about blood.
RAPUNZEL'S PRINCE:	Well, it's sick!
CINDERELLA'S PRINCE:	It's no sicker Than your thing with dwarves.

RAPUNZEL'S PRINCE:	Dwarfs.
CINDERELLA'S PRINCE: Dwarfs . . .	
RAPUNZEL'S PRINCE:	Dwarfs are very upsetting.

This is a riveting display of verbal virtuosity, moving quickly from the "thrall most" / "almost" rhyme to a nearly audible anagram (the thickest of thickets) to a sidebar about the correct pluralization of "dwarf." But the exchange also works dramatically, on several levels. The way in which these verbal twists and turns take shape against the rising tension of a climbing melodic structure perfectly captures the competitive sparring of the two princes. At the same time, the intertwining "thick" rhymes manage to suggest both the denseness of the briar thicket that surrounds Sleeping Beauty's castle (Cinderella's Prince's latest obsession) and, more broadly, the larger thicket of the show's plotting ("the plot thickens"), which has suddenly acquired two additional fairy tales (the other being Snow White, pursued by Rapunzel's Prince). Even more subtle is the way, during the similarly argumentative cut-and-thrust of "Your Fault," that the Witch picks up and manipulates the repeated accusatory refrain "in the first place" in order, with almost casual cleverness, to gain the upper hand through a display of verbal virtuosity fully consistent with her established character (e.g., in "Witch's Rap"):   ♫**3.48**

> BAKER: I'd have kept those beans, / But our house was cursed.
> *(Referring to the Witch)*
> *She* made us get a cow to get / The curse reversed!
> WITCH: It's his father's fault / That the curse got placed
> And the place got cursed / In the first place!

The odd disjuncture between melodic and harmonic structures in the musical language of *Into the Woods* provides another analogue to the mosaic-like assembly of plotlines, physical tokens, and musical motives. Over and over, but especially in his more discursive numbers, Sondheim stratifies his musical textures, typically by supporting the vocal line with a tonally functional bass while filling in the texture with a complex of dissonant chordal structures. The technique has much in common with Kurt Weill's cabaret style, in which stable rhythmic or accompanimental structures are complicated through the application of dissonance within the harmonies. Sondheim often takes this technique a step farther, by effectively springing his vocal line free from its traditional moorings in the accompaniment. This poses a complicated challenge to singers, since achieving a desired sense of vocal naturalness, difficult at times but essential to their presumed folklike simplicity, is also essential to two other effects this technique seems designed to achieve. First, it provides a close musical analogue to an important dramatic dimension of the show, which requires basically simple characters to negotiate their way within a world that seems increasingly rife with unforeseeable and treacherous complexities. And, second, the hard-won effect of vocal

simplicity also helps mask the fact that the vocal lines are often themselves
mosaiclike pieces that do not easily reach conventional melodic closure; thus,
many of the melodic phrases (including the "beans" motive) outline minor
sevenths, providing an emblem for the difficulty the characters have in reaching satisfying psychological closure. Moreover, it withholds from us the seductive assurances of conventional melodic construction until key moments,
when they thereby acquire extraordinary warmth, as in the Witch's final
number, "Children Will Listen," which seems, among other things, to resolve
her earlier complaints about children in musical terms.

Sondheim's ability to extend his mosaic technique into a variety of musical
dimensions provides him, above all, with a suitably fluid environment for
representing the central image of the show, of a psychological "woods" its
characters must all enter, where the rules of society seem not to apply but
whose events, and the moral consequences of choices made and actions
taken, will have tremendous import. The woods—here, as in many works,
in a long tradition of representation—carry an enormous magical charge in
themselves, representing a crisis-ridden "now" of lessened moral responsibility, seemingly offering both random dangers and tremendous rewards. All
possibilities are enhanced by this empowering nowness and by the lack of
clarity about which, if any, moral rules apply within this realm. But there is
also a tone of desperation about the woods, as each character who enters
the woods—even, perhaps, Red Ridinghood—has been driven there by dire
circumstances or deep emotional needs. This "now" dimension of the woods
is made explicit by the Baker's Wife during her final processing song, in
which she considers the value of "Moments in the Woods" after Cinderella's
♪ 3.49   Prince has seduced and abandoned her:

> Oh, if life were made of moments, / Even now and then a bad one—!
> But if life were only moments, / Then you'd never know you had one.
> First a witch, then a child, / Then a Prince, then a moment—
>   Who can live in the woods?

For her, what matters is the psychological disjuncture between the nowness
of moments in the woods and the fact that those moments become vivid,
lasting memories. But the apparent nowness of the woods is misleading in
other ways as well. Although the rules in the woods may not be clear (or
perhaps it is only that they are not obviously enforceable, or that high stakes
make them seem less relevant), they are nevertheless steeped deeply in the
past, providing a place where, within the show, the Baker can meet his father
and, with his wife, secure their mutual future (or not), and where we, collec-
tively, might sense—and perhaps make sense of—our own murky origins
and conceive possibilities for our own futures. Most significantly, the woods
offer a place whose events are charged with a tremendous afterlife of punish-
ments and rewards, which are then carried back to the "real" world to endure "ever after."

That the woods seem not to impose the moral code of society—with its odd mix of goodness and niceness and its apparent disregard (as the Witch points out) for the value of being right—does not give its characters the freedom to operate without such codes but rather demands that they determine their own values, which will then take shape in their actions and will in turn bear real consequences, both material and psychological. Significantly in this context, Lapine and Sondheim, while going back to the Brothers Grimm for their version of the Cinderella story, retrieve her birth mother's final charge to her only in part, retaining "good" but leaving out the equally stressed "pious." Their woods are to be without a moral compass, lacking especially the ready-made compass of religious devotion (although "nice" may well be a code word for Christian values, especially as it is set against both "good" and "right," the latter a code word for justice). It is significant, then, that the first of the two "lessons" laid out in the final two songs (in "No One Is Alone") makes no reference to religion, whether through prayer or the earthly authority of the church, although the subjective centering of this lesson may be understood as an extension of German Idealism, as rooted in Martin Luther and Immanuel Kant (see chapter 4). In this, the show is entirely consistent with the "secular Protestantism" described earlier—tinged, however, with the Liberal sentiment expressed in the song's central admonition:

THE BAKER AND CINDERELLA: Witches can be right, / Giants can be good.
                             You decide what's right, / You decide what's good.

In an important sense, the show asserts that the woods are, in fact, the "real" real world, which fairy tales mystify and bracket off as a place of mythical origins, but which represent better the complexities of our lives and moral responsibilities.

This central conceit of the show, which offers a revisionist alternative to the ways that fairy tales construct a facsimile of the world for children, is not its final message, however; the latter concerns instead the sense of legacy that fairy tales entail. Long before the final song, "Children Will Listen," the function of storytelling has been called into question in a variety of ways. The Narrator, who in the first act is a necessary guide through the complexly woven plot, covering over ellipses and facilitating a kind of cinematic cross-cutting among story lines, is sacrificed in the second act to the giant, leaving the characters to work out their lives on their own. But his role is already suspect in the first act, since he doubles as the Mysterious Man and so seems to have an ambiguous—but certainly not objective—perspective on the proceedings. Moreover, he is scarcely the only narrator even in the first act; the Witch is especially important as a narrator and, in telling the story of the Baker's father in the "Witch's Rap," calls attention to that role by leaving out essential information regarding her own motivations (that is, her wish to restore the beauty she lost when the Baker's father stole her beans): ♪**3.50**

CHAPTER THREE

> I let him go, / I didn't know / He'd stolen my beans!
> I was watching him crawl / Back over the wall—!
> ("Rap")
> And then bang! Crash! / And the lightning flash!
> And—well, that's another story, / Never mind—
> Anyway, at last / The big day came. . . .

Moreover, the many processing songs that follow the opening sequence represent each character's attempt to construct a coherent narrative account, replete with a moral, for the traumas that he or she has undergone. It is, in fact, when the Narrator begins most overtly to perform this kind of processing on a metalevel that the characters turn on him in the second act, in effect demanding their own agency in this realm:

♫3.51

> NARRATOR: It is interesting to examine the moral issue at question here. The
> finality of stories such as these dictates—
> *Narrator turns upstage and notices everyone looking at him
> menacingly. They move towards him. Music stops.*

The Narrator's most important function has by this point disappeared, since the intricate plotting of the first act has been displaced in the second by a single plotline, centered around the giant's wife. Thus, the princes, who continue in the same vein as the first act by singing a reprise of "Agony" and pursuing their respective inaccessible sleeping beauties in parallel disregard for the responsibilities of marriage, become in the process mostly irrelevant. It is precisely the God-like function of the Narrator, and the consequential conceit that the characters are pieces on an elaborate game board (thus both game pieces and pieces of mosaic), that the characters themselves reject midway through the second act, well in line with their later implicit rejection of religion. But in assuming agency over their own lives, they must also assume responsibility for how they tell the tale, precisely because of the magic that such tales hold for children. In the final lines of "Children Will Listen," the Witch's closing admonition is, "Careful the tale you tell, / *That* is the spell. / Children will listen." Indeed, the song's series of equations—between wishes and children, tale and spell—presents the fairy tale as the intersection of our primary paths to legacy and potential immortality (leaving aside the promises of religion): our children themselves and the continued force of our choices and actions, especially as the latter are recounted in stories ostensibly *for* children.

For Further Consideration

(see also the list of Disney classics in note 8)
Babes in Toyland (1903), *The Littlest Rebel* (film, 1935), *The Little Princess* (film, 1939), *Brigadoon* (1947), *Cinderella* (television, 1957; remade for television, 1965 and 1997), *The Sound of Music* (1959, film version 1965),

Once Upon a Mattress (1959), *Oliver!* (1963), *Bedknobs and Broomsticks* (film, 1971); *The Wiz* (1975, film 1978), *Cats* (London 1981, Broadway 1982), *Beauty and the Beast* (animated film, 1991; 1994), *South Park: Bigger, Longer & Uncut* (animated film, 1999), and *Wicked* (2003)

See Also

Among many general and specific discussions of fairy tales, see especially Hilda Ellis Davidson and Anna Chaudhri's rich *Companion to the Fairy Tale*; Bruno Bettelheim's still-controversial classic study *The Uses of Enchantment*; Alan Dundes's folkloristic "casebooks," *Cinderella* and *Little Red Riding Hood*; and J.R.R. Tolkien's thoughtful "On Fairy Stories."

Regarding fairy-tale musicals, see chapter 6 of Rick Altman's *The American Film Musical*.

Regarding Disney animation generally, see especially Frank Thomas and Ollie Johnston's *Disney Animation: The Illusion of Life*.

Regarding *Snow White and the Seven Dwarfs*, see Richard Holliss and Brian Sibley's *Walt Disney's* Snow White and the Seven Dwarfs and *the Making of the Classic Film*; Steve Hulett's "The Making of *Snow White and the Seven Dwarfs*"; and Linda Witowski and Martin Krause's *Walt Disney's* Snow White and the Seven Dwarfs: *An Art in Its Making*.

Regarding *The Wizard of Oz*, see Salman Rushdie's idiosyncratic (and moving) discussion in *The Wizard of Oz* (in the BFI Film Classics series); Aljean Harmetz's *The Making of the* Wizard of Oz; John Fricke, Jay Scarfone, and William Stillman's The Wizard of Oz: *The Official 50th Anniversary Pictorial History*; chapter 5 of Harold Meyerson and Ernie Harburg's *Who Put the Rainbow in* The Wizard of Oz? *Yip Harburg, Lyricist*; Gregory Maguire's revisionist novel *Wicked: The Life and Times of the Wicked Witch of the West*; and chapter 1 in Hugh Fordin's *The World of Entertainment!*

Regarding *Mary Poppins*, see Richard M. Sherman and Robert B. Sherman's "Commentary" in the 1964 vocal score.

Regarding *Into the Woods*, see chapter 12 of Stephen Banfield's *Sondheim's Broadway Musicals*; chapter 10 in Joanne Gordon's *Art Isn't Easy*; chapter 3 of Mark Eden Horowitz's *Sondheim on Music*; chapter 8 of Scott Miler's *From* Assassins *to* West Side Story; S. F. Stoddart's " 'Happily . . . Ever' . . . NEVER: The Antithetical Romance of *Into the Woods*"; the *Performing Arts Journal*'s "Casebook #2: *Into the Woods*," authored and compiled by Nina Mankin; chapter 18 in Meryle Secrest's *Stephen Sondheim: A Life*; and pp. 299–307 in Stephen Citron's *Sondheim and Lloyd-Webber*.

Idealism and Inspiration

THE AMERICAN MUSICAL has long offered inspiring and idealistic perspectives to its audiences, most often within song and/or dance numbers that seek to project and embody qualities of courage, heroic resolve, and the capacity to do the right thing and overcome difficulties. Almost always, these perspectives form an essential part of what makes good outcomes possible and bad outcomes more emotionally wrenching; in the latter case, they help make it clear that such outcomes are first of all failures of personal aspirations.

Because inspiring and idealistic perspectives are set to music in musicals, they are eminently exportable from their immediate contexts as something to be recalled or sung, to similar ends, outside the theater. Numbers of this type inspire well beyond their immediate contexts, taking part in the emotional lives of those who sing, for example, "Old Man River," "You'll Never Walk Alone," or "Climb Ev'ry Mountain" in the shower, who thereby gain a surer sense of their own capacities for heroic perseverance, especially since heroism for most people involves being heroically *vocal* in a central way. Indeed, many Broadway songs with a heroic trajectory, whatever their subject matter, serve this kind of inspirational purpose, through their ability to instill heroic feelings of internalized competency in their singers. Hence the familiar recourse to singing in the shower, with its gratifying acoustic amplifying other positive feelings of renewal often provided in that setting. Singing "If Ever I Would Leave You," "On the Street Where You Live," or "So in Love" in the shower might have specific application, in reinforcing a capacity for long-term romantic commitment, but it first of all affirms the singer's vocal courage, as he or she (mentally) strikes a romantic pose and sustains it through ever higher and longer notes as the song approaches and reaches its predestined climax.[1]

Yet, important as the theme of inspiration and idealism has been to the American musical, and however familiar many of its specific manifestations might be, three dimensions of the theme require some discussion before we take up our slate of musicals that adopt it centrally. First, the many possible meanings of these charged terms (and their close relatives) offer a sometimes useful confusion about both the content of an ideal or inspiration and its perceived relationship to reality; it will be important here to consider briefly how these often blurred terms have evolved, with direct consequences for the American musical. Second, the relationship between this theme and the previous theme, fairy tales and fantasy, requires clarification as to the ways in which they parallel each other and yet differ significantly. Third, there is a large difference between "inspiration and idealism" when it functions as a *secondary* theme, when it might simply support or enhance a larger action (implicitly, the situation described in the first paragraph), and when it functions as a *primary* theme.

Fundamental to idealism is the core concept of "idea"; thus, "idealism" refers specifically to mental constructs understood to be essentially internal—that is, of the mind—although related to the external world at least by aspiration. "Idealism" incorporates some aspects of "ideation," the capacity to imagine or visualize alternatives to the real world, as perceived through the senses. Many common uses of the word "ideal" stem from both this separateness from reality and the aspiration to change reality so as to bring it more in line with an internal vision of what *might* be; thus Utopian visions and ambitious goals have become naturalized associates of the word "ideal," especially when those visions and goals project a better version of the reality we already know. Yet most applications of the term also see the separation from reality as fundamental, so that "of the mind" can seem to mean "*only* of the mind," with "ideal" coming to mean "impractical" or even "useless"; from this perspective, the phrase "impractical idealist" can seem redundant. Nevertheless, idealism—especially when understood to be a personal quality, denoting the capacity to cherish and hold fast to ideals in the face of a hostile reality—is almost universally admired as an attribute that might help pull humanity out of the limitations of the known world and raise it above impulses of sensual gratification or of accommodation to more immediate worldly demands. (In this sense, idealism can function as a form of redemption; often, the two concepts blur in their dramatic presentation.) Fundamental to this validation of the most subjectively intense form of idealism is the strand of philosophy known as German Idealism, which emerged forcefully in the nineteenth century, stemming most immediately from Immanuel Kant (1724–1804) and Johann Gottlieb Fichte (1762–1814), and more distantly from Plato.

German Idealism is both separate from and a fundamental basis for more general notions of idealism as they evolved in the twentieth century. Idealism, in philosophical terms, posits a necessary division between reality and ideas of reality as gained through perception and thought, and places epistemological priority on the ideal world; in its most intense form, Idealism places metaphysical priority there as well. Thus, according to Idealist philosophy, what we *know* is, first of all and perhaps only, the content of our own minds; moreover, what we identify as "reality" is—to the extent that it is "real" in the conventional sense—entirely circumscribed by those dimensions that we may perceive through our senses, so that what we call reality is wholly an internal construct. In its extreme form, Idealism maintains that the development and maintenance of a subjective self is what matters more than achievements in the "real world"; indeed, the subjective self is, in an important sense, the very source of that "real world." Idealism maintains that what you are, and not what you do, carries by far the greater moral and ethical weight. As an important consequence of German Idealist thought, *music*, which has always seemed more removed from reality than the other arts, became for that very reason regarded by many as the highest of the arts. Thus, music, in a formulation that came to be known as absolute music, seemed increasingly to represent an Ideal construct in the strict sense of the term: existing in the mind, mainly bypassing the representational dimension of the other arts, and thereby placing us in closer proximity to the infinite.

Although most Americans tend to think of idealism in terms more of personal qualities and attitudes than of philosophy, German Idealism has nevertheless exerted a powerful if limited influence on how those qualities and attitudes have been formulated and regarded. Idealists are generally taken to be impractical, since they discount practicality in favor of noble ideas and causes, refusing to compromise, and risking life itself for the sake of either the soul or an ideal that has little chance of realization. Yet, even before German Idealism had fully evolved in the nineteenth century, Americans had fought their Revolutionary War based on ideals, inspired by such slogans as "Give me liberty or give me death" (Patrick Henry, 1775) and "I only regret that I have but one life to give for my country" (Nathan Hale, 1776). The success of that war against formidable opposition, and the legendary popularity of these slogans and others (such as New Hampshire's later motto, "Live free or die"), has allowed America—a country that fetishizes practical success above all else—to redeem idealism in terms of its long-range practicality. Americans thus tend to merge notions of idealism with "vision," the ability to foresee long-term consequences, and act accordingly despite the certainty of having to suffer through shorter-term defeats and reverses. In *The Sound of Music*, for example, the Baroness reproaches the Captain in ♪4.1 "No Way to Stop It" (a song dropped for the film version): "You dear attractive dewy-eyed idealist, / Today you have to learn to be a realist." But American audiences who know she is advising the Captain to accommodate to the Nazis will understand that his ability to maintain his idealism—and thus to risk his life, wealth, and family—is his only path to personal salvation, his only means of escape from the taint of association with what is generally regarded as the most evil of an array of totalitarian regimes that emerged during the twentieth century.

The *quality* of idealism, then, becomes a matter of personal courage and the ability to hold on to ideas and ideals against the tide of overwhelming opposition, whether from the mob or from the authorities; yet, importantly, those ideas and ideals must themselves be grounded in a larger practicality, derived from an independent vision of what matters for the longer term. It is this double emphasis that links idealism to inspiration in the formulation of this chapter's theme, since the latter term refers both to the motivating force of the idea and to the creative act that forms the idea in the first place. Thus, ideas must first *arise* through inspiration before they can in turn inspire others; they must take initial shape, as *inspirations*, in an inspired mind. Most typically, then, Broadway inspirational numbers will instill courage, and the capacity to do the right thing and overcome difficulties, through reference to the inspiring idea and ideal that are thereby being served.

Because idealism depends on the capacity to imagine alternatives to the real world, it is inseparably linked to "fantasy," which in some applications is a virtual synonym for "ideation." Yet, fantasy functions differently when linked (through ideation) to idealism and inspiration than when it is linked to fairy tales as in the previous chapter. This difference consists in how fantasy relates to reality in the context of idealism, first because fantasy constitutes an important reality in itself (especially within German Idealism) and second because, within this context, fantasy aspires to compel real change in the world. But fairy tales begin and end by acknowledging their separateness from reality in absolute terms—thus, their formulaic "Once upon a time" and "happily ever after"—creating an alternative world in order to effect escape and, perhaps, indirectly instill values and teach lessons. The two realms of fantasy may be seen to overlap in their shared capacity to project visions of Utopia, but this is dangerous territory for both realms, since Utopian visions detract from the credibility of idealists and may seem too reality-oriented for fairy tales, shading, perhaps, into science fiction. And, apart from their capacity to overlap, fairy tales and idealism differ decisively in their key features: one is oriented toward children, the other toward adults; one seems geared (in recent times, at least) to happy endings, the other to failed (yet somehow not failed) dreams; the one emphasizes the specialness of the world it creates, whereas the other at some point seems to bump up hard against an all-too-familiar reality; and the one seems saturated with doubleness (especially involving a camp dimension), whereas the other seems more directly "sincere." Moreover, among mature American musicals, fairy tales have found their most congenial venue on-screen, and idealist musicals onstage; perhaps decisive among many reasons for this split is the developing capacity for filmmakers to create a more thoroughgoing semblance of a fantasy realm on-screen, counterpoised with the overriding need, within idealist shows, to engage the imagination.

While idealism most easily serves as a secondary theme in a musical, perhaps embodied in a single musical number at a time of crisis, it may also serve as a primary theme; when it does so, it imparts a distinctive profile to the musical. Thus, a musical with idealism as a central theme will typically involve an unsuccessful love story, often with an unhappily resolving love triangle, so that unreturned love may serve as a "reality check" on the ability of the idealistic hero to realize dreams. In this variant of the "marriage trope," the dream does not "marry" reality; in one way or another, the idealized woman, who stands symbolically for the idealistic dimension of the show, fails to live up to the demands of that idealized role. Only in this way can a traditional musical bring dramatic emphasis to bear on dreams and the capacity to dream, and argue through plotting and musical numbers that dreams are more valuable than their potential for realization, and matter beyond the realities that prevent them from coming true. This symbolic function of the woman within an idealistic musical is, to be sure, more than a little old-fashioned today, a discarded remnant of the tradition of courtly love, which accounts somewhat for the prevalent notion that idealism itself risks being regarded as old-fashioned on Broadway. In part to naturalize (or neutralize) this element, idealist musicals tend to be placed in the past and often far away, which at times brings them close to the parallel realms of fairy tale and operetta. Most conducive of all to the symbolic function of the lead woman, as the embodied ideal, are the chivalric codes of medieval knights, as reimagined by later writers, and accessible both through direct representation (as in *Camelot* and *Man of La Mancha*) and metaphor (as in *The Music Man*'s "My White Knight" and elsewhere).

Among its many recurring representational features, idealism is often presented as a youthful phenomenon, a tendency stemming not only from observed reality but also from associations of idealism with innocence and renewal. Thus, in a set of patterns familiar within a wide variety of narrative genres, the youthful, enthusiastic pursuit of lofty goals overcomes obstacles and the worldly cynicism of older figures, often in the process reawakening dormant idealism among the latter. In 1960s America, when the rift between generations was growing wider and idealistic causes were on the ascendant (especially regarding civil rights and the Vietnam War), idealism flowered briefly as a theme in musicals before being effectively snuffed out by *Pippin* (1972), an anti-idealistic musical that was, ironically and almost by assumption, taken by many as proidealist.[2] While appealing strongly to youthful idealism, idealist musicals from the 1960s tended nonetheless to hold fast to older Broadway styles in the face of the actual preference among the young for rock-and-roll, folk music, and other emergent types; in this, they appealed strongly—and still appeal strongly—to nostalgia as well as idealism, making their strongest pitch to those young who remained unaffected by the musical revolutions of the 1950s and '60s and to those in older generations who sought to reclaim their own youthful idealism. To some extent, then, such shows attempted to side-step both the intensifying feeling that adults had betrayed their children by teaching them one thing and doing quite another, and the reality that the music industry catered increasingly to a growing youth market, which conspired, along with an intensifying wave of political protests, to give an increasing sense of empowerment to youth.

Here I will consider two musicals from the 1960s, *Camelot* (1960) and *Man of La Mancha* (1965), which neatly split the decade between the Kennedy years (1960–1963) and the most intense phase of the Vietnam War (that is, beginning in 1965, when the number of draftees increased dramatically). Both shows are structured around a failed marriage trope, as outlined earlier, within the context of a chivalric order in which knights embody idealism and their ladies the ideal itself. Among other intriguing parallels, both also share a prominent ascending triadic motive deployed as an emblem of the heroic,[3] and although both were successes on Broadway, both foundered when they were later brought to the screen as big-budget film musicals.

Neither of these parallels is mere happenstance; the latter, for example, may be traced in both cases to a misguided attempt to bring full filmic reality to projects created specifically for the Broadway stage, where idealistic visions create a more powerful sense of reality than can naturalized settings and "realistic" armor, castles, horses, prisons, and windmills. As in their direct source material—respectively, T. H. White's *The Once and Future King* (1958), drawing on White's earlier writings including the 1939 *The Sword in the Stone*, all based loosely on Thomas Malory's *Le Morte d'Arthur* (published posthumously in 1485); and Miguel de Cervantes's *Don Quixote*, published in two volumes in 1605 and 1615—these shows reimagine their material from the perspective of their audiences. Thus, chivalry represents a Utopian past that might be seen to hold the seeds of a desired future, whereas its specific failures might represent—like our own failures— an opportunity for learning and renewal. Even chivalry, with its essentialized sexism, seems a step in the right direction in this imagined past and provides, in any case, a dramatically useful division between idealizer (man) and embodied ideal (woman).

It is important in both of these shows that the dreamed ideal be impossible (or, at least, that it fail) in order to give dramatic precedence to idealism rather than to the potential realities of achieved happiness. In some engagements with idealism, however, failure is not always mandated. Thus, the two musicals we will consider briefly at the end of this chapter end happily. *The Scarlet Pimpernel* (1997) traces two trajectories of idealism (a strategy taken over from the 1987 import *Les Misérables*), one that is betrayed by the realities of its implementation, the other stepping outside "reality" to avoid its snares and thereby preserving its ideals intact. Here, familiar triangles are traced, but in such a way that it will seem more imperative, in the end, to defeat the failed idealism (of the French Revolution) than to reiterate the point, already well made, that true idealism entails a denial of current realities and their more immediate gratifications. Finally, *Once More, with Feeling* (episode 107 of the television serial *Buffy the Vampire Slayer*, first aired November 6, 2001) takes over in a central way a strategy common to all the other musicals in this chapter, in one way or another, of figuratively placing a part of its audience onstage. Thus, in *Camelot*, King Pellinore and the youth Tom provide contrasting perspectives on the idealist cause, and King Arthur himself learns through the latter that idealism can have an afterlife. *Man of La Mancha* presents its core story to a prison full of cynics, using members of that skeptical group as actors. *The Scarlet Pimpernel*, like *Man of La Mancha*, involves a transformative dimension of playacting; in both shows, skeptics merge their perspectives with that of the more sympathetic parts they are called upon to play. In *Once More, with Feeling*, all the principal characters are compelled against their will to express themselves most revealingly through the conventions of the American film musical.

Among the riches of the latter conceit (apart from the craftsmanship of its execution, extraordinary for a nonmusical television series) is a succinct demonstration of the potential of musicals to enact a transition from the internal world to the real world. This empowering function is related to both the "shower" scenario described earlier and the specific role music came to play among the arts in the wake of German Idealism. Thus, if art more generally represents an ideal realm, in the sense that it creates acknowledged fabrications so as to taste potential realities, then it is no wonder that music, with its built-in removal from reality, emerged during the nineteenth century to be regarded as the highest of the arts. Of all the arts, music merges most easily with the ideal, offering more perfect realities; with ideation, offering a realm of seemingly unfettered imagination; and with idealism, providing a means for projecting more fluidly and perfectly the inner world of the self. It is this latter link, between the inner "truth" of a person and its expression through music, that lends an odd plausibility, in *The Music Man*,[4] to Harold Hill's "think system," which links ideation directly to the activity of making music, whether through whistling, singing, or playing an instrument. But even if we understand that connection to be no more than a convention of the musical stage, the fact that music is *performed*—whether onstage or in the shower—does indeed allow it to serve as a conduit for bringing the ideal out into the open, in a performance of reality that has been made over in the image of the ideal.

Camelot (1960) was written by the experienced team of Alan Jay Lerner and Frederick Loewe, who had been working together since 1944. Because *Camelot* opened while their smash hit *My Fair Lady* was still in the middle of its long run (1956–1962), the many similarities between the two shows stood out in relief—so much so that many critics found *Camelot* wanting in comparison. The parallels were striking indeed: both shows were set in England; both were based on familiar literary properties that were crossbreeds between myth and fairy tale;[5] and both were built around love triangles that shared distinctive ingredients. Julie Andrews formed the vocally stunning apex of the triangle, playing off an older actor known for dramatic diction in the great English tradition (here, Richard Burton), but with little or no musical training so that his songs would be as much recited as sung, and whose character takes on a desexualized "sidekick" as a confidant. In both triangles, the imbalances between the two leads is potentially compensated by the third leg of the triangle, a heroic baritone (here, Robert Goulet) entrusted with the breakaway hit tune.[6] For the critics, the facts that neither love triangle was exactly conventional, and that they worked out much differently from each other, mattered less than these similarities. Even with its fair success, *Camelot* barely outlasted *My Fair Lady* on Broadway (by just over two months). The success it did enjoy owed something to the innovative ploy of having its stars perform numbers from the show on prime-time network television in early 1961 (at that time still a rare marketing stratagem).[7] But its lasting impact probably has as much to do with its association in the public mind with John F. Kennedy, who was an old classmate of Alan Jay Lerner at Harvard, was elected president a month before the show opened, took office about a month after, and (purportedly) sought to align his administration with the show's idealistic tone—an alliance later reinforced by the coincidence of its closing early in the year Kennedy would be assassinated, and through a widely reported interview with his widow in which she recounted Kennedy's especial love for the final lyrics of "Camelot" ("Don't let it be forgot").[8]

What may seem oddest about the show, considering its idealistic outlook and reception, is how few of its musical numbers address that idealism directly. The show begins as if it were a fairy-tale operetta, establishing Camelot as a far-off kingdom ("Once upon a time") where magic rather than human action matters, and where the core story seems to center around the arranged marriage between Arthur and Guenevere.[9] As *Into the Woods* would do much more elaborately, *Camelot* resolves its initial fairy-tale trajectory early on, so that the humanity of its situations might be explored *after* the "happ'ly-ever-aftering" in the final line of the title song, which is reprised at the end of the first scene. Here, however, that humanity is not forced on its characters—as in *Into the Woods*—by an exterior reality that refuses to forgive human fallibility. Rather, the impulse here is an *internal* one, grounded in the emergent idealism of Arthur, who envisions and brings to realization a "new order of chivalry"—whose highest fulfillment, in the person of Lancelot, will, however, destroy the precarious balance between Arthur's idealism, Guenevere's operetta world, and the real humans who in various ways do not fit comfortably within the new chivalric order. Moreover, the event that triggers the destruction is precisely the maturation of Guenevere, who emerges from the world of operetta-based innuendo into the idealized world of chivalry, propelled by her "ideal" love for Lancelot (significantly, in the stage show this love remains unconsummated). But an equally important catalyst for destruction, implied in this development, stems from the realities of human passion and their long-term consequences; it is Mordred, Arthur's bastard son by his half sister and thus the fruit of unchivalrous carnality, who rouses Arthur's knights to revolt against the hypocrisies forced upon them by Arthur's idealistic code. In this codification, the ideal fails simply because, once it becomes real, it is by definition no longer ideal. Accordingly, as an extension of this strict sense of idealism, idealism as such is never made fully "real" in *Camelot*—which means, within the realm of the musical, it is never given full musical expression—except within the realm of idealized love.

Yet, in another sense, the music of *Camelot* is saturated with idealism. It begins in heroic mode, launching the overture with the heroic motive of a rising triad, played first by the horns and then by the trumpets. And the extended musical gesture portends more than mere heroism; it tells us plainly that this is heroism from a bygone era, from deep in the irretrievable past, and that it is saturated, moreover, with magic. The motive emerges out of an opening flourish (harp, cymbals, trilling strings and winds), as if out of the mists, and the militaristic trumpet flourish that answers the motive borrows tropes of musical primitivism, using parallel triads and a lowered leading tone, the latter evoking modal systems that predated the modern tonal system.[10] The glittering past thus evoked is then dipped in magic, using a technique borrowed from the Russian octatonic tradition of the nineteenth century: as shown in example 4.1, the triadic motive, now played by the trumpets, sounds against a backdrop of harmonies shifting upward by minor thirds (E major–G major–B♭ major), a progression that then continues across the next musical phrase (moving beyond B♭ to D♭) before the melody, adapted from the bridge of "Camelot," settles into A major.[11] (A familiar passage from the Russian tradition, which uses precisely this progression with a different starting point, occurs in the slow movement of Tchaikovsky's Fourth Symphony.) Thus, the basically tonal language of the show partakes early on, and will often return to, techniques of enharmonically shifting harmonies, generally by thirds, that evoke a primitive world of magic possibilities, so that the music of the show seems to ride along the edge of a future emergence into the modern era.[12]

♩4.2
♩4.3

Indeed, this "edge" between the eras of magic and human modernity is one important way that the Arthur legends have been traditionally presented, as a parable of humans struggling to create a just and civilized world increasingly divested of magic. In *Camelot*, Merlin disappears early on, although Mordred hints to Arthur that he is the product of his mother's "bewitchment," and then calls upon Morgan le Fay's supernatural assistance to keep Arthur from returning to the castle to warn Lancelot and Guenevere.[13] But access to the sense of "vision" that magic provided Arthur under Merlin's tutelage—ranging from Merlin's tantalizing glimpses of the future, now only dimly recalled, to Arthur's being transformed into a hawk—fuels and sometimes seems to confirm the rightness of Arthur's idealistic innovations. In this way, magic stands behind and informs Arthur's idealism, with music playing a central role in the process, first by evoking a sense of magic and later by providing a thread of ongoing development from that magic to Arthur's idealistic visions of chivalry. As magic slips to the background, it is precisely idealism that displaces it.

The musical mismatch between Arthur and Guenevere is established and resolved wholly within the first scene, with each of them singing a "soliloquy" in turn, followed by Arthur offering the court of Camelot to Guenevere in the form of a song, so that she can sing it back to him as a reprise. Arthur's "speak-singing"—which is notated as such in the score, following the notation Arnold Schoenberg developed earlier in the century for his much differently motivated *Sprechstimme*—quickly establishes vocality as a fundamental difference between them. But other musical disjunctures—and, just as important, connections—between the two soliloquies are also striking. Both songs are relatively complex patterns deriving from standard Tin Pan Alley

Example 4.1. *Camelot*: excerpt from "Overture"

types. In a familiar extension of this type, Arthur's "I Wonder What the King Is Doing Tonight" proceeds from a verse couched in a storytelling, "once-upon-a-time" mode, to a chorus presented as a dialogue between him and his imagined audience (his "people"), which repeats its AABA, thirty-two-bar structure with new lyrics after a more expansive bridge. Even in the first chorus, as Arthur simulates a multitude of his people's voices, the predictable thematic structure modulates freely, with their increasingly pointed questions cascading through a modulatory sequence (based on the descending tetrachord of C) that he silences only with his answer, a decisive return to the tonic that is undercut by the embarrassing nature of that answer:[14]

♪4.4

A	I wonder what the King is doing tonight?	E♭
	What merriment is the King pursuing tonight?	
A	The candles at the Court, they never burn'd as bright.	G
	I wonder what the King is up to tonight?	

B	How goes the final hour	C
	As he sees the bridal bower	B♭
	Being legally and regally prepared?	A♭–G
A	Well, I'll tell you what the King is doing tonight:	E♭
	He's scared! He's scared!	

If Arthur in his soliloquy imagines an audience that isn't really there, Guenevere sings "The Simple Joys of Maidenhood," which follows immediately, in imagined privacy, all the while being overheard by a concealed Arthur. Like his song, hers is complicated formally and by harmonic shifts of a major third; indeed, dovetailing with Arthur's E♭–G, she completes a full cycle of major thirds within the opening verse, shifting from B to G and back again, then dipping into Arthur's key (E♭) for her first vehement outburst ("I won't obey you anymore!"). The first phrase of Arthur's chorus provides the melodic basis for her opening prayer to Saint Genevieve—"I wonder what the King" becomes "Oh, Genevieve, St. Genevieve"—which is then reworked more subtly to launch the chorus ("Where are the simple joys of maindenhood?"), but her chorus is much more stable than his, without real

♪4.5   modulation. As the songs detail, Arthur's and Guenevere's situations are exactly reversed, but with a parallel fear of domestic normalcy: he has already been out in the world and performed heroic deeds (whacking dragons and fighting battles), whereas she desperately wants the feminine counterpart to such adventures, especially in the realm of romance (a wish that will come true, of course, with disastrous consequences).[15]

Continuing the process initiated in these two songs, of borrowing an internal thread from one song to generate another, Arthur launches "Camelot" with the bridge of "The Simple Joys of Maidenhood," so that Guenevere's "Shall I not be on a pedestal, / Worshipped and competed for?" with its opening octave leap and gradual descent, becomes "A law was made a dis-

♪4.6
♪4.7   tant moon ago here." Thus, the series of songs unfolds almost as in a logical syllogism, with each song extending something of the previous song, and with the third in the series providing a sense of resolution through its relatively uncomplicated structural profile (AABA; sixty-four bars, plus extension) after only the scantest of verses. But since Guenevere does not yet know who Arthur is, this potential resolution is premature; when she does learn, and thereafter accepts him as her bridegroom, actual resolution takes the form of a summational twofold reprise (a device more typical for late in the second act than for late in the first scene). Thus, the verse to Arthur's opening song (as underscore) yields to "Camelot," sung as a gesture of acquiescence by Guenevere. The framing gesture in this brief number is twofold, not only embracing and recapping the scene itself but also suggesting a fully framed fairy tale, with the musical "once-upon-a-time" mode of Arthur's song completed by Guenevere, who first paraphrases Arthur's words to the bridge of her own song as Arthur had transformed it ("I hear it never rains till after sundown") and then sings her acceptance of the fairy-tale ending in the final

lines of "Camelot": "In short there's simply not / A more congenial spot / For **happ'ly-ever-aftering** than here / In Camelot."   ♪4.8

Yet, the syllogistic evolution is scarcely complete with this resolution, for "Camelot" also contains the seeds for further elaboration, by introducing the heroic triadic ascent in the bridge, coordinated with a distinctive harmonic shift from D major to F major redolent of similar moves in the overture (the ascending triadic figure is in bold):   ♪4.9

> **Camelot! Camelot!** / I know it sounds a bit bizarre.   (D)
>
> But in **Camelot, Camelot,** / That's how conditions are.   (F)

Though the gesture as initially presented by Arthur is more fanciful than heroic, the non-functional harmonic shift reinforces its latent elemental heroism, providing a ready-made musical introduction for Lancelot one scene—and five years—later. The sequence of events, both dramatic and musical, is deftly plotted. Arthur, inspired by his love for Guenevere and fueled by his military and diplomatic successes, develops two key elements of his new code: "Might *for* Right" to displace "Might is Right" and the idea of the equalizing Round Table. Then, in another reprise of the main musical phrase of "Camelot," Guenevere for the first time responds musically to Arthur in a directly personal way. Until this reprise, she has been his partner and has enjoyed court life at Camelot, but she has not returned or even fully acknowledged the depth of his love for her or recognized the inspirational role that that love has played, until she displaces the song's emphasis on the court with a paean to Arthur himself: "That there is simply not / In all the world a spot / Where rules a more resplendent King than here / In Camelot." Significantly, her substitution does two things besides acknowledging Arthur directly: it removes the key fairy-tale phrase, "happ'ly-ever-aftering," and shifts the emphasis from the court and its governing ideals (which they have been discussing) to the individual who occupies their center. Moreover, she has short-circuited the song itself, leaving out its bridge, and so constructs what is, in effect, a musical cue for Lancelot, who will make his entrance immediately afterward by singing that bridge in heroic style, complete with modulation, as the introduction to his "C'est Moi":   ♪4.10

> **Camelot! Camelot!** / In far off France I heard your call.   (D)
>
> **Camelot! Camelot!** / And here am I to give my all.   (F)

In this way, the succession of songs in *Camelot* simulates with some precision the emergence of the real from out of the ideal, systematically marking each new event in the sequence by building a new song from the bridge material of the last. When Arthur is first inspired by Guenevere, he converts her romantic longings into a description of an achieved wonderland, but he also unwittingly provides the musical seed for Lancelot, who, inspired by Arthur's conception of Camelot, announces his arrival with an interior phrase of Arthur's song. Musically *and* dramatically, then, Guenevere first inspires Arthur, who gives reality to her inner longings and, at the same stroke, inspires Lancelot, the embodiment of Arthur's chivalrous ideal. The logical thread is as clearly drawn as in Arthur's characteristic progression from "proposition" to "resolution" at the end of the first act, after taking due note of the growing love between the end points in this chain of inspira-

♪4.11 tion, Guenevere and Lancelot:

> Proposition: If I could choose, from every woman who breathes on this earth, the face, . . . the smile, the voice, the heart, the laugh, the soul itself, . . . they would all be Jenny's.
> Proposition: If I could choose from every man . . . they would all be Lance. . . .
> Proposition: I'm a king, not a man. And a civilized king. Could it possibly be civilized to destroy what I love? . . .
> Resolved: We shall live through this together, Excalibur: They, you and I! And God have mercy on us all.

Lancelot's entrance song, "C'est Moi," is itself an intriguing set of double images. Put bluntly, the song swaggers, moving from the broadly heroic 4/4 of its "Camelot" calling card to a sense of emphatic resolution, "alla marcia" (in the style of a march), as Lancelot details what a knight ought to be, to a

♪4.12 rollicking 6/8 as he himself lays claim to those virtues ("C'est moi"). But Lancelot, as a character, does *not* swagger (or at least should not swagger), for he lacks sufficient perspective on himself for that. Thus, in the script he is described as having "a stern jaw and burning eyes," with his face "unlined, for he has never smiled." Similarly, the song is verbally clever, loaded with imaginative rhymes and a witty mixing of French and English, and even bordering at times on the sacrilegious ("Had I been made the partner of Eve"); yet, Lancelot is completely disingenuous. In the midst of an operetta that plays wantonly with implied ribaldry and sexual nuance, he insists on taking everything with utmost sincerity. Just as he has taken Arthur's fanciful image of Camelot a shade too seriously, he takes his own recipe for knighthood too literally, and so has made of himself a brittle paragon of both physical and spiritual perfection that clearly cannot hold up to human realities. Indeed, of the song's double images, this is the most important. The song's two verses lay out a complete separation of the physical and the spiritual; yet the song also links them through maintaining a parallel structure and through its claims to an untenable purity that will soon have to confront the urgencies of genuine love.

Coincident with Lancelot's arrival is a parallel arrival in court, of the comic, aging King Pellinore, and with the latter comes another sort of double image that points, however, in the other direction, toward insincerity and ribaldry. Pellinore, whose rusting armor makes him into a kind of Oz-like Tin Man, is, like Lancelot, a caricature; yet, whereas Lancelot has no perspective on himself, Pellinore is all self-deprecation and bawdy humor. On an eighteen-year quest to find his "beast," Pellinore stands in for a core ingredient of the Arthurian legends (although a relatively late addition to

Figure 4.1. The last carefree moment in *Camelot*: Guenevere (Julie Andrews) ca-vorting with the court's knights and ladies in "The Lusty Month of May," just before Arthur introduces her to Lancelot. (Photograph courtesy of Miles Kreuger and the Institute of the American Musical, Inc.)

those legends): the quest for the Holy Grail, which he seems, implicitly, to mock. His addition at this juncture is critical, for his presence allows the show to continue its operetta basis while advancing a strand of tragic ideal-ism that stands in discordant opposition to operetta. He will become Ar-thur's earthy companion just as Guenevere and Lancelot begin their tragic journey into ideal love, a love that effectively prevents Arthur's access to the fruits of his own idealism and will eventually destroy his achievement. Yet, their love also demonstrates the transformative capacities of idealism, espe-cially as Guenevere herself matures into womanhood—capable of both a passion and a sensibility she has only hinted at previously—in response to Lancelot as the embodied ideal.

At various points and in various ways, *Camelot* delineates its categories of ideal and real fairly explicitly, especially in its mapping of the ideal onto the feminine. Early on, in the face of Pellinore's exasperation with him, Lancelot admits that, from an early age, his fanatic idealism has "locked the world out," acknowledging further that "when you lock the world out, you're locked in." Arthur's "How to Handle a Woman" explores

the awkwardness that entails when chivalry's ideal image of womankind
bumps up against the realities of a living, feeling, and especially *thinking*
woman (an awkwardness that extends to the song's broad chauvinism
bumping up against an emergent feminism in the early 1960s). Significantly,
this is nearly Arthur's last song in the show (except for the failed operetta
"rescue" of "What Do the Simple Folk Do?" in the second act and the final
reprise of "Camelot," both discussed later), and it carries his entire idealist
trajectory in musical terms, from an opening Henry Higgins–style rant
against women, in speech song, to a lyric demanding his most tender singing
voice. Early in the last scene, before the final reprise of "Camelot," Arthur
despairingly sums up their situation to Lancelot and Guenevere, "How I
wish I'd never tried to think at all. All we've been through, for nothing but
an idea! Something you cannot taste or touch, smell or feel; without substance, life, reality or memory." And, earlier in the second act, Lancelot's
"madrigal" for Guenevere (the preamble to "If Ever I Would Leave You")
recites the basic tenet of courtly love (with a lowered leading tone at each
cadence to add a touch of medievalism to an otherwise strictly tonal har-
♫4.13   monic treatment):

> Toujours j'ai fait le même voeux, / Sur terre une déesse, au ciel un Dieu.
> Un homme désire pour etre heureux / Sur terre une déesse, au ciel un Dieu.[16]
> Years may come; years may go; / This, I know, will e'er be so:
> The reason to live is only to love / A goddess on earth and a God above.

Understood as an emblem of the ideal, a perfect idea that cannot be realized without destroying its perfection, the unconsummated love between
Lancelot and Guenevere becomes the ache of idealism itself, especially as
expressed in the three songs that delineate that love, "Before I Gaze at You
Again" (Guenevere, end of Act I), "If Ever I Would Leave You" (Lancelot,
beginning of Act II), and "I Loved You Once in Silence" (Guenevere, late in
Act II). In the centerpiece of this trio, that ache is given both special poignancy and a fair measure of heroic posturing (hence its inclusion, at the
beginning of this chapter, in my list of "shower" tunes). In the main section
of the song, major-seventh dissonances, acting as appoggiaturas within the
supporting harmonies (in the last instance involving the actual melodic
pitch), underscore important arrivals at the central climax and across its
♫4.14   dissipation (in bold):

> If ever I would leave you / It wouldn't be in summer;
> Seeing you in summer, I never would **go**.
> Your hair streaked with sun**light** / Your lips red as **flame**.
> Your face with a luster / That puts gold to shame.

When this music returns for the final part of an expanded AABA (with sixteen-bar "A" sections), the energy of the first of these arrival pitches ("Knowing how in spring I'm bewitched by you **so**?") does not dissipate in a descending sequence; rather, that pitch serves first as the top of a harsh augmented

triad near the end of the following line ("Summer, **winter or** fall!"), and then as part of the longest sustained major-seventh of the song, just before the cadence ("No, never could I leave **you** at all").

The special pain of failed idealism is explored in two very different songs in the second act, the first of which represents an abortive attempt to return to a preidealistic moment, when Arthur and Guenevere perform a quintessential operetta number, "What Do the Simple Folk Do?" The song is replete with verbal wit ("When they're beset and besieged, / The folk not nobless'ly obliged," "They obviously outshine us at turning tears to mirth / Have tricks a royal highness is minus from birth"), a full exploration of the inspirational repertoire of musical theater more generally (whistling, singing, and dancing), and a wryly clever ending ("They sit around and wonder / What royal folk would do").[17] The number explicitly refers to the operetta world of the first scene of the show, both in its opening melodic gesture ("I wonder what the king" now becomes "What do the simple folk") and in its basic premise, which, when inverted at the end, exactly reproduces the conceit for Arthur's first song, even reproducing the key verb, "wonder." More basically, the very gesture of Arthur and Guenevere trying to recapture their own shared past derives from operetta (as in the plotting of *The Merry Widow*, or in "Wunderbar," the operetta number recalled near the beginning of *Kiss Me, Kate*). The irony of "What Do the Simple Folk Do?"—vastly amusing to audiences who relish the temporary escape from idealistic angst and frustrated romantic ardor—is underscored by the ending, which for the first and only time in the show brings a potentially romantic couple together to sing in thirds, the traditional emblem for achieved coupling—which here, however, denotes a mutual resigned acceptance of the impossibility of their situation.

"Guenevere" marks the climax of the tragedy and uses ostinato (repetition of musical figures, especially accompanimental figures) as an emblem of the obsessions that have generated this tragedy, as the carrier of the number's sense of inevitable fate, and as the means for shaping its climax.[18] Onstage, the number further enhances its sense of unstoppability by unfolding as description and commentary against pantomimed action, creating an effect similar to that of watching a film of devastating historical events, in this way evoking the history-as-fate trope employed in such shows as *Sweeney Todd* and *Evita* (see chapter 7). The heroic, larger-than-life dimensions of the unfolding, which the pantomimed staging can also support (for example, through the use of enhanced shadowing) stems in part from the main melodic gesture, which is built from a distorted version of the heroic "Camelot" motive, dividing its span of a fifth into a fourth and a second instead of into thirds. Many have found the conception of this number flawed, since it describes action rather than presents it;[19] yet, by so moving realistic action to the background, this number highlights further the show's focus on idealism. The number builds until only violence (or its musical simulation) can provide release for its ostinato repetitions, which become increasingly dissonant as the number proceeds. The intensity with which the number focuses on its central figure, Guenevere, destined to be either burned at the stake or rescued with great bloodshed, also increases until, in the end, the lyric consists mainly in repetitions of her name; this focus is, of course, dramatically to the point, for Guenevere at this stage represents both the ideal and the

♩4.17 destruction of that ideal.

But the finale restores the balance, by reminding us that ideals, and ideas more generally, can live on past present realities. This scene, which begins in despair as Arthur confronts and forgives Lancelot and Guenevere, ends in ecstatic hope, as Arthur meets a youth who has, through stories alone, been inspired to become a Knight of the Round Table. This encounter brings Arthur to the startling realization that his dream does not end with him but will live on through "the stories people tell." Important here are the recurring metaphors of light and fire as emblems of both idealism and destruction. In "Guenevere," we hear that

> In that dawn, in that gloom, / More than love met its doom.
> In the dying candles' gleam / Came the sundown of a dream.

It is this conflation of images of evening and dawn, of light extinguished and light reborn—recalling that Guenevere is herself to be burned at daybreak—that Arthur recasts in the final reprise of "Camelot." In an early dawn setting, just before the final battle, Arthur directs the youth Tom, in a lyric filled with retrospection and implied firesides,

> Each evening from December to December . . .
> Think back on all the tales that you remember
> Of Camelot. . . .
> Don't let it be forgot / That once there was a spot
> For one brief shining moment that was known
> As Camelot.

What matters most in the song's final image is that the moment of Camelot *shines*, and so it casts the inspiring light of its idealism forward to future

♩4.18 generations.

Man of La Mancha (1965) was the lone Broadway success of its creative team, Dale Wasserman (book), Joe Darion (lyrics), and Mitch Leigh (music), although each had some success in separate ventures. In this respect, the show seems fittingly quixotic, an unlikely one-shot success that seems to respond in kind to the oddity of Cervantes's *Don Quixote*: a work reputedly begun in prison and written fairly quickly, the first and only real success of a journeyman writer. Moreover, Cervantes published the first volume of *Don Quixote* in 1605, when he was already fifty-eight, and the second a decade later, a year before his death. Improbably, given these circumstances, the book is now deemed to be the first true novel, is regarded by many as the greatest work of fiction ever written, and is, indeed, the source of the now common word "quixotic." *Man of La Mancha* was, however, based only loosely on Cervantes's *Don Quixote*—which, in the main, was reacting *against* a tide of idealism, much as Voltaire's *Candide* would a century and a half later or Stephen Schwartz and Bob Fosse's *Pippin* would a year after *Man of La Mancha* closed in 1971. Cervantes's tale of a latter-day knight pits itself with biting satire against a deluge of romanticized tales of knight-errantry across the previous century in Spain, along with other fashionable eccentricities such as the pastorale, although a softening of its tone may be detected in the second volume, which appeared in 1615.

It is this softening of tone that the creators of *Man of La Mancha* took to be critical evidence of Cervantes's emergent idealism, a perhaps involuntary response to his own fictional creation. Thus, the show is not so much about Don Quixote, or even the aging Alonso Quijana, who becomes Don Quixote, as about how one responds—as audience, as dramatic player, even as author—to such laughable demonstrations of idealism as Cervantes projects in the face of ridicule and unforgiving realities. The metaphor in *Man of La Mancha* for those unforgiving realities is harsh indeed: all the players, including Cervantes, are in the common room of a Spanish prison, many of them waiting to appear before the Inquisition.

In many respects, *Man of La Mancha* seems more straightforward than *Camelot*. Its music is a Broadway version of "Spanish," which means unabashedly eclectic and ahistorical, using lots of cross rhythms (especially alternating patterns of three and two), a "Spanish" instrumental ensemble (guitar, characteristic percussion, brass, no violins), characteristic dance types such as the bolero, and characteristic melodic figures. Within the practices of Broadway, the resulting exotic idiom also transplants us doubly into the past: to the (real) Spanish Inquisition and to the imagined medievalist world of Don Quixote. The show correspondingly maintains—or seems to maintain—a fairly sharp division between the ideal and the real, with Don Quixote's insistence on his own vision of things—on seeing something other than what everyone else sees—marking him as the idealistic center of the show. Yet this sharp division masks the fact that the reality he refuses to acknowledge is twice mediated, since it has been fabricated by the prisoners under Cervantes's direction, within a prison setting that is in reality a Broadway stage. These circumstances will turn out to matter, since they reflect the broad range of investments in the enacted narrative of Don Quixote: of Cervantes himself, who manages everything and plays the lead role (Quijana/Quixote) so that his manuscript will not be burned; of the prisoners, who play the other parts and observe, with an initial mix of contempt and enthusiasm for the diversion it promises; and of the 1960s Broadway audience—for whom, among other things, the prominent presence of the guitar will betoken a different kind of idealistic content. Despite these complicating factors, *Man of La Mancha* embraces its idealism more fully than *Camelot*, returning to it repeatedly in its musical numbers and transmuting the failure of Don Quixote's idealism to overcome harsh realities into spiritual uplift, with a palpable effect on nearly all the other prisoners.

The songs of *Man of La Mancha* are all part of the show within a show that Cervantes mounts for his fellow prisoners, who will function, in essence, as the audience for an "out-of-town tryout" of his new "musical"—and will, as with tryout audiences for many a Broadway show, play a part in shaping the story. With a few exceptions, the songs of the show set forth either an idealist position or the realities that idealism must confront, all in fairly direct terms; those exceptions generally provide important mediation, by projecting a bridge between the two, often through the human connection of friendship.

The first song, "Man of La Mancha," through which Cervantes introduces Don Quixote and his squire, Sancho Panza, is a combination song in which the relationship between the two is carefully mapped. Central, of course, is Don Quixote himself, whose idealism prevents him from seeing the world as others see it; thus, his contribution carries a sense of a potential clashing of sensibilities through its minor-mode "heroic" motive (the motivic link to *Camelot* discussed earlier) and its insistence on imposing a slower duple meter (6/8) against the basic triple meter of the accompaniment (3/4), in alternation (6/8 rhythms are indicated in bold):

> Hear me **now, oh thou** bleak and un**bearable** world,
> Thou art **base and de**bauched as can be;
> And a **knight with his** banners all **bravely unfurled**
> Now **hurls down his** gauntlet to thee!

With the ensuing line ("I am **I, Don Quixote,** / The **Lord of La** Mancha"), Don Quixote seems to succeed briefly in imposing his vision; the mode changes to major, and the accompaniment now reinforces his metrical alternation between three and two. But the following lines, with their reference to fate, restore the minor mode, and by the end, the accompaniment has returned to its earlier pattern:

♪ **4.19**

> My **destiny** calls and I go.
> And the **wild winds of** fortune will **carry me** onward.
> Oh **whitherso**ever they blow.
> **Whitherso**ever they blow,
> **Onward** to glory I go!

The language here is also significant; as in Cervantes's book, Don Quixote adopts the archaic language of the chivalric romances ("thou art," etc.) that have made his "brains dry up"; indeed, specific phrases of the song derive directly from *Don Quixote* (thus, "winds of fortune"), as do some of the images in "The Impossible Dream" (see note 22). As Sancho adds his melody to the mix, first separately and then overlapping the second half of the Don's, his "normal" language and more straightforward 3/4 rhythms offer a striking contrast to his master's diction, especially when the two sing together. But also important is Sancho's positioning: he neither makes fun of Don Quixote's conceits nor endorses them; he is merely, and proudly, "his friend." Moreover, he sings *above* Don Quixote's melody (although not in the inadequate 1972 film version); figuratively, rather than merely adding support, he thus provides a gloss and perspective through which an audience has sympathetic access to his deranged master.   ♩4.20

Don Quixote's next number, too, places his knightly perspective against a contrasting backdrop, this time one considerably more hostile to his own. "Dulcinea" sounds as a gentle interior to the harsh exterior of "It's All the Same," heard just earlier, and the muleteers' coarse parody of "Dulcinea," which follows immediately. Indeed, all three ostensibly describe the same woman. "It's All the Same" is Aldonza's sullen and contemptuous self-introduction as the inn's resident strumpet, whereas "Dulcinea" is Don Quixote's idealized account of her, as his fair, virginal Lady; in their parody of the latter song, the raucous mockery of the muleteers returns the contempt that Aldonza had earlier lavished on them. As if to underscore their common subject matter, both "It's All the Same" and "Dulcinea" employ a regular accompanimental pattern of alternating duple and triple meters (6/8 and 3/4), and both also involve an element of cynical parody. But the rhythms of Aldonza's song are much more hard-driving, based on a sharp-edged three-measure pattern with complicated subrhythms, breaking into the major mode and a simplified metrical alternation in the bridge, which parodies more elevated ideas of love in its "noble" upward trajectory. "Dulcinea,"   ♩4.21 on the other hand, begins in a deeper register, worshiping from below before reaching upward in all sincerity, and its vocal rhythms maintain a calmly confident 6/8 rhythm against the alternating meters in the accompaniment. "Dulcinea" expresses the familiar chivalric trope of woman as embodied ideal, a Madonna whom Don Quixote addresses as a combination of dream, prayer, and song—even though we know her to be a whore, the other side of that all-too-familiar feminine binary.[20]   ♩4.22

As a kind of way station between acceptance and dismissal of Don Qui-   ♩4.23 xote's delusional idealism, his padre—having already noted with some irony the suspect motives of those who would "cure" him ("I'm Only Thinking of Him")—notes in "To Each His Dulcinea" both the unreality of Don Quixote's idealism and the importance of such escapist dreams as enabling inspirations and as shields against despair. Here, few rhythmic complications contradict the soothing flow of the song's triple meter, but the song's form is stretched in order to lay out the dangerous contradictions. The first two segments of a seemingly conventional AABA elaborate the empowering possibilities of dreams: ♩4.24

> To each his Dulcinea / That he alone can name,
> To each a secret hiding place / Where he can find the haunting face
> To light his secret flame.
> For with his Dulcinea / Beside him so to stand,
> A man can do quite anything, / Outfly the bird upon the wing,
> Hold moonlight in his hand.

But the structure is slightly unbalanced, as each segment is an atypical length of twenty bars and threatens to drift off into a remote key area at the cadence (in bold); hence, as the bridge warns, "A man with moonlight in his hand / Has nothing there at all," it also restores musical rationality within a tidy sixteen-bar phrase that also seems to settle back down to earth melodically. Yet, the lyric and musical profile of the final segment refuses to decide against irrationality, and so it wanders melodically upward and into the harmonic realm of the flat sixth—a traditional emblem of unreality—for the final cadence ("To each his Dulcinea / Though she's naught but flame **and air**"), with the accompaniment returning to the tonic only at the end. In delivery, the song also expresses the delicacy of the balancing act between reality and fantasy: the final word, "air"—the song's highest note—must be sung quite softly and sustained for over six bars, holding to the tonic until the shifting harmonies below confirm it.

♩ **4.25**

Man of La Mancha reaches its crisis point only after the full emergence of Don Quixote's idealistic vision in "The Impossible Dream," when, after Don Quixote, Sancho, and Aldonza surprisingly triumph over the muleteers, things begin to unravel fairly quickly. (It is partly because of the pacing after this dramatic crest that the show has no intermission.) "The Impossible Dream"—the show's one big hit song—is in many respects a traditional Broadway inspirational number and, indeed, functions so as to fuel the short-lived victory that follows it. But it is also of a piece with the show, laying out the tenets of chivalry with the same balanced tension between internal ideals and outward action, as established in Don Quixote's first two numbers, and couched in a characteristic Spanish idiom, in this case the bolero. The latter may seem a strange choice, given the bolero's derivation from the *sequidilla* (most famously, if idiosyncratically, employed in Bizet's *Carmen* [1875], another show that uses an exoticized "Spanish" musical idiom) and its best-known modern example, Ravel's *Boléro* (1928), which have secured its association with salacious sexuality. But the rhythms of the bolero are eminently suitable for the building strategies of the inspirational Broadway number, establishing an ostinato rhythm as an emblem of obsession, yet controlling it through both the dance-based idiom and the referential model of Ravel, whose *Boléro* derives its hypnotic effect above all through an exercise in long-range *control* of its suggestive gestures. Moreover, the bolero rhythms of "The Impossible Dream" are significantly softened from those of Ravel's *Boléro*, with triplet patterns displacing Ravel's duple patterns on the smaller level while maintaining the slow triple meter

♩ **4.26**
♩ **4.27**

basic to the type.[21] Within the show, this emphasis on triplet patterns within a triple meter builds directly on the Padre's "To Each His Dulcinea," which similarly but more simply breaks away from the show's more complex interweavings of triple and duple meters, so that "The Impossible Dream" stands deliberately apart, as an arrival point that will give shape and direction to the whole.

"The Impossible Dream" is in a Tin Pan Alley form expanded tremendously—one is tempted to say heroically—from within: thus, AABA, but
with "B" expanded from eight to fourteen bars, articulating a climax and
dissipation. Within this structure, the lyric at first maintains a careful alternation between inward-directed idealism and the heroic action that inwardness
inspires (the former in italics, the latter in bold):   ♩4.28

> To *dream* the impossible dream, / To **fight** the unbeatable foe,
> To *bear* with unbearable sorrow, / To **run** where the brave dare not go;
> To **right** the unrightable wrong, / To *love* pure and chaste, from afar,
> To **try**, when your arms are too weary, / To **reach** the unreachable star!

As shown, as the lyric progresses, it throws increasing emphasis to action,
shifting action to the leading position with the second section and ending
with a double active verb pointing to the climax to come. The climax within
the bridge extends that outward dynamic, yet reaches its highest climax,
after an initial subsiding, with a return to the internal dimension, which also
brings a more complete dissipation of energies: ♩4.29

> This is my Quest, to **follow** that star
> No matter how hopeless, no matter how far,
> To **fight** for the right without question or pause,
> To be *willing* to **march** into hell for a heavenly cause!
> And I *know*, if I'll only *be true* to this glorious Quest,
> That my heart *will lie* peaceful and calm when I'm laid to my rest.

The final section, which replays the steady rise across the first two sections,
concerns legacy, how the world itself might be transformed through the
image of the inspired, idealist hero.[22] Just before this number, Don Quixote
deprecates this kind of concern as vanity, renouncing his brief indulgence in
considering "how sages of the future will describe" him. Yet, in the context
of the song, these seem to be not "empty boasts" but the acknowledgment
of actual achievement; singing this song has to seem, for this reason, to be
an achievement, and a difficult one. Richard Kiley set the standard in this
regard, with a rough-hewn voice nonetheless capable of climbing from the
opening depths to bellow out the high notes, yet also pull back from the
climax with a confident restoration of calm. Thus, the song works less well
for a singer who too easily manages its climaxes, and not at all for a singer
who cannot do so (not even when he gets "help," as does Peter O'Toole,
with disastrous effect, in the film version).

Besides fueling the immediate success of the idealistic core group, which
through this song expands from Don Quixote and Sancho to include Aldonza, "The Impossible Dream" also lays out the dramatic shape of the rest
of the show, with its double climax, destruction and death of the hero, and
concern for legacy. But the impetus for that trajectory is primarily negative,
and extremely so. After Don Quixote and Sancho leave (having defeated the
muleteers and persuaded the Innkeeper to dub Quixote knight), Aldonza is

raped and beaten by the muleteers and carried off by them, unconscious. Then, as the oblivious knight begins a reprise of "The Impossible Dream," he is interrupted by the "real world" on another level, as the men of the Inquisition descend into the prison to "fetch someone"—in the event, however, not Cervantes, who is nonetheless quite shaken, suffering as well from the taunts of the "Duke," a prisoner who at every opportunity has disparaged Cervantes and his story of a mad knight. It is in response to the Duke that Cervantes gives his most elaborate defense of idealism, based on the harsh realities of his own life (which was, in actuality, even harsher than his description, involving the loss of the utility of his left hand and five years of slavery in Africa):

> My friend, I have lived almost fifty years, and I have seen life as it is. Pain, misery, hunger, cruelty beyond belief. . . . I have been a soldier and seen my comrades fall in battle . . . or die more slowly under the lash in Africa. I have held them in my arms at the final moment. These were men who saw life as it is, yet they died despairing. No glory, no gallant last words, only their eyes filled with confusion, whimpering the question: "Why?" I do not think they asked why they were dying, but why they had lived. [As he continues, he begins to resume the character of Don Quixote, and the music for "Man of La Mancha" begins.] When life itself seems lunatic, who knows where madness lies? Too much sanity may be madness. To seek treasure where there is only trash. Perhaps to be practical is madness. And maddest of all, to see life as it is and not as it ought to be.

But after this recovery completes its trajectory in a reprise of "Man of La Mancha," the devastating setbacks continue: Don Quixote and Sancho are mocked and robbed of all their possessions by a band of Moors and return on foot to the inn; Aldonza also returns after the muleteers are done with her, utterly broken, newly disillusioned, and raging at her inability to make Don Quixote see her as she actually is (in "Aldonza"; see below); and his niece's fiancé (played by the Duke) appears as the Knight of the Mirrors and succeeds in destroying Don Quixote's illusions, by showing him in his "mirror of reality" that he is "Naught but an aging fool . . . a madman dressed for a masquerade" (see figure 4.2). Again, the Inquisition appears, this time warning Cervantes that his time is near. As if this weren't enough, Cervantes's fellow prisoners, unhappy with how his "entertainment" has progressed, are ready to burn his manuscript. It is at this point that Cervantes, in improvising a new ending, completes the promise at the end of "The Impossible Dream"; rather than imagine an unrealistic end with Don Quixote triumphant, he restores authority to Don Quixote's quixotic *vision*, with Aldonza—figuratively, the legacy of his delusional quest—taking his side and, in the end, insisting that her name is Dulcinea.

"Aldonza" is the bleakest number in the show. Like her earlier "It's All the Same," it is couched in the minor mode with only ironic forays into the major, alternating unrelentingly between 3/4 and 6/8. Unlike in her earlier

Figure 4.2.
The beginning of
the end in *Man of
La Mancha*: Don
Quixote (Richard
Kiley) drowning in
the "mirror of real-
ity" wielded by the
Knight of the
Mirrors, who is
actually the fiancé
of his niece, trying
to restore him to his
senses. (Photograph
courtesy of Miles
Kreuger and the
Institute of the
American Musical,
Inc.)

number, however, she is no longer in control of the situation, so that what seems as though it might play out as an AABA structure, with the bridge given over to the ironic major, cycles instead between the two (thus, AAB-AAB-AAB, a kind of "bar form"), with a foreshortened bridge, rising a half step between cycles in simulation of her rising hysteria, and with the end coming only when she finally despairs of reaching Don Quixote, the target of her rant. Yet, even in its bleakness, "Aldonza" lays the groundwork for redemption. Because its melodic rhythm so closely matches Don Quixote's in "Man of La Mancha," she has the unique capacity to function as a reactivating trigger for his resurrection from Alonso Quijana's deathbed. The similarities are obvious, once noted (parallel rhythms are in bold):

♪ 4.30
♪ 4.31

A: I was **spawned in a ditch by a mother who left me there**
DQ: I am **I, Don Quixote / The Lord of La Mancha**

A: **Naked and cold and too hung**ry to cry;
DQ: **My destiny calls and I go;**

A: **I never blamed her, I'm sure she left hoping that**
DQ: And the **wild winds of fortune will carry me onward**

A: I'd have the **good sense to die!**
DQ: Oh whither**soever they blow.**

In the series of reprises that makes up the finale—most of them functioning as remembrances, introduced by Aldonza to jog Quijana's memory—the first two are untexted, segueing almost unnoticeably from "Aldonza" (at her entrance) to "Man of La Mancha" (at the first mention of his knightly name, Don Quixote). Then she sings back the songs he sang to her. Her "Dulcinea" recalls key phrases of his, interspersed with her entreaties for him to remember, to acknowledge the past. Her "Impossible Dream" is his text, recited by her until he takes it up and completes the first (preclimactic) half. Thus empowered, as Don Quixote, he rises from bed, begins "Man of La Mancha" with Sancho and Aldonza supporting him, and dies at the end of the only line in the major mode (ending, "My destiny calls and I go!). But he has in turn inspired *her*; as the Priest intones the Psalm (which begins by echoing the minor-mode ascending triad of "Man of La Mancha"), she insists that her name is Dulcinea. And, finally, Cervantes has inspired the other prisoners, and they (led by Aldonza/Dulcinea) return the gesture, singing "The Impossible Dream" to him as he ascends the stairs to face the Inquisition. This time, the song does not complete itself as originally, but instead, with new lyrics that push only in the direction of outward striving, cycles through repetitions of the first section, ascending by half steps with each "verse" as Cervantes himself ascends the stairs.

♪ 4.32

♪ 4.33

♪ 4.34

If in *Camelot* idealism provides a means to envision a better order, in *Man of La Mancha* it constitutes a defense against reality and, perhaps, a means to face it and to prevail over it. Hence their quite different opening situations:

the one in a fairy-tale operetta, the other in the most oppressive of prisons. Yet, in both shows, idealism fails in a literal sense while succeeding in its mission to inspire—and continues to do so indefinitely. Moreover, in both, remembered song is the ideal vehicle for the ideal, allowing it to continue to inspire each time the song is taken up. Recalling that within German Idealist traditions music emerged as the highest of the arts because of its capacity to evoke both a sense of deep interiority and a sense of the divine, we may note the special capacity of song to both allow us to internalize its encoded emotional and thought patterns and to give external expression to our own emotion and thought. Song, in this sense, and as noted, is an important conduit for negotiating between inner and outer worlds, and it is with this in mind that we turn, more briefly, to our final two musicals, *The Scarlet Pimpernel* and *Once More, with Feeling.*

The Scarlet Pimpernel (1997) did not achieve a long run on Broadway, but it did manage a respectable one after negotiating, like its hero, a series of improbable rescues, each time reopening under a new guise. (I will here refer primarily to the first of its three main versions, since the original song ordering remains, in my view, the most compelling deployment.) A significant factor in its tenacity was the fierce devotion of its fans, many of whom returned to see the show several times and would report back, to e-mail discussion lists and web-based chat rooms, any new changes made (mostly toward the end of its first run, as they prepared the first major overhaul) or particularly effective ad libs by its star, Douglas Sills (see the frontispiece).[23] The strength of the connection between the show and its fans, and its ability to sustain substantial makeovers "on the fly," speak directly to the show's capacity to inspire its audiences in a way that felt both widely shared and intensely personal. There were many specific focal points for the loyalty of the show's fans: besides responding to its charismatic original stars, Douglas Sills, Terrence Mann, and Christine Andreas (or later replacements), many were already fans of the series of books by Baroness Emmuska Orczy or soon became so, or were fans of the various film versions.[24] But the center of their loyalty was the show itself, by Nan Knighton (lyrics and book) and Frank Wildhorn (music). Even the scary intensity of Terrence Mann as Citizen Chauvelin, the risk taking of Douglas Sills's ad libs (as the foppish Percy Blakeney), and the gracious attention its stars lavished on audience members before and after the show seemed extensions of the show's idealism and its inspiring sense of the preciousness of each individual life.[25]

Apart from the air of fervent idealism that surrounded *The Scarlet Pimpernel*, the story explores idealism from a variety of angles. Most centrally, it traces the complicated relationship between one's true self and one's public persona by developing a situation that requires strict secrecy and, on the public side, actual misdirection (part of a "secret-identity" plot device that soon after Orczy's books became extremely popular, particularly in spy novels, comic books, and related genres). This situation is especially familiar to the many Broadway audience members and performers who are closeted gay men maintaining a strict separation between their public and private lives.[26] In fact, *The Scarlet Pimpernel* derives the main part of its humor by precisely inverting the homosexual closet as it conventionally operates: the show's heroes, while privately carrying on clandestine missions at great personal risk, maintain the outer trappings of aristocratic affectation to an exaggerated degree—which means, in effect, that they act "gay" in order to disguise their heroic natures. (The implicit presumption that heroism guarantees heterosexual "normalcy" is, however, belied by the frequency with which their exploits involve dress-up and even cross-dressing.) Moreover, as in *Man of La Mancha*, audiences for *The Scarlet Pimpernel* partake in the actorly dimension of its heroes as *performers* of heroic acts, watching its players transform from one character to another—at least, in demeanor—before their very eyes. The message here is twofold. One may, first of all, be something other than what one seems to be, which allows that all and sundry may, like the "Bounders" that Percy Blakeney (the Scarlet Pimpernel) recruits for his league, redeem themselves through heroic action. And, as a corollary, one may *become* heroic by taking heroic action, which means, in effect, that one may at any moment change one's very nature, or perhaps (depending on one's understanding of how the self is constituted) realize one's true potential. In this sense, it is the transition from inner ideal to outer reality—but not, precisely, the actual realization of ideals—that matters, a transition that can be made only through personal courage and integrity.

If the latter dynamic, of heroism *as performance*, points ahead to the next chapter, where the capacity for musicals to engage with aspects of personal identity will be taken up more directly, *The Scarlet Pimpernel* also engages with tropes of staged idealism resonant with those of *Camelot* and *Man of La Mancha*—most obviously, in the former case, those concerning the triangular relationship among the three leads. Early on, the idealized woman (Marguerite) is cast into shadow, not merely as someone who might betray ideals within the compass of her own person but, very specifically, as someone who poses an active threat, who has already enabled the enemy, and will likely do so again. Important here is how specifically focused Percy's suspicion of her depends on the *results* of her actions, rather than on their full context or her motivation; while those results remove her from idealism's inner circle, what will matter in the end remains for a long time obscurely unreadable: her inner character and her capacity for bravery. Citizen Chauvelin, for his part, is reconceived from his character in the book, continuing a trend that reached an earlier apex with Ian McKellen's Chauvelin in the 1982 film version of the story (for television). In his more modern incarnation, he has become a corrupted idealist who has, ambiguously, either compromised his youthful idealism or remained true to an ideal that was tragically unworthy of the commitment he has given it. Both Percy and Marguerite must endure a troubling disjuncture between appearance and perceived reality: Percy perceives nothing in Marguerite's person to contradict his early idealization of her, yet has learned that she has betrayed a mutual friend to his death, whereas Marguerite continues to see glimpses of the Percy she married even though the persona he presents to all, including her, seems devoid of redeeming features. Both feel betrayed by realities that deny a projected ideal without fully effacing it. With Chauvelin, the connection to Marguerite is more directly idealistic but located in the past (the early stages of the French Revolution), before those shared ideals were translated into the horrific realities of the guillotine and mass murder. Thus, albeit on different scales of culpability and consequence, Chauvelin and Marguerite are implicated both in earlier idealistic motivations and current realities of betrayal and bloodshed.

The conversion of Baroness Orczy's story into an idealist-based love triangle is to some extent a response to conventions of the dramatic musical, in which issues that are raised and resolved in the context of a love story carry more dramatic import than those that are not. Moreover, making Chauvelin a past lover of Marguerite helps give a plausible idealist basis to his obsessive pursuit of death and destruction within a revolution gone bad—even if, in the end, that idealism turns out to have degenerated into a mere pose, to be dropped at the moment of truth. Central to the conversion of the story's central dynamic is the resulting capacity for the show to present its situations and conflicts *in song*; indeed, arguably, the fact that *The Scarlet Pimpernel* was an album of songs long before there was a book explains both how fully those songs advance the key elements of the story and why the framing story and its presentation could be so extensively reworked at a later stage. In the end, the idealist component of the show is almost entirely advanced through song, quite often obliquely, that is, through the songs that express the perspectives of the participants in the love triangle on each other.

Linking many of the songs in the show is a rising-fifth melodic figure introduced at the beginning of the overture and used as a germinating gesture for many of the show's songs. Within the rather concise overture, the figure is a distant horn call, a call to action that is then responded to with a foregrounded show of pomp, converting the horn call into a parade tune, the so-called Pimpernel fanfare, which will appear as a kind of punctuation throughout the show. This fanfare may be heard as either a heroic response ♪4.35 to the call or a pompous parody of it—a useful ambiguity, given the double life of the show's heroes; thus, one of its signal appearances is at the end of "The Creation of Man," a song devoted to the witty foppery that the audience knows is serving as a cloak for heroic idealism. Early in the show, the ♪4.36 germinating motive forms the basis for the crazed obsession of the Parisian mob in "Madame Guillotine," which merges idealism and revenge-driven bloodlust, and soon thereafter helps give Percy and Marguerite's love song, "Believe," an underpinning of idealism.[27] But the core idealist profile associ- ♪4.37 ated with the motive takes shape mainly in the succession of songs that leads ♪4.38 Percy to form the League of the Scarlet Pimpernel, so as to avenge the death of his friend St. Cyr (which he believes to have been engineered by Marguerite). In presenting the formation of the league as a central dramatic element, the show responds directly to the affinity of musicals for such idealist trajectories; in all earlier versions, the Scarlet Pimpernel is already active at the beginning of the story.

In Percy's "Prayer," the rising-fifth motive seems to embody the pain of a lost ideal, at the beginning of the first two "A" phrases within an extended AABA structure ("No, stay. . . . She's gone"); in the course of the song, the motive transmutes into more wrenching two-word phrases ("Come back! . . . Oh Lord, . . . God, no!"). In "Into the Fire," which begins with the horn call from the overture, Percy then answers his earlier "Prayer" with a rousing call to action replete with multiple repetitions of both the melodic fifth (in italics) and transfiguring moments in which an arrival harmony shifts unexpectedly to the flat sixth of the melodic pitch (in bold); along the way, the meter shifts from the common time (duple meter) of the opening to a "traveling" 6/8 meter, a shift emblematic of the difference between the moment of inspiration and the process of taking action on that basis (asterisks mark the transitional phrase):

♪4.39

♪4.40

> David walked into the *valley* with a stone clutched in his hand.
> He was only a boy, but he knew someone must take a **stand**.
> There will always be a *valley*, always mountains one must scale.
> There will *always be perilous waters which someone must* **sail!**
>
> Into valleys, into *waters*, into jungles, into hell!
> Let us ride, let us ride home again with a story to **tell**.
> Into darkness, into *danger*, into storms that rip the night!
> Don't give in, don't give up, but give thanks for the glorious **fight!**

The shift to the flat sixth, a device that continues throughout the rest of the song, is a mainstay of both the "classical" tradition and Broadway, but is here especially redolent of its frequent use in popular music, where it provides both an electrifying moment of harmonic transport and the comfort of a cliché. If the latter feature threatens to cheapen the overall effect of the song, that potential danger is mitigated by the framing structure of the Broadway inspirational number (which, to be sure, carries its own tendency toward clichéd gestures), especially as that structure is enhanced by several things: the rollicking melodic figures in the second half of the song's main structure, borrowed from the swashbuckling films of Errol Flynn and others ("You can tremble, you can fear it, but keep your fighting spirit alive, boys!"); the transformation midway through the song of Percy's library into the heroic prow of a ship (especially impressive in the first two versions of the show); and most important, the dynamic of individual and group, in which Percy rouses the Bounders to join him in the song, but then rises above them at each climax ("Never hold back your step for a moment! Never doubt that your courage will grow!").[28] But the harmonic device also stands out as an emblem of Frank Wildhorn's personal brand of idealism, which involves, as he has explained in numerous interviews, reinfusing Broadway with the

♪4.41

music of its more youthful audience—nearly the opposite impulse as that followed in *Camelot*.

The parallel, triangular situation of the three leads relative to each other is laid out within their individual songs, and more broadly in "The Riddle" (see figure 4.3), a waltz song that serves as first-act finale, where it fails, emblematically, to resolve itself satisfactorily into a single couple. Chauvelin's "Falcon in the Dive" is a song of embittered pride, ambiguous about whether that bitterness is leftover animus against the aristocracy or results from a prideful denial of the realities of the French Revolution as it has degenerated into blood-soaked tyranny. The image of the falcon, as a seemingly independent bird of prey that is nonetheless servant to a human, generally aristocratic master, aptly embodies the contradictions of his position. Figuring into this mix, of jealousy tinged with an embittered idealism, are key earlier roles of Terrence Mann, whose Chauvelin channeled both his Javert (from *Les Misérables*, 1987) and Beast (from *Beauty and the Beast*, 1994). But the restless fervor of the song's basic motives, from which the soaring and swooping "falcon" lines emerge, briefly recalls an important repeated phrase from "Into the Fire" ("He was only a boy, but he knew someone must take a stand" and later), the musical phrase that provides the pivot for Percy's move to 6/8 (see above). This connection is reinforced in "Falcon in the Dive" with a partly parallel lyric (overlapping musical phrase in bold): "How the devil do I **ever prevail when I'm only a man?** / But I'll **never be duped by this scurrilous phantom again.**" The restless energies of "Falcon" return to mark "Where's the Girl?" as uniquely Chauvelin's, but both the song's perspective and its use of the rising-fifth motive in the title phrase ("Where's **the girl?** / Where's **the girl** with **the blaze** in **her eyes?**") link Chauvelin indelibly to Marguerite and Percy, whose "When I Look at You" (sung by each in turn) stands similarly confused by discrepancies regarding a former beloved, and uses the rising-fifth motive in a similarly multiple deployment: "When I **look at you,** / What I **always see** / Is the **face of someone else** / **Who once** belonged to me." And the motive returns in "The Riddle" (figure 4.3) to set the crux of their idealist dilemma:

♩4.42
♩4.43

♩4.44
♩4.45
♩4.46

> Can **I trust** you? Should you **trust me** too? . . .
> 'Til there **comes a** day
> When we **sell our** souls away! . . .
> And **only** fools follow **golden** rules. . . .
> We all are caught in the middle
> Of one long treacherous riddle
> Of **who trusts** who,
> Maybe **I'll trust** you.
> But can **you trust** me?
> Wait and see!

But the latter song's energy comes mainly from its obsessive waltz idiom, which, despite its romantic potential, simply whirls on without resolution. It is this obsessive waltz idiom that is harnessed again in the second act to

Figure 4.3. In "The Riddle," Sir Percy Blakeney (the Scarlet Pimpernel, played by Douglas Sills), stands at the apex of a triangle, between his wife, Marguerite (Christine Andreas), and Citizen Chauvelin (Terrence Mann)—and below Madame Guillotine, who looms above all their heads. (Photograph © Joan Marcus, used by permission.)

set up the final sequence of events; thus, "Storybook" begins by recalling, in waltz rhythm, the musical phrase that "Falcon" shares with "Into the Fire" (most explicitly later in the lyric, with the key line "Come let's believe love can be just as sweet as it seems"), proceeds thence to demand its "storybook ending," and then withholds that ending by concluding in French. Also key ♪4.47 to the final resolution is Marguerite's connection to her brother, Armand, in "You Are My Home," which seems to resolve the rising-fifth puzzlements of "Where's the Girl?" and "When I Look at You" in its title phrase, by first stating the motive (in bold) and then inverting it (in italics): ♪4.48

> You **are my home**. You **make me strong**.
> And in this world of strangers, I belong to someone.
> You are all *I know*. You're all *I have*. I won't let go.[29]

But the ending itself must satisfy a conflicting array of imperatives. Clearly, its default resolution is to follow the original book and the 1934 film version, already familiar to audiences; yet, to do so directly would disappoint. Moreover, while "Storybook" pushes hard for a happy ending, as does the comedic tone of the scenes involving Percy and his men as foppish wits, the idealist tradition in musicals demands, emblematically, that the ideal remain unrealized. Meanwhile, in resolving a central strand of the story, "You Are My Home" merely leaves options for the final denouement wide open. In some ways, the actual ending, which uses trickery and humor to rescue us from tragedy, pulls back from the idealist imperative; yet, arguably, the show's amply demonstrated capacity to inspire audiences depends heavily on Percy's defeating Chauvelin in the end.

The show's central image of the scarlet pimpernel—a "humble wayside flower," which, though seemingly small and insignificant, turns out to make all the difference—deftly suggests both sides of its connotative divide, between escapist foppery and individual heroic action taken against the inexorable tide of historical events. But, like Percy's voice rising above the tumult of "Into the Fire," it also privileges the individual essence—the soul—over both the group and possible mortal consequences. "Into the Fire" carries a similar doubleness of import, implicitly both evoking the individual spark of inspiring idealism and instilling the courage required to carry that spark against the "fire" of a hostile, unforgiving world. Both *Camelot* and *Man of La Mancha* also threaten fire as the consequence of idealism; thus, Arthur's idealistic order, faced with the ideal love between Lancelot and Guenevere, demands that the latter be burned at the stake, while both Cervantes's manuscript of *Don Quixote* and his very person potentially face the flames. Within the idealist equation, humans stand figuratively between Heaven and Hell, nursing the spark of divine inspiration from the former as protection against the threatening, undying flames of the latter. And such is precisely the situation explored, with an intriguing twist, in our final example, however unlikely a choice it may seem initially.

Once More, with Feeling (television, 2001) is the much celebrated "musical" episode from the sixth season of *Buffy the Vampire Slayer*, a television series with a large cult following that overlaps significantly with the fan base for musicals. The conceit for the episode is that a demon summoned by a member of Buffy's cohort, a kind of "Lord of the Dance," causes everyone to behave as though in a musical, expressing her or his innermost feelings in the form of a musical number, replete with all the elements of MERM (Musically Enhanced Reality Mode; see the discussion in chapter 2): singing and dancing, with nondiegetic instrumental support, and so on. This conception was especially audacious considering the starting points: a weekly television dramatic series in which very few of the principals were known for their singing or dancing ability and whose creator, Joss Whedon (writer for many episodes, including this one), was similarly inexperienced as a songwriter. Nevertheless, the episode ranks as one of the most admired in the series; intriguingly, one of its close competitors in that regard is "Hush" (1999), an episode from the fourth season in which everyone is rendered mute. Both shows address the problematic transition from "inside" to "outside," understood as a process of communication in "Hush," and as a matter of personal motivation or self-realization in *Once More, with Feeling*.

One of the bases for the affinity between *Buffy the Vampire Slayer* and the musical, as a genre, is the seemingly pervasive tendency toward doubleness that runs through the latter, in which people and ideas signify within several discourses at once, through metaphor and a web of allusive connections. As most *Buffy* aficionados know, the series also trades heavily in metaphor, often involving sexuality (no stranger to the metaphoric repertory of musicals) and other issues relevant to its basic coming-of-age narrative framework. But more central to this chapter's concerns is *Buffy*'s strong idealist bent. Even in conventional terms, its characters are involved in an ongoing noble struggle against the powers and creatures of Hell; more subtly, following an important strand of German Idealism, the series habitually draws a direct connection between those exterior forces and the demons *within* its characters, through which the former are sometimes empowered and even given birth. Almost pervasively, *Buffy* is already about the problematic transition between "inside" and "outside"; that the series should look to the genre of the musical when such issues become particularly intense reflects the strong association of the musical with inspirational idealism in the popular imagination.

The situation in season six, which *Once More, with Feeling* explores, contains many separate threads, and each of them comes to a head within its musical numbers. The central thread involves Buffy herself, who has died (for the second time) and recently been brought back to life through Willow's magic. As the show will delineate, Buffy's resurrection has not been as joyous as might have been anticipated, and the ambivalence of her situation is reflected in several other ambivalences. Giles, the parental figure for the group, sees his own role as increasingly obstructing Buffy's emergence as an independent adult. Willow has "bewitched" Tara, in the process not only becoming her lover and her source of empowerment, but also exerting an increasing control over her mind (through casting a spell of forgetfulness after an earlier quarrel). Lovers Xander and Anya have become engaged, yet harbor extensive reservations about each other. Spike, the would-be reformed vampire, is caught between his strong attraction to Buffy and her seeming indifference to him. And Dawn, Buffy's younger sister, feels neglected and uncared for (as always). To some extent, the musical numbers simply lay out feelings the characters in the show had not previously been able to express openly or even perhaps to admit to themselves. For example, in "I'll Never Tell," a cutesy "list song" sung by Xander and Anya, they confide their misgivings about each other in specific detail. Yet, in the context of this show, the number also underscores the distinction between private and public, since they are unable to admit such misgivings *except* through a musical number that seems to both state an unpleasantry and take it back within the same gesture—hence the key lyric "I'll never tell," the Cole Porter–inspired verbal fencing between the couples reminiscent of "You're the Top," and the bubbly cheerfulness of the tune and its reassuring retro accompaniment.[30]   ♪ 4.49

Within the central thread, the basic problem is that Buffy has been rescued not from a hellish afterlife as her companions imagine but from Heaven; now back on earth, she understandably lacks the inspiring spark that should support her calling. This is the premise laid out in Buffy's "Going through the Motions," the first song of the episode, during which it also becomes clear that the spark she is missing has a sexual dimension; thus, when a hunky victim she has just rescued turns to her, singing, "How can I repay . . . ?" she turns away with a shrug, interrupting him with a dismissive "whatever" that is impeccably timed to rhyme with her last line, "Sleepwalk through my life's endeavor?" The match of a choreographed musical number with the idea of "routine" amounts almost to a bad pun, but the deadpan, robotic timing of her lyric and her moves—for example, using a wooden stake to dispose of a vampire on the line "Nothing seems to penetrate my heart"—is also directly expressive of her detachment. The latter line is a key one, referring specifically to her lack of inspiration, and it is given special emphasis through comically literal visual support, yet she neither responds to the success of her conquest (not even looking at her victim as she drives the stake home) nor takes any pleasure in her own witticism. Moreover, we identify easily with her detachment, since the tidy choreography of the number makes it abundantly clear that nothing much is actually at stake (so to speak) in the sequence. In the next number, "I've Got a Theory / Bunnies /   ♪ 4.50 We're Together," however, something *is* at stake, and personal involvement from nearly all the characters is abundantly evident, as when Xander forgets himself, inadvertently offending Willow and Tara ("It could be witches"), and Anya flies into an extreme metal-based digression involving her irrational fear of bunnies. But Buffy starts her contribution to the song apatheti-   ♪ 4.51

cally—"I've got a theory, it doesn't matter"—and then has to work hard to reassure the others, who join her, relieved, in obviously phony rhetoric about facing things together. Even Giles is reassured by the end of her solo (specifically, by Buffy's wry joke, "Hey, I've died twice!"), but we know better: for

♪4.52   her, nothing really matters.

As the episode constructs the relationship between its demon-inspired situation and the way "inspiration" plays out according to the conventions of the musical, three key elements, laid out separately within the musical numbers that set up the show's basic situation, are brought to a resolution in the closing numbers. First, the sexual component that often attaches to the act of singing in musicals is most aggressively advanced by Tara, whose "Under Your Spell" traces an associative chain of connections leading from magic to belief to sex—which, as it happens, is not all that different from the progression traced in *Camelot*, from Merlin to Arthur, and thence to Lancelot and Guenevere. The second half of the song—the transition from belief to sex—is especially straightforward, if never quite explicit: after a fair amount of suggestive language and body positioning during the bridge, the ending performs a deft verbal substitution, so that "You make me believe" (which ends the first half of the song) becomes "You make me complete," which Tara repeats, in receding waves, with special emphasis on the first syllable of the final word. Dialogue that immediately follows the number further tightens the metaphoric circle between "singing" and sex, when Xander, resentful that Tara and Willow have so blatantly gone off together, leaving him and the others to pursue the investigation, stops himself from a direct accusation (since the younger Dawn is present): "I'll bet they're—(seeing

♪4.53   Dawn)—singing. They're probably singing right now."

The second core element centers around the metaphor of fire as it pertains to life and death in an idealist context. Shortly after "Under Your Spell," we meet the unnamed demon (identified as "Sweet" in the script) as he watches one of his victims dance himself to death. This is, of course, a standard trope of fairy tales (cf. "The Red Shoes" and some versions of "Snow White");[31] here, it imparts a pointed warning about the coveted spark of inspiration: sparks can ignite fires, and fires can rage out of control and destroy. Significantly, the dancer is (in Giles's words) "burnt up from inside"; it is thus the inner spark itself that poses the danger in this case. Because this development suddenly casts all the episode's musical outbursts of feeling into the category of "life-threatening" (as captured in Xander's succinct summation: "singing and dancing and burning and dying"), it provides an important clarification regarding the episode's plot. But it also complicates things, since what Sweet provides is precisely what Buffy seeks. Spike's "Rest in Peace" makes a similar point in reverse, as his spark of sexual desire for Buffy threatens to consume him and so is to be resisted (and with it, the conventions of musical

♪4.54   comedy), especially since his desire is apparently unreciprocated. Sweet's own song, "What You Feel"—sung to Dawn, who (once again) has gotten her wish to become the center of attention—makes it clear that his power depends absolutely on the inner spark of his victims, that he is, figuratively, the demon whom everyone summons when she or he seeks to unlock that certain inner fire:

♪4.55

> I come from the imagination . . .
> I'm the heart of swing. I'm the twist and shout.
> When you gotta sing, when you gotta let it out. . . .
> Something's cookin', I'm at the griddle.
> I bought Nero his very first fiddle.

That Dawn is not the one who has summoned him is clear enough in their grotesque mismatch of dancing styles, with her "innocent" balletic dancing set against the threatening sexuality of Sweet's tap / soft-shoe. The fact that Sweet is played by a black man (Hinton Battle, who plays the part in "red-face") "taps" uncomfortably into a whole realm of familiar tropes associated with jazz, popular dance styles, and the dynamic between blacks and whites in American culture generally; thus, blacks are often understood to provide whites with access to their own more primitive sexual natures, but at some risk to their souls.[32]

Related to this element (what we might call the "inner fire" idealist trope) is the third: the idea that the "ideal" is by nature personal and private. Accordingly, at least in a strict sense, it is actually impossible for someone to "inspire" someone else, even though inspiration is often conceived—and experienced by the audiences for musicals—in precisely this way (especially when inspiration is sexualized, as it often is in musicals). Giles's "Standing" makes this point fairly explicitly, as voiced from the familiar position of the parent who must allow his child, grown too dependent on him, to stand on her own. Here, however, the setting and filming say at least as much as the words: during a "training" session, he begins to sing while he starts to throw knives at Buffy, an aggressive gesture that provides the means to separate the two into different spheres. Thus, Buffy's defensive maneuvers pull back into slow motion (briefly recalling *The Matrix*, from 1999, although action sequences in slow motion had long since become a cliché), and from that moment, and throughout the rest of the song, slow motion becomes her mode, while Giles remains in real time. This separation into two private realms within the same space then becomes the basis for a combined reprise of "Under Your Spell" and "Standing" (though not fully realized as a combination song), where Giles joins with Tara, who has been led to realize that she can no longer depend on Willow for her own individuating spark. Meanwhile, their counterparts, Buffy and Willow, remain in private conversation, blithely oblivious to them.

♪4.56

♪4.57

The latter two elements of "inspiration"—the separateness of the self and the double nature of fire, as either empowering or destructive—form the basis for "Walk through the Fire," which launches the denouement. Giles sets the number in motion by sending Buffy out alone to save Dawn from the demon, thus splitting the group into separate constituencies: Buffy

Figure 4.4. Nearing the climactic scene of *Once More, with Feeling*, Buffy Summers (Sarah Michelle Gellar) sings "I want the fire back" during the first span of "Walk through the Fire," which will develop from this simple beginning to present four different, musically overlapping perspectives on her upcoming showdown with the demon Sweet: those of Buffy, Spike, Sweet, and the remainder of Buffy's cohort (Giles, Xander, Anya, Willow, and Tara).

herself, Spike, and the group led by Giles. As the number progresses, each of these, plus Sweet, offers a separate perspective on the upcoming battle (recalling not only "Tonight" in *West Side Story* but also "One Day More" in the 1987 *Les Misérables* and the "La Resistance / Tomorrow Night" medley in the 1999 film *South Park: Bigger Longer & Uncut*). Buffy's contribution is, spiritually, a continuation of "Going through the Motions" (see figure 4.4):

♫ 4.58

> I touch the fire, and it freezes me.
> I look into it, and it's black.
> Why can't I feel?
> My skin should crack and peel.
> I want the fire back.

As in her earlier number, which she will later reprise in counterpoint as the number builds in complexity, she adopts the "purposeful-striding" visual motive described in chapter 2 in relation to *Moulin Rouge*, a gesture that should portend both fate and personal involvement, but in this case is held back to a more detached level, with "fate" transmuting into a sense of resignation. As Giles's group and (separately) a comically ambivalent Spike determine to lend their support after all, and Sweet anticipates their arrival, tension builds through the combination of contrapuntal complexity (both musical and visual) and withheld harmonic arrival. Then, just before the parties converge, we finally hear a cadence ("Let it **burn**," with fire trucks speeding by in the background), but it is a deceptive cadence, diverted to the flat sixth, resolving to the tonic only after several repetitions, just as Buffy kicks in the door to the Bronze, the club that Sweet has taken over as his temporary earthly lair. By this point, even though Buffy is unaware that her friends have rallied to join her in battle, their contribution to the song helps fuel the energy of that kick. This kind of spiritual osmosis—a species of MERM—is endemic to musicals, always evident whenever an unseen orchestra lends its support to a singer or (in films, especially) a backup chorus adds its voices (an effect already exploited in "Under Your Spell"). Here, there is no actual connection, or even an imagined one—Buffy still believes she is entirely on her own—yet the growing tide of *musical* support nevertheless has a palpable effect on her, as she gradually quickens her step and then delivers her kick with a vehemence that her emotional ennui would not otherwise sustain (and *Buffy* aficionados will remember that, back in the first season of the series, Buffy herself determined that this very door was too strong to break down). ♩4.59

Buffy's need for the supporting idealism of Giles's group is thus shown to matter in a way possible only in musicals, counterbalancing and, in this moment, overcoming her lack of an inner spark. Clearly, Buffy's transition back to life has made having such a spark and being able to connect with others dual sites of impairment, opposite sides of the same damaged coin. In Buffy's subsequent confrontation with Sweet, in her "Something to Sing About," the title lyric makes it clear that she seeks something both exterior to her being ("Give me something . . .") and an internal capacity (". . . to sing about"). And, when Giles and his group arrive, his deadpan instruction—"She needs backup. Anya. Tara"—works on a deeper level than its surface pun, which equates vocal/dance backup with the more conventional backup Tara and Anya might provide in a fight. It is late in this song that ♩4.60 Buffy, for the first time, tells the group that Willow has brought her back from Heaven, not Hell, and it is an extremely isolating moment; suddenly, as Tara and Anya fade away, her musical style shifts to include a sagging chromaticism reminiscent of Spike's vocal idiom in "Rest in Peace" (the bold-italic combination indicates a chromatic slippage): ♩4.61
♩4.62

> (Buffy, in "Something to Sing About"):
>> There was no pain.
>> No **fear**, no doubt, 'til *they* pulled me out of **heav***en*.
> (Spike, in "Rest in Peace"):
>> I can lay my body down, but I can't **find** my sweet *release*. . . .
>> I **know I should go**-*oh*. . . .

While most of "Something to Sing About," like much else in the episode, is musically generic (and deliberately so, especially in setting Buffy's "through

the motions" mood), it is also schizophrenic, breaking into a chaotic "dou-
ble-time" riff for her fight sequences, shifting among three different meters
(4/4, 7/8, and 6/8). It is during these breaks that she seems figuratively to
"catch fire," and it becomes clear that she will soon *literally* catch fire as she
launches into a final extended break. But, of course, she is rescued. Spike,
having been duly summoned through Buffy's death-evoking shift in musical
style, takes his cue and stops her subsequent dance just as she starts to smol-
der, then sings her sagging chromatic figure back to her, substituting "living"
for "heaven" on the key figure: "Life's not a song. / Life isn't bliss, *life* is
just this: It's liv*ing*.

♫4.63

In this way, *Once More, with Feeling* resolves the apparent oxymoron of
an *imparted*—and thus secondhand—inspiration in two ways: first in terms
of group support, which proves inadequate, but then in terms of sexual connection, which works. It is only Spike who in the end can save Buffy, both
because their perspectives are similar (they've both been dead) and because
he loves her. It is he alone, who "burns" when he doesn't want to, who is
able to answer the call of one who wants to burn but can't. In parallel to
this double presentation of support, which moves from the energizing group
to a sexual connection, the resolution that then takes shape (after Sweet
concedes defeat) initially seems particularly uninspired, as the group, now
saddled with a full set of well-articulated problems, with none of them
solved, starts up a "group sing" finale on the lackluster topic of "Where Do
We Go from Here?"[33] so that it is with some relief that we follow a disgusted
Spike outside. But as Spike leaves, Buffy follows him, having also left the
group; as they sing brief reprises of their signature tunes, intertwining with
telling verbal parallels ("I touch the fire. . . . But I just want to feel" and "I
died. . . . But you can make me feel") and leading to a kiss, the group's final
cadence suddenly "works," since it now supports (if generically) a genuine
resolution in the foreground, conceived specifically in terms of the themes
advanced in *this* musical.

♫4.64

♫4.65

Once More, with Feeling is, of course, more a parody of a musical than a
"true" musical, much like *Little Mary Sunshine* was more a parody of operetta than a "true" operetta (see chapter 1). Yet both are also *affectionate*
parodies, fully enamored of what they parody even as they mock it. As such,
both shows adhere fully to the conventions of the genres they parody; moreover, they provide precisely the same pleasures, if more modestly, since they
honor rather than simply burlesque the core elements of their respective
genres. But *Once More, with Feeling* has one feature that *Little Mary Sunshine* does not have, central to the way it advances the theme of idealism
and inspiration: its characters are acutely aware that they are performing in
a musical. This immediately makes them more like us than is typical for a
musical, in situational terms; moreover, as an extension of this, we may assume that their performance is driven by what they (and we) already know
happens in musicals. As noted, one of the reasons that musicals are so good

at advancing idealist themes is that we may more easily take their idealist substance away with us, in terms that may be counted both internal and external, by joining in their idealism(s) as we sing their songs. In *Once More, with Feeling*, even more than in *Man of La Mancha*, we observe this as a learning process undertaken by the characters in the show, who demonstrate for us the potential benefits (and occasional pitfalls) of assuming roles in a musical. Above all, we see Buffy being empowered by song, even though song might also destroy her.

Even more subtly, and certainly more daringly, the episode strongly suggests that the fire that truly animates her is not divine but diabolical; thus, Buffy returns from Heaven devoid of spark and is restored to genuine "life" only through the pooled agency of a vampire and a demon. How true this might be for inspiration and idealism more generally may be argued (and perhaps resolved through the conceit that Satan stole his fire from Heaven in the first place), but the link between the empowering fire within and the threatening fire without is a strong one, especially when reinforced by song. But then again, "inner fire" is not the only thing about ourselves that musicals help illuminate and shape, for all aspects of self-formation, to the extent that they are performed, are susceptible to their seductively offered instruction.

For Further Consideration

Carousel (1945), *Brigadoon* (1947), *My Fair Lady* (1956), *The Sound of Music* (1959), *Anyone Can Whistle* (1964), *It's a Bird . . . It's a Plane . . . It's Superman* (1966), *Jesus Christ Superstar* (1971), *Godspell* (1971/1976), *Pippin* (1972), *Les Misérables* (1985), *The Phantom of the Opera* (1988), *Joseph and the Amazing Technicolor Dreamcoat* (1993), and *Ragtime* (1998)

See Also

Regarding the legends of King Arthur and their modern enactments, see especially Geoffrey Ashe's *The Discovery of King Arthur*; James J. Wilhelm and Laila Zamuelis Gross's *The Romance of Arthur*; Elizabeth S. Sklar and Donald L. Hoffman's *King Arthur in Popular Culture*; and Kevin J. Harty's *King Arthur on Film: New Essays on Arthurian Cinema*.

Regarding *Camelot*, see chapter 1 of Scott Miller's *Deconstructing Harold Hill*; chapters 14–16 of Gene Lees's *Inventing Champagne*; "Camelot" in Alan Jay Lerner's *The Street Where I Live*; pp. 160–69 in Stacy Wolf's *A Problem Like Maria*; pp. 215–20 in Joseph P. Swain's *The Broadway Musical*; chapter 2 in Ethan Mordden's *Open a New Window*; and pp. 316–28 in Stephen Citron's *The Wordsmiths: Oscar Hammerstein 2nd and Alan Jay Lerner*.

Regarding *Man of La Mancha*, see chapter 10 of Scott Miller's *From Assassins to West Side Story*; pp. 238–41 in John Bush Jones's *Our Musicals, Ourselves*; and pp. 200–204 in Ethan Mordden's *Open a New Window*.

Regarding *Once More, with Feeling*, see the introductory material to the combined script and vocal score (listed in the appendix) and pp. 86–89 in Candace Havens's *Joss Whedon: The Genius Behind Buffy*.

Gender and Sexuality

THE AMERICAN MUSICAL—both inherently and because of the genre's historical development—has proven to be an especially fruitful venue for exploring the dynamic interplay of gender roles and sexuality. Thus, for example, to ground larger themes within personal relationships, a musical might "gender" those themes according to audience expectations and preexisting stereotypes; in chapter 4, I discussed how that has tended to work with the theme of idealism, especially in alliance with codes of chivalry. And, only slightly less often, musicals have deliberately challenged audience expectations in one way or another, making a space for exploring alternative formulations. In this, not surprisingly, they typically run parallel to contemporary societal developments, whether by engaging with emerging ideas and attitudes (either negatively or positively) or by attempting to advance alternatives more aggressively, through bringing them out in the open within a mainstream venue of demonstrated persuasive power.

Indeed, it is the nature of their persuasive power that makes musicals an important site for exploring many aspects of personal identity, since—as noted frequently in earlier chapters—musicals provide material for *performance*, material that may be performed not only by the cast of the show but also, eventually, by those in the audience who might want to appropriate or adapt that material to their own needs. Gender roles and sexuality are, above all, *performed* attributes of personal identity and so constitute a central dimension of how people are defined, both onstage and off.[1] In musicals—that is, *on* stage—frictions between larger themes and the individual characters who embody them are frequently highlighted, providing nuance to those themes and sometimes calling them into question, but always imparting a sense of immediacy to the presented persona *as a person*. Moreover, the specific actress or actor who performs each character will matter tremendously, in a reciprocating relationship, so that the performer's public persona and the specific characters he or she plays will inflect each other in intimate ways. Thus, Julie Andrews's Guenevere in *Camelot*, grounded in both the part as written and her stage persona at that time (post–*My Fair Lady* but pre–*Mary Poppins* and pre–*Sound of Music*), was to a large extent—probably necessarily, and certainly usefully—a modern sensibility blended into an existing mytho-historical character, truly believable as neither but providing more grounding for each perspective than could be achieved through a stricter allegiance to one over the other.

Nearly always in stage portrayals, and especially in musicals, exaggeration is central to how specific attributes of a character or theme are presented, especially regarding gender and sexuality. At the same time, modes of exaggeration (even putting aside the dimension of camp) point vividly and sometimes divisively to different constituencies, among both performers and audience members. Exaggeration in performance has tended, historically, to remove women performers from the accepted boundaries of respectability, often tainting them—if only through the emphasis on personal display that often results from such exaggeration—with associations of sexual license and promiscuity. For male performers as well, this element of unseemly personal display, which is nearly endemic to performance in a musical, not only may lead to presumptions about a performer's promiscuity (historically not as problematic for a man), but also may call into question his "masculinity" (read: heterosexuality); within the more closeted theatrical environment that held sway until the later decades of the twentieth century, presumptions of male homosexuality carried at least the same taint as an actress's presumed promiscuity, so that for a man a reputation for heterosexual promiscuity could actually be an asset, simply because it shielded him from imputations of homosexuality. For an audience, exaggeration in performance, especially in terms of gender roles and sexuality, has functioned in at least three ways. For some, it has provided a liberating model, a demonstration of how one might more aggressively control and challenge the boundaries that traditionally circumscribe one's own gendered, sexual self. For others, it has provided a voyeuristic glimpse into alternatives that may be both relished and—precisely because of the element of exaggeration in their presentation—satisfyingly put aside as morally flawed, however intriguing. And, for still others, exaggerations in these dimensions created a special realm in which performance as such was privileged, sliding easily into camp but not necessarily so; this special realm was centrally important for many closeted gay men, especially pre-Stonewall (that is, before 1969), and became a particular locus of gay affiliation thereafter.

Aside from the ways in which musicals, in general terms, emphasize gender and sexuality through performance and presentation, many musicals take up these elements as particular themes, and it is with these that we will be primarily concerned in this chapter. In broadly historical terms, musicals of this kind have shifted focus, especially since Stonewall, from a preoccupation with what we might think of as "bad girls" to "bad boys," that is, from stigmatized female roles and modes of sexual expression to stigmatized male roles and modes of sexual expression, generally (but not always) reduced to licentious behavior or display for women and the suggestion of homosexuality for men. Standard tropes of representation of sexual deviance in twentieth-century America, in fiction and film as well as onstage, have included some combination of the following, generally drawing to some extent on each:

1. the partial celebration of such alternatives for their spirit of
   independence and liberating effect;
2. a fostering of increased understanding of alternativity, by encouraging audiences to look beyond presumptively defining
   features to the mixtures of good things and bad things that
   define all human beings, considered as individuals; and
3. the ultimate punishment of alternativity.

The latter, in particular, is a distressingly consistent component of the mix,
common to most dramatizations of sexual alternativity and carrying with it
a number of possible rationales and ramifications.

Within mainstream narrative fictional genres in America, bad girls and
homosexuals (especially the latter) tend to die in the end, often but not always as a token of their redemption. There are, of course, exceptions, but
these tend to affirm rather than deny the imperative; thus, if *Camelot*'s
Guenevere is spared the flames for her sexual sins (which are of the heart
only, since they remain unconsummated in the original musical), she is severely rebuked and punished, as is Aldonza in *Man of La Mancha*. More
typical are the fates suffered by Satine in *Moulin Rouge* (see chapter 2),
Frenchy in the 1939 film *Destry Rides Again*, and countless homosexuals as
portrayed in films, even before their homosexuality could be openly identified as such.[2] Often, it is hard to tell precisely *why* they die, only that they
generally *do* die, with their deaths serving as a kind of dramatic purging.
Specific rationales, often only implied, range from

1. a sense of divine justice, since these characters have sinned
   against Heaven and/or nature (thus, perhaps, as a moral lesson, along the lines of "see what happens"); to
2. a sense of realism, since sexual "deviants" of this kind cannot
   survive as such in their respective worlds (thus, perhaps, as an
   object lesson, along the lines of "see how far we still have to
   go"); or, perhaps, to
3. a sense of redemptive Christian sacrifice or saintly martyrdom,
   especially when such characters otherwise occupy the moral
   center of their narratives, so that they die, as did Christ, for
   the sins of others.

Intriguingly, within the latter rationale alternative sexuality functions
much as idealism often does (see chapter 4), especially when that alternative
sexuality is understood to be an essential component of the self, as is increasingly the case in the second half of the twentieth century. Thus, any idealism
centered around the imperative to remain true to one's own self and vision
must logically accord expressed sexuality the highest of moral standings,
even though such consistency flies in the face of specific moral codes (such
as fundamentalist Christianity). In any case, the above mix of rationales is

not always easy to sort out, and probably often deliberately so, since confusion in this regard allows the same artifact to be appreciated and understood from a similar variety of often incompatible perspectives. This is especially true in Hays-era films, which officially had to punish their sinners, or in musicals, which have historically played both sides of a number of attitudinal fences, many of the latter operating on the boundaries that separate diverse categories associated with gender and sexuality.

I have selected the specific musicals in this chapter in response to a number of considerations. I have sought a historical spread across the decades following World War II, a time frame that traverses the historical divide of Stonewall, after which homosexuality comes to some extent to displace feminine promiscuity as the principal carrier for this kind of theme. I have also sought a spread regarding how these issues are understood and dealt with, so that none of the chosen musicals should seem to resemble any of the others too closely. And I have used this opportunity to find a place in this two-volume study for musicals by important contributors to the genre I may have otherwise overlooked (thus, especially, Irving Berlin, Jule Styne, and Cy Coleman). Among the early grouping, *Annie Get Your Gun* (1946) addresses gender roles in charting a path from a "state of nature" to civilization, with its heroine adopting a variety of potential identities along the way; *Gypsy* (1959) explores the ways in which theatrical presentation, and self-presentation more generally, contribute to the formation of self, in the context of a feminized oedipal conflict; and *Sweet Charity* (1966) takes almost the opposite tack from *Gypsy*, first naturalizing identity by casting it as a given thing and inescapable, and then exploring the ways in which that essentialized identity connects and doesn't connect to its outward performance, the visible dimensions of role-playing and expressed sexuality.

Before we then cross the historical divide between the bad girls and the bad boys, I will mark the division with an interlude, to address a number of collateral issues: how key musicals (*Cabaret, Chicago*) have helped us abandon the "bad-girl-always-gets-punished" scenario; how persistent the "homosexuality-must-be-punished" trope proved to be in the mid-1970s (*A Chorus Line*, 1975); and how the long tradition of a closeted camp dimension in musicals figured into the mix (*The Wizard of Oz* and the film version of *Gentlemen Prefer Blondes* [1953]). Finally, after this transitional interlude, I will take up *The Rocky Horror Picture Show* (both the 1975 film and the phenomenon), with its uninhibited celebration of difference couched within a "retro" punishment scenario (with the latter serving as its own site for celebration, since it provides yet another opportunity for outré performance), and consider the postmodern *Hedwig and the Angry Inch* (1998; film version, 2001), which presents its quest for wholeness amid the various fragmentations—of self, of society—that have followed modernity, within both figurative and explicitly sexualized terms.[3]

Annie Get Your Gun (1946), like *Kiss Me, Kate* (1948; see chapter 6) is often understood in terms of the long shadow cast by *Oklahoma!* (1943) and *Carousel* (1945), as part of a scenario in which veteran Tin Pan Alley songwriters Irving Berlin (*Annie Get Your Gun*) and Cole Porter (*Kiss Me, Kate*) attempted to write "integrated" musicals following the lead of Rodgers and Hammerstein.[4] This scenario has perhaps unduly reinforced the mythmaking that has surrounded the team of Rodgers and Hammerstein, who produced *Annie Get Your Gun* and persuaded Irving Berlin to write the songs after Jerome Kern, their first choice, died unexpectedly. Yet it is also true that *Annie* and *Kate* are far and away the most fully realized and frequently performed musicals written by Berlin and Porter;[5] moreover, by the late 1940s, in the wake of Rodgers and Hammerstein's success, both composers felt they had something to prove.

Berlin was semiretired and initially reluctant to take on *Annie Get Your Gun* because, in part, he was uncertain he would be up to the challenge. But star Ethel Merman was already aboard, since it was for her that veteran writers Dorothy and Herbert Fields conceived the show from the beginning, and Rodgers's own deep respect for Berlin provided additional encouragement. Yet, despite the consensus that Berlin rose admirably to the challenge, and despite the huge success of the resulting show both in its initial run and later, *Annie Get Your Gun* is not fully up to the "integrated" standard established by Rodgers and Hammerstein at their best. Berlin's score for *Annie* succeeds admirably on two main fronts, by responding in kind to the "folk-musical" dimension of *Oklahoma!* and *Carousel* and in providing a slate of individually outstanding songs. But the score does not really measure up to the higher aesthetic standard established by Rodgers and Hammerstein, which *Kiss Me, Kate* and many later musicals would continue to advance. Moreover, Berlin's songs, in some important respects, stand apart from the show, often exhibiting a sophistication foreign to the characters who sing them—a criticism especially applicable to many of Annie's songs. Perhaps better "integration" in this sense could have been achieved had Dorothy Fields written the lyrics (as had been the plan when Kern was slated to be the composer), but Berlin—one of Tin Pan Alley's most respected lyricists—always wrote his own lyrics. Nevertheless, this particular flaw also worked to the advantage of the show's presentation of Annie as someone whose brazen, almost masculine self-assurance commands center stage throughout, since her appropriation of verbal tokens of sophistication (rhyming "Vanderbilts" with "kilts" in the early "Doin' What Comes Natur'lly," for example, in combination with a degree of sexual innuendo outside her own experience) combines with the powerfully simple device of the list song to overwhelm all potential challengers.

Like *Oklahoma!*, *Annie Get Your Gun* draws on mythologies of America's West, but those mythologies are not what is at stake in the show, which presents itself, thematically, somewhat more abstractly, as a conflict between an imperiled way of life, reenacted as entertainment, and a number of elements that threaten to destroy it for good.[6] Annie herself becomes the center because she embodies important elements from each side of the conflict. She is, to begin with, already a daunting set of contradictions: a primitive aspiring to civilization, a tomboy aspiring to womanhood, a person of superb capabilities who is abjectly incompetent in the one dimension of her life that seems to matter, and a person who is refreshingly, straightforwardly honest but who ends up being punished for precisely that virtue (along with the virtue of competence). But in pushing Annie to the center of things, the show displaces larger themes with more personal ones, so that we care much more about how reconciling these contradictions will affect Annie herself than about what implications her success or failures might portend for the wider world. Similarly, *Annie Get Your Gun* concerns itself with the principal themes of another of the great models for "book" musicals, *Show Boat* (1927), in probing the relationship between reality and fantasy and in confronting (if fairly weakly) the issue of race in America, offering as well a corrective to *Oklahoma!* in making Indians (rather than blacks, as in *Show Boat*) the principal racial "other" in the show.[7] Yet neither of these themes is sufficiently elaborated, in musical terms, to be anything more than a component of the personal story that occupies the foreground.

For example, Annie—like Magnolia in *Show Boat*—forms an alliance with a disenfranchised group by borrowing its musical styles, a kind of appropriation that is both innocent and respectful in itself, and is taken that way by representatives of that group in the show. Yet those representatives carry different weight in the two shows. The black population in *Show Boat* occupies its own musical space with a persuasiveness that derives additional support from casting policies that avoided blackface for most of the principal roles (but not for the shows within the show). In *Annie*, on the other hand, the Indians do not sing except in a manner approximating the deliberately fraudulent "In Dahomey" number in *Show Boat*, replete with every operative cliché for whites representing Indians in "redface": elaborate, colorful costumes with lots of leather fringe and feathers, face paint, buffalo-horn "jewelry," tribal dances, drum music, and so on. Even in this, the Indians mainly serve as backup for Annie on all levels—vocally, visually, and psychologically. Moreover, the lyric for Annie's "I'm an Indian Too" mixes respect with blatant disrespect, and the song's musical style degenerates easily into parody; indeed, its melody is actually presented *as* a parody, within the conditions set up by the show itself. Thus, the song's opening melody uses repetition and simplification to "dumb down" the musical phrases of the Indians' "Ceremonial Chant," which immediately precedes it (the latter is on the left; boldface indicates a phrase taken up in repetition, and italics a melodic simplification):

♫5.1

Dukta **Dukta**   Like the **Seminole, Navajo, Kickapoo,**
                          Like those **Indians,**

s'na hey mo ring ta	I'm an Indian too.
Cha wa ooh eh	
Hoo eh eh.	A Sioux, ooh-ooh! A Sioux, ooh-ooh!

As for the lyrics—probably the principal reason the song has often seemed too obnoxious in its reductive stereotyping to include in recent revivals—they offend not only through their lists of ridiculous-sounding Indian names ("Big Chief Hole in the Ground," "Falling Pants, Running Nose," "Big Chief Son of a Bear"), but also through their projection of Annie's future life as an Indian ("Looking like a flour sack with two papooses on my back").

While the crux of the show's plotting from an audience's perspective is Annie's presumption, as a woman, to be superbly capable in the hyper-masculine role of trick-shot artist and marksman (markswoman?), the show is structured around her more broadly scaled quest to define her identity in gendered terms.[8] That identity is put into question by the entire set of contradictions listed here, which her "masculine" shooting ability brings into particular focus by highlighting the main barrier to her marrying established marksman Frank Butler. Yet, what he offers seems at first the dullest of alternatives, despite her immediate attraction to him, since he couches his own prescription for marriageable womanhood in language that is doubly quaint and utterly pompous ("The Girl That I Marry"). Even here, however, Annie's attraction is based squarely on *her* needs, since Frank Butler is, with some specificity, everything she is not: masculine yet fancily dressed and attractive, and well at ease with his place in the world, especially regarding sex.[9] But his lyrics are infantilizing in their reduction of women to roughly the status of flowers or pets: his future wife will "have to be / As soft and as pink as a nursery," "wear satins and laces and smell of cologne," "wear a gardenia," "purr like a kitten / [and be] A doll I can carry." And while the rhythmic energy of the show's songs derives, in general terms, from that of ragtime-inspired Tin Pan Alley—thus, using syncopated duple meter, a style of song that Berlin helped refine during the first decades of the century—Butler's "The Girl That I Marry" marks his womanly ideals as sentimental and behind the times even within the *musical* context of the show, simply by presenting them within a straightforward, slow waltz tempo, the very idiom that was being displaced at the turn of the century (and the only example of this type in the show, except for the very end of "Anything You Can Do").[10]

♪5.2

For her part, Annie has already introduced herself as a child of nature, who wears enough of nature on her person that her "Doin' What Comes Natur'lly" can come across almost as a minstrel number. Thus, the dirt on her face (and on the faces of her troupe of younger siblings, who sing backup) substitutes for minstrelsy's blackface—in what Robert Walser calls "hick-face"[11]—and reinforces the other primitivist elements in the song, such as the snap figure on "Doin'" in the title phrase and the song's rudimentary refrain structure (within, however, an AABA Tin Pan Alley structure).[12] On

Figure 5.1. In the first act of *Annie Get Your Gun*, Annie (Ethel Merman) sings "You Can't Get a Man with a Gun" in rueful acknowledgment that she is a far cry from the "soft and pink" girl that Frank Butler has just described in "The Girl That I Marry." (Photograph courtesy of Miles Kreuger and the Institute of the American Musical, Inc.)

the other hand, the song also links her to Frank Butler even before they meet, as his "I'm a Bad, Bad Man," heard just earlier, is couched in a similar form and style, although he interacts differently with his "backup" group of young girls (who would in a later age have been called groupies).[13] But their next set of paired songs, "The Girl That I Marry" and "You Can't Get a Man with a Gun" (see figure 5.1), plays strictly to the contrast between them and sets up her quest to prove herself worthy of his love. As this quest leads her to align herself with a succession of marginalized groups, however, it becomes clear that Annie belongs "natur'lly" to none of them. Her friendship with Sitting Bull and his tribe will provide her support and, eventually, a winning strategy for securing Frank, but her "Indian" song, "I'm an Indian Too," argues against its own ostensible point, being more about how she is *not* an Indian and never could be one. And she is, initially, as uncomfortable with joining the show people, who try hard to sell her on the advantages of show business in what has since become the de facto anthem of that profession, "There's No Business Like Show Business." (Importantly, however, this is precisely the group that will provide her the semblance of a "natural"

♪ 5.3

♪ 5.4

background, perhaps owing to the theatrical tradition for "pants" roles.) But still less is she a natural for the ultrafeminine role she attempts to assume in response to Frank Butler's "The Girl That I Marry."

Oddly, the musical marker for Annie's "true" identity that persists throughout the show is African American in derivation. Late in the first act, she sings a bluesy number as a lullaby for her younger siblings ("Moonshine Lullaby," to be sung in a "Slow Blues Tempo")—not quite a blues, but approximating the genre in style and some aspects of its thirty-two-bar form, harmonies, and melodic inflections.[14] Later, in the second act, she sings a ♪5.5 song that seems to cross-breed two familiar jazz-based Gershwin songs, "I Got Rhythm" (a Merman signature tune from the 1930 *Girl Crazy*) and "I Got Plenty o' Nuttin'" (from *Porgy and Bess*, 1935)—the latter, of course, written for Porgy himself, defining his contented status as a black man, poor in worldly goods but nevertheless rich in blessings (although Annie's "I Got the Sun in the Morning" seems closer to "I Got Rhythm" in terms of its musical profile). Despite its oddness, this peculiar affinity between Annie and ♪5.6 musical styles associated with blacks—never explicit, yet always suggested— ♪5.7 seems vaguely appropriate for several reasons. First, it marks her as a simi- ♪5.8 larly marginalized "primitive," someone unconnected with any particular group in the show (whose main racial "other" is the American Indian), and who thus has difficulty fitting in. Second, the connection offers her access to an idiom that is richer and suppler than most of the other musical styles in the show, making her differences from the other characters as attractive as they are problematic. And, third, the historical blending of these idioms into Tin Pan Alley allows them to occur "natur'lly" in a show that does not otherwise refer substantively to black America.

Of the other musical "identities" in the show, the most encompassing is not Annie's black-derived idiom but rather the brash, often phony, often sentimental idiom of show business. We hear the latter throughout, not only in "There's No Business Like Show Business" but also, most significantly, in the opening number, "Colonel Buffalo Bill" and in the later "Wild West Ballet."[15] In effect, we hear the transmutation of Indianist music into a phony "show business" variety of exotic primitivism when Annie converts their tribal music—which we are seemingly expected to hear as "authentic," at least aspirationally—through parody, into her show song, "I'm an Indian Too." While this dynamic of absorption may seem problematic in an abstract sense, the show endorses this brash "show-business" idiom on at least two levels: as a mode of useful presentation and as mediation between an inner "authentic" self and an outer persona. Thus, "No Business Like Show Business" extols at some length the ability of "show people" to perform no matter what internal turmoil they may be undergoing ("they smile when they are low")—a form of "virtuous dishonesty" whose mastery will eventually allow Annie to "have her cake and eat it, too," to stay more or less who she is, but also marry Frank Butler. Thus, what Annie needs to learn is not quite ♪5.9

as simple as the broad outlines of the plot would indicate. Outwardly, the ruse that she uses to cater to Frank Butler's vanity, of deliberately throwing the culminating shooting match with him after she realizes that Sitting Bull has altered the sights of her guns, is not a capitulation so much as a demonstration that she can manage the separation of inner and outer truths.

The latter is a matter of performance, in two ways. If, as the scene is played, Frank is obviously aware that Annie is throwing the match, and she is equally aware of his awareness, the deception becomes a shared one and helps form the basis for their resumed relationship. The script here is ambiguous; although it is clear that the deception is a shared secret between Annie and Sitting Bull, only Frank's comment to Dolly ("Shut up, Dolly") betrays his possible awareness. In all other respects the scene is written so as to play equally well at various levels of awareness on the part of the principals, although for Frank to believe that Annie misses every shot from lack of skill seems absurd, and this is especially unlikely in the wake of their classic song of one-upmanship heard shortly before, "Anything You Can Do." But performance matters even more here on a deeper level, because outer truth is, in a sense, *performed* truth. Whatever Annie's capabilities as a shooter, her capabilities as a *performer* (in this sense) demand that she miss, and so she does. Nevertheless, this scenario, of a capable woman catering to her male "superiors" (who are nothing of the sort), can be very hard to accept with equanimity, especially in the wake of the women's liberation movement (which began in earnest more than a decade after *Annie*'s first run) and our steadily growing awareness of the "glass ceiling" that has often prevented women from reaching the same level, in many professions, as less accomplished men. Yet, if the scene is played well, Frank will recognize Annie's capitulation as a kind of gendered role-playing, and so, in accepting her gesture, he will seem implicitly to acknowledge both her skill and her overriding love for him.

This difficult point of balance is achieved (although subsequently lost) earlier in the second act, during a number that Berlin added for the 1966 revival (which again starred Ethel Merman as Annie)—"An Old Fashioned Wedding"—which makes it even clearer that their ability to get along as a couple depends ultimately on their using show business as a common ground. The number unfolds as a combination song, with Frank's slower contribution describing a quaintly old-fashioned attitude similar to that of "The Girl That I Marry." But Frank's sincerity in this case is even more suspect than in his earlier waltz song, since he adapts his tune from an interior phrase of "There's No Business Like Show Business" (thus, "Ev'rything about it is appealing" becomes "We'll have an old fashioned wedding"). For her part, Annie seems to offer a brasher version of her "I Got the Sun in the Morning," heard just before, inverting its sentiment and (to some extent) its affect, so that the music of the latter's title phrase sets the most strident part of a lyric that demands glitzy show business as an alternative to Frank's

♪5.10
♪5.11

rustic simplicity (boldface indicates recollections of the repeated-note head of the previous song, "**I got the sun**":

♪5.12
♪5.13

> **A ceremony with a bish**op who will tie the knot and say:
> "**Do you agree to love and hon**or,"
> Love and honor, yes, but not obey. . . .
> **I wanna wedding like the Van**derbilts have, ev'rything big, not small.

Perhaps because Frank's contrasting projection is so obviously an artifice, it doesn't seem to matter that, when the two are combined, Annie's "Love and honor, yes, but not obey" offers an emphatic counterpoint to the last word of Frank's phrase, "You'll vow to love and honor and **obey**." Of course, it actually *does* matter, which is why the song appears long before their final reconciliation; yet, musically, the combination "works," so that while we understand the conflict to be far from resolved at this point, we are also given a concrete demonstration that it can be (and will be) resolved eventually.

♪5.14

The title role in *Annie Get Your Gun* has most often been played by a star considerably older than Annie, whose extended career, typically, has made her an unconventional ingénue. Merman herself had for a long time before the first run succeeded more as a brash comic than as a more conventional romantic lead. Mary Martin, also a star from the 1930s, and who toured in the role to great acclaim following its first run, went on to play the conflicted Nellie in *South Pacific* (1949), the cross-dressing title role in *Peter Pan* (1954, with a celebrated televised version in 1960), and Maria von Trapp in *The Sound of Music* (1959), infusing the latter role with a flavor of unconventional "tomboyish" sexuality.[16] And Bernadette Peters, who successfully revived the role on Broadway in 1999, achieved her definitive stardom in Sondheim's *Sunday in the Park with George* (1984) and *Into the Woods* (1987), both of which involve an elaborate transformation of persona or appearance between the two acts, in the latter case from an ugly witch into a youthful beauty. In each of these cases, within a situation deriving in part from the actress's relative maturity, her Annie has had to convince audiences that advanced maturity and capabilities do not ultimately render unsuitable her coupling with a hunkish and (generally) much younger actor, who is also (generally) much less a star than she. Ironically, it is thus often the actress's very accomplishments in "show business" that set up Annie's abjectness within the show, and thus require her to harness the powers of "show business" anew. Put differently, the role requires a bravura performer who can convincingly—precisely through the bravura of performance turned against itself—depict the denial of that bravura, and present it all as a trajectory of self-discovery.

Gypsy (1959) was based, if loosely, on the self-indulgent *Gypsy: A Memoir*, by Gypsy Rose Lee, the most famous striptease artist ever in America, surpassing even "Little Egypt," who supposedly saved the

Chicago World's Fair from being a financial disaster with her "Hootchy Cootch" act in 1893. Perhaps more relevant here than her fame is the nature of that fame; alone among those in her profession, she became famous *as a personality* and enjoyed some success as an author and television hostess as well, although her sister (June Hovick, appearing as June Havoc) had a more successful career as an actress.[17] From the beginning of the show's development, however, the dramatic emphasis lay not on Gypsy Rose Lee herself but on her ruthless stage mother, Madame Rose (often referred to as Mama Rose), as a role that might provide Ethel Merman another star turn nearly a decade after her last hit (the 1950 *Call Me Madam*), and following up one of her very few flops (the 1956 *Happy Hunting*). Arthur Laurents based the book for the musical to an extraordinary degree on situations and dialogue from the *Memoir*, although much of the plotting and some of the characters were invented, including Herbie—the family's manager and the love interest for Mme Rose—who was pieced together from a succession of similar characters who populate the *Memoir*. Despite initial reluctance, Laurents was attracted to the property both because of Mme Rose's character and because of the book's hints of lesbianism.[18] That the latter element did not find its way into the final show, at least overtly, may have had something to do with Merman's prudishness (recalling her refusal to sing "Kate the Great" twenty-five years earlier, in *Anything Goes*),[19] but it may also reflect sound theatrical judgment, as many other elements in the show probably work better without this added distraction.

Merman herself had a lot at stake in the project and so did not hesitate to exercise her considerable clout in shaping it. Stephen Sondheim, set to compose the songs for a narrative that undoubtedly had special resonance for him (considering his problematic relationship with his own mother), had to settle for another tour of duty as lyricist when Merman refused to allow a then-unknown composer to write the score. Sondheim was reluctant to accept this demotion, fearing it might "typecast" him as a lyricist and make it even harder for him to emerge as a composer on Broadway; moreover, the demotion was in effect twofold, since it also entailed a shift downward from his last project, from being lyricist for Leonard Bernstein on *West Side Story* (1957) to performing the same function for the less prestigious composer Jule Styne. But Sondheim's mentor Oscar Hammerstein II persuaded him to accept the job, since it provided a valuable opportunity to work with a real star and to collaborate with another first-rate team, including Arthur Laurents and director-choreographer Jerome Robbins, who were among his collaborators on *West Side Story*. Moreover, Sondheim's initial disappointment aside, Styne was an eminently reasonable choice to compose the music, with a well-honed ability to write to a singer's strengths, a fecund creative gift for producing musical material on demand, and a distinct affinity for properties featuring quirky female protagonists (*Gentlemen Prefer Blondes*, 1949; *Bells Are Ringing*, 1956; and, later, *Funny Girl*, 1964).

The shift in focus from the *Memoir* to the musical—that is, from daughter to mother—entails a useful ambiguity regarding not only the relative importance of the characters in the show but also the title itself. *Gypsy*, the main title of the *Memoir*, was the only real option for the title of the musical, especially given the author's involvement and personal stake in the project and the *Memoir*'s useful notoriety. But if, going in, audiences might have reasonably expected the show to be about Gypsy Rose Lee, they would have found it to be much more concerned with her mother, who was, after all, the headlining role; many have therefore criticized the title as being to some extent misleading. Yet the show's unusual dramatic structure makes *Gypsy* precisely to the point. The conventional romantic story in *Gypsy*—between Mme Rose and Herbie—is enormously overbalanced in favor of the former, against whom Herbie has no chance, even though he does, in the end, act on a strong sense of morality and personal integrity (by refusing to accede to Rose's pressuring of Louise to perform a striptease). His failure is a noble one: he is utterly sincere in a world in which only show business matters; thus, he is given relatively little to sing and was originally (and is still often) cast with an actor of little or no singing experience. In a musical whose romantic couple is so constituted, the conventional marriage trope cannot satisfy; even if Herbie could convincingly rescue Mme Rose from herself, how could such a rescue ever be expressed in musical terms, without negating either the effect of the rescue or our belief in it? Instead, *Gypsy* is—daringly for a musical—about the "marriage" between mother and daughter, with Herbie functioning as the third leg in the triangle.

At the start of the musical, mother and daughter are poles apart, with Louise desperately needing the approval of Mme Rose, who seems scarcely aware of her older daughter's existence except to criticize her inadequate performance in support of her younger sister, June, the show's star. But at the end, after everyone else leaves them, the two characters merge. According to Laurents, the intent was "that Gypsy *becomes* Rose. The girl becomes the tough mother, and for all of Rose's toughness, she's just a little girl who wants to be recognized."[20] That the two share a name—Louise's birth name is Rose Louise—does not emerge until fairly late in the second act, after which Louise herself is rapidly eclipsed in favor of the stripper personality she will become, a process tracked deftly by the changes made to her name. First, she merges somewhat clumsily with her mother, as "Louise" becomes "Rose Louise" and displaces her mother in the title of the new act, "Rose Louise and Her Hollywood Blondes" (a makeover of the failing "Madame Rose's Toreadorables"). Then, when Rose Louise is preparing to debut as a stripper, she becomes "*Gypsy* Rose Louise," adding the name that describes them both, since "Gypsy" may designate—when it does not refer to a specific ethnic group—either dancers (on Broadway) or all those who, like Rose Louise and her mother, travel the country as independents taking whatever jobs they can get.[21] Finally, "Louise" disappears altogether when the announcer misreads the card, a seemingly random event that carries great significance because it marks the moment when the now-familiar name, "Gypsy Rose Lee," takes its final form.[22] Within this scenario, "Gypsy"—a designation intrinsically hard to pin down—is precisely the name that embraces both mother and daughter, yet belongs legitimately to neither.

If the single name "Gypsy" thus expresses an unusual conjunction of two characters—so that, arguably, mother and daughter have equal claims to being regarded as the title character of *Gypsy*—the larger narrative of the show derives from an utterly familiar situation that is rendered grotesque: the tendency of parents to live through their children, and for children to become like their parents even when they rebel. Thus, as Louise transforms into Gypsy Rose Lee, she becomes a caricature of her mother's ambitions for stardom, and, in response, Mme Rose, in her culminating "Rose's Turn," becomes a caricature of Gypsy Rose Lee, as abjectly unsuited to that role as Louise had earlier been to take over June's routines after the latter had run away with Tulsa. In this way, *Gypsy* becomes the story of identity formation within a family context, told with a heavy emphasis on the negative dimension of generational codependency, so as to intensify the child's need to separate and the parent's difficulty in letting go. It is in part the familiarity of the overall pattern that compels us to believe the story and its denouement; "Gypsy Rose Lee" may not be the only possible outcome when a stage mother's ambition, wedded to her daughter's lack of genuine talent, finds itself confronted with a fading market for vaudeville, but the show's delineation of an all-too-familiar family dynamic makes it an eminently logical one. Moreover, we know this outcome in advance, so that the death of vaudeville—as a victim of both synchronized-sound films and the Great Depression—becomes the fate-driven engine for a doomed trajectory that we know can end in only one terminus: the emergence of a famous stripper from the ruins of vaudeville (that is, from burlesque), seen as both the culmination of a family tragedy and a personal triumph.

Mme Rose is thus not the only one "to blame" for this outcome, even if, at each critical juncture, it is her ruthless pushing that propels Louise toward the abyss. Even Rose's gradually narrowing sensibilities respond crucially to the larger situation. After all, she plays (or makes her daughters play) *to an audience*, and that audience is increasingly less refined in the later stages of the show. For such an audience, considered as a broad spectrum shading off into coarser sensibilities, stripping is but a baby step beyond the emphasis on feminine display that has always lain close to the heart of show business in America, especially when—as is often the case when a young girl is a featured performer—a hint of perverse voyeurism is already part of the package.

That Gypsy Rose Lee can so easily turn Baby June's number, "May We Entertain You" (later, "Let Me Entertain You"), into an ironically deployed strip anthem is thus no mere joke, despite the cleverness with which Sondheim creates seemingly innocent language that may later be effortlessly converted, with virtually every line, into a sexual "come on":

♫5.15

Let me entertain you,
Let me make you smile.
   Let me do a few tricks,
    Some old and then some new tricks—
I'm very versatile!
   And if you're real good,
    I'll make you feel good—
I want your spirits to climb.
So let me entertain you
And we'll have a real good time—yessir!
We'll have a real good time!

The setting for this lyric and its tune undergoes a transition across the show from catering to "child-cute" sensibilities to serving as a stripper's campish "gimmick." In its original form, as a simple waltz song, there is little to indicate its future purpose:

♫ **5.16**

JUNE:	May we entertain you?
	May we see you smile?
	I will do some kicks—
LOUISE:	I will do some tricks.
J:	I'll tell you a story.
L:	I'll dance when she's done. . . .

In this simpler setting, the word "tricks" is deemphasized, sung only once and almost inaudibly ("Sing out, Louise!"), whereas the key lines, "And if you're real good, / I'll make you feel good— / I want your spirits to climb," simply do not appear. Partly, this early version seems designed to draw attention away from the double entendres of the full lyric when it appears slightly later in a somewhat more provocative rhythm. Thus, the familiar device of the reprise, along with the new energy of the number that derives from the addition of the backup group of Newsboys, distracts us, so that we tend not to notice the full implications of the more elaborate lyric, even though nearly all the later melodic "pointers" are already in place (i.e., the upward leaps on the now-repeated word "tricks"). This cloaking effect is reinforced by the brief reprise of the opening of the song later, in its original waltz rhythm, during "If Mama Was Married," so that by the time it reappears in its "stripper" setting, near the end of the show, we feel we've heard the number often—exemplifying Mme Rose's "thrifty" recycling of material and serving as an emblem of the act's stagnation—whereas in fact we've heard it in its full form only once, and then as a reprise buried within a new number ("Baby June and Her Newsboys").

♫ **5.17**

To the extent that this strategy of downplaying the implicit sexualized dimension of June's signature number succeeds, it will seem revelatory that the number is so admirably suited for a stripper's routine, once more raucous orchestration and bump-and-grind rhythms (i.e., a heavy use of dotted fig-

♩5.18 ures, with driving triplets in the accompaniment) are added to the mix. Yet, the "cuteness" of June's earlier performance already has its salacious side. During the opening scene's rehearsal sequence, just before June sings, Uncle Jocko (the host of "Uncle Jocko's Kiddie Show") makes it clear that one particular little girl, covered entirely in balloons, is to be favored above the others, so as to fulfill his promise to her older sister ("Chip off her sister's block. And you ought to see *them* balloons!").[23] Moreover, as the scene ends Mme Rose is pursuing the balloon girl with a hat pin in an oblique reference to the familiar stripper's gimmick, derived from Sally Rand's famous "bubble dance" in the 1930s, which substitutes the popping of strategically worn balloons for the removal of the "seven veils" in re-creations of Salome's famous dance (other familiar devices included feathers and fans). That this salacious side is to some extent built into the genre of the "cute-little-girl" number becomes increasingly apparent as "Baby June" becomes the fully adolescent "Dainty June," pretending to be much younger than she is, yet fooling no one. Whether we see it coming or not, the strip version of the number brings the saucy subtext of the "Baby June" version fully to our attention, if only in retrospect. Moreover, the effect of suddenly revealing the risqué aspect of a lyric we've already heard and accepted as "innocent" makes the full emergence of Gypsy Rose Lee seem all the more inevitable, as something already implicit from the beginning; in a similar fashion, her trademark "conversations" with her audiences—the basis for the real Gypsy Rose Lee's emergence as a "personality"—are also fully grounded in the earlier "child-cute" act (thus: "Hello everybody. My name is Gypsy Rose

♩5.19 Lee. What's yours?").

Louise's formation of her "Gypsy" identity may thus be understood not only in terms of her relationship to her mother but also in terms of societal expectations for the presentation of femininity, similarly carried to grotesque extremes, and thus drawing a *connecting* rather than a *dividing* line between striptease and accepted modes for performing femininity. On this broader scale, the show may also be understood as a perverse version of the "American dream" of success, whose tawdry result in this instance serves as a marker for America's spiritual decline from its cultured European roots, but which is nevertheless based on two basic "American" tenets: self-realization and the idealized family unit. These two ideals converge in three key numbers, each of them appearing in stark contrast to less positive realities unfolding around them: "Some People," "Everything's Coming Up Roses," and "Together, Wherever We Go." The related theme of vaudeville's decline also has some presence, stemming mainly from Jerome Robbins, whose conception of the show diverged somewhat from his collaborators'.[24] And embedded especially in the failed relationship between Rose and Herbie are conflicts between show business and reality that make *Gypsy* resonate with such shows as *Show Boat* and *Annie Get Your Gun*. But feminized oedipal issues trump these other themes, pulling the focus to the personal dimension, with both family dynamics and societal expectations—metaphorically here, whatever succeeds for an audience—serving to emphasize the degree to which achieving a strong personal identity is a matter of performance.

As often with the related theme of idealism, the formation of identity is treated in *Gypsy* as a kind of "quest" narrative, and the deployment of music allows us to trace the evolution of that quest. Two particular devices drive the process, both of them involving the reuse and reinterpretation of musical material, but on different levels. One device corresponds to an inner, "idealist" process, and the other to an externalized process of performance, with different levels of comfort in the latter serving as pointers toward a desired sense of achieved personal identity. Within the bifurcation of mother and daughter, the "idealist" process is carried primarily by the mother ("I had a dream"), and the latter by Louise (*cum* Gypsy), although in the end they merge into something like a double image. Along the way, other double images appear, such as the child-cute / stripper's camp of "Let Me Entertain You," a number that, typically for the show, intertwines with an elaborate process of cross-referencing. Thus, as the act evolves, it adds the "Newsboys" framing material, which carries forward even as "I Have a Moo Cow" displaces "Let Me Entertain You" (see figure 5.2). It is only when this development founders, after its star, June, runs away with Tulsa and Louise proves inadequate as her replacement (in "Madame Rose's Toreadorables"), that a new trajectory emerges from out of the chaos, driven by both Louise's extreme discomfort in performing "June" and her remembered humiliation performing as one of the "boys" behind her sister. In a classic reaction formation based on inversion, Louise becomes the star, but without June's talent, a brunette among blondes who are all imitation Junes, somehow managing to achieve a sense of dignity and self-possession at the center of a laughably ridiculous act barely holding its own in a shabby, second-rate burlesque hall.[25] Tellingly, her emergent but still precarious sense of ladylike dignity, based in her rejection of an adopted identity she cannot perform, will develop into the core of her stripper personality.

But it is Mme Rose's "idealist" trajectory that drives the show, powered by the dynamic "I had a dream" motive, based in triplets, that opens the overture.[26] The deployment of triplets within a duple meter will form its own ♪5.20 core of motivic development across the show, evolving first as a setting for idealist inspiration tinged with a certain cheapness (a virtual archetype for Broadway itself) that will eventually degenerate into the bump-and-grind triplets of the burlesque hall. After the overture, the motive first appears in the bridge of "Some People," set in each of its early presentations to the lofty vision Rose projects in an effort to wheedle money out of her father, but gradually giving way to her more immediate—and much less noble—agenda (the triplet motive is given in bold; faster sections describing the dream's content are omitted): ♪5.21

> I had a dream,
> A **wonderful dream**, Poppa! . . .

Figure 5.2. *Gypsy*'s Madame Rose (Ethel Merman) presents "Dainty June and Her Farmboys," ready for Broadway—all, perhaps, except June's older sister, Louise (the future Gypsy Rose Lee), who has been relegated to the role of Caroline the dancing cow, singing "Moo, moo, moo, moo" in response to June's series of atrocious "moo" puns. (Photograph courtesy of Miles Kreuger and the Institute of the American Musical, Inc.)

> I had a dream,
> Just as real as can be, Poppa! . . .
> **Oh, what a dream,**
> A **wonderful dream,** Poppa.
> And **all that I need** is **eighty-eight bucks,** Poppa.
> **That's what he said,** Poppa,
> Only **eighty-eight bucks.** . . .

Long before the triplets motive appears, the song seems genetically restless, moving between a broadly scaled syncopated tune (a generic "Broadway" style that will reappear in both the "Broadway" segment of the "Dainty June and Her Farmboys" and in Tulsa's "All I Need Is the Girl") and a more urgent, highly repetitive motive that will resurface during the "content" part of the bridge's "dream" (the ellipses in the quotation given above). While

♪5.22

the resulting sense of restlessness fits Rose perfectly, it also serves as a distraction for what is the main point of the song, revealed when the idealistic triplets motive is forced to carry the mundane "eighty-eight bucks"; at the end of the song, Rose simply steals a solid-gold plaque on the wall—her father's most honored possession—to cover her expenses. Within the song, verbal cleverness and deft musical shifts both give content to Rose's assertion of specialness and provide a kind of razzle-dazzle ("Some humdrum people") to distract her father from her real aim.[27] And this is precisely the mix, of idealist drive conjoined with crass amorality, that will define everything Mme Rose touches, culminating in Gypsy's blend of ladylike refinement and blatant pandering. Throughout the show, Rose's many "dreams" are regarded with both dread and enthusiasm by her troupe, as suspect mixtures of genuine inspiration and manipulation that overpower through the sheer force of Rose's will, and whose results will never prove quite as exciting as she dreamed them.

"Ev'rything's Coming Up Roses" is an inspirational anthem that offers an outwardly conventional musical and dramatic profile, as an expression of determination after a devastating setback, whose climax will bring down the first-act curtain. But it also offers one of the most chilling of the show's many chilling moments, because of what it portends for Louise, who at this point is unable to resist her mother's overpowering will. Earlier, with June around, Louise could retreat to the background, becoming one of the "boys," or find some other place of refuge. The latter option, for example, is vividly dramatized for us on her birthday, when the brashly ridiculous "Mr. Goldstone" number preempts her celebration but then evaporates to reveal Louise alone, singing to the live lamb that was her birthday present. "Little Lamb" builds on traditional symbolic tropes in which the lamb represents both childhood innocence and the sacrifice of innocence,[28] vividly evoked in the final haunting lines, "Little lamb, little lamb, / I wonder how old I am." But ♪ **5.23** now, with June gone, there is no one but an equally powerless Herbie to protect Louise from Rose, whose wild ambitions are increasingly tinged with a rising hysteria in response to what she experiences as mutinous betrayal. This time, the song's trajectory is framed by the triplets motive, beginning with "I had a dream" and ending with the title phrase, given in triplets, a phrase that Sondheim devised to sound as if "it had been in the language for years but [which] was, in fact, invented for the show."[29] As the song progresses, it is as if the triplets—the emblem of her "dreams"—are fighting to emerge, to impose themselves on the reality of the duple, generic "Broadway" style of the rest of the song (triplets are in bold; dramatic returns to duple meter are in italics): ♪ **5.24**

> You'll be swell, you'll be great,
> Gonna have the whole world on a plate!
> Starting here, starting now,
>   Honey, **ev'rything's coming up** *roses!* . . .

Set it spinning,
That'll be just the be*ginning!* . . .

You can do it,
All you need is a hand.
We can do it,
Momma is gonna see *to it!* . . .

Honey, ev'rything's coming up roses and *daffodils,*
Ev'rything's coming up sunshine and *Santa Claus,*
Ev'rything's gonna be bright lights and *lollipops.*
Ev'rything's coming up roses for me and for you.

As in "Some People," the rhythmic shifts indicate an edgy restlessness, but here it is less a matter of manipulating others than of self-management. And although Rose seems to succeed in that—in pulling her "self" together—the price is isolation. In terms of the musical quest set up within the song, she successfully imposes her visionary triplets, yet she fails to control what is a more important musical dynamic, that of *connecting* by getting the others to join in. Herbie and Louise are not truly part of her dream/hallucination and can only watch in numb silence as she works herself up to a frenzied climax; they seem equally frightened by both the possibility of her complete disintegration and the prospect of having to help her realize her latest "dream": making a star out of Louise. Yet, while Rose fails to get Herbie and Louise to join in, their recruitment is foregone, since they have no defense against her crazed "dream" mode.[30]

In the early stages of the second act, temporary salvation comes through two key events. After the predictable failure of the new act ("Mme. Rose's Toreadorables," tailored for a mixed audience of Texans and Mexicans), Louise finally stands up to her mother, throwing away the blond wig she has been wearing ("Momma, I am not June!"). Then, in "Together, Wherever We Go," Rose, Herbie, and Louise establish the semblance of a cooperative family unit, achieving what "Ev'rything's Coming Up Roses" could not. Every bit as manipulative as Rose's "Some People," the song nevertheless establishes a rapport based on the fact that the three of them sing *together,* although it is, as always, Rose who sets the terms:

♫ 5.25

Wherever I go, I know he goes.
Wherever I go, I know she goes.
No fits, no fights, no feuds and no egos—
Amigos, together!

The payoff line here is the multilingual "amigos," whose wit was apparently much appreciated by a despondent Cole Porter, for whom Styne and Sondheim performed the song along with many others from the show, in a valiant attempt to cheer him in his failing health.[31] The combination has an almost arithmetic perfection, tracing in its rhymes the formation of their group—

he, she, I (the literal meaning of the Latin "ego"), and friends (amigos)—simultaneously as the music recovers from the tonic minor and a descending sequence to land confidently in the tonic major. Moreover, the Porteresque "amigos" has more than cleverness to offer, since Rose thereby points directly to their failed attempt to merge English and Spanish in their soon-to-be-abandoned act ("Toreadorables"), and subtly invites the others to join her in laughing at themselves. And so they do; by the time the same music comes back around, they are adding rhymed repartee, based again in a kind of arithmetic logic, with Rose again directing her lyrics at their shared perspectives: on travel, farming (implicitly referring to Dainty June's Farm-boys), and accumulating debts. Still, Louise has to struggle for an equal footing, first shifting the rhyme slightly to make room for herself within the group (from "duo" to "trio"), and then acting, playfully, as peacemaker: ♪5.26

ROSE:	Whatever the boat I row, you row—
HERBIE:	A duo!
R:	Whatever the row I hoe, you hoe—
LOUISE:	A trio!
R:	And any IOU I owe, you owe—[32]
H:	Who, me? Oh, No, you owe!
L:	No, we owe—
ALL:	Together!

In the song's final joke, Louise is again a kind of third wheel, requiring correction from her mother: ♪5.27

ALL:	The things we do, we do by threes, A perfect team— *(Louise heads off in the wrong direction)*
ROSE:	—No, this way, Louise!

The song manages to restabilize the group by emphasizing the group's shared perspective, by forgoing the idiosyncrasies of Rose's more typical musical locution for something more easily sung together, and by shifting the arrival point from the narcissistic "Ev'rything's Coming Up Roses" to a multilayered emphasis on the collective. Yet, Louise, as a personality, is at this point still not fully formed, even if her position within the family has improved, so that the sense of stability achieved in this song can be no more than temporary—especially since Louise's renunciation of June, which precipitates the number, is what truly launches her own process of personal growth.

Louise's transformation into Gypsy Rose Lee consists primarily in her integrating the bits and pieces that she has absorbed into the rather unformed person she has otherwise become, and then gradually attaining some level of comfort in performing them. Her shy reserve transmutes into an aloof, ladylike manner. Her sense of secrecy gives credibility to her assumed name, Gypsy. Her sewing skill provides her with elegant clothing, which increases her self-confidence; thus, in dressing for her debut—the first time she wears a dress in the show—she makes a startling discovery: "Momma—I'm pretty—I'm a pretty girl, Momma!" Becoming a stripper gratifies, in rather blatant terms, her desperate desire to be noticed, especially as she suddenly realizes she is well worth noticing. Her "line reading" for burlesque acts, which she has been doing on a fill-in basis, has given her more comfort interacting on the stage (and off). Even so, she falters and falls back almost in panic on the worn-out routines of their old act, only to discover, miraculously, that those routines suit the situation perfectly ("Hello everybody"). Although the transition from "painfully shy" to "commanding presence" is a difficult one to carry off in the time frame of one musical number (incorporating, however, a montage involving several changes of venue and costume), the arrival points are clear cut. The final part of the sequence (Minsky's in New York) serves as an end point by delivering some of the most familiar "Gypsy Rose Lee" material; here, she pretentiously speaks French in elaborate self-mockery and concludes with her famous "ecdysiast" patter:

> An ecdysiast is one who—or that which—sheds its skin. In vulgar parlance, a stripper. But I'm not a stripper. At these prices, I'm an ecdysiast![33]

Dramatically more significant, however, is her speech during the second part of the sequence (Detroit), which refers to her mother in a way that will register as merely playful to her burlesque audience but will seem deeply significant to *Gypsy*'s audience. The key line of her speech (in bold) is at once profoundly true and absolutely false:

♪ 5.28

> My mother—who got me into this business—
> *(She is pulling up her dress)*
> Always told me
> Make them beg for more—
> *(Drops the dress)*
> And then, don't give it to them!
> **But I'm not my mothah!**
> Beg!

True enough, she is for the first time indeed independent of her mother and developing a will and persona that are distinctively her own. Yet her persona—and even her strong will—owes everything to her mother, however outwardly she may seem to be in full-scale rebellion.

   The show's final number, however, is given not to Gypsy but rather to her mother, conceived as a musical representation of a breakdown.[34] To this end, in "Rose's Turn," the restless shifting of tempo and mood, which had marked Rose's numbers before, reappears, careening out of control as she shifts from song to song. Mainly, she sings somewhat surreal versions of "Some People" and "Ev'rything's Coming Up Roses," colored with an admixture of bump-and-grind music (some of it borrowed from the strippers' trio, "You Gotta Have a Gimmick") as she parodies Gypsy's act, and referring briefly to other numbers as well, including one that was eventually cut from the show, "Momma's Talkin' Soft," a counterpoint to "Small World," sung by the girls. Her actual breakdown involves her combination of the "Gimmick" number and "Momma's Talkin'," which breaks down in part because the musical profile already suggests breakdown: a three-beat pattern against the steady duple meter that sounds like a needle stuck in a single groove of a broken record:

> Momma's talkin' loud,
> Momma's doin' fine,
> Momma's gettin' hot,
> Momma's goin' strong,
> Momma's movin' on,
> Momma's all alone,
> Momma doesn't care,
> Momma's lettin' loose,
> Momma's got the stuff;
> Momma's lettin' go—

At this point, she breaks down on the word "Momma," tries to continue, breaks down again, and finally achieves a rhythmic arrival with the dramatically significant declaration "Momma's gotta let go!" ♩5.29

Appropriately, her subsequent recovery comes-through reprising her own material, the restless music from "Some People" ("Why did I do it?") yielding to the visionary "I had a dream" motive. With the latter, a kind of primitive wit rekindles as she regains control, bypassing correct grammar to pivot, midway through, from self-denial to self-assertion (as before, triplets are given in bold): ♩5.30

> **I had a dream—**
> **I dreamed it for you,** June,
> It **wasn't for me,** Herbie.
> And if it **wasn't for me**
> Then **where would you be,**
> Miss **Gypsy Rose Lee!**

Here, the triplets are all about ownership of the dream, if not the achieved success of that dream. And as she recovers, even more stridently than at the end of the first act, she concludes with the final phrases of "Ev'rything's Coming Up Roses," delivered in a dotted bump-and-grind rhythm rather than triplets (which are now in the band, as part of the stripper's music), and ending with desperate repetitions of the final words, "for me!"

The number is thus shaped as a breakdown leading to a partial recovery tinged with desperation, leaving the writers in a quandary as to how to bring it all to an end. Generically, as the star's final number, the song demands a big finish. Dramatically, however, Rose remains broken, with her recovery too desperate to be taken for the real thing. The writers tried to avoid a dramatically dishonest, applause-garnering finish, wishing instead to move directly into the final scene, in which Rose admits to her daughter that she did it all for herself, and the two reconcile within a functionally inverted dynamic. Although they persuaded Merman to go along with this, forgoing her applause, Hammerstein convinced them, after seeing the show during previews, to give Merman her applause for the sake of the audience, who needed that release in order to move on emotionally. Later, for the London production, Angela Lansbury devised with Laurents a way to provide the audience with its needed release without breaking character, by continuing to bow after the applause had ended. Eerily remaining in her own world, she brought them back to the realization that they were in the presence not of a star acknowledging applause but of an unstable woman lost in the emptiness of her "dreams."[35]

♪5.31

Even in this final number, it is through performance—as it has been throughout the show—that identity is to be sought and, perhaps, achieved. Earlier, Louise had tried and failed to be June, yet found a way—midway through performing in front of a live audience—to turn her failed "June" into a successful Gypsy Rose Lee. Similarly, her mother, in "Rose's Turn," tries to perform Gypsy Rose Lee, breaking down in the midst of unfamiliar material, but recovering (to the extent that she does recover) by fusing her most characteristic music to Gypsy Rose Lee's burlesque-house music. Even in musical terms, then, the two characters stabilize their identities by fusing to some extent with the other's distinctive material. And thus, even apart from whatever moral and psychological lessons we might take away from the show regarding the potentially devastating effects of mismanaged family dynamics, we are also vividly shown how identity involves a learning process as well as a quest—through which one observes, imitates, and ultimately owns what one imitates by performing it, thereby making it one's own even though originally it may have been only borrowed.

Sweet Charity (1966) represented a significant milestone for many of those involved in the show. Conceived, choreographed, and directed by Bob Fosse, *Sweet Charity* served as the linchpin for his shift (following the lead of Jerome Robbins) from choreography to directorial control of his projects; he would, in fact, make his debut as a film director with *Sweet Charity* (1969), although with scarcely the acclaim he would achieve with his 1972 *Cabaret*. The show marked Gwen Verdon's triumphant return to Broadway at age forty-one (see the frontispiece), after a six-year hiatus (she had married Bob Fosse in 1960 and given birth to their daughter, Nicole, in 1963). In broad outlines, *Sweet Charity* was clearly intended as a parallel to its inspiration, the 1957 film *Nights of Cabiria* (*Le notti di Cabiria*), written and directed by Federico Fellini as a showcase for his wife, Giulietta Masina.

In basing an American musical on a continental European film, Fosse also established an important precedent for Sondheim's 1973 *A Little Night Music* (see chapter 1) and Maury Yeston's 1982 *Nine*, each of which sought, in its way, to bring a more worldly sensibility to the Broadway musical.[36] Neil Simon's adapted book for *Sweet Charity* helped give him the distinction, still unequaled, of having four plays running on Broadway simultaneously (the others being nonmusicals: *Barefoot in the Park* [1963], *The Odd Couple* [1965], and *The Star Spangled Girl* [1966]). The score is the most distinctive of a handful of Broadway scores by jazz pianist Cy Coleman, including two breakaway hits (by the mid-1960s an increasingly rare achievement for a traditional Broadway show): "If My Friends Could See Me Now" and "Big Spender." And sixty-one-year-old Dorothy Fields came out of semiretirement (following the death in 1958 of her brother and long-time collaborator Herbert Fields, with whom she had written the book for *Annie Get Your Gun*) to write lyrics that deftly extend, into the treacherous linguistic waters of the 1960s, her remarkable gift for endowing vernacular-based lyrics with enough perspective that they rarely seem "dated" to later ears, even though they are quintessentially of their time.[37]

The adaptation of *Sweet Charity* from *Nights of Cabiria* was fairly direct, allowing for a change in setting to New York City and a few corollary adjustments to the main characters and situations. But these changes and adjustments, which seem generically necessary and mainly inconsequential, turn out to matter quite a lot—more, perhaps (or at least in different ways), than the show's creators may have realized. The main character in both the film and the musical derives from the familiar fictional trope, the "prostitute with a heart of gold," with an admixture of Mary Magdalene, the prostitute redeemed by Jesus. Thus, each protagonist (that is, Cabiria and Charity Hope Valentine) attempts to reform herself through an expected marriage to someone who sees past her profession to her essentially innocent soul; yet each in the end seems condemned to playing out her given earthly role. That Charity is not quite a prostitute—she is a dance-hall hostess who does not, like many of her coworkers, turn tricks on the side—may be no more than a concession to American sensibilities, but the change from the film plays out deeper than that, since Charity herself shares those American sensibilities, and thus could not cross the line into prostitution without self-destructing. A less obvious change also involves the American setting, but with an interesting reversal in effect, as Charity's flirtation with a celebrity who is having a fight with his girlfriend plays differently from Cabiria's, despite the outwardly close parallels between these shared episodes. Because the celebrity is an Italian film star in both cases, he is even more exotic for Charity than for Cabiria; moreover, Charity's familiarity with his films (however faulty her account of them) tells us something of her own range of tastes, which more clearly involve a greater thirst for otherness than Cabiria's. The religious episodes, too, play quite differently, since Cabiria's attempt to seek the Madonna's intercession, during ceremonies at a local shrine, represents an attempt to join in mainstream Catholicism, whereas the "Rhythm of Life" number in *Sweet Charity* is, seemingly, a fairly sardonic look at the alternative religions of the mid-1960s. (Additionally, much detail is inevitably lost in the move from film as a result of the broader plotting typical of the musical stage.)

But the most important—and subtlest—change from film to musical resides in the trajectory of the main character. Cabiria undergoes a transformation of sorts, from a hardened prostitute at the beginning to someone who has seemingly reactivated her internal purity (through a hypnotism sequence that has no real parallel in *Sweet Charity*), and is left at the end with that purer self at tragic odds with who she is in the world—although some semblance of hope is suggested by her resiliently warm response to the young partiers who appear after her abandonment by Oscar. *Sweet Charity* is both kinder and more brutal to its heroine than *Nights of Cabiria*. It is kinder because the parallels between the beginning and ending events, in which she is abandoned by the man whom she hopes to marry, are not complete, since Oscar does not rob her and admits that his inability to go through with the marriage is his own failing. Cabiria—who in the beginning of the film has a substantial bank account and owns her own home—is, however, left completely penniless.[38] But *Sweet Charity* is also in one sense more brutal, because Charity herself is not allowed to evolve significantly. While both stories dramatize the distinction between inner and outer selves (a fairly conventional version of the mind-body split), the basic thrust of *Sweet Charity*, and its particular take on identity formation, is that Charity cannot escape who she is, neither inwardly (through evolution or by recapturing something lost) nor outwardly (by leaving her past behind).

In telling the story of someone's futile attempt to escape who and what she is, *Sweet Charity* takes full advantage of its medium to create a sense of a cynical world that holds no legitimate place for Charity and to show her desperate quest to escape. All the collaborators played an important part in this. Neil Simon's wisecracking dialogue—a feature often criticized in his other work as distracting from and sometimes interfering with character development—helps establish the requisite fatalistic cynicism that circumscribes Charity. Thus, in the first scene, after Charlie robs her and pushes her into the lake, she almost drowns while a curious crowd looks on and a sidewalk vendor offers refreshments, until, finally, she is rescued—by a foreigner. Fosse's tightly controlled choreographic style (preserved in the film) underscores that particular brand of cynicism—based, unfortunately, on documented instances of similar behavior in 1960s New York—by embodying a laconic, world-wise, and world-weary "attitude" while expressing a sense of stifling constriction at odds with Charity's generous impulses. (Such numbers starkly contrast with the later "breakout" numbers, "There's Gotta Be Something Better Than This" and "I Love to Cry at Weddings.")

Charity herself, as created by Gwen Verdon onstage and interpreted by Shirley MacLaine in the film, adds a dimension of individual quirkiness that establishes her as both attractively unique and not really "belonging" to any of the alternative settings that she tries on in her quest to escape her life as a dance-hall hostess. But it is in its musical numbers that *Sweet Charity* makes its dramatic points most effectively.

In Charity's opening number, "You Should See Yourself"—which she sings to a silent Charlie, who at the end of the song will rob her and push her into the lake—her inherent, enthusiastic quirkiness deflects a basic conventionality at every turn. Cast as a "jazz waltz," the number is, in broad terms, romantic without being overly sentimental. Formally, it follows a conventional AABA pattern, but with unusual and somewhat unpredictable phrase lengths, incorporating unexpected harmonic and melodic departures. The lyric reveals her sensibilities to be based enthusiastically on commercial culture, so limited in their perspective that she reads Charlie's appearance and sexual focus as tokens of high sensibility: "You're a blockbuster, buster, you got class / And when you make a pass, man it's a pass!" But her lack of perspective on herself is precisely what makes her appealing and gives the song enough perspective that her reliance on clichés becomes an endearing affectation. Particularly effective in rescuing the song from its mundane subject and language are Charity's delivery as written into the song, filled with sexual innuendo in its leaning chromatic touches and adding syllables as an expression of overabundant enthusiasm and in response to the jazzy syncopation: ♪ 5.32

> You're a hundred watt elec-a-tric light. . . .
> And I laugh 'till I'm ga-ga-ga-ga gone!
> When you switch to a seduc-a-tive mood! . . .
> You're a blue ribbon Pul-it-itzer Prize!

"Big Spender" sets the world Charity inhabits yet does not by sensibility really belong to: the jaded atmosphere of the Fan-Dango Ballroom. The number's impact stems in large part from the contrast between its broad musical gestures, all deriving from bump-and-grind stripper's music (thus, with heavy dotting and driving triplets), and the highly stylized and restrained movements of the dancers, who will often move only one body part at a time. Against this restraint, occasional explosive eruptions—"Hey, big spender!" from the dancers or a "growl" from the orchestra—set off, with a heightened, demanding sexuality, the promised intimacy of dancing with a "hostess" in the darkened hall, where such subtle movement carries more sexual charge than the more typically broad movements suggested by the music in generic terms. Thus, at the song's end, loud repetitions of "Hey, big spender!" fall chromatically back to quiet intimacy, with the flattened fifth (one of the "blue notes" of jazz; in italics) suggestively tugging downward toward the tonic with each insinuating repetition of "*Spend* . . . a little *ti*-ime with me." In this song, we also hear evidence of Coleman's classical training, as he sets up and delivers, in the major-mode bridge, a layered, hocketlike contrapuntal effect that becomes, in combination, a transposed

♩5.33   replication of the chromatic opening motive (given in bold):[39]

The **minute you walked** in the joint . . .

Wouldn't you like to have	fun,	fun,	fun?
How's about a few		laughs,	laughs?
I can show you a			good time. . . .

[becoming, in combination:]	fun, laughs, fun, laughs, fun . . .
[and then:]	**fun, laughs, good time.**

The device is sophisticated, yet formulaic enough to be easily accessible—an ideal combination for the bizarre mixture of the exotically titillating and the utterly routine that the number offers more generally.

Two songs in the show detail Charity's determination to escape while at the same time telling us, fairly plainly, that escape is not possible for her. In "Charity's Soliloquy," she recounts the story of her affair with Charlie, a narrative that alternates between her resolve not to be victimized and a series of episodes in which she is, once again, victimized. The number ends with a flourish that seems to harness religious fervor and (in the musical accompaniment) the panache of a tango-dancing toreador (the latter effect apparently inspired by the reference to Florida heard just before; note also the musical "turn" on the word given in bold,[40] another token of Coleman's offhand

♩5.34   musical sophistication):

> [intoned] 'Cause it **turns** out [spoken] the bum wants to go to Florida.
>> C'mon down!
> [sung]
> Now hear this! And get this!
> Oh Susannah! Amen!
> This big fat heart
> Ain't gonna be torn apart
> Ever, ever, ever again! Olé!

Despite these rhetorical flourishes, verbal and musical, we hear throughout the song—and see in the scene immediately thereafter—that it is part of Charity's generous nature to fall for any and every line she hears, however transparently bogus.

After her episode with the Italian film star, she joins with two coworkers in "There's Gotta Be Something Better Than This," in which her friends detail their fantasies of a better life (see figure 5.3). But Charity cannot truly envision an alternative, even along the lines of her friends' comically plebeian fantasies:

Figure 5.3. A striking juxtaposition of determined optimism and habitual cynicism from the 1969 film version of *Sweet Charity*: Charity Hope Valentine (Shirley MacLaine), flanked by confidantes Helene and Nickie (Paula Kelly and Chita Rivera), has a brief prayerful moment during "There's Gotta Be Something Better Than This," framed behind the lineup of dance-hall hostesses waiting at the rail of the Fan-Dango Ballroom.

> [spoken]
> CHARITY: Me too!
> HELENE AND NICKIE: What?
> CHARITY: I'm getting out too!
> NICKIE: But baby—what can you do?
> CHARITY: I dunno. Just get me out of here and I'll figure it out later.

Although Charity delivers her "Soliloquy" while dancing with a client at the Fan-Dango, in "Something Better" the confining set disappears for the duration of the number (in the film they move outside, to the roof), and the dance style gradually becomes more and more exuberantly expansive. As with the ending strains of "Charity's Soliloquy," the music for this number also promises a kind of escape to a southern vacation spot, specifically through its "Tijuana Brass"–style accompaniment and "traveling" tempo (approximating the sound of a contemporary Western film score)[41] and its simultaneous combination of 3/4 and 6/8 meters, deftly evoking "America" in *West Side Story* (the latter referred to also by the performers' Latin dance styles and vocalizing). Coleman and Fields, in the song's distinctive hook, also find another correlative for the "stuttering-exuberance" effect heard earlier in the added syllables of "You Should See Yourself," which provides its own sense of release by retracing and then condensing the song's opening melodic contour: ♪ 5.35

> I'm gonna get up,
> I'm gonna get out,
> I'm gonna get up, get out and live it!

Time and again, the songs of *Sweet Charity* highlight the disjuncture between Charity and the variety of escapes she "tries on" in an attempt to find a legitimizing place for herself, so that much of the show plays as an extended "list aria" of what Charity is not. Three numbers in the sequence involving the Italian film star Vittorio Vidal, for example, provide different dimensions of Charity's disconnection with her setting. "Rich Man's Frug" (subdivided into "The Aloof," "The Heavyweight," and "The Big Finish") is an instrumental number based partly on "Big Spender," establishing the setting in an exclusive nightclub and creating an aura of stylized snobbery that Charity could never take part in. At this point, however, she triumphs over the snobs with a giddy "It's me!" in answer to their offensively pointed questions ("Who's that with Vittorio?"), a line that she repeats at the end of "If My Friends Could See Me Now" ("It's me, Charity"). The latter song, sung in Vittorio's rooms, both celebrates her apparent escape and illustrates vividly that it is no real escape, both through its overall thrust—the entire number is about how out of place she is—and in its language, which describes her expensively furnished surroundings with a decidedly inexpensively furnished ♫5.36 vocabulary. Finally, banished to the closet when Vittorio's lover Ursula unexpectedly returns, Charity watches through the keyhole—as if watching one of Vidal's films from a darkened theater—as he sings the Broadway equivalent of an Italian aria, "Too Many Tomorrows," and reconnects sexually ♫5.37 with Ursula.

In another episode, "The Rhythm of Life" (the current installment of the Religion of the Month Club, to which Oscar belongs), Coleman creates a mixture of jazz, exotic "Eastern" music (in token of the San Francisco origins of the "Rhythm of Life" Church), Protestant organ chorale, and an elaborate, many-leveled counterpoint, the latter deriving from long-standing European traditions of the "sublime" religious style. The number is broadly satirical of religious alternativity—a year before *Hair* would open, with its determination to take such things very seriously—and can seem uncomfortably dated (as it does in the film version, with Sammy Davis Jr. as "Daddy"). But the number succeeds, as satire, even in its datedness, especially through its evocation partway through of the "Swingle Singers," whose sometimes jazzy vocalized versions of instrumental works from the classical repertory enjoyed several years of popularity during the mid-1960s. In thematic terms, the number details and elaborates an organic "growth process" that cyni- ♫5.38 cally blends idealistic inspiration and commercialism:

> Daddy started out in San Francisco,
>   Tootin' on his trumpet loud and mean.
> Suddenly a voice said, "Go forth, Daddy,
>   Spread the picture on a wider screen."

> And the voice said, "Daddy, there's a million pigeons
> Waitin' to be hooked on new religions. . . ."

As in *Nights of Cabiria*, the solution religion offers is a false one, but the point of view here is somewhat confused. *Sweet Charity*, as with its substitution of dance-hall hostess for *Cabiria*'s prostitute, seems unduly timid, unwilling to risk outraging its audience by suggesting that established religion might prove to be a false alternative for Charity. Indeed, in finding alternative religion a fitting object of parody, the show seems to line up on the side of established religion, leading one to wonder why religion in some other form might not have been taken seriously as a solution (as it was for a time in *Nights of Cabiria*). More likely, though, we are expected to notice how similar the constructs of this alternative church are to those of established religion, which were increasingly prone to pandering to changes in taste during the 1960s, especially in the wake of "Vatican II" (1962–1965), which guardedly authorized the use of vernacular idioms in the Catholic service and thereby became the target for rebuke and satire—the latter including Tom Lehrer's "Vatican Rag" (1965). Similarly here, religion's drift in the 1960s toward a Swingle-Singers-like watering down of traditions might be construed as the true object of the song's parody, and so provide a fuller explanation for why religion is not a viable alternative for Charity.[42]

But respectability—here, as so often, represented by marriage—is also no viable alternative. In "Baby Dream Your Dream"—a song that may well have been modeled on the narrative strategy of Cole Porter's "It's Delovely"—Helene and Nickie narrate the full trajectory of a romance, including the disillusionment that follows the wedding.[43] Here, the device of holding a single note over shifting harmonies both inspires a dreamlike harmonic succession and depicts a certain tenacity of image in the many returns to the head of the tune, beginning with and returning to the warm third of the tonic triad (melodic repetitions of E are given in bold; each line carries a different harmony, as noted):[44]

♪ 5.39

Baby, dream your dream.	(C major)
Close your **eyes** and **try** it.	(C-augmented)
Dream of furniture;	(A minor)
Dream that I can **buy** it.	(V₇/F)

But even in its hopeful moments, the song admits to being only a dream, a setup for the inevitable disillusionment to follow. Later in the act, in the seemingly climactic "I Love to Cry at Weddings," we are confronted with a discordant double image when Oscar shows up for the surprise shower thrown by Charity's coworkers at the Fan-Dango. With a visibly discomfited Oscar present, the irony is almost viscerally painful: the more celebratory the number becomes, the clearer it is that the wedding they are anticipating will never happen.

♪ 5.40

Yet the irony of this musical climax remains invisible to those who know the show only from recordings. This is particularly true for the original cast album, in which Charity's "I'm a Brass Band" follows "I Love to Cry at Weddings" (out of order), so as to give the impression of a conventional happy ending. Even "I'm a Brass Band"—a seemingly celebratory number Charity sings directly after accepting Oscar's proposal—finds Charity unable to settle on an appropriate musical mode for performing her happiness, oscillating wildly among alternatives: brass band, harpsichord, clarinet, Philadelphia orchestra, Modern Jazz Quartet, Count Basie, cathedral bells, and
♪5.41   tissue paper on a comb. By ending with "I Love to Cry at Weddings," the musical trajectory of the show "lies," which may have been why, in the film, Charity's "Where Am I Going?" is delayed until near the end, after her abandonment by Oscar. In the stage show, the latter number marks Charity's despairing realization that her profession has doomed her as far as marrying Oscar is concerned, leading her to quit the Fan-Dango with no hope of holding on to Oscar (who, as it happens, has already learned what she does for a living and will soon propose to her anyway). And yet, her despair is more existential than circumstantial; even if she can somehow escape from the
♪5.42   Fan-Dango, she cannot escape from herself:

> Run to the Bronx, or Washington Square,
> No matter where I run, I meet myself there,
> Looking inside me.
> What do I see?
> Anger and hope and doubt.
> What am I all about?
> And where am I going?
> You tell me!

Charity's fatalistic failure to escape may be interpreted in many ways. It may betoken the ways in which one's self remains apart from one's situation; thus, Charity cannot truly adapt to fit into a different life, just as she cannot efface the tattooed "Charlie" on her arm, which serves as a permanent declaration of her failure. Or her failure may, considering her show of resiliency in the final scene, be taken as a strange kind of victory, so that the show celebrates her undefiled difference, as a person whom an inadequate world (i.e., Oscar) cannot accept. In this sense, her failure to adapt is actually a sign of self-loyalty; although she may be incapable of the kind of "performance" that allows Annie to win Frank in *Annie Get Your Gun*, this is more to her credit than not. Or her failure—taken as ambivalently open-ended— may simply be a reflection of 1960s America, so full of what Charity sees inside herself: "anger and hope and doubt." More broadly, however, her failure stems from the conditions of the Broadway stage, which were not all that different in the mid-1960s from those of Bizet's *Carmen*, nearly a century earlier.[45] However acceptable it might have been to build a story around a fully and frankly sexualized woman, it was far less acceptable to show her succeeding in the world. By the 1960s, this may have been widely seen as more a failure of the world than of the woman in question, but the salient fact remains that *Sweet Charity*'s ending upholds the image of sexual otherness as an abject position, regardless of how, in other ways, that image might simultaneously be admired.

———————

If we take the designation "bad girls" to refer only to heroines whom an audience might be expected to disapprove of in at least one important sense, then, in the musicals discussed earlier, only Gypsy Rose Lee and her mother really qualify. Annie Oakley is particularly innocent, although she transgresses gendered boundaries. Charity is pure of heart, and even her sexual indiscretions arise from her innate generosity and naïveté. Moreover, both of these shows provide us with significant models for how we should respond to them; "good" characters (Sitting Bull and Oscar) respond positively to Annie and Charity, who bring out the best in more dubious sorts, such as Frank Butler and Charity's friends Nickie and Helene. Indeed, a central strategy in musicals for making at least some kinds of "badness" acceptable and even laudable is to provide a model for our expected response in this way, or in intricate variations of it. For example, late in *Gypsy*, even though we expect it and even understand it, we are invited through Herbie's censure to regard Madame Rose's pushing of Louise to strip as the moment she crosses the line. Yet, until that moment, because Herbie goes along with everything else, we are given permission to enjoy at least the audacity of Rose's amorality when she steals, sabotages other acts, lies, and browbeats her way through life. But Louise escapes Herbie's censure altogether, even though the decision to strip is ultimately hers. Perhaps our attitude is expected to change as Louise becomes Gypsy Rose Lee, since that is the moment she loses her status of being only a victim and chooses freely to enter a tainted profession. Yet, if we are expected to feel critical of her for that choice, the crucial moment comes, ambiguously, with the later reconciliation of mother and daughter. This reconciliation may be understood in at least two ways: as Rose's partial redemption, because she is accepted by a "good" person (to the extent that Gypsy Rose Lee is still Louise); or as Gypsy Rose Lee's implicit admission that there is little to choose between them, in moral terms. In any case, however subtly their relative "badness" may be cast, all of these "bad girls"—even the innocently bad ones—are punished to varying degrees, although none of them dies.

Cabaret, another "moral fable" that opened the same year as *Sweet Charity*, follows this general pattern to some extent: the bad girl (Sally Bowles) remains before us as an admired free spirit until Clifford (Brian in the 1972 film) leaves her behind at the end; we know, implicitly, that she will not survive in Nazi Germany. If Sally Bowles ends up worse off than Annie, Gypsy, or Charity, however, we don't see her bad end; rather, we see only someone who is a genuine diva throughout the show, misbehaving in a grand style, both onstage and off. Thus, what Gypsy Rose Lee does only at the end of *Gypsy*, Sally Bowles does throughout: she *performs* "badness." Moreover, by the end of *Cabaret*, that performance has developed sufficient roots so that she can no longer seem innocent (that is, according to "our" reaction as performed by Clifford/Brian). Less than a decade later, after Fosse had already intensified this corruptive dimension of Sally Bowles's divahood in the 1972 film version of *Cabaret*, his 1975 *Chicago* offered up a world that contained no conventionally "good" perspective with which audiences could identify, so that what counts as good is generally something between naïveté and stupidity (thus, Roxie at times and her husband throughout), which can hardly be expected to provide a reliable moral compass. Indeed, conventional notions of morality seem simply beside the point in *Chicago*. In one important sense, this marks a kind of historical division point, after which, within a certain line of theatrical development, the idealist notion of self is eclipsed by performance as such.

Many things contributed to that development, but the threshold event was, arguably, the 1969 Stonewall Rebellion, whose aftermath saw homosexuality increasingly acknowledged in several arenas, especially in personal terms ("outing") and in theatrical venues. The increased emphasis on Brian's homosexuality in the film version of *Cabaret* clearly reflects this changed environment. Post-Stonewall, it becomes more evident (even to mainstream audiences) that his admiration of Sally Bowles stems in large part from her divahood, and that his being in Berlin at all has less to do with his work than with his recreation, since Berlin—like Morocco for an earlier generation—was widely known as a place one could indulge in homosexuality without fear of official censure, particularly in the years immediately preceding June 1934, at which point the Nazis cracked down on homosexuality, beginning with their own (in the "Night of Long Knives"). Within the closeted gay theatrical context of pre-Stonewall Broadway, the badness of "bad girls," especially in the sexual realm, frequently served as a stand-in for homosexuality, and no more so than when the bad girl in question was an unabashed diva. While Broadway's penchant for indulging sexual license held appeal across orientations—Fosse, after all, was himself a notorious womanizer, although operating, as a dancer and choreographer on Broadway, within a world populated by a high percentage of gay men—the importance of many sexualized female stars to gay subculture became increasingly evident in more mainstream culture. Stonewall, in this sense, "outed" the diva as a trope of homosexuality.

To a significant extent, the specific features and the reception histories of many earlier film musicals, such as *The Wizard of Oz* and the 1953 *Gentlemen Prefer Blondes*, revolve around their playing in part to a closeted gay community while seeming to target mainstream audiences. I discuss how this works for *The Wizard of Oz* in chapter 2; in *Gentlemen Prefer Blondes* (and here I refer only to the film version), the constellation of elements that play, often blatantly, to a gay audience is staggering, particularly considering that its director, Howard Hawks (who, however, had little if anything to do with the musical numbers), is widely considered among the most heterosexually "masculine" of that generation of Hollywood directors.[46] Those elements include Marilyn Monroe's fragile divahood and campish portrayal of femininity as Lorelei Lee; Jane Russell's broad-shouldered mannishness as Dorothy Shaw, which enables her parody of Monroe in a blond wig to play almost precisely like male drag; their glitzy production numbers, "Two Little Girls from Little Rock" and "Diamonds Are a Girl's Best Friend" (among the few songs retained from the 1949 Broadway score by Jule Styne and Leo Robin); their strangely emasculated admirers, Tommy Noonan's Gus Esmond, Elliott Reid's Ernie Malone, George "Foghorn" Winslow's Henry Spofford III, and Charles Coburn's "Piggy," none of whom sings and only the latter of whom had any real currency at the box office; and, of course, the all-male Olympic track team, famously featured as a nearly nude beefcake chorus line in Russell's "Ain't There Anyone Here for Love" (by Hoagy Carmichael and Harold Adamson; added for the film).

Post-Stonewall, the gay dimension of these and other films became more and more accessible to mainstream audiences, and open treatment of homosexuality grew increasingly common on stage and in film. For example, in the hugely successful *A Chorus Line* from 1975 (conceived, directed, and choreographed by Michael Bennett, with book by James Kirkwood and Nicholas Dante, music by Marvin Hamlisch, and lyrics by Edward Kleban), one of the finalists (Paul) is given an extensive monologue detailing his experiences as a gay dancer.[47] Whereas many saw this frankness as a breakthrough, others faulted the show for the timid conventionality of its overall treatment of this issue, especially given its daring treatment of other frankly sexual themes (e.g., in "Dance Ten, Looks Three," better known by its hook, "Tits and Ass"). Thus, after Zack (the director) pressures Paul into telling his story against his own wishes, Paul falls and injures himself; while this allows him to assume greater dramatic importance, it also eliminates him from contention and thereby excuses the musical from having to clarify how much, if at all, his being a "tortured gay" might have mattered in the selection process. (The other openly gay character, Greg, does not make the final cut.) Moreover, his elimination through what may well be a career-ending injury lies uncomfortably close to the familiar "punishment" scenario long associated with portrayals of gay men on stage and screen.[48]

In some ways, this episode plays as a miniature version of the basic strategy of the show, which is to make each person matter tremendously as such, with particular focus on his or her deepest fears and vulnerabilities, and then to efface his or her individuality completely as each dancer either fades away through elimination or becomes absorbed into the uniformity of the chorus line. For example, Cassie, a former star (a diva?), must hold herself in check so as not to stand out among the group, whereas the ambiguously titled "One"—the number they are learning to perform—seems at first to be a celebration of the uniqueness of each individual but ends up celebrating the oneness of the ensemble, which moves with such uniform mechanical perfection that it becomes difficult to tell one dancer from another.

In a deep sense, then, *A Chorus Line* runs counter to, or at least hedges around, the very reason that performance—especially in its heightened form, the performance of a *star*—is central to theatrically centered gay culture, which is that such performance is above all about making difference *matter*. This is not to deny the very important work that *A Chorus Line* performed for many gay men in giving Paul one of the most moving monologues of the show. But it may well be argued—and his monologue supports this, if obliquely—that Paul's appearance at an audition for a "normal" show marks his desperate need to deny his own difference so as to blend in. This is why it is particularly painful for him to have to recount his story at this moment, to "come out" just when he is in the process of trying to go back into whatever closet might be left for him. Moreover, with this speech the show also seems to suggest that Paul's prior theatrical venues were indeed something for him to be ashamed of; thus, he elicits ready sympathy by describing the Jewel Box Revue—a much-acclaimed, racially integrated drag show that ran for well over three decades—as "the asshole of show business." Needless to say, this opinion would hardly have been shared by the large number of the Revue's fervent devotees. But such judiciously mainstream positioning was, as we will shortly see, scarcely the only means by which musicals could, by the mid-1970s, engage with the phenomenon of gay divadom.

The Rocky Horror Picture Show (film, 1975) was based on the experimental rock musical *The Rocky Horror Show*, by actor-composer Richard O'Brien, which he developed in early 1973 with director Jim Sharman for a three-week run at the experimental Theatre Upstairs in the Royal Court Theatre of London's King's Road.[49] Its success there allowed them to move it to a larger theater in King's Road, the Classic Cinema, for a slightly longer and even more successful run beginning in August. By November, it had settled into the King's Road Theatre, where it would play until March 1979.[50] In early 1974, Los Angeles–based record producer Lou Adler arranged to bring the show to his Roxy Theater on Sunset Boulevard, where the pace of many musical numbers became faster, and the basic style—apart from the frequent use of pastiche—shifted from glam (a development that had been less successful in America than in London) to an early version of punk;[51] it was during this run that audience members began dressing up as if they were in the show. The successful run closed in January 1975 to prepare for the move to Broadway, by which time the film version, based on Jim Sharman's adaptation, had already been shot within a tight schedule and under conditions so dreary that many participants were left discouraged or sick (or both; Susan Sarandon would suffer a nervous breakdown while battling pneumonia over the next nine months).

By the time the film was ready for screening, however, the stage show had opened and closed at the Belasco Theater on Broadway after only forty-five performances and predominantly negative reviews, seemingly bringing the positive trajectory of the show in America to an abrupt end. Without the expected wave of anticipation from a successful Broadway run, and despite the film's great success in Los Angeles, Fox decided not to give the film wider distribution. Indeed, many *Rocky Horror* fans who saw the film at this stage found it disappointing, whether because it left behind the seedy cinematic setting of the stage show, because it toned down some of the show's sexual references, because it left out a fair amount of the show's dialogue, or because it seemed to be much slower paced than the stage version (as is often the case with film adaptations of stage musicals). After some minor editing,[52] Fox attempted, without much success, to market the film in college venues and then decided to try it out with midnight cult-film audiences in New York. So, on the midnight following April Fool's Day in 1976, the film opened at the Waverly in Greenwich Village—which marks the true beginning of the *Rocky Horror* story in America, notwithstanding its success as a stage show earlier in Los Angeles.

The revolutionary dimension of the *Rocky Horror* "phenomenon"—as it came to be called—was not just that it continued to draw audiences over a very long time or that many people came back again and again to see the film (all of which was unusual but not unprecedented),[53] but rather that members of the audience began *participating* in the film, a practice that evolved into a regular feature of midnight screenings across the country. Several factors contributed to this development, based variously in the sub-genre of rock musicals, then-current trends in rock concert behavior, and long-developing habits of television viewing. The groundwork for activating these factors was well laid. Many of the principals in *Rocky Horror* had participated in the *Hair* "phenomenon" a few years earlier—*Hair* being, of course, the first "rock musical," which had tried in various ways to break down the boundaries between stage and audience. It was in the 1970 London touring company of *Hair* that O'Brien met Tim Curry, who would originate *Rocky Horror*'s Frank-N-Furter (variously punctuated) in London and America before playing the role in the film; and Jim Sharman worked with Brian Thomson on the Sydney *Hair* (also 1970), where Thomson had the idea to distribute participatory "kits" to the audience at each show. Shifts in the ways in which audiences and performers interacted at rock concerts (especially within the emergent "punk" community) had contributed to the audience-dress-up trend already noted with regard to the Los Angeles stage production. But aside from props and accessories, such as costumes, makeup, rice, and toast, the most startling development in audience behavior was its engaging the film in a semblance of conversation.

Louis Farese Jr. is most often given credit for the first call out, on Labor Day weekend in 1976, at the Waverly,[54] but it didn't take long for others to join in, as audiences found that the relatively slow pace of the film, with its

242   CHAPTER FIVE

often stylized, portentous line delivery, replete with internal "method"-style gaps, made it a particularly congenial property in this regard. Audience members could easily "respond" to the film's characters and their behavior, or interject questions or commands that ensuing dialogue or action would seem to respond to. Or, as part of an ongoing "floor show," audience members already dressed to resemble the film's cast could perform musical numbers either before the screening or along with the film. Many newspaper and magazine articles and, eventually, several books were written to document the various experiences of *The Rocky Horror Picture Show*'s devotees. The Waverly received the most media attention, which indirectly led to the show's closure there in January 1978, after such publicity led not only to huge crowds but also to street-gang harassment of those crowds, threatening and sometimes delivering violence. But by then, in early 1978, *The Rocky Horror* phenomenon had long since become an ongoing national event that has yet to run its full course.

The practice of talking back to the screen, or performing along with it, probably devolves most directly from television, and in particular the screening and rescreening of certain films or film genres to somewhat specialized audiences in late-night slots, often (in those days) broadcast from local UHF stations. Familiarity with particular films or their predictable devices, or even with the recycling of a handful of (typically) really bad advertisements, undoubtedly led to a variety of homegrown verbal practices whose motivation might have ranged from "defense mechanism" to genuine (if sometimes patronizing) affection. Those verbal practices were like primitive versions of the elaborate "scripts" that would evolve for *The Rocky Horror Picture Show*, less imaginative and ritualistic but similar enough to confirm the significant overlaps between late-night-television viewers and the audiences for *The Rocky Horror Picture Show*. The informal late-night party atmosphere that developed around the film's screenings thus led to a process of mutual discovery. Audience members who might have found echoes of their own private viewing habits in others who were talking back to the film felt uninhibited enough to join in, and through a cult-based folklike process evolved an oral tradition that both hardened into ritual and, paradoxically, liberated its participants into a quasi-improvisatory space. At the same time that the practice of talking back to *Rocky Horror* provided a way of asserting control over the unresponsive medium of film more generally, the film itself became, in part, a vehicle for something else: *performance*.

Any performer of someone else's material—especially in a musical—undergoes something very like this negotiation between the prescribed dimension of performance and a liberating feeling of agency. This feeling stems both from the physical aspects of performance and the process of adapting the material to one's own person and situation (thus making it one's own in some sense), which may or may not involve overt improvisation or riffing on what is already given. Moreover, as I have noted several times (see especially the beginning of the previous chapter), audience members often perform material from a musical privately (with or without the assistance of "original cast" record albums), which both helps to internalize a musical's characters, emotions, attitudes, and so on, and makes possible a kind of "acting out," ambiguously either expressing one's "true self" or stepping outside oneself to assume an entirely different persona. Part of the liberating experience that this kind of performance provides lies in that ambiguity, in the difficulty (often even for the performer) in distinguishing between what is real and what is put on. "Trying on" roles in this way could allow private performers either to "find themselves" or "lose themselves"—or, in another seeming paradox, both at once.

Participating in screenings of *The Rocky Horror Picture Show*, then, allowed audiences to merge this fairly private sphere of performance with the public arena of theatrical performance. What requires further explanation, however, is why this film, and only this film, has served this purpose so well, notwithstanding the proliferation of highly successful derivative events in recent years, including "sing-along" screenings of such films as *Mary Poppins*, *Evita*, and *The Sound of Music*.

Part of the reason is that the show was conceived and written by someone who shared many obsessions with this future audience base, including late-night genre films on television (especially science fiction), the theatrical dimension of rock concerts and rock musicals, *The Wizard of Oz* (after it began airing on television), and comic books. And here, the specifics matter tremendously. The predominant trope of the science-fiction/horror films to which O'Brien refers—those of the 1950s, when television first evolved into a mass media, and of the 1930s, especially those of the Frankenstein / King Kong / haunted-house varieties—was cultural paranoia, allegorically expressed. In the 1930s, much of that paranoia centered around political issues, so that, as a reaction to the xenophobic regimes that would form the Axis powers in World War II, America and its future (mainly English-speaking) allies, already suffering under the Great Depression, easily warmed to catastrophic or near-catastrophic scenarios involving uncontrollable monsters of one kind or another. The 1930s saw the best of the Frankenstein series (James Whale's 1931 *Frankenstein* and 1935 *Bride of Frankenstein* and Rowland Lee's 1939 *Son of Frankenstein*), *The Old Dark House* (Whale, 1932), and *King Kong* (Merian Cooper and Ernest Schoedsack, 1933); the decade also heard Orson Welles's panic-inspiring *War of the Worlds* radio broadcast on Halloween 1938. Moreover, *The Wizard of Oz* (1939), like this parade of horrific strangeness, found renewed life on 1950s and 1960s television, albeit at a more respectable hour. After viewing these films repeatedly against the backdrop of evolving standards of presentation, aficionados began to relish the artificialities of situation and performance that many today would identify as camp, but which also stem in part from their allegorical basis.

In the 1950s, that allegorical basis would have seemed to address one or more of three main targets of cultural paranoia: communism (with focal points ranging from simple xenophobia to communism's atheistic basis), science (seen as either unnatural or against nature, or perhaps atheistic in its aspirations to God-like powers, but above all the suspect source of atomic power's various dangers, such as radiation-driven mutation), and an increasingly rebellious youth (manifest in specific elements of pop culture, commonly expressed in the triad of "sex, drugs, and rock and roll"). That the latter would provide the primary (but not only) focus for O'Brien has to do with the confluence of artificiality and performance. Sex, drugs, and rock and roll have always been about performing in some sense, offering opportunities for individual release and more generally constituting a rebellion of one generation against its predecessor. The lines of division were mostly a matter of performance: either you did these things or you didn't. Whatever person you were "inside," you were still a virgin, by definition, if you didn't take part (and it is no accident that the term "virgin" carried over into the *Rocky Horror* film cult to describe first-time viewers). Even O'Brien's response to rock was heavily mediated by issues of performance. Early on, before he moved back to London from rural New Zealand (where he had been raised), he was fascinated by an Elvis imitator;[55] later, the ready-made personae of *Hair* and the androgynous element in glam clearly held enormous appeal for him. In all three cases, despite the mythology of authenticity that has dominated a lot of discourse on rock music, it was the performative dimension that mattered for O'Brien, the ways in which rock created situations and personae for performance. Above all, then, *The Rocky Horror Show* was conceived as an opportunity—brazenly artificial because constructed of bits and pieces of familiar characters and situations—to perform those characters as experienced through the prism of the evolving rock scene in the early 1970s, in which everything revolves around sexual identity and its performance.

What follows is a partial accounting of the assemblage of situations and characters in *Rocky Horror*:

> **Frank-N-Furter** (see the frontispiece) collapses the androgynous glam rock star and the God-like presumption of Dr. Frankenstein (Colin Clive in Whale's Frankenstein films) into one rock diva, channeling also some of the amoral and sexually aggressive qualities of Alex in *A Clockwork Orange* (as played by Malcolm McDowell in the 1971 Stanley Kubrick film). At the end of the film, Frank also recalls Billy Wilder's *Sunset Boulevard* (1950), in both his tearful "diva-farewell" scene in front of an imaginary audience (Gloria Swanson's Norma Desmond) and his ending position, as a discarded corpse facedown in the pool (William Holden's Joe Gillis, *Sunset Boulevard*'s narrator). Besides being a mocking derivation from the familiar "Frankenstein," Frank's name is promiscuously suggestive in sexual terms. In a mix of Freudian associations and then-current British slang, "frank" and "fur" refer to the male and female genitalia, respectively, with Frank's middle initial blurring the distinctions between "and" and "in," so that the name suggests both

heterosexual copulation (frank *in* fur) and hermaphroditic qualities (frank *and* fur). Moreover, the familiar image of the frankfurter, of a "frank" in a "bun," has often been used to suggest male homosexuality.

Riff Raff is also a combination character, deriving most clearly from the dwarflike or hunchbacked servants of the Frankenstein films (variously, Fritz, Albert, or Ygor) and, with his sister, **Magenta**, the odd hosts of *The Old Dark House*. With the latter, the suggestion of incest between Riff Raff and Magenta probably stems from a more covert intimation of sexual deviance invoked by the hosts' family name (Femm) and the quirkily creepy performing style of Ernest Thesiger (Horace Femm; also Dr. Pretorius in *The Bride of Frankenstein*).[56] Additionally, Magenta takes on aspects of Morticia Addams (Carolyn Jones in the 1960s television series), Marlene Dietrich (especially in her monotonic singing style in her verse of "Time Warp"), and, completing the circle back to Frankenstein, Elsa Lanchester's "bride" in *Bride of Frankenstein* (with her hairdo at the end of the film).

The Criminologist (the "Narrator" in the stage version) was modeled most directly on Edgar Lustgarten,[57] who hosted *Scotland Yard* (1953–1961), *Mysteries of Edgar Wallace* (1960–1965), and *Scales of Justice* (1962–1967), British crime-program "featurettes" from Merton Studios, which were also syndicated for airing on British and American television; more generally, he serves (especially for those unfamiliar with Lustgarten) to parody stuffy authority figures of all kinds.

Brad Majors and **Janet Weiss**, like the first couple in *The Old Dark House*, are young (sexual) innocents stranded on a stormy night who seek help at the "haunted castle"; they also evoke the generic "good" kids tempted by the wilder ways of their peers in youth-oriented films, and the potential young victims/heroes of science-fiction and horror films. To betoken their relative lack of sophistication, they are played by Americans, whereas the rest of the cast are European (mostly English, following the tradition of the Whale films). They are also versions of Dorothy Gale from *The Wizard of Oz*, who, like them, travels during a catastrophic storm to a strange, unearthly place. Original plans were to imitate the *Oz* film by casting the framing sequences in black and white (or sepia) and by prefiguring future Oz characters among those in Kansas/Denton; following that plan, color would have arrived with Frank.[58] *Oz* is also evoked when, as Brad and Janet approach the haunted castle, they encounter a sign reading "Enter at your own risk," recalling the sign read out by the Cowardly Lion as they approach the castle of the Wicked Witch of the West.

Columbia is a rock groupie (of Frank), modeled specifically on tap-dancing stars of film musicals from the 1930s to the 1950s. She and rock and roller **Eddie**—whose knuckles read "l-o-v-e" and "h-a-t-e," recalling Robert Mitchum's creepy Rev. Harry Powell in Charles Laughton's *Night of the Hunter* (1955)—are discarded sexual conquests of Frank.

Rocky Horror is the creature created by Frank, referring most obviously to the Frankenstein monsters of 1930s films (all played by Boris Karloff) in being brought to life on a stormy night through electricity, being virtually mute (at least in the original 1931 film), showing an affinity for music (here he sings but does not speak), fearing fire, and escaping captivity after being tormented with fire by the servant. Like King Kong, he will attempt, late in the film, to ascend a tower carrying his beloved, in this case the RKO Tower rather than the Empire State Building (recalling, perhaps, that *King Kong* saved RKO from bankruptcy), and carrying Frank rather than Fay Wray (whom Frank has just identified with in song). Rocky differs from Karloff's monsters (and King Kong), however, in conforming physically more to the Charles Atlas bodybuilding ideal touted in ads at the back of 1950s-era comic books, or to Steve Reeves, a former Mr. Universe who made several films in the 1950s (Frank's songs refer to both); he has been created, after all, to serve Frank's sexual needs.[59]

Transsexual, Transylvania (the planet and galaxy of origin for Frank, Riff Raff, and Magenta, as well as many of the guests in the film version) connects the obligatory central European location for horror films with the gender bending that became increasingly mainstream in the 1970s, thanks in part to glam and a more general tendency toward gothic creepiness. In temporal terms, this constellation of "places" brings the relative innocence of the early 1960s (Brad and Janet) face to face with early 1970s presentations of alternative sexual identities, giving an explicitly sexual profile to the more allegorically presented strangeness of earlier science-fiction/horror films.

Significantly, each of the above combines elements from less than reputable cultural artifacts familiar from late-night television, makes their sexualized dimension explicit and dominant over other elements (such as science and politics), and provides the basis for elaborately artificial performance. Performance itself thus becomes, like the learning of dance crazes ("The Time Warp") and sexual experience (Frank's separate seductions of Brad and Janet, and Janet's seduction of Rocky in "Touch-a Touch-a Touch-a Touch Me"), a rite of passage, seen both in individual and in cultural terms. In this way, Frank's rampant sexuality encompasses and infiltrates all the stranger elements of genre film, making them seem, in retrospect, to have been mainly about weird sex in the first place.[60]

In this context, *Rocky Horror*'s music provides a means for regulating and facilitating the performances of these eclectically assembled personae, using exaggerated pastiche to emphasize both their artificiality and their adherence to generic archetypes.[61] Brad and Janet's "**Dammit Janet,**" for example, exaggerates rock and roll's tendency to repeat simple chord progressions by repeating the progression I–iii–vi (not uninteresting in itself, but relatively simple and without a strong direction) to support a lyric that revels in its own uninspired inadequacies.[62] And, indeed, the score has many similar numbers that tread the boundary between pastiche and parody, so that they might be enjoyed as examples of their genres while emphasizing, with affectionate indulgence, their generic limitations. Just as important as these con-

♪5.43

structed inadequacies, however, are the score's many instances of intriguing and subtle sophistication, so that the show does not simply wallow in the predictabilities of the generic but also engages its possibilities.

For example, Frank's pretensions to a God-like mastery of life itself—creating Rocky and manipulating, seducing, and physically controlling the other characters—resonates readily with both the Frankenstein stories and familiar tropes of divahood, a connection that is encapsulated in Frank's oft-quoted line (when he discovers Rocky with Janet), "I made you . . . and I can break you just as easily." The same trope, of "making" someone in both figurative and literal terms (with a suggestive undercurrent of what it means to "make" someone in sexual terms), provides the hook for "I Can Make You a Man," which Frank sings to Rocky after he emerges from his birth tank.[63] But here there is an additional layer to the "make" pun, as the song pushes hard against the Charles Atlas promise to make weaklings into "real men" through a crash exercise program (familiar from ads at the back of comic books). Even more fundamental to the scene, however, is the God-like pose Frank assumes, recalling Colin Clive's line at a similar moment in the 1931 *Frankenstein*, "Now I know what it feels like to *be* God!" The full line of the song's hook is "In just seven days, I can make you a man," alluding, with subtle blasphemy, to the original seven-day creation story from Genesis and evoking tropes of religious expression in the elaborate plagal conclusion to the line, delivering a full-scale "Amen" cadence (IV–I, with intervening harmonies) over "a man" (a near homophone of "amen"):[64] ♪ 5.44

> In just seven days,
> I can make you a **ma-aa-aa-an**.
> [Ame-ee-ee-en.]

(Another evocation of the creation story occurs in the later "floor show" sequence, when the "creation-of-man" image from the Sistine Chapel is revealed on the bottom of Frank's pool; Frank floats above the image, situated between God and Adam, buoyed by a life preserver labeled "Titanic"; see figure 5.4)

Although *Rocky Horror* is flagrantly eclectic, O'Brien's score retains some aspects of the "integrated" score fostered in "book" musicals, mostly by drawing important harmonic materials out of the opening number, "Science Fiction—Double Feature," which was, indeed, one of the important generators for the show, both conceptually and literally. In the film, the song is sung by a pair of disembodied lips belonging to Patricia Quinn, the original Magenta, who sang the song in the original play dressed as an usherette. But the voice we hear is Richard O'Brien's, pitched so as to sound at times masculine and at times feminine. (The idea for this presentation was Brian Thomson's—production designer for the film and longtime collaborator with Jim Sharman—who found Sharman's idea for a montage of science-fiction film clips too boring.)[65] The resulting combination of androgynous sexuality and general campy creepiness is ideal, and this function of the

Figure 5.4. Blasphemous images from *The Rocky Horror Picture Show*: the disembodied lips of the opening credits fading into the cross above the Denton Episcopalian Church after "lip-synching" "Science Fiction—Double Feature" (top panel); and the "cross"-dressing Frank-N-Furter (Tim Curry) singing "Don't Dream It, Be It" while floating between the Sistine Chapel's images of Adam and God, as reproduced on the bottom of his pool. Easily missed in the latter, but evident in this juxtaposition, is how closely Frank-N-Furter—with some help from the "SS Titanic" life preserver and his brightly painted lips—reproduces the earlier image's constellation of smile, oval, and cross (thus also anticipating his own imminent "crucifixion").

song—that is, to set a context for the show/film—carries forward on many fronts. Most obvious are the song's lyrics, which point to the quaintly exotic world of filmic science fiction. But the disembodied presentation itself points in two directions, toward the objectification of body parts encouraged by pornography and other overtly sexualized presentations, and toward the free-floating idealist "dream world" that the song suggests in its free-floating intermingling of situational "images" from roughly a dozen films (including *Rocky Horror*). Even more subtly, the musical profiles for verse and chorus point very specifically to significant musical moments late in the show, and less specifically to important material in between.

The chorus of "Science Fiction—Double Feature" plays out against one of the few really standard chord progressions in the show, especially familiar from doo-wop music from the 1950s, looped as an ostinato (as is typical for both rock and roll generally and this score in particular): I–vi–IV–V. But the progression is kept oddly off-balance by beginning in the middle (rectified by a two-bar extension of IV near the end) and by a device of musical phrasing common to most of the show's songs, of deemphasizing the opening harmony of a phrase in favor of the subsequent harmony (thus, V and vi in this case), by beginning after the former is struck and leaning syntactically into the latter:[66]

♩ 5.45

IV	V	I	vi
Science	fiction,	double	feature.
Doctor	X	will build a	creature.
See androids	fighting,	Brad and	Janet
Anne Francis	stars in	"Forbidden	Planet." Oh, oh, oh,
Oh, oh, oh, oh,			
At the late night,			
Double	feature picture	show.	

During the extended "Floor Show," this progression returns, but in a gradually normalized phrasing, to set Frank's "soliloquy" and then his repeated mantra, "Don't dream it, be it" (figure 5.4), which is eventually taken up by everyone as they join him in the pool in a stylized, dreamlike orgy:

♩ 5.46

I	vi	IV	V
Whatever happened to	| Fay Wray, that	| delicate satin draped	| frame, as it
		| Clung to her	| thigh, how I
Started to	| cry, 'cause I	| wanted to be dressed just the	| same.
. . .			
Don't	| dream it,	| [vocal rest]	| be it

Not only is the progression itself regularized into its more satisfying conventional shape (a kind of resolution), but the words of the mantra, as well as the preceding words, are also especially well aligned with the harmonies, drifting toward the minor and softer realm of the subdominant ("Fay Wray, that delicate satin draped . . ."; "Started to cry"; "Don't dream it") and then coming around with a strong assertion of will on the dominant (in italics) ("I wanted to be dressed just the *same*"; "*be it*").

The verse for "Science Fiction" follows a different four-chord ostinato harmonic pattern based on the descending tetrachord from tonic to dominant (in this case, E♭–D♭–C♭–♭), and this progression, too, forms an important part of the concluding scene, as one of the traditions associated with this shape, the "lament" tradition, takes over in "Super Heroes." Although the lyrics do not lament, precisely, the song itself functions as a lament in musical terms; as the bass traces a fully chromatic descending tetrachord (see note 14 in the previous chapter), the song suggests a profound sense of loss even as its lyrics provide different modes of "processing." Thus, Brad remains fixated on his inadequate performance as a conventional strong male ("down inside I'm bleeding"), Janet on the insatiable sexual desires still fully awake within her ("still the beast is feeding"), and the Criminologist on the "larger picture" in suitably clichéd terms ("lost in space and meaning"). But the music mourns Frank, and it also offers a segue back to a concluding reprise of "Science Fiction," a segue that is both thematic (in its dreaminess) and musically specific.

Somewhat less literally, the opening harmonic progression in the chorus of "Science Fiction," a strong move from a major chord to the major chord a whole step above, forms the basis for many of the more aggressive rock numbers, particularly those with a strong sexual component. "Time Warp," for example, the most elaborate "strangeness" that Brad and Janet encounter in the early stages of their "haunted-castle" adventure, evokes a kind of visceral strangeness in its opening progression, each time cycling safely back to the tonic through a series of plagal resolutions (descending harmonically by fourths):

I (A)		II (B)	♭VII (G)	IV (D)
It's astounding, time is		| fleeting,	| madness	| takes its
toll, / Listen closely, not for very much		| longer	| I've got to	| keep con-
trol, / I remember doing the		| Time Warp	| drinking	| those moments,
when / The blackness hit me				
	and the void would be	| calling		

melody:	F	E	G	F♯	F♯–E
harmonies:	♭VI (F)	♭III (C)	♭VII (G)	IV (D)	I (A)
	Let's	| do the	| Time	| Warp a-	| gain,
	Let's	| do the	| Time	| Warp a-	| gain.

As shown, the refrain initially jumps even farther afield (to F, the ♭VI of A and a tritone leap from B) before an extended plagal progression completes the cycle back home, while the melody maintains a tight, quasi-hysterical circle of control. The overall progression is a decidedly odd one, despite its familiarity, a combination that perhaps holds the key to the song's irresistibility. Importantly, while the initial harmonic impetus may be traced to "Science Fiction," the song is more concerned with controlling something that seems initially strange, so that it begins by bringing out the strangeness of its "Science Fiction" source progression, and then proceeds to control that strangeness. In literal terms, this fits the "instructional-dance" mode of the song, borrowed from similar numbers of the 1950s and early 1960s (a trope that Brad recognizes and acknowledges in his suggestion that they do the "Madison"), but it also suggests very strongly, through its surreal party setting, a realm of both drugs and strange sexuality ("But it's the pelvic thrust that really drives you insa-a-ane")—which can, however, be similarly learned and controlled.

"Sweet Transvestite" (Frank's entrance number), along with several later numbers with strong sexual implications or specific connections to Frank, takes its fundamental progression from the more extended progression of "Time Warp"; thus, "Sweet Transvestite" (I–♭III–IV) and the chorus of Eddie's "Hot Patootie—Bless My Soul" (I–II–IV), while partaking of different segments of the extended "Time Warp" progression, also bear a strong familial resemblance to each other.[67] Perhaps most elaborate in this regard is Janet's "Touch-a Touch-a Touch-a Touch Me," which extends a minor-mode version of the referential progression to the dominant, thereby creating a strong charge of urgent desire (dominant arrival is in bold):

 ♫5.50
♫5.51

♫5.52

> I was feeling done in, couldn't win,
> I'd only ever kissed before,
> I thought there's no use getting into heavy petting,
> **It only leads to trouble and seat wetting.**
> Now all I want to know, is how to go,
> I've tasted blood and I want more,
> I'll put up no resistance, I want to stay the distance,
> **I've got an itch to scratch, I need assistance.**

The harmonies of the verse (i–♭VII–III–iv, etc.) set up this moment of desire twice before the release into the major mode and Eddie's "Hot Patootie" progression:

♫5.53

I	II	IV	I
Touch-a, touch-a, touch-a,	touch me.	I want to be	dirty.

In its eclectic and fragmented recycling of the past, and in its breaking down of the boundaries between a fixedly performed "work" and a newly empowered audience, *The Rocky Horror Picture Show* seems quintessentially postmodern. Only its status as doggedly *not* aspiring to high-art status would seem to bar it from becoming the poster child of postmodernism in its most pretentious form. Yet this point of resistance is crucial; for all its irreverence, *The Rocky Horror Picture Show* is dead serious about valuing its tokens of low art *as such*—that is, as found, recycled objects that belong to us all. In this sense, *Rocky Horror* is not at all postmodern but rather a kind of modernist reconstitution of devalued and discarded artifacts, deftly aligned into gratifyingly performable personae. Probably, it makes greater sense to think of the film as post-Stonewall, created during a time in which sexual identities seemed fragmented and nebulous, in which it could seem only natural and right to play freely with the combinatorial possibilities, both in fantasy and in the more fully realized domain of role-playing and performance.

Hedwig and the Angry Inch (1998), despite outward similarities with *Rocky Horror*, is aggressively postmodern, as it resolutely confronts us with the postapocalypse of the European-based modernist trajectory. The apocalypse in question is World War II and the Holocaust, and its "post" phase is the enforced splintering of cultures and societies represented most vividly by the Berlin Wall (1961–1989) and its aftermath. In *Hedwig*, the Wall and the conflicts it symbolizes are embodied within the person of Hedwig Robinson (né Hansel Schmidt), whose sex-change operation has left him/her in both gender and sexual limbo. While *Hedwig* seems to have been intended as a kind of follow-up to *Rocky Horror*, and though its mode of presentation is decidedly unorthodox (a mixture of standup comedy and low-budget rock concert), it is also, in the way it interweaves its political and personal themes, a much more conventional musical than *Rocky Horror*.

The parallels between the two shows are important. Both are situated in America and feature a non-American, cross-dressing male diva of somewhat ambiguous sexuality who pays a steep price for his/her deviance. Both scores are based in a sometimes retro rock idiom that partakes generously of punk—specifically, *Rocky Horror* is based in 1950s pastiche within a glam-derived protopunk, and *Hedwig* in what might be described as neoglam and postpunk, with a substantial admixture of heavy metal. Indeed, in Hedwig's monologue, the musical influences she cites overlap significantly with Richard O'Brien's, including *Jesus Christ Superstar* (not mentioned in the film version) and those whom Hedwig terms "the crypto-homo rockers: Lou Reed . . . Iggy Pop . . . David Bowie" (ellipses in original). *Hedwig* includes many direct and oblique allusions to *Rocky Horror*, referring early on to a doctor's operating table as a "slab" and incorporating verbal images of Frankenstein's creature in "Exquisite Corpse" (thus, "I'm all sewn up"), a song that also evokes the title of a key song in *Rocky Horror* during the bridge ("As *time* collapses and space *warps*"; emphasis added). More externally, there has been some effort to duplicate the *Rocky Horror* phenomenon through midnight screenings of the 2001 film of *Hedwig* in selected venues. But there is above all the sense of a shared *attitude* between the two shows, to some extent coming from their shared musical basis. In its unusual and flagrantly low-budget mode of presentation in particular, *Hedwig* seems to thumb its figurative nose at established ways of staging a narrative musical show, especially considering the hugely expensive productions that dominated Broadway during its development in the mid-1990s. Indeed, in this respect *Hedwig* is probably more daring than *Rocky Horror*; certainly its format allows it to indulge its music according to more normative standards of rock authenticity, mostly eschewing the often distancing effect of campy parody that runs through *Rocky Horror*'s songs.

One particular parallel, however, points vividly to how very different the two shows actually are. *Hedwig* went through a longer period of development than *Rocky Horror*, dating from early 1994, when actor John Cameron Mitchell created the central character, backed by Stephen Trask's songs and his band Cheater, at Don Hill's Squeeze Box in Greenwich Village, as part of a series of live-singing drag queens. As a full-fledged theater piece, *Hedwig* began in earnest in February 1997 at the Westbeth Theatre Center (considered off-off-Broadway) before moving a year later to an off-Broadway venue, the Jane Street Theatre, where it ran for a little over two years after a slow start. Once it achieved success as a show, its trajectory grew more parallel to that of *Rocky Horror*. In particular, the creative team for each show was quick to try to expand on the success of its initial American run (neither of them on Broadway, where *Rocky Horror* failed and *Hedwig* never ventured) by producing a film version, and each—like Hansel becoming Hedwig—had to "leave something behind" in order to make that move. In dropping its evocation of a seedy theater in favor of a more "natural" setting, *Rocky Horror* brought itself closer to the science-fiction films that were its inspiration, increasing the degree to which its central figures could be readily understood as composites created solely for the pleasure of performing them. The film version of *Hedwig* seems to move in the same general direction, away from the artificialities of the stand-up stage (sacrificing some of John Cameron Mitchell's often quite funny shtick in the process) toward something like the real world, by projecting believable if slightly surreal versions of pre-1989 East Berlin, a trailer park near Junction City, Kansas, and America as experienced by a band on a road trip. More to the point, perhaps, it tells its story along more conventional narrative lines than the stage version. Importantly, however, this strategy—while producing a film that acquired quick and deserved recognition when it appeared at the Sundance Film Festival in 2001—took the show away from the most unusual features of its initial presentation and brought it closer to what it was at heart: a Broadway musical whose characters resonate in vivid ways with the world of its time.

The world of *Hedwig*'s time was, of course, very much in flux, a situation that remains true as of this writing. Despite the widespread jubilation that greeted both the destruction of the Berlin Wall in 1989 and, slightly later, the collapse of the Iron Curtain, when both the Soviet Union and Yugoslavia broke apart into constituent nations and ethnic groups in 1991, the reality of liberation was quite grim. The figurative Iron Curtain—so named by Winston Churchill in a famous speech in March 1946—had been erected between Soviet-controlled (or Soviet-influenced) Europe and the West just after World War II, whereas the more literally termed Berlin Wall was erected in 1961, as part of a failed attempt to isolate and then absorb West Berlin into the Soviet bloc. Partly because both institutions seemed, throughout the many decades that they remained in place, destined to endure for the foreseeable future, their sudden removal was felt with particular force. Yet, the extreme and prolonged violence that accompanies political repression tends to cast a long shadow, and it became clear across the 1990s that the removal of these long-enforced political barriers had activated (and in some cases reactivated) a large number of disturbing problems, both ethnic and economic. Throughout the 1990s, the former East Germany drained the resources and patience of the more prosperous West Germans, and ethnic- and nationalist-driven violence flared with barbaric ferocity in the Balkans and elsewhere, recalling for many the horrors of World War II and the Holocaust. The process of East European liberation was, all in all, a messy operation.

In thematic terms, *Hedwig* maps this unhappy political situation onto the body of its title character and relates it as well to ancient myths of origin, both of humanity and of sexual orientation. Thus, most obviously, the "messy operation" is performed on Hansel Schmidt's person, effacing his very identity as part of a process of liberating him politically and sexually. While Hansel acquiesces, by agreeing to the operation and assuming his mother's name as a necessary means for marrying the black American sergeant Luther Robinson, it is equally clear that his choices are closely circumscribed by political realities in East Berlin in the years before the wall came down. Despite frequent interpretive assumptions to the contrary,[68] there is little in the script (or in performances I've seen, which have in some ways deviated from the script) that confirms that *Hedwig*'s Hansel is in fact gay, although he does seem confused regarding his sexual orientation. As Hedwig makes very explicit, Hansel allows himself to be seduced by Sgt. Robinson specifically because of the taste of *power* that it gives him, and his agreeing to the unsuccessful sex-change operation is not driven by his sense of being a woman trapped within a man's body but by political necessity, since it appears to be the only way that he can use Sgt. Robinson as a ticket to the West. Many transsexuals have understandably felt betrayed by *Hedwig* because it problematizes Hedwig's sexual identity in any number of ways without providing any perspective whatever on how or why someone in a position to choose freely might decide to change her or his gender. But the show's fundamental frame of reference, politically, is not sexual politics in the United States but rather postmodern global politics, enacted in sexualized terms; from *Hedwig*'s perspective, it is thus crucial that Hansel's decisions and their consequences reflect basic truths about the chaotic, postmodern, and soon-to-be post-Soviet world he inhabits, in which promised freedoms prove elusive, choices are often few and onerous, and most attempts to improve things seem to make them worse.

But the depressing state of world politics is not the only larger frame of reference for *Hedwig*, for the show is also grounded, as noted, in ancient myths of origin, which offer important perspectives on both current world politics and Hedwig's situation. The most central of these myths comes from Plato's *Symposium* and is laid out in the second song of the show, "The

Origin of Love," cast as a recollection of one of Hansel's mother's rare bed-time stories. According to this myth (which has its Judeo-Christian counter-part in Eve's creation from a part of Adam), and as recounted in the song, people were formed by the gods splitting us in two as punishment for our presumption; previously, we were double size (four legs, four arms, two heads, etc.), sometimes two men (Children of the Sun), sometimes two women (Children of the Earth), and sometimes mixed (Children of the Moon). In splitting us, the gods created the pain of love, understood as the desire to reunite with our severed other half. In Hedwig's song, the myth assumes universalized status through her naming of a variety of gods drawn from among different mythologies (see figure 5.5): Norse/Germanic (Thor), Greek (Zeus), Egyptian (Osiris), Roman (Jove), and Indian (unspecified). Moreover, the myth naturalizes homosexuality and even speculative bisexu-ality, since, although none of us can know whether his or her other half is female or male, we are nevertheless impelled through the painful urges of love to seek to reunite with that other half.

The myth has obvious application to both the political situation outlined here and to Hedwig's own personal quest. Despite the widespread urge to put things back together, whether politically or personally, it is a fairly hope-less quest to efface the violence of initial separation and the passage of time. As the first song, "Tear Me Down," states in fairly aggressive terms, the Berlin Wall that is Hedwig—at times suggesting that he represents the broken human legacy of the wall, at other times the wall itself—remains defiant of those who would simply remove it. Yet the song also holds out some hope, substituting in its final strophe the image of a bridge for that of the infamous wall. Being in between—Hedwig's position, both culturally and sexually—is, however, a decidedly mixed blessing, for it not only facilitates connection but also clarifies and reinforces the essential separateness of the two sides, neither of which represents home.

"Tear Me Down," like most of the "angry" songs in *Hedwig*, uses the musical language of metal, dominated by successions of "power chords" (that is, chords that are missing the mode-defining third, often overamplified to produce distortion and add rawness to the tone). Part of what gives power ♪5.54 chords their "power" is their evocation of the primitive, which includes a seeming antipathy for the more refined subtleties of the major and minor modes. It is probably appropriate to hear this aggressive disregard for the basic binary categories of tonal harmony, which have dominated music for three centuries, as a parallel to Hedwig's—and the world's—situation in the mid-1990s: as something in between, and thus at the same time either-or and neither-nor. While this congruence between technical features and the show's basic themes may be a matter of instinct or happenstance, it goes a long way toward explaining why metal makes up an essential part of *Hed-wig*'s idiom. Moreover, two things indicate that Trask's musical choices in this regard are neither casual nor merely reflex driven. Later in the show, after Hedwig spits beer into the audience, she explains: "That was a rock

Figure 5.5. Two images from Emily Hubley's animated sequence for "The Origin of Love," in the 2001 film version of *Hedwig and the Angry Inch*. In the upper panel, gods representing four different mythologies—from left, moving clockwise, Thor, Durga (or Devi; the song does not identify precisely which Indian god), Osiris, and Zeus—plot how to punish humanity; in the lower panel, Zeus splits the compound humans in half with his thunderbolts, forming the two-legged species we know. This fundamental act of irreparable mythical violence serves in the show as the metaphorical basis for both Hedwig's quest for wholeness and postmodern political realities.

and roll gesture. Actually that was a heavy metal gesture. Want to see a punk rock gesture? *(Fills mouth with beer; a threatening pause; then she spits it over herself.)* It's the direction of the aggression that defines it." This theatrical demonstration of gesture and attitude underscores generic conventions without either choosing among them or denying their value as authenticating expression; even here, Hedwig remains in between. Moreover, such distinctions also have a specifically musical profile in *Hedwig*, worked out as part of the show's basic musical strategy of alternating anger (metal, power chords) and comfort (often retro, with full harmonies).

Thus, "The Origin of Love" begins with a gentler but still "primitive" style, with chords consisting mainly of empty fourths and fifths and an off-the-beat tonic motive that seems a more tranquil echo of the screaming, off-the-beat tonic power chords heard during the instrumental portions of "Tear Me Down." This faint hint of the violent idiom of the previous song soon gives way to a warmly sophisticated treatment of fuller harmonies when the vocals enter, emphasizing the major-mode third in a repeated melodic figure, but then shifting the harmonies beneath. The effect is a kind of harmonic shape-shifting, which sets a child's view of the origin myth, brilliantly captured in Emily Hubley's animation (see figure 5.5), which accompanies this song in the film (in the following, boldface indicates melodic repetitions of $F_\sharp$, the third of the tonic D):   ♪ 5.55

When the **earth** was still flat / And	D
clouds made of fire / And	Bm
mountains stretched up to **the** sky,	A (added sixth)
Some**times** higher. . . .	G^4_3 (inverted G_7, or G/D)

Especially poignant is the final line of this introductory "once upon a time," with its aching major-seventh combined with an image that suggests both Olympus and a child's perspective on mountains. But besides setting up these warmly expressive harmonies, the emptier harmonies of the opening also look ahead to the angry explosion of power chords that will erupt as the gods perform their cataclysmic surgery on humanity. If the connection to Hedwig's own cataclysmic surgery is only implicit, the final return places the myth firmly within the context of Hedwig's personal quest, a matter now of personal pronouns, beginning with "Last time I saw you."   ♪ 5.56

The next song, "Sugar Daddy," inverts that progression toward the personal, moving in its three verses from a craving for sugar to a craving for the surge of experienced power, a transition mounted against a series of dominant-tonic cadences late in the verse, moving from V to I both melodically and harmonically (italics are for the melodic dominant, bold is for the tonic arrival):   ♪ 5.57

> v. 1: *Oh, the thrill* of **control**, like *the rush* of rock **and roll** . . .
> v. 2: *Oh, the thrill* of **control**, like *a blitz*krieg on **the roll** . . .
> v. 3: It's *our tradition* to **control**, like E*rich Hon*ecker and He**lmut Kohl**. . . .[69]

But in the angriest song from the first part of the show, the subsequent song, "Angry Inch," with its wall-to-wall power chords and stuttering vocal delivery, the personal-exteriorized profile becomes a kind of sandwich, with all personal hurt on the outside, slaked with some bitter humor, and with only the hint along the way of how Hedwig's personal and at times physical pain reflects a larger situation ("I'm from the land where you still hear the cries").   ♪ 5.58

This kind of negotiation, between the personal dimension and its larger context, partakes of an integrative strategy typical of musicals, usually assuming some aspects of the marriage trope, and it is worthwhile to sort out the dimensions of the latter in *Hedwig*. To begin with, there is the question of gender and its potential for "bending." Significantly, for example, the makeup of her band (the "Angry Inch") undergoes a shift in gender while reflecting both Hedwig's real need to scavenge as best she can and her apparent desire to move along the borders; thus, she first uses "Korean sergeants' wives" and later switches to fellow East European political refugees, Jacek, Schlatko, Krzyzhtof, and Skszp (according to the script, pronounced "SKSHP"). In the show's original staging, *Hedwig*'s band provided most of the needed vocal backup, although in some later productions a separate vocal group also assumes some of the roles in Hedwig's stories, perhaps as a compromise with the more naturalistic approach of the film. Originally, Hedwig's only onstage collaborator is her current husband, Yitzhak, another refugee who is a former drag queen from Zagreb, Croatia, where he was (according to Hedwig's monologue) billed as "the Last Jewess in the Balkans," appearing under the name "Krystal Nacht" (referring to the infamous "Night of the Broken Glass" in 1938 Nazi Germany, when Jews were beaten and their property was destroyed all over Germany).[70]

The extremity of Yitzhak's marginalization is underscored by his being played by a woman (Miriam Shor) in both the original production and the film. This casting stemmed partly from musico-dramatic needs: to have higher notes available in some of the ensemble singing, and to allow Yitzhak more easily to upstage Hedwig on occasion, as required by the plotting of the show. Arguably, this casting also moves the show somewhat closer to the mainstream casting of musicals, which have traditionally benefited from the blending of female and male vocal types, especially as integrated within a romantic plot. But the choice also carries deeper thematic significance, both by providing a balancing reversal for Hedwig's profile as a man imperfectly presenting as a woman, and by underscoring the tendency to align marginalized populations with feminine characters. Hedwig's own emasculation reflects this tendency as grounded in the political realities of East Germany after World War II, when it had come to occupy the more feminine position of disenfranchised "Other" in relation first to the Soviet Union and then to West Germany. The legacy of World War II and the Nazi era also inflects Hedwig's view of things; thus, as she notes the visual parallel between Sgt. Robinson and his proffered Gummy Bears, she concludes with a brief but chilling reference to the Nazi gas chambers, disturbingly resonant as well with her descriptions of her childhood experiences, when, as a boy, and on his mother's insistence, he listened to rock and roll with his head in the oven: "His expression is echoed in scores of tiny faces pressing against clear plastic. Painted faces of every imaginable color, creed and non-Aryan origin, fogging up the bag like the windows of a Polish bathhouse. It's only a shower. Absolute power!" But notwithstanding the complementary gender-bending aspects of Hedwig's pairing with Yitzhak, that relationship is clearly destined to be no more permanent than her marriage to Sgt. Robinson, for it is constantly being eclipsed by her past relationship with Tommy Gnosis, né Tommy Speck, the son of a general who, after gratefully receiving Hedwig's love and tutelage, has built a successful career as a rock star on the songs she taught him and with the name she bequeathed to him ("Gnosis," the Greek word for knowledge).

The film and some later stage versions of *Hedwig* efface the delicious possibility that Tommy (or perhaps only his relationship to Hedwig) is a phantom, a mere projection on Hedwig's part. Since in the original all of the characters are channeled through the same actor's monologue, the strong suggestion persists throughout that they are but dimensions of one complex personality, embracing not only Hedwig herself but also Hedwig as a boy (Hansel), his mother, Luther Robinson, and Tommy, all of whose voices emanate from Hedwig. Moreover, this interpretation, or something like it, is eminently consonant with the show's governing myth of separation and possible recombination through love—from which, however, Yitzhak stands somewhat apart, both because he is literally present and because he resists assimilation into Hedwig's encompassing psyche. The original show is thus much more ambiguous about the boundaries of the self, and it seems plausible to see Hedwig's inadequacies—the neither-nor dimension of her in-betweenness—as powerful facilitators, allowing her to transcend neither-nor and even either-or to become, simply, *all*. As such, drawing on Christian imagery, her story lies close to that of Christ, whose abjectness transmuted into the universal and all-encompassing; there are, indeed, rather broad hints that this is an intended deep reading of the show. Hence, early on, Hansel's mother draws a shocking, cryptic analogy between Jesus and Hitler (both of whom "died for our sins");[71] Hedwig later alludes to the Shroud of Turin, whose ghostly image many believe to be the imprint of Christ's face (in this case, the "Shroud of Hedwig" consists of the imprint of her overdone makeup on a hand towel); and the show encourages a close identification, especially in "Exquisite Corpse," between Hedwig and the martyred creature of Dr. Frankenstein,[72] who is often seen as Christ-like, born without original sin and martyred to humanity's imperfections.

Hedwig's assumption of different personae in telling her story is brought to a musical focus in "Wig in a Box," the "comfort" song that follows "Angry Inch," and which details Hedwig's ritual of assuming identities as a mode of escape, admittedly temporary (since each verse but the last ends with Hedwig alone: "I put myself to bed" and "I turn back to myself"). The ritual dimension is carried by a calming descending sequence, dropping fairly conventionally from tonic to subdominant by way of the submediant, in an expansion of the familiar doo-wop progression (first verse given; later lyrics vary slightly):

I put on some makeup   (I–V)
Turn on the tape deck   (vi–iii)
And put the wig back on my head   (IV–I–V)

At this point, the ritual accomplishes its magic, and Hedwig (now fully
"head-wig") becomes someone else over transporting harmonies:

> Suddenly I'm Miss Midwest Midnight Checkout queen . . .
> . . . Miss Beehive nineteen sixty-three . . .
> . . . Miss Farrah Fawcett from TV . . .
> . . . this punk rock star of stage and screen. . . .

All of these identities are retro, transfixing images from Hedwig's youth as
Hansel, and so are both all the more tantalizing and all the more unattain-
able. The final identity—"this punk rock star"—is not relinquished, however; perhaps because of the "angry" bridge, an empowered Hedwig
insists at the end of the final verse, "And I ain't never, I'm never turning
back." In its ritualized, transformative performance of clichéd characters,
this number comes the closest in *Hedwig* to the world of *Rocky Horror*, and
it is no coincidence that this number has lent itself most readily to audience
participation.

Yet, despite this number and the untraditional device of enacted narration,
with its enticing interpretive avenues, the show may also be read less
obliquely, as a more traditional deployment of key songs underpinning a
story of romantic reconciliation. "Wicked Little Town," which doesn't appear until midway through the show, provides the linchpin, positioned by
Hedwig as "the first song I've ever written" and left hanging, incomplete, at
the end. The song is, in effect, the show's "Science Fiction—Double Feature"
(that is, its musical and thematic wellspring) while at the same time functioning as its "Send in the Clowns," appearing fairly late, but still early enough
so that its reciprocated reprise can complete the drama. Hedwig sings it to
Tommy shortly after they meet, and it is through his singing it back to her
with a new lyric of conciliation that the show achieves some sense of closure.
Like *Rocky Horror*'s "Science Fiction—Double Feature," "Wicked Little
Town" begins with a prominent instrumental descending line that will later
be elaborated as a lament bass (in "Hedwig's Lament"). Like "Send in the
Clowns," the song proffers an invitation that alternates between hopeful
and hopeless, in this case evoking a context that mandates escape as a first
priority, implicitly conflating both Junction City and Berlin with Sodom, the
original "Wicked Little Town." But between the invitation and its eventual
acceptance (however ambivalent and partial) comes Hedwig's complete
breakdown, as her exquisitely rendered "Lament," with shifting minor-
mode harmonies over a chromatically descending bass, segues into what is
another aria type borrowed, like the lament, from opera: the "mad" scene.
"Exquisite Corpse" ferociously inverts the chromatic descents of the "Lament," screams out its stream of power chords, and breaks mood incoher-

ently ("A random pattern with a needle and thread"), while the lyric speaks directly to the ways that the world's madness has literally been mapped onto Hedwig ("I'm all sewn up, a hardened razor-cut scar map across my body"). As this number concludes, Hedwig removes her wig and smashes the tomato breasts from her bra against her bare male chest. Now fully abject and defeminized, she is able to become Tommy, and does so, singing the reprise of "Wicked Little Town."

♩5.61

Hedwig offers an intriguing constellation of the "authentic" dimension of rock—its capacity to enact raw, ugly violence and emotional depth in seemingly direct terms—and the acknowledged artificialities of performance. At the same time, it develops its themes in such a way that personal identity is conceived as only and always partial, so that a deep sense of self is necessarily also partial, driven to seek its completion in others. The divided world, divided Europe, divided Berlin, and Hedwig's divided self are all aspects of the possibly redemptive tragedy of human existence, the impossible quest for a stable, embracing unity that must inevitably be denied to any sexual being. But redemption is nonetheless possible, through abjection and perspective, both of them familiar tropes of religion. Hedwig and Tommy achieve individual redemption through Hedwig's failure, Tommy's recognition of her, and Hedwig's subsequent gesture of release to Yitzhak, the latter delivered during the benedictory "Midnight Radio"—another reference to *Rocky Horror* in its acknowledgment of a community that achieves spiritual union through the air waves at the "in-between" time of midnight.

"Midnight Radio" adopts a "traveling" tempo in a 6/8 meter but begins starkly, in barely related chords and isolated melodic pitches, so that the more secure flow of the evolving song will emerge as part of a process that will later include an honor roll of female divas (Patti, Tina, Yoko, Aretha, Nona, and Nico),[73] and culminates in the familiar harmonic token of redemption and religious acquiescence, the plagal "Amen" cadence (on the final syllables of "radio" and "rock and roll"):[74]

♩5.62

> And you're shining like the brightest star,
> A transmission on the midnight radio.
> And you're spinning like a forty-five,
> Ballerina dancing to your rock and roll. . . .
> And you're spinning your new forty-fives,
> All the misfits and the losers.
> Well, you, you know you're rock and rollers
>   Spinning to your rock and roll.

In paying homage to other female divas, Hedwig effectively abandons her divahood by joining perspectives with the "misfits and the losers" she is singing to. As when she left East Berlin, she progresses here by thus leaving part of him- or herself behind. The process of stripping away the trappings of her divahood made a particularly strong effect in the prefilm stage productions, when the process also implicitly depleted her of her supporting cast, most of whom were channeled through John Cameron Mitchell as he enacted Hedwig's story with the mix of real life and exaggeration familiar to us from stand-up comedy. But even in the more conventionally narrative film version, and in many postfilm stagings of the show, which tend toward greater narrative realism, Hedwig is able to redeem something of herself in the end only by renouncing her own divahood and becoming part of the audience, part of the world at large, for whom rock and roll is something heard over the airwaves, at midnight. To be sure, the world she thereby embraces is broken, perhaps beyond repair. But by joining it—and here she again recalls Christ, in his renunciation of divinity to become human—she enables a sense of transcendence that is confirmed by one of music's most powerful and traditional symbols of transcendence: the flat sixth, which is why the number (and the show) ends with a cycle of alternations between tonic and flat sixth ("Lift up your hands").

♩5.63

For Further Consideration

The Wizard of Oz (1939), Carousel (1945), Gentlemen Prefer Blondes (1949; film, 1953), Bells Are Ringing (1956), Funny Girl (1964), Mame (1966), Thoroughly Modern Millie (film, 1967), Applause (1970), A Clockwork Orange (film, 1971), Seesaw (1973), A Chorus Line (1975), The Wiz (1975), La Cage aux Folles (1983), Beauty and the Beast (1994), Howard Crabtree's "When Pigs Fly" (1996), Rent (1996), A New Brain (1998), The Full Monty (2000), Bat Boy (2001), Hairspray (2002), Avenue Q (2003), and Wicked (2003)

See Also

Regarding Annie Get Your Gun, see chapter 5 of Andrea Most's Making Americans; pp. 218–28 in Philip Furia's Irving Berlin: A Life in Song; pp. 235–46 in Edward Jablonski's Irving Berlin: American Troubadour; pp. 233–40 in Michael Freedland's A Salute to Irving Berlin; and pp. 111–18 of Ethan Mordden's Beautiful Mornin'.

Regarding Gypsy, see Keith Garebian's The Making of Gypsy; chapter 6 of Scott Miller's From Assassins to West Side Story; chapter 4 of Craig Zadan's Sondheim & Co.; pp. 375–400 in Arthur Laurents's Original Story By; pp. 105–28 in Stacy Wolf's A Problem Like Maria; pp. 69–121 in D. A. Miller's Place for Us; pp. 244–51 in Ethan Mordden's Coming Up Roses and pp. 276–78 in his Better Foot Forward; pp. 132–43 in Meryle Secrest's Stephen Sondheim: A Life; and chapters 14, 16, and 17 of Theodore Taylor's Jule: The Story of Composer Jule Styne.

Regarding Sweet Charity, see pp. 219–22 of Ethan Mordden's Open a New Window and, concerning the film version, Richard Dyer's "Sweet Charity."

Regarding Rocky Horror, see (among a large quantity of writings about the show and film) especially Jim Whittaker's Cosmic Light: The Birth of a

Cult Classic; Scott Michaels and David Evans's *Rocky Horror: From Concept to Cult*; Sal Piro's *"Creatures of the Night": The Rocky Horror Picture Show Experience* (including an introduction by Richard O'Brien and some of the audience "scripts"); Bill Henkin's *The Rocky Horror Picture Show Book*; and Richard J. Anobile's *The Official Rocky Horror Picture Show Movie Novel*.

Regarding *Hedwig and the Angry Inch*, see Scott Miller's "Inside *Hedwig and the Angry Inch*" and pp. 233–51 of Judith Peraino's *Listening to the Sirens*.

Relationships THE AMERICAN MUSICAL has been most consistently successful when its stories and themes resolve through the formation of conventional romantic relationships. Nor has that success been merely commercial. The project of reconciling opposites has long provided narrative drama a reliable means to generate and sustain dramatic tension and has also served the more abstract dramas of instrumental music as a fundamental organizing principle (especially within what is usually called sonata form). The presentational logic, for musical theater, is persuasive. To present opposites in human terms, one tries, "naturally," to embody those opposites within fundamental existing differences, which come ready-made in the two sexes, male and female. And to reconcile such opposites, so embodied, one wants, "naturally," to weld them into a union that will be in human terms most convincing and in musical terms most satisfying—which is to say, a romantic, heterosexual union. Putting aside for now the rather improbable premise of this line of reasoning—that it is with the "natural" that one is automatically most concerned in a musical drama—we may readily see that it applies whether one is primarily interested in the actual characters in a musical or in the larger themes they partly embody.

To be sure, not all opposites lend themselves to sympathetic reconciliation, least of all the fundamental categories of "good" and "bad," critical to many if not most mainstream musicals. The bad may perhaps be redeemed or forgiven *by* the good but not reconciled *with* the good, at least not if one wishes to retain the sympathies of most audiences. But the formula still operates; as with any complications or obstacles along the way to some kind of reconciliation, the dramatic crux will lie not in the larger trajectory (which is probably a given) but in the ways in which the relationships between and among the principals are delineated in musical and dramatic terms. When it comes to relationships in musicals, the magic—whether angelic or devilish—is in the details.

Through most of the history of the American musical, the "natural" has, of course, been taken to be heterosexual, despite the proportionally substantial numbers of homosexuals who have always been part of the audience for musicals and most often part of the creative team and among the performers as well. There are several ways to make sense of this. One way is to understand homosexuality as unnatural, and there is no denying that many audience members and probably many on the other side of the curtain have felt this way, although, surely, their numbers are diminishing. Another is to understand the relationships one creates and/or sees onstage both in fairly literal terms and in figurative or symbolic terms, as standing in for a range of possible relationships, including homosexual ones. Still another, which will come into play in some of the musicals in this chapter, is to understand heterosexuality as normative, at least in terms of societal notions of respectability, but with homosexual practices and inclinations understood—most often obliquely and implicitly within the show's action—as both natural and to be negotiated in terms of familiar patterns of accommodation. Perhaps also, delineating conflict and its romantic resolution along gendered lines has an inherent appeal for musical drama, because of the resulting mixture of vocal types. (This argument applies less convincingly to dramatic types outside a musical context, which are often no more than stereotypes, based less in nature than in conventional modes of presentation.) In any case, the resoluteness with which American musicals have reified heterosexual norms, except very occasionally and mainly in the last few decades, is as astonishing as it is understandable; it is no aberration that three of the five resolutely heterosexual musicals under consideration here were composed by homosexual men.[1]

The musicals in this chapter occupy a rather privileged position in this larger study, in representing a thematic dimension basic to nearly all musicals. Indeed, I have elected not to provide a list of works "for further consideration" at the end of this chapter, since that would require a nearly comprehensive listing of all musicals. Moreover, I have assumed that the musicals I choose to discuss cannot truly represent the full gamut of how musicals treat relationships. This is less troubling than it might be, since the variety of ways in which musicals treat relationships has been a frequent concern for me throughout this two-volume study, beginning especially with my discussion of *Anything Goes* in chapter 4 of the previous volume. Thus, I have made my selection according to three main criteria. I've tried for some kind of chronological spread, but tried also to balance that criterion against the requirements that each selected musical should make relationships matter in an unusual way, and that musical presentation should be a central component of how relationships are elaborated, problematized, and (when relevant) presented as dramatic resolution.

Lady in the Dark (1941), for example, views its existing and potential relationships as touchstones for a woman's quest for psychological wholeness, and it is thus a particularly interesting show to consider immediately after *Hedwig and the Angry Inch*; moreover, its musical profile is among the most unusual in American musicals. *Kiss Me, Kate* (1948), in elaborating two separate but parallel musical worlds for its principals, allows us to consider more fully how performance as such contributes to the success of a relationship. *My Fair Lady* (1956) presents contrasting modes of vocality as both the problem and the rationale for its central relationship. *Company* (1970) is about relationships as such, considered within the context of late-

1960s sensibilities; thus, the show highlights the importance of commitment, following a decade in which the acceptable options for relationships had been strenuously reconsidered and to some extent reformulated. And *Passion* (1994)—which we will consider here as a kind of postscript—not only is one of the most unusual relationship-based stories ever to be told within an American musical but also finds, like *Lady in the Dark*, an appropriately unusual musical mode for telling its story, and so usefully completes this chapter's frame.

Lady in the Dark (1941) is more a serious play than a musical comedy. Its central dramatic situation concerns a successful career woman, Liza Elliott, the editor of *Allure* (a thriving fashion magazine), who is undergoing psychoanalysis as she battles psychological problems that have increasingly disrupted her life, both professionally and personally. Although the play does involve music centrally, it does so in a heavily circumscribed way, mainly providing a surreal setting for three dream sequences, which together offer important insight into the nature of her neurosis. More naturalistically, music holds the key to unlocking traumatic events of her childhood, which are associated with a half-remembered song whose opening melodic phrase continues to haunt her.

The premise for *Lady in the Dark* reflects both playwright Moss Hart's deep respect for psychotherapy (he dedicated the book to his own psychotherapist, Lawrence S. Kubie)[2] and his determination not to write a conventional musical comedy as he set out on his own after his decade-long period of collaborating with George S. Kaufman and such Tin Pan Alley stalwarts as Irving Berlin, Richard Rodgers and Lorenz Hart, and Cole Porter. This determined move toward the unconventional was shared by his principal collaborator, Kurt Weill, who nevertheless objected when Hart's advance publicity gave the impression that Weill's contribution would be no more than "incidental music."[3] For his part, Kurt Weill had fled Nazi Germany to avoid persecution (or worse), after both earning prestige for his concert music and achieving success and notoriety for his theatrical collaborations with Bertolt Brecht in the late 1920s (their *Zeitopern*, or "operas of the time"). Weill continued to be caught between "serious" music and a more accessible musical theater, and had yet to catch his stride on Broadway. Moreover, and strangely, his music for *Lady in the Dark* and *One Touch of Venus* (1943)—his two most commercially successful Broadway shows (not counting the Marc Blitzstein translation of *Threepenny Opera* in the 1950s, originally written with Brecht in the 1920s)—went mostly unused in their respective film versions. As a result, Weill's contributions to Broadway before the critically acclaimed *Street Scene* (1947) have been remembered—as with most other pre-*Oklahoma!* shows—more for including a handful of memorable songs than as complete shows. For these and other reasons, Weill's Broadway career has managed to detract from his overall stature as a composer without its being taken as seriously as it warrants on its own, despite unstinting devotion from a number of highly regarded scholars.[4] For the other main collaborator on the show, Ira Gershwin (lyrics), *Lady in the Dark* was a break with convention in another sense, since it marked the beginning of his comeback after the death of his brother and most frequent collaborator, George Gershwin, in 1937.

There are many explanations for the relative neglect that *Lady in the Dark* has suffered over time.[5] Today it is often regarded as a show that pointed in the direction of a more ambitious Broadway musical theater but had the misfortune of being eclipsed two years later by *Oklahoma!* which established an entirely different direction. It is also often regarded, somewhat unfairly, as naive or dated in its depiction of neuroses and their treatment, but this aspect of its reputation is a product of a number of elements, some native to the show and some not. There is undoubtedly a tendency in the musical "dream" sequences to reduce to comic absurdity what are, for Liza herself, frightening experiences, although this is to some extent also a matter of performance (but not always; there is no dramatic excuse for the "Tschaikowsky" interpolation in the "Circus Dream" sequence). More important for some is the fact that the resolution comes too quickly and too completely to satisfy any sense of psychological realism, although this is partly a matter of following dramatic conventions and adhering to necessities of the musical stage. And, perhaps also, the resolution itself is too conventional; depending on how it is played, the ending may seem uncomfortably close to an antifeminist comeuppance on the order of Annie's in *Annie Get Your Gun*, so that what Liza has to learn is not so much to face the fears of her childhood but to realize that she has been too much the career woman (read: too much the man) and too little the woman (read: too little accepting of men's historic prerogatives, both in personal and professional terms).[6] Certainly, the film version (1944, dir. Mitchell Leisen) does little to counteract this reductive view of the show's themes and their resolution. But such a view fails to take into consideration the stage show's extended treatment of her various symptoms and their childhood cause, and it cannot be sustained against the guarded, actually quite understated, resolution itself when played as written.

The basic strategy of placing Liza's dreams within musical settings, besides separating them from "reality" and enabling the free play of fantasy, also gives her dreams a *heightened* sense of reality, particularly since, in musicals, that's what music generally does. Liza's dreams may not be "real," but they are based in a stage version of MERM (Musically Enhanced Reality Mode; see chapter 2), which is a kind of reality, and the kind that counts in musicals; thus, it is significant that we see some of the people in Liza's life first through her dream images of them, before we even know their names. Immediately striking is her own appearance in her dreams, since she appears in each of these, at least for a time, considerably more glamorous and confident than the woman we see entering Dr. Brooks's office at the beginning of the show. But even more striking in the first dream (the "Glamour Dream") is the position of the Marine (corresponding to Charley Johnson), whose *unglam-*

orous painting of Liza brings her previously gratifying dream to a harrowing conclusion. Thus, Charley, even before we know who he is, appears in her dream as a relatively unimportant figure whose ability to see through her gives him enormous power over her.

Of the three musical dreams, the most impressively realized is the third,[7] the "Circus Dream," which combines a trial setting with aspects of Charley Johnson's proposed "circus" cover, which Liza has been hesitating to choose over a more traditional Easter cover (see figure 6.1). The Ringmaster/Judge in the dream is her magazine's photographer, who stands apart from her romantic dilemmas as an obviously gay man and provides comic relief throughout—especially as originally played by relative newcomer Danny Kaye, whose "Tschaikowsky" would, in fact, bring down the house, despite its dramatic irrelevance. The common device of using homosexuality in this way is both useful and potentially offensive; in this case it is particularly advantageous (while being only mildly obnoxious) because both the circus and courtroom settings require a person of authority who is not involved directly in the action.[8] At this point, Liza has not fully ruled out marrying her long-term married lover, Kendall Nesbitt (who is finally getting divorced), although her second dream sequence, the "Wedding Dream," has left that possibility hanging by a thread; film star Randy Curtis has also recently come forward as a possible romantic partner, whereas Charley is set to leave the magazine. While Liza is "on trial" for her inability to make up her mind what cover to use, the larger issues are her similar inability to decide her own future, given a range of romantic options, and to resolve a long-festering childhood trauma. Thus, the prosecuting attorney (and trapeze artist) is her seeming nemesis Charley Johnson, and her defense attorney (and bareback rider) is the insecure "dreamboat" Randy Curtis. As in all her dreams, Liza has an extended song during which the dream's trajectory seems basically to be running in her favor, only to be deflated in connection with a recollection of the childhood melody.

It is, perhaps, the special emphasis placed on Liza's inability to make up her mind that more than anything else distracts from the overriding quest to uncover the *cause* of this indecision (along with Liza's other problems), which is by far the more interesting psychological issue. By some accounts, the element of indecision in her neurosis (rather than, say, her depression, her inability to control her anger, or her uncharacteristic desire to sleep) became a prominent feature of the show because of Hart's exasperation over Gertrude Lawrence's hesitation to sign a contract to play Liza—even though he himself had been waffling, having earlier offered the part to someone else.[9] In musical terms, devoting an extended number to this particular symptom—and (as will be seen) the most effective number, at that—inevitably reduces the overall problem of the show to Liza's indecision, solved a shade too conveniently by having her cede authority to a strong male. Moreover, this shift in emphasis is reinforced by the show's recorded music, which represents our principal means for remembering the show, since it is only rarely

Figure 6.1. Gertrude Lawrence, the original Liza Elliott in *Lady in the Dark*, appears in the third of the show's dream sequences, the "Circus Dream," inspired by the cover design that Charley Johnson, her apparent nemesis and future romantic partner, has proposed for *Allure*, the magazine Liza edits (bottom left). (Photograph courtesy of Miles Kreuger and the Institute of the American Musical, Inc.)

revived and since the film version is particularly inadequate (especially regarding the play's psychological dimension).[10]

Within the "Circus Dream," Weill sets this quality of indecision with consummate skill. The opening "Circus" music is built around two particularly "indecisive" chords, the so-called French-sixth chord (which points decisively enough, but to two incompatible resolutions, a dissonant tritone apart) and the diminished-seventh chord, which has any number of potential resolutions (French-sixth is in boldface, diminished-seventh is in italics):

♪6.1

> Tarara, **tszing, tszing, tszing,**
> Tarara, tszing, tszing, tszing,
> Tarara *tszing, tszing, tszing, tara*ra,
> Tarara **tszing, tszing, tszing,**
> Tarara, tszing, tszing tszing,
> Tarara, **tszing, tszing, tszing, tara**ra!
> The Greatest **Show on Earth!**
> **It's full of** thrills and mirth!
> You get your *money's worth!*
> *Come one, come* all!
> Come see the midgets and the bushmen from Australia,
> Come see the cossacks in their dazzling re**galia,**
> The flow'r of **womankind who can't make** up her mind
> Is a *feature you will always re*call!
> You get your **money's worth!**
> **It's full of** thrills and mirth!
> The Greatest **Show on Earth!**
> Come one come all!

After the prosecutor lays out his case in "He Gave Her the Best Years of His Life"—a pastiche waltz song that inverts gendered stereotypes, as suggested by the title—and after the Ringmaster's "Tschaikowsky," Liza delivers her own showstopper in defense, "The Saga of Jenny," which sets out the perils of decisiveness by relating the story of someone whose impulsive decisions all end badly. In musical terms, the song is "sexy" not only in its jazzy rhythms and instrumentation but also in the tendency for its harmonies to slide chromatically downward from its "strong" pitches. Each verse ends with a descending sequence as the lyric recounts the tragic results of each of Jenny's "decisions" (creating a feeling of inevitability oddly blended with a somewhat insincere "lament"), coming to an emphatic "decision point" in the repeated-note cadential formula setting the words "But she would make up her mind." Of course, Jenny's decisions turn out badly in part because she is wanton, and many of the verses are quite ribald in their descriptions of her sexual indiscretions ("she got herself a husband, but he wasn't hers"; or, "in twenty-seven languages she couldn't say no"). In this sense, Liza's defense, in which she acts out Jenny's sexy disregard for decorum, comes across as a kind of longing—similar in kind to her self-projection

♪6.2
♪6.3

♪6.4

in the "Glamour Dream"—to have Jenny's confidence, if not her black heart (and even the latter apparently holds some appeal, given Liza's exuberant performance).

But before any of these ambivalences can be brought out, the prosecutor zeroes in on a key aspect of the song, if only implicitly. Like all of Liza's "Dream" songs, "The Saga of Jenny" presents a holistic view of a human life. Thus, both "One Life to Live" from the "Glamour Dream" and "The Princess of Pure Delight" from the "Wedding Dream" are directly concerned with achieving happiness. The tendency across the show is for these holistic life views to become increasingly narrative in approach, moving from considering how one ought to live in the first to charting a fairy-tale path to happiness in the second to describing the disastrous life course of a reprobate in "Jenny." Significantly, the latter is the only one of the three that begins in childhood—specifically, with a traumatic childhood event (three-year-old Jenny's burning down her house and orphaning herself on Christmas). With compelling if obscure logic, the prosecutor calls attention immediately after "Jenny"—seemingly as a way of changing the subject—to the "circus" cover, with its strong appeal to childhood, which the jury then "sings" as the haunting melody that has plagued Liza throughout the show. In this moment, which terrifies Liza, the "circus" cover (referring to Charley Johnson) and the half-remembered childhood song (referring to her childhood trauma) merge. ♫6.7

The opening phrases of "My Ship"—the song that Jenny can't quite remember—spell out a standard chordal configuration of American popular music, the major tonic triad with added sixth. Significantly, the first half of the melody is therefore also pentatonic, a scale without half steps that is frequently used to evoke the folklike. Although there is a slight oddness in the way the melody occasionally leaps and dips, creating an ambiguous modal orientation (thus, in F, but with an emphasis on the note D), its initial presentation at the beginning of the "Glamour Dream," over a single sustained D, emphasizes its simplicity until, gradually in the continuation, half steps are added, bringing the melody into sharper focus just before it breaks off. As the initially hummed melody then gets passed into the orchestra, it modulates along a cycle of minor thirds and acquires a gradually accumulating level of chromatic dissonance. This fairly rapid process of developing ♫6.8 complexity, established at the outset, becomes a larger shaping principle as the melody continues to reappear throughout the show; whenever the melody reappears to challenge Liza, it thereby seems to acquire an additional "edge." At the end of the "Glamour Dream," for example, C is added to the singly sustained D of the opening, intensifying the modal conflict. Liza herself begins the melody during the "Wedding Dream," initially set to a sustained C; later in the dream, when it seems to turn against her, it sounds against a mocking simulation of wedding bells. Finally, when the melody ♫6.10 appears just after "Jenny" in the "Circus Dream," it carries the nasty underpinning of a rapid, repeating chromatic figure that eventually erupts into

(Marginal music cues: ♫6.5, ♫6.6, ♫6.9)

simulated laughter, as the chromatic figure becomes an extended series of augmented triads moving chromatically up and then down the scale. The "Circus Dream" then ends with the jury's chanted exhortation to Liza, "Make up your mind!" repeated over a reprise of the French-sixth progressions that had opened the dream sequence.

♩6.11

Part of the ambition of *Lady in the Dark* is to counterbalance the general tendency in musicals to move toward a specifically musical climax; instead, *Lady in the Dark* wants to return to the simplicity of childhood, to pull out the other end of the psychological narrative string. Ultimately, the show will end in a musical understatement, with Charley and Liza singing "My Ship" together (it turns out that he, too, remembers the song, so that in a much less traumatic way he is also rejuvenated through a remembered youth). But the true musical climax of the show occurs somewhat earlier and is in its way even simpler.

The pivotal stage of Liza's treatment is a succession of recalled childhood memories that together explain the recurring images of her dreams and allow her to work through the choices that have befuddled her. As in the dream sequences, these memories are presented as surreal vignettes, but without the disorienting musical collages of the dreams. During this sequence, Liza remembers four childhood traumas (see the appendix), involving rejections by her father and schoolmates. Her fourth remembered trauma is the most devastating, because it seems at first to dispel the first three, but then reaffirms them with a vengeance; it is here, for the first and only time in the show, at the positive emotional peak of this memory, that Liza sings "My Ship" in its entirety. Liza, now seventeen, has been chosen most popular senior at her high school and is approached romantically by the boy chosen as most handsome (who is having a fight with "most beautiful"); she responds, accepts his kiss, and sings "My Ship" at what appears to be the happiest moment in her life. But then "most beautiful" returns to reclaim "most handsome," leaving Liza to naively await his return until she realizes she has been abandoned.

"My Ship," in Weill's full setting, is deceptively simple. Its form is a standard thirty-two-bar Tin Pan Alley form, AABA with coda. Its melody gets no more complicated than what we've heard of it already, and there is only the hint of a key change midway through the bridge. But the harmonic underpinning is richly chromatic, guiding each phrase to a comforting, seemingly inevitable arrival. In this way, Weill's setting constitutes a careful—and necessary—balancing of sophistication and simplicity. Emblematically, the chromatic richness of the song's setting may be understood to represent the complexities of the world, unknowable to the child Liza but seemingly justifying her belief that the world is basically benevolent and may be trusted to shepherd her through to a happy adulthood. Emblematically, as well, the song's simple melodic profile represents her trusting simplicity as a child. It is, of course, Liza's trust in the world that her now-recalled traumas consistently betrayed, with devastating effect on her chances for happiness, and only the

haunting simplicity of the melody remains to remind her of her folly and
perhaps also to help rescue her. Moreover, Weill's rich but simple setting   ♩6.12
also contributes to another important metaphoric function of "My Ship,"
in which the process of remembering how a song "goes" requires a retracing
from memory, much as the process of recovering childhood memories
through psychoanalysis facilitates drawing a direct line from past to present,
and from there to an optimistic projection of the future.[11] In this case, Liza
first recalls the opening melody; then, finally recalling the words that fit that
melody, she is able to follow through to the satisfying end of the song. Weill's
setting thus fulfills a difficult assignment: although necessarily simple, the
completed song must also seem worthy of the process. "My Ship"—particularly because it turns out to be a song Charley also remembers with similar
approbation—relates to the "secret song" or "mysterious melody" songs in
Moulin Rouge and *Naughty Marietta* and thus functions within a traditional
paradigm (see pp. 37–38 and 108–09, respectively). The fact that "My Ship"
is in this case both literally and figuratively connected to the recovery of
childhood memories, however, both separates it from that paradigm and
draws attention to why that paradigm carries such persuasive power.

Understood well, *Lady in the Dark* is not fundamentally about Liza's relationship to the particular men who present themselves to her as romantic
options, and least of all is it about her acquiescence to Charley, the man
who will become her husband. This is why Charley is, throughout, such an
enigmatic figure, whose true nature does not emerge until quite late, coincident with the advanced stages of Liza's process of self-discovery. Rather,
Lady in the Dark more fundamentally concerns Liza's relationship to her
own self, rooted within her experienced life, and of that self to the world
more broadly; put another way, it is about her relationship, as an adult, to
her own past. In this sense, the show stands somewhat apart from the concerns of this chapter, belonging perhaps more to the previous chapter than
to this one. Yet, because *Lady in the Dark* grounds its personal quests within
romantic options, it is in its way an ideal beginning point from which to
launch a consideration of the following two shows, considerably more mainstream than *Lady in the Dark* in their approach to relationships.

Kiss Me, Kate (1948) is often understood to be Cole Porter's response to the "integrated" musicals of Rodgers and Hammerstein, in
parallel to Irving Berlin's *Annie Get Your Gun* two years earlier.[12] It is certainly his most ambitious show, encompassing not only Broadway sophistication regarding sexuality, but dramatic, literary, and musical sophistication
as well, albeit lightly worn. While to some extent Porter's ambitions may be
understood in terms of the new standard raised by *Oklahoma!* and *Carousel*,
the derivation of *Kiss Me, Kate* from Shakespeare's *The Taming of the Shrew*
seems to speak also to a somewhat different order of ambition, more in line
with the operatic ambitions of George Gershwin in the 1930s or of Leonard
Bernstein and his cohort in the 1950s—yet it is altogether less assuming, a

resounding echo, perhaps, of Rodgers and Hart's more modestly successful setting of a Shakespeare comedy a decade earlier, *The Boys from Syracuse* (1938, based on *A Comedy of Errors*). Perhaps the most remarkable aspect of *Kiss Me, Kate* is that it is an anomaly, an example of Cole Porter—believed by many in the late 1940s to be over the hill—rising spectacularly to the challenge of setting a property both extremely ambitious and essentially comedic, and extending it in both realms. To be sure, the show's anomalous status should not surprise overmuch, given Porter's abysmal and gradually deteriorating physical condition after his catastrophic riding accident in 1937. Nevertheless, he had continued throughout the 1940s, and would continue even more energetically well into the 1950s, to compose admirable songs for successful films and shows—none of them, however, comparable to *Kiss Me, Kate* in terms of either artistic achievement or box office success.[13]

Perhaps the best way to characterize *Kiss Me, Kate* is to note that it is, at its core, *not* anomalous, except in how consistently it draws on Porter's unusual array of talents, on all fronts. In my first volume I wrote of how subtly the songs of *Anything Goes* (1934) define that show's intertwining and shifting relationships,[14] and Porter's facility in this realm is again the cornerstone of his success in *Kiss Me, Kate*, particularly as his songs convey both the deep affection and the surface skirmishing that mark the kind of relationships *Kiss Me, Kate* is built around. But the show also taps into Porter's rather casually deployed erudition, both literary and musical, gaining enrichment from his easy blending of Shakespearean diction with modern American English, couched within a similarly conceived blend of Tin Pan Alley with archaic musical styles prevalent during Shakespeare's time (or, more subtly, in *Italy* during Shakespeare's time, acknowledging the setting for *The Taming of the Shrew*). And, of course, there is Porter's ability, as a cosmopolitan sophisticate, to draw other languages into his songs as appropriate, often so as to suggest a more "continental" attitude regarding sexual mores. Thus, the intermingling of German and English in "Wunderbar" refers to the carefree inebriation of Viennese operetta ("Let us drink, Liebchen mein"); the French climax to "Always True to You in My Fashion" points to the easy sexuality associated with Paris ("Bébé, Oo-la-la! Mais je suis toujours fidèle"); and Kate's exclamations in Italian during the show's finale, with each impetuous term followed by its own superlative ("Caro! Carissimo! Bello! Bellissimo! Presto! Prestissimo!"), evokes the passionate natures often ascribed to Italians—which is, after all, the prevalent temper of *The Taming of the Shrew*.

♩6.13

♩6.14

♩6.15

The basis for *Kiss Me, Kate*'s presentation of relationships, in which nearly every dramatic element has a relevant "double," whether presented as an opposite or a parallel, was a famous 1935 Theatre Guild performance of *The Taming of the Shrew* by the Lunts, Alfred Lunt and Lynn Fontanne, whose offstage and onstage bickering was nonstop, the one mirroring and at times bleeding into the other. Arthur Saint-Subber, a stagehand for the production, determined years later, when he was an out-of-work stage manager, to produce a show based on the situation, and so, with his partner Lemuel Ayers, recruited Bella and Sam Spewack, a married writing team whose work on the show would bring them back together after a separation (in close parallel to the show's main action).[15] It was then Bella Spewack who persuaded a reluctant Cole Porter to take on the project; Porter's task would be to write songs for *both* the backstage action and what was now to be a musical version of *The Taming of the Shrew*.[16]

In converting *The Taming of the Shrew* into *Kiss Me, Kate*, Bella Spewack imposed a variety of "doubles" on the play, especially between the onstage and offstage personalities of the principals, at the same time condensing it to a length and content suitable for its purpose, able both to accommodate the addition of musical numbers and to work well as a "play within a play" (a device already present in *The Taming of the Shrew*, although not essential to the action). Her most important large-scale adjustment was to redefine and rearrange Shakespeare's characters so as to follow the theatrical convention, especially common in musicals, of complementing the leading dramatic couple with a second couple, conceived in part as a more comic version (or inversion) of the principals. Coordinated with this simplification of plot were important shifts in the nature of the principal characters themselves, so that Shakespeare's Kate (played by *Kiss Me, Kate*'s Lilli Vanessi) is a man hater rather than merely a shrew, and Bianca (Lois Lane) is more her obverse—a shameless flirt—than the innocent ingénue of Shakespeare's original, as signaled by her name ("Bianca" means "White," a traditional symbol of virginal purity). Their counterparts were similarly reconceived in opposing terms, with Shakespeare's thrifty and calculating Petruchio (*Kiss Me, Kate*'s Fred Graham) offset by a poor and carefree Lucentio (Bill Calhoun)—the latter quite different from Shakespeare's wealthy student in disguise. For the onstage/offstage dynamic to work, the "actors" playing these parts had to be similar in kind if not in degree. Thus, Lilli is somewhat softer than Kate, distrusting rather than hating men (more, in fact, like Shakespeare's Kate); whereas Bianca can't choose, Lois chooses much too often; Fred is a manipulative control freak, not quite as smart as he likes to think, capable (like Petruchio) of resorting to force but ultimately appealing to love; and Bill is a compulsive gambler, unable to exercise sufficient self-control.

It is above all the habitual, repetitive behaviors of the four offstage characters that bind them together despite their arguments: both Lois and Bill give in too freely to their compulsions (sex and gambling), and both Lilli and Fred play their cards too close to the vest, Lilli because she is innately distrustful and Fred because he is a control freak. With both couples, the success of the relationship will prove to be centered around performance—indeed, roughly equal parts of performance, and of believing (or performing belief) in the other's performance, so that, for them, a successful relationship resembles a game played for extraordinarily high emotional stakes. Although the game seems, at first, to be about winning in the conventional sense, it turns out to be much more about allowing the other to believe that she or he has won, as part of a self-reinforcing cycle and as an expanded version of performing, in public, the self one would like to be. What ups the ante in the case of *Kiss Me, Kate* is the public-private dimension of its central gimmick, which brings additional pressure to bear on the element of performance, augmenting what is already an important dimension in most relationships: that one is often forced by circumstances to "perform" a relationship on two tracks at once, both for one's partner and for a readily curious larger circle of friends and acquaintances. Perhaps even more obviously, this works in reverse as well, since it is equally a commonplace that actors often carry their onstage performances with them offstage; this is, as noted in previous chapters, a central dynamic in how musicals themselves "perform" for their audiences (that is, by providing material for offstage performance, as well as onstage).

Porter's songs for *Kiss Me, Kate* comprise a comprehensive set of "doubles," including every sung number in the show (with two reprises and one song—"Always True to You in My Fashion"—that doubles with two other songs; italics indicate a song that takes place in *The Taming of the Shrew*, and numerals indicate the act):[17]

Another Op'nin', Another show (1)	//	*We Open in Venice* (1)
Why Can't You Behave (1)	//	Always True to You in My Fashion (2)
Wunderbar (1)	//	Brush Up Your Shakespeare (2)
So in Love (1)	//	So in Love (reprise; 2)
Tom, Dick or Harry (1)	//	*I've Come to Wive It Wealthily in Padua* (1)
I Hate Men (1)	//	*I Am Ashamed That Women Are So Simple* (2)
Were Thine That Special Face (1)	//	Bianca (2)
I Sing of Love (1)	//	Too Darn Hot (2)
Act I Finale (*So, Kiss Me, Kate*)	//	Act II Finale (*So, Kiss Me, Kate*)
Where Is the Life That Late I Led? (2)	//	Always True to You in My Fashion (2)

These doubles seldom duplicate the ways in which other paired songs relate to or oppose each other; they do, however, display in each case a combination of mutual reflexivity and stark contrast (even in the reprises) and fall into some fairly distinct categories.

Some song doubles, for example, pair a *Shrew* song with a backstage song. "We Open in Venice" repeats the gesture of "Another Op'nin' ": in each, the nonprincipals and stage crew introduce themselves, first as members of Fred Graham's company in "Another Op'nin'," and then as the players within *Shrew*, dressed in colorful period costumes, in "Venice." Each song also locates itself geographically: the first through the American "tryout" cities of Philly, Boston, and "Baltimo'e," and the second through the Italian touring towns of Venice, Verona, Cremona, Parma, Mantua, and Padua. And each song expresses a general attitude about the enterprise, the one contrasting sharply with the other, as the hopeful, nervous excitement of the first is displaced in the second by routine boredom (the fate of virtually any show that survives the first, more exciting stage). Indeed, in "Venice," even the pleasures and trials of a touring company become merely routine; each time the chorus of "Venice" repeats and cycles through its parade of towns, we learn that Parma may be expected to negate each specific pleasure offered by Cremona, which offers laughs, bars, dough, and quail (fast women, probably prostitutes), whereas Parma is, in turn, a "dopey, mopey" / "beerless, cheerless" / "stingy, dingy" / "heartless, tartless" menace. Moreover, Porter's musical means for setting the opposed attitudes of the two songs are as balanced as Cremona's virtues and Parma's faults, as he employs dramatically rising melodic sequences in "Another Op'nin' " and falling melodic sequences in "Venice."[18]

    ♩6.16

    A similar kind of opposition governs the pairing of "I Sing of Love" and "Too Darn Hot" on either side of the intermission. The former sets a benign folk-based pastoral (with a regrettably weak lyric, although its simulation of Italian folk musical styles is creditable), and the latter offers contrasts on every level even given its obvious situational parallel: urban jazz dance rather than pastoral; overt sexuality (in style and through innuendo if not according to the lyric) rather than benign, idyllic love; and modern behavioral science (that is, referring repeatedly to the "Kinsey Report")[19] rather than folk-based traditions of courtship.

    ♩6.17

    Whereas these ensemble numbers act as a kind of musical scene setting, helping to keep the two worlds of the show separate, three of the song doubles underscore instead significant parallels between and among the characters—all, as it happens, involving Petruchio. Most striking is the first of these, involving Bianca's ensemble number with her three suitors ("Tom, Dick or Harry") and Petruchio's "I've Come to Wive It Wealthily," both of which use the "canzona" rhythm prominently in the accompaniment (a repeated duple-meter pattern of long-short-short, long-short-short, etc.), a rhythm specifically associated with Italian instrumental music during Shakespeare's time.[20] Petruchio's song is one of several instances of Porter's drawing inspiration directly from Shakespeare, although he often merely imitates his language (as he admits during the internal verse of "Were Thine That Special Face": "I wrote a poem / In classic style / I wrote it with my tongue / In my cheek / And my lips in a smile"). Here, four lines from one of Petruchio's early speeches (Act I, Sc. II, 73–76) inspire the song's hook and one of its many colorful similes:

    ♩6.18

    ♩6.19

> . . . were she as rough
> As are the swelling Adriatic seas:
> I come to wive it wealthily in Padua;
> If wealthily, then happily in Padua.

While the latter two lines provide the song's starting and ending points, Porter expands the previous two into a lively contrast between hot and cold that, as in Shakespeare's speech, is adroitly "grounded" in Italy:[21]

    ♩6.20

Do I mind if she fret and fuss,
If she fume like Vesuvius,
If she roar like a winter breeze
On the rough Adriatic seas. . . .

Both songs partake of an easy flow between modern American English and Shakespearean diction, although only Petruchio's is actually derived from Shakespeare. (Here Porter is fairly consistent in taking more care to derive Petruchio and Katherine's songs from Shakespeare, perhaps responding to the hierarchy of characters.) While both songs are also quite ribald, and free with their wordplay (as befits *The Taming of the Shrew*, which is stuffed with atrocious puns), "Tom, Dick or Harry" is the more audacious of the two, initially rhyming its faux-Shakespearean "I'm a maid who would marry / And will take with no qualm" with the more colloquial "Any Tom, Dick, or Harry" (a familiar phrase only a century and a half younger than Shakespeare), but then continuing with the risqué variant—ostensibly to complete the rhyme scheme—"Any Harry, Dick, or Tom." If the recast phrase suddenly turns the supposedly "pure" Bianca into some kind of nymphomaniac, the wordplay on "hairy dick" is nevertheless eminently deniable, an essential feature of much of Porter's wordplay.[22] Besides its canzona rhythmic basis, "Tom, Dick or Harry" also evokes its time period with "archaic" modulations (in the introductory verse by the three suitors, each of whom shifts down a whole step, harmonically, after his entrance) and a simulated "madrigal" section, intended to be performed a cappella ♪6.21 (that is, without accompaniment), but rarely performed that way. But the songs reflect each other most of all in their playfully cynical approach to sexual relationships; both Petruchio and Bianca, albeit for quite different reasons, will need to learn to love more genuinely—or perhaps merely to display their true feelings.

Indeed, midway through the second act, both of them explicitly acknowledge a libertine past that will surely need to be forsworn, Petruchio in "Where Is the Life That Late I Led" and Lois Lane (that is, the offstage Bianca) in "Always True to You in My Fashion." In completing a double set of doubles, this pairing also clarifies that each song fits its associated onstage and offstage characters equally. Again, saucy wordplay provides a link between the two songs, along with their parallel functions as formulaic "catalog songs" of previous romantic conquests.[23] Contrasts between the two come principally on two fronts. "Where Is the Life" provides another deft survey of Italian landmarks, each now bearing some ribald association (easiest, perhaps, with Pisa: "You gave a new meaning to the leaning tow'r of ♪6.22 Pisa"); "Always True to You" contrasts this with a similar map of the modern world, referring, with seemingly endless saucy variations, to both the professions and the native towns of Lois's sexual partners (making it clear that she favors her men to be away from home, presumably in town for conventions or business). But the most striking difference is the contrast

Lois offers to Petruchio/Fred's rueful look back on past behavior no longer acceptable; she obviously hopes to continue her "hobby," justified by a rather mystifying distinction that allows her sexual exploits not to "count," since in some unspecified way she remains true to Bill in her own "fashion." (Lois's curious standards are, furthermore, entirely double. "Always True to You" connects not only to Petruchio's "Where Is the Life" but also, and more directly, to her own "Why Can't You Behave" at the beginning of the show, which she reprises briefly as a lead-in to "Always True to You.")   ♩6.23

If Bianca/Lois does not precisely join Petruchio in accepting the idea that love ought to rein in promiscuous sexuality, however, Petruchio's pangs over what seems to be an unreciprocated love—as expressed in "Were Thine That Special Face," which Porter derived from a line delivered by Bianca in the original play (see note 21)—do find reflection in "Bianca," the one solo song given to Lois's suitor, Bill.[24] Each frustrated suitor presents his song as defective (using a fairly common device of Porter's), whether because it was originally written in jest—in the case of Petruchio (thus, in the verse quoted earlier: "with my tongue / In my cheek / And my lips in a smile")—or through inexperience—as in Bill's case ("Though I'm just an amateur"). And each song enacts an intensification true to the character of the singer, as Petruchio's initially sedate presentation suddenly becomes an amorous beguine (another Porter specialty) after he acknowledges during the internal verse that his jesting poem has come true, and Bill segues into a specialty dance number after singing through "Bianca" with chorus backup. True to the parallelism common to comic characters, Bill also invokes Petruchio's strategies as a possible way to "tame" Bianca (in the process offering an exceptionally inadequate rhyme for Bianca that reflects a lower-class imitation of Italian speech patterns): "Bianca, Bianca, / You'd better answer yes / Or poppa spanka."   ♩6.24

Like these two fairly modest songs of loving devotion, the show's major love song, "So in Love," is sung each time without the beloved's being present, an effect intensified through its being sung, each time, without any on-stage audience at all, so that it stands as close as possible for "inner truth," much as a Shakespearean soliloquy might do.[25] It is this setting—in isolation—that allows Fred's reprise to act almost as a separate song doubling Lilli's earlier version, in part because the situation has progressed, yet it has not resolved (indeed, it has moved in the other direction), and in part because Fred sings it at a more desperate moment in the second act than Lilli's in the first, which, because of their different perspectives, brings out a different profile from the song itself.[26] Thus, when "Taunt me and hurt me" launches the final return to the low register in which the song begins (the final "A" of a typical AABA structure), Lilli's subsequent gratifying move to a soaring higher register seems a celebratory transcendence ("I'm yours till I die"). When sung by a despairing man, all this changes, as he will more naturally indulge the riches of the lower register, bringing out the reality (rather than the pastness) of being taunted and hurt, and converting the upper register into a realm of heroic resolve. Even the phrase "till I die" shifts its meaning, from Lilli's projection of their consummated love (via the centuries-old trope of equating "dying" with orgasm; here the melody simulates orgasm by achieving climax and subsiding in waves) to Fred's heroic defiance at the ♪6.25   prospect of a life spent *without* that consummation.

The song is expertly crafted, not only so as to bring out this subtle shift in emphasis according to register, but also in the way it manipulates motive, registral climax, and modal shifts between minor and relative major. Beginning with its lowest notes, the song's melody leaps upward by fifths (C to G, F to C) before falling back after a weaker leap reaches only slightly higher ♪6.26   (B♭ to D♭). Again, with the second "A" phrase, the melody strives upward, this time reaching slightly higher, but not yet to a full fifth in its final ascent ♪6.27   (B♭ to E♭)—enough, however, to break into the major mode for the bridge. The bridge's passionate memory shades slightly higher (to F♭, on the word "joy") before fading back to the opening when, finally with the last "A" phrase, the upward-fifth motive carries through to the song's melodic peak (B♭ to F), descending more gently to settle into the relative major, colored ♪6.28   by its own parallel minor (on the final repetition of the title phrase). Significantly, whereas the upward-fifth leaps in the first two "A" phrases point outward, seeking the beloved, in the final "A," with its enhanced awareness of the singer's aloneness, they point inward, expressing love as a privately held emotion, still unexpressed to the beloved (upward fifth-leaps are in bold):[27]

> Strange, dear, but true, dear,
> When **I'm close** to **you, dear,**
> The stars fill the sky, . . .
> Even without you
> My **arms fold about you,**
> You know darling why, . . .
> So taunt me and hurt me
> **Deceive me** desert **me,**
> I'm **yours** 'till I die. . . .[28]

Lilli's own transformation—for it is much more hers than Kate's, although it is Kate who sings—is expressed in the paired opposites "I Hate Men" and "I Am Ashamed That Women Are So Simple," the latter taken nearly intact form her final speech in the original play (Act V, Sc. II, 161–68, 177–79). Here, similar melodic figures are put to opposing uses. While in each song a basic descent is shaped as a pattern of alternating ascents and descents, the minor mode and close intervals of "I Hate Men" (at least at the beginning) evoke the darkness of the Dies Irae,[29] whereas the major mode and wider intervals of "I Am Ashamed" dispel that darkness and replace it with the musical language of home truths, simply expressed, whether we are meant to believe those "truths" or not (parallel descending phrases from each song ♪6.29   as described):

I hate men,
I can't abide 'em even now and then. . . .

I am ashamed that women are so simple
To offer war where they should kneel for peace.

It is the contrasting energies of these songs that carries over into the two finales, which are alike in evoking the dramatic excesses of Italian opera. But those excesses here come also in two distinct flavors: the exaggerated passions in the second-act finale (with Kate's interjections, quoted earlier: "Caro . . . Prestissimo") and, in the first-act finale, as a standard trope of Italian opera, the "mad scene" (referring to insanity rather than anger). Porter here is in effect punning on the word "mad," alluding directly, in Kate's vocal cadenza and ensuing dialogue with a flute, to one of the most famous mad scenes in all opera: that of Gaetano Donizetti's *Lucia di Lammermoor* (1835), where the bride Lucia returns to the wedding celebration, in blood-stained dress, after having murdered her bridegroom (perhaps, then, the allusion also serves as Lilli's warning to Fred not to push things too far).[30] ♪6.30

Oddly, the linchpin for the successful outcome laid out in these elaborately gestured milestones of Fred and Lilli's restored offstage relationship is a virtual throwaway pastiche song, "Wunderbar," a campish parody of an old-fashioned operetta waltz song (in fact, derived from a "trunk" song that had been discarded from three shows in the 1930s)[31] that is subtly recalled through its comic counterpart, "Brush Up Your Shakespeare," a "Bowery" type of waltz song sung late in the show by the gangsters, just before they leave. This is a critical moment, since Fred has made them his allies—despite their insinuating insistence on calling him Mr. Gray-ham (thus, not only a ham, but also an old one)—in order to keep Lilli from leaving the show midway through the first performance;[32] with them gone, Fred fully expects that Lilli will leave as threatened. The comic nature of the song is probably what most assures us of a happier resolution, but, more subtly, the waltz idiom provides at least a faint echo of "Wunderbar." ♪6:31

As with "My Ship" in *Lady in the Dark*, "Wunderbar" acts as a healing and enabling "memory" song, with Fred and Lilli tracing precisely the same path as Liza had to the song's restoration: a bit of remembered melody, a grasping for the key opening words that will unlock the entire song, and an exuberant rendition of the song that is both a triumph of restored memory and a renewed delight in the song's ridiculously dated conceits and generic exaggerations (see figure 6.2). It is this song that convinces us, in dramatic terms, that the couple had a past relationship worth reviving. It is also what allows us to see how close beneath the surface that revival lurks, in the easy way the two first fall into the comic play at enacting the "loving couple" familiar from Viennese operetta, then yield to the seemingly inevitable moment when the masks slip and their play becomes real (a demonstration of one of the great secrets of camp more generally: its capacity to turn brazen artificiality into the real thing). Without this number, "So in Love" would seem mere posturing and Lilli's return completely out of character.

The capitulation of Kate/Lilli at the end can, of course, seem appalling, both because it is so easily assumed and because of its reification of a woman's subordinate position in marriage and in life more generally. One may well believe that even Shakespeare's audience would have understood this resolution—especially given its immoderate elaboration in Kate's final speech—to be a matter of exaggerated playacting, as Kate's way of gaming the marriage system, reciprocating Petruchio's "method" of defeating her through deprivation while pretending to be excessively attentive.[33] But this reading, even well performed, will escape enough of an audience that the ending will remain unsettling, especially given Kate/Lilli's spanking in the first act—an officially sanctioned act of domestic violence enacted in public (and the distinction blurs regarding who exactly is getting spanked, Lilli or Kate). Nevertheless, what remains true, and will come through in most performances, is that by capitulating and acting the part of the subservient wife—that is, by *performing* obedience—Kate secures the upper hand in their relationship, or at least achieves a more balanced power structure, since, after all, Petruchio must also continue his performance of dutiful attentiveness. Important too is the implicit acknowledgment from each that the other's (onstage) performance is based on something genuine (offstage), so that Lilli, by returning, has shown that she has seen through Fred's manipulations to the love beneath, and Fred, in turn, might reasonably believe that Lilli has, indeed, "come around," even though what he sees is no more than Kate playing the part as written. As onstage and offstage personae and situations thus merge—as Fred expresses his feelings through Petruchio and Lilli expresses hers through Kate—the distinction between the performed relationship and the actual relationship fades, replicating the kind of merger we have seen, in previous chapters, between the self and the enactment of self through performance.

Kiss Me, Kate draws powerfully on the ways in which the American musical traditionally "performs" romance and points to the ways music can seem indispensable to the success of a relationship. In this, it parallels real life, where a couple's connection is often secured through a favorite song; hence, the common phrase "they're playing our song" or the situational dynamic of "You and I" in *Meet Me in St. Louis* (see pp. 100–01). Music, as a vehicle for performance, especially through song and dance, and quite apart from the many ways it might otherwise align itself with sexuality, can in fact (and in fantasy) make all the difference. How else to explain how one of Shakespeare's least palatable plays can serve as the basis for the delightful evening that *Kiss Me, Kate* has reliably provided? Like Fred and Lilli's dressing room scene before they remember how "Wunderbar" goes, *The Taming of the Shrew* now seems incomplete and dramatically unsatisfying without Porter's music, through which—and only through which—we can truly believe in

Figure 6.2. After sparring verbally, *Kiss Me, Kate*'s acting couple Lilli Vanessi (Patricia Morison) and Fred Graham (Alfred Drake), long since divorced, try to overcome opening-night jitters by reminiscing, and inadvertently rekindle old romantic feelings while performing "Wunderbar," a number from the operetta that first brought them together. (Photograph courtesy of Miles Kreuger and the Institute of the American Musical, Inc.)

the romantic viability of the central couple. The show thus joins Mozart's *The Marriage of Figaro* and Rossini's *The Barber of Seville* in making its original dramatic bases seem incomplete—a distinction also shared by the next of this chapter's musicals.[34]

My Fair Lady (1956) was adapted directly from George Bernard Shaw's best-known play, *Pygmalion* (1913; first staged in English in 1914), by the veteran team of Alan Jay Lerner (book and lyrics) and Frederick Loewe (music). Since it is rare for a highly regarded play to become a similarly highly regarded musical, the exceptional few that do so become especially interesting. Arthur Laurents, in adapting Shakespeare's *Romeo and Juliet* for *West Side Story* (which opened after a long gestation period in 1957, a year after *My Fair Lady*), reworked the story so as to eliminate coincidence and demystify the workings of fate; in many respects, the result, although necessarily simpler than the original, is dramatically stronger, at least by twentieth-century standards (and this not even counting the brilliant contributions of Bernstein, Robbins, and Sondheim). Moreover, Laurents's adaptation avoids direct comparison to Shakespeare's play through its change of setting, from warring families long ago and far away to warring gangs on contemporary New York streets. Similarly, even apart from its music, the many ways that *Kiss Me, Kate* riffs on *The Taming of the Shrew* provide useful plot complications that appeal to more modern sensibilities; moreover, those parts of *Kiss Me, Kate* that derive directly from Shakespeare are even more obviously meant as a partial realization of the play, mediated both by how little of it we actually see and by the conceit that, as a musical version, it is already compromised, the more so for having been devised and overseen by actor-impresario Fred Graham, whose artistic credentials are highly suspect.[35]

Unlike these roughly contemporary adaptations, however, *My Fair Lady* is extremely faithful to Shaw's original, or at least to the original as Shaw adapted it for the 1938 film at the behest of producer Gabriel Pascal and codirectors Anthony Asquith and Leslie Howard. Most of the dialogue in *My Fair Lady* is Shaw's, and key phrases from many of the songs derive from Shaw as well. Thus, to its seeming discredit, *My Fair Lady* is unabashedly a musical version of a play that plays extraordinarily well *without* music. Nevertheless, the musical version in this case, despite its broader pacing, *also* plays extraordinarily well, and many prefer it to the play. What makes Lerner and Loewe's achievement all the more impressive is that Gabriel Pascal had offered the play to many other successful Broadway teams in the early 1950s, who either rejected it outright (i.e., Betty Comden and Adolph Green, Noël Coward, and Cole Porter, among others) or soon gave it up in frustration. Lerner and Loewe themselves had abandoned the project after a brief struggle in 1952, and when they returned to it two years later, they had enormous difficulty evolving the score's now-classic suite of songs, rejecting countless efforts along the way. Reportedly, Rodgers and Hammerstein spent a year working on it unsuccessfully before they admitted defeat, although they ended up much later with an appropriate consolation prize when their *Cinderella*—whose familiar story is often assumed to have been the basis for *Pygmalion*—aired in March 1957 as the first made-for-television musical, a little over a year after *My Fair Lady* opened with the same star, Julie Andrews, in the role of Eliza Doolittle.[36]

Arguably, the reason *My Fair Lady* has triumphed over its situational difficulties is that Lerner and Loewe, by adding music to the play in a particularly strategic way, moved it away from Shaw's conception and closer to what its casts and audiences had always been predisposed to take it for: a version of *Cinderella*.[37] But the differences between Shaw's original *Pygmalion* and *Cinderella* are profound. Implicit in the respective emphases of their titles, *Pygmalion* is *his* story, whereas *Cinderella* is *her* story. Shaw, in his preface to the play, takes great pains to emphasize the derivation and importance of Henry Higgins, paying homage both to his profession and, to some extent, his namesake, a brilliant but arrogant expert in phonetics, Henry Sweet. There is also quite a bit of Shaw himself in Higgins, enough so that when some of Shaw's prose from the preface finds its way into Higgins's first song, "Why Can't the English?" there is no real change in tone (the quotation from Shaw's preface is given above that from "Why Can't the English?"):

♩ 6.32

> The English have no respect for their language, and will not teach their children to speak it. . . . It is impossible for an Englishman to open his mouth without making some other Englishman hate or despise him. German and Spanish are accessible to foreigners: English is not accessible even to Englishmen.[38]
>
> An Englishman's way of speaking absolutely classifies him.
> The moment he talks he makes some other Englishman despise him. . . .
> Why can't the English teach their children how to speak?
> Norwegians learn Norwegian; the Greeks are taught their Greek.
> In France ev'ry Frenchman knows his language from "A" to "Zed." . . .

Moreover, in his lengthy sequel (a prose addendum to the published play), Shaw denies his Cinderella her prince with great force of logic and within an elaborate scenario designed in part, it would seem, to make us feel better about it all. But, of course, we tend not to. The character of Eliza has, from the beginning, been so appealing that the play has seemed to audiences to be, in the end, more about her than about Higgins, with an expectation that she will triumph not only in her quest to master speech and decorum but also in her need to get romantic recognition from her prince (that is, Higgins).

Shaw himself contributed to the play's drift toward *Cinderella* with three significant additions he made in adapting it for the screen. Specifically, he added (or authorized), in order: a training sequence, missing from the original play, in which we get a more vivid sense of how Eliza's lessons were run (an "earning" process comparable to Cinderella picking the lentils out of the ashes);[39] a ball scene that brings Eliza's fairy-tale performance closer to Cinderella's; and a reconciliation scene between Eliza and Higgins at the very end, in which Eliza returns to Higgins's home in time to take the place of her own voice playing on his phonograph. Moreover, the particular focus on Higgins's slippers after their victory, already in the original play, recalls Cinderella's much-fetishized slippers; this connection is amplified when Higgins refers to them again in the final line of the brief "Cinderella-coda" added for the film (and retained for the musical), to convey his smug acceptance of Eliza's gesture of capitulation ("Where the devil are my slippers?"). The allusion underscores an important reversal from the fairy tale, for Higgins's slippers become the symbol not of Eliza's rescue but of her servitude, similar in kind to the symbolic gesture Kate describes in "I Am Ashamed That Women Are So Simple" at the end of *Kiss Me, Kate*: "So wife, hold your temper and meekly put / Your hand 'neath the sole of your husband's boot."

♪6.33

Yet there are many obstacles to a *Cinderella* ending, beyond those that Shaw points out in his sequel. In the Pygmalion myth—parallel in this respect to the Frankenstein stories—the created being, Galatea, is first of all an egotistical extension of her creator and only secondarily an independent person (and scarcely that, as the myth is usually recounted). To the extent that Galatea is a genuine person, her father is the sculptor Pygmalion and her mother the goddess Aphrodite (who brings her to life), which adds a whiff of incest to her union to Pygmalion.[40] But overriding this suggestion of incest—always a potential adjunct to a teacher-student romantic relationship—are Higgins's own inclinations. While there is always deniability about such things, Higgins's and Pickering's shared domestic situation and status as "confirmed old bachelors," coupled with Higgins's frequently expressed contempt for women (particularly during his rant songs in *My Fair Lady*, "I'm an Ordinary Man," "A Hymn to Him," and parts of "I've Grown Accustomed to Her Face"), strongly suggest homosexuality or its second cousin, a variation of the "buddy" trope discussed with regard to *Singin' in the Rain* (see chapter 2), although sexual repression (presumably the basis for the situation's "deniability") is also a possibility.

Higgins's possible homosexuality must be understood in relation to a developmental trope particularly common in England, in which homosexual relations are understood to be a phase within a longer process of a young male's maturation into a normal heterosexual man. Higgins thus becomes a case of arrested development, and it is in this light that Shaw's elaborate descriptions of Higgins near the beginning of Act II might fruitfully be read:

> He is, in fact, but for his years and size, rather like a very impetuous baby "taking notice" eagerly and loudly, and requiring almost as much watching to keep him out of unintended mischief.... The only distinction he makes between men and women is that when he is neither bullying nor exclaiming to the heavens against some featherweight cross, he coaxes women as a child coaxes its nurse when it wants to get anything out of her.[41]

Elsewhere, we hear Mrs. Higgins rebuke her son and Pickering (in Act III), "You certainly are a pretty pair of babies, playing with your live doll."[42] And, back in Act II, we might well consider why Higgins owns a collection of Japanese dresses ready for Eliza to step into (certainly a convenience after Higgins orders Eliza's clothes burned; but that awkwardness could be quite easily glossed over—as it is in *My Fair Lady*, which omits any reference to Higgins's dresses, but which later does include Higgins's readily volunteered knowledge of where to buy women's gowns: "Whiteley's, of course").[43]

Because Higgins's possible homosexuality is deniable (as it must be at this juncture of dramatic history), his disinclination to marry a young woman must be couched differently, either as it is in the play (thus, to his mother in Act III: "My idea of a lovable woman is something as like you as possible") or, as Shaw's sequel further elaborates it, as a form of Higgins's narcissism. Thus, in a line from *Pygmalion* dropped in *My Fair Lady*, during his final confrontation with Eliza, he overtly likens his position to that of God: "Would the world ever have been made if its maker had been afraid of making trouble? Making life means making trouble."[44]

The proximity of *Pygmalion*'s story to that of Frankenstein underscores a particular irony about the play and its gradual transformation, in that Shaw—like Frankenstein, like Higgins, and like Pygmalion himself were we to reimagine his experience credibly—loses control of his creation once he creates it. A play exists as such only when it is *played*; and once it takes the stage, its characters belong mainly to those who play them. And the process unfolds almost as though it were inevitable; in this case, seemingly, *Pygmalion* becomes *Cinderella* because it must, to honor the reality of Eliza Doolittle as created by an actress onstage. And yet, *My Fair Lady* is not *simply* a Cinderella story, for her would-be Prince is far too well developed a character for it to be that. Rather, the show is about a *relationship*, seen—as the musical's title suggests with some irony—from Higgins's perspective, with Eliza as a possessed and transformed object. An earlier candidate for the title, "Lady Liza," would have thrown the emphasis more completely onto her; indeed, an alternative ironic reading of "My Fair Lady" retains that emphasis ("Mayfair Lady," with the first word pronounced in a cockney accent). More obviously, the title phrase comes from the familiar nursery song "London Bridge Is Falling Down" (quoted by the orchestra during the opening scene in Covent Garden), often serving as the basis for a children's "capturing" game in which two individuals (Higgins and Pickering?) form a "bridge" with their arms, lowering them to capture their victim (Eliza?) at the key phrase; in this sense, the title describes the basic situation of the show more broadly. In the event, as a literal reading of the title would have it, *My Fair Lady* focuses attention on Eliza, but initially from Higgins's perspective; to this end, Lerner and Loewe give musical precedence to Higgins's perspective (in "Why Can't the English"), which we hear before Eliza's (in "Wouldn't It Be Loverly?").[45]

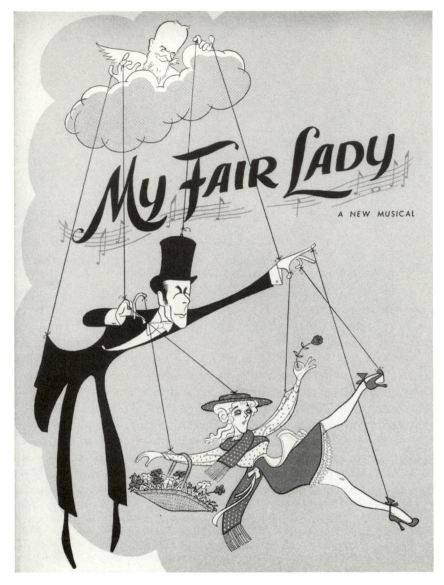

Figure 6.3. Broadway's definitive caricaturist Al Hirschfeld's drawing for the original souvenir program book of *My Fair Lady* (frequently adopted for use with different stars) traces the hierarchy of control, with Shaw (on high) manipulating his puppet creation Henry Higgins (Rex Harrison), who in turn manipulates *his* puppet creation Eliza Doolittle (Julie Andrews)—thus also retracing the flow of titles, from Shaw's *Pygmalion* to Pygmalion's *Fair Lady*. Notwithstanding the smug expressions on the two men's faces, neither remains in control of "his" creation. By sheer force of personality (with Shaw's partial complicity and, later, with additional help from Lerner and Loewe's songs), Eliza over time has managed *both* to rebel against Higgins and to insist on converting Shaw's story—against his vehement opposition—into a version of Cinderella. (Reproduction courtesy of Miles Kreuger and the Institute of the American Musical, Inc.)

But the songs matter in *My Fair Lady* far more than as tokens of hierarchy or even for their important verbal content, because the central relationship in the show is defined above all by *vocality*. Put simply, Higgins can talk but can't sing, and Eliza can sing but can't talk. The genius of Lerner and Loewe's adaptation centers on its deliberate pairing of a fiercely verbal actor who could not sing with Julie Andrews, the possessor of what is arguably the finest vocal instrument ever heard on a Broadway stage.[46] In a literally visceral way, then, they affirm Rick Altman's description of how relationships in film musicals tend to function:

> As a preliminary formulation, we can thus state not only that each character is double, made up of both a surface and a repressed personality, but that *the surface personality of each member of [a] couple corresponds to the repressed personality of the other.*[47]

If we are to believe in the Cinderella story, then, we need to believe that Higgins longs for a musical lyricism (that is, figuratively, an expressible emotionality) as deeply as Eliza longs for Higgins's locutionary skills (and empowering reason)—a situation that treads extremely close to an archetypal binary division between the sexes, which contrasts the rational man with the feeling woman, and which sets each out to recover what she or he lacks by forming a bond with the other. That *My Fair Lady* expresses this binary in purely vocal ways may explain why it has sometimes been seen as the most perfect of musicals, at least within a tradition that accepts such archetypes implicitly. Clearly, then, both Eliza and Higgins have something to learn from each other. The real question of the show is thus not whether Eliza will learn to speak properly—which may be assumed as part of the story's basic premise—but whether Higgins will learn to "sing." In literal terms, of course, Rex Harrison never had a chance against Julie Andrews, but the show's status as a version of the Cinderella story depends absolutely on whether he moves convincingly in her direction *at all.* This is a daunting requirement, for to do so, he has first to take due note of her (and not just of her pronunciation)—the supreme test of a narcissist in an incipient relationship.

Their opening positions are well articulated in their first numbers. Higgins's "Why Can't the English?" establishes his verbal prowess, his lack of musicality (through a kind of speech-song, often called *Sprechstimme* or *Sprechgesang*), his alignment with privilege (especially in the song's stylistic affinities to "Rule Britannia"), and his penchant for edgy, petulant rants that underscore his wit at the expense of his aristocratic pose. For the latter, he may approach a cadence only to interrupt himself by heading in a new direction, both rhythmically and harmonically, then grinding to a musical halt before he can continue in his original vein:

♪ 6.34
♪ 6.35

> Oh, why can't the English learn to
>   set a good example to people whose English is painful to your ears?
>   The Scotch and the Irish leave you close to tears.

There even are places where English completely disappears.
[*spoken, as music stops*] In America, they haven't used it for years!
Why can't the English teach their children how to speak?

Eliza's "Wouldn't It Be Loverly?"—parallel to Higgins's introductory song in being mounted as a speculative question—establishes her, on the other hand, as supremely musical but verbally deficient, lower class but able to dream of something better, and beguilingly easygoing, the latter due to the offhand, soft-shoe style of the number, redolent of the English music hall (a more raucous version of which we hear in her father's numbers, "With a Little Bit of Luck" and "Get Me to the Church on Time"). Eliza's syllabic interpolations are particularly telling, as they add to the easy flow of the melody. In the first phrase of the bridge (within a conventional AABA structure), for example, measured repeated notes over shifting harmonies frame the melodic line, with the lilting interior of the line informally adding syllables as required by the rhythm (repeated notes are in bold, syllabic interpolations in italics):

♪ 6.36

♪ 6.37

Oh, so lov*er*ly sittin' abso-*bloomin'*-lutely still!

Particularly subtle here is the use of "bloomin'," a bowdlerized rendering of what Lerner actually heard on the streets of London while researching for the show: "abso-bloody-lutely," roughly equivalent in force to the American "abso-fucking-lutely."[48] Much of the publicity surrounding the premiere of Shaw's play focused on Eliza's use of the word "bloody" in her first scene with Higgins's mother, with Freddy Eynsford-Hill and family in attendance.[49] Eliza's early delicacy thus defines the starting point for a progressively daring locution, held in check when we first encounter her, but later to be unlocked by her exposure to Higgins's profanity. At the comparable moment to Shaw's famous "Not bloody likely," as Eliza loses her composure while exhorting a horse running at Ascot, she stays with "bloomin' " but puts her foot in her mouth with a word calculated to register more strongly with American audiences: "Come on, Dover!! Move your bloomin' arse!!!!" When she does finally get around to "bloody," she does so coolly and deliberately, at the melodic peak of her triumph over Higgins, in the final phrase of "Without You": "So go back in your shell, / I can do bloody well without" (at which point, however, she is interrupted by Higgins's self-congratulatory reprise of "You Did It").[50]

♪ 6.38

The target of Higgins's petulant ranting, once Eliza enters his household, shifts from bad pronunciation to women, as expressed especially in two songs that indulge their rants within overarching assertions of masculine reasonableness.[51] The first of these, "I'm an Ordinary Man"—which he will recall in his final song, "I've Grown Accustomed to Her Face"—contrasts its rant against women with a musical depiction of the sedate life he leads when safely insulated from them, a modest strolling song that is then cast aside in favor of a sputtering declamation alternating with raucous

interjections from the orchestra. Late in the second act, when he and Picker- ♪6.39
ing discover that Eliza has disappeared, his "A Hymn to Him" substitutes a
suitably manly 6/8 march tempo for this casual stroll, occasionally broken
for a digressive side rant.[52] At the same time, he returns to the speculatively
questioning mode of his first song, a sign of the genuine desperation he is
experiencing (thus: "Why can't a woman be more like a man?"). As the
target of this rant comes to focus more narrowly on Eliza, so also does the
contrasting focal point narrow, across three strophes, from the initial
question to (addressing Pickering) "Why can't a woman be like us?" and,
finally, to "Why can't a woman be like me?" (This final line to the song is ♪6.40
not only a nakedly narcissistic moment—even in his rage, Higgins manages
to pat himself on the back—but also the motivational basis for the original
Pygmalion story. As a whole, the song confirms at least Higgins's latent
homosexuality.)

Not surprisingly, one of the principal things Eliza learns from Higgins
is how to rant. Even before she learns to speak properly, her "Just You
Wait" provides, like Higgins's rants, its own internal contrasts of placid
self-sufficiency ("One day I'll be famous"), so as to set off the subsequent
explosion: "All I want is 'enry 'iggins 'ead!" "Show Me," with which she
rebukes Freddy Eynsford-Hill for his ineffectualness midway through the
second act, manages to combine a rant that would do Higgins credit, with— ♪6.41
owing partly to its aggressively fast waltz tempo—an insistent sexuality
that seems more directed toward Higgins than Freddy, who nevertheless
bears the brunt of it. But if these earlier rants occasionally fly out of control,
her final rant, "Without You," maintains its sense of measured control
throughout, until Higgins asserts himself at the final cadence. But the most
revealing moment in Eliza's rants occurs in the first one, when she imagines
herself, à la Salome, demanding Higgins's head as tribute from the king. If
Salome's demand for the head of John the Baptist stands as the archetypal
response of "a woman scorned," we may infer that Eliza's rant is inspired
less by her ill-treatment than by her need to occupy Higgins's awareness as
a person.

Indeed, what facilitates her linguistic breakthrough soon after this particular rant is precisely that kind of recognition. Because such recognition must
derive from Higgins's more generous and eloquent nature, it cannot be sung,
but is instead a speech delivered, according to the stage directions, "with
sudden gentleness":

> Eliza, I know you're tired. I know your head aches. I know your nerves are as
> raw as meat in a butcher's window. But think what you're trying to accomplish.
> Think what you're dealing with. The majesty and grandeur of the English lan-
> guage. It's the greatest possession we have. The noblest sentiments that ever
> flowed in the hearts of men are contained in its extraordinary, imaginative and
> musical mixtures of sounds. That's what you've set yourself to conquer, Eliza.
> And conquer it you will.[53]

♩6.42

The celebration that follows, in "The Rain in Spain," has a quality of improvisation, riffing on bits of pronunciation exercises. But the song's choreography is fully elaborated in the stage directions, which dictate Pickering's playing the bull to Higgins's matador, Eliza's and Higgins's brief tango, Pickering's and then Higgins's flamenco steps, and a wild "jig" dance with all three at the end (the latter based on the jota, traditionally an athletic Spanish dance for men). As described, and as rendered in the film, this scene plays much like "Good Mornin'" in *Singin' in the Rain* (see pp. 76–77)— that is, as a negotiation within a mixed triangle, spurred by a moment of exhilaration during which a woman is suddenly admitted into the tight circle of bonded male buddies. Here, however, the lingering private celebration that ensues is performed not by the lead male (cf. Gene Kelly's "Singin' in the Rain," discussed on p. 77), but by the woman.

For anyone unfamiliar with the story of *My Fair Lady* but familiar with the show's songs, the dancing to which Eliza refers in "I Could Have Danced All Night" will surely be understood as taking place at a *Cinderella*-like ball (which happens only much later, and with nearly the opposite effect on Eliza). Moreover, the song's seemingly predestined popularity, along with that of Freddy's "On the Street Where You Live," makes them seem as though they must provide the centerpiece for a conventional *Cinderella*-like romance. And this is no accident, for their presence in the score is prompted by generic necessities regarding the Cinderella archetype; this is why they appear side by side in the overture. But the romance imagined in these songs is, for each singer, wholly an idealization. Eliza's perception of the breakthrough evening is that it has launched a romantic adventure, even though the homosexually charged byplay between Pickering and Higgins during "The Rain in Spain" has signaled—to a perceptive audience, if not to Eliza— a very different situation. And Eliza will have none of Freddy's idealization of her, although the possibility that she will end up with him is never fully put aside, even given Lerner's rejection of Shaw's sequel (in a brief note introducing the published libretto).

Yet, in the end, Higgins *does* respond to "I Could Have Danced All Night," and in specifically musical terms. While his "I've Grown Accustomed to Her Face" begins with a rant derived from "An Ordinary Man," it soon gives way to something like genuine song, which seems—and surely deliberately—to be a cross between the ranting portions of "An Ordinary Man" and Eliza's "I Could Have Danced All Night." The connection between the two songs is, in fact, circumstantially close. As Lerner relates, regarding the "I Could Have Danced All Night" slot, "every song we wrote—we wrote seven—said too much. . . . Finally, we were only able to write the song when we . . . had written "I've Grown Accustomed to Her Face." We said, 'There's the ballad. We don't have to worry about a ballad. We'll just go back and write a happy song.' " Although Lerner, as lyricist, may not have wanted to draw particular attention to it, the two songs are also musically closely related.[54] We hear that relation in the sequential lyrical portions of "I've Grown Accustomed to Her Face," which come across as a registrally compressed version of the similarly sequential phrases of "I Could Have Danced All Night," but with the melodic appoggiaturas (on "Danced" in the latter song) elaborated into the repeated-note figure of Higgins's contrasting rant (melodic pitches are given above the appoggiatura figures):   ♪6.43

A♭   G   G
I could have **danced** all night!

G   F   F
I could have **danced** all night!

E♭   E♭ E♭ E♭ D♭
She almost **makes the day be**-gin.

G   G   G G   F
I've grown **accustomed to the** tune

F   F   F   F   E♭
She **whistles night and** noon.

A♭ A♭ A♭   A♭   A♭
But I shall **ne-ver take her back!**

The gesture of this song—that he *has* noticed her and is even trying to approximate "the tune / She whistles night and noon"—nearly convinces us that the reciprocal needs of Higgins and Eliza might be met through each other. Crucially, then, the song doesn't truly end, as such. Instead, it drifts into a violin-solo version of "I Could Have Danced All Night," which confirms both the musical connection and that the tune, representing Eliza, is on his mind. The tune continues to play as Higgins then seeks solace in his recordings of her voice, until—as if by sheer force of his will, or by generic imperative—Eliza returns, with the reality of her presence confirmed by a full-tutti conclusion of her song. It is thus the fulfilling reality of Eliza's idealizing romance—her song—not Higgins's final words, "Where the devil are my slippers?" that closes the show.[55]

Company (1970) marked the beginning of Stephen Sondheim's full emergence as a major player on Broadway. Although his talents as a lyricist had long been near legendary, he had only twice composed the complete score for a Broadway show, resulting in one hit (*A Funny Thing Happened on the Way to the Forum*; 1962) and one disastrous flop (*Anyone Can Whistle*; 1964). Like *Forum*, *Company* won Tony Awards for Best Musical, Author, Production, and Direction; this time, however, Sondheim himself also won, for both lyrics and score.[56] With this stronger start in the 1970s, he followed up with *Follies* (1971) and *A Little Night Music* (1973), both of which were mostly admired by the critics and won multiple Tony Awards (including Best Original Score for both), even if neither enjoyed an exceptionally long run.[57] Sondheim's three shows from the early 1970s for many years remained the cornerstone of his career and reputation; together, they helped cement his extraordinarily fruitful working relationship with producer-director Harold Prince and launched his collaborations with orchestrator Jonathan Tunick. Significantly, all three shows are intimately concerned, each in a very different way, with interwoven sets of relationships. *Company* is grounded in the specific milieu of 1960s-style urban sophistication, from which one may then trace a progression backward, through the dramatic situations of *Follies* and *A Little Night Music*, first to an earlier generation of American urban sophisticates and thence to an Old-World sophistication of a still-earlier generation. (Interestingly, Sondheim's later shows from the 1970s, *Pacific Overtures* [1976] and *Sweeney Todd* [1979], although less centrally concerned with romantic relationships, would continue this progression back in time and, in general terms, geographically outward.)

Company is often cited as the first successful "concept" musical—that is, an integrated book musical that is essentially nonnarrative, or at least nonlinear in its narrative approach, and that often takes on some aspects of a revue.[58] Others, however, would give that distinction to *Hair* (1968), which came slightly earlier and enjoyed considerably greater commercial success.[59] Indeed, *Company* and *Hair* are strikingly parallel even though they operate within separate spheres, as each attempts to come to terms with the changing urban landscape of the 1960s regarding both relationships and prevalent musical styles; moreover, to the extent that either show has a central narrative, it concerns a critical decision that must be made by someone who stands somewhat outside the main cohort of characters: Claude (in *Hair*) and Bobby (in *Company*). In *Company*, however, that cohort is scarcely as seductive as its counterpart in *Hair*, consisting not in the latter's youthful dropouts, who seem to have forged a viable alternative lifestyle outside the strictures of society, but rather in five married couples whose relationships all seem deeply flawed yet who try to convince Bobby that he should join them, if not in marrying, then at least in committing to a life partner. Thus, *Company*'s ensemble cast of established couples urges basic conformity to a societal norm, whereas *Hair*'s "Tribe" urges the reverse. The specific problems of *Company*'s couples, and of Bobby's inability (or reluctance) to commit, may easily be understood as representing a set of issues especially relevant to the "silent generation" of urban professionals, born between 1924 and 1945, who were too old for the counterculture; not coincidentally, as Stephen Banfield points out, this generation happened to include Sondheim, Prince, and Furth.[60] Nevertheless, Bobby's cohort, though older than that of *Hair* (who belonged to the first generation of post–World War II baby boomers), shares much of the latter's ambivalence regarding traditional family and societal structures, and so they try in various ways to respond to the new, more liberating alternatives that emerged during the 1960s.

It is entirely plausible to see many of the couples in *Company* as part of the broad audience base for *Hair*, many of them eager to submit to the liberating influence of the various revolutionary movements then on the ascendant, so long as they didn't actually have to drop out to do so. This helps explain why they are so desperate to recruit Bobby, who seems to operate closest to the kind of freedom the counterculture would have represented to them; getting Bobby to commit himself to a stable, partnered lifestyle would go a long way toward validating their own circumstantial compromises as both practical *and* idealistic. The list of revolutionary movements that emerge in *Company* is by no means exhaustive (notably absent are the civil rights and the Vietnam antiwar movements),[61] but they do include, at least by implication, women's liberation (Sarah's karate expertise, Joanne's jaded independence, and Amy's and Susan's ambivalent attitudes toward marriage), drugs (Joanne's references to Librium, and Jenny and David's experimentation with marijuana, provided by Bobby), and changing notions regarding the relationship between sex and marriage (Susan and Peter's decision to divorce without separating, Amy's reluctance to marry long-time partner Paul, and Joanne's speculative cynicism, which leads her to flirt with one of the married men at Bobby's surprise birthday party and, later, to proposition Bobby at a nightclub while Larry, her third husband, is paying the check).

More subtle are the musical parallels between *Hair* and *Company*. *Hair* is, famously, the first rock musical and wears the contemporary derivation of its musical style quite openly. *Company*, on the other hand, has often seemed more conventional in its music, in part because it engages in pastiche (although not to the extent of *Follies*), relying on such divergent reference points as "girl groups" from the 1930s–1950s (the Andrews Sisters, especially in "You Could Drive a Person Crazy"), "Latin" nightclub music ("Little Things" and the bossa nova sections of "The Ladies Who Lunch"), the cakewalk/soft-shoe/tap-based production number (in "Side By Side" and "What Would We Do Without You?"), and the Broadway traditions of combination songs and patter songs ("Getting Married Today"). Yet *Company*'s music is scarcely conventional, despite its congenial relationship with traditional Broadway. On an obvious level, the orchestration by Jonathan Tunick is quite contemporary, including a full range of reeds, brass, and percussion, two guitars, electric piano (swapping out for organ), and a reduced string section, with which Tunick creates a kind of symphonic-rock sound with admixtures of urban folk (especially through the guitar figurations),[62] while mostly avoiding the obvious rock gesture of the backbeat.

But the specific sound world of *Company* is first of all dictated by Sondheim's score, which uses, as a central "mantra" for the show, a quasi-minimalist texture involving layered, pulsed repetitions of words and phrases ("Bobby . . . Bobby . . . Bobby baby . . . Bobby bubi" and, later in "Company," "You I love and you I love and you and you I love and you" superimposed on repetitions of "Isn't it?"). Moreover, Sondheim derives his often dissonant musical motives from specific sounds associated with urban modernity circa 1970, all associated with a kind of overabundance of mechanized communication (or its obverse, mechanized disconnection): the busy signal, door chimes, trains, and car horns.[63] Sondheim thus draws a direct link between the energies of modern urban music as represented by his score and the musical (and sometimes cacophonous) energies of modern urban life; even the basic busy-signal motive, with its abrupt stops on the second and fourth beats, creates a nervous facsimile of the backbeat, otherwise missing from the score.[64]

♩6.44

Company's evocation of musical minimalism is perhaps its most pointed gesture toward what would have passed for musical sophistication in 1970. Minimalism was then a fledgling "movement" whose ostensible adherents were at great odds with each other, straddling several "cutting-edge" frontiers, among them the avant-garde, trance music, offshoots of rock music (especially in the "psychedelic" direction), "happenings," and a return to chord-based harmonic structures as an attempt to reverse the direction of modernism's harshest developments (such as the "total serialism" of Pierre Boulez or Milton Babbitt—the latter having been one of Sondheim's teachers). Indeed, in one of the early minimalist classics, *Come Out* (1966), Steve Reich used phased repetition to manipulate what we might now call a sound bite—in this case, like Sondheim's busy signal, a negatively charged "found object" from urban life—as the sole basis for a substantial musical composition.[65] Other specific musical developments in the 1960s that *Company* incorporates, apart from its basic rock sound, include the Swingle Singers' popularizing renditions of contrapuntally complex classical music (overlapping to some extent with *Company*'s evocations of minimalism, made possible by the syllabic propensities of the "Bobby" motive and other repeated words and word patterns)[66] and the reemergence of Mahler's music after decades of neglect, spearheaded in America by Sondheim's sometime collaborator Leonard Bernstein, in a project that spanned most of the 1960s. Joanne refers to Mahler in her caustic drinking song, "The Ladies Who Lunch," along with "intense" playwright Harold Pinter, in a lyric that mocks the self-imposed difficulties of faddish sophistication (Jonathan Tunick obligingly provided a quotation from Mahler's Fourth Symphony immediately after the passage quoted below):[67]

♩6.45
♩6.46

> Another long, exhausting day,
> Another thousand dollars,
> A matinée, a Pinter play,
> Perhaps a piece of Mahler's—
> I'll drink to that.
> And one for Mahler.

In a notable triangulation, Mahler and the Swingle Singers were brought together (along with another "difficult" playwright, Samuel Beckett) by Luciano Berio in the third movement of his 1968 Sinfonia,[68] as part of a tribute to Leonard Bernstein and the New York Philharmonic. Berio composed this movement out of the scherzo of Mahler's *Resurrection* Symphony (a central work in Bernstein's conducting career) and Beckett's 1953 novel *The Un-*

namable, to whose basic structures Berio adds a disorienting welter of musical and textual quotations. The exhortation to "keep going," which is given repeated emphasis throughout this movement, also plays a key role in *Company*'s "Being Alive," calling subtle attention to the common thematic strand connecting all of these artifacts of the 1960s, including *Company*, and for which Mahler provided pathbreaking musical precedents: the alienation of the individual soul within a modern urban environment. Moreover, Sondheim's interweaving of voices during the "Bobby baby" portions of the score bears a striking resemblance to the overabundance of Berio's Mahler movement (an intensification of an effect already present in Mahler's original), so that the subjective position (Bobby) becomes overwhelmed by the multitude of attempts to connect with him, which in turn, and ironically, thus form a major part of his sense of alienation—all of which is expressed in directly musical terms. Even Mahler's original programmatic basis for this, the most famous of his "alienation" movements—a man observing the wedding celebration of his beloved from a distance who finally, near the end of the movement, screams his protest—finds echoes in *Company*, in the first instance when Bobby learns Kathy is planning to marry someone else (Act I, Sc. V), and when an exasperated Joanne observes, "You were always outside looking in the window while everybody was inside dancing at the party" (Act II, Sc. IV). Even Mahler's scream finds its correlative in *Company*, when Bobby finally protests against the repeated sonic onslaught of his friends at the beginning of "Being Alive," by interrupting their "Bobby" chorus and demanding to know "What do you get?" (see also the later discussion of "Being Alive").

Whereas many of the show's numbers reinforce Bobby's alienated perspective, often through reprises of the "Bobby" music, many others articulate other perspectives as well.[69] Joanne's "Little Things," for example, provides a jaundiced view of couple interactions, which perhaps overlaps with Bobby's as he endures Sarah and Larry pecking away at each other's foibles (hers for eating, his for drinking), a dynamic that seems to form the heart of their relationship and erupts finally in an impromptu karate match. This "list song" combines, appropriately, a basic calypso style (a type traditionally used to engage romance in a humorous fashion) with the barest hint of a fast tango beneath it, resonating well with Joanne's later Latin number, "The Ladies Who Lunch."[70] Many of the song's lists illustrate the tendency, within couples, for things to progress too far and too rapidly along well-worn patterns of (in this case) negative interaction:

> The concerts you enjoy together,
> Neighbors you annoy together,
> Children you destroy together,
> That keep marriage intact. . . .
> It's sharing little winks together,
> Drinks together,

> Kinks together,
>> That makes marriage a joy.
> It's bargains that you shop together,
> Cigarettes you stop together,
> Clothing that you swap together,[71]
>> That make perfect relationships. . . .
> It's things like using force together,
> Shouting till you're hoarse together,
> Getting a divorce together,
>> That make perfect relationships.

As with many calypso numbers, the lead singer is joined by a backup group, in this case the other couples entering to make what is perhaps the key point ♩6.54 of the song:

> It's not talk of God and the decade ahead that
> Allows you to get through the worst.
> It's "I do" and "You don't" and "Nobody said that"
> And "Who brought the subject up first?"

With their sly dig at the marriage vows ("I do"),[72] these lines make the familiar point that it is process, rather than substance, that matters in a couple's interactions, but the song uses only negative examples of the "tit-for-tat" variety. Although "Little Things" mirrors some aspects of Bobby's perspective, it nevertheless concludes—like the barely contained marital squabble he leaves behind him—with something that confirms a shared attitude of the singers, who know that reconciliation always follows marital arguments, ♩6.55 and that this part of the pattern will inevitably redeem the rest: "Uh-huh . . . / Kiss, kiss . . . / Mm-hm."

Other numbers even more obviously establish non-Bobby perspectives, such as the hilarious pastiche number "You Could Drive a Person Crazy" or "Another Hundred People." The first of these also raises, rather obnoxiously, an interpretive window on Bobby that Sondheim has tried since to close: the suggestion here and elsewhere that part of Bobby's problem is that ♩6.56 he is gay or perhaps bisexual:

> I could understand a person
> If it's not a person's bag.
>> Doo-doo doo-doo doo
> I could understand a person
> If a person was a fag.
>> Doo-doo doo-doo doo

While the lyric is easily (and now almost always) rendered less offensive, the insistence of the show more broadly on a normative heterosexuality just a few months after Stonewall may seem surprising; despite Sondheim's protestations, thoughtful recent performances of the show have managed to raise the suggestion that Bobby may be conflicted about his sexual orientation (or at least, quite reasonably, to suggest that those close to him might suspect as much) without overwhelming the basic arch of the show.[73]

As Stephen Banfield has shown, "Another Hundred People" uses a layered technique deriving from guitar accompaniments, in a way that again suggests minimalism in its phased repetitions of highly profiled patterns. Significantly, Sondheim's "rapprochement with minimalism"[74] in this song occurs in connection with a layered representation of mostly anonymous city life, with motor rhythms describing the people (who thus seem to phase in and out of sync with each other), and a slightly slower commentary that rises "above" the noise ("It's a city of strangers") amid recurring simulations of incessantly repeating city noise (hence, Tunick's simulation of car horns through the trumpets' rendition of the "Bobby" motive). The verbalized images are familiar from 1960s folk rock,[75] raising hopes while simultaneously complaining of the city's unrelieved ugliness and relentless stew of humanity: ♩6.57

> And ev'ry day
> The ones who stay
> [key change]
> Can find each other in the crowded streets and the guarded parks,
> By the rusty fountains and the dusty trees with the battered barks,
> And they walk together past the postered walls with the crude remarks.
> [key change]
> And they meet at parties through the friends of friends who they never know.
> Will you pick me up or do I meet you there or shall we let it go?
> Did you get my message 'cause I looked in vain?
> Can we see each other Tuesday, if it doesn't rain?
> Look, I'll call you in the morning or my service will explain—
> [key change, back to original key]
> And another hundred people just got off of the train.

Critical to the song's despairing insistence on hope (hence all its shifts in key) is a figure that will return in "Being Alive," a melodic striving upward to the major seventh above the tonic (the "leading tone"), here held without resolution ("Look, I'll **call you in** the morning or my ser**vice will explain**"), which reduces, at the end of the song, to a leap upward of a major seventh, sustained in strident protest against the tonic resolution: ♩6.58

> And another hundred people just got off of the train—
> And another hundred people just got off of the train!

A number of songs highlight, through simulated conversation (or phone messages), the failure of attempted connection. This device is already employed in the overlapping voices of the "Bobby" music; in "Getting Married Today," the disconnect among the three perspectives provides a more traditionally realized example. The "conversations" that introduce "Poor Baby," in the second act, are behavioral gems, as husbands Harry and David insert their one-syllable reactions into the occasional gaps of their wives' monologues, who demonstrate through their own self-preoccupied delivery that it is somehow not Bobby's happiness they are thinking of. (The latter becomes explicit as the song shifts from its conclusion that "Robert ought to have a woman" to a series of overlapping put-downs regarding April, his actual choice for a lover.)

♩6.59

Meanwhile, Robert's own sense of desperation has gradually increased, especially in the wake of his rejected proposal to Amy at the end of Act I ("Marry me! And everybody'll leave us alone!")—which brings Amy to her senses just after she has refused to go through with her wedding to Paul. Act II then opens with a production number that exposes the awkward position of Bobby as the "third wheel" in each of the others' relationships ("Side by side . . . by side"), whose concluding tap breaks leave Bobby stranded without a partner, almost as in a game of musical chairs (see figure 6.4).[76] A similar effect follows his tryst with April ("Tick-Tock"), as we hear an echoing chorus of "I love you" from the married couples just after Bobby has found himself unable to utter the phrase beyond the first word. "Barcelona" then provides the climax of Sondheim's conversation-song manner (in *Company*), ending in what is, for Bobby, an unmitigated disaster of miscommunication. The song proceeds as a sleepy good-bye—April is an airline stewardess who has a flight to catch—in which Robert pushes his give-and-take protests too far, so that they seem enough like a commitment to April that she decides to stay (this despite his inability to say "I love you" or even to remember her name—which failures have, in fact, led him to augment his protests in compensation).

♩6.60

♩6.61

♩6.62

Famously, Sondheim wrote four different ending songs for *Company*.[77] Two of them, "Marry Me a Little" and "Multitudes of Amys," depended on Amy's not marrying Paul at the end of Act I, and so no longer worked when the plotting of the show changed.[78] The third attempt, which was performed at tryouts in Boston, was "Happily Ever After" and echoes Amy's desperation in "Getting Married Today" without the saving grace of comic hysteria.[79] Backed by a driving, incessant rhythm in triple meter, sounding almost like a three-legged march (or, perhaps, a regimented waltz), it bitterly indicts marriage and relationships in general:

♩6.63

♩6.64

> Someone to hold you too close,
> Someone to hurt you too deep,
> Someone to love you too hard,
> Happily ever after.
> Someone to need you too much,
> Someone to read you too well,
> Someone to bleed you of all
> The things you don't want to tell—
> That's happily ever after,
> Ever, ever, ever after
> In Hell.

Figure 6.4. Bobby (Larry Kert, far right), through his fear of commitment, remains the odd man out in *Company*'s kick line, the only one without a partner. (Photograph courtesy of Miles Kreuger and the Institute of the American Musical, Inc.)

In some respects, this is no resolution, but rather an insistence on Bobby's part that his inability to commit is well grounded in human experience. What resolution the song did offer was a committed resolve not to commit—the final return replaces "Someone" with "No one"—coupled with a sense of completing the show's overall dramatic shaping, in which the final outcome structurally reverses the outcome of the first act, when Amy relents and marries Paul. Despite the song's dramatic force, its harsh truths seemed too negative following the insistent comic tone of the show as a whole. Yet, in writing a replacement song that effected a transition, from a starting point derived from "Happily Ever After" to an ambivalent acceptance of human needs that override the drawbacks of relationships, Sondheim did not simply cave in to convention.[80] Rather, recognizing that Bobby's basic problem all along—first identified in the opening scene, when he blows out his birthday candles without making a wish—has been his inability to allow himself to experience genuine desire (easily readable as repressed homosexual desire), Sondheim wrote a song that compels Bobby to experience desire, in musically specific terms, and to recognize desire as the quality that most defines "being alive."

"Being Alive" begins with the same lyric as "Happily Ever After," but against a softened musical background—a slower tempo established through a repeated, comforting guitar lick—signaling that the singer genuinely wants to know the answer to the question he has just hurled at his friends ("What do you get?"). And because of this softer tone, there is room for them to help him seek his own answer. Three times, as the song develops, he breaks off after climbing up to the dissonant seventh degree of the scale (recalling the strategy of "Another Hundred People"), the third time more insistently than the others (leading-tone iterations are in bold):[81]

♩6.65

> Someone to hold you too close,
> Someone to hurt you too deep,
> **Some**one to sit in **your chair,**
> To ruin **your sleep.** . . .
> Someone to need you too much,
> Someone to know you too well,
> **Some**one to pull you **up short**
> And put you **through hell.** . . .
> Someone you have to let in,
> Someone whose feelings you spare,
> **Some**one who, like it **or not,**
> Will want you **to share**
> A little, **a lot.** . . .

In between, his friends urge him on (thus, Jenny's "Don't stop now! Keep going!") as the music confirms that the continuation will allow Bobby to reach his implied goal. And so, the fourth time through, he does achieve his release, on the title phrase, "being alive," although not securely, and not all at once (thus, requiring ever-more secure repetitions of the phrase). After this extended breakthrough, Bobby's linguistic syntax changes, shifting from the infinitive in "Someone to hold you too close" to the imperative plea in "Somebody hold me too close" (thus reversing the directional shift from that

♩6.66

of "Happily Ever After," where "Someone" shifts to "No one"). Clearly, what empowers him at last to feel and express genuine need is that he now knows how the whole thing "goes," and so understands that he won't be left hanging, so to speak, on the leading tone but will be allowed instead to carry through to a resolution. Indeed, as his confidence increases, he is even able to weather an elaborate deceptive cadence, when the expected harmonic resolution is pulled away, leaving him stranded briefly in a remote key

♩6.67

("Make me con**fused**").

Whether the conclusion represented by this song is the "truth" about Bobby may be contested, but it is a conclusion well grounded in the show, based as it is on the need for Bobby to experience firsthand what the others have known all along: the comfort of resolution absorbs and heals the pain of actually needing it in the first place. And in its way, this conclusion is less "compromising" than the grim realities of "Happily Ever After" because it allows for the humanity of the embodied characters to have its say beyond what *Company*'s "concept" might have required. In this, the revisions to *Company* resemble those to Shaw's *Pygmalion*, since they are grounded within the long-standing compacts that exist, implicitly, between author and actor, and between actor and audience—the latter perhaps the only relationship in the theater that truly matters.

Passion (1994) derives jointly from *Fosca*, an epistolary novel by Iginio Ugo Tarchetti left incomplete when he died in 1869,[82] and the 1981 film based on *Fosca*, Ettore Scola's *Passione d'amore*, first screened in America in 1983. The film provided the initial impetus for Sondheim, but his collaborator James Lapine preferred to work directly with the book, which was translated from the original Italian expressly for this purpose.[83] Taking place in one act (although it has also been performed in two), the show relates the story of an unattractive woman (Fosca) in a remote army post, physically unhealthy and mentally unstable, who inspires, through her own obsessive devotion over a protracted period, the love of a young, handsome officer (Giorgio), who is already deeply in love with a married woman living in Milan (Clara). The intensity of the show, in particular the relentless obsession of Fosca (in Donna Murphy's extraordinary performance), proved problematic for some members of early Broadway audiences, who refused to take its premise seriously; despite these problems and its relatively short run, *Passion* won several Tony Awards (Best Musical, Book, Score, and Actress) and has gradually built a strong following, partly because of a handsomely produced video—originally shot on film rather than videotape—that was made just after the show closed in 1995. Rather than address the show as a whole, I wish here to address more narrowly its central device—the epistolary song—in terms of how Sondheim uses it to delineate romantic relationships.[84]

Although the epistolary musical seems to have been Sondheim's innovation—and certainly there is nothing else remotely like this musical, taken as a whole—there are several important precedents for the ways in which Sondheim realizes the concept.[85] Perhaps the most immediately important background may be found in his own techniques, already well developed in *Company* (as discussed earlier), both for rendering dialogue in song and for overlapping vocal lines within a song. Nevertheless, combining the two techniques within a sexually charged romantic situation was—despite Sondheim's own experiments along these lines (e.g., in *Company*'s "Barcelona")—an innovation of Richard Wagner, whose *Tristan und Isolde* (completed in 1859 but first performed in 1865, and so roughly contemporaneous with *Fosca*) provoked scandal through its musical simulations of sexual encounters. The latter included, like Sondheim's "Happiness" (*Passion*'s opening number), passages of overlapping dialogue reaching moments of special intensity when the two lovers sing in unison. In Wagner these moments, especially as shaped through their wavelike preparations, simulate simultaneous orgasm, whereas in Sondheim they echo the simulated orgasm that launches the number; like "Barcelona," "Happiness" is thus postcoital

♪6.68 (whereas almost the entirety of *Tristan* is, at least in some sense, *precoital*).[86]
♪6.69 But if Wagner's *Tristan* may be seen as providing the basis for the opening
scene of *Passion* (even if we might find faintly ridiculous the prospect of
traditional Wagnerian singers performing, like Giorgio and Clara, in the
nude), that scene is itself preparation for the interactive presentations of the
letters, mostly in song, between Giorgio and Clara (eventually involving
Fosca as well), which will form the heart of the show.

What is established dramatically through "Happiness" is a level of intense
yet natural intimacy (which is why the nudity matters),[87] in which the singers
are singing much more directly into each other's faces than would typically
be the case in a musical, even in a conventional love duet. This degree of
closeness is then what their correspondence will attempt to preserve; the
conceit is that by reading each other's letters, they might be transported
into each other's presence. Prior to *Passion*, the most powerful extended
suggestion of this conceit, realized in musical terms, is in Beethoven's *An die
ferne Geliebte* (To the Distant Beloved, 1816), a collection of six songs with
piano accompaniment, to be sung without interruption and representing the
first significant example of what would become an important nineteenth-
century genre, the song cycle. Indeed, the song cycle, especially within the
German *Lied* tradition, relates in interesting ways to the epistolary novel;
both evolved as adjuncts to bourgeois life in the late eighteenth century, more
specifically as oblique narrative devices whose individual "artifacts" (the
individual poems, songs, or letters) would carry both the stamp of authenticity and the immediacy of expressed feeling.[88] The poetic conceit of *An die
ferne Geliebte*, which closely resembles that of *Passion*, is that song could
provide the medium through which the poet might reunite with his "distant
beloved";[89] in the final song, the poet assures his beloved that, through her
singing of his songs, time and distance will collapse, and they will be re-
♪6.70 united.[90] In *Passion*'s staging, while this conceit remains figurative, Giorgio
and Clara do sometimes come together onstage while singing their own and
each other's letters, occasionally merging their voices and even sometimes
looking directly at each other.[91] And because the mode of delivery so closely
resembles that of "Happiness," the letters become, as vividly as possible, a
mode of lovemaking. (All of this is foretold by Giorgio's declaration in the
first scene: "And after I leave, we'll write each other daily. We'll make love
♪6.71 with our words. You'll be with me every day, Clara.")

Letters sung together by writer and reader, who are nevertheless understood to be far removed from each other, extend the privacy of the individual
expression—the letter, the song—into the space shared by an intimately engaged couple. In *Passion*, virtually all possible permutations of sung letter-
writing and letter-reading occur: separately and simultaneously, and often
moving between these modes, restructuring operatic conventions in fundamental ways. Ordinarily, in an operatic aria or solo song in a musical, a
character sings directly of his or her feelings and thoughts, sometimes as a
soliloquy and sometimes to declare those feelings to another character or

characters. In a conventional love duet, there is generally a period of negotiation before the couple sings together in perfect alignment, without which it is no true duet. With Sondheim's sung letters, a variety of things happen, which are both related to these types and distinct from them. Because the text is already analogous to an operatic aria, in being the singular expression of one individual to be read by another, temporality is readily effaced through the act of involving both the writer and the reader in its singing. When Clara and Giorgio sing their own letters, distance as well as time collapses: the voice and even the person of the letter's writer become an immediate reality for the letter's reader. Yet, even when reader and writer sing together, the origin of what they sing remains clear, although a special response from the reader is implied by her or his reading of particular passages "aloud." The text remains, however, a singular expression, partaken of by two individuals in a way that is both facilitated by their intimacy and gives that intimacy expression. In this way, the singing of the letters recalls those passages in "Happiness" when the two lovers interrupt each other, anticipating each other's thoughts slightly and, in a sense, giving voice to them:[92]   ♩6.72

CLARA: That we ever should have met is a miracle.   Then, in - evitable, . . .
GIORGIO: No, inevit - a - ble.

CLARA: When we glanced at each other in   the   park.   Unhappiness can be seductive.
GIORGIO: We were both unhappy. . . .

Sondheim's virtuosity is stunningly casual, as when the separate strands of their contributions suddenly weave together, become more urgent, and come together (here, on the traditionally charged words "I do"):   ♩6.73

CLARA: All the time we lost. . . .
GIORGIO: I thought I knew how much I could feel.   I didn't

CLARA: I've never known what love was.   And now I do.
GIORGIO: know what love was.   But now   I do.

While singing their letters, their voices merge in similar fashion, and they recall these urgent simultaneities of shared feeling, which in "Happiness" already register as aftershocks of shared orgasm, understood to be moments of perfect anticipation of the other's thoughts and feelings. The core of musically expressed relationships, in *Passion*, thus becomes the transmutation of dialogue into shared monologue.   ♩6.74

It is this process of shared intimacy that Fosca must force on Giorgio, first by writing to him (even though they are stationed in the same remote outpost) and then by insisting that he write to her as he goes to visit Clara on leave. The latter tactic backfires initially, since it is through Giorgio's letter, which Fosca sings in counterpoint to Clara and Giorgio's reprise of "Happiness," that Fosca first learns that Giorgio's "heart belongs to someone else."   ♩6.75
But she takes advantage of an opportunity to push this avenue of communication further when Giorgio visits her sickbed (after the post's doctor con-

vinces him he must do so in order to give Fosca the hope necessary for her recovery), and he even accedes to her request that he join her on her bed (see figure 6.5). In a scene that is chilling both for the coercion involved and for the ways in which it reveals Fosca's capacity for insight, despite her seeming mental incapacities, she pressures Giorgio into writing out a dictated letter to her that is, in fact, in his voice and very close to what he feels (or will come to feel), even if he still lacks the courage to admit it ("I Wish I Could ♪6.76 Forget You").[93] In parallel to this, Fosca also finds opportunities to impress Giorgio with the force of her own being and capacity for self-awareness ("I read"), with how alike they are spiritually ("They Hear Drums [we hear music]," sung before Fosca learns of Clara), and with how completely her ♪6.77 love for Giorgio has taken over her own being ("Loving You").

♪6.78   Sondheim wrote the latter song late, and reluctantly, in order to make clear to audiences something he felt should already have been clear enough in the action of the play, which at this juncture was rapidly approaching the point when Fosca would, in a sense, *become* Clara, fully eclipsing the latter in Giorgio's eyes.[94] But the song matters dramatically, despite Sondheim's reservations, because it registers strongly with Giorgio, allowing him to see the limitations of Clara's love in comparison with Fosca's. "Loving You," like Fosca herself, is breathtakingly and painfully direct, and quite short considering its pivotal position in the narrative. As with "Being Alive" in *Company*, its melody pushes hard, and even more obsessionally, against the melodic major seventh, yet it accepts that repeated, painfully dissonant mo-♪6.79 ment as a simple fact of life:[95]

> Loving **you** is not a **choice**,
> It's who I **am**.
> Loving you is not a choice,
> And not much reason to rejoice,
> But it gives me **pur**pose,
> Gives me **voice** to say to the **world**.

Moreover, the "breakthrough" (which follows immediately here) is couched in language, both musically and verbally, very similar to the parallel moments in "Being Alive," except that here everything is tempered by an overriding acceptance of inevitable unhappiness. As with the first two iterations of Bobby's breakthrough phrase, "being alive," Fosca's two iterations of "why I live" sequence downward, releasing the pressure, and, as Bobby does in his extended phrase, she reaches decisive resolution on her final syllable, although to a new key: "This is why I live. / You are why I live."[96] In a show so saturated with reflexive singing—of one singer responding in the most immediate terms to another, often interrupting—it should come as no surprise that the breakthrough enacted in this song is not the singer's but the hearer's (that is, Giorgio's).

It is tempting to see *Passion*, especially given its nineteenth-century provenance and intricate leitmotivic work,[97] as a version of Wagner's *Tristan und*

Figure 6.5. At the insistence of his post's doctor, Giorgio (Jere Shea) caters to the absurd demands of Fosca (Donna Murphy), agreeing to sleep beside her in her bed. As he falls asleep, his beloved Clara (Marin Mazzie) recites a letter: "Dearest Giorgio, It is three in the morning, and I've just arisen from a dream of you, a dream so real I could swear you were there at my side." The superimposition shown here occurs in the filmed version of *Passion*'s original stage show, during a scenic dissolve to Clara as she recites these first lines; a similar superimposition occurs near the end of her letter, with her lines "How I wish I could just lie by your side and watch you sleep"; seemingly taking her cue from Clara's letter, Fosca awakes and begins to watch Giorgio as Clara's image fades. After Clara's letter, when Giorgio gets up to leave, Fosca insists that he write a love letter to her, which she then dictates ("I Wish I Could Forget You").

Isolde, yet *Passion* forgoes something that *Tristan* shared with Tarchetti's *Fosca*, the conviction that obsessional love is an incurable sickness, resolved only in death. True enough, this belief is given voice in *Passion*, as when, at the end of the flashback sequence, the ensemble repeats the dictum "Beauty is power, / Longing a disease." Yet, in the best idealist way, love in *Passion* also survives death, not in the sense of *Tristan* (where the lovers unite in death), but in the sense reiterated in the final repeated lines of the show, drawn from Fosca's dictated letter: "Your love will live in me." The phrase, ♩6.80 which becomes a kind of mantra stretching into a projected future, makes explicit that relationships provide the cornerstone for the most gratifying variety of immortality, because one survives death, according to this formulation, only through one's capacity to love and to instill love. But it is important to note, too, that the manner in which Fosca survives is specifically through the enabling power of her passion. If at the beginning of the show Giorgio can easily believe he has found the most perfect love possible in his relationship with Clara, by the end he has acquired something infinitely more empowering, however sick the process of acquiring it has made him: he has experienced the full force of Fosca's love for him. And, characteristically, this is expressed by Giorgio's reading (singing) Fosca's last letter to him: ♩6.81   "Now at last / I see what comes / From feeling loved."

See Also

Regarding *Lady in the Dark*, see chapter 7 of Geoffrey Block's *Enchanted Evenings*; Bruce D. McClung's "Art Imitating Life Imitating Art"; chapter 10 in Foster Hirsch's *Kurt Weill on Stage*; chapter 21 in Ronald Sanders's *The Days Grow Short*; chapter 9 in Philip Furia's *Ira Gershwin: The Art of the Lyricist*; pp. 59–68 in Ethan Mordden's *Beautiful Mornin'*; pp. 258–65 in Ronald Talyor's *Kurt Weill: Composer in a Divided World*; Matthew Scott's "Weill in America: The Problem of Revival"; David Drew's *Kurt Weill: A Handbook*, pp. 315–18; pp. 138–40 in John Bush Jones's *Our Musicals, Ourselves*; and pp. 276–82 in Jürgen Schebera's *Kurt Weill: An Illustrated Life*.

Regarding *Kiss Me, Kate*, see chapter 9 of Geoffrey Block's *Enchanted Evenings*; chapter 6 of Joseph P. Swain's *The Broadway Musical*; Robert Lawson-Peebles's "Brush Up Your Shakespeare: The Case of *Kiss Me, Kate*"; chapter 21 of Charles Schwartz's *Cole Porter: A Biography*; chapter 14 of George Eells's *The Life That Late He Led: A Biography of Cole Porter*; chapter 9 of David Grafton's anecdotal *Red, Hot & Rich: An Oral History of Cole Porter*; pp. 251–61 of Ethan Mordden's *Beautiful Mornin'*; and pp. 215–19 and 306–9 of Stephen Citron's *Noel and Cole: The Sophisticates*.

Regarding *My Fair Lady*, see "Pygmalion" in Randolph Goodman's *From Script to Stage: Eight Modern Plays* for an account of its evolution from preplay to musical; pp. 195–214 in Geoffrey Block's *Enchanted Evenings*; chapter 8 of Joseph P. Swain's *The Broadway Musical*; chapter 13 of Scott Miller's *From* Assassins *to* West Side Story; pp. 153–60 in Stacy Wolf's *A Problem Like Maria*; chapter 10 of Ethan Mordden's *Coming Up Roses*; chapters 7–12 of Gene Lees's *Inventing Champagne: The Worlds of Lerner and Loewe*; "My Fair Lady" from Alan Jay Lerner's memoir, *The Street Where I Live*; and pp. 241–48 and 261–80 of Stephen Citron's *The Wordsmiths: Oscar Hammerstein 2nd and Alan Jay Lerner*.

Regarding *Company*, see chapter 5 of Stephen Banfield's *Sondheim's Broadway Musicals*; chapter 4 of Scott Miller's *From* Assassins *to* West Side Story; chapter 3 in Joanne Gordon's *Art Isn't Easy: The Achievement of Stephen Sondheim*; chapter 22 in Harold Prince's *Contradictions*; chapter 12 in Craig Zadan's *Sondheim & Co.*; pp. 190–202 in Meryle Secrest's *Stephen Sondheim: A Life*; pp. 85–92 in Foster Hirsch's *Harold Prince and the American Musical Theatre*; chapter 3 of Dan J. Cartmell's "Stephen Sondheim and the Concept Musical"; Eugene K. Bristow and J. Kevin Butler's "*Company, About Face! The Show That Revolutionized the American Musical*"; John Olson's "*Company—25 Years Later*"; pp. 183–85 in Jim Lovensheimer's "Stephen Sondheim and the Musical of the Outsider"; pp. 318–20 of Ethan Mordden's *Better Foot Forward* and pp. 25–33 of his *One More Kiss*; pp. 275–78 in John Bush Jones's *Our Musicals, Ourselves*; and pp. 228–30 in Barbara Means Fraser's "Revisiting Greece: The Sondheim Chorus."

Regarding *Passion*, see chapter 20 of Meryle Secrest's *Stephen Sondheim: A Life*; chapter 4 of Steven Swayne's *Hearing Sondheim's Voices* (" 'Teach Me How to Sing': Sondheim and the World of Opera"); chapter 1 of Mark Eden Horowitz's *Sondheim on Music*; chapter 6 of Scott Miller's *Deconstructing Harold Hill*; Gary Konas's "*Passion*: Not Just Another Simple Love Story"; Sandor Goodhart's " 'The Mother's Part': Love, Letters, and Reading in Sondheim's *Passion*"; and Shoshana Milgram Knapp's "Difference and Sameness: Tarchetti's *Fosca*, Scola's *Passione d'Amore*, and Sondheim's *Passion*."

EPILOGUE

Operatic Ambitions and Beyond

THE AMERICAN MUSICAL has long suffered from a kind of inferiority complex, with many of its critics and practitioners decrying a perceived gap in value between musicals and opera, its "high-art" counterpart. Ironically, in the last few decades, many shows that bring operatic sensibilities to the American-musical stage—quite often as part of the so-called British invasion—have contributed to a widespread belief that the heyday of the American musical is over (or, perhaps, "over for good," for those who believe Broadway's "Golden Age" ended long ago, in the mid-1960s). In this final chapter, I will first consider three shows that have, in different but related ways, advanced the musical in the direction of opera; this main part of the chapter will complete the cycle of three important twentieth-century influences on the genre, addressed separately in the first two chapters of this book. I will then consider briefly where the operatic impulse, more generally and when combined with other (sometimes related) developments, has left the Broadway musical as an institution.

The American musical has not been the only American art form to suffer from an inferiority complex. Similar feelings of inadequacy have also bedeviled jazz and Hollywood film, which, especially at earlier stages of their developments, were found wanting in relation to concert music and staged drama, respectively. But if jazz and American film grew significantly in prestige during the second half of the twentieth century, the musical has been less upwardly mobile, although its gestures in that direction—*Show Boat* (1927), *Porgy and Bess* (1935), *Oklahoma!* (1943), *Street Scene* (1947), *The Most Happy Fella* (1956), and so on—have been lauded, nurtured, and even (in the case of *Oklahoma!*) much imitated. Notably, however, the shows on this list that achieved the least initial commercial success—*Porgy and Bess* (124 performances) and *Street Scene* (148 performances)—aspired most vigorously to extend the musical and its idiom into the realm of opera.[1]

Nevertheless, ambitious impulses have not been lacking among those who make musicals, and many of them responded after the Second World War to the challenges of bettering their product, most specifically in the directions indicated by *Oklahoma!* and the variety of "integrated" musicals that followed. For some relative newcomers to Broadway during the aspirational phase of the postwar period, Irving Berlin's Americanist response (*Annie Get Your Gun*, 1946; see chapter 5) provided an important model; thus, for example, both Frank Loesser's *Guys and Dolls* (1950, based on Damon Runyan's stories) and Meredith Willson's *The Music Man* (1957), discussed in chapter 6 of my first volume, use iconic American characters and settings. For others, Porter's adaptation of a venerated Old-World theatrical property (*Kiss Me, Kate*, 1948; see chapter 6) seemed a more appealing option, pursued in Lerner and Loewe's *My Fair Lady* (1956, based on George Bernard Shaw's *Pygmalion*; see chapter 6) and Bernstein and Sondheim's *West Side Story* (1957, based on *Romeo and Juliet*; discussed in chapter 8 of my first volume). But none of these, however ambitious, aimed for an operatic alternative to the new Broadway being created by and in response to Rodgers and Hammerstein. To be sure, Leonard Bernstein had ambitions for something altogether grander, patterned to some extent on earlier attempts by Marc Blitzstein to create an American form of *Zeitoper* along the lines of Bertolt Brecht and Kurt Weill's *Dreigroschenoper* (thus, Blitzstein's 1937–1938 *The Cradle Will Rock* and his more operatic *Regina* of 1949). But the relative failure of Bernstein's own one-act opera *Trouble in Tahiti* (1952) taught him to move more cautiously beyond the considerable success he achieved with his more mainstream shows *On the Town* (1944) and *Wonderful Town* (1953).[2]

Centrally at issue with Bernstein was his strong desire not just to elevate the Broadway musical but also, and more generally, to efface the increasingly sharp boundary between high and low art as it had evolved in American music across the first half of the twentieth century. His own separate career as a concert musician, pursued most vigorously in his long association with the New York Philharmonic, was deeply concerned with extending the market for and appreciation of "classical" music. Thus, he used his charismatic persona, and his gifts as an informally eloquent lecturer and writer, to advocate for the music he performed on the concert stage, achieving particular success with his series of Young People's Concerts (1958–1972). As a composer for Broadway, Bernstein added modernist techniques such as serialism to traditional "classical" techniques of musical integration, as a way to organize and enhance an equally sophisticated use of a wide variety of popular idioms. In these respects, Bernstein was the archetypical "crossover" composer of his age, a successor of sorts to George Gershwin, but more obviously grounded within the "classical" tradition.

Just after *Trouble in Tahiti* and *Wonderful Town*, Bernstein and Lillian Hellman began work on a show whose evolution would intertwine significantly with that of *West Side Story*. Like the latter, it was based on a venerated literary property, but with much stronger political overtones: Voltaire's *Candide*, originally published in 1759, partly in response to the devastating Lisbon earthquake of 1755 and the religious and philosophical controversies spawned by that event. The literary bases for both shows were chosen for their contemporary relevance, but the setting for *West Side Story* was from the beginning to be changed to contemporary New York City, where its original political dimension (which pitted the power struggles between feuding families against the romantic inclinations of two of their members) could assume greater relevance for contemporary audiences, whereas

Candide remained (mainly) within Voltaire's original story and settings. This is significant, since the specific *political* relevance for *Candide* in the 1950s was its depiction of the Inquisition, to which Senator Joseph McCarthy's anti-Communist campaign was often compared (especially by its victims, which included Hellman). But bringing out this element required a significant adjustment in emphasis from Voltaire's original in order for the point to register, resulting in an Inquisition scene that has no real parallel in Voltaire, the most egregious example of the original show's sometimes heavy hand in its treatment of political issues. Partly because of this underlying political agenda and its consequences, and partly owing to personal friction among its collaborators, the show's development was painful and beset with delays, and the final result did not have a long original run (seventy-three performances). But its music was quite successful, because of both its captivating overture, which became a standard concert piece, and its "original-cast" album.

Thus, *Candide* stands as one of the more noteworthy examples of a show kept alive and increasingly venerated by virtue of its cast album, demonstrating what an important stand-in and advertisement for shows the cast album had by then become. In general terms, the cast album was capable of reaching huge numbers of people unable to see the show on Broadway, and thus helped to build audiences for revivals and community-based performances, especially in the wake of the hugely successful album for *Oklahoma!*—often hailed as the pioneer in this medium.[3] Indeed, the perceived "integration" of musicals starting with *Oklahoma!* owed much to the increasingly automatic issuance of a cast album, which in itself asserted (or, perhaps, demonstrated) an organic coherence to a show's music, and also added to the incentive for composers to *achieve* such coherence in their scores. Thus, in its way, the cast album, as an institution, played a significant role in encouraging the aspirations of Broadway composers who were determined to elevate their art.

The story of *Candide*'s many transformations after its original Broadway run is a central narrative within what we might well term the American musical's operatic quest, a persistently recurring theme within its historical development. *Candide*'s position in this ongoing quest stems partly from the way its history as a show seems to replicate the intertwined questing narratives of its central characters, since the show's complicated history of revision and revival involved the similarly intertwined efforts of many individuals who sought to realize the show's musical and dramatic potential. The quest to realize the specifically musical potential of *Candide*, however, entails a striking irony, for its musical score does not constitute a single integrated whole. Rather, it is—strangely for a score so venerated in its own right—audibly related to *West Side Story*, a project with which it would otherwise seem to have no vital connection. Besides the oddly anachronistic importation into *Candide* of contemporary Latin music and the use in both shows of modern twelve-tone techniques,[4] their musical images of potential redemption—"Somewhere" in *West Side Story* and "Make Our Garden Grow" in *Candide* (along with its many antecedents in the show)—are extraordinarily similar, both technically and gesturally. Beyond this, the musical profile of *Candide* seems considerably more eclectic than for most shows, incorporating elements of modernism, operetta, religious chorale, and a wide range of exotic musical types—although, to be sure, such eclecticism has often been taken to be one of the score's virtues, providing a musical richness that is managed *within* a governing musical sensibility and style.[5]

But more basic than either of these ironies are two simple facts. First, the actual practices of opera have nearly always readily tolerated the compromising of the very musical integrity that many, with idealized visions of opera, have insisted that the American musical aspire to; Mozart's *The Magic Flute* (1791), for example, is famously eclectic. And, second, *Candide* is more an operetta than an opera, as acknowledged in its original subtitle (*A Comic Operetta Based on Voltaire's Satire*)—which in practical terms offered Bernstein precisely the way station between mainstream Broadway and idealized opera that he needed.

The central involvement in the later stages of *Candide*'s revisions of Harold Prince, who by the mid-1960s was one of Broadway's most ambitious producers and directors, is particularly significant. Prince brought in frequent collaborators Hugh Wheeler to rewrite the book and Stephen Sondheim to revise the lyrics as needed. Sondheim's contribution, though relatively circumscribed, underscores the importance of Bernstein's operatic ambitions to his own career, especially considering their collaboration on *West Side Story* while the original *Candide* was still playing, and Prince's subsequent role as an important instigator in Sondheim's most ambitious projects. Given the importance of this collaborative team to Broadway's aspirational profile, it seems imperative to include here, as Sondheim's own principal contribution to Broadway's "operatic quest," his *Sweeney Todd* (1979, in collaboration with both Prince and Wheeler), produced after his involvement in revising *Candide* but a decade before *Candide*'s "final revised version, 1989."[6] And, indeed, *Sweeney Todd* shares important features with *Candide*, including its basis in a European property and setting, its musical sophistication, and its concern for political and social problems attendant on what in other contexts has been viewed as "progress" (thus, the Enlightenment for *Candide*, the Industrial Revolution for *Sweeney Todd*). Although the juxtaposition of *Sweeney Todd* here with Andrew Lloyd Webber's *Evita* at a later stage in this chapter may seem curious—even if the two shows did appear in the same year, and even if *Evita* also benefited from Hal Prince's involvement—it is important to note that the latter also has intriguing ties to Bernstein's *Candide*. It is, like *Candide*, highly political, and considers anew the relationship between Europe and its South American colonial adventures—specifically, Buenos Aires. More basically, however, it shares with the later versions of *Candide* (along with Lloyd Webber's shows more generally) the distinction of being a show whose development and production were profoundly affected by the prior success of a record album.

Moreover, both *Sweeney Todd* and *Evita* line up with each other—and against *Candide*—in one important respect. *Candide*'s music is often wantonly anachronistic, to the extent that it becomes one of the principal ways in which the story, two centuries old at the time of its first presentation, becomes palpably *our* story as well. Thus, *Candide*'s musical profile seems designed in part to allow us to connect its world to our own more readily. Yet, in both *Sweeney Todd* and *Evita*, the music functions largely to create a world apart from ours; indeed, the heavy use of music in these shows—the principal hallmark of their operatic profile, especially since the music itself is in neither case quite operatic in a conventional sense—is owing precisely to this function. We must therefore take note of two distinct strands in Broadway's operatic ambitions, which a consideration of these three shows will enable us to do. One aspect of those ambitions concerns a *prestige*-oriented enhancement, a desire to elevate the genre by presenting its musical sophistication in high profile; both Sondheim and Bernstein exemplify this approach. But another dimension also emerges, brought out by the otherwise odd pairing here of Stephen Sondheim and Andrew Lloyd Webber, a dimension indebted equally to film music and to the indebtedness of film music, in turn, to Richard Wagner's operatic works: a desire to use music more pervasively so as to create the sense of a world different from our own, and to manage the idiosyncrasies of that world and its inhabitants through the persuasive force of an integrated score.[7] The progression between the two strands, with *Sweeney Todd* partaking in both, may be seen in another way, in parallel to the three principal twentieth-century influences on the musical considered in this book, moving from Bernstein's operetta-based *Candide*, through Sondheim's cinematic *Sweeney Todd*, to Lloyd Webber's more purely operatic *Evita*.

Yet, if *Evita* is the more purely operatic of the three, its status as an *elevated* extension of the American musical has seemed, to most, questionable at best. And it is within that paradox that I will, in the concluding part of the chapter, try to situate some of the more recent developments in the American musical.

Candide (1956) is based directly on the original episodic novella by Voltaire, which may be seen as both one of its great strengths and one of its most basic problems as a comic operetta. Voltaire's *Candide* resonates quite well with many features common to modern culture, working itself out as a serial in which, whatever dire circumstances befall its central characters, they survive for the next episode (as in, for example, *The Perils of Pauline, Flash Gordon, Star Trek*, or in most situation comedies). And, as in many modern satirical comedies, its situations and events are drawn from some of the grimmest contemporary realities. Yet, it is also shaped as the story of its title character's development from a naïf to a realist, and it offers what seems to be a seriously intended model for getting past what Voltaire saw as one of the Enlightenment's most pernicious illusions: the optimistic belief that—as voiced by Voltaire's contemporary Gottfried Wilhelm von Leibniz and echoed by Candide's teacher, Dr. Pangloss—"all is for the best in this best of all possible worlds."[8]

As in such familiar episodic tales as *Gulliver's Travels, Alice's Adventures in Wonderland,* and *The Wizard of Oz* (all satiric and presented as if only for children), the main character in *Candide* undertakes a fantasy journey, on the way learning valuable lessons about what matters in his native setting by experiencing settings quite different from it.[9] What sets *Candide* apart, however, is that Candide's "native setting" is untenably fanciful, whereas his experiences in the real world are based entirely on the most horrifying realities familiar to the mid-eighteenth century: devastating natural disasters (earthquakes, fires, storms at sea, and the like), the plague, syphilis, war (including forced conscription, multiple rape, dismemberment, and other brutalities), slavery (including multiple rape, punitive dismemberment, and other brutalities), piracy (including rape, dismemberment, and other brutalities), partial cannibalism (including partial dismemberment and other brutalities), public torture and execution, murder, speculative castration in the service of opera's castrato tradition, religious conflict and persecution, racial conflict and persecution, class-based exploitation, political corruption, prostitution and other more direct forms of sexual slavery, sexual bestiality, avarice leading to thievery and swindles, power lust, blackmail and extortion, ignorance (leading to life-threatening bloodletting, bad art, bad critics, and other follies), and everyday cruelties such as poverty, hunger, the repayment of kindness with betrayal, and a general lack of human charity toward those who suffer. If this seems a grim list, it is nevertheless by no means complete, for Voltaire's *Candide* is unrelenting in its detailed parade of human misery. It is, in fact, one of the most unpleasant classic texts available, invaluable for its critique of a time that others insisted on seeing more positively, yet for the most part expressing no credible hope for its embattled cohort of characters whose sufferings are elaborated as the core of nearly every episode.

In itself, Voltaire's *Candide* poses a strange conundrum regarding its attitude on human possibilities. That it is against blind optimism is clear enough. But some of its characters seem genuinely good (rather than just naive) and are in the end at least partly rewarded for their goodness. That the main characters do not die may be taken either as a perverse celebration of human perseverance or as a cynical manipulation designed to make them continue to suffer. And the final resolution that, in Candide's words, "We must cultivate our garden" offers thin consolation for what has come before. Indeed, since within the book's narrative every previous attempt to achieve some kind of stable outcome meets with utter failure, wouldn't we be as naive as Candide has been throughout were we simply to accept this conclusion at face value? Certainly, the revisers of the Bernstein operetta vacillated on this issue; in some versions (but not in all performances) the concluding number, "Make Our Garden Grow," is disrupted by the death of Candide's cow from the pox.

A particularly strange episode in Voltaire's novella (left out of the original stage show, except by narration, but restored in revision) takes place in El Dorado, an almost inaccessible paradise that serves oddly as a more conventional fantasy journey within the extended "real-world" journey that makes up the bulk of *Candide*. Here, too, it is clear that the primary thrust of the episode is its satirical refutation of Leibniz, since Candide and company resolve in short order to leave this place where, apparently, everything truly *is* for the best—but also hopelessly and endlessly boring. The episode also forms part of a critique of basic Christian constructs, presenting El Dorado as a kind of Heaven, however implausible, to serve as a complement for the initial Westphalian Garden of Eden. When Candide rejects this "Heaven" and returns to "earth," we are presumably to understand this as confirmation that life on earth is what truly counts, rather than an anticipated paradise beyond. But Voltaire's attempt at the end of the novella to rescue a viable potential for happiness on earth, in the face of his overwhelming account of what stands in the way of such happiness, is not entirely convincing in dramatic terms. Perhaps we are unconvinced simply because not enough direct attention has been paid before the end to how some types of behavior support human contentment and others do not; without any preparation of this kind, the ending seems unsupported from within the drama, however convincing it may be in the abstract.

As if all this were not enough, there was a further circumstantial awkwardness in adapting Voltaire's *Candide* for America in the 1950s. The justified outrage that Hellman and others felt at the conduct of the congressional hearings led by Senator McCarthy simply fails to find adequate footing in the book. Indeed, the requisite Inquisition scene had to be invented (for the 1956 version), since it was not part of Voltaire's original.

GRAND INQUISITOR:	What is the charge?
FIRST PROFESSOR:	The overbuying of candles for the overreading of books in subversive association with associates.
OLD MAN:	Great judge, I learned to read as a very young man. I can see now that I was a tool and a fool. I was poor, I was lonely—
FIRST PROFESSOR:	Who are your associates? Be quick.
OLD MAN:	Yes, sir. Well, there was Emmanuel, Lilybelle, Lionel, and Dolly and Molly and Polly, of course. And my Ma and my Pa and my littlest child. A priest, deceased, and my uncle and my aunt. The president, his resident, and the sister of my wife—
GRAND INQUISITOR:	All right. All right. Thank you for your splendid cooperation.

The scene was obviously meant to resonate with the McCarthy hearings, concerned as they were with the naming of names. But even locally, the interrogation stands well apart from the horrors of the actual Inquisition. While the victims of the McCarthy hearings genuinely suffered, they were not burned alive or flogged as public entertainment. And in the context of Voltaire's book, the indignity of being forced to name names (or even of being blacklisted or serving jail time) would scarcely register within its teeming catalog of misery. Nor, after all, was the world at a lack, in the early 1950s, for truly Voltairean miseries, so recently after the Second World War and its unique legacies—the Holocaust and the destruction of entire cities through fire bombing (Dresden) and dropping atomic bombs (Hiroshima and Nagasaki). Yet, despite the effect of breast-beating in Hellman's heavy-handed emphasis on the Inquisition, her general adherence to Voltaire left open a promising approach to revision, whereby the score might be rescued simply by revising the book.[10]

The many attempts to revise *Candide* constitute a hopelessly convoluted tale that may, however, be readily condensed to its essentials. Already with the first staging, the divided lyrics credit spoke to a general dissatisfaction for how the constituent parts fitted together, as Richard Wilbur (the principal lyricist, who took over the job relatively late) shared the credit with earlier contributors John LaTouche and Dorothy Parker; before Wilbur had gotten involved, both Bernstein and Hellman had also contributed lyrics, some of which would remain in the show, uncredited. Following *Candide*'s initial run, there were attempts to revive and revise the show, both as a show and in concert, but the most successful series of revisions began when Hal Prince took on the job of directing a one-act off-Broadway version in 1973.[11] Prince reconceived the show in carnivalesque terms (to avoid the ponderous weight of the original), hired Hugh Wheeler to write a new book, cajoled a reluctant Sondheim into adding and revising some of the lyrics (especially necessary for the reconceived opening), secured the permissions of the principal earlier collaborators, and achieved a run sufficiently successful that he was able to move quickly to Broadway with an expanded version. Encouraged by these successes, Prince continued to work with his collaborators to restore as much of the excised material as seemed feasible; the result was given a fully operatic mounting by the New York City Opera in 1982, in a version that was televised nationally. Despite the elevated theatrical setting, however, the show in this form presents itself as a fairly lighthearted romp that doesn't take its string of catastrophes all that seriously; many regretted a perceived substitution of flippancy for the gravity of the original. A further revision was thus undertaken in 1988 for the Scottish Opera, this time with Bernstein's involvement. For this revision, in which comedy and seriousness were held more in balance, John Wells adapted Wheeler's book so as to restore some of the settings and musical numbers from the original conception, in some cases adding back early material that would be staged for the first time.

I cannot, of course, do justice here to all the possible angles on the show suggested by this web of revisions. But I can usefully take my cue from Stephen Sondheim's appraisal of the original show when he was called upon to critique it just before it opened (he was in the midst of working on Bernstein's *West Side Story*, for which Bernstein had already provided some lyrics): "The book didn't belong with the score, the score didn't belong with the direction, and the direction didn't belong with the book. I thought Lillian's book was wonderful, but it's very black. The score is pastiche, with bubble and sparkle and sweetness. The direction was wedding cake, like an operetta."[12] Given this (undoubtedly accurate) assessment, while remembering also that it was not Hellman's "black" book nor the direction that kept the property alive past its abbreviated initial run, the primary task here reduces to one of considering how Bernstein's bubbling "pastiche" makes itself felt above all else, and more especially of how it interacts with the larger property, in whatever specific form it has taken.

That larger property opens, like the original book, in a complacent Westphalia (a region of western Germany), introducing a set of characters who will somehow survive the series of calamities that make up the main action of the show: the upper-class siblings Cunegonde and Maximillian, taught by Dr. Pangloss (a stand-in for Leibniz), the serving girl Paquette,[13] and Candide, a bastard relative. Although the show eliminates a great many of Voltaire's episodes, we nevertheless witness Candide's eviction from Protestant Westphalia for daring to fall in love with Cunegonde (left panel of figure 7.1),[14] his abduction by the Bulgars (in various accounts understood to be either Gypsies or Prussians, but equally plausible as Catholics, Islamics, or Eastern Orthodox), who force him to fight against the Abars (Arabs?) in a war that sees Cunegonde multiply raped and left for dead, and their Westphalian home and its inhabitants destroyed and killed with her. Candide's subsequent travels eventually take him to Lisbon just in time for the great earthquake, where he is—after being flogged nearly to death at an auto-da-fé meant to prevent further earthquakes[15]—reunited with Cunegonde, who is being shared as the sexual property of the Grand Inquisitor and a rich Jew (in the Prince-Wheeler version, which in this instance follows Voltaire more closely than the others; see right panel of figure 7.1, and the discussion of "Glitter and Be Gay" below). Candide rescues Cunegonde, in the process killing both the Grand Inquisitor and the Jew, and they set sail for the New World with renewed hope. In the New World, however, Cunegonde takes up with the corrupt governor of Buenos Aires, who soon tires of her. Meanwhile, Candide, fleeing for his life, finds El Dorado, but then leaves it and sets sail for Europe to find Cunegonde. Finally (with some variations regarding how), after Candide rescues Cunegonde (and her brother) from a Turkish harem, the surviving cast settles on a small farm.

Even in the reduced form of the Prince-Wheeler revision, *Candide* is stiff medicine, pushing a comic tone very hard while depicting horrible brutality. We see all the religious-cultural conflicts that beset Europe in the eighteenth

Le Baron...voyant cette cause & cet effet, chassa Candide
du Château à grands coups de pied dans le derriere;
Candide chap. 1er

"Whereby the house and I belong to both in common."

Figure 7.1. That *Candide* has meant different things to different audiences may be seen vividly by comparing illustrations among the many editions of the story. In a 1778 French edition (left [Paris: Bouillon], illus. Daniel Chodowiecky), Candide is banished after "experimenting" with Cunegonde; even the portrait in the background seems to take part in his ejection. In an American edition of 1930 (right [New York: Book Collectors Association], illus. Mahlon Blaine), Cunegonde has become a jaded "modern girl," a bored bystander waiting impassively as the Jew and Grand Inquisitor argue over her. Here, she comes across as a version of Wedekind's Lulu, whose story had just been filmed (*Pandora's Box*, 1929, dir. Georg Pabst, with Louise Brooks) and would soon be set to music by Alban Berg (*Lulu*, left incomplete at his death in 1935). Both illustrations indulge the opportunity to undress Cunegonde while casting aspersion on her character, suggesting in the first that she is the cause of Candide's downfall—the Eve who has caused Candide's Adam to be banished from Eden, albeit without her—and in the second that, through her amorality, she bears at least some responsibility for the rampant sin and corruption that surround her. Although neither is really to the point of Voltaire's text, the 1956 musical and its various reincarnations do even more violence to Voltaire's vision by allowing Cunegonde's function as an operetta ingénue to preserve her from being genuinely tainted by her long series of misdeeds and misadventures.

century (explicitly involving Protestants, Catholics, Muslims, and Jews), along with the false promise of the New World, the latter represented most vividly by syphilis. We are treated to the spectacle of war, mass rape, natural disaster on an epic scale, public torture and execution, sexual slavery, and a woman who has lost her buttock through cannibalism. Yet, throughout, and especially at the end, the music conveys a different message, reassuring us even more surely than Pangloss that everything will work out, that it ought not to be Candide's—or our—fate to be endlessly miserable. In part, this kind of reassurance is one of the principal functions of music in any musical, but it is especially vital in this one, where its capacity to reassure is crucially important to the precariously balanced "tone" of the story, poised between bitter, barely comic satire and a serious, somehow hopeful perspective on human possibilities for sustainable happiness.

One of the most effective changes to the original show restored Voltaire's opening situation, in which Candide's awakening lust for Cunegonde betrays him and precipitates his fall from grace, in parallel to humankind's fall from the Garden of Eden. Musically, this decision meshed easily with the desire to provide a more conventional opening musical number to introduce the main characters; for this, Sondheim wrote new lyrics for "Venice Gavotte," the penultimate number in the original show. The choice allows, within Bernstein's original combination-song format, the delineation of an internal contrast among the three youths. Candide and Cunegonde—in clear expression of their compatibility—sing their verses of "Life Is Happiness Indeed" to the same relatively sedate melody, whereas the solipsistic Maximillian sings his verse paired only with his reflection in the mirror, in what seems to be a wholly different style and tempo, but which combines neatly with the other two as a frenetic countersubject. The original opening num- ♪7.1
ber, "The Best of All Possible Worlds," then follows, with much-revised lyrics.[16] Although the revisions to "The Best of All Possible Worlds" seem mostly motivated by the removal of marriage as a principal topic (now irrelevant at this point), they also point out more vividly the emptiness of the central argument. Thus, the new lyric for the refrain (or its slight variants), ♪7.2

> Once one dismisses / The rest of all possible worlds,
> One finds that this is / The best of all possible worlds,

replaces a variety of alternatives, including ♪7.3

> None have more grace in this best of all possible worlds.
> No finer race in this best of all possible worlds.

This clearer presentation of the Leibniz tautology is especially important because a recurring chorale that embodied it (setting Bernstein's own lyric) had been dropped even before the original show, not to be restored until the 1989 revisions: ♪7.4

> We have learned, and understood, / Everything that is, is good;
> Everything that is, is planned, / Is wisely planned, is right and good.

Following the opening ensemble, Candide and Cunegonde discover that their attraction for each other is mutual, while imitating an "experiment" regarding the juxtaposition of bodies that Cunegonde had seen Dr. Pangloss performing with Paquette. The ensuing duet, "Oh, Happy We," manages to express both how very different they are in their expectations for marriage and how little such differences matter.[17] Thus, from their opening words they blatantly contradict each other while perfectly complementing each other in musical terms (lyrics from the 1989 version):

CANDIDE: Soon, when we feel we can afford it,
             We'll build a modest little farm.
CUNEGONDE: We'll buy a yacht and live aboard it,
             Rolling in luxury and stylish charm.

As a rhythmic correlative for this discrepancy, the graceful tune fits somewhat awkwardly within a seven-beat measure structure, a metrical foreshortening that also seems to betoken a certain lustful impatience on the singers' ♪7.5 parts. Thus, the next segment foreshortens these units even further, into alternating three-beat patterns; here, their verbal disagreement expresses itself harmonically as well, with each phrase in a different key, but returning deftly ♪7.6 to the original key for the end:

CAN. *(G Major):*   Cows and chickens.
CUN. *(A♭ Major):*   Social whirls.
CAN. *(A Major):*   Peas and cabbage.
CUN. *(G Major):*   Ropes of pearls.

After additional repetitions of this pattern within a traditional AABA structure (where the "B" reproduces the same overall metrical structure, but in a different key), the song concludes in a stretto (or cabaletta), a traditional operatic device for concluding a slower number (often a cavatina) with a fast closing section. In this case, metrical confusion and rhythmic foreshortening produce a close canon, in which one voice follows immediately behind the other, "chasing" it but never catching it (the following repeats several times):[18]

CUN.:   Oh, happy pair! / Oh, happy we! / It's very rare / How we agree!
CAN.:   Oh, happy pair! / Oh, happy we! / It's very rare / How we agree!

In the second half of the pattern, the internal rhymes ("It's **very rare** / How **we agree!**") line up within the canonic treatment, yet another way in which the music registers the disjointed nature of their "agreement" that also provides one final foreshortening before the final buildup. At the end of the number, Candide does indeed "catch up" with Cunegonde, so that they achieve (musical) climax together—just in time to be caught in the act by Cunegonde's outraged family.

♪7.7

Bernstein's sure hand with his musical materials, here blending sophisticated rhythmic and harmonic manipulations within a traditional Tin Pan Alley structure that then gives way to the operatic—all exquisitely expressive of the situation and lyric—reaches into every corner of his score. Even the overture, which might have been little more than an agreeable combination of tunes from the show, is integral to the overall musical profile. The overture uses the two opening numbers (as they were then; thus, "The Best of All Possible Worlds" and "Oh, Happy We") as the framework for a foreshortened sonata form. Sonata form—the central structure for instrumental music since about the time of Haydn and Mozart—provides a structural basis that is particularly adept at setting up and resolving conflicts that can be rendered as contrasting themes, by initially presenting those themes in contrasting keys but eventually playing the second of them in the key of the first. In this case, the skewed "rationalizing" music of "The Best of All Possible Worlds" establishes the home key, with the lyrical alternative of love, "Oh, Happy We," presented first in conflict with the opening key, and then eventually resolved within it. In this way, the sonata form performs the kinds of musical reassurances generally performed more immediately by the use of conventional song forms within the show: we know (or think we know) from this overture that everything will work out. But the overture also tells us other important information: that it won't be easy, albeit fast paced (thus all that scurrying activity, taking us rapidly and with random abandon through various keys); that it will involve carnivalesque exaggeration (in the episode between the two main themes); and that the ending may not be quite as expected, since the resolution of the "love" theme does not bring the overture to a close but yields instead to a stretto conclusion based on a later number from the show (the "laughing song" portion of "Glitter and Be Gay"; see below), which, like the concluding section of "Oh, Happy We," proceeds in close canon. In all of these features, Bernstein borrows deftly from various operatic overture traditions, most notably from Mozart for the scurrying activity within a preset frame (the overtures to Così fan tutte and The Magic Flute); from Berlioz—by way of Smetana, by way of Stravinsky—for the carnivalesque episode (Roman Carnival, The Bartered Bride, Petrushka); and from Rossini for the stretto conclusion, which reproduces Rossini's trademark effect of presenting a crescendo over a repeated orchestral figure.

♪7.8

The virtuosic showcase of the show is Cunegonde's "Glitter and Be Gay," which was, in the original show, part of an extended Paris sequence in which she is the shared sexual property of two brothers who have somehow become a marquis and a sultan, a conceit absent in Voltaire's novella. Wheeler's revision restores Voltaire's original situation, in which she is shared between the Grand Inquisitor and a rich Jew in Lisbon—which of course also carries a higher political charge—but at the price (for purists) of moving a Parisian *operette* number somewhat incongruously to a Portuguese setting. (The compromise solution, for the 1989 version, returns the number to Paris, with Cunegonde shared between the Cardinal Archbishop and a rich Jew, but thereby loses the special religious-political charge of Voltaire's Inquisition setting.) The number is also a showcase for Bernstein, who marshals all the ingredients of musical high drama, even if such serious content is contradicted by the larger context and the number's eventual evolution into operetta-based frivolity.

"Glitter and Be Gay" proceeds twice through a trajectory that moves from an opening melancholy to frivolity, beginning with a droopy, minor-mode aria introduced and accompanied by a melodramatic shawmlike figure. The shawm is an older reed instrument, whose modern correlatives, the English horn or oboe, are often used both as an expression of loneliness and to suggest an exotic location (often removed also in time); here both uses combine, evoking Cunegonde's misery within the harem atmosphere of the Sultan (in the original stage version). Throughout the slow first section, Cunegonde seems continually to try to pull away from the opening C-minor melodic phrase, only to be pulled back repeatedly, as one who can't escape her unfortunate situation; in the second time through, her attempt to escape becomes even more melodramatic, as she recites her lines with exaggerated feeling over the

♪7.9   music, rather than singing them. Each time, with a great show of resolve, she "resigns" herself to enjoying the gilded part of her "gilded cage"; the number then shifts to the major mode for a fairly typical "laughing song" in the best operetta tradition,[19] deriving (and also implicitly contradicting) its fiercely resolute "joy" by requiring the singer to pull apart into a close canon with the oboe after an initial unison presentation. In this faster section, which the second time around yields to an even faster and more virtuosic cabaletta, the key shifts suddenly to the flat-sixth degree (in this case A♭ major), a key relationship that is, as noted in previous chapters, often used to signify "escape" to a "better place" through its sudden transport to a fresh and exotic-sounding remote key. That we are indeed to understand this as escape seems clear, given the lyric that carries Cunegonde to the extended "Ha ha ha ha

♪7.10   ha!" episode (and with it the first full arrival in A♭):

> Enough, enough, / Of being basely tearful!
> I'll show my noble stuff / By being bright and cheerful!
> Ha ha ha ha ha! / Ha!

Within the tradition of the flat sixth and its treatment, reality normally returns as we inevitably shift back to the here and now (the original key). And, indeed, "Glitter and Be Gay" does so the first time through. But in the end, the promised escape is made "real" through the song's ending in the remote alternative key, maintained through the cabaletta; from this we may assume that Cunegonde has managed to talk herself into enjoying her situation,

♪7.11   whatever her remaining protestations to the contrary.

The score of *Candide*, especially with the restoration of much of its previously discarded material, is extraordinarily rich in associations, a feature that has always made it a particularly attractive object of study. "Auto-da-fé," for example, makes grim use of the "echo-song" device, a venerated song type popular from the earliest operas, in which an echo of the final syllables of a question sometimes provides a surprising answer.[20] ♪7.12

INQUISITORS:	Are our methods legal or illegal?	CHORUS:	Legal!
	Are we judges of the law, or laymen?		Amen!
	Shall we hang them or forget them?		Get them!

The cabaret-style jaded-waltz type provides a fitting vehicle for "What's the Use," which describes the futile circle through which the money circulates in a Venice casino, enriching no one. "Bon Voyage" seems to offer a nod to ♪7.13 Gilbert and Sullivan in the cynical asides of the Governor ("Oh, but I'm bad") as the populace sends Candide on his doomed way (cf. Bunthorne's sly asides as *Patience*'s bridesmaids sing "In a Doleful Train").[21] The quartet ♪7.14 finale for the first act (although with variant words and situations in the ♪7.15 original and 1989 versions, both by Wilbur) offers an elegantly conceived combination song that serves equally as an ensemble finale after the Italian opera buffa tradition, with the parts deftly arranged so that each singer's words might emerge clearly from the complex texture so as to detail four distinctly different perspectives. As noted earlier, Bernstein even indulges in ♪7.16 a bit of twelve-tone music (in "Quiet"), surely offered as yet another dimension of his musical erudition, yet also recalling, in its situational dynamic, "Conversation Piece" from Bernstein's 1953 *Wonderful Town*. ♪7.17

Among the most personal of the score's riches is "I Am Easily Assimi- ♪7.18 lated," with two oft-noted autobiographical references: "My father came from Rovno Gubernya. . . . My father spoke a High Middle Polish" (both of which were true for Bernstein, although the reference to High Middle Polish is no more than a humorous reference to High Middle German). In this song Bernstein fuses (assimilates?) obvious tokens of a South American tango idiom (appropriate for Buenos Aires, the locale for the song as it appears in the show) with melodic and instrumental references to klezmer music. That the mix is intentional is well documented; as Elizabeth Wells relates, "the composer's facsimile [of the song] reads 'Old Lady's Jewish Tango' with the marking 'Moderato Hassidicamente.' "[22] Moreover, given the multilingual wordplay within the song, for which Bernstein himself wrote the lyric, we may assume that the unstated assonance between "Hispanic" and "Hassidic" would have provided as much private pleasure as the more public rhyme of "Me muero, me sale una hernia!" (I'm dying, I'm getting a hernia!) with "A long way from Rovno Gubernya!" The setup line—a throwaway joke that underscores that the singing Hispanics are simultaneously working very hard—apparently came from Bernstein's collaboration on the song with his Chilean-born wife, Felicia, which further grounds the song's ethnic blend within Bernstein's personal life.[23]

But the song's wordplay, if sometimes obscure, is gesturally fairly obvious even without access to this personal background. When the Old Lady repeats back the Spaniards' "Tus labios rubí dos rosas que se abren a mí, Conquistan mi corazón, Y sólo con una canción" (Your ruby lips (are) two roses that open themselves to me, and conquer my heart with only a song) in a confused mess of Spanish, French, English, German, and Russian, it becomes abundantly clear that this is someone who has learned how to say yes in a wide variety of languages (and the French phrase "Je ne sais quoi," a common euphemistic reference to sex appeal, makes it equally clear what she is in the habit of saying yes to):

♩7.19

Mis labios rubí, /	Dreiviertel Takt,	mon très cher ami,
My ruby lips, /	three-quarter time,	my very dear friend,
(Spanish)	(German)	(French)

Oui oui,	sí sí,	ja ja ja,	yes yes,	da da. /	Je ne sais quoi!
Yes yes,	yes yes,	yes yes yes,	yes yes,	yes yes. /	I don't know what!
(French)	(Spanish)	(German)	(English)	(Russian) /	(French)

Moreover, it is altogether appropriate that a song about assimilation—especially one from Bernstein—should hide a Jewish core within an outwardly South American idiom.

Among the most striking of *Candide*'s many associative links to various musical traditions is the recurring "calling song," "You Were Dead, You Know," built around a favorite device of American operetta, the song of recognition (e.g., the "mysterious melody" in *Naughty Marietta* that becomes "Ah, Sweet Mystery of Life," or "Indian Love Call" from *Rose-Marie*; see chapter 1, pp. 37–38). When this song is first heard, at the reunion of Candide and Cunegonde in the first act, it enacts the gesture of culmination, as if the lovers have won out, even though they have a lot more trials to undergo. It thus serves as an exaggerated joke, dramatically misplaced and foretelling the opposite of its optimistic dramatic and musical profile. As we have surely realized by this point in the action, these people do not see the big picture, at least not yet. An opening orchestral splash—the musical equivalent of a flash of illuminating light—signals the lovers' simultaneous discovery of each other, and their first calls, echoing between them the generic calling figure of a falling third, sound in full consonance with the orchestral background. But this profile shifts for the second phrase, as the voices sing at that point in sharp dissonance to the supporting harmonies (falling E–C against an F-minor triad), leading to an intense effect of "winning out" when the key they insist on (C) is finally embraced by the full orchestra, in an arrival that brings the couple together both literally (stage center) and musically, with their close canon resolving simultaneously on the word "love" (recalling, and thus completing, the cabaletta of "Oh, Happy We"):[24]

♩7.20

CUN.:	Oh.	Is it you?	Candide!	Candide!	Can . . .
CAN.:	Oh.	Is it true?	Cunegonde!	Cunegonde!	Cunegonde!

CUN:	Oh.	Is it you?	Candide!	Dear,	my	love!
CAN:	Oh.	Is it true?	Cunegonde!	Oh my	love,	dear love!

The question of how Candide and company do eventually see the bigger picture is addressed primarily through music, for it is only in this realm and on this level that we might plausibly believe it. With *Candide*, the musical problem is particularly daunting because we already know that the overture has lied to us, or at least tricked us, by substituting the cynical laughter of "Glitter and Be Gay" for the cabaletta conclusion of the more innocent "Oh, Happy We." And the culmination that "You Were Dead, You Know" offers to "Oh, Happy We" is palpably false even when we first hear it late in the first act, and *especially* so when we hear it repeated—this presumably is a one-of-a-kind culmination—in the second act. Innocence—even *restored* innocence—won't do here; only wisdom will serve. But how exactly does Candide acquire wisdom, and how do we recognize its happening?

The key element for this process is the capacity of musical numbers to allow us to "see" a character thinking and feeling simply by taking us away from the action. For Candide, this reflective mode occurs especially within his solo meditations, "It Must Be So," "It Must Be Me,"[25] and "Nothing More Than This." In the first of these, Candide accepts his fate as "for the best" when he is first expelled from Westphalia; in the second, he begins to question his teachings after he barely survives his flogging at the auto-da-fé, yet he still blames himself for the cruelty with which the world treats him. But in the third number, which stands musically apart from the other two, he has reached full disillusionment, finally seeing even his idealized Cunegonde for the brazen opportunist she has always been.[26] Equally relevant to this musical "thought journey" are the series of chorales sung by the chorus, which run in parallel to Candide's emergent disillusionment; these chorales (restored only in the 1989 version) trace a progression from "We have learned, and understood / Everything that is, is good" (quoted earlier) through a more questioning version—"Have we learned?"—at the beginning of the second act, and reaching a final realization that "Life is neither good nor bad. / Life is life, and all we know" just after Candide's "Nothing More Than This," and before the final number, "Make Our Garden Grow."[27]

♪7.21

♪7.22

Two processes contribute to making the final number at least potentially convincing as the realistically hopeful hymn it is trying to be. First is the emptying out that these earlier numbers trace, detailing a full renunciation of naive optimism. Only after this process has been completed—and only the 1989 version includes their entire trajectory—can the musical groundwork laid in these numbers emerge, newly constituted, as a reasonably hopeful closing number. And the reasonability here is crucial; we can believe this hope only because its expression is grounded in the here and now, because it derives from individual labor, and because it specifically rejects both Eden ("Those Edens can't be found") and the "sugar cake" of a promised hereafter. Yet even with this preparation fully restored (along with a more balanced diet of perspectives along the way, particularly with the restoration of the complete pessimist Martin, the inverted image of Pangloss), the show's ability to convince depends in the end on a single masterstroke within the closing chorale, when the orchestra falls away suddenly, leaving the choir to continue on its own. The gesture works in part because it builds on traditions of a cappella singing as an emblem of community and as the expression of common feeling (as in barbershop quartets or church choir singing). But even more important is the visceral effect of removing all external foundations, all props, from the singers, who must then do their best without help, a musical correlative for the characters' own situation. In this inspired moment, the cast stands before us suddenly naked, at least in musical terms, and Bernstein's thorny counterpoint ensures that we hear them struggle a bit before they emerge together on the culminating phrase, "And make our ♪7.23   garden grow."[28]

Yet the show remains fundamentally flawed, however well realized this core musical elaboration of its redemptive theme may be. And the reason for this has everything to do with the ways in which the overture has lied to us and why it has done so; in similar ways, both the overture and the music more generally (especially the cast-album selections) indelibly imprint a world in which innocence—Candide's, Cunegonde's, and ours—somehow *can* be preserved through it all. Voltaire knew better. And so, in his way, surely did Bernstein—why else would he have so carefully nurtured a convincing musical narrative that entails first the complete *disillusionment* of Candide's opening innocence? But the show, in all its versions, tries too strenuously to have its sugar cake and eat it too, which simply can't be done. Emblematic of how thoroughly disjunct the world of Bernstein's *Candide* is from Voltaire's is the simple matter of Cunegonde's appearance at the end of the show. On Broadway and the opera stage she remains enduringly youthful even then, but Voltaire renders her, more realistically, as having grown old and ugly before her time, so that Candide resolves in the end to marry her *anyway*, both to keep his earlier promise and (perhaps more important) to spite her brother.

That this more complex resolution seems untenable for the Broadway stage may be put down to genre limitations, but it is not entirely clear whether those limitations stem from audience expectations and predilections, or misjudgments or failure of nerve among the show's creative team when faced with an intractably problematic property. Both, perhaps. But even more basically, they stem from the tautological assurances endemic to popular genres, most of all to popular *musical* genres, which tend much more often than not to reaffirm optimistic perspectives. Popular musical genres are based, most fundamentally, on eighteenth-century tonal practices, and—as Susan McClary has eloquently argued—like those forms they reinscribe over and over again the conviction that things *will* work out for the best, at least in some sense.[29] Because popular musical genres were a necessary constituent element not only of American musicals but also of any truly "American" operatic form as it might have been conceived in the 1950s, it should not surprise us that *Candide*'s music will seem to be more on Pangloss's side than Martin's. Even Bernstein's ready recourse to classical traditions does not avail him; one may well argue, following McClary, that *Candide*'s overture lies because it *has* to lie, since its very language and forms—themselves developed according to the same Enlightenment sensibilities that Voltaire mocked—stand in the way of the kind of story it ostensibly prepares. Perhaps, then, the musical languages of 1956 Broadway, even augmented by Bernstein's musical sophistication and his ambitions for a truly Americanized opera, were inadequate, *fundamentally*, to the challenges posed by Voltaire's *Candide*.

Sweeney Todd (1979) grew out of Stephen Sondheim's response to Christopher Bond's play *Sweeney Todd, the Demon Barber of Fleet Street* (also the musical's full title), which he had seen and admired in London in 1973. Sondheim's original idea was to set it to music without substantially altering its text, which would have required that it be to a large extent "through-composed," with continuous music; thus, from the beginning, the show was conceived in operatic terms. The subject for Bond's play had by then acquired the status of legend, with many believing that it had at least some basis in fact (like the later stories about Jack the Ripper, which were based on a series of unsolved murders in 1888). But it actually came out of an early nineteenth-century tradition of macabre stories, which were often called penny dreadfuls, and are often lumped together with their own twentieth-century offspring, the Grand Guignol in France.[30] Yet, as Sondheim put it,

> It turned out to be not Grand Guignol but this charming melodrama. . . . But [it was] also a legend, elegantly written, part in blank verse which I didn't even recognize till I read the script. . . . It had a weight to it and I couldn't figure out how the language was so rich and thick without being fruity; it was because he wrote certain characters in blank verse. . . . [This was how] he was able to take all these disparate elements that had been in existence rather dully for a hundred and some-odd years and make them into a first-rate play.[31]

This reads as a particularly "Sondheimesque" rationale for why he undertook the project, with himself so captivated by the language of the original play that he was inspired to turn it into an opera. Ironically, however, few operas are renowned for the literary value of their librettos, which under ordinary circumstances might make his account either implausible or beside the point. Yet, Sondheim's own enormous gifts for language had been widely recognized ever since Bernstein brought him in to finish the lyrics of *West Side Story* and eventually gave him full official credit as the show's lyricist. Indeed, for many years thereafter Sondheim's reputation as a lyricist seemed to impede his ability to make his way as a composer, and even when he did begin to compose his own shows with some regularity, his specifically musical skill of making his lyrics as effective as possible often led critics to undervalue his music as such. Thus, Sondheim's profile, as a composer of some sophistication who knew how best to value and serve language through music, would have enhanced tremendously the plausibility of the project from the outset. In the event, however, *Sweeney Todd* is not fully an opera by most standards, however operatic it may be, although it does preserve the quality of "weight" that Sondheim so admired in the play.[32]

In some ways, however, Sondheim's connection to the project ran deeper than his admiration for Bond's language.[33] The themes and character relations in *Sweeney Todd*, although not of Sondheim's invention, uncannily reflected his own life, which had been similarly torn apart in many ways. As Sondheim's biographers have frequently noted in trying to trace the development of his prodigious talent, his parents were unhappily married; his father left when he was ten, and his mother attempted to transfer her bitterness about men to Stephen, at the same time requiring him to fulfill some spousal functions (biographers have seen in this an undercurrent of behavioral incest, although not actual incest). His personal savior was Oscar Hammerstein II, a close neighbor who like Sondheim's father had also remarried and was at that time just starting his celebrated collaboration with Rodgers after ten years of virtually treading water in his own career.[34] Although differently configured, much of this biographical terrain—the broken home, the resulting bitterness, the sense of lostness, the fear of institutions, and the thirst for redemption—appears in *Sweeney Todd*, spread among its many characters and situations.[35]

The show opens as Benjamin Barker (now named Sweeney Todd) returns to London many years after he was sent to a penal colony in Australia on a trumped-up charge,[36] so that the crooked Judge Turpin could "move in" on his young wife, Lucy. Barker/Todd finds no trace of Lucy, and Mrs. Lovett, the baker below his shop, tells him that Lucy took poison after the Judge's ill use of her, but that his daughter, Johanna, survives as the Judge's ward. Meanwhile, Anthony, the sailor who rescued Sweeney and has accompanied him to London, forms an attachment to Johanna, and Tobias, the assistant to Pirelli (a blackmailing rival barber), forms an attachment to Mrs. Lovett. Sweeney lives for two things: to revenge himself on the Judge, along with the Beadle Bamford, who assisted him, and to see his daughter again. Both of these seem about to happen at the end of Act I, when suddenly both are simultaneously pulled impossibly out of reach. Already unstable and wound tightly by the proximity of his desires, Sweeney snaps from the intense frustration (see figure 7.2), declaring that "we all deserve to die" in the disturbingly powerful "Epiphany." In the second act, he has become a killing machine, and by the end he has managed, almost inadvertently, to kill the Judge, the Beadle, his wife Lucy (whom he has not recognized because she has become a crazed beggar woman after surviving her suicide attempt), Mrs. Lovett, and (almost) his daughter disguised as a sailor. On this very basic level, the story concerns the dehumanizing and tragic effects of seeking revenge above all else.

Equally important, however, is the dimension that Hal Prince sought to bring to the story. Prince saw the story as symptomatic of the dehumanizing effect of the Industrial Revolution, realizing also that presenting it in this light would make the show more politically relevant for Americans. Thus, the story becomes a morality play of sorts, decrying the dangers of industrialization and big business, whereas the main British emphasis had been on class difference (which may help explain why the musical did not succeed at first in London, although it did later). To this end, the property seemed tailor-made, with its central image of a "factory" whose purpose is to process human bodies by killing them and baking them into pies for the consumption of others who might themselves later serve the same function. In *Sweeney Todd*, people—and Sweeney makes no distinctions among them, despite the macabre humor of "A Little Priest"—become both the ultimate commodities and the ultimate consumers.

The dramatic strategy of the show provides a simple and effective means to blend melodrama with farce (which Sondheim claims as his "two favorite forms of theatre because . . . they are obverse sides of the same coin").[37] Starkly put, the show develops a pattern of first scaring the hell out of its audience and then rescuing the situation through humor, each time by introducing Mrs. Lovett into a situation saturated with Sweeney Todd's wrenching angst. This scare-rescue pattern happens twice to great effect, at the beginning and end of Act I, but its real payoff is the devastating conclusion, where there is no comic rescue. The denial of this previous pattern greatly intensifies the darkness of the supremely bleak ending, making the show's musical profile seem operatic to Broadway audiences even though, ironically in this respect, the denouement unfolds with only intermittent singing.[38]

But the musical dimension of the show is also deliberately operatic, as it interweaves, Wagner-like, a host of recurring motives, mostly related to each other through a common origin in the Dies Irae, from the Catholic requiem mass. The Dies Irae (literally, "Day of Wrath"; see example 7.1) was taken up as a symbol of death and retribution in music throughout the nineteenth century and continuing into the twentieth (the most important early such use was by Berlioz in his 1830 *Symphonie fantastique*). Most scene changes ♪7.24 bring back "The Ballad of Sweeney Todd," which includes both fast and slow versions of the Dies Irae (example 7.1) and builds up to a frenetic, obsessive chorus of "Sweeney, Sweeney."[39] The music of the show is not ♪7.25 continuous, but it is considerably more so (at about 80 percent) than in most Broadway shows; enough of the show has at least some musical accompaniment that its music registers as pervasive even though it isn't. Indeed, in its flow of music, often with spoken dialogue above it (as opposed to the traditional recitative of Italian opera), the show is doubly evocative of Wagner, in that its music seems more than anything else to behave like classic American film music, whose composers derived their own leitmotivic technique from Wagner.[40]

Much of the leitmotivic work in *Sweeney Todd* is contained within the orchestra and so tends to operate, as it does in Wagner and in classic film

Di - es i - rae, di - es il - la sol-vet   sae - clum   in fa-vil la te - ste   Da-vid   cum sy - bil - la.

Example 7.1a. Dies Irae: first phrase

At - tend   the   tale   of   Swee - ney Todd.

Free - ly   flows   the   blood   of   those   who   mor - al - ize.

Example 7.1b. *Sweeney Todd*: excerpts from "The Ballad of Sweeney Todd"

scores, on less than a fully conscious level, intimately binding one scene to a related scene without the audience's really knowing how. But Sondheim also incorporates his leitmotivs into his vocal lines (much more so than Wagner), which adds another dimension to the dramatic action.[41] For example, within the fractured Barker family—Johanna, the beggar woman, and Sweeney himself—a network of vocal allusions underscores their affinity, helping us realize something we might otherwise only partly sense early on (perhaps from familiarity with conventions of melodramatic plotting) or discover only at the end: that the beggar woman is Todd's wife, Lucy, who has been driven mad.

With her first appearance, although we are given a verbal clue to her identity ("Hey, . . . don't I . . . know you, . . . Mister?"),[42] we also see and hear palpable evidence of her derangement, since in one moment she is begging piteously ("Alms . . . alms . . . for a mis'rable woman") and in the next obscenely coming on to Anthony (" 'Ow would you like a little muff, dear, / A little jig jig, / A little bounce around the bush?"). Moreover, Sweeney is no stranger to London, and it seems at least plausible—and potentially dangerous to him—that he might be recognized on the street (as, indeed, he is shortly thereafter, by Mrs. Lovett, and later by Pirelli, who becomes his first victim). But the suggestion of a prior relationship nevertheless remains, and each phrase of the beggar woman's music (example 7.2a) will appear later, providing subtle confirmation of familial connection. The orchestra plays the "obscene come-on" motive as a minuet when Mrs. Lovett begins to describe her undoing at the Judge's ball during "Poor Thing" (example 7.2b),[43] while ghostly images reenact the scene. Johanna then recalls the "Alms" motive in "Green Finch and Linnet Bird" as she sings about the lark who won't sing in captivity, getting stuck within the referential groove as an expression of both her own parallel captivity and her melancholy moment of inner reflection (example 7.2c). Sweeney himself pushes through a similar groove at particularly anguished moments in "Epiphany" while recalling

♫7.26

♫7.27

♫7.28

Example 7.2a. *Sweeney Todd*: excerpts from "No Place Like London"

Example 7.2b. *Sweeney Todd*: excerpt from "Poor Thing"

Example 7.2c. *Sweeney Todd*: excerpt from "Green Finch and Linnet Bird"

first Johanna and then Lucy and, in between, demanding vengeance (example 7.2d).[44] Perhaps most remarkable in this motivic family affair is the Judge's participation, in "Johanna" (a number cut from the stage show but included on the cast album), which periodically recalls, as part of his own personal torment, the halting delivery of "Don't I know you, Mister?" (thus, his final lines, with ellipses indicating gaps: "You'll . . . deliver me, . . . Johanna, . . . / From this . . . / Hot . . . red . . . devil . . . / With your . . . soft . . . white . . . cool . . . virgin . . . palms").

The kind of musical fabric heard throughout *Sweeney Todd*, in which a continuous, often formless musical flow carries referential motives, and which I've already likened to both Wagner and classic film scoring, serves in all three of these contexts to represent two things in a seemingly unmediated way: the sensibilities of a single mind or worldview and the world itself. Within this kind of texture, leitmotivs seem to represent, from one perspective, the emergence of individual thoughts and feelings within a flow of consciousness, and from the other, the deep connection of objects we perceive directly to the world's essence, itself invisible except through such manifestations. This ability for music—and especially "background" music, or underscoring—to evoke simultaneously an individual consciousness and the world's essence resonates strongly with both nineteenth-century thought

♪7.29

♪7.30

Example 7.2d. *Sweeney Todd*: excerpts from "Epiphany"

about the relationship between consciousness and the world (deriving from Kantian notions of subjectivity) and the simultaneously emergent view of music as a conduit between the two.[45]

In *Sweeney Todd*, the dominant consciousness is, of course, Sweeney's; although it does not constitute the whole world, it sets its tone, or at least merges with it to such an extent that we cannot fully separate them. This is why, after many of the passages of dialogue in which the music stops, it resumes as underscoring for a sudden moment of awakening on Sweeney's part, with him thereby reasserting his domination over the world's tone. Such moments represent significant turns in his—and the show's—psychological drama: when he "reconnects" with his razors early in Act I ("My Friends"), when he begins to prepare Judge Turpin for a shave ("Pretty Women"), when he reacts in rage after being denied his victim ("Epiphany"; see figure 7.2), when—more subtly—his finally "getting it" allows "A Little Priest" to acquire momentum, when he awakens from his obsessive reverie to learn of Johanna's removal to a madhouse ("Wigmaker Sequence"), and when, at the end, he recognizes the beggar woman, whom he has recently killed, as his wife, Lucy.

In providing access to Sweeney's inner life, the music of *Sweeney Todd* fuses with and expresses *his* sense of the world above all else. In effect, when the opening prologue conjures Sweeney from his grave (the first of many versions of "The Ballad of Sweeney Todd," sung by the entire company in lieu of an overture), it does so by re-creating the world in his image, with that image being above all a musical one, sustained through an incessant flow of leitmotiv-saturated music. With such a fusion between Sweeney's sensibilities and the world he inhabits, it seems virtually inevitable that his death at the end does not truly finish him. As in countless horror films— which work essentially in the same way, and often just as carefully coordinated with music—the dominant malevolent presence cannot die at the end, so deeply intertwined is it within the world we have come to know. Even after his death, Sweeney's ongoing music asserts that the world has fully become *his* world, and once again conjures him from the grave, with the force of inexorable fate ("The Ballad of Sweeney Todd," final reprise).[46]

Besides this "conjuring" function, "The Ballad of Sweeney Todd" does a number of things for the show. First, it introduces the subject for American audiences, who otherwise might not know the story. This is particularly important because *Sweeney Todd* depends heavily on sustaining a sense of fate; we need to have some foreknowledge of the story, at least in its broad outlines, if its specific events are to carry that kind of weight. Also helping to achieve a sense of malevolent fate—and, as noted, allowing Sweeney to dominate the story—are the many returns of the song, serving in part as a reminder that this "tale" is being narrated and in part to embody the idea of fate itself, through its seeming omnipresence and through its thorough absorption of the ultimate "fate" motive, the Dies Irae. The number takes a firm grip on us from the outset, as its first line, "Attend the tale of Sweeney Todd," reformulates more familiar story openings in poetic terms, reinforcing its iambic rhythm with a striking alliteration, at the same time exhorting us to pay attention, both literally and through its economy, brevity, and the quaintness of its language.[47]   ♪ 7.31

To carry its full dramatic weight, "fate" must also be reinforced by setting, and that is established in the following number, "No Place Like London," which opens with a bell figure that sounds like a distorted version of Big Ben.[48] This association is confirmed by arresting returns of this figure to set the title phrase, sung with opposite meanings by Anthony and Sweeney, who see London as a place of wondrous excitement and deplorable depravity, respectively. As the show progresses, versions of this bell figure will gradually   ♪ 7.32 restore it to its more familiar contours (cf., for example, the beginnings of "No Place Like London"; "Pirelli's Miracle Elixir," where it introduces the marketplace scene; and "Johanna" in its second-act reprise, where it again sets a London street scene; see example 7.3). Meanwhile, in "No Place Like   ♪ 7.33 London," Sweeney's bleak view of London overwhelms Anthony's, thanks   ♪ 7.34 to the internal monologue of the song, beginning "There was a barber and his wife," which sets up the first "comic rescue" immediately after. In Mrs.   ♪ 7.35 Lovett's "The Worst Pies of London," as in "No Place Like London," the title phrase is set to a significant musical phrase, a waltz motive that will

Example 7.3a. *Sweeney Todd*: excerpt from "No Place Like London"

Example 7.3b. *Sweeney Todd*: excerpt from "Pirelli's Miracle Elixir"

Example 7.3c. *Sweeney Todd*: excerpt from "Johanna" (Act II sequence)

establish Mrs. Lovett's affinity for the music of the nineteenth-century London music hall (like the score's Big Ben chimes, somewhat before its time in this early nineteenth-century setting), a venue that featured broad humor and popular music, much like American vaudeville.

♩7.36

As the first act proceeds, it ripples freely between comedy and menace. The former is especially evident in the Pirelli marketplace sequence (beginning with "Pirelli's Miracle Elixir"), but also receives impetus from Mrs. Lovett's jaundiced perspective and Johanna's quirky flirtation with madness (a side to her that also, more darkly, hints at her kinship with the crazed beggar woman). Menace comes from both sides, from Sweeney's obsession with revenge and in his haunting "My Friends,"[49] and from the Judge and his Beadle, who directly threaten the incipient romance of Anthony and Johanna. This smoldering alternation finally explodes in "Epiphany," after the protracted foreplay of "Pretty Women," sung by Sweeney and the Judge as the latter sits unsuspecting beneath Sweeney's razor. "Pretty Women" is a long setup for a climactic slash of the knife that never comes, owing to Anthony's unexpected appearance, which warns the Judge and scares him off—without, however, his learning just who Sweeney is or what his precise intentions are.

Figure 7.2. "I *had* him!" shouts an enraged Sweeney Todd (George Hearn) near the end of the first act of *Sweeney Todd*, as Mrs. Lovett (Angela Lansbury) tries in vain to calm him down. Suddenly denied his long-anticipated revenge against Judge Turpin, his still-bloodless razor in hand, Sweeney snaps, vowing in "Epiphany" to "practice on less honorable throats" while continuing to plot his revenge against the Judge and the Beadle Bamford. (Still reproduced from the 1982 video recording, made for television.)

Part of what makes "Epiphany" so scary is the way it cascades chaotically through its various stages. The opening blind rage—"I had him! His throat was bare beneath my hand" (figure 7.2)—comes to its first focal point in a recollection from "No Place Like London": "There's a hole in the world like a great black pit / And it's filled with people who are filled with shit / And the vermin of the world inhabit it. . . ." In "No Place Like London," these lines led to Sweeney's ironic repetition of the title phrase, but here, they lead to a foreboding motive even more directly derived from Big Ben,[50] to which Sweeney intones his resolute "But not for long!" and proceeds to explain with equally resolute conviction, "They all deserve to die!"—what Ethan Mordden aptly describes as "the sound of a mind unhinged yet working out a logic all its own."[51] Even this frenzied resolution is not yet enough to hold ♪7.37 his world together, as his thirst for revenge caves into, then merges with, his realization that Johanna and Lucy are to be withheld from him forever (see example 7.2d), interrupted only by the manic and maniacally improbable recollection of a classic music-hall routine ("Who, sir? You, sir?"). ♪7.38

Once again, Mrs. Lovett provides the comic rescue, folding even Sweeney's bloodthirst into her own practical needs: if he's really going to murder all those people, it will at least solve her pie problem, which will in turn assist him in disposing of the bodies. The callous humor of this notion finally brings Sweeney out of his obsession enough to enjoy the delicious irony of her suggestion. As he puts it within her increasingly confident waltz tune, replete with her music-hall interjections:[52]

♪ 7.39

TODD:	The history of the world, my love . . .
MRS. LOVETT:	Save a lot of graves, / Do a lot of relatives favors . . .
TODD:	Is those below serving those up above.
MRS. LOVETT:	Everybody shaves, / So there should be plenty of flavors . . .
TODD:	How gratifying for once to know . . .
BOTH:	That those above will serve those down below!

The most disturbing dimension of this number—for those who can see past its undeniable humor and the relief it provides for the dramatic intensity that has just passed—is that it presents the first real human connection in the show, the first meshing of sensibilities within what passes for genuine community in musical terms. And we are so starved for that musical gesture that we embrace it despite the fact that what they are contemplating is the establishment of a factory for killing, baking, and selling human beings as food for other human beings.

In Act II, we see that factory in full operation, both from within and without. Again we have every reason to be appalled yet every *musical* reason to be reassured, for we watch Sweeney's now-casual murders against the backdrop of the most lyrical number of the show, the reprise of Anthony's "Johanna," to which Todd adds his own detached reverie: "Johanna. / And are you beautiful and pale, / With yellow hair, like her?" Outside, however, there is increasing panic, with the beggar woman's "City on fire" providing an unsettling counterpoint to "Johanna," a cry that will eventually provide the foreground for the escape of the lunatics from Fogg's Asylum, where Johanna is being held. As the second act unfolds and the plot slowly takes shape, the music again sustains an uneasy alternation, with Mrs. Lovett's music-hall assurances and parlor songs balanced against the interpolations of the opening ballad, which point inexorably forward to unknown but certain horrors.

♪ 7.40

Whether we regard *Sweeney Todd* as a musical, an opera, or some kind of mixed genre based also on film music and operetta, it presents itself with a potentially perplexing problem: by the end of the show, its principals, except for Anthony and Johanna, who are barely salvaged from the wreckage, are either dead or insane. Who, then, to sing a finale? As noted, however, the preservation of the show's musical world virtually impels the resurrection of its cast, most of all Sweeney himself. On the most mundane level, the cast's resurrection merely completes the structure established at the beginning, reminding us of the narrative frame with Tobias's introductory words to the finale, "Attend the tale of Sweeney Todd," and encouraging us to notice that the exhortation to "attend" now includes as well the admonition to "heed," to learn from the tale. But learn what exactly? Some of the lyrics in the finale, repeated precisely from the prologue, actually rule out what would seem to be its formulaic function, to find a moral:

♩ 7.41

> Swing your razor wide, Sweeney!
> Hold it to the skies!
> Freely flows the blood of those
> Who moralize!

A constellation of images emerges from the text, which otherwise recycles material already heard. First is the reminder, with a slightly higher profile than in the prologue, that "Sweeney heard music that nobody heard," here recast as part of a refusal to let go of the past:

> Sweeney wishes the world away
> Sweeney's weeping for yesterday,
> Hugging the blade, waiting the years,
> Hearing the music that nobody hears.

The "music that nobody hears," it would seem, refers to the music that defines Sweeney's world, the music of revenge lust, the music that keeps the past alive and holds sway over the present. But the finale also warns us that Sweeney may be beside us, that he lives within anyone who hears his music—the "music that nobody hears"—who might savor the truly stunning, orgasmic moment of Sweeney's revenge over the Judge, or who might forget that it came by way of his killing his beloved wife, Lucy, just to get her out of the way, and that nothing, save nihilism and the abyss, lies ahead of this moment. What we must "attend" in Sweeney's tale is the close proximity of its more satisfying content—achieving a goal rooted in a past best forgotten—to the utter desolation that must inevitably follow.

♩ 7.42

Both *Candide* and *Sweeney Todd* cut against the grain of the American musical as a genre: the first by calling into question the affirmative function of music within the tradition, the second by being an out-and-out tragedy. In each, music functions as a kind of drug, in *Candide* deadening us to the reality that things are really quite bleak, and in *Sweeney Todd* representing the title character's addiction to blood and his druglike obsession with revenge. The shared contrariness of these shows toward the traditions of American musicals stems in large measure from the fact that both recount rather grimmer stories than musicals tend to, which is, of course, part of their aspirational profile and part and parcel with the urge toward a more operatic musical profile. Together, they suggest an interesting paradox: seemingly, only by working against the genre can it be elevated. But this is after all no real paradox, for the opposite alternative to "elevating" musicals to the level of opera is not to renounce the genre but to celebrate it for what it is, perceived limitations and all. While neither of these shows celebrates the musical as such, they also do not betray it; rather, they extend its capacities in intriguing ways—as it happens according to the possibilities suggested in the first two chapters of the book, by evoking the musical procedures of operetta (*Candide*) and film (*Sweeney Todd*).

Evita (London, 1978; New York, 1979) followed Andrew Lloyd Webber's controversial but highly successful *Jesus Christ Superstar* (1971, studio album in 1970), and preceded his monster hit, *Cats* (1981). Although *Evita*, too, was first released as a studio album (1976), the show was conceived as an opera from the beginning and helped create a subgenre often referred to as pop opera. As Lloyd Webber put it in an essay released just before the show reached the stage:

> But, possibly because I am a composer, I find a snag with the musical. I find worrying that awkward moment when . . . [you sense] the impending approach of music. . . . I have a nagging feeling that the best musicals ultimately give you a sort of exhilarating experience like being in second gear in a fast car: incredibly exciting but hardly very profound. Not that there is anything mere about mere entertainment. It's just that I like to write something where the music and words can get uninterrupted attention without jolts from one style to another. That is why Tim [Rice, his lyricist] and I chose to write *Evita* with continuous music.[53]

Lloyd Webber's grudging "thanks, but no thanks" approbation for the American musical, as a play with songs,[54] has been answered in kind: *Evita*, and Lloyd Webber's shows more generally, have been widely criticized in America. The most frequently heard complaint about *Evita* is that it makes do with only a very few tunes, over which new words are layered to suit the dramatic situation, a process sometimes called *contrafactum*, in reference to much older musical traditions of setting new words to existing melodies (the term carries almost the same pejorative sense as the English "counterfeit," its closest cognate).[55] Especially in its seemingly wanton recycling of music and inadequate attention to text setting, *Evita* is seen as lacking two perceived strengths of the more traditional Broadway stage: musical variety and an oft-demonstrated capacity for marrying words and music so intimately that neither seems sufficient without the other. According to this ideal, Lloyd Webber's use of the same music for quite different songs seems fundamentally inadequate. Yet, as I shall argue later, there is a substantial trade-off for this procedure, both in terms of individual numbers and the long-range impact of the music involved.

Hal Prince's involvement in *Evita*'s staging had a pronounced effect on its political profile, especially when he brought the show to New York (by way, unusually, of Los Angeles and San Francisco).[56] The original album version of *Evita* was criticized for promoting fascism because it seemed to be an uncritical celebration of its central character, Eva Perón, who rose from humble beginnings to a position of great prominence in Argentina following the

Second World War, as "first lady" in a corrupt government redolent of the Axis powers in World War II. Although glorifying Evita was neither Lloyd Webber's nor Rice's intention—their depiction of her is, after all, far from flattering—it was Prince who gave their critical perspective on her more dramatic impact, by moving the character of Che to a more central position, where he could point at every turn to the grim realities behind the more positive image she presented to her worshipful admirers.[57] This was especially important because most of the other criticism Eva receives in the show, however justified, stems from characters who are much less sympathetic than she. Indeed, even Che is given ulterior motives in the earlier version, which had the unfortunate effect, in the aftermath of *Jesus Christ Superstar*, of making him seem to be playing Judas Iscariot to Evita's Jesus. The enhanced and more sympathetic presence of Che in Prince's version allows *Evita* to have things both ways, to present both fantasy and reality side by side while taking both seriously.

Eva Perón died in 1952, at a time when her husband's hold on power, as president of Argentina, was becoming increasingly tenuous. Much of what *Evita* presents to us is, in broad outlines, based on fact: she arose from humble, illegitimate beginnings, using men as stepping-stones to become a public personality, and was thereby well positioned at the time of the devastating San Juan earthquake in early 1944—which is probably also when she met Juan Perón—to help the future president politically. Both of them used the political unrest that followed the earthquake to their advantage, he through heavy-handed political maneuvering combined with outright thuggery, and she through speeches on the radio. Although it is highly unlikely that she was as instrumental as *Evita* indicates in managing Perón's spectacular reversal of fortunes in October 1945—from being forced to resign and imprisoned by the military to being appointed vice president one week later—she certainly played a large role in his subsequent successful run for the presidency in 1946. Her tour of postwar Europe, beginning in mid-1947, went pretty much as "Rainbow Tour" in *Evita* describes: she was hugely successful in Franco's Spain, but increasingly less so in Italy (where the Peróns were widely perceived to be Fascists—as, indeed, they essentially were) and France (where she wasn't taken seriously), with official England simply snubbing her. Back home, she accomplished much good through her charity foundation while enriching the family coffers, but she withdrew from her bid to become vice president in 1951, whether from political pressure or from increasingly bad health. After an unsuccessful operation and a period of lingering (milked by Perón, who kept the nature of her illness from her and the press but used it to shore up his political position and to secure his reelection), she died and became an occasion for national mourning. Left out of *Evita* is the precise cause of her death, which was cervical cancer—a disease that, coincidentally or not, had also claimed Juan Perón's first wife—and what was probably her signal political achievement: securing Argentine women the right to vote.

Evita, even more forcefully than *Sweeney Todd*, uses our knowledge of the "endgame" to maintain a tragic, fateful undercurrent throughout; in this it is helped tremendously by its basis in known historical figures. But even if Eva Perón had been a fictional creation, the story is told within a framework that ensures that its audience knows she died young and was beloved by her country's people, and that there is some reason (thanks to Che) for us to believe she was less than worthy of their adoration. Che's function as privileged spectator recalls the figure of Voltaire in the revised versions of Bernstein's *Candide*; he—like Voltaire—provides us with an audience-friendly perspective. Like *Sweeney Todd*, *Evita* reuses its central musical themes rampantly, yet not quite according to the Wagnerian leitmotivic model, since Lloyd Webber reuses whole melodic constructs rather than building new ones from smaller motives. Nevertheless, the effect of musical saturation, of creating a continuous musical fabric out of a handful of musical ideas, and so to create a "world" within which to tell the story, is similar in kind to that of *Sweeney Todd*, since, in musical terms, consistency and continuity are the key elements, not effective text setting.

It is a vexing question whether it is truly important in opera for otherwise effective music to set otherwise serviceable words well. According to at least some operatic standards (namely, Stravinsky's), music *should not* be placed in the direct service of text setting and should even work against our hearing the text "naturally," that is, in a way analogous to how it would be delivered in speech.[58] Less extremely, operatic traditions clearly support the idea that music matters a great deal more than words, especially when an opera is in a foreign language (as is generally the case in America), which means that it will either not be directly understood by a large percentage of the audience or will have been translated, with generally inadequate results regarding standards of text setting. In this respect, however, *Evita* must be judged according to two frames of reference: not only operatic standards but also Broadway standards, by which many of Tim Rice's lyrics for *Evita* fail to satisfy; often enough, they border on the inadequate even on their own, but especially so when they cut against the grain of the music, as they frequently do. Yet operatic standards also matter for *Evita*, however much they conflict with Broadway standards; this becomes especially evident whenever *Evita* is compared favorably with *Sweeney Todd*—as it often is, and often enough as part of a general comparison between Lloyd Webber and Sondheim. The pro–Lloyd Webber position generally points to his tunes as being more likable and persuasive than Sondheim's, whose obsession with words is, from this perspective, seen to be his downfall. And there is no denying that *Evita*'s success is based directly on how receptive people have been to its tunes and the way they carry the story—and continue to do so even as the story and lyrics have been reworked in various ways, most recently for the 1996 film version. Thus, oddly, and at least according to familiar critical responses, the ideal Broadway fusion of words and music seems to bifurcate between these two composers, the one emphasizing words over (inadequate) music, and the other emphasizing music over (inadequate) words.

Nevertheless, and without giving credence to this negative critique of Sondheim, we may answer at least some of the criticisms leveled at Lloyd Webber. First, we may extend the claims made earlier, that the music does indeed support the story in highly effective ways, precisely through the way its repetitions and more transformative recyclings create the sense of a musically based narrative; beyond this, such reuses of music inevitably carry specific dramatic meaning (whether intentionally or not), since they impel us to relate the corresponding moments of the drama to each other.

Thus, for example, Joseph Swain objects to the reuse of the tango singer Magaldi's "Eva Beware of the City" in Eva's "Goodnight and Thank You."[59] In the former, Magaldi warns Eva first to "beware of the city / It's hungry and cold, can't be controlled," and later to "beware your ambition / It's hungry and cold—can't be controlled." By using the same music to set quite different perspectives on Eva, first as inadequate to the city's dangers, but then as someone oblivious to the dangers of her own cravings, Magaldi relates the "monster outside" to the "monster inside," unwittingly underscoring for us that the city and Eva are, in fact, made for each other. Now, this kind of opposition, in itself, has a much venerated past, perhaps most relevantly in the thesis-antithesis songs of Gilbert and Sullivan (thus, "Is Life a Boon" in *Yeomen of the Guard*). And in this case, the musical reminder, when we see Eva enacting Magaldi's fears in the very setting he described (in "Goodnight and Thank You"), is right in line with Wagnerian leitmotivic practice (which one may well call, in many instances, a species of contrafactum).

♩7.43

Or, taking an example of a tune serving two different songs, we might consider how "Oh What a Circus" seems to borrow—in advance, as it were—from the later song "Don't Cry for Me Argentina," precisely an example of the kind of contrafactum so often objected to in *Evita*.[60] In this case, we hear the derived song first, as "Oh What a Circus" fragments *Evita*'s well-known "big tune," presenting it sarcastically, almost in caricature. Here, too, the rationale may be easily discerned simply by noticing the enhanced effect when Eva sings the tune "right"—that is, gracefully and emotively, and for a sympathetic audience. As in many extended musical works both onstage and off—works as diverse as Kurt Weill's *Lady in the Dark* (1941; see chapter 6), Wagner's *Die Meistersinger von Nürnberg*, and Beethoven's Ninth Symphony—a melody acquires a sense of "rightness" by reassembling in more pleasing fashion what we have heard before in more fragmented form. But the musical borrowing also has a thematic point to make. Che sings passionately of Evita's phoniness while the rest of Argentina mourns the loss of a national saint: "As soon as the smoke from the funeral clears / We're all going to see—and how!—she did nothing for years!"[61] And phoniness is precisely the undertone we are thus invited to notice—however prone audiences are *not* to notice it—when Evita delivers her number from

♩7.44

the balcony of the presidential palace. Moreover, if (as argued later) it is in "Don't Cry for Me Argentina" that Evita claims an indestructible bond with the Argentine people, Che's preempting her song is almost obligatory, since this is precisely the basis of his conflict with her: it is after all *he*, not she, who best represents their interests.

And, of course, sometimes repetition is precisely the point, as in "Goodnight and Thank You," where it underscores the interchangeability of Eva's succession of stepping-stone lovers. In the film version, a verse is added to this song that subtly, if laughably, underscores the song's point that all seductions are essentially the same, as Eva is seen singing a soap commercial into a radio microphone with female backup singers. Beneath this throwaway joke is a specific reality alluded to already in the original version of the song: Eva actually did get her break into radio through soap commercials, and her early radio career owed everything to her extensive promotion by the soap manufacturer with whom she was then having an affair.

Evita insists most heavily on its operatic dimension in two related numbers. At the very opening, after the announcement of Evita's death interrupts the film in the cinema ("Eva Peron, the spiritual leader of the nation, entered immortality at 20.25 hrs. today"), the grandiose hymn "Requiem for Evita" presents us with the spectacle of a nation in mourning, merging religious and operatic expressive gestures in a suitably grand manner. The conceit here, vividly represented, is that Evita is regarded on the one hand as a saint, and on the other as one with the Argentine people, and it is the latter conceit that forms the core, as well, of "Don't Cry for Me Argentina." What may be most remarkable about this number, around which the show was written in a literal sense, is that audiences tend to respond to it in precisely the way that the Argentinean crowd below the balcony does, even though Lloyd Webber intended the number from the beginning to be phony at its core, a "romantic theme tune for Eva which would sum up the technique she used to get sympathy," a "slightly cynical use of sentimentality" whose authenticity is blatantly undercut once Eva is out of sight of the crowd ("Just listen to that! The voice of Argentina! We are adored! We are loved!").[62] It is, it would seem, deliberately a pop song in the guise of an aria, and a particularly easy one to sing at that, so that it has entered culture, broadly speaking, as accessible, eminently performable, and "beautiful" in a high-art way, much like the first movement of Beethoven's *Moonlight* Sonata, and serving more or less the same function. And yet, the lyric slips occasionally into incoherence and even incompetence, so that it undermines the carefully constructed musical gesture, while the song's verbal "hook" contradicts what the song is actually saying with its every note: "*Do* cry for me." Yet perhaps the latter is a strength rather than a weakness, for it shows us an Eva capable of adroit manipulation, not least because she has personalized her relationship with the people, addressing them as one would a revered lover and singing in a style that somehow manages to combine the hymnic with tango.

Figure 7.3. In the 1996 film version of *Evita*, Eva (Madonna) sings "Don't Cry for Me Argentina" to the people of Argentina (top panel), while Che (Antonio Banderas) watches with skepticism (middle panel). Later, in "Waltz for Eva and Che" (bottom panel), the two confront each other, sometimes violently, across a sequence of changing backdrops. As they spar verbally, their waltz frequently takes on aspects of the tango, combining on each side a sexualized fascination with a sense of violence barely held in check.

What "Don't Cry for Me Argentina" asserts most vividly is a version of the marriage trope, in which Eva's identification with the people allows her to function in their stead; when Juan marries her, he joins forces with the people of Argentina as surely and vividly as when he symbolically removes his coat (recalling the name of their populist movement, the "shirtless ones"). After Evita stumbles through the sometimes halting lyric of the verse, the melody of the chorus extends the title phrase out over her audience as the first of two arching, broadly ascending gestures, then pulls them inward to her with two similarly arched phrases on a smaller scale, reassuringly presented in falling sequence, before broadening the gesture once again across the final two phrases. In deliberate stages, the music thus embraces the crowd, caresses them, draws them to her, and offers them comfort. But the lyrics do not follow this gestural series particularly well. True enough, the first two phrases do accomplish what they need to, asserting a connection between Evita and her people in a way that can be applied equally to her ascension to power and wealth and to her death ("The truth is I never left you").[63] But the two sequential phrases that follow, designed to pull the crowd inward, are set to lyrics that would fit better with more outward-reaching musical gestures—"All through my wild days / My mad existence"—moreover (a minor flaw, but it does matter), the musical rhyme between these two phrases does not match up with the textual rhyming pattern. Then, with the final two phrases needing to be pulled together, the lyric does the opposite, springing them apart by jumping perspective halfway through (thus, "I kept my promise / Don't keep your distance). And it is not just that the words don't fit well; they actually make the melody seem disjointed and slightly incompetent in the process.

♩7.48

Yet, paradoxically, it is finally in this light that the song "works," through its very abjectness as a song. Clearly, what the onstage audience hears and responds to is the musical gesture; when Evita breaks down, they hum the melody back to her, returning her gesture, but wordlessly. And when, at the end of the song, she wonders—as well she might—"Have I said too much?" it is a moment of extremely public self-doubt, and thus of extreme vulnerability. And therein lies the song's power. In this moment, she places herself completely in her audience's hands, asking only that they believe her sincerity: "But all you have to do is look at me to know that every word is true." And who would have the heart to doubt someone willing to make herself so abjectly vulnerable?

The casting of the title role in *Evita* has always occasioned speculation and controversy, ever since Julie Covington (who sang the role on the original album) declined to play the role onstage. Hal Prince established an early tradition of casting a relatively unknown actress to play the role so as to reinforce the situation in the show itself; thus, Elaine Page introduced the role on the London stage, and Patti LuPone on Broadway, where she was joined by another soon-to-be-famous newcomer, Mandy Patinkin, as Che. The scramble to cast Eva for the on-again, off-again film seemed to reverse this dynamic, as major stars—the most often named are Barbra Streisand, Meryl Streep, Michelle Pfeiffer, and Madonna—vied for the honor. In a curious way, the final casting of Madonna, despite the many who found this choice mystifying and mistaken, accorded precisely with the persona of Evita, a quite ordinary talent with "just a little touch of star quality" (to borrow Eva's self-descriptive phrase in "Buenos Aires"). Here was perhaps the perfect embodiment of the *Evita* promise, that any woman, however unremarkably talented, can become an opera diva, given the drive and the willingness to brave potential humiliation. After all, how much talent does it really take to sing "Don't Cry for Me Argentina"?[64]

Evita lays claim to opera in a profoundly different way from *Sweeney Todd*. In the latter, music represents the larger logic of fate and seems to participate fully in the traditional dialectic that pits motivational passion (music) against the control exercised through words—and here, it is significant that Sweeney is master in both realms. *Evita*, however, asks that one surrender fully to the music, an emblem of the operatic axiom that passion matters above all else. While both shows require an operatic approach to the music, *Evita* makes the closest approach to opera. At the same time, however, it removes itself most decisively away from the musical as a genre in a way that neither Bernstein in *Candide* nor Sondheim in *Sweeney Todd* was willing to do.

The strange tension between the operatic ambitions of *Evita* and *Sweeney Todd* has persisted and grown stronger over the years, with their composers coming to represent opposing forces that now seem poised like giant pincers over what remains of the older Broadway mainstream. Sondheim's presence on Broadway has seemed, from different perspectives, either a lethal threat to what remains of that mainstream or its last best hope. Thus, from one perspective, Lloyd Webber's tuneful scores seem a welcome antidote to Sondheim's continued questing march into difficult musical and dramatic terrain, even if they do lack the incisive verbal dimension that for decades was the mainstay of Broadway musicals.[65] Yet, demonstrably, Sondheim is himself a strong development *from within* that mainstream, tutored by Oscar Hammerstein II—the man who for decades was its dominant visionary—and a collaborator early on with not only Hammerstein's longtime partner, Richard Rodgers, but also a steady stream of the most ambitious talent in Broadway's then emergent generation: Leonard Bernstein, Jerome Robbins, Arthur Laurents, and Hal Prince. Moreover, Sondheim's particular facility for pastiche has kept his musical style close to the bone of traditional Broadway, even if his musical language has also in some important ways evolved beyond Broadway's standard Tin Pan Alley blend of romantic-era tonality and jazz-based idioms.[66] From this perspective, Lloyd Webber's shows on Broadway come across as a glib "dumbing down" of a rich tradition that has grown yet richer through Sondheim's contributions.

Although both Lloyd Webber and Sondheim have enjoyed substantial support among performers, audiences, and critics, only Lloyd Webber has provided a practical model for emulation, most notably through the efforts of British producer Cameron Mackintosh and French composer Claude-Michel Schönberg. There are probably two main reasons that Sondheim's musicals have not fostered a parallel development.[67] He is, of course, a "tough act to follow." It is rare for other lyricists even to approach his thoroughgoing mastery of the craft. Moreover, it is even rarer for other composers to manage (or even attempt) his rapprochement between modernist musical sensibilities and conventional Broadway intelligibility, even though in this he may be understood as deriving from Bernstein, Weill, and Blitzstein. And, although many other composers have engaged in pastiche, they generally do not enjoy the success or scope of Sondheim's stylistic imitations and almost never match the contextual depth that he brings to the practice. But there is another, more fundamental reason that Sondheim has been a tough act to follow. As noted, he has tended more often than not to establish a retrospective position with regard to particular genres and traditions, so that his shows (especially after *Company*) tend more to culminate traditions than to provide the basis for an easily identified "new direction," not only because extending a culminating statement is a difficult business (since the gesture of culmination must first be denied), but also because each of his shows seems either to look back on a decidedly different tradition or to stand apart as a one-of-a-kind experiment (e.g., *Pacific Overtures* and *Passion*).[68] Presumably, then, to follow in Sondheim's footsteps would require one to write shows as different from his—and everyone else's—as possible.

Meanwhile, there are those among Broadway's composers and critics who resist both of these forces, clinging to what remains of Broadway's "golden age," most often understood to extend from *Oklahoma!* to the mid-1960s. Accounts from this point of view see the achievements of this era falling victim to key aspects of a changing theatrical world: amplification, the encroachment of rock styles, increased catering to a younger generation, a sharpened and more contentious political dimension, and the opening of the homosexual closet after Stonewall, which helped launch a long slide into an "anything goes" that Cole Porter could never have imagined.[69] From this perspective, Lloyd Webber's "rock operas" and Sondheim's difficult progressiveness have been equally unwelcome. Complicating the picture still further is the advent of the so-called megamusical, spawned by the British Invasion but including also the influx of Disney films turned into elaborate stage musicals,[70] the latter development facilitated in part by the conversion of Times Square, under Mayor Giuliani, from its former potpourri of iniquities into a squeaky-clean tourist magnet.[71] Broadway, it would seem, has changed, and few who loved the old Broadway have been willing to embrace the new.

However resonant this situational sketch may seem with current realities, it is far from the whole truth about the current state of the American musical, which does not reduce to a war whose only remaining warriors are Mackintosh, Lloyd Webber, Schönberg, Sondheim, Disney, and various holdouts from and throwbacks to an earlier generation. But these players (the named ones, at any rate) have changed the rules of the game in important ways, each ferociously embodying a separate thread of the tradition and pushing hard on some aggrandizing dimension of the genre's potential. Smaller players, and even Sondheim, have been pushed away from Broadway's main strand, leaving room there only for shows of a relative handful of reliably successful profiles. Many observers point to the ever-stronger presence of revivals on Broadway as important evidence either that new shows cannot compete with the best of Broadway's "classics" (a circumstance that has, in this view, increased the market value of older shows) or that only the sure bet of an established success justifies the risk of mounting a new show in the face of today's escalating costs.[72]

It is probably important at this juncture, however, to note the ways in which "Broadway" and "the American musical," as descriptive terms, have increasingly become less than synonymous. Certainly, it seems odd to regard many of Broadway's most successful shows of the last two decades as American musicals (apart from revivals); many of these originated in Europe, and Broadway's "homegrown" megamusicals (apart from Stephen Flaherty's 1998 *Ragtime* and a very few others) have tended neither to engage American topics nor to ground their treatment of non-American topics in American experience. Paul Prece and William A. Everett argue convincingly that the megamusical, as a concept and as a development, "constitutes a reinvigoration of nineteenth-century French grand opera," with many of its key features recovered for modern stages and sensibilities.[73] Even Jonathan Larson's *Rent* (1996), an apparent exception to the tendency to move away from the specifically "American" in musicals, stems largely from a venerated European classic (Puccini's *La bohème*).[74] And, among Frank Wildhorn's shows, by far the least successful has been his most obviously American: *The Civil War*, which opened and closed in 1999 after sixty-one performances. Which is not to say that an "American musical" need focus on America in this strong sense; if that were the critical issue, the American basis of *Wicked* (2003—another important exception) would perhaps compensate much more than it does for the way the show compromises its starkly original source material.[75] But, a handful of exceptions aside, an important shift away from American sensibilities has accompanied the advent of the megamusical.[76]

I have, in my two-volume historical survey, been concerned almost exclusively with shows written specifically for American audiences. Aside from early operetta imports (Gilbert and Sullivan's *HMS Pinafore* and *The Mikado*, in the previous volume; and *The Merry Widow* in this one), only three shows I discuss at any length have originated elsewhere. Of these three, two are principally considered here as films with targeted American audiences (*Moulin Rouge* and *The Rocky Horror Picture Show*), and *Evita* was, as noted earlier, importantly reshaped in anticipation of its move to America by Hal Prince. At the same time, I have also tended, in this second volume, to locate the center of what has mattered for the genre somewhat outside of Broadway. The list for the first volume, apart from its imports, included only two non-Broadway shows, *Hair* and *Assassins*, both of which moved to Broadway (the former within a year, the latter not until 2004, more than a decade after it originally opened). Of the thirty-one shows discussed in this book, however, almost half, by origin or because of my focus, do not belong to Broadway: I discuss eleven films (two of them adaptations of stage shows), two off-Broadway shows (not counting *Man of La Mancha*, which quickly moved to Broadway), two imported stage shows (which, perhaps coincidentally, frame the book), and one television show. Implicitly, and now explicitly, I thus claim that although Broadway has historically been centrally concerned with issues of both American identity and personal identity, in recent decades the former concern has been much effaced and the latter has increasingly been better served in other venues—film, off-Broadway, and television—which have thus become to a much larger extent core for the American musical as a genre. Part of this shift stems from my revisionist desire to consider film musicals not as a separate genre but rather as a subgroup within the American musical. But two other important realities are at work, as well: the globalization of Broadway (and of Manhattan more generally), which has increasingly argued against specifically Americanist perspectives, and the steady diffusion of the ways in which musicals have mattered to their audiences and of the venues in which those ways have blossomed. If the former claim seems too weighty to argue here at any length—although surely globalization has also helped maintain Broadway as the definitive location for "making it" as a performer—the latter may be more usefully probed.[77]

For a long time, traditions for performing Broadway shows in schools and communities have consolidated a community-based interest in the genre that, while looking to Broadway for material and models, has been more a matter of civic and parochial pride than national pride.[78] Moreover, film has also always been experienced most regularly within communities of filmgoers. Even the ways in which films have been marketed have acknowledged this, although, to be sure, films have often achieved broadly based, large-scale success through skillful management of local markets. And television—like the original-cast album, which achieved its heyday in television's early years—has targeted the most intimate audience space, the home; it is after all through this medium that most Americans, through the *Ed Sullivan Show* and countless other musical variety shows in television's early decades, were most often and regularly exposed to new performances by practitioners of the American musical.[79] In important ways, Broadway has gradually become the least personally involving of venues, especially as—to borrow central arguments of the "golden-agers"—amplification and size have made the stage seem more and more remote from most audience seats.[80]

While Broadway has continued to appeal strongly to specific communities and through specifically American topics, it has steadily had to compete with other venues that more reliably give audiences the sense of personal relevance they seek. To be sure, the last few years have seen a number of Broadway successes for distinctly American musicals, albeit mainly on a different order from that of the megamusical; among these one may count (beyond those already counted) *The Producers* (2001), *Urinetown* (2001), *Hairspray* (2002), *Avenue Q* (2003), *Little Shop of Horrors* (2003), and *Caroline, or Change* (2003). This is a short list, however, and seems an unsuitable foundation for the genre's continued success across the full range of its potential.

Yet this view of things is uncomfortably pessimistic, and youthful perspectives certainly do not confirm such pessimism. Drawing on fewer and only indirect experiences of old Broadway, younger generations are finding in many of the new Broadway's offerings, whatever their point of origin or scope of ambition, much that matters to them, and they are fired as easily as earlier generations with the excitement of live performance. To some older perspectives, that seems the worst possible news; anyone who would like to see the reimposition of earlier standards and values will take scant pleasure in how intensely many young people are moved by (for example) *Phantom of the Opera* or *Rent*.[81] But this kind of response is clearly the dominant reality of today's Broadway. However difficult it may be for older sensibilities to either fathom or accept, the new Broadway is powerfully relevant to large numbers of people, and specifically to those people who will provide the basis for Broadway's future audience. It is, in truth and despite lingering reservations, the best situation that could be hoped for. That the young would rather look forward than backward ought properly to be seen as the basis for optimism, not the reverse. Broadway and the American musical will surely continue their interlocked trajectories, but time runs only in one direction, and what comes next can never be seen clearly, only anticipated.

For Further Consideration

Show Boat (1927), *Dreigroschenoper* (1928; on Broadway as *Threepenny Opera*, 1954), *Four Saints in Three Acts* (1934), *Porgy and Bess* (1935), *Carmen Jones* (1943), *Song of Norway* (1944), *Carousel* (1945), *Street Scene* (1947), *The Telephone / The Medium* (1947), *Regina* (1949), *The Consul* (1950), *Amahl and the Night Visitors* (for television, 1951), *Trouble in Tahiti* (1952), *Kismet* (1953), *The Golden Apple* (1954), *Fanny* (1954), *The Saint of Bleeker Street* (1955), *The Most Happy Fella*

(1956), *West Side Story* (1957), *Jesus Christ Superstar* (1971), *Cats* (1981/ 1982), *Les Misérables* (1985/1987), *Sunday in the Park with George* (1985), *Phantom of the Opera* (1986/1988), *Aspects of Love* (1990), *Miss Saigon* (1991), *Sunset Boulevard* (1993/1994), *Beauty and the Beast* (1994), *Passion* (1994), *Rent* (1996), *The Lion King* (1997), *Jeckyl & Hyde* (1997), *The Scarlet Pimpernel* (1997), *Titanic* (1997), *Ragtime* (1998), *The Civil War* (1999), *Aida* (2000), and *Wicked* (2003).

See Also

Regarding *Candide*, see chapter 12 in Ethan Mordden's *Coming Up Roses: The Broadway Musical in the 1950s* for a lively account of what made each version of the show either work or fail; chapter 25 in Humphrey Burton's *Leonard Bernstein*; pp. 201–11 in Meryle Secrest's *Leonard Bernstein: A Life*; pp. 247–53 in Joan Peyser's *Leonard Bernstein: A Biography*; chapter 26 in Harold Prince's *Contradictions*; pp. 146–56 in Foster Hirsch's *Harold Prince and the American Musical Theatre*; pp. 189–91 in John Bush Jones's *Our Musicals, Ourselves*; and pp. 212–25 in Carol Ilson's *Harold Prince: From* Pajama Game *to* Phantom of the Opera.

Regarding *Sweeney Todd*, see chapter 22 ("Murder, He Wrote") in Craig Zadan's *Sondheim & Co.*; chapter 9 in Stephen Banfield's *Sondheim's Broadway Musicals*; chapter 14 ("The Thriller as Musical") in Joseph Swain's *The Broadway Musical: A Critical and Musical Survey*; chapter 7 in Joanne Gordon's *Art Isn't Easy: The Achievement of Stephen Sondheim* (particularly useful in its comparison of the Wheeler-Sondheim adaptation with Bond's original play); chapter 15 in Meryle Secrest's *Stephen Sondheim: A Life*; chapter 15 in Scott Miller's *From* Assassins *to* West Side Story: The Director's Guide to Musical Theatre; chapter 17 of Carol Ilson's *Harold Prince: From* Pajama Game *to* Phantom of the Opera; and chapter 6 in Mark Eden Horowitz's *Sondheim on Music: Minor Details and Major Decisions*. For more specialized studies, see Judith Schlesinger's "Psychology, Evil, and *Sweeney Todd*; or, "Don't I Know You, Mister?"; Joseph Marchesani's Lacanian reading "Arresting Development: Law, Love, and the Name-of-the-Father in *Sweeney Todd*"; pp. 118–30 in Foster Hirsch's *Harold Prince and the American Musical Theatre*; pp. 290–93 in John Bush Jones's *Our Musicals, Ourselves*; and pp. 228–32 in Ethan Mordden's *One More Kiss*.

Regarding *Evita*, see Andrew Lloyd Webber and Tim Rice's *Evita: The Legend of Eva Peron, 1919–1952*; Stephen Citron's *Sondheim and Lloyd Webber: The New Musical* ("A Rainbow Goddess," pp. 221–36); chapter 12 ("History as Musical") in Joseph Swain's *The Broadway Musical*; chapter 16 of Carol Ilson's *Harold Prince: From* Pajama Game *to* Phantom of the Opera; and pp. 157–66 in Foster Hirsch's *Harold Prince and the American Musical Theatre*.

Regarding the causes and import of recent developments on Broadway, see Paul Prece and William A. Everett's "The Megamusical and Beyond";

Mark Grant's *The Rise and Fall of the American Musical*; Jessica Sternfeld's "The Megamusical: Revolution on Broadway in the 1970s and 80s"; chapters 5–7 in David Walsh and Len Platt's *Musical Theater and American Culture*; Ethan Mordden's *One More Kiss*; and Barry Singer's *Ever After: The Last Years of Musical Theater and Beyond*.

APPENDIX

Additional Resources   IN THIS APPENDIX, I provide supplementary material for each musical covered separately in the main text, including a plot summary (unless I have provided a summary in the text, in which case I provide a page-number reference) and a list of readily available published written source materials, including the book and musical scores. The items listed here are not generally repeated in the main bibliography. For a list of songs (in almost all cases according to the original production) and a list of other available source materials, including recordings, films, and video recordings, see the book's website (http://epub .library.ucla.edu/knapp/americanmusical/).

Chapter One

The Merry Widow (1905, 1907 in New York)
Book: Victor Léon and Leo Stein (after Henri Meilhac); standard
    English translation by Adrian Ross
Lyrics: Victor Léon and Leo Stein
Music: Franz Lehár

Plot: see pp. 20–22

Book
Partial libretto is available in German and English in the program booklet to
    Deutsche Grammophon 439 911–2, 1994, with Cheryl Studer, Boje Skovhus, Bar-
    bara Bonney, Rainer Trost, and Bryn Terfel; John Eliot Gardiner conducts the Wie-
    ner Philharmoniker and Monteverdi Choir.

Musical Scores
Franz Lehár, Victor Léon, and Leo Stein. *Die lustige Witwe*. Vienna: Musikverlag
    Doblinger, 1906 (vocal score).
Franz Lehár, Victor Léon, Leo Stein, and Adrian Ross. *The Merry Widow*. London:
    Chappell, 1907 (vocal score).
Franz Lehár, Victor Léon, Leo Stein, and Christopher Hassall. *The Merry Widow*.
    London: Glocken Verlag, 1959 (vocal score).
Franz Lehár, Victor Léon, Leo Stein, and Sheldon Harnick. *The Merry Widow*. Bryn
    Mawr, PA: Theodore Presser Company, 1977 (vocal score).

Naughty Marietta (1910)
Book and Lyrics: Rida Johnson Young
Music: Victor Herbert

Plot: New Orleans, just before the French Revolution, prepares for the arrival of a boatload of "casket girls," sent with a small dowry by the king of France to provide wives for his subjects in the New World. Meanwhile, Richard Warrington and his band of freelance rangers are seeking the notorious pirate Bras Piqué, who is actually Etienne Grandet, the son of the lieutenant governor, secretly working for independence from France. One of the casket girls is Marietta, the mysterious source of a mysterious melodic fragment heard repeatedly throughout the show; she is really Countess d'Altena, running away from an arranged marriage in Italy. Captain Dick discovers her and, although they agree that "It Never, Never Can Be Love," he arranges for her to join a marionette group as its leader's "son." Meanwhile, Adah, Etienne's slave and lover, worries that he has lost interest in her; indeed, he has conceived a plan to find the runaway countess and marry her as a form of protection against prosecution as Bras Piqué. At the less than respectable Quadroon Ball, Etienne, angry at Adah's jealousy and needing her out of the way in order to pursue Marietta, threatens to auction her off and finally does so. Captain Dick buys her, with the result that both Adah and Marietta feel spurned, prompting the quartet "Live for Today." But Captain Dick has bought Adah in order to set her free. In the end, he rescues Marietta, who has heard him singing her melody, now completed as "Ah, Sweet Mystery of Life." When Etienne escapes, Captain Dick lets him go, content to have won Marietta.

Musical Score
Victor Herbert and Rida Johnson Young. *Naughty Marietta*. New York: M. Witmark & Sons, 1910 (vocal score).

Little Mary Sunshine (1959)
Book, Music, and Lyrics: Rick Besoyan

Plot: Little Mary Sunshine, the adopted daughter of Chief Brown Bear of the Kadota Indians and the proprietor of the Colorado Inn (threatened with foreclosure by the United States government), welcomes Captain "Big Jim" and the forest rangers, who are pursuing an Indian renegade, Yellow Feather (Brown Bear's son, whom he believes to be dead). Other guests at the inn include Ernestine von Liebedich, a retired opera singer from the Old Country, and young ladies from the Eastchester Finishing School; the latter are courted by the rangers while Captain "Big Jim" courts little Mary and Corporal Billy Jester "courts" free-spirited Nancy Twinkle. On a mission to capture Yellow Feather, Billy Jester allows himself to be adopted by Chief Brown Bear in order to acquire a suitable costume; Nancy also disguises herself as Yellow Feather to find and protect Billy. Meanwhile, while the rangers are out hunting him, the real Yellow Feather returns and ties Mary up, but she is rescued in the nick of time by Captain "Big Jim" and his men, who determine to reform Yellow Feather and return him to society. Meanwhile, General Oscar Fairfax has arrived and, having flirted with the young ladies and courted Ernestine von Liebedich, finally delivers his message: the Kadota Indians have won their suit against the United States, granting them one-quarter of the state of Colorado, which Chief Brown Bear gives to his adopted children so that Little Mary may continue to run the inn and Billy can establish a national park.

Book
Rick Besoyan. *Little Mary Sunshine*. In *Theatre Arts*, December 1960 (complete text).

Musical Score

Rick Besoyan. *Little Mary Sunshine*. Los Angeles: Sunbeam Music, 1960 (vocal score).

A Little Night Music (1973)
Book: Hugh Wheeler
Music and Lyrics: Stephen Sondheim

Plot: (See also main text, pp. 51–54) Mme Armfeldt tells her granddaughter Fredrika about the three "smiles" of the summer night (which in Sweden is mainly a long twilight): for the young (Fredrika), the fools, and the old. Meanwhile, sexual tension in the Egerman household is high: middle-aged lawyer Fredrik's eleven-month-old marriage to eighteen-year-old Anne has not been consummated; his son, Henrik, a divinity student smitten with Anne, unsuccessfully diverts his amorous attentions to Petra (the maid); and Anne overhears Fredrik say the name Desirée as he naps. The Desirée in question is Fredrika's mother, Fredrik's former lover and a famous actress who now tours, whose show Anne and Fredrik are to attend that evening. At the theater, Anne insists on leaving after she sees the connection between Desirée and her husband. Later that evening, Fredrik visits Desirée and renews his affair with her, only to be interrupted by Desirée's current lover, Count Carl-Magnus Malcolm, whom they manage to put off with a flimsy story. The next day, Carl-Magnus sends his wife, Charlotte, to tell Anne (her sister's childhood friend) of Fredrik's nocturnal visit to Desirée; as she does so, an invitation arrives for the Egermans to spend a weekend at the Armfeldt country mansion. After much indecision, the Egermans decide to go, but so does the uninvited Carl-Magnus (as a "birthday present" to Charlotte). The weekend unfolds as a series of fiascos, as Charlotte tries unsuccessfully to make her husband jealous by flirting with Fredrik; Henrik, who has publicly embarrassed himself and his family, determines to kill himself; and Fredrik finds himself unable to forsake Anne (and his lost youth) for Desirée, who in turn cannot seem to shake off Carl-Magnus. But suddenly (in the second of the night's smiles) things start to work out. Henrik, seeing Petra together with the Armfeldt butler (Frid), fails in his suicide attempt and declares himself to a very receptive Anne; Fredrik and Charlotte see them running off together; Carl-Magnus sees his wife consoling Fredrik and challenges the latter to play Russian roulette (Fredrik loses, but he only grazes his ear); Charlotte is overjoyed to see her husband defending her honor; and Desirée and Fredrik are left with no alternative but to accept their happy ending. The night smiles for the third time as Mme Armfeldt dies.

Books

Hugh Wheeler and Stephen Sondheim. *A Little Night Music*. New York: Dodd, Mead, 1973.

Hugh Wheeler and Stephen Sondheim. *A Little Night Music*. New York: Applause Theatre Book Publishers, 1991. Additional material: introduction by Jonathan Tunick, additional lyrics and dropped songs, with commentary by Stephen Sondheim.

Stephen Sondheim, Hugh Wheeler, James Lapine, Burt Shevelove, and Larry Gelbart. *Four by Sondheim*. New York: Applause Theatre Book Publishers, 2000 (includes *A Funny Thing Happened on the Way to the Forum*, *A Little Night Music*, *Sweeney Todd*, and *Sunday in the Park with George*).

Musical Score

Stephen Sondheim. *A Little Night Music*. New York: Revelation Music Publishing & Beautiful Music, 1974 (vocal score).

Chapter Two

Singin' in the Rain (1952)
Screenplay: Betty Comden and Adoph Green
Director: Gene Kelly and Stanley Donen
Lyrics: Arthur Freed
Music: Nacio Herb Brown

Plot: After the 1927 film *The Jazz Singer* creates a demand for "talkies," film producer R. F. Simpson determines that his studio's current project, *The Dueling Cavalier*, starring the silent-film stars Lina Lamont and Don Lockwood, should be made into a sound film. When the results are disastrous (due to technical failings, Lockwood's inept ad-libbing and ham acting, and most of all Lamont's grating voice), Lockwood and aspiring actress Kathy Seldon, conspiring with musical director Cosmo Brown, decide to turn the film into a musical (*The Dancing Cavalier*), with Seldon dubbing Lamont's songs and dialogue. At the successful premiere, when Lamont demands that Seldon continue dubbing her voice without credit, the others unmask her in front of the live audience, paving the way for Seldon to become a star on her own, teamed with Lockwood both publicly and privately.

Book

Betty Comden and Adolph Green. *Singin' in the Rain*. New York: Viking Press, 1972 (with an introduction by the authors; includes credits, cast list, and stills).

Stormy Weather (1943)
Screenplay: Frederick Jackson and Ted Koehler
Director: Andrew Stone
Lyrics and Music: various (see song list at http://epub.library
.ucla.edu/knapp/americanmusical/)

Plot: see pp. 86–87

Bamboozled (2000)
Screenplay: Spike Lee
Director: Spike Lee
Music and Lyrics: various

Plot: A black television writer (Pierre Delacroix), disgusted with himself and his job, seeks to get fired by proposing *The New Millennium Minstrel Show*—to be performed in blackface. Expecting outrage from the public, he instead achieves his first true success, in the process making stars of the ragtag performers he has recruited from the street. Over time, his female assistant (Sloan) sickens of him and the project, whereas he convinces himself it has been a brilliant, liberating experiment. In the final series of events, one of his two principal stars quits (Sleep'n Eat), the other refuses to get into blackface (Mantan), a black revolutionary gangsta rap group (the

Mau-Maus) kidnaps Mantan and kills him on live TV, and Sloan shoots Delacroix, who has become obsessed with racist paraphernalia; as he lies dying, he watches a montage of film and television clips detailing disturbing images of blackface minstrelsy, prepared by Sloan.

Meet Me in St. Louis (1944)
Screenplay: Irving Brecher and Fred F. Finklehoffe (various uncredited)
Director: Vincente Minnelli
Songs: Hugh Martin and Ralph Blane; Arthur Freed and Nacio Herb Brown; Conrad Salinger and Roger Edens; various turn-of-the-century standards

Plot: see pp. 94–95

Moulin Rouge (2001)
Screenplay: Baz Luhrmann and Craig Pearce
Director: Baz Luhrmann
Lyrics and Music: various (see song list at http://epub.library .ucla.edu/knapp/americanmusical/)

Plot: Christian, a young would-be writer from London at the turn of the last century, comes to the Moulin Rouge in Paris to live the Bohemian lifestyle, and is recruited by Toulouse-Lautrec and his fellow Bohemians (including Satie and a narcoleptic Argentinean) to write a musical to be called *Spectacular Spectacular*. Christian pitches the still-unwritten show to Satine, the star and principal courtesan of the Moulin Rouge, run by Harold Zidler. Satine (who we realize early on is dying of tuberculosis) believes Christian to be the wealthy Duke of Worcester and so falls readily in love with him, and he with her. With Zidler and the Bohemians' help, Christian and Satine persuade the Duke to finance the show, which will require remodeling the Moulin Rouge as a theater. During rehearsals, everyone but the Duke realizes that the star and writer are in love, yet he senses enough to overrule the happy ending of the play—whose plot parallels the main story's—in which the courtesan marries the penniless sitar player rather than the rich Maharajah (played by Zidler), and to insist on the removal of the lovers' "secret song" ("Come What May"). When their affair can no longer be hidden, Satine (who now knows she is dying), to save Christian from being killed by the Duke's bodyguard, convinces Christian that she does not love him. He returns to renounce her, onstage, during the first performance, but she responds by singing their "secret song," and they are reconciled, in the process changing the ending of *Spectacular Spectacular* back to its happy ending. Meanwhile, the furious Duke tries to kill Christian, but Zidler and the Bohemians intervene; at the end of the show, Satine collapses and dies. Much later, Christian, alone in his hotel room near the Moulin Rouge, begins to write the story we have just seen.

Musical Score
Songs from Baz Luhrmann's Film Moulin Rouge! London: Wise Publications, 2001 (vocal score).

Chicago (2002)
Screenplay: Bill Condon
Director: Rob Marshall
Original Book: Fred Ebb and Bob Fosse, based on the play by
    Maurine Dallas Watkins
Lyrics: Fred Ebb
Music: John Kander

Plot: (Note: some details of the film's plot differ from that of the stage show.) In 1920s Chicago, nightclub star Velma Kelly awaits trial for the double murder of her husband and her sister (the other half of her sister act) after catching them having an affair. Roxie Hart, who dreams of being a star, joins her in prison after she murders her lover just as he is set to leave her, having almost—but not quite—duped her slow-witted husband, Amos, into taking the rap. Roxie learns how to get by even though Velma spurns her, cozying up to Matron ("Mama") Morton and hiring shady lawyer Billy Flynn, who is also defending Velma. Flynn takes her case to the press, creating a "back story" to elicit sympathy. Velma, whose case is postponed and now has little press, approaches Roxie as a potential replacement for her murdered sister, but is spurned in turn. When a new (and wealthy) murderess threatens to take Billy's and the media's attention away from Roxie, as well, she fakes being pregnant, and her case is quickly brought to trial. At the trial, Billy seems to have the upper hand until Velma appears with Roxie's incriminating diary, having cut a deal with the DA. But the diary has been doctored with lawyerly language (by Billy, of course), and Roxie is acquitted. Released from prison, neither Roxie nor Velma has much luck finding work until they team up as a double bill, as "Chicago's own killer-dillers."

Book
John Kander and Fred Ebb. *Chicago*. New York: Samuel French, 1976.

Musical Scores
John Kander and Fred Ebb. *Chicago*. New York: Chappell Music, 1975 (vocal score).
John Kander and Fred Ebb. *Chicago*. Milwaukee: Hal Leonard, 2002 (vocal score from film version).

Chapter Three

Snow White and the Seven Dwarfs (animated film, 1937)
Story adaptation: Ted Sears, Otto Englander, Earl Hurd, Dorothy Ann Blank, Richard Creedon, Dick Rickard, Merrill De Maris, and Webb Smith
Music: Frank Churchill (songs), Leigh Harline and Paul Smith (additional music)
Lyrics: Larry Morey

Plot: A queen who deals in evil magic, obsessed with her own beauty, learns from her magic mirror that her stepdaughter, Snow White, is the fairest in the land and so orders her huntsman to take Snow White into the forest and kill her. Meanwhile, Snow White, in rags and hard at work, has wished for her true love to find her, which he does. When the huntsman takes her into the forest, he is unable to carry out his orders. Warning her not to return to the castle, he leaves her in the forest, where, with the help of her animal friends, she finds the empty cottage of the seven dwarfs and sets about tidying it up. The dwarfs (Doc, Happy, Dopey, Sneezy, Grumpy, Bashful, and Sleepy), returning that evening from their diamond mine, discover a clean cottage, a hot meal, and a sleeping Snow White. As the dwarfs accept her into their household, the Queen discovers through her magic mirror that she has been tricked; enraged, she uses magic to transform herself into an ugly peddler woman and to poison an apple, whose only antidote is "love's first kiss." While the dwarfs are on their way to work, the disguised Queen/Witch tricks Snow White into taking a bite of the poisoned apple. During the ensuing storm, the dwarfs chase the Queen up to a precipice, from which she tries to roll a huge boulder down on them; instead, lightning strikes the precipice and she falls to her death. Unable to bring themselves to bury Snow White, the dwarfs enshrine her in a glass coffin, where she is found by the Prince and awakened by his kiss.

The Wizard of Oz (film, 1939)

Screenplay: Noel Langley, Florence Ryerson, and Edgar Allan Woolf (and many more uncredited), after L. Frank Baum's novel

Direction: Victor Fleming (and many more uncredited, including King Vidor for the Kansas scenes)

Lyrics: E. Y. (Yip) Harburg

Music: Harold Arlen (scoring by Herbert Stothart)

Plot: Dorothy Gale, an orphaned farm girl in sepia-toned, turn-of-the-century Kansas, dreams of a better place "Over the Rainbow" after she finds that none of the adults on the farm (Auntie Em, Uncle Henry, and farmhands Hunk, Zeke, and Hickory) seems to have time for her. When her dog, Toto, escapes Miss Gulch, who is taking him to be destroyed, Dorothy runs away but soon encounters the kindly humbug fortune-teller Professor Marvel, who sends her back home just as a tornado hits, knocking her unconscious on her bed. She awakens in colorful Munchkinland, in the land of Oz, where she learns from Glinda, the (good) Witch of the North, that her falling house has killed the Wicked Witch of the East. When the latter's sister, the Wicked Witch of the West (Miss Gulch in green makeup) appears for vengeance and to claim her sister's ruby slippers, Glinda magically transports them to Dorothy's feet; then, after the Wicked Witch departs, she and the Munchkins send Dorothy off to the Emerald City via the yellow-brick road, to consult with the Wizard of Oz. Along the way, she acquires three companions, the Scarecrow (Hunk in makeup), the Tin Man (Zeke), and the Cowardly Lion (Hickory), who plan to ask the Wizard for a brain, a heart, and courage, respectively. Despite the Witch's efforts to stop them, they reach the Emerald City, where a reluctant Wizard (who, along with the Doorman, Cabbie, and Guard, is a version of Professor Marvel) agrees to help them if they deliver the broomstick of the Wicked Witch of the West. En route to the Witch's castle, Dorothy is captured and appears doomed, but her companions manage to get to her in time, through the Scarecrow's planning, the Lion's courage, and the Tin Man's concern for her. In a final confrontation, the Witch sets fire to the Scarecrow but is herself melted by the water thrown to douse the flames. Returning to the Emerald City, Dorothy and her companions confront the Wizard and find him to be a kindly fraud, but then he is unexpectedly helpful in providing tokens of the brain, heart, and courage, which they have already shown they possess through their able assistance to Dorothy. The Wizard, attempting to take Dorothy home in his balloon (which is how he had arrived in Oz from Kansas) after appointing her companions to rule in his absence, ends up leaving without her. Glinda appears and reveals that the ruby slippers can return Dorothy to her home. Awakening in bed, back in sepia-toned Kansas, Dorothy tries to tell everyone of Oz and recognizes the people around her as her companions there, but they can only nod in sympathy, grateful she has returned to consciousness.

Musical Score
E. Y. Harburg and Harold Arlen. The Wizard of Oz *Vocal Selections*. Miami: Warner Bros. Publications, 1995 (vocal score).

Mary Poppins (film, 1964)
Screenplay: Bill Walsh and Don Da Gradi, from P. L. Travers's Mary Poppins books
Direction: Robert Stevenson
Music and Lyrics: Richard M. Sherman and Robert B. Sherman

Plot: In 1910 London, George Banks (a banker) and his wife (a suffragette) have had trouble retaining nannies for their precocious children, Jane and Michael. Mr. Banks takes on the job of hiring the new nanny but discards the advertisement his children compose. The following morning, as the other applicants are literally blown away by the new easterly wind, Mary Poppins descends from the clouds with the discarded notice, cows Mr. Banks, and proceeds to captivate the children through music and magic, agreeing to stay only "until the wind changes." With Mary's friend Bert (alternately a street musician, a screever, a chimney sweep, and a kite salesman), they enter one of his chalk pavement pictures for an outing and the following day have a tea party on the ceiling with her Uncle Albert. Disturbed by how flighty his household has become, Mr. Banks then attempts to fire Mary Poppins, but finds instead that she has manipulated him into taking the children to the bank the following day. At the bank, the children start a "run" when Michael refuses to deposit the tuppence he has brought along to feed the birds at Saint Paul's Cathedral. Escaping the bank, the frightened children run into Bert (now a sweep), who brings them home, then agrees to mind them while he cleans the Banks's chimney. When Mr. Banks returns home, he interrupts a riotous impromptu party involving Bert, Mary, the children, and Bert's fellow sweeps; after everyone but Bert leaves, Mr. Banks expresses his dejection at how rapidly his career has just been cut short, receiving Bert's sympathy but also his rebuke that Mr. Banks has allowed his work to distract him from his own children. Later that evening, Mr. Banks returns to the bank; as he is being fired, he suddenly seems to snap with the giddy realization that Bert is right. The following morning, as a concerned household wonders at his absence, he emerges from the basement with the children's kite, broken at the beginning of the film but now mended. As the wind changes (both literally and figuratively), Mary ascends back to the clouds, unnoticed by anyone but Bert and Andrew (the dog) as the family heads out to the park to fly the kite. There they meet the other bankers, also flying kites, and learn that the senior partner has died laughing at Mr. Banks's "capital piece of humour" (a joke the children had repeated from their tea party), leaving room for Mr. Banks to return as a full partner.

Musical Score

Richard M. Sherman and Robert B. Sherman. *Mary Poppins.* Buena Vista, CA: Walt Disney Productions, 1964 (vocal score).

Into the Woods (1987)
Book: James Lapine
Music and Lyrics: Stephen Sondheim

Plot: The familiar stories of Cinderella (and her Prince), Rapunzel (and her Prince), Little Red Ridinghood (and her Wolf), and Jack (and his Beanstalk) intertwine with each other, linking also to a newly invented story involving the Baker, his wife, and the Witch who lives next door—all presided over by the benevolent and slightly pompous Narrator. The Witch informs her neighbors that she has cursed them, as punishment for the Baker's father's having stolen magic beans from her, so that now they cannot have children (the thievery has also resulted in the Witch's being made ugly). She promises the Baker and his wife to lift the curse if they acquire certain items for her in three days: a white cow, a red cape, a golden slipper, and a shock of yellow hair. The action commences with most of the cast headed "Into the Woods," Red Ridinghood to visit her Granny, Jack to sell his cow, Cinderella to go to the ball, the Baker and his wife to collect the Witch's color-coded ingredients, and, later, the two Princes, pursuing Cinderella and Rapunzel (the Baker's sister, whom the Witch has been raising in a secluded tower). In the first act, all of these stories end happily, with the Baker furnishing Jack his magic beans and rescuing Red Ridinghood along the way. Even the Witch is successful; although she has lost Rapunzel and her power, she restores her beauty by drinking the milk of the cow, after it has been fed the other ingredients.

The second act unravels much of what the first act so carefully sewed up. The Giant's Wife appears, seeking revenge for the death of her husband and laying waste to the Witch's garden, the castle, and both Red Ridinghood's and her Granny's houses as she vents her rage. The princes, aware of the crisis, are nevertheless pursuing prospective romantic adventures in the woods (with Sleeping Beauty and Snow White). The other characters, returning to the woods to respond to the crisis, confront the Giant and try to appease her by sacrificing the Narrator, to no avail. Jack's mother is then killed by the Prince's steward as she argues with the Giant, and Rapunzel is trampled as the Giant leaves to find Jack. The Baker's Wife, after being seduced and abandoned by Cinderella's Prince, also falls victim to the Giant. The main survivors—the Witch, the Baker, Cinderella, Jack, and Red Ridinghood—argue over who is to blame; then, after the Witch leaves, the others concoct a plan to kill the Giant, exploiting Cinderella's magical way with birds. When they succeed, they plan to face the future together, since Cinderella has left her Prince and the others have lost their remaining family members. The Baker, urged on by the spirit of his dead wife, begins to tell the tale of his adventures to their infant child.

Book

Stephen Sondheim and James Lapine. *Into the Woods.* New York: Theatre Communications Group, 1987.

Musical Score
Stephen Sondheim. *Into the Woods*. New York: Rilting Music, 1989 (vocal score).

Chapter Four

Camelot (1960)
Book and Lyrics: Alan Jay Lerner
Music: Frederick Loewe

Plot: On the eve of their arranged marriage, King Arthur and Guenevere meet for the first time after escaping from their attendants. He persuades her to stay in Camelot and—after she discovers who he is—to marry him, although the affection she feels for him clearly falls short of love. After the magician Merlin (Arthur's tutor) is spirited away by the nymph Nimue, Arthur conceives a new order, based not on "Might Is Right" but on "Might for Right," whose nobly inspired knights will assemble at the Round Table. Lancelot arrives from France to join the Knights of the Round Table, nearly killing Arthur when he first meets him but then quickly becoming his dear friend. Meanwhile, however, his superior air completely alienates the rest of the court, especially Guenevere, who champions three of Arthur's best knights to joust with him. Lancelot wins all three jousts, killing the strongest but reviving him through prayer. Guenevere and Lancelot then fall deeply in love but refrain from acting on it; for his part, Arthur is keenly aware of their feelings, although they try to hide them. Meanwhile, Arthur's illegitimate son, Mordred, appears, determined to use the love between Arthur's wife and his best friend as a weapon with which to destroy Arthur and the Round Table and thereby to assume the throne. His machinations work, but Lancelot escapes when he is caught with Guenevere and returns to rescue her just as she is about to be executed for treason. On the eve of the resulting battle between Arthur's and Lancelot's armies, Guenevere—now with the holy sisters—returns with Lancelot to beg for Arthur's forgiveness, which he readily grants. A young boy arrives to join the Round Table, giving Arthur hope that his dream will have an afterlife, capable of inspiring future generations.

Book
Alan Jay Lerner and Frederick Loewe. *Camelot*. New York: Random House, 1961.

Musical Score
Alan Jay Lerner and Frederick Loewe. *Camelot*. New York: Chappell Music Company, 1962 (vocal score).

Man of La Mancha (1965/1968)
Book: Dale Wasserman
Lyrics: Joe Darion
Music: Mitch Leigh

Plot: Prisoners in the "common room" of a Seville dungeon in the late sixteenth century "welcome" two new arrivals—Miguel de Cervantes and his servant, both slated to appear before the dreaded Spanish Inquisition—by conducting a mock trial and confiscating Cervantes's goods: a trunk of theatrical props and the incomplete manuscript of his book *Don Quixote*. Pleading guilty to the charge of being "an idealist, a bad poet, and an honest man," Cervantes proposes, in his defense, to put on an "entertainment," using fellow prisoners as actors. Cervantes and his servant then transform themselves into Alonso Quijana and his neighbor, the former an aging and half-crazed "man of La Mancha" who becomes a latter-day knight errant—Don Quixote—seeking, with his squire, Sancho Panza, to restore the lost age of chivalry. As they ride out, they do battle with a windmill that Quixote insists is a giant who at the last minute has been transformed by his nemesis, the Enchanter. Defeated, they proceed to an inn that Quixote insists is a castle. At the inn, the serving girl / whore Aldonza is propositioned by a rough gang of muleteers just before Quixote and Sancho arrive in their bedraggled state. Quixote "recognizes" Aldonza as his ideal Dulcinea, despite Aldonza's angry attempt to make him see her as the whore she is. Quijana's Padre and his niece's learned fiancé, Dr. Carrasco, arrive to try to bring him back to his senses, only to see him expropriate a barber's basin as the lost "golden helmet of Mambrino," after which the Padre concedes that the old man might be better off left to his dreams. Meanwhile, Aldonza, gradually intrigued and even won over by Quixote and his mad vision, is rebuked for her budding idealism by the muleteers, but, somehow, Quixote, with the help of Sancho and Aldonza, manages to defeat them. After Quixote and Sancho leave, however, the muleteers retaliate by beating and raping her; meanwhile, Quixote and Sancho are robbed by a band of Moors and so return to the inn even more bedraggled than before, where they find a freshly disillusioned Aldonza. Carrasco then appears as the Knight of the Mirrors, using the substance of Quixote's mad visions as a way to return him to his senses. At this low point in the narrative, with Quixote a defeated and broken man, the prison guards warn Cervantes to make ready. Seeing he is losing the sympathy of his fellow prisoners, Cervantes improvises a different ending: the dying old man, having been restored to his senses, becomes Don Quixote once again in response to Aldonza's entreaties. After he dies in midsong, a transfigured Aldonza insists her name is Dulcinea. The Inquisition arrives, and the prisoners restore Cervantes's precious manuscript to him, sending him on his way with a reprise of his anthem, "The Impossible Dream."

Books

Dale Wasserman and Joe Darion. *Man of La Mancha*. New York: Random House, 1966.
Dale Wasserman and Joe Darion. *Man of La Mancha*. Introduction by John Bettenbender. New York: Dell, 1968.

Musical Score

Mitch Leigh and Joe Darion. *Man of La Mancha*. New York: Sam Fox Publishing Company, 1965 (vocal score).

The Scarlet Pimpernel (1997)
Book and Lyrics: Nan Knighton
Music: Frank Wildhorn

Plot: (Original version.) In Paris, 1794, the Marquis de St. Cyr and his family are executed. When his English friend Sir Percy Blakeney hears the news, he also learns that Marguerite St. Just, a French actress he has just married, is responsible for betraying St. Cyr to Chauvelin, a French official. Percy forms the League of the Scarlet Pimpernel (using his family crest as a symbol), dedicated to saving French aristocrats from the guillotine; among their members is Armand, Marguerite's brother. Meanwhile, to keep the operation secret, the league members pretend to be frivolous fops, interested only in fashion and wit. Chauvelin arrives in London to discover the identity of the Scarlet Pimpernel, whose men have been very successful in their work. Chauvelin enlists Marguerite's help through blackmail, using the fact that her brother, Armand, has been arrested. But Marguerite betrays Chauvelin by arranging a secret rendezvous with the Scarlet Pimpernel, to whom she confesses her earlier betrayal of St. Cyr to Chauvelin, her former lover, who had promised St. Cyr's safety. Percy, still unable to tell her his identity, is nevertheless overjoyed to learn of her basic innocence. Marguerite and Percy, in separate attempts, try to save Armand, but Chauvelin seems to have gotten the upper hand through his spy Grappin (who is actually Percy in disguise). But their execution is staged; the future Madame Tussaud (a friend of Marguerite's) has arranged a deception, so that when they are guillotined, their severed heads will in fact be her wax replicas. In the end, Percy and Marguerite, reconciled and reunited with her brother, sail back to England, with Chauvelin— wearing the ring of the Scarlet Pimpernel—tied up and awaiting discovery by the French authorities.

Musical Score
Frank Wildhorn and Nan Knighton. *The Scarlet Pimpernel*. Miami: Warner Bros.
   Publications, 1998 (partial vocal score).

Once More, with Feeling (television, 2001)
Book, Music, and Lyrics: Joss Whedon

Plot: Buffy Summers, the "Vampire Slayer," has recently been restored to life (through witchcraft) by Willow, a member of Buffy's "Scooby gang," a group who support her in her fight against vampires and other demons in Sunnydale. A demon inadvertently summoned by Xander (another member of the gang, engaged to Anya) has caused everyone in Sunnydale to perform as if in a musical and begins to accumulate victims who combust from within as they perform out of control. His actual mission, however, is to claim the person who has summoned him, to make her join him in the Underworld as his Queen. When Dawn (Buffy's younger sister) steals the charm that summoned him and puts it on, she is kidnapped, but she forestalls the demon by telling him that her sister is the Slayer. In a final showdown, Buffy nearly combusts, but is rescued by Spike, a somewhat reformed vampire who is in love with her. The demon elects not to take Xander when he admits that it was he, and not Dawn, who activated the charm. Buffy, who has been listless since returning to life, is suddenly animated by her growing attraction to Spike, and the episode ends with their kiss as the rest of the cast contemplate having to deal with the various secrets revealed under the "musicals" enchantment. (For more details, consult the main text.)

Book and Musical Score
Joss Whedon. *Buffy the Vampire Slayer: "Once More, with Feeling."* New York:
   Simon Pulse, 2002 (shooting script and vocal score).

Chapter Five
Annie Get Your Gun (1946)
Book: Herbert and Dorothy Fields
Lyrics and Music: Irving Berlin

Plot: Sharpshooter Annie Oakley, an unknown from the backwoods, bests professional showman Frank Butler in a shooting contest but also falls in love with him despite his swaggering disregard for women. She joins Buffalo Bill's Wild West Show as Frank's assistant. Frank, returning her love but unable to handle her rapidly rising stardom, joins Pawnee Bill's rival show. Meanwhile, Sitting Bull, the famous Sioux warrior who is also now part of Buffalo Bill's show, befriends Annie and adopts her as his daughter. When the Wild West Show returns nearly bankrupt from a triumphant European tour, they join forces with Pawnee Bill. Reunited with her beloved Frank, but with neither able to accept the other as his or her superior in shooting, Annie "loses" a showdown match between them (somewhat differently in various versions of the show), which leads to their reconciliation.

Book
Irving Berlin, Herbert Fields, and Dorothy Fields. *Annie Get Your Gun*. New York: Irving Berlin Music, 1967.

Musical Scores
Irving Berlin. *Annie Get Your Gun*. New York: Irving Berlin Music, 1947 (vocal score, original version).
Irving Berlin. *Annie Get Your Gun*. New York: Irving Berlin Music, 1967 (vocal score, revival version).

Gypsy (1959)
Book: Arthur Laurents
Lyrics: Stephen Sondheim
Music: Jule Styne

Plot: Quintessential stage mother Rose pushes her two daughters, Louise and "Baby June," into Uncle Jocko's Kiddie Show, and then takes them on the road trying to break into the vaudeville circuit. Louise, whether from shyness or lack of talent, fades into the shadow of June, the star of the act. Teaming up with Herbie, who becomes the act's theatrical manager, Rose scrambles to keep the act going as the young girls grow into adolescence and vaudeville gradually degenerates into burlesque. Meanwhile, the girls hope their mother will marry and settle down, but she keeps putting off Herbie's marriage proposal. When June elopes, Rose determines to start over with Louise, but their spiral downward ends in a Wichita burlesque hall. In an act of desperation, the shy Louise becomes a stripper; paradoxically, in overcoming her shyness, she learns to connect with her audience and develops into the world-famous Gypsy Rose Lee, a stripper known for her elegance of manner and sophisticated "conversation" with her audience. Rose, appalled at the reality of her realized dream and bitter at her rejection by her two daughters, breaks down while imagining herself in the stage career she never had, but she reconciles with Gypsy Rose Lee in the final scene.

Book
Arthur Laurents and Stephen Sondheim. *Gypsy*. New York: Random House, 1960; reprint, New York: Theatre Communications Group, 1994.

Musical Score
Jule Styne and Stephen Sondheim. *Gypsy*. New York: Chappell, 1960 (vocal score).

Sweet Charity (1966)
Book: Neil Simon
Lyrics: Dorothy Fields
Music: Cy Coleman

Plot: Charity Hope Valentine, a dance-hall "hostess" at the Fan-Dango Ballroom, on a date with her current boyfriend (Charlie, a married man), suggests they throw something into the park lake for luck; eager to oblige, he throws *her* in, in the process stealing her bag, which contains her life savings. Determined not to be taken advantage of any longer, Charity finds herself suddenly with Vittorio Vidal, an Italian film star who needs a date when his girlfriend, Ursula, leaves him stranded. Although Vidal is charmed by Charity, she ends up spending the night in his closet when Ursula returns unexpectedly. Seeking to improve herself, Charity attends a cultural event at the local "Y" but gets stuck in an elevator with a claustrophobic accountant, Oscar Lindquist. They begin dating, going to an alternative church and Coney Island, where they get stuck on one of the high rides. In despair about telling Oscar what she does for a living (he thinks she is a bank teller), Charity quits the Fan-Dango; to her surprise, however, Oscar already knows what she does and proposes marriage to her anyway. But in the end, he can't go through with it and pushes her into the same lake as Charlie had. When Charity emerges, she sees a "good fairy," who tells her, "Tonight, it will all happen tonight"—then turns away, revealing an advertisement for a television program that evening.

Book
Neil Simon and Dorothy Fields. *Sweet Charity.* New York: Random House, 1966.

Musical Score
Cy Coleman and Dorothy Fields. *Sweet Charity.* London: Campbell Connelly, 1994 (vocal score).

The Rocky Horror Picture Show (film, 1976)
Book, Lyrics, and Music: Richard O'Brien

Plot: On the way to visiting an old college professor (Dr. Scott), a clean-cut young couple (Brad Majors and his fiancée, Janet Weiss) develop car trouble and take refuge at an obviously "haunted" mansion (later revealed to be a spaceship), presided over by Dr. Frank-N-Furter, a transvestite from the planet Transsexual in the galaxy of Transylvania. With the assistance of the hunchbacked Riff Raff and his incestuous lesbian sister, Magenta, along with a fantastical cohort of partiers, Frank creates Rocky Horror (a perfect male specimen designed for Frank's sexual pleasure), kills the party-crashing motorcyclist Eddie, then proceeds to seduce Janet and Brad, in succession. In the denouement, Frank "transduces" (immobilizes) his guests and Dr. Scott—a later arrival at the mansion, who is searching for his nephew Eddie—and then proceeds to put on a floor show with his living statues. Riff Raff and Magenta turn on him, killing him and releasing his guests before taking off in their mansion-spacecraft.

Books
Richard O'Brien. *The Rocky Horror Show.* New York: Samuel French, 1983.

Richard O'Brien. *The Official Rocky Horror Picture Show Movie Novel*. Edited by
   Richard J. Anobile. New York: A&W Visual Library, 1980 (a transcription of the
   film, interwoven with images).

Musical Score
Richard O'Brien. *The Rocky Horror Show*. London: Wise Publications, 1998 (piano/
   guitar/vocal score).

Hedwig and the Angry Inch (1998; film, 2001)
Book: John Cameron Mitchell
Lyrics and Music: Stephen Trask

Plot: Hedwig tells her story as a stand-up monologue with songs, assisted by Yitzhak
and a backup band, the Angry Inch: Hedwig grows up as Hansel Schmidt with his
mother in East Berlin. Seduced by Luther Robinson, a black American sergeant, he
undergoes a botched sex-change operation in order to marry him (using his mother's
name, Hedwig) and to emigrate to America. By the time the Berlin Wall comes down,
one year later, Luther has abandoned Hedwig in Junction City, Kansas, and she has
to earn her living as a babysitter and prostitute. Hedwig forms a band, the Angry
Inch, and tutors Tommy Speck (a general's son she meets while babysitting his
younger sibling) in both rock music and sex. Just before they are estranged, Hedwig
rechristens him Tommy Gnosis with a silver cross on his forehead, and then watches
as he rockets to stardom using her songs. Later, a chance meeting results in disaster
and notoriety, as Tommy's limo runs into a bus of deaf schoolchildren. Meanwhile,
Hedwig is with Yitzhak, a drag queen he has rescued from the former Yugoslavia,
whom Hedwig has forbidden to appear in drag. As Hedwig's narrative nears completion, Hedwig breaks down, stripping off her feminine guise; in the aftermath, Hedwig
enacts a reconciliation of sorts with her alter ego, Tommy Gnosis, and releases Yitzhak by offering him one of her wigs. (Note: some details of the story are changed for
the film version.)

Books
John Cameron Mitchell and Stephen Trask. *Hedwig and the Angry Inch*. Woodstock,
   NY: Overlook Press, 1998 (includes pictures and biographies and an excerpt from
   Plato's *Symposium*).
John Cameron Mitchell and Stephen Trask. *Hedwig and the Angry Inch*. New York:
   Dramatists Play Service, 2003 (includes excerpts from the Gnostic Gospel of
   Thomas and Plato's *Symposium*).

Musical Score
Stephen Trask. *Hedwig and the Angry Inch*. Milwaukee: Hal Leonard, 1999 (piano/
   guitar/vocal score).

Chapter Six

Lady in the Dark (1941)
Book: Moss Hart
Lyrics: Ira Gershwin
Music: Kurt Weill

Plot: Liza Elliott, the unglamorous editor of a successful glamour magazine, *Allure*, consults Dr. Brooks, a psychiatrist, because she seems to be on the verge of a breakdown, susceptible to fits of rage, a compulsion to sleep, disturbing dreams brought on by a half-remembered tune, and an inability to make up her mind either in her personal life or as an editor. Specifically, she must choose, on the one hand, between two suggested magazine covers, a traditional Easter cover or a daring circus-themed cover recommended by her competent but irascible colleague Charley Johnson, and, on the other, whether or not to marry her long-term lover, Kendall Nesbitt, an older man who has financed the magazine and is finally getting a divorce. Meanwhile, Randy Curtis, an impossibly handsome but insecure movie star, is beginning to pursue her. Liza's dreams reveal a strong desire for the glamour she denies herself in real life and gradually hint at the traumatic events of her childhood. As matters at *Allure* disintegrate rapidly without Liza's secure control, Charley Johnson prepares to quit. The pivotal phase in her treatment occurs when Liza recalls a series of childhood events; through these memories and Dr. Brooks's guidance, she begins to see her way out of her depression. These memories are her father describing her as plain in comparison with her mother as she prepares so sing "My Ship" to her parents' friends (age 10); her rejection by the male lead after she has been selected to play the female lead in a school play (age 7); her inability to cry when her mother dies and her father's rebuke when he finds her dressed in her mother's clothes (age 10); and the interruption of her romantic interlude with a boy in high school when he abandons her for a prettier girl (age 17). During the last of these, before she is abandoned, she finally remembers "My Ship"; thus liberated, she returns to work, turns down proposals from Kendall and Randy, and makes it up with Charley, with whom, she suddenly discovers, she shares a deep bond.

Book

Moss Hart, Ira Gershwin, and Kurt Weill. *Lady in the Dark*. With a preface by "Dr. Brooks" (probably Lawrence S. Kubie). Cleveland: World Publishing Company, 1944.

Musical Score

Kurt Weill and Ira Gershwin. *Lady in the Dark*. New York: Chappell, 1941 (vocal score).

Kiss Me, Kate (1948)
Book: Sam and Bella Spewack
Lyrics and Music: Cole Porter

Plot: A divorced theatrical couple—Fred Graham and Lilli Vanessi—have reunited to perform the starring roles of Petruchio and Katherine in a musical version of Shakespeare's *Taming of the Shrew*, under Graham's direction. Their affair seems about to be rekindled when flowers that Fred intended for the ingénue Lois Lane (a girlfriend of Bill Calhoun, a dancer in the show) are delivered to Lilli—until she discovers the card that came with the flowers. Meanwhile, Calhoun, a compulsive gambler, has signed Graham's name to an IOU. When two thugs arrive to collect the debt, Graham manipulates them into preventing Lilli from leaving the show. The story then unfolds on two parallel tracks, on stage and off, around parallel musical numbers. Like the lead couple, Lois and Bill also have a falling out, over her promiscuousness and his gambling. In the second act, the thugs discover that their boss has been killed, rendering the IOU invalid. This frees Lilli to leave the show, which she does, only to return unexpectedly to finish the play. The play's reconciliation between Kate and Petruchio thus signals the reconciliation of Lilli and Fred as well.

Book
Bella Spewack, Sam Spewack, and Cole Porter. *Kiss Me, Kate.* New York: Knopf, 1953.

Musical Score
Cole Porter. *Kiss Me, Kate.* New York: T. B. Harms, 1951 (vocal score).

My Fair Lady (1956)
Book and Lyrics: Alan Jay Lerner (after Shaw's *Pygmalion*)
Music: Frederick Loewe

Plot: Professor Henry Higgins, a brilliant English phonetician and "confirmed bachelor," encounters Eliza Doolittle, a Cockney flower girl in Covent Garden, where he also chances on Colonel Pickering, a fellow linguistic expert who has just arrived from India to meet him. In a spurt of generosity, Higgins gives money to Eliza as he leaves with Pickering, who has agreed to accept Higgins's hospitality. Eliza, having overheard Higgins's address, appears at his home offering to pay for English lessons so that she might get a job in a florist's shop; Higgins, intrigued, and encouraged by Pickering, accepts the challenge. When after a protracted struggle Eliza at last seems to "get it," they decide to try her out in front of Higgins's mother's guests at Ascot—where, however, Eliza forgets herself in the excitement of the race. Although disgraced by her outburst ("Move your bloomin' arse!!!!"), she has attracted the romantic attention of Freddy Eynsford-Hill. Undeterred by the Ascot fiasco, Higgins and Pickering resolve to take Eliza to an embassy ball, where she performs so well she is taken for Hungarian royalty by a rival phonetician, Zoltan Karpathy. Following this triumph, the two men congratulate themselves and ignore Eliza, and are then stunned when she gets angry and leaves. After Higgins confronts Eliza at his mother's home the day after the ball, he also confronts his own feelings for her on his way home, contemplating with dismay what life will be like without her. Meanwhile, Eliza has turned down Freddy, who, like Higgins, seems to be all words and no action. The ending is ambivalent: Eliza returns to Higgins with the implicit promise of reconciliation between them, but Higgins's immediate reaction is to ask her to fetch his slippers.

Book
Alan Jay Lerner. *My Fair Lady.* New York: Coward-McCann, 1956.

Musical Score
Frederick Loewe and Alan Jay Lerner. *My Fair Lady.* New York: Chappell, 1956 (vocal score).

Company (1970)
Book: George Furth
Lyrics and Music: Stephen Sondheim

Plot: Framed by birthday celebrations for Bobby, a bachelor who has just turned thirty-five, the show proceeds in brief vignettes centering around five sets of Bobby's married friends and his occasional girlfriends. Seen mainly through his eyes, these episodes reveal that all of his friends' relationships have severe problems, which confirms him in his own bachelorhood. These episodes include an evening watching Harry and Sarah needle each other about their respective addictions (drink and food), ending in Sarah's demonstrating karate on Harry; Peter and Susan announcing their plans for a nonacrimonious divorce; Bobby with Jenny and David experimenting with marijuana, with Bobby rationalizing his half-pursued relationships with April, Kathy, and Marta; Bobby with Amy and Paul on their wedding day as Amy struggles to decide whether or not to go through with it; Bobby "dating" his current girlfriends (with Kathy announcing she is leaving New York to get married); another (or, perhaps, the same) birthday celebration; Bobby's tryst with April; his "double date" with Marta, Peter, and Susan (the latter pair now divorced); and Bobby with Joanne and Larry in a nightclub, where Joanne propositions him. In the end, he finally recognizes that relationships are an essential part of life and sees that through his fear of commitment, he is missing out on something valuable. A final "surprise" birthday party finds his friends assembled, but without Bobby, leaving us with the implication that he is finally getting on with his life.

Books
George Furth and Stephen Sondheim. *Company.* New York: Random House, 1970.
George Furth and Stephen Sondheim. *Company.* In *Ten Great Musicals of the American Theatre.* Edited by Stanley Richards. Radnor, PA: Chilton, 1973.

Musical Score
Stephen Sondheim and George Furth. *Company.* New York: Valando Music and Beautiful Music, 1970 (vocal score).

Passion (1994)
Book: James Lapine
Lyrics and Music: Stephen Sondheim

Plot: Giorgio, a captain in the Italian army, is having an affair with a married woman, Clara, when he is reassigned to a remote post. His boredom is broken only by their letters to each other, until he meets his colonel's niece, Fosca, an ugly, sickly woman who develops an obsessional love for him. Fearing her attachment to him, Giorgio arranges a leave to visit Clara and writes to Fosca, hoping to break it off. Their estrangement weakens Fosca until she is near death. The post's doctor persuades Giorgio to visit Fosca to try to restore her to health, and she coerces him into writing a letter to her, professing his own obsession with her. Fosca recovers and pursues Giorgio to a remote setting on a stormy night, where, spurned once more, she collapses. Giorgio becomes so ill from carrying her back in the storm that the doctor sends him on an extended leave, but Fosca follows him on the train and makes him see that Clara cannot love him as completely as she does. Giorgio and Clara break up after she refuses to leave her husband; meanwhile, the doctor has arranged to have Giorgio transferred, and the colonel challenges Giorgio to a duel when he finds the letter Fosca had dictated to him. Giorgio declares his love for Fosca, wounds the colonel in their duel the next morning, and learns, as he is recovering several months later, that Fosca died shortly after their night together.

Book
James Lapine and Stephen Sondheim. *Passion*. New York: Theatre Communications Group, 1994.

Musical Score
Stephen Sondheim and James Lapine. *Passion*. Miami: Warner Bros. Publications, 1996 (vocal score).

Chapter Seven
Candide (1956)
Book: Lillian Hellman (principal revised versions: Hugh Wheeler; John Wells's adaptation from Wheeler's version)
Lyrics: Richard Wilbur, John LaTouche, Leonard Bernstein, Dorothy Parker, Lillian Hellman (additional lyrics contributed by Stephen Sondheim for the Hugh Wheeler version)
Music: Leonard Bernstein

Plot: see pp. 317–18 and 321

Book
Lillian Hellman, Leonard Bernstein, Richard Wilbur, John LaTouche, and Dorothy Parker. *Candide*. New York: Avon, 1970 (first published 1957 by Random House).

Musical Scores
Leonard Bernstein, Richard Wilbur, John LaTouche, Dorothy Parker, and Lillian Hellman. *Candide*. New York: G. Schirmer, 1958 (vocal score of original version).
Leonard Bernstein, Richard Wilbur, John LaTouche, Stephen Sondheim, and Hugh Wheeler. *Candide*. New York: Schirmer Books, 1976 (vocal score and book for the 1974 Broadway version, with an introduction by Harold Prince).
Leonard Bernstein, Richard Wilbur, John LaTouche, Lillian Hellman, Dorothy Parker, Stephen Sondheim, and John Wells. *Candide*. New York: Jalni Publications, Boosey & Hawkes, 1994 (1989 Scottish Opera version; orchestrations by Bernstein, Hershy Kay, and John Mauceri).
Leonard Bernstein, Richard Wilbur, John LaTouche, Lillian Hellman, Dorothy Parker, Stephen Sondheim, and John Wells. *Candide*. New York: Jalni Publications, Boosey & Hawkes, 1994 (vocal score of 1989 Scottish Opera version).

Sweeney Todd (1979)
Book: Hugh Wheeler
Music and Lyrics: Stephen Sondheim

Plot: see p. 332

Books
Stephen Sondheim and Hugh Wheeler, after Christopher Bond. *Sweeney Todd: The Demon Barber of Fleet Street*. New York: Dood, Mead & Company, 1979.

Stephen Sondheim and Hugh Wheeler, after Christopher Bond. *Sweeney Todd: The Demon Barber of Fleet Street*. Introduction by Christopher Bond. New York: Applause Theater Books, 1991.

Stephen Sondheim, Hugh Wheeler, James Lapine, Burt Shevelove, and Larry Gelbart. *Four by Sondheim*. New York: Applause, 2000 (includes books of *A Funny Thing Happened on the Way to the Forum*, *A Little Night Music*, *Sweeney Todd*, and *Sunday in the Park with George*).

Musical Score

Stephen Sondheim. *Sweeney Todd: The Demon Barber of Fleet Street*. Revelation Music Publishing Corporation & Rilting Music, 1981 (vocal score).

Evita (1979)
Book and Lyrics: Tim Rice
Music: Andrew Lloyd Webber

Plot: see p. 343

Books

Andrew Lloyd Webber and Tim Rice. *Evita: The Legend of Eva Peron, 1919–1952*. London: Elm Tree Books, 1978 (contains lyrics for songs as rewritten for the stage show, but before it opened).

Andrew Lloyd Webber and Tim Rice. *Evita: The Legend of Eva Peron, 1919–1952*. New York: Avon, 1979 (the "official edition" of the libretto).

Musical Scores

Andrew Lloyd Webber and Tim Rice. *Evita*. London: Evita Music and Leeds Music, 1977 (vocal score with complete libretto, prestage version).

Andrew Lloyd Webber and Tim Rice. *Evita*. Melville, NY: Leeds Music and MCA Music, 1979 (vocal score with complete libretto, stage version).

Andrew Lloyd Webber and Tim Rice. *Evita*. Milwaukee: MCA Music Pub. and H. Leonard, 1997 (vocal score, film version).

NOTES

Entr'acte

1. *The American Musical and the Formation of National Identity* (Knapp1). As there, I am here following the convention of using the term "American," in both its adjectival and noun forms, to refer specifically to the United States, in full awareness that the term slights the rest of the Americas—Canada, Mexico, Central America, and South America—by exclusion. There is, however, no widely recognized alternative, and there are many common combinations—such as "American musical"—that can scarcely be avoided.

2. See, among other discussions, Riis2 and Graziano.

3. Nate Salsbury's *The Brook* (1879), which established a short-lived vogue for farce-comedy, was the most notable success of this kind before Cohan, although Salsbury's "composing" was mainly a matter of adaptation. Among Salsbury's other shows were *Green-Room Fun* in 1883 and *The Humming Bird* in 1887. He is best known today for his association with William F. Cody's *Wild West Show*, which he managed from 1883 until his death in 1902, along the way helping to make Annie Oakley an international star. Notably, as well, in 1895 he produced *Black America*, a variety show featuring a large cast of African Americans. Initial advertisements for *Black America* (then at Brooklyn's Ambrose Park) claimed 500 performers, although that number shrank to 300 when the show moved to Madison Square Garden later in the year. The *New York Times*'s advance article (May 25, 1995), which confirms the figure of 500, also makes it clear that while the show sought to celebrate its subject and was taken this way by both audiences and performers, it also included many traditional minstrel routines, along with sentimentalized re-creations of antebellum plantation life (as the *New York Times* article put it, "befo' the wah").

4. This agenda was advocated most vigorously by Leonard Bernstein; see Bernstein, pp. 178–79.

5. The difficulty of fully disengaging the American musical from its various models and influences is especially evident in the case of operetta, as exemplified in some of the arguments Gerald Bordman has advanced concerning the operetta basis of many mainstream musicals after *Oklahoma!*; see Bordman2 and further discussion in chapter 1.

6. The characteristic Viennese inflections to the waltz rhythm survive more as a continuous performing tradition than as clearly notated instructions in the music. Although most modern performances of *The Merry Widow* in English will attempt to incorporate a Viennese rhythmic inflection, we cannot be sure that this is what Americans heard in 1907. Plausibly, because both the Viennese waltz and the American waltz song became distinctive types during the later nineteenth century, their distinctive stylistic differences would have been brought out in performance. My own conviction in this was reinforced many years ago from hearing a fine American Gilbert and Sullivan repertory company perform Johann Strauss's *Die Fledermaus* with a particularly leaden effect; it had none of the characteristic Viennese "lilt." Surely,

a similarly leaden performance of *The Merry Widow* would have undermined the success of the show in its first American run.

7. In a celebrated scene, *Blazing Saddles* draws comic attention to how easily we accept the filmic convention of mood-setting or accompanimental orchestral music, whatever the setting. As Bart (Cleavon Little) rides to his new post as sheriff to the accompaniment of a full orchestra, we are meant to assume that the music is nondiegetic (that is, not originating in the world of the film), until the incongruity of this assumption is given visual expression, when the camera pans outward to reveal a full orchestra playing on the prairie. Brooks may have derived this gag from a scene in Woody Allen's *Bananas* (1971), in which a daydreaming Fielding Mellish (played by Allen) gets off his bed to open a door, revealing the source of what we have taken to be nondiegetic "mood" music: a harpist practicing in his closet.

8. See MEYER for an extended presentation of the view that "[c]amp is solely a queer (and/or sometimes gay and lesbian) discourse" (p. 1).

9. And, as I will argue later, this dual receptive mode may well have been in place from the beginning; see chapter 1, pp. 32–34.

10. KNAPP1, p. 283.

11. Cf. ALTMAN: "The marriage which resolves the primary (sexual) dichotomy also mediates between two terms of the secondary (thematic) opposition" (p. 50).

12. This is not to say that the dominant *meanings* of recorded artifacts do not change from one receptive context to another, as, for example, when the audience's perspective shifts from child to adult, or the interpretive mode from straight to camp.

13. See this book's appendix and website for listings of the principal available material along these lines. The website also provides audio clips of illustrative musical examples, musical notation when useful, and additional pictures; see "Explanatory Note about Audio Examples" on page xi.

Chapter One
The Viennese Connection: Franz Lehár and American Operetta

1. See BORDMAN2 and chapter 5 of BORDMAN1 (pp. 230–296).

2. See chapters 2 and 7 of MORDDEN5 regarding the stagnation and rebirth of operetta in the 1920s, from "fat-and-besotted operetta" early on (p. 36) to its reinvention in the second half of the decade; see also EVERETT.

3. Operetta has appealed to a variety of constituencies, and from a variety of perspectives. See, for example, chapter 6 of ALTMAN for a discussion that places many of its filmic reincarnations under the broad rubric of fairy-tale musical.

4. This version, though it uses many of Lehár's tunes, and only a few that aren't his, puts them to often drastically different uses, with new lyrics by Lorenz Hart and (officially, at least) Richard Rodgers.

5. There were Broadway revivals in 1921, 1929, 1931, and 1943; besides the two film versions already noted, an earlier silent version was filmed in 1925 by Erich von Stroheim, whose plot was related to the operetta only in broad situational terms.

6. "Danilowitsch" is an example of a patronymic commonly used in Russian and some related cultures, in this case meaning "son of Danilo." In the 1934 Lubitsch film, which for the most part follows Ross's name changes, Danilo is captain of the guard.

7. "Women" is given as a march and actually performed as a march in both the 1934 and 1952 films (near the beginning), thus making it conform after the fact to a very different operetta trope; see the later discussion of "Tramp, Tramp, Tramp" (from *Naughty Marietta*). Also conforming to a different operetta trope is a plot device common to both the 1934 and 1952 versions, in which it is the disguised heroine that the hero first falls in love with.

8. In Sheldon Harnick's later adaptation of the show, in most respects closer to the original than Adrian Ross's, the country is called Petrovenia, an apparent reference to Petrovic. Erich von Stroheim's 1925 silent film version, with its much-changed plot, makes the connection to Montenegro the most explicit, renaming the kingdom Monteblanco (White Mountain).

9. *The Merry Widow* derives from *The Ambassador's Attaché*, written in 1861, shortly after Danilo's assassination. Its Parisian author, Henri Meilhac, worked frequently with Halévy and Offenbach; their 1872 collaboration *Le réveillon* was the basis for Johann Strauss's 1874 *Die Fledermaus*. Thus, the two most famous of the Viennese operettas were in part Parisian imports—as was, of course, the genre itself.

10. The mazurka comes from the region of Mazovia, the likely reference point for Ross's change from Pontevedro to Marsovia; many of the other name changes also seem to follow from the implicit geographic shift north. The impulse to change locations probably stemmed specifically from English rather than American sensibilities since enmity for the Balkans was widespread in England just after the turn of the century. The Lubitsch film offers an additional wrinkle to the shifting location of this "fictional" land: the film opens with a map of 1885 Europe, panning to a tiny country wedged in a corner between Roumania (*sic*)and Austria-Hungary, somewhat east of Serbia, whose name (now Marshovia) is readable only with the help of a magnifying glass.

11. Notably, the second Danilo secured his secession through an endorsement from the Russian czar. Russia's interest in Montenegro was partly historical but more vitally political and religious, since Montenegro, with Serbia, helped them maintain an Eastern Orthodox "wedge" between the Muslim Turks and the Catholic Austrians that reached all the way to the Mediterranean Sea.

12. The kolo is actually a round dance, not a couple dance ("kolo" means "circle"), and is often danced without accompanying music—according to legend so as not to alert the Turks to the Montenegrans' presence. Probably, the "Mi velimo dase veslimo!" dance is also meant to be a kolo, with its characteristic interpolations of "Hei!"

13. For an extended discussion of orientalism in the American musical, see chapter 10 of KNAPP1. The defining text on the subject of orientalism more generally is SAID.

14. This snap, over open-fifth drones (that is, a set of sustained pitches an open fifth apart, as commonly found in simple folk-music accompaniments), will transmute easily into one of the standard tropes of American operetta: its indulgence in "Indianist" music, such as that of *Rose-Marie* and *Little Mary Sunshine* (discussed below). Both here and in the later tradition, the dramatic function is the same, as the musical gesture serves as a marker for an exoticized primitivism that will exert an inexorable pull on the lead characters and ground their romance in something deeper than the familiar world around them.

15. Many performances begin with a rewritten overture that features the waltz prominently, but this was not Lehár's conception.

16. Ross's translation reads: "Though I say not what I may not / Let you hear, / Yet the swaying dance is saying, / Love me, dear! / Ev'ry touch of fingers / Tells me what I know, / Says for you, It's true, it's true, / You love me so! // And to the music's chime, / My heart is beating time, / As if to give a sign, / That it would say, Be mine, be mine! / Though our lips say no word, / Yet in the heart a voice is heard. / You cannot choose but know / I love you so."

17. These are Mozart's operatic masterworks in the Italian "buffa" tradition, *The Marriage of Figaro* (1786), *Don Giovanni* (1787), and *Così fan tutte* (1790). As befits the "domestic" theme, Lehár's treatment of the exchanges in this number is extremely formulaic, however engaging; elsewhere in Act I, in both the earlier duet for Camille and Valencienne, and in Hanna's flirtatious engagement with her would-be suitors, Lehár finds suitable occasions to indulge in more musically sophisticated contrapuntal textures.

18. Most other "Merry Widows"—such as a 1908 special delivery stamp, various cocktail recipes (beginning around 1930), and a brand of condoms—do not foster as literal a connection to the character as these, although obviously referential. The illicit pleasures suggested in the phrase "merry widow" probably have more to do with its appropriations in detective fiction (e.g., Hitchcock's 1943 *Shadow of a Doubt*, the 1997 "Merry Widow Murder" episode in the television series *Diagnosis: Murder*, Richard Hunt's 1998 *Death of Merry Widow*, and Meagan McKinney's 2000 *The Merry Widow*) than anything specific to the show itself.

19. Mahler, a converted Jew from the provinces, left anti-Semitic Vienna for New York City in 1907, partly in response to Vienna's ill-treatment of him. He thus arrived in New York in near synchronicity with *The Merry Widow*.

20. Adorno writes of Mahler's allusive tune: "It saunters to the rhythm of the 'Women' song in the *Merry Widow*, which at that time squeaked from the brass horns of phonographs. Thus does Proust deport himself in those photographs showing him as a bon vivant with top hat and jauntily flourished cane: the incognito of the genius who destroys himself by mingling in the shallow life of others" (ADORNO, pp. 162–163). In MAHLER (p. 120), Alma Mahler describes her and her husband's clandestine affection for *The Merry Widow* and recounts their visiting a music shop, not to buy the music (which would have been embarrassing) but to study it on the sly.

21. Although Bartók is often understood here to satirize Shostakovich, this seems inconsistent with his character. More likely, both composers were satirizing the pretensions of Germanic culture by calling attention to one of its most widely known and seemingly trivial artifacts. Both composers were fierce nationalists whose native countries were, at the time these two works were written, being brutalized by Nazi Germany. Significant also is that Lehár remained in Europe to be much celebrated by the Nazis, for which many did not forgive him; see, for example, LERNER2, p. 41.

22. For a concise exposition of Lehár's deft compositional touch, see LAMB2. Another roughly contemporary "high art" response to the success of *The Merry Widow* is Richard Strauss's 1911 *Der Rosenkavalier*.

23. Yet, there is more to this "crude joke" than might be suspected; see KNAPP3.

24. A quadroon is a person who is one quarter African and three quarters European; the term derives from the Spanish "cuarterón." Thus, quadroon music might be expected to have a sensuous, exotic inflection, in this case carried by a suggestive chromaticism in parallel thirds. Related terms used to indicate a mixed-race heritage are "mulatto" and "Creole." With the former, the insulting analogy (not generally noted) is to mules, nonreproductive work animals with a horse for a mother and

sired by a donkey. The term "Creole" (which did not necessarily indicate mixed ancestry) could refer, variously across the Gulf of Mexico region, to mixtures of Spanish and black (especially in the islands), or French and black (especially in New Orleans), so long as the dominant cultural influence and language base were European or European derived; the term refers specifically to heritage, which in New Orleans could redeem even mixed-race parentage.

25. The introduction to "Who Will Buy?" from *Oliver!* (1964) is a well-known modern re-creation of this tradition, within a London setting quite in keeping with the roots of the tradition. Another striking twentieth-century example may be found in the 1935 *Porgy and Bess* (the cries of the Strawberry Woman and Crab Man), where the evocation serves in part to mark Catfish Row's separation from mainstream white America. The specific association of street cries with a London setting has been reinforced, within symphonic settings, by Haydn's *London* Symphony (no. 104, 1795) and Vaughan Williams's *A London Symphony* (1911–1914). Despite the traditional understanding of Haydn's finale theme as deriving from the cry of a street vendor, however, the tune has been more securely traced to a Croatian folk song; this was scarcely the last time such an "obvious" signpost would be misread by Londoners: the *Alphorn* theme in the finale of Brahms's First Symphony (1876) was heard by contemporary Londoners as a reference to Big Ben. Regarding Big Ben itself, see my discussion of *Sweeney Todd* in chapter 7. Regarding other ways of evoking London in musical terms, see my discussions of "Feed the Birds" in chapter 3 and "Wouldn't It Be Loverly" in chapter 6. (I wish to thank Philip Gentry for bringing Haydn's *London* Symphony to my attention in this regard.)

26. Other significant changes in the 1935 film include a larger amount of time spent on the "back story" of Marietta's European predicament and flight to America (which results in the elimination of the title song) and a virtual elimination of the secondary plot involving the pirate Bras Piqué. In the much-shortened television version, Captain Dick is American; intriguingly, the American-French marriage trope is evoked in that production, only to be rejected as irrelevant. Historically, the marriage trope makes little sense, since, in the years following the creation of the United States, France controlled New Orleans only between 1801 and 1803, although the city remained culturally tied to its French heritage.

27. A particularly flagrant historical inaccuracy of *Naughty Marietta* concerns the fact that by 1780 (the stipulated date of the operetta's events) New Orleans was under Spanish control, not French. According to the librettist, Rida Johnson Young, the date was changed from the original 1750 (originally to 1775, which improbably placed its events near the outbreak of the American Revolutionary War) at the insistence of the costume designer (see WATERS, p. 356). Still, restoring the 1750 date would erase only some of the show's most obvious ahistoricisms, including the strong implication that its action occurs *before* the American Revolution, not after. Moreover, some performances place the date even later; thus, the 1958 televised version is set in 1790. Underlying the show's confusion of dates is the fact that the closest historical approximation to its scenario of a pirate friendly to American interests took place during the Battle of New Orleans (1814–1815), when Jean Laffite supplied Andrew Jackson with munitions and men in exchange for amnesty; Jackson's forces also included a group of "Kaintucks" (i.e., itinerant rifleman from Kentucky).

28. The standard ploy for achieving this kind of historical vagueness in operetta traditions is placing the action in the imagined kingdom of Ruritania, somewhere in Eastern Europe. Thus, for example, Ruritania is the setting of both Stroheim's 1925

film version of *The Merry Widow* and—perhaps most famously—of Anthony Hope's 1894 novel, *The Prisoner of Zenda*, which has been often filmed, most successfully by John Cromwell in 1937.

29. This characteristic feature of Viennese waltz is nicely described by Stephen Banfield in reference to *A Little Night Music*: "[The *Luftpause*] is an archetypal waltz feature, the point of silence or rhythmic hiatus like the moment of stillness and latent energy at the end of a pendulum's swing; it implies the thrill of physical motion, of hovering for a moment in midair, on the turn, rolling yet poised in suspense, that is part of the waltz's propensity for ecstasy" (BANFIELD2, pp. 243–44).

30. In the 1935 film, " 'Neath the Southern Moon" is sung by Captain Dick (Nelson Eddy), a direct appropriation of the song into the main love story—a maneuver that is based, however, on what was already at least implicit in the original. As noted, "Naughty Marietta" is not used in the film.

31. BELL, p. 621.

32. Grant appeared as an acrobat in an English comedy troupe from about 1918 until he was discovered by Arthur Hammerstein (son of Oscar and uncle of Oscar II), for whom he appeared—still as Archie Leach, his real name—in the 1927 stage operetta *Golden Dawn* (book and lyrics by Oscar Hammerstein II and Otto Harbach, music by Emmerich Kalman, Robert Stolz, and Herbert P. Stothart, and set in Africa with white performers in blackface; given the retrogressive racial profile of *Golden Dawn*, it is shocking to realize that Hammerstein and Kern's *Show Boat* would open less than a month later). Before he became a first-rank star, Grant also appeared in supporting roles in a few early Hollywood musicals, most notably in the Mae West vehicle *She Done Him Wrong* (1933). As George Chauncey notes, Grant's follow-up line in *Bringing Up Baby*, to "I just went *gay*, all of a sudden!" is also significant. Grant, who by this point is sitting on the stairs but still in the negligee, mutters, "I'm sitting in the middle of 42nd Street waiting for a bus" (in answer to the question, "What are you doing?"), which ties his use of "gay" directly to the New York City theater district, and in particular to forty-second Street's function as "the primary cruising strip for the city's male prostitutes, including transvestite prostitutes," a situation in which "waiting for a bus" could serve both as a legitimizing excuse and a euphemism (CHAUNCEY, p. 18).

Elsewhere, Chauncey discusses the prominence (and relative tolerance) of homosexuality on Broadway during this era (see, especially, pp. 301–4). And, in a particularly valuable discussion of terminology (pp. 14–23), he traces the emergence of the euphemistic use of the word "gay" in the 1940s against a backdrop of more familiar designations for male homosexuals (i.e., "fairy," "queer," "faggot," and "pansy"), noting that the term's value early on derived from its wide currency as an uninflected term, so that it could retain an ambiguity denied these other, more familiar terms. For earlier decades, this very ambiguity makes usage of the term harder to pin down; Chauncey cites its inflected use in novels already in the late 1920s, which would suggest that the word had already acquired this meaning some time before. Jonathan Ned Katz speculates on the possibility that the coded use of "gay" may have had some currency "as early as 1908–1912" (KATZ, p. 405)—the first years of the American response to *The Merry Widow*, and encompassing the inception and first run of *Naughty Marietta*. Elsewhere, Katz notes the lines from the 1929 Noël Coward operetta *Bitter Sweet* (sung by a male chorus): "We are the reason for the nineties being gay" (p. 437), a daring appropriation of a commonly used designation, which implicitly claims (without evidence, of course) that the word already had a double meaning even in the "Gay Nineties." See also Russo, regarding *The Gay Brothers* (an experimental film of 1895) and Grant's negligee scene in *Bringing Up Baby* (pp. 6 and 47, respectively).

33. Dumont's work with the Marx Brothers began with her 1925 stage appearance in *The Cocoanuts* and ended with the 1941 film *The Big Store*, although she continued to play similar roles for many years. The suggested parallel to MacDonald is deeper than might be supposed; Dumont was an opera singer and thereby had acquired the requisite "presence"—and a seeming capacity to take herself seriously however loopy the situation—to serve as an effective foil for Groucho.

34. Verbal play on terms that intersect with the word "gay" is, of course, a common source of humor; thus, in Mel Brooks's *Robin Hood: Men in Tights* (1993), when Robin introduces his merry men to Rabbi Tuchman (played by Mel Brooks), the latter asks, "Fageles?"—to which Robin replies, "No, we're straight. Just merry."

35. Miller-Da1, p. 119. Miller's explanation of how connotation works in signaling homosexuality is worth quoting at length, in part because it also applies to my earlier discussion of the development of "gay" as an inflected term: "Yet if connotation . . . has the advantage of constructing an essentially insubstantial homosexuality, it has the corresponding inconvenience of tending to raise this ghost all over the place. For once received in all its uncertainty, the connotation instigates a project of confirmation. In cases where nothing prevents what is connoted from being denoted as well, confirmation is easily provided. . . . But when, with homosexuality as with nothing else, what is connoted may not be denoted, whoever would establish a given connotation can only support it through other connotations equally precarious. . . . Needing corroboration, finding it only in what exhibits the same need, . . . connotation thus tends to light everywhere, to put all signifiers to a test of their hospitality. . . . Connotation . . . excites the desire for proof, a desire that, so long as it develops within the connotative register, tends to draft every signifier into what nonetheless remains a hopeless task" (pp. 119–20 and 123).

36. In both the 2002 film *Chicago* and *Roxie Hart*, the 1942 film based on the same story, the role of Mary Sunshine is played by a woman. It is entirely possible that Maurine Watkins, the *Chicago Tribune* reporter who wrote the original play in 1926, intended the character as a caricature of herself.

37. The lyrics of this song are as follows (allowing for many slight variants): "Good morning, merry sunshine, / How did you wake so soon? / You've scared the little stars away, / And shined away the moon. / I watched you go to sleep last night, / Before I stopped my play, / How did you get way over there, / And, pray, where did you stay? // I never go to sleep, dear, / I just go 'round to see / My little children in the East, / Who rise to watch for me. / I waken all the birds and bees, / And flowers on my way, / Then last of all, the little child / Who stayed out late to play." I wish to thank Rose Rosengard Subotnik for pointing out this song and its associated rituals to me, and Byron Adams and Mitchell Morris for their insights more generally into the possible connotations of the name.

38. The full list is trustworthy, loyal, helpful, friendly, courteous, kind, obedient, cheerful, thrifty, brave, clean, and reverent. The first three are not listed explicitly in the song, which adds "grave" to "reverent" and substitutes "honest" for "trustworthy," and "thoughtful" for "helpful." Only "loyal" is left out, with "healthy" serving as its curious substitute, providing an odd assonance with the missing "helpful." Presumably, each substitution has a point, since "He's loyal and he's brave" would

have scanned just as well as "He's healthy and he's brave"—perhaps we may infer that health matters more than loyalty in this particular troop.

39. Specifically, the sequence seems meant to recall the combination of the men's "We Sail the Ocean Blue" with the women's "Gaily Tripping" in *Pinafore*; and that of the women's "Welcome Gentry" with the men's "When Thoroughly Tired of Being Admired" in *Ruddigore*.

40. Nancy's evocation of Mata Hari is an anachronism, since the (probably wrongly accused) exotic dancer was executed by the French as a spy much later, during World War I, although her fame as a dancer (1905–1912) was roughly congruent with the time frame of *Little Mary Sunshine* (early in the twentieth century).

41. For a somewhat different elaboration of the relationship of *A Little Night Music* to operetta, see chapter 5 in GORDON1 (pp. 123–56).

42. See SWAYNE, pp. 244–51, for an extensive discussion of this problematic term and its (mis-?)application to *A Little Night Music*.

43. See TUNICK, p. 3, and SWAYNE, pp. 278–99, especially p. 282.

44. One of the most puzzling decisions made in adapting *A Little Night Music* for its film version (1977) was to move its location to Vienna (which according to Craig Zadan was purely for financial reasons; see ZADAN, p. 195). Although this shift acknowledges the Viennese operetta basis (sort of—*The Merry Widow*, after all, takes place in Paris), it removes the core conceit of the original film, of inhabiting a time suspended between day and night.

45. For an extended discussion of the interrelationships among *A Little Night Music*, *Smiles of a Summer Night*, and *A Midsummer Night's Dream*, see PUCCIO. Another point of relevance for Bergman's scenario is Arthur Schnitzler's notorious 1900 *Der Reigen* (The Round Dance), filmed by Max Ophuls in 1950 (*La Ronde*); see BANFIELD2, p. 227, and SECREST2, p. 256.

46. The most familiar examples of this type generally involve only two mismatched couples (as in *Così fan tutte*); as a filmic genre, they are usually grouped within the general category of screwball comedy. Among many classics of this type from mid-1930s Hollywood are *Sylvia Scarlet* (George Cukor, 1935), *Libeled Lady* (Jack Conway, 1936), and *The Awful Truth* (Leo McCarey, 1937). A latter-day evocation of the type, meant also to celebrate the legacy of Cole Porter, is Peter Bogdanovich's *At Long Last Love* (1975), which also tried, with mixed success, to bypass the lip-synching conventions of film musicals by recording the actual singing on the set (but not the instrumental arrangements, which were laid down ahead of time and played back to the singers through earphones). The 2004 Mike Nichols film *Closer*, from the 1997 Patrick Marber play, demonstrates the aptitude of the type to move beyond comedy to something approaching tragedy. *Closer* resembles *Così fan tutte* both in some details of its plotting and in its overriding focus on the emotional realities of romantic betrayal, and acknowledges its debt with ample helpings from the opera's beguiling score, used as diegetic background music. Regarding *Così fan tutte* and the capacity of this kind of story more generally to undermine what Robin Wood terms the "ideology of the couple," see WOOD-R2, pp. 85–93; see also his related discussions of *Jean Renoir*'s 1939 film, *The Rules of the Game*, pp. 60–85.

47. Banfield attempts a more radical redrawing of Tunick's diagram, with the latter's triangles forming the points of an incomplete star (simulating dancers on a schematic dance floor, in a round dance with the men on the outside); his chart is topographically the same as Tunick's without the latter's horizontal lines (BANFIELD2, p. 227). Puccio provides a less comprehensive chart showing parallels between *A Midsummer Night's Dream* and *A Little Night Music* (PUCCIO, p. 136), adding vec-

tor arrows to the lines of connection used here; see also his commentary on "mathematical" texts (or "narrative cartology"), p. 163n9.

48. Specifically, she states a preference for fall over summer, and then, with a meaningful look at Fredrik, refines her preference to "early fall" over "late fall." While implicitly acknowledging Fredrik's advanced age relative to her own (fall), her refined preference is for *younger* older men (*early* fall)—that is, roughly Fredrik's age.

49. As noted by Banfield (BANFIELD2, p. 234), the conceit of a young girl being tutored in the (sexual) ways of the world by an older "expert" relative seems to have been borrowed from Lerner and Loewe's 1958 *Gigi*, which similarly takes place at the turn of the century and similarly cast Hermione Gingold in the role of the older tutor. (*Gigi*, originally a film musical, was staged on Broadway in 1973, the same year as *A Little Night Music*.)

50. At an early stage of development, the show was to unfold as a series of manipulations by Desirée, each failing to achieve the desired result, with Mme. Armfeldt's reshuffling of the cards serving to indicate a point of starting over. From this extended exploration of Bergman's conception of Desirée as a stage manager, however, Wheeler did an about-face, drafting a scenario in which Desirée's seeming control simply disintegrates, leaving the characters at the mercy of the summer night and its smiles. For Sondheim's description of the earlier plan, see ZADAN, p. 182; see also BANFIELD2, p. 226.

51. Frid's full list for the recipients of the third smile includes the sad, depressed, sleepless, confused, frightened, and lonely.

52. This set of questions was particulary pressing in 1973, after Sondheim's two previous shows: *Company* (1970), with its disturbing view of modern relationships, and *Follies* (1971), with its unsuccessful quest, in parallel to that of *A Little Night Music*, to recover a romanticized past.

53. The reference in "A Weekend in the Country" is courtesy of Jonathan Tunick, the orchestrator (see TUNICK, p. 7). Regarding the others, see BANFIELD2, pp. 223–25.

54. The term "Liebeslieder" (love songs) refers most obviously to two sets of waltz songs by Johannes Brahms (his *Liebeslieder Waltzes*, opp. 52 and 65, composed 1868–1874), set for vocal quartet and four-hand piano, through which he codified a "Viennese" style that embraced both Schubert and Johann Strauß. Sondheim's pointed addition of a fifth singer, as Steven Swayne has pointed out, prevents the ensemble from subdividing into couples without leaving someone out; in pragmatic terms, they cannot all dance the waltz at the same time. As Swayne argues, the primary function of waltz in the show is as a *de*coupler, in effect making the show an *anti*-"waltz musical" (SWAYNE, pp. 281–82). The removal of this group for the film version of *A Little Night Music* deprives the film of the otherworldly aura of the stage version.

55. Another way in which *A Little Night Music* has seemed to imitate *The Merry Widow* is in the late placement of its most famous tune, which many in the audience will have come especially to hear, in this case "Send in the Clowns." This is by all accounts an unintended consequence, however, stemming from the unexpected popular success of the song.

56. As Carl-Magnus explains to Desirée when he appears unexpectedly later in the first act, he has divided his twenty hours of leave time strategically and strictly according to the numbers: "Three hours coming here, nine hours with you, five hours with my wife and three hours back."

57. Banfield provides a useful chart of the binary choices Fredrik considers in "Now" (BANFIELD2, p. 218).

58. Banfield's suggestion of a Bach influence here is particularly apt, not only because of the musical connections (slow sarabande rhythm and inverted counterpoint between voice and cello), but also because of the connection to Lutheranism, of whom Bach is the greatest musical representative, his music being understood as both pious and richly introspective (see BANFIELD2, pp. 222–25; see also SWAYNE, pp. 275–76).

59. For a somewhat different view of the interpersonal dynamic in this combination song, see YOUNG, pp. 77–88. In particular, Young argues that the three singers "become engaged in individuating themselves from one another, declaring their difference, and ultimately declaring their resistance/attraction to each other" (p. 85).

60. See SWAYNE, pp. 259–61, on the appropriateness of this dance type to Carl-Magnus and to this moment in the plot.

61. Gordon characterizes this song as a hunting song, a genre to which it clearly alludes at times, especially when Jonathan Tunick adds horns to the mix (GORDON1, p. 144). Adding to this suggestive mix of types, Swayne identifies elements of the Italianate saltarello in this number, as part of a general "Mediterranean topos" (SWAYNE, p. 300), whose orientation toward sexual pursuit is typical of the show's many songs in compound meter (pp. 299–308). Tunick himself identifies the song as a gigue (TUNICK, p. 3), an identification supported by its frequent hemiolas, a common feature of eighteenth-century gigues (as argued by Marcus Desmond Harmon, personal communication).

62. Both Banfield and Swayne have explored the richness of musical types alluded to in this song, one of the more subtle ways that it "looks back." See SWAYNE, pp. 308–16, who quotes extensively from an unpublished paper by Banfield (pp. 314–15).

63. See Banfield's discussion of Sondheim's manipulation of the *Luftpause* in this number BANFIELD2, pp. 244–45. As reported by Meryle Secrest, the song's many pauses were the result of Sondheim writing to accommodate Glynis Johns's short-windedness (SECREST2, pp. 252–53).

64. See KNAPP1, pp. 141–42.

65. BANFIELD2, p. 214.

66. And this may well have been the original rationale for having five singers rather than four. Despite the clear relevance of this grouping to the staging, as noted, staging was not Sondheim's concern; in fact, he had the quintet in place months before producer-director Hal Prince figured out how to deploy them onstage (see GORDON1, p. 127; see also PRINCE, pp. 174–75).

Chapter Two
The Movie Musical

1. *The Jazz Singer* was not the first sound film, but it was the first commercially successful film with significant sections of synchronized sound.

2. SARRIS, p. 32, in specific reference to *The Jazz Singer*.

3. With color, the principal challenges of synchronization were "front end" only, involving the need to produce two films (after 1932, three films) simultaneously through the same lens, each filtered for a different part of the color spectrum, so

that when they were dyed and recombined, they would produce a single strip of colored film. The process had been available since 1922 but was quite expensive, often produced unsatisfactory results, and seemed to have no commensurate commercial payoff.

4. For more on the music of the "silents" era, see MARKS and chapter 1 of MARMORSTEIN. Robinson provides a particularly useful guide to the practice of accompanying "silent" film.

5. In 1932 this trend began to reverse itself, with a decisive tendency toward more pervasive "background" music.

6. This kind of culture shock about the casualness of blackface is by no means associated only with *The Jazz Singer*. As I noted in chapter 8 of the first volume (KNAPP1), Hollywood films continued for some years to indulge a taste for blackface, which was in fact a trademark of some stars, such as Al Jolson and Eddie Cantor; the latter, for example, appeared on Broadway doing a blackface medley as late as 1941 (*Banjo Eyes*) and continued to appear in blackface roles throughout the 1940s (e.g., in *If You Knew Susie*, 1948). More mainstream stars appearing in blackface during this period included Fred Astaire (*Swing Time*, 1936), Irene Dunne (*Show Boat*, 1936), Judy Garland alone (*Everybody Sing*, 1938) and with Mickey Rooney (*Babes in Arms*, 1939, and *Babes on Broadway*, 1941), Bing Crosby and Marjorie Reynolds (*Holiday Inn*, 1942), and Betty Grable (*The Dolly Sisters*, 1945). *The Jazz Singer* was remade in a wide variety of guises; see the first chapter of GABBARD1 for an extended consideration of these films. For a contextualization of the complex racial dimension of blackface, as one path toward Jewish assimilation in the early sound era in Hollywood, see ROGIN1 and ROGIN2. See also chapters 1–3 of MELNICK, regarding how the practice affected evolving Black-Jewish relations across the twentieth century; and the first two chapters of MOST1, which focus on the 1925 stage version of *The Jazz Singer*.

7. See LAING for a useful discussion of what I am calling MERM.

8. Thus, for example, in the gag from *Blazing Saddles* discussed in "Entr'acte," the diegetic music we are ostensibly hearing from the on-screen orchestra that accompanies Cleavon Little's riding across the prairie was recorded in a studio.

9. See ALTMAN for one example of how a book-length typological treatment of the film musical might proceed: first through a variety of perspectives (genre, components, structure, style) and thence through broad types, of which he defines three: "the fairy-tale musical," "the show musical," and "the folk musical." For Altman, these are the three principal modes of make-believe, the stock and trade of musicals; thus, these three, respectively, allow key displacements: to another place, another body, and another time (p. 127).

10. One striking difference between film and stage versions directly involves MERM, as, for example, when many otherwise straightforward adaptations of stage musicals take the action "outside" while leaving the production of the film's musical component to the more gratifying and consistent acoustic world of the studio. This is especially evident in films that try to give more consistent reality to their scenic dimension (as in the 1955 *Oklahoma!*) or offer a fully elaborated scenic dimension that is nevertheless highly stylized (as in the 1955 *Guys and Dolls*). Yet, arguably, these adaptations do not on this account necessarily betray their stage versions any more than does the simple decision to turn them into films. Nor do other aspects of fidelity, such as remaining true to the original musical score, offer adequate measures of what is a much more complex relationship than it is generally understood to be,

although they can make a substantial difference. *The Music Man* (1962) is nearly faithful to its original musical score, yet it seems overall to be no more or less faithful than the film version of *Oklahoma!* which eliminates the critically important "Lonely Room." On the other hand, *Guys and Dolls*, which more obviously caters to the needs of its stars, might for this reason be judged by some as less than faithful. (I discuss all three of these, as stage shows, in chapter 6 of KNAPP1.) In some respects, however, translation between media is simply inadequate, rendering faithful adaptation difficult or impossible. However well realized, for example, the "Rock Island" train number in the filmed version of *The Music Man* cannot escape the generic realism of film to re-create the magic of a train's visualized rhythms forming the basis of a staged musical number. Despite these very important differences and difficulties, however, most audiences want to see—and will thus be predisposed to see—adaptations more as versions of the original stage versions than as independent artifacts.

11. Regarding the Freed Unit, see FORDIN and chapter 9 in MARMORSTEIN.

12. It would be some years before sound films caught up with the silents in terms of profitability, at least on the high end. According to a 1932 *Variety* article, four silent films—*Birth of a Nation* (1915), *The Big Parade* (1925), *Ben Hur* (1925), and *Way Down East* (1920)—had by that time equaled or out-grossed *The Singing Fool* ("Biggest Money Pictures," *Variety*, June 21, 1932). Claims of this kind are notoriously problematic, however, since much depends on how one defines the category, how accurate the information is, and when the measure is taken.

13. Berkeley's career in Hollywood as a choreographer (or "dance director") began in 1930, but he wasn't given the chance to direct until 1933, after the success of *42nd Street* (for which he was only choreographer). Regarding Berkeley's career and significance, see RUBIN-M.

14. The precise role of *The Merry Widow* in this renaissance remains in dispute. Some claim the film lost money, marking the end of European-style operetta films and setting up the American alternative, beginning with *Naughty Marietta*; others, however, see the success of *The Merry Widow*, after an earlier decline, as the beginning of the renewed success of operetta films. For a concise account of both views, see SARRIS, pp. 39–41.

15. Regarding the fall and rise of the movie musical in the 1930s, see chapters 5–9 of FEHR/VOGEL. The falloff in the popularity of film musicals did not mean, of course, that memorable musicals did not continue to be made. Among noteworthy examples from the early 1930s are a few operetta-based films by Lubitsch and Rouben Mamoulian, including the former's *The Smiling Lieutenant* (1931, with Maurice Chevalier and Claudette Colbert) and *One Hour with You* (1932, with Maurice Chevalier and Jeanette MacDonald, and codirected by George Cukor) and the latter's *Love Me Tonight* (1932, also with Maurice Chevalier and Jeanette MacDonald, and songs by Rodgers and Hart). Mae West began her film career in 1932, and the Marx Brothers continued to produce reasonably successful films throughout this period, although these all stood at some remove from the mainstream Hollywood musical. Within that mainstream, Busby Berkeley choreographed five musical films in 1932, and Frank Tuttle's *The Big Broadcast* (1932, with Kate Smith, Bing Crosby, the Mills Brothers, Cab Calloway, and the comedy team of George Burns and Gracie Allen) launched the subgenre of radio musicals, helping to establish the groundwork for the resurgence in the larger genre the following year.

16. *Singin' in the Rain* has many intriguing parallels with an earlier film that purports to tell the history of this era from an opposing standpoint: that of vaudeville's

demise, crushed by the onslaught of cheaper and more accessible Hollywood musicals and the Great Depression. The 1939 *Babes in Arms* (bearing almost no resemblance to the stage show by Rodgers and Hart, beyond borrowing three of its songs), directed by Busby Berkeley, was conceived as a vehicle for Mickey Rooney and Judy Garland and seems to celebrate a shade too raucously the latter's displacement of Shirley Temple as the most bankable "child star" of the day; the latter is directly parodied in the film as an obnoxious has-been. Like *Singin' in the Rain*, *Babes in Arms* was produced by Arthur Freed and uses many of the same tunes to establish the late-1920s time frame (all by Freed and therefore entailing no payments of royalties): "Broadway Melody," "Singin' in the Rain" (including a brief clip of the "raincoat" sequence—directed by Berkeley—to which the credit sequence of *Singin' in the Rain* pays homage), "Good Morning," "You Are My Lucky Star," and "Broadway Rhythm." Unlike *Singin' in the Rain*, *Babes in Arms* makes no attempt to underplay the importance of minstrelsy to this era and includes a painfully long blackface sequence with Rooney and Garland playing Mr. Tambo and Mr. Bones; this scene, coupled with Rooney's frenetically mugging performance throughout, makes the film such an embarrassment that its appearance in the same year as *The Wizard of Oz* seems incongruous, even if Margaret Hamilton plays much the same villainous role in each. Regarding the connection between *Singin' in the Rain* and minstrelsy, see my discussion of *Stormy Weather* later in this chapter.

17. Regarding the film's critical elevation, see WOLLEN, pp. 52–53.

18. Comden and Green hint rather broadly that Simpson is based on Freed in the introduction to COMDEN/GREEN (pp. 1–10), by making a big point of Freed's habit of calling them kids (p. 2), a habit shared by Simpson in the film. The "best feet forward" line—which would normally be "best foot forward"—if it had been given to a less earnest character such as Cosmo, might have come across as witty byplay, especially had it occurred in reference to the later conversion of *The Dueling Cavalier* to *The Dancing Cavalier*. Sam Goldwyn's "colorful" use of English included a penchant for unconsciously twisting common phrases, perhaps most famously in his oft-recounted phrase, "Include me out," which also evokes the image of ruthlessly—and often crudely—exercised dictatorial power.

19. Another fairly obvious parody figure in the film is Olga Mara (played by Judy Landon, described in the script as "an exaggeratedly exotic woman of the Jetta Goudal–Nita Naldi variety," but whose name more clearly recalls Theda Bara and Pola Negri). The male lead was conceived as a John Gilbert type, whose career was salvaged (unlike Gilbert's) from the wreckage of a badly improvised love scene ("I love you, I love you, I love you") through his reincarnation as a star of musicals. The original "It Girl" was Clara Bow. Possible models for Lina's combination of elegant appearance and fishwife accent include Norma Talmadge and Clara Bow.

20. Louise Brooks (1906–1985) was an American silent-film star who appeared in a brief series of European films between 1929 and 1930, most notoriously as Lulu (a prostitute) in *Der Büchse der Pandora* (Pandora's Box, G. W. Pabst, 1929, based, like Berg's unfinished 1935 opera *Lulu*, on Frank Wedekind's Lulu plays). Consigned to virtual exile by the Hollywood studio system in the 1930s, Brooks gradually became something of an intellectual's pinup girl and, for some, an icon of feminist defiance when she reemerged as a writer on film from the 1950s on. Her trademark page-boy hairstyle, copied here to establish Charisse's sluttish persona, would surface again in Liza Minnelli's portrayal of Sally Bowles in the 1972 film *Cabaret* (dir. Bob

Fosse) and Catherine Zeta-Jones's Velma Kelly in the 2002 film *Chicago*—the latter is discussed later in this chapter.

21. See KREUGER for an account of this era as distilled from *Photoplay*, including descriptions of the technologies of synchronized sound (e.g., pp. 2–3, 8–9, and 12–13) and accounts of "voice doubling" (what we now call dubbing or overdubbing; pp. 34–35). For a useful, somewhat revisionist account of the transition era between "silents" and "talkies," see part 1 of CAMERON.

22. As given in the script: "What's wrong with the way I talk? What'sa big idea—am I dumb or somethin'?"

23. The slowing down at the end, which seems to deepen Lina's final "Yes, yes, yes," could happen with both technologies. It would probably also make little difference that the sound-on-film technology at that time was magnetic (as in audiotapes) rather than optical, as in later technologies.

24. COMDEN/GREEN, p. 42. Although Berkeley didn't direct films until 1933, his first turn as film choreographer, in *Whoopee!* (1930), already introduced some of his trademark effects.

25. Taps in dancing sequences, however, were often overdubbed after they were filmed, as "Foleys" (that is, sound effects added after filming, named after sound-effects pioneer Jack Foley).

26. WOOD-R1 was the first major study to identify this trope in Hawks's films.

27. Interesting exceptions in mainstream Hollywood musicals are the Frank Sinatra roles, as sidekick to Gene Kelly, in *Anchors Aweigh* (George Sidney, 1945), *On the Town* (Stanley Donen and Gene Kelly, 1949), and *Take Me Out to the Ball Game* (Busby Berkeley, 1949). But the exception is mainly apparent; in each of these, while the sidekick dimension is safely grounded in an all-male occupation (armed forces or professional sports), and while the Sinatra character ends up heterosexually coupled, he begins the film as a sexual "innocent" who in effect "comes of age" (i.e., achieves heterosexual union) during the course of the film. But the Sinatra roles also point to the derivative status of the desexualized sidekick tradition, which forms a subset of the longer narrative tradition of flanking the main romantic story with one or more secondary stories, often offered as a comic version of the main story.

28. TINKCOM provides a broader consideration of a gay presence in Hollywood musicals, specifically within the Freed unit. In a related discussion in the same volume, COHAN discusses the "feminization" of dancing film stars, focusing on Fred Astaire.

29. Babington sees Levant's persona as deriving from his uncomfortable situation between classical and popular music (BABINGTON, pp. 33–34). The rueful narcissism of Levant's character in the film is especially evident in his imagined performance of the finale of Gershwin's Concerto in F, with himself playing each instrument, a conceit that may have had its origins in Buster Keaton's *The Playhouse* (1921), in which Keaton simultaneously takes on all the roles in a minstrel show.

30. The script reads, "Yes, Lina, you looked pretty good for a girl."

31. "Moses Supposes" is the only number in the film for which Comden and Green wrote the lyrics (Roger Edens wrote the music); it is not, however, a complete song by Tin Pan Alley standards.

32. Peter Wollen's observation that the story of the film derives in part from Hans Christian Andersen's *The Little Mermaid*—whose heroine also could sing but not dance, and whose voice was similarly at risk of being taken from her—provides an intriguing perspective on this dynamic; see WOLLEN, pp. 54–55. In "Body Talk"

(chapter 2 of SILVERMAN), Kaja Silverman takes the various dubbing episodes in the film as a point of departure for an extended discussion of "voice" in film. For a more practically oriented account of Reynolds's unpreparedness to dance opposite Kelly, see HIRSCHHORN, pp. 180–81.

33. "Make 'em Laugh" was newly written by Freed as a substitute for "Wedding of the Painted Doll" (which remains in the film as part of the "Hollywood Montage") and is rather obviously based on Cole Porter's "Be a Clown," sung by Gene Kelly and Judy Garland in Vincente Minnelli's *The Pirate* (1948). There are two famous stories concerning this number, both possibly apocryphal. When Kelly first heard the song, he reportedly asked, "Who's responsible for that bit of plagiarism?" (See CLOVER, p. 167n3, for a useful account of the song's "borrowing" from Porter.) And O'Connor, for whom the number became career defining, reportedly had to perform his bravura performance over again when it was discovered after the shoot that there was no film in the camera. Clover (CLOVER, p. 160) finds some components of this number symptomatic of whites' appropriation of blacks' dance moves (especially O'Connor's back flips off the wall, which are especially redolent of the Nicholas Brothers); see also GOTTSCHILD. The routine as a whole, however, derives from O'Connor's athletic vaudeville dancing, which included this kind of maneuver, and he recounts asking permission of one of the Three Stooges for another part of the routine (HIRSCHHORN, p. 184), which indirectly undermines Clover's claim that he "stole" from the Nicholas Brothers (who were, coincidentally, backup dancers for Kelly in *The Pirate*).

34. See p. 86 for a possible basis for this "step" in *Stormy Weather*. Peter Wollen argues for the more obvious "adolescent" interpretation (WOLLEN, pp. 17 and 27). Carol Clover discusses the stomping as part of the escalating violence of the scene, cut short by the appearance of a policeman, and relates this element to later filmic references to the number, in Kubrick's *A Clockwork Orange* (1971) and Michael Jackson's "Black or White" (*Dangerous: The Short Films*, 1993); see CLOVER, pp. 165–67 and 172–73, especially n53. My characterization of this moment as one of "dancing sublime" speaks to the substitution of a primitive ugliness for a conventional dancing grace or virtuosity, much as Beethoven's "sublime" moments are often his ugliest and most brutal.

35. Wind machines were not enough, however, to produce the phallic image of the upswept train; for that, they had to use airplane motors, against which Charisse had trouble keeping her balance; see HIRSCHHORN, p. 188.

36. This was a somewhat awkward solution to the problem that Reynolds simply could not have danced an extended ballet number; in practical terms as well as figurative, Charisse was indeed Reynolds's stunt double (see HIRSCHHORN, p. 186).

37. See WOLLEN, p. 55, for another account of Hollywood's role as a fantasy world. Wollen sees Hollywood as the linchpin that allows *Singin' in the Rain* to combine Rick Altman's three subgenres of film musicals: the show musical, the fairy-tale musical, and the folk musical (see note 9).

38. The references include, in order, a blackface "cannibal" scene as part of a pan across a variety of silent films being shot (Kelly actually speaks to one of the "cannibals," as if to clarify that he is in blackface), Cosmo's brief song snippet "my darling little mammy / Down in Alabamy" when Simpson mentions *The Jazz Singer* soon after, and Cosmo's later comic suggestion of "The Dueling Mammy" for the new musical title of *The Dueling Cavalier*. CLOVER cites these as emblems of a larger

guilt given covert voice in the film, pointing especially to its "borrowing" of specific African American dance tropes; see note 33 and further discussion later.

39. See KNIGHT for an analysis of black representation in American film during this period.

40. See chapter 10 in WOLL2 for a description of this practice.

41. A brief but useful account of this period and its effects on the American film industry may be found in WOLLEN, pp. 44–52.

42. See chapter 4 in KNIGHT for an extended discussion of these films. This short list does not include Disney's *Song of the South* (largely animated, and coming under heavy fire for its romanticizing of the South under slavery) or such mixed-race films as *Emperor Jones* (1933, dir. Dudley Murphy, with Paul Robeson) and *Imitation of Life* (1934, dir. John Stahl, with Claudette Colbert and Hattie McDaniel). Confirming Hollywood's expectations, such films either did not play in the South or had very short runs there. Intriguingly, Queenie's role in the 1936 *Show Boat* (dir. James Whale), eventually given to Hattie MacDaniel, may well have gone to a white woman in blackface (as it had been performed on Broadway) except for the fear of potential public outrage if a white actress were to be paired with Paul Robeson—this despite the show's concern for the brutality of miscegenation laws (see STANFIELD). For a general discussion of the persistence of blackface films in the 1930s, see ROGIN2. For a discussion of the ghettoizing of black performers within Hollywood films, see DYER1. For a discussion of the backlash against blacks in Hollywood that occurred after *Cabin in the Sky* and *Stormy Weather* (along with related films such as *The Negro Soldier, Crash Dive, Sahara,* and *Bataan,* all made in 1943), see LOTT2, p. 89.

43. Minnelli was an uncredited director on *Panama Hattie* (1942).

44. On the whole, however, *Cabin in the Sky* tends to temper its deployment of racially demeaning stereotypes; thus, the film also features Mantan Moreland in a minor role that eschews his usual "quivering coward" film persona, discussed later in the chapter.

45. Donald Bogle, following a standard set of conventions, identifies black players in Hollywood films according to stereotypical relational patterns to whites; see BOGLE. The particular designation for blacks who collaborated with and were obsequious to whites as "Uncle Toms" (or, as in Bogle, just "Toms") stems from Harriet Beecher Stowe's 1852 novel *Uncle Tom's Cabin.*

46. For an interesting analysis of "indefinite talk" routines, and in particular this one (but from a somewhat different perspective), see KNIGHT, pp. 110–19.

47. For another consideration of the connections between *Bamboozled* and *Stormy Weather* (along with other references in the former film), see KNIGHT, pp. 241–48. Among the seemingly odd omissions in *Bamboozled* and its voice-over commentary by director Spike Lee on the DVD is any reference to *Stormy Weather,* either as a model or as something to be satirized; see KNIGHT, pp. 243–44, for a discussion of this and other curious omissions.

48. Another odd contributor to the perseverance of minstrelsy was radio. According to Timothy D. Taylor, "advertising agencies, who produced most of the programs until after World War II, were so leery of offending audiences that they turned to older musics that they thought would be uncontroversial, unlike what they called jazz, which was controversial" (personal communication). Regarding the role of advertising in radio programming during this era more generally, see TAYLOR-T1.

49. Jews, especially in the 1920s and 1930s, also played a role in both perpetuating blackface and displacing blacks in the practice, as they, like the Irish in the nine-

teenth century, laid claim to an assimilated American whiteness by blacking up; see note 6.

50. BOGLE, pp. 47–48.

51. For a brief discussion of Robinson's dancing style (including this critique, which was first voiced by Fred Astaire), see DELAMATER, pp. 79–81.

52. See Stearns/Stearns, p. 183.

53. This was, however, cynically managed by the American command; the all-black 369th Infantry Regiment, the "Hellfighters," to which Jim Europe belonged, was the first American unit sent over. Europe's own career was tragically ended when, shortly after his triumphant return to America, he was killed by a disgruntled member of his band. For a concise account of Europe's salutary impact on the emergence of jazz into the mainstream, both in America and in France, see MAGEE, pp. 404–5. See also JACQUES, pp. 70–71; Jacques (somewhat oddly) sees *Stormy Weather* as "based loosely on Europe's life," and continues, regarding the film as a whole: "In my view it is the best film on a jazz musician ever made by Hollywood" (p. 70).

54. There is a curious assonance here between "Selina Robins" and "Serena Robbins," the latter a character in *Porgy and Bess*. Selina's decision to try for a career in Paris also reflects the latter's infatuation with American jazz and other black performing artists, part of the legacy of Jim Europe's performances there during the First World War. Oddly, *Stormy Weather* makes nothing of the principal reason Selina would have returned to America by the time America entered World War II: since mid-1940, Paris had been under the control of Nazi Germany.

55. This song, like "Diga Diga Do," was introduced in the stage revue *Blackbirds of 1928*, one of Robinson's greatest successes onstage.

56. Cf. Krin Gabbard's description of Waller's performance: "singing, playing, and feverishly exercising his lips and eyebrows, Waller proves that he can do several things at once while seeming to be involved with none. Everything seems to be an ironic aside about something else, including the solos of his drummer. . . . Throughout the film Waller maintains this trickster quality, never actually advancing the plot, always commenting from the side" (GABBARD1, p. 244). Gary Marmorstein, also writing about this scene, is more explicit about the sexual overtones: "few men of such girth have exuded such sexiness, a growling, mocking, eyebrow-bouncing sensuality that was ripe for the movies" (MARMORSTEIN, p. 309). Waller died shortly after the film was released, and this was his only featured appearance in a major film.

57. Calloway's performance style here, which also anticipates Sammy Davis Jr. in his appearances with the "Rat Pack," seems to derive its "feminine" dimension (as it will tend to appear to more recent audiences) both from a more fluid gestural vocabulary grounded in American black culture and from an ingratiating obsequiousness associated with "Toms" within Donald Bogle's categories of blackness as performed for whites (see BOGLE).

58. Calloway's commanding presence is greatly enhanced by the oversize "zoot suit" he wears through much of the extended number.

59. For another discussion of "Stormy Weather," see FRIEDWALD, pp. 280–307.

60. The most important example of this trend, as it affected the American musical, was probably Agnes de Mille's choreography for Rodgers and Hammerstein's *Oklahoma!* which opened in the same year that *Cabin in the Sky* and *Stormy Weather* were released. Dunham's style, dubbed early on as "*Ballet negre*," was informed by Caribbean and Brazilian dance.

61. Another vivid image of discomfiture—and another unacknowledged link to *Stormy Weather*—occurs when Dunwitty presents Mantan with Bill Robinson's dancing shoes and points out how unusual they are (Robinson used wooden soles, which is part of how he achieved his distinctive sound).

62. On this topic, see WOLL2 and JENKINS.

63. See KAUFMAN for an extended discussion of the film's stylized visual dimension (for example, the color scheme, discussed on p. 50).

64. Although the original consisted of eight stories, Benson added four more to make it an even dozen (covering a full year, month by month), publishing the lot as *Meet Me in St. Louis* in 1942 (New York: Random House). Although the book predated the film by two years, it nevertheless took its name from the anticipated film, which was then already in development. For a discussion of the "greeting-card" dimension of the film, especially as it extends to the framing of individual scenes, see KAUFMAN, p. 60.

65. Probably, this practice of trading verses of a song stems from staged opera and operetta; the device became a familiar feature of the late nineteenth-century American stage, when it became known as the vaudeville finale, although earlier examples may be found (for example, in Mozart's comic operas). Within filmic traditions, this kind of infectious "trading" of a song among many characters was a regular feature in Lubitsch's early operetta films, as, for example, in his 1929 *The Love Parade* and 1930 *Monte Carlo*; by then, it had dropped its earlier closing function and often took on the role of exposition. Already in 1932, the device was both roundly parodied by the Marx Brothers, who trade verses of "Everyone Says I Love You" (by Bert Kalmar and Harry Ruby) in Norman McLeod's *Horse Feathers*, and used to particularly good effect in Rouben Mamoulian's *Love Me Tonight*. The latter, with songs by Rodgers and Hart, uses the device three times: "Isn't It Romantic" is transmitted from a tailor (Maurice Chevalier) to a princess (Jeanette MacDonald) by way of the former's customer, a cab driver, a composer, a band of soldiers, and a Gypsy violinist; later, a reprise of Chevalier's "Mimi" is traded among several others in the princess's household; and, near the end, "The Son-of-a-Gun Is Nothing but a Tailor" is traded among most of the principals, a process that is then extended to include a framed bas-relief portrait and various groupings of the household domestics. What marks *Meet Me in St. Louis* as a departure is the degree of naturalness the device assumes, since all those who sing the title song might well have been singing it in just such circumstances as the ones being portrayed, albeit without the light orchestral underscore.

66. Tootie's two songs are actually linked thematically, since "Brighten the Corner" was a standard of the Women's Christian Temperance Union (WCTU). Thus, among Tootie's macabre interests is an apparent fascination with drunkenness.

67. In reality, of course, *The Merry Widow* came *after* the St. Louis Fair; see note 70 regarding more overt jumbling of dates in the film's re-creation of turn-of-the-century America.

68. Regarding the roles of "Little Egypt," the Chicago Fair, and the "Hootchy Cootch" in the development of American striptease, see SHTEIR, pp. 41–45.

69. To be sure, the song's composers, Bob Cole and J. Rosamond Johnson, stand somewhat apart from this tradition, as among the pioneering black writer-performers who strove to establish a viable African American presence on Broadway around the turn of the twentieth century. The song, too, is a cut above typical "coon" songs, being sophisticated in both its witty lyrics and its unusual musical derivation (from the spiritual "Nobody Knows the Trouble I've Seen"). For more on this pair and

their context, see RIIS1, pp. 26–28, 33–37, and 52–53. For an insightful appreciation of the song itself, see MAGEE, p. 393. Regarding its derivation from "Nobody Knows" and its emergence as a hit song, see WOLL1, pp. 19–21.

70. Nor does it really matter that a few of the songs weren't written yet, including the title song (which was introduced with the fair itself, in 1904), and "Brighten the Corner" (1912).

71. See the filmed interview footage included as part of the 1994 documentary *Meet Me in St. Louis: The Making of an American Classic* (Turner Home Entertainment), in the VHS tape release of *Meet Me in St. Louis* (Turner Entertainment Co. and Warner Home Video, 2000).

72. This cut results in a minor awkwardness in the final segment, since John's line in response to seeing the fair—"I liked it better when it was just a swamp"—has no earlier point of reference.

73. Both texts are given in KAUFMAN, p. 9, but rearranged to show substitutions. In a later, more familiar version, "From now on" replaces "Next year . . . all" in the second and fourth lines, "Here we are" replaces "Once again" in the fifth line, "are" and "gather" replace "were" and "will be" in the sixth line, "Through the years" replaces "Some day soon" in the seventh line, and the eighth line becomes "Hang a shining star upon the highest bough."

74. As recounted by Hugh Martin in *Meet Me in St. Louis: The Making of an American Classic*.

75. As interviewed in *Meet Me in St. Louis: The Making of an American Classic*.

76. Hitchcock used this term frequently to refer to the ostensible object of the characters' striving in his films, which is both central and entirely irrelevant to the dramatic action—hence, for example, the exact meaning of the coded snatch of melody in his 1938 *The Lady Vanishes* or the treaty clause in his 1940 *Foreign Correspondent*.

77. Especially in musicals; see KNAPP1, pp. 167, 193, and 332 (note 10).

78. The cancan from the latter is especially famous, and here it provides the musical basis for the song "Spectacular Spectacular."

79. The song had originally been intended for Luhrmann's *Romeo + Juliet* (1996) but wasn't used until *Moulin Rouge*.

80. The official lyric for the song is "Listen to my heart, can you hear it sing? / Telling me to give you everything."

81. At least, such was my observation at early screenings of the film.

82. Indeed, among recent discussions, David Savran's identification of a "postnaturalistic performance" dimension in queer theater resonates well with my extension of camp categories into a realm of exaggerated reality; see SAVRAN, p. 68.

83. Tinkerbell (from Disney's 1953 *Peter Pan*, made just before Marilyn Monroe became a star) was in fact modeled on Margaret Kerry. "The green fairy" (*La fée verte*) was a familiar codename for absinthe, the favorite intoxicant of fin-de-siècle Bohemians.

84. Woody Allen achieved a similar effect in his 1996 *Everyone Says I Love You*; the point there seems almost the opposite, however, since Allen attempts to naturalize song-based MERM, whereas the film version of *Chicago* draws a sharp distinction between "reality" and its razzle-dazzle variety of MERM.

85. Other models for Minnelli's portrayal, whether consciously or unconsciously chosen, included Marlene Dietrich's nightclub singer in *Der blaue Engel* (dir. Josef von Sternberg, 1930) and her own mother, Judy Garland (see MORRIS).

86. The "real-life" referent for "Roxie" is Roxie's conversation with Mama Morton (Queen Latifah), in which, curiously, Mama drops three names associated with "coon shouting": "You can be bigger than Sophie Tucker . . . bigger than Cantor and Jolson combined." The first of these names figures into the song and is surely the most relevant, since the character of Mama Morton derives partly from Sophie Tucker, who billed herself as the "last of the red-hot mamas." Thus, implicitly, Roxie conflates Mama and Sophie Tucker and sees her own future star billing as a triumph over the prison matron whom she must now bribe and otherwise kowtow to ("And Sophie Tucker will shit, I know, / To see her name get billed below / Roxie Hart"). But the casual dropping of Cantor's and Jolson's names, by a black performer (Queen Latifah) and in this context, seems gratuitous, except perhaps to underscore, however subtly, that Sophie Tucker's own persona was modeled directly on that of black blues singers, even if she dropped blackface from her act at a relatively early stage of her career.

87. Camp has many forms and dimensions, but on the most general level it nearly always involves a disjuncture between subject matter and performance, whether deliberate or the result of incompetence. By "extreme forms of camp," I mean those in which modes of performance swamp all other considerations.

88. See my discussion of *Cabaret* in chapter 9 of KNAPP1; see also MORRIS.

Chapter Three
Fairy Tales and Fantasy

1. I do not engage here with the more general questions of definition, origin, and dissemination of fairy tales; an excellent overview of those issues and their attendant controversies may be found in the introduction to DAVIDSON/CHAUDHRI.

2. See my discussion in KNAPP1, chapter 2. The fairy-tale component in *The Black Crook* derives from its two European models, Weber's *Der Freischütz* (1821) and *La biche au bois* (1865), the latter an imported *féerie* set to open in New York when its scheduled venue burned down. The féerie, a French ballet tradition based on fairy tales, was also an important tributary to the late nineteenth-century Russian ballet tradition; from the latter, Tchaikovsky's fairy-tale ballets *Swan Lake* (1875), *The Sleeping Beauty* (1888), and *The Nutcracker* (1891) rank among the most enduring of repertory works.

3. Gilbert and Sullivan, whose operettas were the first to enjoy widespread success in America, sometimes relied for their plots on magic or the supernatural (as had many of their French models), although only *The Sorcerer* (1877), *Iolanthe* (1882), and *Ruddigore* (1887) deal directly with such forces (along with *Thespis*, an early collaboration for which the music has been lost). More often, they relied on comic manipulations of language and reversals of social convention to manufacture their happy endings, conceived as a kind of dramatic double negative within their imagined kingdom of topsy-turvydom. Judging by Gilbert's persistence with his "lozenge" plot, there would have been a great deal more of the supernatural in their shows if Sullivan had not resisted.

4. See ALTMAN, chapter 6. Since operetta and dance musicals dominate his discussion of this type, actual fairy tale has almost no presence within the broader category that bears that name in Altman's typology.

5. Also figuring into this background was the contemporary American vogue for Wagner, whose operas trade heavily in the supernatural (see HOROWITZ-J).

6. Between 1929 and 1939, Disney released seventy-five of these short animated films, for which the guiding principle was that the musical score determined the action, rather than the reverse. It was especially in this series that the Disney studios developed a wide variety of techniques that prepared them to produce their full-length animated films. Regarding cartoon music in general, see GOLDMARK.

7. THOMAS/JOHNSTON.

8. This early series, although now much venerated, yielded diminishing returns at the box office, owing in large part to the onset of World War II. Later animated features from Disney that would eventually compete with the long-standing popularity of this early series include *Cinderella* (1950), *Alice in Wonderland* (1951), *Peter Pan* (1953), *The Lady and the Tramp* (1955), *Sleeping Beauty* (1959), *101 Dalmatians* (1961), *The Sword and the Stone* (1963), *The Jungle Book* (1967), *Robin Hood* (1973), *The Many Adventures of Winnie the Pooh* (1977), *The Little Mermaid* (1989), *Beauty and the Beast* (1991), *Aladdin* (1992), and *The Lion King* (1994).

9. *The Perils of Pauline* was a silent-film serial (a series of short episodes) in 1914, perhaps the most famous filmic damsel-in-distress narrative. "Dudley Do-Right" episodes were regular features of the television series *Rocky and His Friends* and its continuation as *The Bullwinkle Show*, whose framing spy narratives and "Fractured Fairy Tales" (narrated by film-musical veteran Edward Everett Horton) also contributed to its double appeal to children and to fetishized camp tastes.

10. This is not to deny the appeal of these types to women and children, who were, after all, their principal market audience.

11. I discuss *The Sound of Music* from a very different perspective in chapter 9 of KNAPP1.

12. The first gap reflects the dwarfs' consternation when they return home after Snow White's arrival; the second follows the elaborate sneeze with which Sneezy ends the celebratory "Silly Song."

13. Regarding the operetta basis for *Snow White*, see BANFIELD1, pp. 332–33.

14. At one stage in the planning, this was to have been made even more explicit, with Snow White's Prince as the Queen's newest victim (after he refuses to marry her or to acknowledge her as the most beautiful in the land); see HOLLISS/SIBLEY, p. 14.

15. The "answering-echo" device shows up occasionally in dramatic scenes, as well; thus, for example, when a despairing Alvin York in *Sergeant York* (Howard Hawks, 1941) shouts, "I can't do it!" he hears the resounding echo "Do it! Do it!"

16. The Grimm brothers (Jakob and Wilhelm) compiled their fairy tales in the early nineteenth century (1812, with many later additions and editions) in part as an expression of a budding German nationalism based on a mythologized medieval past. The two would also produce additional instruments to codify and preserve Germanic culture, including the *Deutsche Grammatik* (1819–1837, by Jakob) and, perhaps most important, the *Deutsches Wörterbuch* (1852–1860, with revisions still continuing today), a vast compendium of German words and expressions that explores how they are rooted in culture and legend. Although the Brothers Grimm have achieved the status of authority, their beliefs regarding the origin of fairy tales, and their significance for nationalist thought, were largely erroneous, even if highly influential; see BLAMIRES.

17. *Snow White*'s more actively involved birds may have been borrowed from *Cinderella*, where they act in part as a conduit between Cinderella and her mother.

This is a traditional role for birds, who often seem to bear cryptic messages "from above" or have other religious significance; thus, in the Brothers Grimm version of *Snow White*, the birds are implicitly a token of divine intervention. Notably, all the musicals considered in this chapter involve interactions with animals, although only *Snow White* and *Into the Woods* follow older traditions (the latter because it, too, goes back to the Brothers Grimm).

18. "Music in Your Soup" is another interesting exception that tends—because the song was dropped—more to prove this point than to dispute it; clever as the song is, the timing for the sequence is overwhelmed by the fact that the song comprises a full AABA structure, completing itself before Snow White even reacts to the dwarfs' uncivilized behavior. It thus presents uncivilized behavior within a "civilized" structure that is generally reserved for Snow White herself or to show her influence. (This partly animated sequence is included in the "Platinum Edition" DVD release of 2001.)

19. We see Snow White's death only indirectly, reflected in the storm that breaks as she bites into the apple and through the reactions of the Queen-Witch as she watches Snow White die.

20. Disney animated films have often been thought to include subliminal messages; many seem a plausible "acting out" by animators unable to resist the temptation, but many others seem far-fetched. Among the most commonly noted "messages" from Disney animators are the spelling of "sex" by a dust cloud in *The Lion King*, Jessica Rabbit's "flashing" in *Who Framed Roger Rabbit* (1988), and a sexually aroused clergyman in the first wedding scene of *The Little Mermaid*.

21. I wish to thank Elizabeth Upton for sharing her paper, "Music and the Aura of Reality in Walt Disney's *Snow White and the Seven Dwarfs*" (UPTON2), prior to publication. The "uncanny valley" was first observed in 1978 by Masahiro Mori at the Tokyo Institute of Technology and is succinctly described by Dave Bryant in BRYANT; see also MORI and REICHARDT.

22. Implicitly, and completely consistent with the events of the story, Glinda is cynically using Dorothy, setting her up either to kill the Wicked Witch of the West or die trying. The film's apparent endorsement of this reprehensible strategy is appalling, even if neither the strategy nor the film's endorsement of it is stated explicitly.

23. Gregory Maguire's moving novel *Wicked: The Life and Times of the Wicked Witch of the West* (MAGUIRE) has served to reinforce this switch of sympathies from Glinda to the Wicked Witch of the West, by making the latter seem the victim of magic, genetics, and the Wizard's Fascistic despotism, with Glinda devolving into little more than a boot-licking "good little girl." This reworked dynamic was only partly retained in the recent musical version of the novel (Stephen Schwartz and Winnie Holzman, 2003).

24. The Stonewall Rebellion was a three-day riot that began as a routine confrontation between police and homosexuals at the Stonewall Inn on Christopher Street, New York City, and became the locus for gay activism in major cities across America. It is generally seen as a decisive moment in the then-emergent gay rights movement.

25. The Winkies' deepness of voice, like the Munchkins' high-pitched voices, was produced by recording at one pitch and replaying at another, at that time a highly innovative technique; see HARMETZ, pp. 97–98. The indistinctness of the Winkies' chant undoubtedly stems from this process; their chant (according to the script, "O—Ee—Yah! Eoh—Ah!"), however memorable, is in any case not supposed to be intelligible, although it sounds vaguely like the sailors' (or boatmen's?) "Yo, heave ho."

26. During the Munchkinland sequence, flowers open to reveal concealed Munchkins (thus, "flower children"), and during the Emerald City sequence, a horse changes color several times.

27. This device was itself borrowed from Ted Eshbaugh's 1933 short animated version of *The Wizard of Oz*.

28. For a more extended discussion of "Over the Rainbow," see FORTE1, pp. 231–36.

29. "Home, Sweet Home," also known as "There's No Place Like Home," comes from English composer John Howard Payne's opera *Clari, the Maid of Milan* (1823).

30. Another frequently offered explanation for the number being dropped is that the reference was unintentional, since the jitterbug dance craze supposedly occurred only after the song was written. But such claims are simply false. Cab Calloway recorded "The Jitterbug" in 1934, and the dance craze itself dates back to at least 1932 (it was basically a rechristening of the 1927 "Lindy Hop," named after Charles Lindberg's solo "hop" across the Atlantic that year; the name "Jitterbug" had effectively replaced "Lindy Hop" well before 1937). Although the number was cut, the Witch's later instructions to her flying monkeys incongruously include the line "I sent a little insect on ahead to take the fight out of them."

31. Ironically, the animators of *Snow White and the Seven Dwarfs* had worked in the opposite direction, trying to achieve a more naturalistic coloring than was typical of cartoons.

32. This kind of saucy wordplay has some history also in musical comedy; thus, in Ernst Lubitsch's *Monte Carlo* (1930): "He's an ass / he's an ass / he's a nasty-tempered brute." More generally, the device relates to the more "adult" tradition of the echo song, discussed earlier in relation to "I'm Wishing" (in *Snow White*; see note 15), but attaches its puns and other verbal wit to the first syllables of phrases rather than the last.

33. "Over the Waves" (from the 1891 collection *Sobre las olas*) is the only piece by the Mexican composer Juventino Rosas (1868–1894) that still has currency today (sometimes as "George Washington Bridge"); ironically, its very familiarity leads many to assume it to be by a better-known composer, such as Strauss or Waldteufel.

34. While it may be assumed that the clarification of Mr. Banks's line of work (unclear in the books) responds first of all to his surname, the film's resonance with *It's a Wonderful Life*, which in the early 1960s had yet to emerge as a perennial "Christmas" film, is greatly enhanced by the importance of Mr. Banks's profession to the plotting of *Mary Poppins*. Given Mr. Banks's centrality to the denouement, reinforced by this resonance with *It's a Wonderful Life*, it is worth noting that the 2004 London stage adaptation of *Mary Poppins*, based on the Disney film but with additional songs by George Stiles and Anthony Drewe (produced by Cameron Mackintosh and directed by Richard Eyre and Matthew Bourne), greatly expands on Mr. Banks's back story.

35. *It's a Wonderful Life* cheats as shamelessly as *Mary Poppins* in allowing George's personal redemption to be echoed professionally, even if in the former film that redemption is more obviously earned by a demonstrated professional competency.

36. Hidden in this lyric is one of *Mary Poppins*'s many oblique references to Christianity, in the "transubstantiation" of bread and water into tea and cakes; see related discussions below. I wish to thank Elizabeth Morgan for bringing this connection to my attention.

37. The echoing "Tuppence" evokes the concluding line of what is probably the most familiar folk song based on street cries, "Molly Malone": "Cockles and mussels, alive, alive-o." Regarding the costermonger or "street cries" musical tradition, see chapter 1, p. 35 and p. 381, note 25.

38. Ann Hould-Ward, who designed the costumes, balanced the aims of James Lapine, Tony Straiges (whose set was inspired by traditional fairy-tale book illustrations), and the quality of Sondheim's music: "Stephen [Sondheim] took ideas for songs from the characters he saw in my renderings. In the same way, I can often know what a costume needs to be by listening to what his music is doing" (quoted in MANKIN, p. 59). Stephen Banfield hears the influence of "Ravel's Beast in *Ma mère l'oye*" ("Mother Goose") in "Hello, Little Girl"; see BANFIELD2, p. 385. The "foreboding" music that introduces the Wolf and reappears when Red Ridinghood arrives at her Grandma's cottage evokes (partly through Jonathan Tunick's orchestration) the "wolf" music from Prokofiev's *Peter and the Wolf*. Regarding the sexual dimension of "Hello, Little Girl" and "I Know Things Now" (with Little Red Ridinghood) and Jack's "Giants in the Sky," see MILLER-S3, pp. 116–18. As is commonly noted, the story of Little Red Riding Hood (along with many a fairy tale) is, at bottom, a parable about sex.

39. With a number of the stories, there are several different versions, but allegiance to some kind of authority is taken to be necessary in order for *Into the Woods* to remain true to its premise. Its version of Cinderella, for example, follows the story as told by the Brothers Grimm, with a three-evening festival and gold slippers (although her dress and footwear change each night in Grimm) and with her stepsisters mutilating their feet and, in the end, being pecked blind by Cinderella's birds. The now more familiar version, involving only one evening and glass slippers, and with a more benign treatment of the stepsisters, owes its popularity largely to the 1950 Disney film. The notions of "authenticity" and "definitive" as applied to fairy tales, though widely believed in, are highly problematic, since it is in their nature, owing to varied means of transmission and dissemination, to change considerably over time. Cinderella has been traced back to ninth-century China and even further (i.e., Herodotus); already in the nineteenth century Marian Roalfe Cox (in her 1893 *Cinderella*) identified "345 variants [of Cinderella] from every part of the world, summarized and systematically arranged according to the various redactions" (Reidar Th. Christiansen, as quoted in SCHAEFER, p. 145; see also ANDERSON).

40. This assumed profile of fairy tales, which regards them as primarily for children and involving moral lessons, is of fairly recent vintage, which becomes obvious when one reads more deeply into the many older collections, that is, beyond the more familiar stories. It is precisely because most fairy tales were *not* originally meant to carry this kind of moralizing weight that Lapine and Sondheim find such easy purchase in calling this dimension of the genre into question. For a cogent discussion of modern mutations of fairy tales, see SHIPPEY.

41. Sondheim reports that these songs were part of Lapine's concept: "Jim had this notion of 'psychological songs,' that instead of dealing with the facts, these songs should describe the psychological changes they were going through as a result of their adventures" (MANKIN, p. 64). Scott Miller notes the tendency of these songs to be in the second person, which he identifies as a means of pulling the audience into the action; see MILLER-S3, p. 113.

42. His death coincides with—and is a convenient distraction from—the Witch's transformation into a beautiful young woman. In case this latter-day "transformation scene" might have kept us from paying proper attention to its supporting distractions, the Narrator's first words immediately following are "And so the old man died."

43. For more extended discussions of "No More," see BANFIELD2, pp. 390–92 and 409–10.

44. According to Sondheim, Cinderella's "I wish" was the originating motive for the entire show, not because Cinderella is the main character, but because "*wishing* is the key character"; see HOROWITZ-M, pp. 81–83 (quotation from p. 83).

45. See also BANFIELD2, pp. 285–87, regarding the interrelationships among these songs; MILLER-S3, pp. 111–12, provides a useful summary of the show's central motives and their recurrences. Sondheim explains the way his initial plan to identify each character with a theme and instrument grew into this less tidy interweaving of related motives as an outgrowth of his decision to use "I wish" as an initiating gesture (see the previous note): "Once you do that, it dictates a lot. . . . They all have little echoes of each other. This turned out to be a very valuable decision, because Lapine really wanted many of the songs not to end, but to drift into dialogue. So to prevent a truly frustrated feeling of coitus interruptus, when you hear something you've heard before there's a certain satisfaction, even if it doesn't end" (HOROWITZ-M, p. 84). Perhaps even more to the point are his comments quoted in MANKIN, p. 60: "I decided to use musical ideas not as developmental *leit motifs,* but in the functional way you would use modular furniture. The same theme becomes an inner voice, an accompaniment, a counterpoint. It may be fragmented, but it is not really developed."

46. Despite its varied uses in the show, Sondheim in an early interview referred to this motive as the "bean theme," and the designation has stuck; see, for example, HOROWITZ-M, pp. 81–90 (especially p. 84), and BANFIELD, p. 395. Scott Miller calls this motive the " 'danger' leitmotive" (MILLER-S3, p. 111); while his ability to link the motive to either danger or potential danger works to some extent, it does not really hold up under scrutiny, since everything in the show links readily to potential danger, and not all references to danger involve this motive.

47. See BANFIELD2, pp. 395–99, regarding further permutations of this motive. Again, Sondheim's motivation for manipulating this theme, and for calling attention to it, is revealing; for him, as related in HOROWITZ-M, pp. 84–86, the important thing is the interconnectivity itself, deriving mostly from simply recalling motives, rather than those motives' actual signification (which he flatly denies, for example, regarding the inversion of the motive for the line "People make mistakes" in "No One Is Alone," p. 86). Making performers aware of this kind of process, he believes, will give them focus: "And just that awareness will affect how they approach the show, even if they don't utilize it in any way. I mean, how are you going to utilize that knowledge if you're an actor, or whatever? But to know it is important" (p. 85).

48. For a cogent discussion of this fragmentary dimension of the score, see BANFIELD2, pp. 406–7.

49. To be sure, sometimes this kind of reconsideration happens in a way consistent with leitmotivic conventions, as when the Baker's Wife, being seduced by Cinderella's Prince, sings "This is ridiculous, / What am I doing here? / I'm in the wrong story" to the "festival" motive—which, indeed, belongs specifically to Cinderella's story and not to hers.

Chapter Four
Idealism and Inspiration

1. "Old Man River" is from Kern and Hammerstein's *Show Boat* (1927); "You'll Never Walk Alone" from Rodgers and Hammerstein's *Carousel* (1945); "Climb Ev'ry Mountain" from the latter's *The Sound of Music* (1959); "If Ever I Would Leave You" from Lerner and Loewe's *Camelot* (1960); "On the Street Where You Live" from the latter's *My Fair Lady* (1956); and "So in Love" from Cole Porter's *Kiss Me, Kate* (1948). For an extended treatment of how performance matters in inspirational numbers (whether heard or performed, publicly or privately), see MILLER-DA2; for a related discussion regarding the inspirational and self-actualizing dimension of musicals, see WALL.

2. *Pippin* (music and lyrics by Stephen Schwartz) begins with the beguiling "Magic to Do" and the idealism of youth, but proceeds as a series of disillusionments, partly rescued in the end through Pippin's escape to a simple rural life. *Pippin*, whose trajectory as described is nearly identical to that of *Candide* (1956, discussed in chapter 7), was initially a much greater success than *Candide* and probably helped pave the way for the growing success of *Candide* in revival.

3. Elizabeth Upton has traced the tradition for brass fanfares similar to this triadic motive to serve, if anachronistically, as the modern sound track for evocations of the courtly and heroic medieval. I wish to thank her for sharing a copy of her paper, "Hollywood Knights: Film Music and Medievalism" (UPTON1).

4. I discuss *The Music Man* in chapter 6 of KNAPP1.

5. Hence, George Bernard Shaw's *Pygmalion*, based dually on Cinderella and the Greek myth of Pygmalion and Galatea; and T. H. White's *The Once and Future King*, a latter-day retelling, in a child-oriented idiom, of the myriad stories that had long been accumulating around the figure of King Arthur. For discussions of *Camelot*'s derivation from White, see MILLER-S2, pp. 3–4, and SWAIN, pp. 215–16.

6. Respectively, the sidekicks were Colonel Pickering and King Pellinore (both originally played by Robert Coote), and the hit tunes were "On the Street Where You Live" and "If Ever I Would Leave You"; for other parallels between the shows, see MILLER-S2, pp. 1–2, and MORDDEN7, pp. 24–25.

7. In fact, the impetus seems to have come from Mr. Television himself, Ed Sullivan, and happened to coincide with substantial revisions to the show just after its director Moss Hart had recovered from a serious illness; see LERNER3, pp. 244–46; LEES, pp. 201–2; and MORDDEN7, p. 28.

8. For a moving account of how *Camelot* became identified with Kennedy's presidency, and of how that ultimately affected the show's reception, see LERNER3, pp. 250–52. Because Jacqueline Kennedy's interview is the first public record of the connection, there are some grounds for thinking that she may have exaggerated Kennedy's special attachment to the show, making his association with *Camelot* little more than a retrospective wish.

9. The opening operetta basis aligns the show with the Camelot projected in Rodgers and Hart's 1927 *A Connecticut Yankee*, a commercially successful crossbreed between musical comedy and operetta based on Mark Twain's *A Connecticut Yankee in King Arthur's Court* (1889), which was revived (with only modest success) in 1943.

I follow the show's nonstandard spelling, "Guenevere," which may have been chosen for phonetic reasons, and which seems to be a cross between the more common "Guinevere" and "Guenever," the spelling T. H. White uses in *The Once and Future King.*

10. Precisely this harmonic configuration, combined with ceremonial bagpipe effects, military drums, and "primitive" grace-note figures, will return at the end of the overture, which closes, in full majestic pageantry, with the ceremonial music in the first-act finale (where Lancelot is knighted; the act closes, however, with Arthur's propositions/resolution quoted later in the text).

11. Octatonic music employs a collection of eight pitches, derived by alternating whole steps and half steps; octatonicism (although so named only much later) played an important role in Russian music of the nineteenth and early twentieth centuries (especially in the music of Rimsky-Korsakov, Musorgsky, Tchaikovsky, and Stravinsky) and also for the French "Impressionists" (most notably, Ravel and Debussy) and the composers they influenced in both England and America. Loewe here uses the collection consisting of the eight pitches, E, F, G, G♯, B♭, B, D♭, D; the three statements of the triadic motive use precisely seven of these pitches (E–G♯–B, G–B–D, B♭–D–F), capturing the eighth (D♭) with the subsequent modulation to that key. The phrases that follow the triadic motive do not stay within the octatonic collection, although they briefly continue its characteristic sequential motion.

12. The harmonic language of *Camelot* derives directly from procedures that evolved in the late nineteenth and early twentieth centuries, across many traditions (including, besides the already-mentioned Russian and French composers, Wagner, Brahms, Dvořák, and Grieg) that sought to merge advanced harmonic practice with evocations of the primitive, the past, and the supernatural. Enharmonic relations—in which, for example, an A♯ might suddenly become a B♭, the same basic pitch but with a different significance—lie at the heart of such "magic" or transformative harmonic manipulations.

13. Originally, the latter involved erecting an invisible wall around Arthur; this use of magic is often eliminated in revivals, where instead Mordred, as in the 1967 film version of the show, tricks Arthur into staying in the forest in order to "prove" to Mordred that there is nothing between Lancelot and Guenevere.

14. The descending tetrachord is a familiar bass figure, often used as an ostinato, or (as here) to simulate harmonic motion without actually going anywhere. The figure most typically moves down from the tonic to the dominant and comes in three main "flavors": major mode (e.g., C–B–A–G), minor mode (C–B♭–A♭–G), and chromatic (C–B–B♭–A–A♭–G). This instance uses the minor-mode tetrachord in a major-mode context, a fairly common device that heightens the effect of harmonic motion. As an ostinato and in a minor-mode context, and especially in its chromatic or partly chromatic varieties, the descending tetrachord provides a traditional basis for laments.

15. As Scott Miller notes, a further link between the two opening songs is the chromatic series of parallel triads that both ends Arthur's song and begins Guenevere's (MILLER-S2, p. 17); in each case, the gesture clearly relates to the fact that both have taken flight from their responsibility to go through with their planned marriage.

16. This madrigal—one of the few songs in the show actually to address chivalric idealism, yet ironically left off the cast recording—has little, if anything, to do with the historical genre of madrigal, which flowered in England during Shakespeare's time, a period much later than that of Arthur, but which has long stood, like lowered

leading tones, for a fondly remembered musical past. Although the French lyric seems meant to be understood as equivalent to the English, it corresponds only to the final part of the English "translation": "Always I've made the same wishes, / On earth a goddess, in heaven a God. / A man desires for his happiness / On earth a goddess, in heaven a God."

17. Cf. Scott Miller's discussion in MILLER-S2, p. 20.

18. Much of the achievement for shaping this number belongs to the orchestrator, Robert Russell Bennett, just as Ravel's orchestration lies behind the success of similarly shaped works such as *La valse* and *Boléro*. Bennett, whose sure hand with the Broadway pit orchestra was central to the achievements of the so-called golden era of the Broadway musical, singles out this number in his discussion of the show in BENNETT, p. 237.

19. See, for example SWAIN, p. 218, and MILLER-S2, pp. 21–22; for a nearly opposite view, see MORDDEN7, p. 25.

20. In *Don Quixote*, Aldonza is a peasant girl, not a whore, although whores are not lacking among those whom Don Quixote addresses as "Lady." Moreover, *Don Quixote* explicitly critiques the substitution of a knight's Lady for the Christian God in prayer, both from the standpoint of its violation of Christian tenets and for the impossible demands it places on its objects of veneration. While *Man of La Mancha* (like *Camelot*) addresses the latter objection to the tenets of chivalrous love (i.e., in the lyrically off-balance 7/8 of Aldonza's "What Does He Want of Me?"), it does not address the former. In "Dulcinea," Don Quixote repeatedly equates his Lady with the divine: "Half a prayer, half a song. . . . I see heaven when I see thee. . . . And thy name is like a prayer an angel whispers." Moreover, this idealization is later endorsed, if obliquely, by the Padre, in "To Each His Dulcinea"; see further discussion in the text.

21. Perhaps also, the turn to Ravel as a model may have stemmed from Ravel's larger concern for Spanish subjects late in his career; after *Boléro*, he contemplated writing music for a film based on Cervantes's life before turning instead to write *Don Quichotte à Dulcinée*, which was his last completed composition.

22. The idealist images of this song stem directly from *Don Quixote*, from the unaccompanied songs sung, just before dawn, by a love-struck muleteer's boy, as Quixote himself stands knightly vigil in the inn's courtyard (book 1, chapter 43). In the first of the boy's two songs, his "mariner of love" is "Guided by a distant star," knowing "not where she leads" and sailing "perplexed, confused"; in the second, "sweet hope" tames "th'impossible," inspiring the singer to "strive to reach [his] heaven" from earth. In blending the two, and placing the resulting song within the sensibility of Quixote rather than the boy, *Man of La Mancha* also replaces the basic image of the guiding star, as a navigational tool, with the "unreachable" star. This perhaps unconscious shift makes the image more relevant for 1960s audiences, who would have been less familiar with an earlier age's navigational reliance on stars and more familiar with the rather quixotic quest, just under way in the mid-1960s, to conquer space—a quest emblematically as important to the United States' world positioning as Spain's waning dominance of the seas during Cervantes's lifetime (Spain's vaunted armada was defeated by the British in 1588). Quotations here are from Edith Grossman's translation (New York: Harper Collins, 2003, pp. 374–76); an annotation after the second poem reads: "Martín de Riquer indicates that this lyric (and other poems inserted in the text) was composed by Cervantes years before he wrote *Don Quixote* and set to music in 1591 by Salvador Luis, a singer in the

chapel choir of Philip II." I wish to thank Elisabeth LeGuin for bringing these songs to my attention.

23. Many online fans belong to a group called the League of the Scarlet Pimpernel, whose website is still operational as of this writing; see http://www.thepimpernel.com, especially http://www.thepimpernel.com/html/league.shtml (accessed July 2, 2004).

24. Baroness Orczy (1865–1947), the Hungarian-born daughter of composer-conductor Felix Orczy, was both an artist and a writer. *The Scarlet Pimpernel* began its public life in 1903 as a play coauthored by her husband, Montague Barstow, whose success facilitated publication of the first of a series of books beginning in 1905, later made into a successful film starring Leslie Howard, Raymond Massey, and Merle Oberon (1934, with several spin-offs and remakes). Fondness for the kind of double role in *The Scarlet Pimpernel*, involving a hero who plays the fool, became a familiar operetta trope, as, for example, in Romberg, Hammerstein, and Harbach's 1926 *The Desert Song*. Baroness Orczy's books—unlike the Broadway show and the earlier films—took for granted a pro-aristocracy bias, from which arises the premise of English aristocrats helping French aristocrats escape the excesses of the uncivilized masses, who had seized control of Paris during the French Revolution. Later versions of the story, especially in America, tend to ignore this bias, sometimes substituting an anti-French sentiment while focusing mainly on the clever ruses by which its hero rescues imperiled innocents deep in enemy territory. Although America's response to the French Revolution has been a complicated affair, many of the latter's ideals (if not its realities) have generally been understood as reasonably compatible with those of the American Revolution; among these is a democratic, anti-aristocratic impulse (even if the help the Revolutionaries in America received from France—specifically from the Marquis de Lafayette—was aristocratic in origin).

25. Concerning the show's fans, Douglas Sills reported, "I was very willing to spend whatever energy it took to make the audiences feel respected, regarded, accommodated, enjoyed, cared after, and that means spending an hour, an hour and a half outside the stage door every night on top of my job." And, concerning the fans' devotion to the show, he went on, "I guess . . . they must feel regarded, otherwise why would they come back? You don't go to someplace where you're being disregarded or disrespected. . . . I'll try to make time for them backstage, make exceptions to the rules, make the boundaries of my personal life flexible so that I will talk to them afterwards, make eye contact, remember their names, remember what they're doing in their lives . . . you try and remember them as you would want to be remembered if you were making repeat visits. I think that's why they come back." And, finally, he explained his often risk-taking ad libs in terms of "Danger. That's what . . . people that are coming back more than once want to see. . . . Why do we want to hear the tenor sing those high notes? 'Cause you want to know if he's going to crack. . . . It's a high wire. . . . I think that's the whole point." (Quoted from an interview with Nancy Rosati, http://www.talkinbroadway.com/spot/sills1.html; accessed July 2, 2004.)

26. Post-Stonewall, the homosexual closet surrounding Broadway musicals has, of course, been opened considerably, but this complicated process still seems, thirty-five years later, only well begun. Part of the reason for the tenacity of the closet concerns the pleasures it offers, which are presumably at risk as the need for the closet dissipates. These pleasures include the closet's indulgence in camp, its air of

secrecy, its sense of aesthetic superiority, and so on—all of which *The Scarlet Pimpernel* exploits shamelessly.

27. "Believe" was replaced by a reworked "You Are My Home" in later versions of the show.

28. Later versions of the show reverse this dynamic in a later reprise of "Into the Fire," in which the group rouses a dispirited Percy back to action.

29. Both "Storybook" and "You Are My Home" were moved to the beginning of the show in the later versions, with "Storybook" reprised in the second act and, as noted, "You Are My Home" reworked as a wedding song, replacing "Believe."

30. I discuss the intertwining of compliment and insult in "You're the Top" in KNAPP1, p. 92.

31. Although folk based rather than fairy based, Stravinsky's ballet *The Rite of Spring* (1913), subtitled *Pictures from Pagan Russia*, also uses this trope, ending with a "Sacrificial Dance" in which the Chosen One dances herself to death.

32. Even more troubling are the parallels between the implied racial dynamic in *Once More, with Feeling* and that of the Disney cartoon short *The Goddess of Spring* (1934), in which the title character, who dances in a balletic style, is abducted by a devil-like character dressed in red and forced to become Queen in Hades, where fierce black creatures dance to jazz music. As for Sweet's oversize "Zoot suit," it, too, recalls tropes of black American musical styles; cf. Cab Calloway in *Stormy Weather*, discussed in chapter 2.

33. This song alludes to both *Hair*'s "Where Do I Go" and *Sweet Charity*'s "Where Am I Going?"; like the latter, it offers a blend of confusion and despair ultimately rescued by a shift of focus to something more hopeful.

Chapter Five
Gender and Sexuality

1. Judith Butler has made a particularly influential case for the centrality of performance in gender formation; see BUTLER, especially pp. 16–25 and 134–41.

2. RUSSO is a particularly useful resource on this subject; see also the related 1995 documentary (*The Celluloid Closet*). As Russo states regarding a period spanning most of the two decades around Stonewall, "In twenty-two of twenty-eight films dealing with gay subjects from 1962 to 1978, major gay characters onscreen ended in suicide or violent death" (p. 52).

3. For accounts of *Rocky Horror* and *Hedwig* that are mostly consonant with those given here (but which appeared only after I had completed this book), see PERAINO, pp. 233–40 and 246–51.

4. See, for example, Geoffrey Block's discussion of Berlin and Porter in the wake of Rodgers and Hammerstein (BLOCK2, pp. 179–80).

5. Although Porter's *Anything Goes* has also been much revived, it has been much *revised* in the process, to the extent that the show has become little more than a pretext for reviving the show's songs, most often with an admixture of additional songs from other shows.

6. Andrea Most sees the dialectic between *Annie Get Your Gun* and *Oklahoma!* in even starker terms: "As if in direct response to *Oklahoma!*, [*Annie Get Your Gun*] rejects claims of naturalness, instead firmly and unequivocally insisting that America

is *theater*, and that only those who understand and embrace America's inherent theatricality are destined for success" (Most1, p. 119; italics hers).

7. See Knapp1 for discussions of these two themes in *Show Boat* (pp. 185–94) and of *Oklahoma!*'s disregard for the state's American Indian heritage (pp. 122–34).

8. Cf. Andrea Most's discussion of the gendered component of identity-formation in the show (Most1, pp. 140–52). Most convincingly places Annie's gender crossings in the context of the post–World War II era, when women who had during the war taken on jobs traditionally understood as men's (working in factories and the like) were returning, often unwillingly, to more traditional feminine roles and behavior (pp. 142–43).

9. Depending on how this scene is played, Frank is either oblivious to Annie's attraction to him or teasing her unmercifully about it; in either case, his subsequent behavior confirms that what he sings is consistent with his actual feelings.

10. Although the precise dates for the action of *Annie Get Your Gun* are not specified, they would most likely not mesh well with this stylistic division, since Annie Oakley joined Cody's Wild West Show in 1885, at the age of twenty-five. Even if none of the songs in the show actually *is* in ragtime—mostly, they use a fairly generic march-derived idiom—we are clearly meant to think of the waltz idiom of "The Girl That I Marry" as old-fashioned, which it would not have been in 1885.

11. Personal communication.

12. The effect of blackface in this number is especially apparent in the mostly inadequate 1950 film version of the show. To some extent, poking fun at "hillbillies," or poor southern or Appalachian whites, served functionally, along with cartoons, to displace blackface minstrelsy as the latter's use gradually declined across the 1930s and 1940s. In the latter development, Al Capp's popular comic strip *Li'l Abner* (1934–1977) figured prominently and may be seen as a specific influence behind this number and others in *Annie Get Your Gun*; it would later serve as the direct basis for a musical in Gene de Paul, Johnny Mercer, Norman Panama, and Melvin Frank's 1956 *L'il Abner*. Philip Gentry sees the thrust of such films as *Annie Get Your Gun* and the derivative *Calamity Jane* (1953, with Doris Day) as describing a path toward whiteness, which becomes a matter of both visual and vocal presentation. In "Doris Day, *Calamity Jane*, and the Sound of Whiteness" (unpublished paper), Gentry usefully extends the ground-breaking work of Richard Dyer on this subject; see especially Dyer5 and Dyer1.

13. This song, like "I'm an Indian Too," is often cut in revivals.

14. Annie sings "Moonshine Lullaby" with train porters as backup, which both helps "naturalize" the faux-blues idiom and serves once again to demonstrate her easy affinity with marginalized groups.

15. Andrea Most demonstrates how thoroughly this element penetrates the action and dialogue of *Annie Get Your Gun* as well, in a wide-ranging discussion that touches also on the close relationship posited by the show between pose and identity; see her "The Apprenticeship of Annie Oakley, or, 'Doin' What Comes Natur'lly,'" in Most1. See also her related discussions of the scene when Annie concedes defeat (pp. 148–52), discussed later in the text.

16. See Wolf1 for an excellent discussion of the myriad ways in which Merman and Martin, along with Julie Andrews and Barbra Streisand, have, through their careers, performing personae, and private lives, often run against the grain of expected heterosexual normality; regarding speculations that either might have been lesbian or bisexual, see especially pp. 76–84 and 97–99.

17. The circumstances and subject matter of Rodgers and Hart's *Pal Joey* (1940, revived in 1952 and filmed in 1957) intertwine intriguingly with those of *Gypsy*. *Pal Joey* daringly presented its lead player as an irredeemable manipulator—as would *Gypsy*, albeit with a reversal of gender. *Pal Joey*'s Melba (a savvy reporter) refers to Gypsy Rose Lee and then performs a parody of the latter's act (in "Zip"). The original cast for the show included June Havoc, Gypsy Rose Lee's sister, playing a blackmailing lead dancer. Originally only a modest success, *Pal Joey* did much better in its 1952 revival, produced by Jule Styne, *Gypsy*'s composer. And, probably, the distinctive personalities of the dancers in *Pal Joey* helped inspire *Gypsy*'s "You Gotta Have a Gimmick." See SHTEIR regarding the Chicago fair (pp. 41–44), Gypsy Rose Lee (pp. 177–92 and *passim*), *Pal Joey*'s "Zip" (pp. 222–23), and the evolution of striptease in America more generally.

18. For Arthur Laurents's account of how this dimension intrigued him, to the point of persuading him that there was a musical in Gypsy Rose Lee's story, see LAURENTS, pp. 376–77; see also SECREST2, p. 132. WOLF1 offers an insightful argument for a strong lesbian sensibility in the show (pp. 105–28; see especially pp. 118–25). Among the more amusing hints in this direction is Sondheim's lyric to "I Have a Moo Cow": "She loves a man cow"—a line that, as with many of *Gypsy*'s child-act lyrics, may be read either as sexual innuendo or childish naïveté.

19. I discuss this song and its homoerotic content in KNAPP1, pp. 90–92.

20. ZADAN, pp. 49–50.

21. Another plausible derivation centers around Louise's palm reading, established in her scene with Tulsa, one of the male dancers in the act, just before he runs away with June.

22. This is not how the name arises in the *Memoir* (LEE), where Louise is inspired to change from Rose Louise to Gypsy Rose Lee while watching her name being put up on the marquee just before her first appearance as a stripper (pp. 226–27). The rationale for the change in name given there also involves a two-step process: first, a shift from "Louise" to "Lee" (in an attempt to shield her new identity from her grandfather), and then the addition of "Gypsy" because "Rose Lee" "didn't sound like enough of a name."

23. In the 1962 film version, this line is dropped and the sexual dimension of the rigged contest is downplayed, in part because Uncle Jocko is really Herbie (and thus not involved in any corruption)—the first in a succession of (mostly unfortunate) changes from the stage show.

24. See LAURENTS, pp. 45–46.

25. A reaction formation, according to psychological usage, occurs when a person enacts the opposite of his or her true (and often repressed) desires; the term originates with Freud. Here, Louise's desire to be June, in order to receive recognition from her mother, leads her to enact an inversion, in which she—remaining as opposite of June as she can be—has become the star, while stand-ins for June occupy the secondary position, to which she was formerly relegated.

26. Rose's "dreaming" is important as well in providing yet another link between her and Louise, who later confesses to Tulsa that she makes up dreams.

27. See ZADAN, p. 42.

28. In Jewish traditions, the Paschal Lamb is slaughtered and eaten at Passover, which came to represent, in Christianity, the sacrifice of Christ (the "Lamb of God").

29. SECREST2, p. 136.

30. The particular "crazed" quality of this number stems in part from its melodic profile. As Todd Decker has shown, in "Rose's (Interminable) Turn: Jule Styne's *Gypsy* and the Ironies of Playing Mama Rose" (paper presented at the Society for American Music Annual Conference, Eugene, Oregon, February 2005), Rose's general pattern has been, until this point in the show, to climb heroically from a very low pitch to a high pitch, often using prominent stepwise ascents; here, however, the chorus starts near the top of her range, and, having no place to go, she remains poised throughout the rest of the number between heroic arrival and hysteria.

31. Sondheim relates the line's effect on Porter: "I heard him go 'Ah!' right in the corner of the room. And it's a very Cole Porter line, because he would use these foreign languages for rhyme, for effect, and he didn't see it coming" (SECREST2, p. 136). What Sondheim does not point out is that Porter was always sensitive—as Sondheim is here—to the context and associations for foreign-language interpolations; see my discussions of *Kiss Me, Kate* in chapter 6.

32. Surely not by accident, this line trumps the first lines in this verse, based on a punning use of "row," by replicating the children's game of forming words from letters; thus "And NEIOUIOUO."

33. Gypsy Rose Lee did not coin the term "ecdysiast," but rather borrowed it from critics H. L. Mencken and George Jean Nathan, who derived it from "ecdysis," the process by which snakes and other animals shed their outer skins.

34. Scott Miller likens this number to an operatic "mad scene"; see his discussion in MILLER-S3, pp. 92–94. Regarding its composition—more by Sondheim in collaboration with Laurents and Robbins than by Styne—see SECREST2, pp. 138–40.

35. LAURENTS, pp. 395–96.

36. *Nine* is based on Fellini's *8½*; another attempt to base a musical on Fellini, the 1969 *La strada*, closed after one night. Fellini and Ingmar Bergman are, of course, the most celebrated in that generation of continental European filmmakers.

37. As Ethan Mordden puts it, "As for Dorothy Fields, this wonderful talent may be the only lyricist in musical-theatre history who sounded more youthful as time ran on" (MORDDEN7, pp. 221–22).

38. The ending of the film version of *Sweet Charity* differs from the stage version, which introduced a "good fairy" who turns out to be an advertisement for a television show; the film reverts to something like that of *Nights of Cabiria*, substituting flower children for the latter's partying youths. In an alternative ending for the film, included in the DVD release, Oscar realizes his mistake and returns to Charity.

39. A hocket is an old contrapuntal device, dating from the thirteenth and fourteenth centuries, in which one combining melody fills in the gaps left by another. In the later "catch," which was a kind of round (in which the same melody is sung by each part but starting at different times) popular in England from Shakespeare's time well into the eighteenth century, hockets were used to produce combinations of lyrics that could be merely humorous or, often, obscene. Peter Schickele (P.D.Q. Bach) offers a modern replication of the ribald hocket tradition in "The Art of the Ground Round" (*The Intimate P.D.Q. Bach*, Vanguard CD 79335–2, originally released as LP 79335, 1974).

40. The turn figure here is actually an extended turn, moving to *two* notes below the starting pitch after an opening ascent; turns generally circle the starting pitch, visiting first the upper and then the lower neighbor.

41. Herb Alpert and the Tijuana Brass, who specialized in a Latin-tinged sound with mariachi overtones, enjoyed a huge popularity in the 1960s. Regarding this and other contributions by Ralph Burns, the show's orchestrator, see MORDDEN7, p. 219.

42. Despite their popularizing agenda, the Swingle Singers were an accomplished group who performed a sometimes difficult repertory with precision—enough so that Luciano Berio used them in his 1968 Sinfonia, dedicated to Leonard Bernstein; see chapter 6, pp. 296–97. The popularity of this (originally Paris-based) group in America seems inevitable, given the dually American derivation of its style. Ward Swingle was himself an American, and the style he developed for performing classical repertory derived fairly directly from jazz vocal styles such as scat-singing. But their sound also recalls that of the extremely popular German group the Comedian Harmonists, whose highly distinctive style emerged about thirty years earlier as an admiring extension of American barbershop harmonizing.

43. The extended version of Porter's "It's De-lovely" (not always heard in performances) details the arrival of a baby, which occasions decidedly different reactions from the mother and the father.

The theme of disillusioned hopes that pervades *Sweet Charity* is structural and pervasive; as Richard Dyer points out (about the film version), *Sweet Charity* "indicates *after* 'There's Gotta Be Something Better Than This' the futility of employment aspirations for hookers, and *after* 'I Love to Cry at Weddings' the futility of the institution of marriage" (DYER4, p. 63; see also the further discussion below in the text). Thus, the show, as a whole, conforms to what Marcus Desmond Harmon calls the "retrospective reveal," a characteristic Bob Fosse device in which an audience is first seduced and then disillusioned, as when the boy singing "Tomorrow Belongs to Me" in *Cabaret* (film, 1973) is only gradually revealed to be dressed in a Nazi uniform ("When the Film Just Doesn't Love You Back," unpublished paper).

44. The harmonic logic of this progression derives from the "hopeful" internal line that rises chromatically from G to B♭ against the original chord's C and E.

45. For related discussions, see McCLARY2, especially pp. 60–61.

46. But see chapter 5 of WOOD-R1, and also the "Retrospect" he added for the 1981 edition, especially regarding "male bonding" and the buddy trope (see also my related discussions in chapter 2, pp. 75–76).

47. *Applause* (Charles Strouse and Lee Adams, 1970) and *Seesaw* (Cy Coleman and Dorothy Fields, 1973) were two earlier shows with openly homosexual characters; the former, based on the classic Joseph L. Mankiewicz film *All About Eve* (1950), ran for 896 performances, the latter for 296; neither, of course, had nearly the commercial success of *A Chorus Line*, which ran from 1975 to 1990.

48. Paul is also Puerto Rican, a choice that seems meant either to call up the dance ensembles of *West Side Story* in historical terms or merely to problematize his identity even further.

49. Much of the information in this and the following two paragraphs is culled from WHITTAKER.

50. The show would make one more move during its initial run—prompted by plans to tear down the King's Road Theatre—to the Comedy Theatre in the West End, where it ran until September 1980.

51. Glam rock, which took off around 1971 with David Bowie as one of its central figures, was in part an attempt to move away from the machismo of rock through cross-dressing, applying feminine makeup, and adopting more direct, less virtuosic modes and forms of expression. Punk rock is generally understood to have been

launched by the Sex Pistols in 1975 as a hard-edged extension of glam, but many have argued for its roots in the 1960s (i.e., Lou Reed and the Velvet Underground), as an existing movement that moved to the mainstream in the mid-1970s, with the American groups Ramones and Iggy Pop anticipating the Britain-based Sex Pistols.

52. The most drastic edit was the removal of the first two verses of "Super Heroes" near the end of the film, sung by Brad and Janet, cutting directly to the final verse, recited rather than sung by the Criminologist. The cut segment is available on the DVD release's "UK Version."

53. *The King of Hearts*, for example, ran for more than four years at the Central Square Theater in Cambridge, Massachusetts, in the early 1970s, a run sustained in part by those who returned many times to see the film.

54. WHITTAKER, pp. 180–81.

55. Ibid., p. 6.

56. "Femm" seems designed to recall its homophone "femme" (or "fem"), a term used to describe the more feminine member in a same-sex relationship when gendered role-playing is evident.

57. WHITTAKER, p. 18.

58. While the sepia-to-color plan was scrapped, key "Oz" characters are prefigured in the opening Denton sequence, along with several Transylvanian party guests. Thus, of the former, Frank is the preacher, and Riff Raff and Magenta (in a parody of the painting *American Gothic*) are apparently church employees.

59. Mel Brooks's *Young Frankenstein*, released in 1974 (thus, between the opening of *The Rocky Horror Show* and the filming), overlaps significantly with this multireference to the 1930s Frankenstein films, including the stormy night, the monster's musical proclivities, the sexual liaison between the monster and the hero's fiancée, and the replication of the bride's hairdo at the end of the film. For further discussion of this connection, see KNAPP3.

60. For another elaboration of the "weird sex" dimension of *Rocky Horror* and other "midnight movies" (specifically, *Pink Flamingos* and *Liquid Sky*), see STUDLAR. Provocatively, Studlar finds Frank less transgressive than he appears, because he holds on to male prerogatives and, despite appearing in drag throughout, is never truly feminized.

61. The show's use of these archetypes also contributed to an ongoing recovery in the early 1970s of 1950s rock and roll—as in, for example, George Lucas's 1973 *American Graffiti* or the television series *Happy Days* (1973–1984).

62. I follow the convention here of designating major-mode harmonies with upper-case numerals, and minor-mode with lower-case.

63. Hitler is also evoked in this scene; in an allusion to Leni Riefenstahl's 1934 *Triumph of the Will* (which Frank either ignores or doesn't get), Riff Raff contemptuously compliments Frank's Rocky: "He's a triumph of your will."

64. In the film, the final cadence of the song transmutes into the even more elaborate plagal cadence that begins Mendelssohn's famous "Wedding March" from his Incidental Music for Shakespeare's *A Midsummer Night's Dream*. Another superimposition of Mendelssohn's "Wedding March" over the concluding cadence of a song figures prominently in what is, among the many marriages of sexual and religious imagery in the film, perhaps the most shocking. As the opening credit sequence ends with this substituted cadence, the disembodied lips that have been lip-synching "Science Fiction—Double Feature" (discussed later in the text) disappear into the crotch

of a Christian cross, which is then revealed to be atop the Denton Episcopalian Church's steeple (see figure 5.4).

65. WHITTAKER, p. 130.

66. I thank Elizabeth Upton and Mitchell Morris for calling the latter phrasing peculiarity of *Rocky Horror* to my attention. This vocal mannerism seems of a piece with the film's method-style verbal delivery more generally, especially in songs that are more recited than sung, such as "Sweet Transvestite," in which this kind of phrasing seems to play almost like an elaborate setup for Tim Curry's famous delay midway through "antici- . . . -pation."

67. The progression for "Sweet Transvestite" might also have been derived from Deep Purple's 1972 "Smoke on the Water," a huge hit whose chord changes quickly became common currency among guitarists. Although similar to those of "Sweet Transvestite" (and a likely inspiration for O'Brien), Deep Purple's riff is played much faster, without the thirds, and with the fifth of each chord played below the root. This famous riff also played its part in the evolution of heavy metal's "power chord," discussed later in relation to *Hedwig and the Angry Inch*.

68. As, for example, in Scott Miller's provocative essay "Inside *Hedwig and the Angry Inch*" (MILLER-S4).

69. Erich Honecker and Helmut Kohl were at that time the leaders of East and West Germany, respectively.

70. This casual reference to a key event leading up to the Holocaust, along with other similar references identified later, is hard to read precisely. The line is surely calculated to offend—or, perhaps, to dare us to take offense at this reference in particular, with so much else in the show that might offend in one way or another. In this, it simply extends the show's strategy of aggressive tastelessness, offered up as an emblem of our deeply broken world. Yet, we may well wonder whether this and later references to Hitler and the Holocaust are part of a generational reflex that wants to "get over" the past, and so makes them the subject of casual jokes and throwaway lines. That would be more deeply offensive than the show seems on the whole to intend, however, and runs counter to its thematic claim that we cannot fully move past devastating events. Perhaps, then, these references may be best understood as part of Hedwig's abjectness, of a piece with the self-deprecating humor of her monologue; thus, they implicitly underscore that she and her disfigured body represent the grotesque residue of Germany's past sins.

71. In a situation similar to the one I discuss in the previous note, this shocking pairing of Jesus and Hitler, as fellow martyrs, can seem offensively casual. Yet its central paradox lies at the heart of Hedwig's problematic position, as a descendant of those who perpetrated the Holocaust (thus, it is Hedwig's mother who makes the connection) who seems at times to aspire to a Christ-like martyrdom.

72. See MILLER-S4 for another discussion of Hedwig's connection to Frankenstein.

73. As Scott Miller notes, "most of these divas led lives similar in some details to Hedwig's. . . . It wasn't until [Patti Smith] left behind the influences of the men in her life that she became a force to be reckoned with, as one of the leaders of the New Wave movement. Tina Turner . . . in 1984 . . . staged a rock and roll comeback like few had ever seen, and she became a bigger star than she had ever been with Ike. . . . It wasn't until [John Lennon's] murder in 1980 that [Yoko] Ono . . . was finally taken seriously. Aretha Franklin . . . considered leaving the music business [, but when] given almost complete artistic control of her work . . . she soared to the top. Nona Hendryx had success for years singing back-up . . . and found her greatest success

in her solo career. . . . Nico was a model, film actress, and singer with The Velvet Underground before going on to her own solo career." Miller also notes the significance of Hedwig's earlier reference to LaVern Baker (in "Wig in a Box"); Baker was an R & B singer from the 1950s who—being barred from white-run radio stations and venues because she was black—had to endure others' achieving fame and fortune from singing her songs. Another especially plausible point of reference Miller cites is Marlene Dietrich, a self-exiled German national who became notorious for her gender-bending performances (MILLER-S4).

74. The plagal effect here is only partial, using the familiar guitar figure of a 4–3 appoggiatura on the arrival chord.

Chapter Six
Relationships

1. For an astute analysis of the heterosexual paradigm and its bases in film musicals, with a somewhat different emphasis, see DYER2. For a discussion of the paradigm in film narratives more generally, see WOOD-R2, pp. 77–80. For related discussions, see also SEDGWICK, WOLF1, and WOLF2.

2. McCLUNG, p. 4. Hart drew not only on his own experiences in psychotherapy but also on Kubie's 1936 book, *Aspects of Psychoanalysis: A Handbook for Prospective Patients and Their Advisors* (New York: Norton), and, regarding some of Liza Elliott's specific neurotic predilections, Gertrude Lawrence (whose capacity to put off making decisions was legendary); see McCLUNG, pp. 4–6.

3. McCLUNG, p. 4; see also HIRSCH2, pp. 181–82.

4. For good accounts of Weill's reception and critical reputation relative to his Broadway shows, see BLOCK2, pp. 133–37, and McCLUNG/LAIRD, pp. 167–74.

5. See HIRSCH2, pp. 202–3, for a thoughtful alternative appraisal of this neglect. In his view, *Lady in the Dark* "reads like a strictly conventional period piece . . . an old-fashioned Cinderella romance sprinkled with a dusting of simplistic psychoanalysis," with the possibility of the show's revival being further undermined by its main character's "strychnine personality," its "brittle theatrical diction of yesteryear" and "now-dated treatment of psychoanalysis," and its too conventionally gendered ending. See also BLOCK2, pp. 153–55; Block identifies its naive take on psychoanalysis, its chauvinistic plotting, and Charley Johnson's characterization as the main barriers to the show's successful revival. See JONES, pp. 138–40, for an almost completely laudatory account of the show, which finds the "only false note [to be] the brevity of Liza's course of analysis" (p. 140).

6. In Ronald Sanders's dismissive summation, "she wants to be submissive rather than bossy, after all" (SANDERS, p. 303).

7. See, however, Ronald Sanders's assessment of "Circus Dream" as "musically inferior to the other dream sequences by a considerable margin" (SANDERS, p. 307).

8. Ethan Mordden reads the presence of homosexuality in *Lady in the Dark* at an even deeper level, likening the entire scenario to a "gay coming-out parable"; thus, he sees in Liza's " 'lady executive' . . . a likeness of a gay man," notes the introduction of a "Hollywood beauty" (Randy Curtis) as "more gay imagery," and observes further that Moss Hart "intended his play for Katharine Cornell, a real-life lesbian wedded to a gay man, Guthrie McClintic" (MORDDEN1, pp. 60–62).

9. McClung, pp. 4–6. As McClung delineates, much of the show was drawn from a particular case study involving a transvestite teenage girl.

10. As David Drew succinctly puts it, "The film owes nothing to the Broadway show apart from the title, the basic plot idea, and the opportunity it wasted" (Drew, p. 318).

11. This process corresponds closely to the fascinating psychological project laid out in Reik, which begins with the question, "What does it mean when some tune follows you, occurs to you again and again so that it becomes a haunting melody?" (p. vii). Part 1 traces the potential of unbidden melody to provide a link to the unconscious (pp. 9–14), notes that "tone images are grasped earlier than word images, and that the memory for the first is more tenacious than for the latter" (p. 22), recounts instances when remembered tunes have proven useful aids in pschoanalysis (pp. 29–37 and later), and analyzes Reik's own experiences in interpreting his spontaneous musical recollections (much of pp. 39–147). After considering additional cases in part 2, involving more persistent instances of melodic "haunting," which often involve paradoxical inversions of mood (as in *Lady in the Dark*), Reik's part 3 analyzes at greater length his own involuntary preoccupation with the chorale melody of Mahler's *Resurrection* Symphony. (I thank Rose Rosengard Subotnik for pointing this connection out to me.)

Despite the deftness of Weill's setting, Ira Gershwin's lyrics for the song have been found wanting, as unimaginatively sentimental (see, e.g., Furia3, p. 150).

12. See, for example, Block2, pp. 179–81. Porter himself was acutely aware of how Rodgers and Hammerstein had become the center of Broadway's solar system, and of how this had affected the general perception of old-timers such as Berlin and Porter; in a discarded verse for "Bianca," Bill Calhoun claims to be a ghostwriter for Irving Berlin, who is struggling to compete with Rodgers and Hammerstein, knowing that if Berlin "thinks / My ballad stinks, / He'll sell it to Oscar and Dick" (the entire alternative lyric is given in Citron1, p. 218n). As noted, it was Rodgers and Hammerstein who recruited Berlin to write the score for *Annie Get Your Gun*.

13. There are, to be sure, many who would deny the show's artistic achievement; see especially Mordden1, pp. 255–59; see also Swain, p. 164. However differently they might be expressed, most complaints revolve around the observation that the characters in *Kiss Me, Kate* don't sing "themselves" so much as they sing Cole Porter songs, so that on this level the show does not really subscribe to the "integrated" model of Rodgers and Hammerstein. Yet, in an interesting way, Porter's "presence" in the show's songs puts a useful emphasis on the element of performance, as such— which, as we shall see, is fundamental to how relationships work in the show.

14. See chapter 4 in Knapp1.

15. This was scarcely the first time the team would approach this kind of material with success; besides *Kiss Me, Kate*, for which they won a Tony Award, they are perhaps best known today for *My Favorite Wife* (1942, dir. Garson Kanin), another story involving a couple's sometimes stormy reconciliation (based on a story by director Leo McCarey).

16. See Schwartz, pp. 230–31. The Spewacks had earlier collaborated with Porter on *Leave It to Me* (1938), which included "My Heart Belongs to Daddy," generally regarded as Mary Martin's breakthrough song, and "From This Moment On," which was interpolated into the 1953 film version of *Kiss Me, Kate* and is often included in revivals of the show (including the 1999 Broadway revival).

17. These pairs include all of the songs in Porter's published score. Although Porter had been content to leave Harrison Howell, Lilli's "other man," without a song (as he had done with Sir Evelyn in *Anything Goes*), "From This Moment On" was added for the 1953 film, as noted. "I Sing of Love" is often dropped in revivals (it was also left off the original-cast recording); in the 1999 revival, the music provides the occasion for a modest Bacchanalia.

18. In the 1999 revival, the latter device was carried over onto another level, with each repetition of the chorus of "Venice" dropping in pitch, tempo, and dynamic level.

19. Alfred Kinsey's *Sexual Behavior in the Human Male*, released in 1948, is commonly referred to as the Kinsey Report. Porter here was right up-to-date, even to his hints regarding masturbation as an alternative to sex with a partner ("But pillow, you'll be my baby tonight"), since the prevalence of masturbation was one of the more shocking findings of the Kinsey Report. The song also refers fairly openly to homosexuality ("A marine / For his queen"), perhaps the most significant among the practices that Kinsey reported as much more widespread than it was then believed to be.

20. For more extensive discussions of Porter's use of Italian and Renaissance musical styles, see BLOCK2, pp. 183–89, and SWAIN2, pp. 142–52. Both Block and Swain also discuss the intermingling of the distinctively contemporary American and the deliberately archaic.

21. The most elaborate of Porter's borrowings from Shakespeare are in Kate's "I Am Ashamed That Women Are so Simple" (discussed later in the text). Other borrowed phrases include:

> "Rage like an angry boar" (Pet., Act I, Sc. II, 203, which becomes "fight like a raging boar" in "I've Come to Wive It Wealthily";
> "I never yet beheld that special face" (Bianca, Act II, Sc. I, 11), which Porter takes over as the germ for Petruchio's "Were Thine That Special Face";
> "And kiss me, Kate, we will be married o' Sunday" (Pet., Act II, Sc. I, 326), the source for the show's title phrase, which occurs at roughly the same initial place in the action (at the end of the first act) and is then repeated at the climax of the second, more or less duplicating Shakespeare's later repetitions, in Act V, Sc. I, 148, and especially Act V, Sc. II: "Why, there's a wench! Come on, and kiss me, Kate" (Pet., 180); and
> "[*Singing*] Where is the life that late I led" (Pet., Act IV, Sc. 1, 143), which Porter elaborates into a full-scale song.

Another Shakespearean borrowing, though not from *Shrew*, has been identified in "So in Love," whose "So taunt me, and hurt me, deceive me, desert me" may derive from *A Midsummer Night's Dream*'s Helena's "Use me but as your spaniel—spurn me, strike me, Neglect me, lose me" (FURIA3, pp. 178 and 287n20). Bella Spewack's script draws even more heavily on Shakespeare, of course, as do, less specifically, Sam Spewack's comic speeches for the gangsters and Porter's song for them in the same vein, "Brush Up Your Shakespeare." For a deft discussion of how the latter song expresses attitudes about cultural divisions, specifically regarding "low-culture" appropriations of Shakespeare (as part of a broader consideration of the 1953 film version of the show), see LAWSON-PEEBLES1.

22. This is particularly true here, since the song continues with a third, less problematic permutation of names: "I'm a maid mad to marry / And will take double quick / Any Tom, Dick or Harry, / Any Tom, Harry or Dick"—even though this

ending sets up, eventually, an extended riff on the very word that serves as the focal point for the double entendre ("A-dick-a-Dick, Dick, Dick").

23. A more subtle link between "Where Is the Life That Late I Led" and "Always True to You in My Fashion" is the homage each pays to the third stanza of Ernest Dowson's 1860 poem "Non Sum Qualis Eram Bonae sub Regno Cynarae" (better known as "Cynara"), which provided both a phrase for Petruchio's song ("gone with the wind"; this is the source also for the title of Margaret Mitchell's celebrated 1936 book, but rhymed in Dowson and Porter, à la Shakespeare, with "mind" and "find," respectively) and the recurring punch line from Lois's song (all four stanzas of "Cynara" end with the same line):

> I have forgot much, Cynara! gone with the wind,
> Flung roses, roses riotously with the throng,
> Dancing, to put thy pale, lost lilies out of mind;
> But I was desolate and sick of an old passion,
> Yea, all the time, because the dance was long;
> I have been faithful to thee, Cynara! in my fashion.

Regarding Porter's acquaintance with "Cynara," see SPEWACK/SPEWACK, p. xii, and EELLS, p. 242. For an analysis of "Where Is the Life That Late I Led," see CITRON1, pp. 307–9.

24. According to a popular anecdote, Porter wrote this song quickly and under some pressure, in order to accommodate Harold Lang's contract (according to George Eells, on an elevator of the Waldorf Towers between the first and forty-first floors [EELLS, pp. 248–49]). As the story is sometimes told, Porter's annoyance led him to write a deliberately weak song in the hopes it would be cut (this version derives from Patricia Morison; see BLOCK2, p. 190). Weak or not, however, the song perfectly encapsulates Bill's naïveté.

25. I thank Lauren Sanchez for pointing this connection out to me (personal communication).

26. See, however, BLOCK2, which faults this reprise both for its logic (how does Fred know this song, since he wasn't there when Lilli sang it in Act I?) and its violation of the dramatic integrity of an otherwise "integrated" musical (pp. 192–93). Yet, few have minded when, in the context of a Broadway musical or opera, a singer recalls another's music, even absent an explanation. An easy way of offering such an explanation in this case might have been to have Lilli "remember" the song from the same operetta as "Wunderbar," although, to be sure, this kind of explanation would have undermined the soliloquy dimension of the song. Truer to most people's understanding, I suspect, is to regard Lilli's and Fred's expressing their private thoughts through the same song as evidence of their being inwardly compatible, despite their squabbling. Understood in this way, the device is a fairly modest extension of the aesthetic, operative in most musical-theatrical traditions, that allows choruses to sing and dance together in musical numbers that purport to be spontaneous responses to particular dramatic moments. For a related discussion of a similar situation in Verdi's *La traviata*, see CONE, pp. 126–28.

27. For related discussions of the melodic structure of "So in Love," see SWAIN, pp. 154–58, CITRON1, pp. 306–7, and FORTE1, pp. 140–46.

28. In the 1999 revival, both singers extend the melodic climax higher, rising on "I" in an échappée figure before descending on "die." In my view, this modern Broadway gesture, as applied to the melodic climax of this song, unnecessarily distorts

Porter's structure, although it retains and even reinforces the more subjective orientation of the final lines by giving increased emphasis to the word "I."

29. The Dies Irae derives from the requiem mass and is traditionally used to represent death or the diabolical; see my discussion of *Sweeney Todd* in the epilogue.

30. Joseph P. Swain notes an additional archaism that is not consistent with the time period of *The Taming of the Shrew*: the eighteenth-century arietta style he adopts for "I Am Ashamed That Women Are so Simple" (SWAIN, pp. 159–63). Another point of reference for the flute duet may be found in another parody of *Lucia*'s mad scene: Mad Margaret's "Cheerily Carols the Lark" in Gilbert and Sullivan's *Ruddigore*.

31. See SCHWARTZ, pp. 232–33.

32. This kind of play with names, although most obvious with Fred "Gray Ham," is evident throughout; thus Lilli is "Vain as he" (Vanessi), Lois Lane is (in vulgar terms) a "loose lay" (while also incongruously borrowing the name from the Superman comic books), Harrison "Howl" is a hoary windbag, Lilli's maid's name, Hattie, points especially to her mistress's headgear, which will be a contentious issue both onstage and off (Hattie McDaniel, the blues singer who played many maid/mammy roles in Hollywood, may be another intended point of reference), and "Bill" Calhoun cannot pay his bills (his gambling debts).

33. See BLOCK2, pp. 193–96, for a good summation of changing attitudes about the end of Shakespeare's play (particularly regarding the wager scene, which was once to be played more extensively in *Kiss Me, Kate*) and for a contrasting discussion of how these play out in *Kiss Me, Kate*.

34. I thank Rose Rosengard Subotnik for pointing out to me the parallels among these now-favored musical versions of Shakespeare, Shaw, and Beaumarchais.

35. Who exactly within the show is to take credit for the adaptation is a bit murky, although in the first scene Fred Graham refers offhandedly to Shakespeare and "the six other fellows who've been sitting up nights rewriting him."

36. See LERNER3, especially p. 38. For additional accounts of the various attempts to musicalize the play, see BLOCK2, pp. 228–31, and RIIS/SEARS, pp. 148–49.

37. Another story that Shaw's *Pygmalion* seems to shadow is that of George Du Maurier's 1894 novel *Trilby*, with Higgins playing Svengali to Eliza's Trilby. Despite the hint during the training sessions that Eliza might be susceptible to hypnotism, and notwithstanding her trancelike state at the embassy ball, the basic dynamic between Higgins and Eliza is vastly different in most respects. To the extent that the Trilby story speaks to the possibility of unlocking an ideal self, however, it is indeed consonant with much of *Pygmalion*, albeit with a very different conclusion.

Still another relevant dimension of the play is its treatment of the theme of "passing"; if set in America, *My Fair Lady* might well have included racialized settings or brought its submerged references to sexual orientation out in the open, since these are the most common American situations in which passing is a common dramatic trope.

For a valuable comparison of Shaw's play to both the Pygmalion myth and Cinderella, see BERST, pp. 3–14.

38. Preface to SHAW, p. ix.

39. Many of the details of this training sequence were developed by the filmmakers, specifically David Lean (film editor, but acting as a de facto assistant director) and Asquith; see GOODMAN, p. 313. For other discussions of the film adaptation, see BLOCK2, pp. 228–35, and COSTELLO.

40. Regarding the "incest" interpretation of Shaw's play, see SILVER, pp. 198–99, and REYNOLDS, p. 120. Part of the issue regarding this dimension has to do with what aspect of the story one engages with. Shaw's play is concerned, from the beginning, with what happens (or will happen) *after* the success of the experiment, an emphasis almost completely absent in the original myth. This concern for the aftermath of "happily ever after" resonates in obvious ways with the larger sense of reality that Sondheim and Lapine imposed on fairy tales in *Into the Woods* (see chapter 3), but it also partakes of a recurring trope in Lerner and Loewe's collaborative work, whether in the real world/fantasy conflict of *Brigadoon* (1947) or, as discussed earlier, in the nested operetta structure of *Camelot* (chapter 4).

41. SHAW, pp. 12–13.

42. SHAW, p. 43. Regarding Higgins's childishness, see also MILLER-S3, pp. 179–80. Autobiographical resonances here are also revealing, not only the oft-observed similarity between Shaw and Higgins, but also Lerner's attraction to the property, his tailoring of the role to Harrison's character and behavior, and Lerner and Harrison's evolving friendship, the latter based in part on their similar difficulties with women (both were much married and divorced), a condition that once led Harrison to exclaim to Lerner, on a public sidewalk, "Alan! Wouldn't it be marvelous if we were homosexuals?" (LERNER3, p. 92; regarding the tailoring of the role to Harrison, see LERNER3, pp. 56–59, 70, 79–80, and 92; and LEES, chapters 9–10).

43. For a more extended discussion of the homosexual dimension of the show, see WOLF1, pp. 153–60.

44. These lines are followed by the particularly Shavian lines "Theres only one way of escaping trouble; and thats killing things. Cowards, you notice, are always shrieking to have troublesome people killed" (SHAW, p. 68).

45. See LERNER1, p. 329.

46. The courage that this approach required of Lerner, Loewe, and especially Rex Harrison makes the cowardly dropping of Julie Andrews from the 1964 film version all the more unforgivable, especially since Audrey Hepburn—otherwise quite wonderful in the role—was in the end so audibly dubbed with someone else's voice (Marni Nixon's) that the entire point of Eliza's lyrical vocality is lost. Marcie Ray has argued, however, that this apparent weakness becomes a strength of sorts, since, among other things, it underscores the separateness of Eliza's singing voice, which Higgins does *not* have on his wax cylinders ("The Phantom Voice and Invisible Feminism in the 1964 Film of *My Fair Lady*," unpublished paper).

47. ALTMAN, p. 81.

48. LERNER3, p. 60.

49. For an extended account of this aspect of the play's early reception, see HUGGETT, pp. 49–54 and 122–59, and BERST, pp. 15–25.

50. This interruption was added to keep a reluctant Rex Harrison onstage to bear the full brunt of this song; see LERNER3, pp. 99–101.

51. Interestingly, each of Higgins's three rant songs contains a grammatical or usage error. Generously, we might imagine the error to be deliberate, as a way of drawing attention to Higgins's lack of restraint. Indeed, because the final error is not in the lyrics as written but was supplied by Rex Harrison in the height of fury, we might be tempted to indulge this notion—were it not for the fact that the other errors are of a kind Americans are particularly prone to making. Thus, in the introductory verse to "Why Can't the English?" Higgins declares, regarding Eliza, "By rights she should be taken out and hung [hanged] / For the cold-blooded murder of the English

tongue!"; in "I'm an Ordinary Man," he states, "I'd be equally as willing for a dentist to be drilling than [as] to ever let a woman in my life!"; and Harrison substitutes "was" for "were" in the final stanza of "A Hymn to Him": "If I were a woman who'd been to a ball, / Been hailed as a princess by one and by all; / Would I start weeping like a bathtub overflowing?"

52. For related discussions of the march idiom of this song, see MILLER-S3, p. 183, and LERNER1, p. 333.

53. The importance of this speech is also noted by Geoffrey Block (BLOCK2, p. 235) and Joseph P. Swain (SWAIN, p. 201, where it is quoted in full, along with some of the surrounding dialogue).

54. Scott Miller identifies another song that the music of "I've Grown Accustomed to Her Face" recalls: Higgins's revenge scenario ("How poignant it will be") borrows from the melody of Eliza's parallel song from Act I, "Just You Wait" (MILLER-S3, pp. 185–86). Miller also identifies the lyrical strain of "I've Grown Accustomed to Her Face" as deriving from the rants of "I'm an Ordinary Man," which he takes as additional evidence of Higgins's deeper feelings for Eliza, because he has, indeed, "let a woman in his life" (p. 186). Geoffrey Block details several motivic parallels between Higgin's and Eliza's songs, involving "Just You Wait," "Without You," "I'm an Ordinary Man," and "I've Grown Accustomed to Her Face," some of which are taken up here (BLOCK2, pp. 236–40). See also SWAIN, pp. 210–14, for a related discussion.

55. Scott Miller also finds in this concluding quotation from "I Could Have Danced All Night" a sense that Eliza has the last word, after all (MILLER-S3, p. 187).

56. Specifically, Burt Shevelove and Larry Gelbart won in the author category for *Forum*, and George Furth for *Company*; Harold Prince won for production for both; and George Abbott won for direction for *Forum* and Prince for *Company*. Sondheim's double win for *Company* occurred when, for a brief time, there were separate categories for lyrics and score; partly because of this, *Company* set a new record for most Tony Awards, at seven.

The project that became *Company* grew out of a set of one-act plays and sketches by Furth, which had lost its funding. Originally, each situation involved a central couple, to be performed by the same actors; as the musical evolved, the stories and situations were interwoven around the central figure of Bobby.

57. Indeed, both shows fell short of *Company*'s 706 performances, with *Follies* running for 522 performances, and *A Little Night Music*—calculated to be a moneymaker after *Follies*'s losses—for 600.

58. This fairly common view of *Company*'s historical position is most elaborately presented in CARTMELL; see especially chapter 3 (pp. 132–76) and, for an account of the concept musical's defining features, pp. 94–105. Some take issue with this view, citing earlier experimental musicals such as Rodgers and Hammerstein's *Allegro* (1947) and Alan Jay Lerner and Kurt Weill's *Love Life* (1948), which may be seen as important precedents for not only *Company* but also *Follies* and *Merrily We Roll Along* (1981); see, for example, MILLER-S1, pp. 187–91, and MILNER, pp. 158–67. Stephen Banfield finds the designation of "concept" musical both problematic and of little real use; see BANFIELD2, pp. 147–49.

59. Another show sometimes cited as the first successful concept musical is the 1966 *Cabaret*, produced and directed by Harold Prince. Although *Cabaret* does not really satisfy the generally accepted criteria for a concept musical, it certainly leans that way (Prince himself considers *Company* the major departure in this direction; see PRINCE, p. 149). More importantly for *Company*, however, *Cabaret* was the show

that convinced Sondheim that he might be able to work well with Prince as a director (see SECREST2, pp. 185–90).

60. See BANFIELD2, p. 161.

61. Bobby's lack of interest in politics is made evident in his conversation with Marta, who implicitly is. When she asks him how many Puerto Ricans or blacks he knows, he confesses, "I seem to meet people only like myself" (Act I, Sc. 5), a comment more revealing than he realizes, as Marta's response—"Talk about your weirdos"—indicates.

62. For related discussions of the various popular musical styles that influenced *Company*, see CARTMELL, pp. 159–70, and BANFIELD2, pp. 151–57, 161, and 170.

63. For a provocative discussion detailing how musical minimalism relates to modern urban experiences during this time period, sometimes quite specifically, see FINK, chapter 2. For an extensive discussion of *Company*'s motivic work, see BANFIELD2, pp. 149–50 and 152–60. Among Banfield's many astute observations is that Sondheim tends to extend his musical motivic work into his lyrics, not only within the "Bobby" music but also elsewhere—as, for instance, in "Sorry-Grateful," where the reflexive oscillations of musical motives are matched verbally by syllabic patterns in the opening lyrics: "You're sorry—**grateful, Regretful**—happy" (p. 159).

64. As Banfield notes, the busy signal is actually sped up as it transfers to the orchestra (BANFIELD2, p. 149), which adds to its sense of nervousness.

65. Specifically, Reich used the final five words of a black teen's harrowing explanation of what he had to do to receive medical treatment after being beaten during the 1964 Harlem riots: "I had to, like, open the bruise up and let some of the bruise blood come out to show them."

66. At one point, Sondheim planned a more elaborate overture based in this style, which Stephen Banfield describes as "a cappella–style wordless voices" (BANFIELD2, p. 158); the final version of the (rather short) overture offers a slower, dreamlike version of the vocalizing "Bobby" music with orchestral accompaniment.

67. Tunick inserted the phrase to impress Sondheim and, he hoped, Bernstein, but Sondheim apparently didn't notice it (or didn't comment), and Bernstein never heard it because of a missed cue on the night he attended; see SECREST2, p. 198.

68. Berio later expanded the 1968 version from four to five main sections; this later version was performed in October 1970, many months into *Company*'s run.

69. Sandor Goodhart and Scott Miller argue, separately, that the entire show may be understood as Bobby's perspective (GOODHART1, p. 19, and MILLER-S3, pp. 57–60). Yet, while Bobby's perspective is surely the crux, it is by no means that of the entire show, since we must also be able to see Bobby's perspective itself in perspective. The question of perspective may hinge on whether we think we are seeing the same or different birthday parties for Bobby as the evening moves forward, and in this the show seems deliberately ambiguous. As Prince notes, after describing the device of a recurring birthday celebration as "Pinteresque in feeling," "I am certain they were one. I wouldn't be surprised if George Furth believes they were four. It doesn't matter" (PRINCE, pp. 149 and 150). See also BANFIELD2, pp. 164–70.

70. For a related discussion of Sondheim's use of Latin styles in *Company*, see BANFIELD2, p. 157.

71. These two lines may refer, in the first instance, to the familiar (if now dated) association of smoking cigarettes and making love (thus, smoking after intercourse, or within the ritual familiar from Hollywood films of a couple lighting cigarettes for each other and then putting them down to kiss), and in the second, to either the

fetish of cross-dressing or the relaxed carelessness of postcoital attire. Alternatively, "Cigarettes you stop together" might refer to the repeated cycle of a couple's failed attempts to quit smoking, especially given the setting (where the unshakable habits are overeating and drinking, however, not smoking) and in the aftermath of the series of Surgeon General Reports, beginning in 1964, that linked smoking to a variety of health problems, leading to the 1965 passage of a federal law requiring that cigarette packages include health warnings, which thereafter became both more specific and more definite, by increments.

72. As Sandor Goodhart points out, this lyric may be read as a very specific cycle leading from "marriage contract ('I do') to accusation ('You don't'), to denial ('Nobody said that'), to scapegoating ('Who brought the subject up first?')"; see GOODHART1, p. 19.

73. A simple oft-used "fix" for the lyric is, "I could understand a person / If he said to go away / . . . I could understand a person / If he happened to be gay." For related discussions of Bobby's orientation, see BANFIELD2, p. 162, and ZADAN, pp. 360–61 (within an extended quotation from Arthur Laurents); among the most strenuous arguments against this line of interpretation is Ethan Mordden's (MORDDEN6, p. 30). Given the theatrical history of disguising tropes of gayness within contexts of heterosexual "normalcy," the attempts by Sondheim and others to shut down this particular mode of reading the show can come across as oddly disquieting.

74. BANFIELD2, p. 155. Scott Miller provides another description of the layered phasing in the accompaniment for "Another Hundred People"; see MILLER-S3, p. 61.

75. For example, similar images form the basis for Simon and Garfunkel's 1964 "The Sound of Silence," which helped launch the "folk-rock" genre in 1965 when its original acoustic version was overdubbed with electric guitar and a rock beat, and in that form it quickly rose to the top of the charts. Simon's lyric speaks to loneliness and alienation (thus, "silence") within the noisy crowds of a city: "And in the naked light I saw / Ten thousand people, maybe more. / People talking without speaking, / People hearing without listening, / People writing songs that voices never share / And no one dare / Disturb the sound of silence" (*The Paul Simon Song Book* [New York: Charing Cross Music, 1966], p. 3). Simon's references to graffiti in this song ("the words of the prophets are written on the subway walls / And tenement halls"; p. 4) and in "The Poem on the Underground Wall" (1966) find their echo in the "crude remarks" referred to in "Another Hundred People."

76. This staging, which one can "hear" in the cast recording only if one knows what is happening, is nicely described in MILLER-S3, pp. 66–67.

77. The alternatives these songs pose have been much discussed. See, for example, BANFIELD2, pp. 163–73; GOODHART1, pp. 16–20; MILLER-S3, pp. 69–71; and SECREST2, pp. 200–202.

78. For later productions, "Marry Me a Little" was added at the end of Act I, with Sondheim's approval.

79. Cf. Scott Miller's comment that at the end of the first act "Amy 'becomes' Robert for a moment" (MILLER-S3, p. 65). Sondheim himself saw the song as "a scream of pain . . . it was a fellow trying to convince himself that committing oneself to one person leads to grief, anguish, loss of privacy, loss of individuality" (quoted in ZADAN, pp. 124–25). Ethan Mordden's pithy explanation for the song is that it represents Bobby's "savage attempt to unlearn what he can't face having learned— that he is in fact lonely" (MORDDEN2, p. 319).

80. Sondheim himself has stated, however, that "the ending of the show was a cop-out"; see ZADAN, p. 125.

81. Here, however, the harmonies shift under the stranded leading tone, descending by thirds (a typical "searching" maneuver, appropriate for the song's "questing" profile). Thus, while the first two false starts end dissonantly, with the leading tone over a subdominant harmony, the third pushes one step further ("A little, a lot"), so that the resulting dissonance is already slightly less sharp and mitigated by a multivoiced appoggiatura, which briefly superimposes a full triad (iii), including the voice's leading tone, over the fundamental ii. (This happens the previous times, as well, in the accompanimental continuation, but the vocal line has stopped by then.)

82. The novel was completed by his friend Salvatore Farini, then languished in obscurity for more than a century until it was republished in 1971.

83. Shortly after, and independently, another translation, by Lawrence Venuti, became commercially available. For an account of how Lapine and Sondheim's adaptation relates to the original novel and later film, see KNAPP-S.

84. For a concise account of how letters—written, received, read, and acted upon—permeate the action of *Passion*, see GOODHART2, pp. 228–29. Goodhart also delineates a way in which the entire musical might be understood as a letter of understanding to Sondheim's own mother, citing a large number of parallels involving biography, plotting, and specific language (pp. 241–56).

85. The 1969 musical *1776* offered an odd foretaste of *Passion*'s central device, in the sung letter exchanges between John Adams and his wife, Abigail, while he is in the nearly all-male company of the Second Continental Congress. As Steven Swayne has pointed out, there are also occasional operas that give letters a central role in the discourse, such as Verdi's *La traviata* (1853) and Tchaikovsky's *Eugene Onegin* (1878); see SWAYNE, p. 160.

86. The postcoital situation of *Passion*'s opening scene parallels the opening to Richard Strauss's *Der Rosenkavalier* (1911)—another bedroom scene between a married woman and her young lover—but with a very different profile, since Octavian in the latter scene is a "pants" role (a woman playing the part of a young man), and their encounter is disrupted by the appearance of an intruder. I thank Rose Rosengard Subotnik for pointing out this connection to me.

87. For a more extensive consideration of *Passion*'s nude scene, see MILLER-S2, pp. 123–24.

88. Significantly, one of the books Giorgio lends Fosca is a landmark of the genre of epistolary novel, Jean-Jacques Rousseau's *Julie, ou La nouvelle Héloïse* (1761).

89. For Beethoven, the "distant beloved" in question was most likely his own "Immortal Beloved," Antonie Brentano, with whom he had parted in 1812; regarding this convincing (although still not universally accepted) identification of the "Immortal Beloved," long a mystery for biographers of Beethoven, see chapter 15 of SOLOMON.

90. Although this is perhaps not to be taken as more than figurative, Beethoven's music, especially in the final bars of the cycle, provides such a powerful simulation of that projected reunion that one must almost conclude that Beethoven believed that music could have the power to overturn reality; see KNAPP4.

91. See MILLER-S4, p. 105, for a useful discussion of how the readings of the letters are staged.

92. Yet, as Shoshana Milgram Knapp notes, in the overlapping dialogue of "Happiness," Giorgio and Clara often contradict each other, even if their differences get absorbed into a shared melodic and verbal arrival point (KNAPP-S, pp. 109–10).

93. For similar observations, see MILLER-S4, pp. 104 and 113.

94. Subtle indications of this identity transference are carried by dress, understood in the context of their opposing names. Thus, "Clara" means light; significantly, her affair with Giorgio is conducted as a series of "matinees," as she wryly observes. "Fosca," on the other hand, means dark, and, of course, she is just that. That their names are opposites may be confirmed by the related English verbs "to clarify" and "to obfuscate." As the show progresses, Clara is seen in progressively darker dresses, whereas Fosca gradually emerges from darkness.

95. As Scott Miller observes, the principal motive in "Loving You," a rising triad, resembles a bugle call; Miller connects this to Fosca's ruthlessness and the fact that until Giorgio arrives at the post, she has been reading military handbooks (MILLER-S4, p. 111).

96. Two other intriguing parallels between *Passion* and *Company* consist, first, in the recurrence of the number three, which in *Company* points to Bobby's position as a "third wheel" ("Side by Side by Side") and here to the introduction of an improbable alternative to a commitment already made. Thus, Fosca's first letter begins with the thrice-repeated "Three days" (the only words of the letter that she sings); Giorgio's letter on his return begins with the phrase "Three weeks" (sung twice by Clara—again, the only words from this letter that are sung rather than read aloud); Clara's letter to Giorgio, read while he sleeps in Fosca's sick bed (see figure 6.5), just prior to his writing the dictated letter to Fosca, begins, "It is three in the morning"; and, as reported in the doctor's letter to Giorgio at the final scene, "Fosca died three days after the night you two last saw one another." Regarding the importance of the number three to *Passion*, see KONAS.

Perhaps the most significant component of this shared "threeness" is a related parallel between the shows: the ways in which the "differences" manifest by their respective "third wheels"—Bobby and Fosca—relate to familiar tropes of homosexuality. Thus, Fosca's "Loving you is not a choice, / It's who I am" may be read as an extension of "being gay is not a choice," particularly since, as Geoffrey Block has pointed out, the latter claim is better grounded in recent psychological thought (personal communication).

97. Leitmotivs in *Passion* have been much discussed but rarely made full dramatic sense of. Steven Swayne (SWAYNE, pp. 228–33) provides a significant exception, however, as he details the interplay of two central motives in the show, which he terms "happiness" and "obsession." Particularly intriguing is Swayne's compelling argument that the "infection" of the latter motive is carried by the letters Clara reads (sings) from Giorgio.

Chapter Seven
Operatic Ambitions and Beyond

1. Regarding *Porgy and Bess*, see KNAPP1, chapter 8. We may note, as further evidence for the commercial folly of indulging operatic ambition on the Broadway stage, that *Porgy* achieved its first real success as a more conventional musical, and that *Porgy*, *Street Scene*, and even *The Most Happy Fella* have enjoyed their most lasting success when mounted as operas rather than as musicals.

2. Bernstein also argued this agenda offstage, both on television and in print (BERNSTEIN). Lehman Engel (ENGEL, pp. 137–38), however, argues that many mainstream shows already fit Bernstein's stated criteria for opera. For a wide-ranging

discussion that considers operatic musicals within the context of canon formation along the lines of the European operatic canon, see BLOCK1.

3. See "The Cast Album" in Mordden1 regarding the emergence of the cast album in the 1940s.

4. Hence, the twelve-tone fugue in *West Side Story*'s "Cool" and the more sinuous—and insinuating—twelve-tone "row" in *Candide*'s "Quiet."

5. For a discussion of Bernstein's general eclecticism and its manifestation in *Candide*, see LAIRD.

6. So billed in the London Symphony recording, conducted by Bernstein, released by Deutsche Grammophon in 1991 (429 734–2).

7. Not surprisingly, this "integrated" function of music may be traced to the Rodgers and Hammerstein collaborations. See, for example, Rodgers's "theory about musicals," redolent of Richard Wagner both in its central argument (cf. Wagner's *Gesamtkunstwerk*) and in the way Rodgers's theorizing, however modest compared to Wagner's, provides a platform for self-promotion: "When a show works perfectly, it's because all the individual parts complement each other and fit together. . . . In a great musical, the orchestrations sound the way the costumes look. That's what made *Oklahoma!* work. . . . It was a work created by many that gave the impression of having been created by one" (RODGERS, p. 227). It is telling, however, that Rodgers seems to locate this integrative dimension specifically within orchestration—which was something done to "flesh out" a composer's piano score, or "short score," in parallel to the function of costumes and scenery in relation to a show's book—rather than more directly within the composer's work. Arguably, even on this basis, Bernstein's and Sondheim's musico-dramatic ambitions were of a different order.

8. Leibniz was a philosopher-scientist-mathematician whose principal claim to fame today is his invention, along with Newton but working separately, of the calculus, one of the foundations of modern mathematics and physics. In many respects, Voltaire's vehement refutation of Leibniz was based on a simplistic view of what the latter argued, yet it also represented an attempt to take his ideas seriously, by trying—and failing—to find them resonant with the world as humans actually experienced it.

9. For the Bernstein-Hellman collaboration, Stravinsky's *The Rake's Progress* (1951), in which Robert Rounseville (their eventual Candide) had starred, was undoubtedly another important point of reference, as it similarly skews the episodic *Bildungsroman* through satire, and similarly refers to a variety of musical traditions in a bravura show of erudition.

10. Hellman eventually became the scapegoat for the show's failure, and, with her urging, her work and name were completely absent from the Wheeler version, although some of her material was restored for the 1989 opera version (after her death, in 1984). See PETERS for a brief and lively account of her involvement with the show. Her book receives its most ardent defense in MORDDEN4.

11. For useful accounts of Prince's renovation of *Candide*, see PRINCE, chapter 26; ILSON, pp. 212–25; and HIRSCH1, pp. 149–56.

12. Quoted in SECREST2, p. 120. Lyricist Richard Wilbur provides a similar account of the show's failure: "There was no single villain. Lillian Hellman doesn't really like musicals. Lenny's music got more and more pretentious and smashy—the audience forgot what was happening to the characters. Lillian's book got to be mere connective tissue" (BURTON, p. 263).

13. The character of Paquette, central to the original novella, is not in the original stage production but was restored for the revisions.

14. Confusedly, the original show opens on what is to be the wedding day of Candide and Cunegonde.

15. The auto-da-fé was an instrument of the Inquisition, which featured, in public, the execution or other punishment of heretics.

16. In the main, this revision restored John LaTouche's original lyric, although with some retouching by Sondheim.

17. The title of this duet may pay homage to "Happy we!"—the lovers' duet that ends the first act of Handel's 1718 masque *Acis and Galatea*. The situations are, indeed, somewhat parallel, as each duet celebrates an early exuberant coupling between lovers with mismatched pedigrees (Galatea is part goddess); moreover, both sets of lovers are separated immediately thereafter by force, in *Candide* by Cunegonde's outraged family, and in *Acis and Galatea* by the jealous Cyclops Polyphemus, who crushes Acis beneath a boulder. I thank Rose Rosengard Subotnik for pointing out this possible connection to me.

18. This canon is inexplicably not performed as such on the original cast album, where the two sing in unison.

19. A more direct point of reference, at least situationally, is the "Jewel Song" of Gounod's *Faust*; see BURTON, p. 260. From the operetta tradition, the most important nineteenth-century model for the type is probably the famous "Laughing Song" from Johann Strauss's *Die Fledermaus*; see also the discussions, in chapter 1, of "In the Modern Style," from *The Merry Widow* (p. 31), and the title song from *Little Mary Sunshine* (pp. 48–49).

20. See also the discussion of "I'm Wishing," from *Snow White and the Seven Dwarfs*, in chapter 3, p.126.

21. Pangloss's "Dear Boy"—a song about syphilis—offers another apparent reference to Gilbert and Sullivan in its musical presentation of skewed logic; see BURTON, p. 260.

22. See WELLS for further discussion of this musical blend of ethnicities.

23. Even so, Bernstein was concerned that the line might offend Spanish speakers, but this was partly an outgrowth of a general nervousness about the show's political content, especially those parts that refer to the McCarthy hearings.

24. Besides evoking the operetta-based "song of recognition" more generally, "You Were Dead, You Know" also evokes, with some specificity, a well-known model for the type: Papageno and Papagena's duet near the end of Mozart's *The Magic Flute*. Both numbers begin with their paired lovers repeating back versions of their mates' lines in overlapping imitation, before coming together in a concluding declaration of love. I thank Rose Rosengard Subotnik for pointing this connection out to me.

25. This second meditation is left out in the 1976 revision.

26. This number, which appears only in the 1989 version, comes as close as the musical seems willing—probably for generic reasons—to Voltaire's more realistic reduction of Cunegonde to an ugly hag by the time Candide marries her at the end.

27. In the first of these chorales, *Candide* echoes the concluding line of the chorus that ends Act II of Handel's 1752 oratorio *Jephtha* ("How dark, O Lord, are Thy decrees"). With insistent vehemence, Handel's chorus repeats the final words, "Whatever is, **is right**," to the point that he seems more to question than to confirm belief in the maxim. The literal darkness of the chorus's text—thus, the opening phrase,

and the line "As the night succeeds the day"—points to the special significance these final words may have held for Handel, since by 1752 he was rapidly losing his sight (*Jephtha* would be his last-completed large-scale work). Taken as a whole, *Jephtha* is remarkably bleak for an oratorio and seems at times to be the musical equivalent of Voltaire's *Candide*—which was, after all, written only a few years later. The possibly direct relationship between *Candide* and Handel's oratorio seems, confusedly, both confirmed and undermined by the fact that both texts have a common source in the final six lines of Alexander Pope's *An Essay on Man: Epistle One*, first published in 1733: "All Nature is but art unknown to thee; / All chance, direction, which thou canst not see; / All discord, harmony, not understood; / All partial evil, universal good; / And, spite of pride, in erring reason's spite, / One truth is clear, Whatever is, is right."

28. Paul Laird finds echoes of both Copland ("The Promise of Living" from *The Tender Land*) and Mahler's choral style in this number; see Laird, p. 37. Regarding Copland and Bernstein's evolution of a generally accepted American "sound" and its relationship to their sexual orientations, see Hubbs. Regarding Copland's situation as a gay Jewish composer who nevertheless contributed centrally to this distinctive sound, see Pollack.

29. McClary provides her most extended argument along these lines in McClary1.

30. The Grand Guignol was a theater in the Montmartre district of Paris from 1897 to 1962, specializing in shocking special effects and lifelike gore, having much of the appeal of today's slasher films, but in a more intimate space. In its day, the theater was a tourist attraction on a par with the Louvre and Eiffel Tower. For a useful contextualization of the legendary character Sweeney Todd within the "penny dreadful" literature, see Smith. As Smith lays out (pp. 21–28), Sweeney first made his appearance in *The String of Pearls*, 1846, and received his definitive treatment in *Sweeney Todd, the Demon Barber of Fleet Street* in about 1878 [*sic*; Hazleton's story was published in 1862], but antecedents for the character may be found in *The Tell-Tale* (1824), *The Murderous Barber* (1825), and *Joddrel, the Barber* (1844); the character had enough currency that "Tom Pinch in *Martin Chuzzlewit* [by Charles Dickens] in 1843–44 hopes he will not be turned into meat pies" (p. 23).

In both his introduction to Hazleton and his book-length treatment of the subject (Haining), Peter Haining also notes the lineage back to *The Tell-Tale* and the reference in *Martin Chuzzlewit*, relates the story unsatisfactorily to the legend of Sawney Bean, a cannibalistic Scot from the time of James I, and finally argues that the story must have had some basis in fact, perhaps traceable in the so-far-unverified *Newgate Calendar* 1802 account of a Sweeney Todd executed in 1785 (pp. 42–43 in the former source). Cf. Meryle Secrest's discussion of precedents (including Shakespeare's *Titus Andronicus*, replete with meat pies) in Secrest2, p. 289. An unpublished theatrical treatment by George Dibdin Pitt has apparently circulated in various versions from 1847 on, which helps explain the story's tenacious currency. Regarding the play's provenance, see Swain, pp. 360–61, and Gordon1, pp. 207–10.

31. Quoted in Secrest2, p. 290. It was apparently Hugh Wheeler who showed Sondheim that much of the play was in blank verse, since it is not obvious from the conventional layout of the printed play; see Banfield2, p. 282. Bond's play started out as a "doctoring" of the nineteenth-century Pitt version, but in his words, "It didn't need doctoring, it needed a heart transplant, and preferably new lungs and balls as well. . . . I crossed Dumas's *The Count of Monte Cristo* with Tourneur's *The*

Revenger's Tragedy for a plot; added elements of pastiche Shakespeare in a sort of blankish verse for Sweeney, the Judge, and the lovers to talk; borrowed the name of the author of *The Prisoner of Zenda* for my sailor boy; remembered some market patter I'd learnt as a child; and adapted the wit and wisdom of Brenda, who ran the greengrocer's shop opposite my house, for Mrs. Lovett's rumination upon life, death, and the state of her sex life" (introduction to *Sweeney Todd* [1991], pp. 3–4). In his preface to the play (BOND), Bond also lists *The Spanish Tragedy* among his "inspirations" (p. v); the latter—by Thomas Kyd, a slightly older contemporary of Shakespeare and Christopher Marlowe—is a revenge tragedy written (like much of Bond's play) in blank verse.

32. For an interesting speculation on the operatic dimension of *Sweeney Todd*, and its compositional basis in Sondheim's early attempt simply to set the play to music, see BANFIELD2, pp. 285–92. Although I will consider a variety of ways that the show might or might not be understood as operatic, or even opera, it does not conform well to any specific opera tradition, and—in terms of how its music supports the central action—often shows much more affinity with old-fashioned melodrama and film.

33. Regarding Sondheim's adroit conversion of Bond's text into song lyrics, see BANFIELD2, pp. 87–89 and 283–85.

34. Regarding Sondheim's artistic debt to Hammerstein, see MILNER. Sondheim has consistently credited Hammerstein for teaching him the craft of integrating lyrics and drama. A good account of Hammerstein's often harsh criticism of Sondheim's early work may be found in SECREST2, pp. 50–53 and 89–91, along with a moving account of Sondheim's gratitude (pp. 142–43).

35. Most prescient in this regard is the reaction of Judy Prince (Hal's wife) when Sondheim played through some of his work on *Sweeney Todd*: "It's nothing to do with Grand Guignol. It's the story of your life" (quoted in SECREST2, p. 295).

36. Britain began establishing penal colonies in Australia in the wake of the American Revolution and continued to do so until 1868. Before the American Revolution, petty criminals had been sent to the American colonies as indentured labor.

37. Quoted in SECREST2, p. 290.

38. For a related discussion of this deployment of the serious and comic in *Sweeney Todd*, see HIRSCH1, pp. 124–27. See also Joanne Gordon's somewhat different account of this dynamic in GORDON1, pp. 218–21. Sondheim describes the effect of the first such rescue ("The Worst Pies in London"): "The audience has just gone through five to ten minutes of intense and very brooding and creepy atmospheric stuff, and I wanted the contrast to be sudden and sharp, just the way the contrast between the two characters is sudden and sharp—Todd, the brooding, totally involved, obsessive man and Mrs. Lovett, the cheerful, totally amoral, practical, chatty lady" (ZADAN, p. 249). At the end of Act I, it is Mrs. Lovett who again tempers Sweeney's excesses, this time with macabre humor. The denial of this pattern at the end of the show is thus in an important sense "embodied": when Todd kills Mrs. Lovett late in the second act, he also kills abruptly the possibility of a third comic rescue engineered by her, a process already seemingly under way with a (soon-aborted) reprise of "A Little Priest."

39. Regarding Sondheim's use of the Dies Irae in *Sweeney Todd*, see BANFIELD2, pp. 297–301.

40. Thus, although Wagner (and sometimes Britten) have stood in for the operatic tradition in accounts of *Sweeney Todd*, it is the film composer Bernard Herrmann whom Sondheim foregrounds as his musical inspiration in this score; see BANFIELD2, pp. 305–7; HOROWITZ-M, pp. 127–28; SECREST2, p. 295; and SCHLESINGER, p. 127. See also ZADAN, who quotes Sondheim as follows: "What I wanted to write . . . was a horror movie. The whole point of the thing is that it's a background score for a horror film" (p. 246); and later, "It's because something is *promised* [by the music]. Hitchcock and all of the people who've ever done suspense used music in that way. Music is what holds it together. That's why so much of *Sweeney Todd* is sung and underscored—not because I wanted to do an opera, but because I realized that the only way to sustain tension was to use music continually, not to let the heat out, so that even if they're talking, there's music going on in the pit" (pp. 247–48). As Steven Swayne argues, however, opera remained an important frame of reference for *Sweeney Todd*, evident in the deployment of vocal types according to operatic traditions, regarding both musical features and dramatic associations; see SWAYNE, pp. 181–88.

41. Among various discussions of Sondheim's motivic manipulations in *Sweeney Todd*, cf. especially SWAIN, pp. 363–80, and BANFIELD2, pp. 300–305.

42. Ellipses are added to indicate gaps in delivery.

43. Sondheim describes the intended effect of this musical reminiscence: "The beggar woman is in disguise, . . . and the audience is supposed to be surprised in the end when they find out who she is. A few, very alert people caught on right away though, and knew that the beggar woman was Sweeney's wife, because when the young wife appears and is raped, the minuet they're playing is the beggar woman's theme in a different guise. The justification for this is that the lady's gone crazy because of the rape and the symbol of that rape is the music which is always playing in her mind" (quoted in ZADAN, pp. 251–52; for related discussions, see BANFIELD2, pp. 295–96, and CITRON2, p. 249).

44. See the discussion of this motivic family in BANFIELD2, pp. 295–96.

45. For a related discussion, see KNAPP5.

46. See also Joseph Swain's discussion of how Sondheim's complex musical language helps to achieve a distinctive "atmosphere" in *Sweeney Todd*, as well as in his other shows (SWAIN, pp. 350–60).

47. Hazleton's original story also begins with a prologue, perhaps a crude model for Sondheim's; Hazleton's first words are "Listen, oh listen, to a story of deep demoniac dread, / A narrative heaped with horrors, all piled upon horror's head; / Such a terrible tale you'll never discover where'er you plod / As this, of a Demon Barber, whom people called Sweeney Todd" (HAZLETON, p. 51). Bond's play, on the other hand, begins with the arrival of Anthony and Sweeney in what is a clear model for what follows Sondheim's prologue; thus,

> ANTHONY: I have sailed the world, beheld its fairest cities, seen the pyramids, the
>   wonders of the east. Yet it is true—there *is* no place like home.
> TODD: None.
> ANTHONY: What's the matter?
> TODD: You are young. Life has been kind to you.

(BOND, p. 1).

48. The chimes of Big Ben, the bell clock atop the tower at Westminster, consist of one to four phrases in even note values, repeating the same four notes in different

orders, depending on which quarter of the hour is being struck. The most distinctive (and much-quoted) phrase consists of two subphrases, but this segment is never heard separately (numbers refer to degrees of the scale, with 5 below 1):

3–1–2–5 / 5–2–3–1

(This is as given in the top line of example 7.3c in a different rhythm). The actual chimes are:

3–2–1–5 (quarter hour)
1–3–2–5 / 1–2–3–1 (half hour)
3–1–2–5 / 5–2–3–1 / 3–2–1–5 (three-quarter hour)
1–3–2–5 / 1–2–3–1 / 3–1–2–5 / 5–2–3–1 (full hour)

When Big Ben was completed in 1858, it was the largest clock in the world; its chimes were patterned after the Saint Mary's chimes in Cambridge (installed in 1793), which were in turn based, reportedly, on a phrase from "I Know That My Redeemer Liveth" from Handel's *Messiah*. In Hazleton's 1862 story, Big Ben is the "Tower warder," uncle to Johanna, who finds Toby Ragg just after his discovery of a dismembered arm and later helps apprehend Todd.

49. As noted by Citron2, p. 250, "My Friends" is based on an inversion of the Dies Irae.

50. Specifically, the motive moves 2–5–2–3, with 5 in the upper octave rather than the lower.

51. Mordden6, p. 229.

52. Cf. the discussions of this passage in Banfield2, p. 9, and Puccio/Stoddart, pp. 125–26.

53. Andrew Lloyd Webber, "The Music of Evita," in Lloyd Webber/Rice. This unusual resource presents the songs and action from the then-projected stage show alongside a reasonably accurate historical account of its people and events. The quoted passage follows Lloyd Webber's praise for the direction that the American musical had taken after *Oklahoma!*

54. To some extent, Lloyd Webber's prejudice against the musical undoubtedly derived from his recent failed attempt at a more conventional mix of comedy, dialogue, and song, in the 1975 *Jeeves*.

55. See, for example, the discussion in chapter 12 of Swain, especially pp. 322–26.

56. Regarding Prince's modifications to the show's politics, see Ilson, pp. 265–68 and 271; and Hirsch1, pp. 159–65.

57. Che adopts the persona of Che Guevara, then a young Argentinean revolutionary who had no known contact with Eva Perón, except as he opposed the Perón regime from relative obscurity, but who would later become famous as an associate of Fidel Castro.

58. Stravinsky's *The Rake's Progress* is perhaps the best exemplar in English for this aesthetic; regarding how Stravinsky developed this approach, see Taruskin.

59. See Swain, p. 325.

60. See ibid.

61. Che's song refers to Eva's burial ("Demand to be buried like Eva Peron"), but her body, although well preserved through embalming, was in fact buried not in Argentina but in a humble grave under another name in Italy. Nearly two decades later, it was restored to Juan Perón. Shortly thereafter, he returned to assume the presidency of Argentina, but his term in office was cut short by his death; he was

succeeded by Isabel Perón, the woman Perón married while in exile, who, unlike Eva (but clearly owing to her example and courageous advocacy of women's rights), had by then been elected vice president.

62. Quoted from LLOYD WEBBER/RICE, "The Music of Evita."

63. Even here, it was a near miss, as the first line—and thus the title—was in flux right through the making of the studio recording with Julie Covington. The earlier line for which the title substitutes—which would have had the virtue of making the second line a more obvious consequent, but which would perhaps have announced too loudly that she was addressing them as one would a lover—was, "It's only your lover returning." See CITRON2, pp. 226–29, for a useful account of the development of this song.

64. This promise of ready-made divahood is of course a false one; while the familiar "Don't Cry for Me Argentina" may practically sing itself, much of the score is quite difficult, with frequent meter and tempo changes.

65. Although Sondheim has seemed to triumph over his critics, having acquired an enduring and increasingly secure reputation, as well as having inspired a large literature celebrating him and his achievements, his support among commentators remains far from universal. See, for example, chapter 9 in LEWIS-DH. Despite Lewis's occasional grudging compliment, his summation of Sondheim's career early in the chapter, as an "act of mutiny" (p. 108), remains his dominant theme throughout, and his portrait of Sondheim, as having willfully betrayed both his inheritance and his own talent, represents a now-typical profile of negative Sondheim criticism. Lewis also well represents the other component of this position, in his subsequent paeans to Andrew Lloyd Webber, Cameron Mackintosh, and Claude-Michel Schönberg (chapters 12 and 13 of the same volume).

66. I have argued more extensively and specifically for Sondheim's grounding in traditional Broadway in KNAPP2.

67. See GRANT, p. 99, for an account of those he terms "Sondheimistas," composers who imitate some of Sondheim's mannerisms (such as ostinato-based accompaniment supporting a recitative-like melodic declamation), in which category Grant places Jonathan Larson, Michael John LaChiusa, and Bill Russell.

68. For a discussion of this dimension of Sondheim's work, see chapter 43 in McLAMORE.

69. The most extended critique along these lines is GRANT. Because the period Grant laments—his "belle époque"—is considerably longer than the post-*Oklahoma!* golden age, extending from 1927 (that is, from *Show Boat*) to 1966, he is able to ground each of his complaints in a description of a more extended evolutionary process. His list is not wholly congruent with my list of conventional complaints; specifically, he does not mention Stonewall's impact, and he includes an extended section in which he traces (and bemoans) the rise of the director-choreographer as a controlling creative force on Broadway. The first extended discussion of the impact of amplification on Broadway is BURSTON. The demise of the golden age is a central theme in the final volume of Ethan Mordden's series of books on the musical (MORDDEN6); Mordden sees that demise as primarily a combination of increasing expense and the shift to a rock-based sound. For a more enthusiastic critique of the last twenty years, as (to paraphrase and drastically simplify) a partial resurfacing of golden-age values and qualities in more modern dress, see LEWIS-DH, chapters 12–17; see also chapter 12 in GÄNZL.

70. Although some will be more inclined than others to see Disney's move to Broadway as ironic, it followed a growing awareness that the Disney animated films had become, in Rose Rosengard Subotnik's phrase, "the last repository of the old-fashioned, mainstream Broadway type of musical" (personal communication). Regarding Disney's reliance on operetta styles, in particular, see BANFIELD1, pp. 332–33.

71. For an excellent, extended discussion of the megamusical and how it evolved, especially between *Jesus Christ Superstar* (1971) and *Phantom of the Opera* (1988), and including major discussions of both *Cats* (1982) and Claude-Michel Schönberg's *Les Misérables* (1987), see STERNFELD. In her final chapter, on the 1990s, Sternfeld also discusses, among others, Lloyd Webber's *Aspects of Love* (1990) and *Sunset Boulevard* (1994); Schönberg's *Miss Saigon* (1991); Disney's *Beauty and the Beast* (Alan Menken, 1994), *The Lion King* (Elton John and others, 1997), and *Aida* (Elton John, 2000); and Frank Wildhorn's *Jeckyl & Hyde* (1997), *The Scarlet Pimpernel* (1997, discussed here in chapter 4), and *The Civil War* (1999).

72. In the event, however, few revivals actually turn a profit, and one of those few that continue as of this writing to make money—*Chicago*—was originally only moderately successful; see "Hey, Let's Not Put on a Show!" by Jesse McKinley, *New York Times*, August 21, 2005.

73. See PRECE/EVERETT; quoted phrase from p. 246. The principal dramatic features of French grand opera scarcely needed resurrection, however, since they have long been the basis of epic movies.

74. *Rent* is also somewhat anomalous as a show; like *Hair* (to which it is most frequently compared), it initially positioned itself apart from Broadway, yet its stylistic affinities place it somewhere between the "pincers" of Sondheim and Lloyd Webber, drawing inspiration from both.

75. Stacy Wolf argues persuasively that what I term the show's "compromises" actually extend a vital strand of Gregory Maguire's original novel: its lesbian subtext. This extension requires—usefully for a musical, and in a way especially relevant to *Wicked*'s largely feminine fanbase—that Elphaba's relationship with Glinda *not* devolve into an isolating opposition, even though the latter development is central to the devastating effect of the novel's tragic trajectory (Wolf, " 'We're Not in Kansas Anymore': The Broadway Musical, Women, and *Wicked*" [article in development]; I thank the author for sharing a preliminary draft of this essay with me).

76. It is, of course, possible to find "Americans" within European subjects and stories. Thus, for example, the heroine of Disney's 1994 *Beauty and the Beast*, like many a Disney heroine, seems nothing so much as a transplanted American despite her ostensibly foreign roots (cf. my discussion of *Snow White* in chapter 3).

77. For an account of how globalization has fed and shaped the growth of the megamusical, see chapter 6 ("Modernity, Globalization, and the Megamusical") of WALSH/PLATT.

78. How exactly community musical theater articulates with Broadway and its traditions is difficult to pin down. Graham Raulerson argues that, while the "text" for such performance traditions is itself a complicated affair, and differently constituted for each venue, its social function comes much closer in many cases to ritual than to entertainment ("Establishing Texts, Canonizing Texts: Theater and Ritual in the Performance Contexts of the American Musical," unpublished paper).

79. In yet another way—through sitcoms—the living-room television often became a venue for musical performance much like that found in stage and film musicals; see STILWELL.

80. For a discussion of the alienating effect of amplification, in particular, see BURSTON, especially his discussion of the "audio-visual split," pp. 209–12. The term "audio-visual split" was coined by John Corbett to describe a fetishized ideal of modern audiophiles; see CORBETT, p. 38.

81. The kind of reaction to *Phantom of the Opera* and *Rent* described here is wholly typical of many students I have taught, and several colleagues who teach courses on the musical report similar preferences among their students. *Phantom* seems a particular locus of identification for young women, which a recent contribution to the "New Voices" feature of *Newsday*, by high school junior Caroline Brody, helps to explain. In "Seeing a Broadway Show Can Change Your Life" (November 8, 2004), she admits to seeing the show fifty-two times and describes both how its situation and story continue to inspire her and how she learns from details of its actors' performances, from "the way [they] breathe, or the way they hold their mouths, . . . the way that the dancers move their feet." I thank Rose Rosengard Subotnik for bringing this item to my attention.

BIBLIOGRAPHY

(See Also Appendix)

ADORNO: Adorno, Theodor W. *Mahler: A Musical Physiognomy.* Translated by Edmund Jephcott. Chicago: University of Chicago Press, 1992. Originally published as *Mahler: Eine musikalische Physiognomik.* Frankfurt am Main: Suhrkamp Verlag, 1971.

ALTMAN: Altman, Rick. *The American Film Musical.* Bloomington: Indiana University Press, 1987.

ANDERSON: Anderson, Graham. "Old Tales and New: Finding the First Fairy Tales." In *A Companion to the Fairy Tale,* edited by Hilda Ellis Davidson and Anna Chaudhri. Cambridge: D. S. Brewer, 2003, pp. 85–98.

ANOBILE: Anobile, Richard J. *The Official Rocky Horror Picture Show Movie Novel.* New York: A&W Visual Library, 1980.

ASHE: Ashe, Geoffrey. *The Discovery of King Arthur.* New York: Henry Holt, 1985.

BABINGTON: Babington, Bruce. "Jumping on the Band Wagon Again: Oedipus Backstage in the Father and Mother of All Musicals." In *Musicals: Hollywood and Beyond,* edited by Bill Marshall and Robynn Stilwell. Exeter: Intellect Books, 2000, pp. 31–39.

BANFIELD1: Banfield, Stephen. "Popular Song and Popular Music on Stage and Film." In *The Cambridge History of American Music,* edited by David Nicholls. Cambridge: Cambridge University Press, 1998, pp. 309–44.

BANFIELD2: ———. *Sondheim's Broadway Musicals.* Ann Arbor: University of Michigan Press, 1993.

BELL: Bell, Matthew. "Musical Theater." In *Gay Histories and Cultures: An Encyclopedia,* edited by George E. Haggerty. New York: Garland, 2000, pp. 621–24.

BENNETT: Bennett, Robert Russell. *"The Broadway Sound": The Autobiography and Selected Essays of Robert Russell Bennett.* Edited by George J. Ferencz. Rochester, NY: University of Rochester Press, 1999.

BENSON: Benson, Sally. *Meet Me in St. Louis.* New York: Random House, 1942.

BERGSTEN: Bergsten, Staffan. *Mary Poppins and Myth.* Stockholm: Almqvist & Wiksell International, 1978.

BERNSTEIN: Bernstein, Leonard. "American Musical Comedy." In *The Joy of Music.* New York: Simon and Schuster, 1959, pp. 152–79.

BERST: Berst, Charles A. *Pygmalion: Shaw's Spin on Myth and Cinderella.* New York: Twayne Publishers, 1995.

BETTELHEIM: Bettelheim, Bruno. *The Uses of Enchantment: The Meaning and Importance of Fairy Tales.* New York: Knopf, 1977.

BLAMIRES: Blamires, David. "A Workshop of Editorial Practice: The Grimms' *Kinder- und Hausmärchen.*" In *A Companion to the Fairy Tale,* edited by Hilda Ellis Davidson and Anna Chaudhri. Cambridge: D. S. Brewer, 2003, pp. 71–83.

BLOCK1: Block, Geoffrey. "The Broadway Canon from *Show Boat* to *West Side Story* and the European Operatic Ideal." *The Journal of Musicology* 11, no. 4 (Autumn 1993): 525–44.

BLOCK2: ———. *Enchanted Evenings: The Broadway Musical from* Show Boat *to* Sondheim. New York: Oxford University Press, 1997.

BOGLE: Bogle, Donald. *Toms, Coons, Mulattoes, Mammies, & Bucks; An Interpretive History of Blacks in American Films.* 4th edition. New York: Continuum, 2001. First published 1973.

BOND: Bond, C[hristopher] G. *Sweeney Todd, the Demon Barber of Fleet Street.* London: Samuel French, 1974.

BORDMAN1: Bordman, Gerald. *American Musical Theatre: A Chronicle.* New York: Oxford University Press, 1986.

BORDMAN2: ———. *American Operetta from* H.M.S. Pinafore *to* Sweeney Todd. New York: Oxford University Press, 1981.

BRAUDY: Braudy, Leo. "Musicals and the Energy from Within." In *The World in a Frame: What We See in Films.* Chicago: University of Chicago Press, 2002 (first published 1976), pp. 139–63.

BRISTOW: Bristow, Eugene K., and J. Kevin Butler. "*Company,* About Face! The Show That Revolutionized the American Musical." *American Music* 5 (1987): 241–54.

BRYANT: Bryant, Dave. "The Uncanny Valley: Why Are Monster-Movie Zombies so Horrifying and Talking Animals so Fascinating?" http://www.arclight.net/~pdb/nonfiction/uncanny-valley.html (accessed May 30, 2005).

BURSTON: Burston, Jonathan. "Theatre Space as Virtual Place: Audio Technology, the Reconfigured Singing Body, and the Megamusical." *Popular Music* 17, no. 2 (May 1998): 205–18.

BUTLER: Butler, Judith. *Gender Trouble: Feminism and the Subversion of Identity.* New York: Routledge, 1990.

BURTON: Burton, Humphrey. *Leonard Bernstein.* New York: Doubleday, 1994.

CAMERON: Cameron, Evan William, ed. *Sound and the Cinema: The Coming of Sound to American Film.* Pleasantville, NY: Redgrave Publishing Company, 1980.

CARTMELL: Cartmell, Dan J. "Stephen Sondheim and the Concept Musical." Ph.D. dissertation, University of California, Santa Barbara, 1983.

CERVANTES: Cervantes, Míguel de. *Don Quixote.* Translated by Edith Grossman. New York: Harper Collins, 2003.

CHAUNCEY: Chauncey, George. *Gay New York: Gender, Urban Culture, and the Making of the Gay Male World, 1890–1940.* New York: Basic Books, 1994.

CITRON1: Citron, Stephen. *Noel and Cole: The Sophisticates.* Oxford: Oxford University Press, 1993.

CITRON2: ———. *Sondheim and Lloyd Webber: The New Musical.* Oxford: Oxford University Press, 2001.

CITRON3: ———. *The Wordsmiths: Oscar Hammerstein 2nd and Alan Jay Lerner.* Oxford: Oxford University Press, 1995.

CLOVER: Clover, Carol J. "Dancin' in the Rain." In *Hollywood Musicals: The Film Reader,* edited by Steven Cohan. London: Routledge, 2002, pp. 155–73.

CLUTTER: Clutter, Timothy. "Alone: The 'Outsider' in Sondheim's Works." *The Sondheim Review* 6, no. 3 (Winter 2000): 26–29.

COCKRELL: Cockrell, David. *Demons of Disorder: Early Blackface Minstrels and Their World.* Cambridge: Cambridge University Press, 1997.

COHAN: Cohan, Steven. " 'Feminizing' the Song-and-Dance Man: Fred Astaire and the Spectacle of Masculinity in the Hollywood Musical." In *Hollywood Musicals: The Film Reader,* edited by Steven Cohan. London: Routledge, 2002, pp. 87–101.

COMDEN/GREEN: Comden, Betty, and Adolph Green. *Singin' in the Rain*. New York: Viking Press, 1972.

CONE: Cone, Edward T. "The World of Opera and Its Inhabitants." In *Music: A View from Delft*, edited by Robert P. Morgan. Chicago: University of Chicago Press, 1989, pp. 125–38.

CORBETT: Corbett, John. "Free, Single, and Disengaged: Listening Pleasure and the Popular Music Object." In *Extended Play: Sounding Off from John Cage to Dr. Funkenstein*. Durham: Duke University Press, 1994, pp. 32–55. Essay originally published in *October* 54 (Fall 1990): 79–101.

COSTELLO: Costello, Donald P. *The Serpent's Eye: Shaw and the Cinema*. Notre Dame, IN: University of Notre Dame Press, 1965.

DAVIDSON/CHAUDHRI: Davidson, Hilda Ellis, and Anna Chaudhri. *A Companion to the Fairy Tale*. Cambridge: D. S. Brewer, 2003.

DECKER: Decker, Todd. "Rose's (Interminable) Turn: Jule Styne's *Gypsy* and the Ironies of Playing Mama Rose." Society for American Music Annual Conference, Eugene, Oregon, February 2005.

DELAMATER: Delamater, Jerome. *Dance in the Hollywood Musical*. Ann Arbor: UMI Research Press, 1981.

DiMAGGIO: DiMaggio, Paul. "Cultural Boundaries and Structural Change: The Extension of the High Culture Model to Theater, Opera, and the Dance, 1900–1940." In *Cultivating Differences: Symbolic Boundaries and the Making of Inequality*, edited by Michèle Lamont and Marcel Fournier. Chicago: University of Chicago Press, 1992, pp. 21–57.

DREW: Drew, David. *Kurt Weill: A Handbook*. Berkeley: University of California Press, 1987.

DUNDES1: Dundes, Alan, ed. *Cinderella: A Folklore Casebook*. New York: Garland Publishing, 1982.

DUNDES2: ———, ed. *Little Red Riding Hood: A Casebook*. Madison: University of Wisconsin Press, 1989.

DYER1: Dyer, Richard. "The Colour of Entertainment." In *Musicals: Hollywood and Beyond*, edited by Bill Marshall and Robynn Stilwell. Exeter: Intellect Books, 2000, pp. 23–30. Originally published *Sight and Sound*, 1995.

DYER2: Dyer, Richard. " 'I seem to find the happiness I seek': Heterosexuality and Dance in the Musical." In *Dance, Gender and Culture*, edited by Helen Thomas. London: Macmillan Press, 1993, pp. 49–65.

DYER3: ———. *Only Entertainment*. Expanded from the 1992 edition. London: Routledge, 2002.

DYER4: ———. "Sweet Charity." In *Only Entertainment*. London: Routledge, 2002, pp. 60–63. Originally published *The Movie, 1981*.

DYER5: ———. *White*. London: Routledge, 1997.

EELLS: Eells, George. *The Life That Late He Led: A Biography of Cole Porter*. New York: G. P. Putnam and Sons, 1967.

ENGEL: Engel, Lehman. *The American Musical Theater: A Consideration*. New York: Macmillan, 1967.

EVERETT: Everett, William A. "Romance, Nostalgia and Nevermore: American and British Operetta in the 1920s." In *The Cambridge Companion to the Musical*, edited by William A. Everett and Paul R. Laird. Cambridge: Cambridge University Press, 2002, pp. 47–62.

EVERETT/LAIRD: Everett, William A., and Paul R. Laird, eds. *The Cambridge Companion to the Musical*. Cambridge: Cambridge University Press, 2002.

EWEN: Ewen, David. *Complete Book of the American Musical Theater*. New York: Henry Holt, 1959.

FEHR/VOGEL: Fehr, Richard, and Frederick G. Vogel. *Lullabies of Hollywood: Movie Music and the Movie Musical, 1915–1992*. Jefferson, NC: McFarland, 1993.

FEUER: Feuer, Jane. *The Hollywood Musical*. Bloomington: Indiana University Press, 1982.

FINK: Fink, Robert. *Repeating Ourselves: American Minimal Music as Cultural Practice*. Berkeley: University of California Press, 2005.

FORDIN: Fordin, Hugh. *M-G-M's Greatest Musicals: The Arthur Freed Unit*. New York: Da Capo Press, 1996. Previously *The World of Entertainment! Hollywood's Greatest Musicals*. Garden City, NY: Doubleday and Company, 1975; and *The Movies' Greatest Musicals, Produced in Hollywood USA by the Freed Unit*. New York: F. Ungar, 1984.

FORTE1: Forte, Allen. *The American Popular Ballad of the Golden Era, 1924–1950*. Princeton: Princeton University Press, 1995.

FORTE2: ———. *Listening to Classic American Popular Songs*. New Haven: Yale University Press, 2001.

FRANK: Frank, Rusty E. *Tap! The Greatest Tap Dance Stars and Their Stories, 1900–1955*. Revised edition. New York: Da Capo Press, 1994. Originally published 1990.

FRASER: Fraser, Barbara Means. "Revisiting Greece: The Sondheim Chorus." In *Stephen Sondheim: A Casebook*, edited by Joanne Gordon. New York: Garland Publishing, 1997, pp. 223–49.

FREEDLAND: Freedland, Michael. *A Salute to Irving Berlin*. London: W. H. Allen, 1986.

FRICKE/SCARFONE/STILLMAN: Fricke, John, Jay Scarfone, and William Stillman. *The Wizard of Oz: The Official 50th Anniversary Pictorial History*. New York: Warner Books, 1989.

FRIEDWALD: Friedwald, Will. *Stardust Melodies: A Biography of Twelve of America's Most Popular Songs*. New York: Pantheon Books, 2002.

FURIA1: Furia, Philip. *Ira Gershwin: The Art of the Lyricist*. New York: Oxford University Press, 1996.

FURIA2: ———. *Irving Berlin: A Life in Song*. New York: Schirmer Books, 1998.

FURIA3: ———. *The Poets of Tin Pan Alley: A History of America's Great Lyricists*. New York: Oxford University Press, 1990.

GABBARD1: Gabbard, Krin. *Jammin' at the Margins: Jazz and the American Cinema*. Chicago: University of Chicago Press, 1996.

GABBARD2: ———, ed. *Representing Jazz*. Durham, NC: Duke University Press, 1995.

GÄNZL: Gänzl, Kurt. *The Musical: A Concise History*. Boston: Northeastern University Press, 1997.

GANS: Gans, Herbert. *Popular Culture and High Culture*. New York: Basic Books, 1974.

GAREBIAN: Garebian, Keith. *The Making of Gypsy*. Toronto: ECW Press, [1994].

GOLDMARK: Goldmark, Daniel. *Tunes for 'Toons: Music and the Hollywood Cartoon*. Berkeley: University of California Press, 2005.

GOODHART1: Goodhart, Sandor. "Introduction: Reading Sondheim; The End of Ever After." In *Reading Stephen Sondheim: A Collection of Critical Essays*, edited by Sandor Goodhart. New York: Garland Publishing, 2000, pp. 3–33.

GOODHART2: ———. " 'The Mother's Part': Love, Letters, and Reading in Sondheim's *Passion*." In *Reading Stephen Sondheim: A Collection of Critical Essays*, edited by Sandor Goodhart. New York: Garland Publishing, 2000, pp. 221–58.

GOODHART3: ———, ed. *Reading Stephen Sondheim: A Collection of Critical Essays*. New York: Garland Publishing, 2000.

GOODMAN: Goodman, Randolph. *From Script to Stage: Eight Modern Plays*. San Francisco: Rinehart Press, 1971.

GORDON1: Gordon, Joanne. *Art Isn't Easy: The Achievement of Stephen Sondheim*. Carbondale: Southern Illinois University Press, 1990.

GORDON2: ———, ed. *Stephen Sondheim: A Casebook*. New York: Garland Publishing, 1997.

GOTTFRIED1: Gottfried, Martin. *Broadway Musicals*. New York: Harry N. Abrams, 1979.

GOTTFRIED2: ———. *More Broadway Musicals: Since 1980*. New York: Harry N. Abrams, 1991.

GOTTLIEB: Gottlieb, Jack. "The Music of Leonard Bernstein: A Study of Melodic Manipulations." DMA dissertation, University of Illinois, 1964.

GOTTLIEB/KIMBALL: Gottlieb, Robert, and Robert Kimball. *Reading Lyrics*. New York: Pantheon Books, 2000.

GOTTSCHILD: Gottschild, Brenda Dixon. *Waltzing in the Dark: African American Vaudeville and Race Politics in the Swing Era*. New York: St. Martin's Press, 2000.

GRAFTON: Grafton, David. *Red, Hot and Rich: An Oral history of Cole Porter*. New York: Stein and Day, 1987.

GRANT: Grant, Mark. *The Rise and Fall of the Broadway Musical*. Boston: Northeastern University Press, 2004.

GRAZIANO: Graziano, John. "Images of African Americans: African-American Musical Theatre, *Show Boat* and *Porgy and Bess*." In *The Cambridge Companion to the Musical*, edited by William A. Everett and Paul R. Laird. Cambridge: Cambridge University Press, 2002, pp. 63–76.

GREEN1: Green, Stanley. *Broadway Musicals Show by Show*. Milwaukee: Hal Leonard Books, 1985.

GREEN2: ———. *The World of Musical Comedy: The Story of the American Musical Stage as Told through the Careers of Its Foremost Composers and Lyricists*. New York: Ziff-Davis Publishing Company, 1962.

HAINING: Haining, Peter. *The Mystery and Horrible Murders of Sweeney Todd, the Demon Barber of Fleet Street*. London: Frederick Muller, 1979.

HAMM1: Hamm, Charles. *Music in the New World*. New York: Norton, 1983.

HAMM2: ———. *Yesterdays: Popular Song in America*. New York: Norton, 1983.

HARMETZ: Harmetz, Aljean. *The Making of* The Wizard of Oz: *Movie Magic and Studio Power in the Prime of MGM—and the Miracle of Production #1060*. New York: Dell Publishers, 1977.

HARTY: Harty, Kevin J. *King Arthur on Film: New Essays on Arthurian Cinema*. Jefferson, NC: McFarland, 1999.

HAVENS: Havens, Candace. *Joss Whedon: The Genius Behind Buffy*. Dallas: Benbella Books, 2003.

HAZLETON: Hazleton, Frederick. *Sweeney Todd, the Demon Barber of Fleet Street*. Introduction by Peter Haining. London: W. H. Allen, 1980. Story originally published 1862.

HENKIN: Henkin, Bill. *The Rocky Horror Picture Show Book*. New York: Hawthorn Books, 1979.

HILL: Hill, Constance Valis. *Brotherhood in Rhythm: The Jazz Tap Dancing of the Nicholas Brothers*. Oxford: Oxford University Press, 2000.

HIRSCH1: Hirsch, Foster. *Harold Prince and the American Musical Theatre*. Cambridge: Cambridge University Press, 1989.

HIRSCH2: ———. *Kurt Weill on Stage: From Berlin to Broadway*. New York: Alfred A. Knopf, 2002.

HIRSCHHORN: Hirschhorn, Clive. *Gene Kelly: A Biography*. New York: St. Martin's Press, 1984.

HOLLISS/SIBLEY: Holliss, Richard, and Brian Sibley. *Walt Disney's* Snow White and the Seven Dwarfs *and the Making of the Classic Film*. New York: Simon & Schuster, 1987.

HORN: Horn, Barbara Lee. *The Age of* Hair: *Evolution and Impact of Broadway's First Rock Musical*. New York: Greenwood Press, 1991.

HOROWITZ-J: Horowitz, Joseph. *Wagner Nights: An American History*. Berkeley: University of California Press, 1994.

HOROWITZ-M: Horowitz, Mark Eden. *Sondheim on Music: Minor Details and Major Decisions*. Lanham, MD: Scarecrow Press, 2003.

HUBBS: Hubbs, Nadine. *The Queer Composition of America's Sound: Gay Modernists, American Music, and National Identity*. Berkeley: University of California Press, 2004.

HULETT: Hulett, Steve. "The Making of *Snow White and the Seven Dwarfs*." In *Walt Disney's* Snow White and the Seven Dwarfs, edited by Jack Solomon Jr. New York: Viking Press, 1979, pp. 215–25.

HUGGETT: Huggett, Richard. *The Truth about* Pygmalion. New York: Random House, 1969.

ILSON: Ilson, Carol. *Harold Prince: From* Pajama Game *to* Phantom of the Opera. Ann Arbor: UMI Research Press, 1989.

JABLONSKI1: Jablonski, Edward. *Harold Arlen: Rhythm, Rainbows, and Blues*. Boston: Northeastern University Press, 1996.

JABLONSKI2: ———. *Irving Berlin: American Troubadour*. New York: Henry Holt, 1999.

JACQUES: Jacques, Geoffrey. "Listening to Jazz." In *American Popular Music: New Approaches to the Twentieth Century*, edited by Rachel Rubin and Jeffrey Melnick. Amherst: University of Massachusetts Press, 2001, pp. 65–92.

JASEN: Jasen, David A. *Tin Pan Alley: The Composers, the Songs, the Performers and Their Times*. New York: Donald I. Fine, 1988.

JENKINS: Jenkins, Jennifer R. " 'Say It with Firecrackers': Defining the 'War Musical' of the 1940s." *American Music* 19 (2001): 315–39.

JONES: Jones, John Bush. *Our Musicals, Ourselves: A Social History of the American Musical Theater*. Hanover, NH: Brandeis University Press, 2003.

KANTER: Kanter, Kenneth Aaron. *The Jews of Tin Pan Alley: The Jewish Contribution to American Popular Music, 1830–1940*. New York: Ktav Publishing House, and Cincinnati: American Jewish Archives, 1982.

KATZ: Katz, Jonathan Ned. *Gay/Lesbian Almanac*. New York: Harper & Row, 1983.

KAUFMAN: Kaufman, Gerald. *Meet Me in St. Louis*. London: BFI Publishing, 1994.

KISLAN: Kislan, Richard. *The Musical: A Look at the American Musical Theater*. Revised, expanded edition. New York: Applause Books, 1995.

KLEINHANS: Kleinhans, Chuck. "Taking Out the Trash; Camp and the Politics of Parody." In *The Politics and Poetics of Camp*, edited by Moe Meyer. London: Routledge, 1994, pp. 182–201.

KNAPP1: Knapp, Raymond. *The American Musical and the Formation of National Identity*. Princeton: Princeton University Press, 2005.

KNAPP2: ———. "*Assassins, Oklahoma!* and the 'Shifting Fringe of Dark Around the Campfire.'" *Cambridge Opera Journal* 16 (2004): 77–101.

KNAPP3: ———. "Music, Electricity, and the 'Sweet Mystery of Life' in *Young Frankenstein*." In *Changing Tunes: The Use of Pre-existing Music in Film*, edited by Phil Powrie and Robynn Stilwell. Aldershot, UK: Ashgate, 2006, pp. 105–18.

KNAPP4: ———. "Reading Gender in Late Beethoven: *An die Freude* and *An die ferne Geliebte*." *Acta musicologica* 75, no. 1 (2003): 45–63.

KNAPP5: ———. " 'Selbst dann bin ich die Welt': On the Subjective-Musical Basis of Wagner's *Gesamtkunstwelt*." *19th-Century Music* 29 (Fall 2005): 142–60.

KNAPP-S: Knapp, Shoshana Milgram. "Difference and Sameness: Tarchetti's *Fosca*, Scola's *Passione d'amore*, and Sondheim's *Passion*." In *Reading Stephen Sondheim: A Collection of Critical Essays*, edited by Sandor Goodhart. New York: Garland Publishing, 2000, pp. 101–19.

KNIGHT: Knight, Arthur. *Disintegrating the Musical: Black Performance and American Musical Film*. Durham, NC: Duke University Press, 2002.

KONAS: Konas, Gary. "*Passion*: Not Just Another Simple Love Story." In *Stephen Sondheim: A Casebook*, edited by Joanne Gordon. New York: Garland Publishing, 1997, pp. 205–22.

KOWALKE: Kowalke, Kim H., ed. *A New Orpheus: Essays on Kurt Weill*. New Haven: Yale University Press, 1986.

KRASNER: Krasner, Orly Leah. "Birth Pangs, Growing Pains and Sibling Rivalry: Musical Theatre in New York, 1900–1920." In *The Cambridge Companion to the Musical*, edited by William A. Everett and Paul R. Laird. Cambridge: Cambridge University Press, 2002, pp. 29–46.

KREUGER: Kreuger, Miles, ed. *The Movie Musical from Vitaphone to* 42nd Street *as Reported in a Great Fan Magazine*. New York: Dover Publications, 1975.

LAING: Laing, Heather. "Emotion by Numbers: Music, Song and the Musical." In *Musicals: Hollywood and Beyond*, edited by Bill Marshall and Robynn Stilwell. Exeter: Intellect Books, 2000, pp. 5–13.

LAIRD: Laird, Paul R. "The Best of All Possible Legacies: A Critical Look at Bernstein, His Eclecticism, and *Candide*." *Ars musica Denver* 4, no. 1 (1991): 30–39.

LAMB1: Lamb, Andrew. *150 Years of Popular Musical Theatre*. New Haven: Yale University Press, 2000.

LAMB2: ———. "*Die lustige Witwe (The Merry Widow)*." In *The New Grove Dictionary of Music Online*, edited by Laura Macy. http://www.grovemusic.com.

LAUFE: Laufe, Abe. *Broadway's Greatest Musicals*. Revised edition. New York: Funk & Wagnalls, 1977.

LAURENTS: Laurents, Arthur. *Original Story By: A Memoir of Broadway and Hollywood*. New York: Alfred A. Knopf, 2000.

LAWSON-PEEBLES1: Lawson-Peebles, Robert, ed. *Approaches to the American Musical*. Exeter: University of Exeter Press, 1996.

LAWSON-PEEBLES2: ———. "Brush Up Your Shakespeare: The Case of *Kiss Me, Kate*." In *Approaches to the American Musical*, edited by Robert Lawson-Peebles. Exeter: University of Exeter Press, 1996, pp. 89–108.

LEE: Lee, Gypsy Rose [Rose Louise Hovick]. *Gypsy: A Memoir*. New York: Harper & Brothers, 1957.

LEES: Lees, Gene. *Inventing Champagne: The Worlds of Lerner and Loewe*. New York: St. Martin's Press, 1990.

LERNER1: Lerner, Alan Jay. "Lyrics for *My Fair Lady*." In Randolph Goodman. *From Script to Stage: Eight Modern Plays*. San Francisco: Rinehart Press, 1971, pp. 328–34.

LERNER2: ———. *The Musical Theatre: A Celebration*. New York: McGraw-Hill, 1986.

LERNER3: ———. *The Street Where I Live*. New York: Norton, 1978.

LEWIS-DH: Lewis, David H. *Broadway Musicals: A Hundred Year History*. Jefferson, NC: McFarland, 2002.

LEWIS-DL: Lewis, David L. *When Harlem Was in Vogue*. New York: Vintage Books, 1982.

LHAMON: Lhamon, W. T., Jr. *Raising Cain: Blackface Performance from Jim Crow to Hip Hop*. Cambridge, MA: Harvard University Press, 1998.

LLOYD WEBBER/RICE: Webber, Andrew Lloyd, and Tim Rice. *Evita: The Legend of Eva Peron, 1919–1952*. London: Elm Tree Books, 1978.

LONEY: Loney, Glenn, ed. *Musical Theatre in America: Papers and Proceedings of the Conference on the Musical Theatre in America*. Westport, CT: Greenwood Press, 1981.

LOTT1: Lott, Eric. *Love and Theft: Blackface Minstrelsy and the American Working Class*. New York: Oxford University Press, 1993.

LOTT2: ———. "The Whiteness of Film Noir." In *Whiteness: A Critical Reader*, edited by Mike Hill. New York: New York University Press, 1997, pp. 81–101.

LOVENSHEIMER: Lovensheimer, Jim. "Stephen Sondheim and the Musical of the Outsider." In *The Cambridge Companion to the Musical*, edited by William A. Everett and Paul R. Laird. Cambridge: Cambridge University Press, 2002, pp. 181–96.

MAGEE: Magee, Jeffrey. "Ragtime and Early Jazz." In *The Cambridge History of American Music*, edited by David Nicholls. Cambridge: Cambridge University Press, 1998, pp. 388–417.

MAGUIRE: Maguire, Gregory. *Wicked: The Life and Times of the Wicked Witch of the West*. New York: Regan Books, 1995.

MAHLER: Mahler, Alma. *Gustav Mahler: Memories and Letters*. Revised and edited by Donald Mitchell. Translated by Basil Creighton. London: John Murray, 1968. Originally published Amsterdam, 1940.

MANKIN: Mankin, Nina. "Casebook #2: *Into the Woods*." *Performing Arts Journal* 11, no. 1 (1988): 46–66.

MARCHESANI: Marchesani, Joseph. "Arresting Development: Law, Love, and the Name-of-the-Father in *Sweeney Todd*." In *Reading Stephen Sondheim: A Collection of Critical Essays*, edited by Sandor Goodhart. New York: Garland Publishing, 2000, pp. 171–85.

MARKS: Marks, Martin. *Music and the Silent Film: Contexts and Case Studies, 1895–1924*. New York: Oxford University Press, 1997.

MARMORSTEIN: Marmorstein, Gary. *Hollywood Rhapsody: Movie Music and Its Makers, 1900–1975*. New York: Schirmer Books, 1997.

MARSHALL/STILWELL: Marshall, Bill, and Robynn Stilwell, eds. *Musicals: Hollywood and Beyond*. Exeter: Intellect Books, 2000.

MAST: Mast, Gerald. *Can't Help Singin': The American Musical on Stage and Screen*. Woodstock, NY: Overlook Press, 1987.

MATES: Mates, Julian. *America's Musical Stage: Two Hundred Years of Musical Theatre*. Westport, CT: Greenwood Press, 1985.

McCLARY1: McClary, Susan. *Conventional Wisdom: The Content of Musical Form*. Berkeley: University of California Press, 2000.

McCLARY2: ———. *Georges Bizet:* Carmen. Cambridge: Cambridge University Press, 1992.

McCLUNG: McClung, Bruce D. "Art Imitating Life Imitating Art: *Lady in the Dark*, Gertrude Lawrence, and *Star!*" *Kurt Weill Newsletter* 19, no. 2 (Fall 2001): 4–7, 12.

McCLUNG/LAIRD: McClung, Bruce D., and Paul R. Laird. "Musical Sophistication on Broadway: Kurt Weill and Leonard Bernstein." In *The Cambridge Companion to the Musical*, edited by William A. Everett and Paul R. Laird. Cambridge: Cambridge University Press, 2002, pp. 167–78.

McLAMORE: McLamore, Alyson. *Musical Theater: An Appreciation*. Upper Saddle River, NJ: Pearson Prentice Hall, 2004.

MELNICK: Melnick, Jeffrey. *A Right to Sing the Blues: African Americans, Jews, and American Popular Song*. Cambridge, MA: Harvard University Press, 1999.

MEYER: Meyer, Moe. *The Politics of Camp*. London: Routledge, 1994.

MEYERSON: Meyerson, Harold, and Ernie Harburg. *Who Put the Rainbow in* The Wizard of Oz? *Yip Harburg, Lyricist*. Ann Arbor: University of Michigan Press, 1993.

MICHAELS/EVANS: Michaels, Scott, and David Evans. Rocky Horror: *From Concept to Cult*. London: Sanctuary Publishing, 2002.

MILLER-DA1: Miller, D. A. "Anal *Rope*." *Representations* 32 (Fall, 1990): 114–33.

MILLER-DA2: ———. *Place for Us [Essay on the Broadway Musical]*. Cambridge, MA: Harvard University Press, 1998.

MILLER-S1: Miller, Scott. "*Assassins* and the Concept Musical." In *Stephen Sondheim: A Casebook*, edited by Joanne Gordon. New York: Garland Publishing, 1997, pp. 187–204.

MILLER-S2: ———. *Deconstructing Harold Hill: An Insider's Guide to Musical Theatre*. Portsmouth, NH: Heinemann, 2000.

MILLER-S3: ———. *From* Assassins *to* West Side Story: *The Director's Guide to Musical Theatre*. Portsmouth, NH: Heinemann, 1996.

MILLER-S4: ———. "Inside *Hedwig and the Angry Inch*." http://www.geocities.com/newlinetheatre/hedwigchapter.html, 2003 (accessed August 27, 2004).

MILLER-S5: ———. *Rebels with Applause: Broadway's Groundbreaking Musicals*. Portsmouth, NH: Heinemann, 2001.

MILNER: Milner, Andrew. " 'Let the Pupil Sow the Master': Stephen Sondheim and Oscar Hammerstein II." In *Stephen Sondheim: A Casebook*, edited by Joanne Gordon. New York: Garland Publishing, 1997, pp. 153–69.

MORDDEN1: Mordden, Ethan. *Beautiful Mornin': The Broadway Musical in the 1940s*. New York: Oxford University Press, 1999.

MORDDEN2: ———. *Better Foot Forward: The History of the American Musical Theatre*. New York: Grossman Publishers, 1976.

MORDDEN3: ———. *Broadway Babies: The People Who Made the American Musical.* New York: Oxford University Press, 1983.

MORDDEN4: ———. *Coming Up Roses: The Broadway Musical in the 1950s.* New York: Oxford University Press, 1998.

MORDDEN5: ———. *Make Believe: The Broadway Musical in the 1920s.* New York: Oxford University Press, 1997.

MORDDEN6: ———. *One More Kiss: The Broadway Musical in the 1970s.* New York: Palgrave Macmillan, 2003.

MORDDEN7: ———. *Open a New Window: The Broadway Musical in the 1960s.* New York: Palgrave, 2001.

MORI: Mori, Masahiro. *The Buddha in the Robot.* Translated by Charles S. Terry. Tokyo: Kosei Publishing, 1981.

MORRIS: Morris, Mitchell. "*Cabaret*, America's Weimar, and the Mythologies of the Gay Subject." *American Music* 22 (2004): 145–57.

MOST1: Most, Andrea. *Making Americans: Jews and the Broadway Musical.* Cambridge, MA: Harvard University Press, 2004.

MOST2: ———. " 'We Know We Belong to the Land': Jews and the American Musical Theater." Ph.D. dissertation, Brandeis University, 2001.

NICHOLLS: Nicholls, David, ed. *The Cambridge History of American Music.* Cambridge: Cambridge University Press, 1998.

OLSON: Olson, John. "*Company*—25 Years Later." In *Stephen Sondheim: A Casebook*, edited by Joanne Gordon. New York: Garland Publishing, 1997, pp. 47–67.

OSTROW: Ostrow, Stuart. *A Producer's Broadway Journey.* Westport, CT: Praeger Publishers, 1999.

PERAINO: Peraino, Judith. *Listening to the Sirens: Musical Technologies of Queer Identity from Homer to* Hedwig. Berkeley: University of California Press, 2006.

PETERS: Peters, Brooks. "Making Your Garden Grow: Lillian Hellman and *Candide.*" *Opera News* 65, no. 1 (July 2000): 38.

PEYSER: Peyser, Joan. *Leonard Bernstein: A Biography.* New York: Beech Tree Books, 1987.

PIRO: Piro, Sal. "*Creatures of the Night*": The Rocky Horror Picture Show *Experience.* Redford, MO: Stabur Press, 1990.

POLLACK: Pollack, Howard. *Aaron Copland: The Life and Work of an Uncommon Man.* New York: Henry Holt, 1999.

POPE: Pope, Alexander. *An Essay on Man.* 4 vols. London, 1733–34.

PORTER: Porter, Cole. *The Complete Lyrics of Cole Porter.* Edited by Robert Kimball. New York: Alfred A. Knopf, 1983.

POWRIE/STILWELL: Powrie, Phil, and Robynn Stilwell, eds. *Changing Tunes: The Use of Pre-existing Music in Film.* Aldershot, UK: Ashgate, 2006.

PRECE/EVERETT: Prece, Paul, and William A. Everett. "The Megamusical and Beyond: The Creation, Internationalisation and Impact of a Genre." In *The Cambridge Companion to the Musical*, edited by William A. Everett and Paul R. Laird. Cambridge: Cambridge University Press, 2002, pp. 246–65.

PRINCE: Prince, Hal. *Contradictions: Notes on Twenty-six Years in the Theatre.* New York: Dodd, Mead, 1974.

PUCCIO: Puccio, Paul M. "Enchantment on the Manicured Lawns: The Shakespearean 'Green World' in *A Little Night Music.*" In *Reading Stephen Sondheim: A*

Collection of Critical Essays, edited by Sandor Goodhart. New York: Garland Publishing, 2000, pp. 133–69.

PUCCIO/STODDART: Puccio, Paul M., and Scott F. Stoddart. " 'It Takes Two': A Duet on Duets in *Follies* and *Sweeney Todd*." In *Reading Stephen Sondheim: A Collection of Critical Essays*, edited by Sandor Goodhart. New York: Garland Publishing, 2000, pp. 121–29.

REICHARDT: Reichardt, Jasia. *Robots: Fact, Fiction, and Prediction*. London: Thames & Hudson, 1978.

REIK: Reik, Theodor. *The Haunting Melody: Psycholanalytic Experiences in Life and Music*. New York: Grove Press, 1960. Originally published Farrar, Straus & Cudahy, 1953.

REYNOLDS: Reynolds, Jean. Pygmalion's *Wordplay: The Postmodern Shaw*. Gainesville: University Press of Florida, 1999.

RIIS1: Riis, Thomas. *Just Before Jazz: Black Musical Theater in New York, 1890–1915*. Washington, DC: Smithsonian Institution, 1989.

RIIS2: ———. *More Than Just Minstrel Shows: The Rise of Black Musical Theatre at the Turn of the Century*. New York: Institute for Studies in American Music, 1992.

RIIS/SEARS: Riis, Thomas L., and Ann Sears. "The Successors of Rodgers and Hammerstein from the 1940s to the 1960s." In *The Cambridge Guide to the Musical*, edited by William A. Everett and Paul R. Laird. Cambridge: Cambridge University Press, 2002, pp. 137–66.

ROBERTS: Roberts, John Storm. *The Latin Tinge: The Impact of Latin American Music on the United States*. 2nd ed. New York: Oxford University Press, 1999.

ROBINSON: Robinson, David. *Music of the Shadows: The Use of Musical Accompaniment with Silent Films, 1896–1936*. Pordenone, Italy: Giornate del cinema muto, 1990.

RODGERS: Rodgers, Richard. *Musical Stages: An Autobiography*. New York: Random House, 1975.

ROFFMAN: Roffman, Frederick S. [Record-album notes.] *Naughty Marietta*. The Smithsonian American Musical Theater Series N 026, 1981.

ROGIN1: Rogin, Michael. *Blackface, White Noise: Jewish Immigrants in the Hollywood Melting Pot*. Berkeley: University of California Press, 1996.

ROGIN2: ———. "New Deal Blackface." In *Hollywood Musicals: The Film Reader*, edited by Steven Cohan. London: Routledge, 2002, pp. 175–82.

ROSENBERG/HARBURG: Rosenberg, Bernard, and Ernest Harburg. *The Broadway Musical: Collaboration in Commerce and Art*. New York: New York University Press, 1993.

ROWSE: Rowse, A. L. *Homosexuals in History: A Study of Ambivalence in Society, Literature and the Arts*. New York: Carroll & Graf Publishers, 1977.

RUBIN-J: Rubin, Joan Shelley. *The Making of Middlebrow Culture*. Chapel Hill: University of North Carolina Press, 1992.

RUBIN-M: Rubin, Martin. *Showstoppers: Busby Berkeley and the Tradition of Spectacle*. New York: Columbia University Press, 1993.

RUBIN/MELNICK: Rubin, Rachel, and Jeffrey Melnick, eds. *American Popular Music: New Approaches to the Twentieth Century*. Amherst: University of Massachusetts Press, 2001.

RUSHDIE: Rushdie, Salman. *The Wizard of Oz*. London: British Film Institute, 1992.

Russo: Russo, Vito. *The Celluloid Closet: Homosexuality in the Movies*. Revised ed. New York: Harper & Row, 1987. Original version 1981.

Said: Said, Edward. *Orientalism*. New York: Vintage Books, 1994. Originally published: Pantheon Books, 1978.

Sanders: Sanders, Ronald. *The Days Grow Short: The Life and Music of Kurt Weill*. New York: Holt, Rinehart and Winston, 1980.

Sanjek: Sanjek, Russell. *Pennies from Heaven: The American Popular Music Business in the Twentieth Century*. Updated by David Sanjek. New York: Da Capo Press, 1996. Originally published 1988.

Sarris: Sarris, Andrew. *"You Ain't Heard Nothin' Yet": The American Talking Film; History & Memory, 1927–1949*. Oxford: Oxford University Press, 1998.

Savran: Savran, David. *A Queer Sort of Materialism: Recontextualizing American Theater*. Ann Arbor: University of Michigan Press, 2003.

Schaefer: Schaefer, Pat. "Unknown Cinderella: The Contribution of Marian Roalfe Cox to the Study of the Fairy Tale." In *A Companion to the Fairy Tale*, edited by Hilda Ellis Davidson and Anna Chaudhri. Cambridge: D. S. Brewer, 2003, pp. 137–47.

Schebera: Schebera, Jürgen. *Kurt Weill: An Illustrated Life*. Translated by Caroline Murphy. New Haven: Yale University Press, 1995. Originally published as *Kurt Weill: Eine Biographie in Texten, Bildern und Dokumenten*. Wiesbaden: Breitkopf & Härtel, 1990.

Schlesinger: Schlesinger, Judith. "Psychology, Evil, and *Sweeney Todd*; or, 'Don't I Know You, Mister?' " In *Stephen Sondheim: A Casebook*, edited by Joanne Gordon. New York: Garland Publishing, 1997, pp. 125–41.

Schwartz: Schwartz, Charles. *Cole Porter: A Biography*. New York: Dial Press, 1977.

Scott: Scott, Matthew. "Weill in America: The Problem of Revival." In *A New Orpheus: Essays on Kurt Weill*, edited by Kim H. Kowalke. New Haven: Yale University Press, 1986.

Sears: Sears, Ann. "The Coming of the Musical Play." In *The Cambridge Companion to the Musical*, edited by William A. Everett and Paul R. Laird. Cambridge: Cambridge University Press, 2002, pp. 120–36.

Secrest1: Secrest, Meryle. *Leonard Bernstein: A Life*. New York: Alfred A. Knopf, 1994.

Secrest2: ———. *Stephen Sondheim: A Life*. New York: Alfred A. Knopf, 1998.

Sedgwick: Sedgwick, Eve Kosofsky. *Between Men: English Literature and Male Homosocial Desire*. New York: Columbia University Press, 1985.

Shaw: Shaw, George Bernard. *Pygmalion*. New York: Dover Publications, 1994. Reprint of the London edition of 1916, by Constable and Company.

Shippey: Shippey, Tom. "Rewriting the Core: Transformations of the Fairy Tale in Contemporary Writing." In *A Companion to the Fairy Tale*, edited by Hilda Ellis Davidson and Anna Chaudhri. Cambridge: D. S. Brewer, 2003, pp. 253–74.

Shteir: Shteir, Rachel. *Striptease: The Untold History of the Girlie Show*. Oxford: Oxford University Press, 2004.

Silver: Silver, Arnold. *Bernard Shaw: The Darker Side*. Stanford: Stanford University Press, 1982.

Silverman: Silverman, Kaja. *The Acoustic Mirror: The Female Voice in Psychoanalysis and Cinema*. Bloomington: Indiana University Press, 1988.

SIMON: Simon, Paul. *The Paul Simon Song Book*. New York: Charing Cross Music, 1966.

SINGER: Singer, Barry. *Ever After: The Last Years of Musical Theater and Beyond*. New York: Applause Theatre & Cinema Books, 2004.

SKLAR/HOFFMAN: Sklar, Elizabeth S., and Donald L. Hoffman, eds. *King Arthur in Popular Culture*. Jefferson, NC: McFarland, 2002.

SMITH/LITTON: Smith, Cecil, and Glenn Litton. *Musical Comedy in America*. New York: Theatre Arts Books, 1950 and 1981.

SMITH: Smith, Helen R. *New Light on Sweeney Todd, Thomas Peckett Prest, James Malcolm Rymer and Elizabeth Caroline Grey*. London: Jarndyce-Bloomsbury, 2002.

SOLOMON: Solomon, Maynard. *Beethoven*. 2nd ed. New York: Schirmer, 1998.

SPEWACK/SPEWACK: Spewack, Samuel, and Bella Spewack. "Introduction: How to Write a Musical Comedy; An Esoteric Analysis of a New Art Form." In *Kiss Me, Kate*. New York: Knopf, 1953, pp. vii–xix.

STANFIELD: Stanfield, Peter. "From the Vulgar to the Refined: American Vernacular and Blackface Minstrelsy in *Show Boat*." In *Musicals: Hollywood and Beyond*, edited by Bill Marshall and Robynn Stilwell. Exeter: Intellect Books, 2000, pp. 147–56.

STEARNS/STEARNS: Stearns, Marshall, and Jean Stearns. *Jazz Dance: The Story of American Vernacular Dance*. New York: Da Capo Press, 1994.

STERNFELD: Sternfeld, Jessica. "The Megamusical: Revolution on Broadway in the 1970s and 80s." Ph.D. dissertation, Princeton University, 2002.

STEYN: Steyn, Mark. *Broadway Babies Say Goodnight: Musicals Then and Now*. New York: Routledge, 1999.

STILWELL: Stilwell, Robynn J. "It May Look Like a Living Room . . . : The Musical Number and the Sitcom." *Echo* 5, no. 1 (Spring 2003).

STODDART: Stoddart, S. F. " 'Happily . . . Ever' . . . NEVER: The Antithetical Romance of *Into the Woods*." In *Reading Stephen Sondheim: A Collection of Critical Essays*, edited by Sandor Goodhart. New York: Garland Publishing, 2000, pp. 209–20.

STUDLAR: Studlar, Gaylyn. "Midnight S/excess: Cult Configurations of 'Femininity' and the Perverse." *Journal of Popular Film and Television* 17, no. 1 (Spring 1989): 2–14.

SWAIN: Swain, Joseph P. *The Broadway Musical: A Critical and Musical Survey*. 2nd ed. Lanham, MD: Scarecrow Press, 2002.

SWAYNE: Swayne, Steven. "Hearing Sondheim's Voices." Ph.D. dissertation, University of California, Berkeley, 1999.

TARUSKIN: Taruskin, Richard. "Stravinsky's 'Rejoicing Discovery' and What It Meant: In Defense of His Notorious Text Setting." In *Stravinsky Retrospectives*, edited by Ethan Haimo and Paul Johnson. Lincoln: University of Nebraska Press, 1987, pp. 162–200.

TAYLOR/JACKSON: Taylor, John Russell, and Arthur Jackson. *The Hollywood Musical*. New York: McGraw-Hill, 1971.

TAYLOR-TH: Taylor, Theodore. *Jule: The Story of Composer Jule Styne*. New York: Random House, 1979.

TAYLOR-TI: Taylor, Timothy D. "Music and Advertising in Early Radio." *Echo* 5, no. 2 (2003).

THOMAS/JOHNSTON: Thomas, Frank, and Ollie Johnston. *Disney Animation: The Illusion of Life*. New York: Abbeville Press, 1981. Released in a "popular edition" in 1984, revised 1995.

TINKCOM: Tinkcom, Matthew. " 'Working Like a Homosexual': Camp Visual Codes and the Labor of Gay Subjects in the MGM Freed Unit." In *Hollywood Musicals: The Film Reader*, edited by Steven Cohan. London: Routledge, 2002, pp. 115–28.

TOLKIEN: Tolkien, J.R.R. "On Fairy-Stories." In *Monsters and the Critics and Other Essays*, edited by Christopher Tolkien. London: Allen and Unwin, 1983.

TUNICK: Tunick, Jonathan. "Introduction." In *A Little Night Music* by Hugh Wheeler and Stephen Sondheim. New York: Applause Theatre Book Publishers, 1991.

UPTON1: Upton, Elizabeth. "Hollywood Knights: Film Music and Medievalism." Talk sponsored by the Center for Medieval and Renaissance Studies, UCLA, April 21, 2005.

UPTON2: ———. "Music and the Aura of Reality in Walt Disney's *Snow White and the Seven Dwarfs*." Society for American Music Annual Conference, Eugene, Oregon, February 2005.

VOGEL: Vogel, Frederick G. *Hollywood Musicals Nominated for Best Picture*. Edited by Mary Vogel. Jefferson, NC: McFarland, 2003.

WALL: Wall, Carey. "There's No Business Like Show Business: A Speculative Reading of the Broadway Musical." In *Approaches to the American Musical*, edited by Robert Lawson-Peebles. Exeter: University of Exeter Press, 1996, pp. 24–43.

WALSER: Walser, Robert. "The Rock and Roll Era." In *The Cambridge History of American Music*, edited by David Nicholls. Cambridge: Cambridge University Press, 1998, pp. 345–87.

WALSH/PLATT: Walsh, David, and Len Platt. *Musical Theater and American Culture*. Westport, CT: Praeger, 2003.

WARFIELD: Warfield, Scott. "From *Hair* to *Rent*: Is 'Rock' a Four-Letter Word on Broadway?" In *The Cambridge Companion to the Musical*, edited by William A. Everett and Paul R. Laird. Cambridge: Cambridge University Press, 2002, pp. 231–45.

WATERS: Waters, Edward N. *Victor Herbert: A Life in Music*. New York: Macmillan, 1955.

WELLS: Wells, Elizabeth. "*West Side Story* and the Hispanic." *Echo* 2, no. 1 (2000).

WHITE: White, T. H. *The Once and Future King*. London: Collins, 1958.

WHITTAKER: Whittaker, Jim. *Cosmic Light: The Birth of a Cult Classic*. Altoona, PA: Acme Books, 1998.

WILDER: Wilder, Alec. *American Popular Song: The Great Innovators, 1900–1950*. Edited by James T. Maher. New York: Oxford University Press, 1990. Originally published 1972.

WILHELM/GROSS: Wilhelm, James J., and Laila Zamuelis Gross, eds. *The Romance of Arthur*. New York: Garland Publishing, 1984.

WILLETT: Willett, Ralph. "From Gold Diggers to Bar Girls: A Selective History of the American Movie Musical." In *Approaches to the American Musical*, edited by Robert Lawson-Peebles. Exeter: University of Exeter Press, 1996, pp. 44–54.

WINTZ: Wintz, Cary D. *Black Culture and the Harlem Renaissance*. Houston, TX: Rice University Press, 1988.

WITOWSKI/KRAUSE: Witowski, Linda, and Martin Krause. *Walt Disney's* Snow White and the Seven Dwarfs: *An Art in Its Making.* New York: Hyperion Press, 1995.

WOLF1: Wolf, Stacy. *A Problem Like Maria: Gender and Sexuality in the American Musical.* Ann Arbor: University of Michigan Press, 2002.

WOLF2: ———. " 'We'll Always Be Bosom Buddies': Female Duets and the Queering of Broadway Musical Theater." *Gay and Lesbian Quarterly* 12, no. 3 (2006): 351–375 (forthcoming).

WOLL1: Woll, Allen L. *Black Musical Theatre: From* Coontown *to* Dreamgirls. Baton Rouge: Louisiana State University Press, 1989.

WOLL2: ———. *The Hollywood Musical Goes to War.* Chicago: Nelson-Hall, 1983.

WOLLEN: Wollen, Peter. *Singin' in the Rain.* London: BFI Publishing, 1992.

WOOD-G: Wood, Graham. "Distant Cousin or Fraternal Twin? Analytical Approaches to the Film Musical." In *The Cambridge Companion to the Musical,* edited by William A. Everett and Paul R. Laird. Cambridge: Cambridge University Press, 2002, pp. 212–30.

WOOD-R1: Wood, Robin. *Howard Hawks.* Garden City, NY: Doubleday, 1968, and London: British Film Institute, 1981.

WOOD-R2: ———. *Sexual Politics and Narrative Film: Hollywood and Beyond.* New York: Columbia University Press, 1998.

YOUNG: Young, Kay. " 'Every Day a Little Death': Sondheim's Un-musicaling of Marriage." In *Reading Stephen Sondheim: A Collection of Critical Essays,* edited by Sandor Goodhart. New York: Garland Publishing, 2000, pp. 77–88.

ZADAN: Zadan, Craig. *Sondheim & Co.* 2nd ed. New York: Harper & Row, 1986. Greatly expanded from the 1974 edition.

INDEX

Note: Page numbers in italics refer to figures.